THE PRAISEWORTHY ONE

This book is a publication of

Indiana University Press
Office of Scholarly Publishing
Herman B Wells Library 350
1320 East 10th Street
Bloomington, Indiana 47405 USA
iupress.indiana.edu

This book is printed on acid-free paper.

Manufactured in China

Cataloging information is available
from the Library of Congress.

ISBN 978-0-253-02526-5 (hardback)

2 3 4 5   24 23 22 21

Erdem'ciğim için
Evvelimsin, ahirimsin

CONTENTS

This book was more than a decade in the making. Over those many years, I have had the pleasure of traveling around the globe (several times over) and working with Islamic paintings and manuscripts held in international museums, libraries, and other repositories.

Along the way, many colleagues helped me make new discoveries, facilitated access to collections, and shared their expertise and resources with me. For their generosity and kindness, my heartfelt thanks go most especially to Fariba Afkari, Jere Bacharach, Jake Benson, Hülya Bilgi, Evrim Binbaş, Sally Bjork, Ali Boozari, Sheila Canby, Zeynep Çelik Atbaş, Michael Cook, Maryam Ekhtiar, Sebastian Encina, Aslıhan Erkmen, Massumeh Farhad, Paul Flemming, Kjeld von Folsach, Jürgen Frembgen, Fawzia Ghafoor Khawaja, Navina Haidar, Marianne Stecher, Tobias Heinzelmann, Renata Holod, James Impoco, Andreas Isler, Benoit Junod, Said Khoddari, Pedram Khosronejad, Linda Komaroff, Evyn Kropf, Ulrich Marzolph, Charlotte Maury, Mary McWilliams, Nahla Nassar, Shahpour Pouyan, Elizabeth Puin, Christoph Rauh, Scott Redford, Yael Rice, Francis Richard, András Riedlmayer, David Roxburgh, Yousef Saeed, Irvin Schick, Mirjam Shatanawi, Michael Shenkar, Shreve Simpson, Eleanor Sims, Pooyan Tamimi Arab, Richard De Unger, Peter Wandel, Stefan Weber, Elaine Wright, Suzan Yalman, Mohamed Zakariya, and Noorashikin Zulkifli.

I also owe a debt of gratitude to Hadiye Cangökçe for her stunning photos of manuscript paintings held in the Topkapı Palace Library; Sheida Riahi for her research assistance; and Omid Safi, Barry Flood, and John Tolan, who read and provided feedback on the first draft of the book manuscript. Their constructive comments allowed me to chisel and expand my text, while Janet Rauscher added her Midas touch throughout. I also wish to thank Carl Ernst for our lively conversation about publicly engaged scholarship. His article calling upon academics to avoid jargon and forgo transliteration in favor of "stealth analysis" inspired the bare-bones prose I decided to adopt for this project.[1] While this book is geared toward scholars and students in the arts and humanities, it is my hope that it will prove accessible to a general readership.

I also have benefited from the logistical and financial support provided to me by my academic institutions. This project first began while I was faculty at Indiana University (2005–2010). At that time, a New Frontiers Grant in the Arts and Humanities allowed me to launch my research and acquire images, and it provided the first half of the publication subvention. At the University of Michigan (since 2010), I was fortunate to receive a fellowship granted by the Associate Professor Support

Fund, which enabled me to complete my research and writing. A second publication subvention, provided by the History of Art Department at the University of Michigan, capped the process and ensured the inclusion of full-color images in the book. At Indiana University Press, I extend my thanks to Robert Sloan, Dee Mortensen, Paige Rasmussen, and the production team for their hard work on this collective endeavor. Above all, I thank the Press for taking on this project with such eagerness—and without any hesitation whatsoever.

Last but not least, I wish to dedicate this book to my husband, Erdem. He has been by my side and has had my back for over a dozen years. He put up with me while I was on the road and during my stints of "writing quarantine." For some odd reason, he even found it satisfying to polish all my footnotes and bibliography in the wake of publishing his own book and securing tenure. We interspersed our edits with latte dates, squirrel and bird feedings, and running around in circles at the gym. I could not imagine a more blessed and peaceful life than with my co-çapulcu and much better half right next to me.

NOTES

1. Ernst, "It's Not Just Academic."

THE PRAISEWORTHY ONE

أَسْمَاءُ سَيِّدِنَا وَ مَوْلَانَا مُحَمَّدٍ صَلَّى اللّٰه
عَلَيْهِ وَسَلَّمَ مِئَتَانِ وَوَاحِدٌ وَهِيَ هٰذِهِ

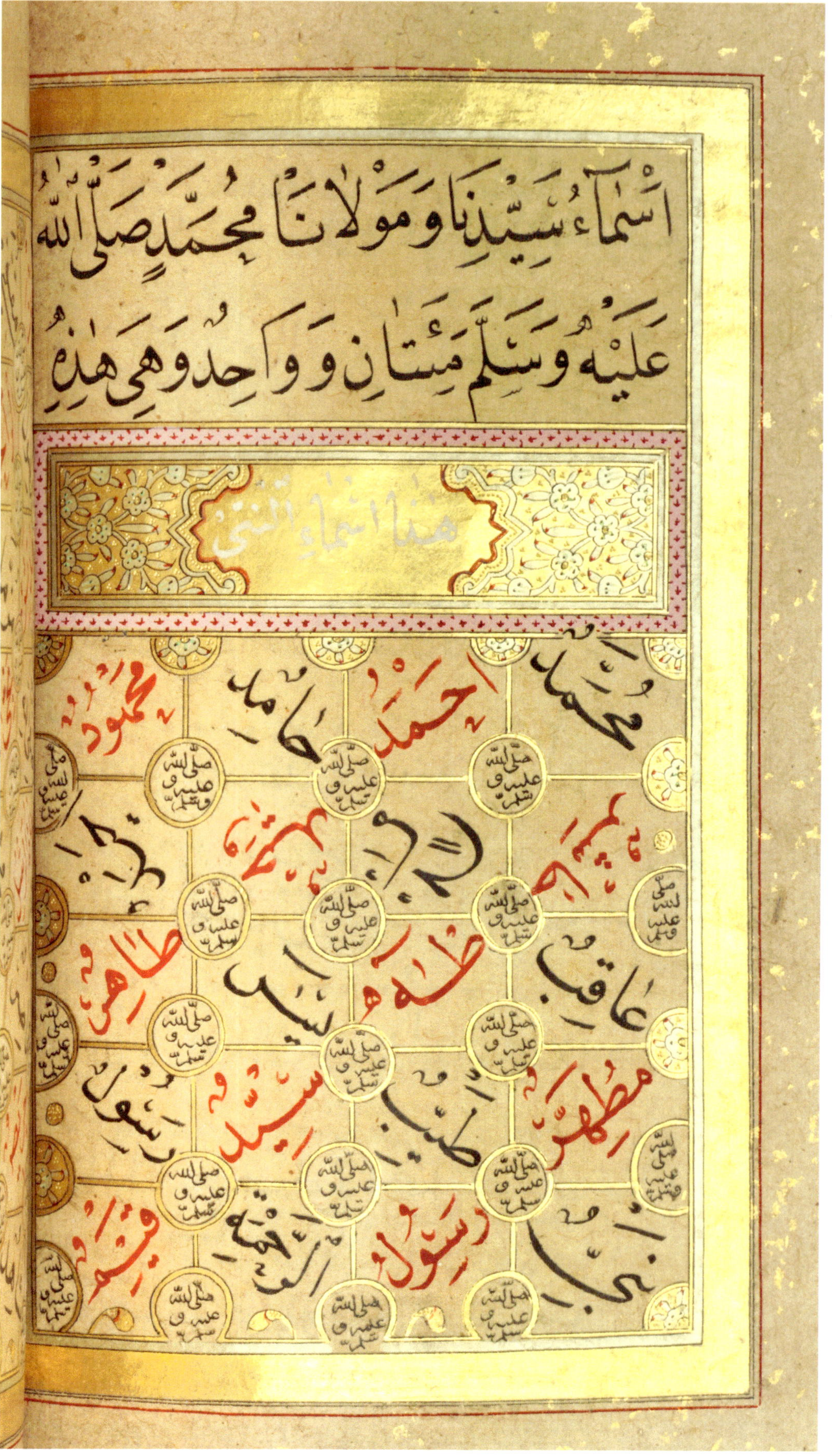

INTRODUCTION

Certainly in God's Messenger you have a beautiful model.

Qur'an 33:21

The apostle of Islam is known in Arabic as Muhammad, or "The Praise-worthy One." While Muhammad has long been used in Islamic sources as the Prophet's personal name, it also functions as an honorary epithet that was conferred on him at the beginning of the revelation of the Qur'an.[1] This anointment or appointment name is, however, only one of many praise terms by which Muhammad is called. Classified as the "names of the Prophet" (*asma' al-nabi*), Muhammad's many appellations encompass nouns and adjectives that collectively pay tribute to his supreme prophetic standing and impeccable moral character.[2] Sometimes numbering in the hundreds, these names adorn religious manuscripts and talismanic objects; they also are recited aloud as a way of remembering and invoking the Prophet within various Islamic devotional practices (fig. I.1).

Intriguingly, the Qur'an mentions Moses 136 times, Abraham 69 times, and Jesus 25 times. There exist hundreds of mentions of "messenger" (*rasul*) and "prophet" (*nabi*), but Muhammad appears only four times in Islamic scripture.[3] As Tarif Khalidi stresses, Muhammad's personal name (if Muhammad is to be considered a personal rather than a praise name) retreats behind his qur'anic image as a "divinely appointed universal missionary."[4] Within the Qur'an, Muhammad's illustrious position indeed is promoted by his other titles and soubriquets, including "seal of prophets" (*khatam al-nabiyyin*), "bearer of glad tidings" (*bashir*), and "warner [of hell and calamities]" (*nadhir*).[5] Moreover, Muslim exegetes contend that the Qur'an records Jesus foretelling Muhammad's status as "Ahmad," that is, "The Most Praiseworthy One," who serves as the ultimate comforter and intercessor.[6] This type of qur'anic prophetology, catalyzed by Muhammad's many names, without a doubt laid the ground for elaborations of his personal attributes in a variety of Islamic textual sources, including the Sayings of the Prophet (Hadith), biographies, historical narratives, and mystical poems.

Muhammad's many names follow the pattern of God's "beautiful names" (*al-asma' al-husna*), aligning them with notions of the divine.[7] In Islamic traditions, both God and Muhammad are believed to necessitate an expansive nomenclature in order to fully capture the multifaceted ontological reality of each. As a complex totality, the many names of Muhammad thus construct a range of conceptual images via the power of linguistic articulation. Through the use of terminology alone, at times Muhammad is described as a mere mortal being who serves as the human carrier of God's message, while at others he is lauded as an ineffable, transcendental, metahistorical, and everlasting flux of light emitted into the world.[8]

FACING, I.1. The "names of the Prophet" (*asma' al-nabi*) inscribed in a checkerboard, al-Jazuli, *Dala'il al-Khayrat* (Proofs of Good Deeds), calligraphed by Mustafa al-Halimi, Ottoman lands (possibly Istanbul), 1214 AH/1799–1800 CE. Special Collections, Hatcher Graduate Library, University of Michigan, Ann Arbor, Isl. Ms. 249, p. 274.

At first glance, expressive strategies praising Muhammad's human and his superhuman characteristics may seem mutually exclusive. However, they coalesce into a colorful mosaic of images, some of which were especially popular in particular times and places. Such creative imaginings of the Prophet—whether through the crafting of praise names, textual descriptions, or the visual arts—have proved a hallmark of many Islamic cultures from the seventh century to the present day.

This book's primary aim consists in exploring this textured miscellany, in the process highlighting the fact that Muhammad, "The Praiseworthy One," has served as the beating heart of his followers' devotional energy for well over a millennium. Its second goal is to emphasize Islam's rich literary and artistic heritage by illuminating the many pivotal roles Muhammad has played in Muslim constructions of self and community in various religious, political, and cultural contexts. In exploring the Prophet's significance in Muslim life, thought, and creative activity, this study pays particular attention to processes of narration and imagination, stressing that a fruitful approach to both textual and visual materials emphasizes Muhammad's personhood as a larger metaphor that helps to explain both past and present events, to build and delineate a sense of community, and to help individuals conceive of and communicate with the realm of the sacred.

This book is also defined by what it is not: it is not concerned with unearthing an ostensibly historical Muhammad, especially due to the fact that the Prophet gained mythical status already during his lifetime.[9] In other words, it does not attempt to parse myth from fact in order to delineate what may have been, or may have happened, in actuality. To the contrary, this study highlights the ways in which writers and artists developed their own symbolic lexicon in order to conjure a more metaphorical Muhammad, whose larger-than-life persona often transcended historical specificity.[10] From such intellectual and creative efforts emerged rather malleable prophetic images, which could be tinged and tailored to suit the various cultural and devotional needs of their epochs. More often than not, Muhammad thus has served as a polyvalent symbol rather than a fixed empirical datum. Unshackled from the confines of verifiable truth, he has thrived as a capacious repository of meaning, largely within the domains of mythmaking, allegory, and creative imagination.

The man and the metaphor have yielded many "praiseworthy" images—cerebral and aural as well as textual and visual—within Islamic expressive traditions.[11] Such conceptual imaginings, or pious "picturations" (*tasawwurat*), of the Prophet began very early and have flourished throughout the centuries.[12] At times, Muhammad is described in quite literal ways: he is said to be neither too tall nor too short; his eyes are almond shaped, and his hair is black. However, even the most mimetic of sketches incorporate descriptions that are allegorical or otherworldly. Biographies of the Prophet, texts that record his physical and moral "characteristics" (*shama'il*) or enumerate his "proofs of prophecy" (*dala'il al-nubuwwa*), eulogistic poems, and verbal icons (*hilyes*) are all studded with embellishments. We are told that Muhammad's flesh shone like white light and that he bore a "seal of prophethood" (*khatam al-nubuwwa*) on his physical body; that he had supernatural gifts and powers, including the ability to ascend through the heavens and split the moon in half; and that trees, animals, and even pebbles miraculously walked toward or talked with him, singing his praises and attesting to his apostleship.

In almost every case, the Prophet emerges as a mortal man overlaid with formulas of allusion befitting his exalted status as God's messenger. He thus is compounded as the "historical" and the "imagined" Muhammad in the hearts and minds of his devotees,[13] for whom he acts as both exemplar and foil.[14] This more emblematic—one could even say parabolic—Prophet emerged early on, per the qur'anic exultation "Certainly in God's Messenger you have a beautiful model" (33:21). For members of the faith community, this beautiful paradigm (*uswa hasana*) invited an attempt to mimic Muhammad's manners and deeds, which themselves provide an exemplary moral code.[15] Even efforts to emulate the Prophet's dress and quotidian practices, including hygiene, have been deemed helpful to individuals seeking to cultivate an "attitude of piety and blessedness"[16] in their everyday lives.

To no small extent, the Hadith codified Muhammad's behavior, practices, and statements on various social and religious issues. This body of literature—which in essence acts as Muhammad's verbal relics passed down posthumously through the generations—paints a larger prophetic "tradition," or *sunna*, which provides a more detailed picture of Islam's messenger than the Qur'an. Collated but not seamless, the Hadith record Muhammad as a narrator who directs and records his own life story, in which he offers ethical teachings to promote good and inhibit evil. Within this authoritative framework, Muhammad's sayings include narrative elements that both educate and entertain its readership.[17] Collectively, they serve as a guidebook that provides instruction on proper behavior.[18]

Memories of Muhammad and his recorded deeds have enabled the faithful to grasp and appreciate his role and significance in both past and present life.[19] Whether Muhammad is praised as a divinely sent apostle, eschatological messiah, political revolutionary, statesman and community leader, military strategist and commander, arbiter of disputes, dispenser of justice, or quintessential mystic, in the end his character and deeds have yielded a highly variegated "Prophet-image" that functions as an expressive or experiential model of what is good and, hence, beautiful.[20]

As Annemarie Schimmel maintains, within Islamic literature "Qur'anic remarks were elaborated and spun out into long tales and wondrous legends, which slowly illuminated the outlines of the historical Muhammad with an array of color."[21] Indeed, early Arabic-language biographies (*siras*) of the Prophet and historical narratives—especially those penned by Ibn Ishaq (d. ca. 761–70 CE) and al-Tabari (d. 923 CE)—reveal a number of strategies for amplifying Muhammad's sacred import according to larger heroic tropes. These and other Muslim authors assembled rather opaque qur'anic data in order to sculpt a story around a number of key words, phrases, and verses, and their narrative impulse discloses a larger drive to give order and meaning to the story of the Prophet, about whom so little information (including his personal name) is provided within Islam's holy book. As exegetical forms of storytelling, then, both biography and history aim to order historical information even as they mythicize and dramatize history's dramatis personae, among whom Muhammad serves as both founding father and prime example within the history of Islamic civilization.

Biographies, histories, poems, and festivals in praise and honor of the Prophet blossomed across the Islamic world from the tenth century onward. Some prophetic vitas did more than recount Muhammad's birth, characteristics, deeds, battles, and death. In a manner similar to coeval "characteristics" (*shama'il*) and "proofs" (*dala'il*) texts, they focus on his many miracles, which served as irrefutable evidence of his prophetic selection. At times, the prophetic biography also was considered a form of therapy (*shifa*). For example, the medieval judge (*qadi*) 'Iyad al-Yahsubi (d. 1129 CE) penned a *sira* of the Prophet titled *Kitab al-Shifa bi-Ta'rif Huquq al-Mustafa* (The Book of Healing by the Recognition of the Rights of the Chosen One).[22] Much as the faithful direct their blessings and prayers to the Prophet in order to seek cure and salvation, this biography was believed to carry thaumaturgic power, especially if placed in a house and recited by (or on behalf of) someone who was ill.

Additionally, al-Yahsubi's prophetic vita acted essentially as a logbook of Muhammad's miracles, thus falling within the literary genre of magical realism.[23] In his text, the author speaks of the Prophet's various water and milk miracles, in which his fingers caused the gushing of springs and the flowing of a dry sheep's udders. At times, Muhammad miraculously replenishes food supplies, including barley and lamb, during moments of want or starvation; at others he heals the sick through his *baraka*-filled saliva. Indeed, Muhammad's prophetic *baraka*, or blessings, were many and included several wondrous occurrences. To give just one example, al-Yahsubi records an individual requesting proof of Muhammad's prophecy, whereupon suddenly a "tree leaned to the right and left, in front and behind, pulled up its roots and came splitting the earth, dragging its dusty roots until it stood by the Prophet, saying: 'Peace be Upon You, O Messenger of God.'"[24] In sum, many natural organisms and phenomena are said to follow in Muhammad's footsteps, protecting him from harm while confirming his prophetic standing.

This spiritualized approach to the Prophet of Islam can be detected within Islamic textual sources written during and after the medieval period (i.e., the ninth through fourteenth centuries) in particular. Although Muhammad remains the paradigm of charismatic rule, wielding

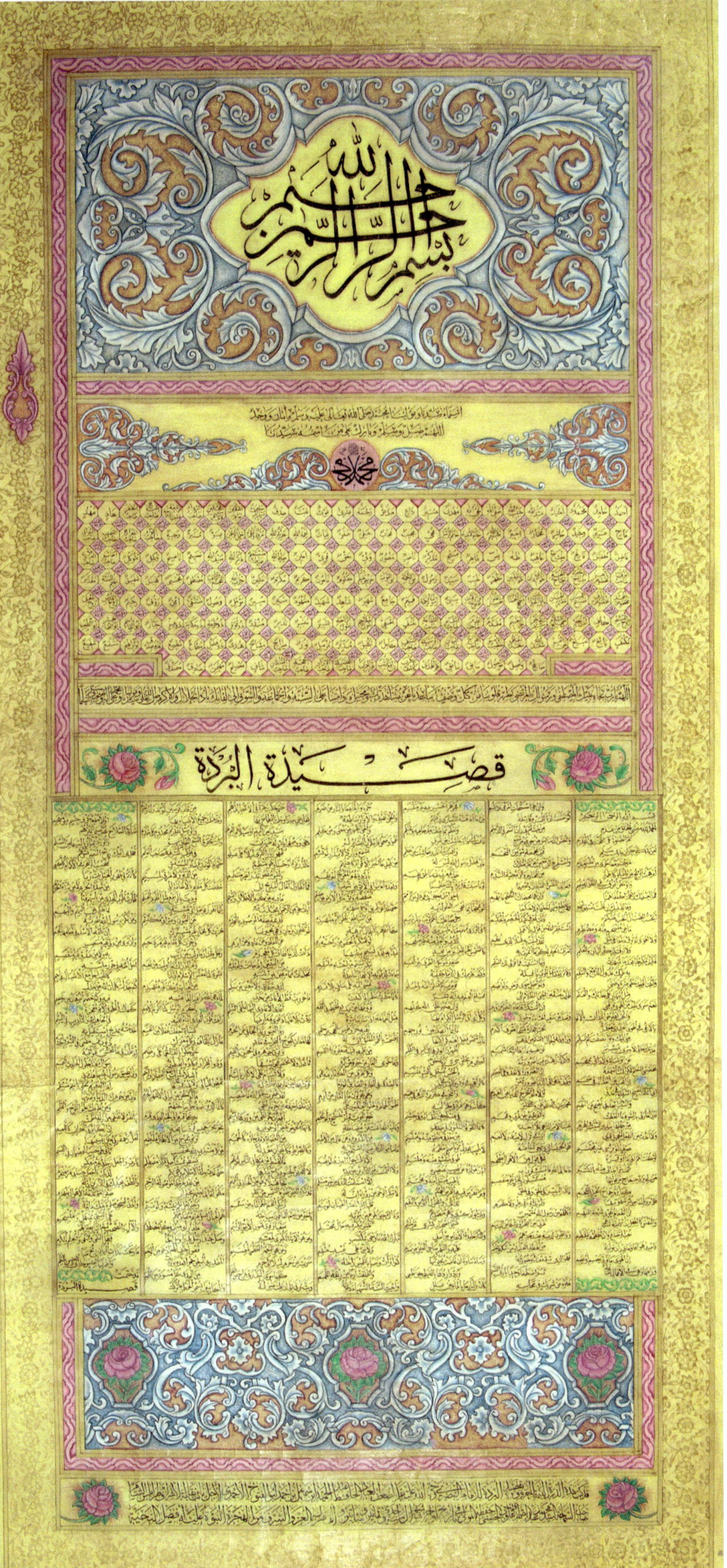

1.2. Painting of the "names of the Prophet" (*asma' al-nabi*) and al-Busiri's *Qasidat al-Burda* (Mantle Ode), Tripoli, Lebanon, 1860 CE (Ottoman period). Frederick de Jong Collection, National Museum of World Cultures, Amsterdam, 7031–22.

supreme authority and enacting worldly and divine dispensation, he also provided the archetype for mystics who embarked on their own journeys toward oneness with God. Beyond Arab lands, mystical works in the Persian and Turkish languages eulogized Muhammad's character and attributes, the poetic plaudits revealing an increasing lyricism in Islamic discursive methods of visualizing the Prophet. Such expressions, which elevated allegory over dogmatic literalism, proved a natural outgrowth of Sufism, Islam's more personal and gnostic form of religious thought and practice. Within more mystically inclined spheres, the faithful have imagined Muhammad as the first spiritualist, sojourner, and teacher—as well as the principal channel and guide toward divine unity—in the process crafting a larger "Muslim mystical prophetology."[25]

The panegyric poem (*madh* or *na't*) offers one important realm of textual production in which Muhammad emerges as if a supernatural figure, shedding his human condition and reaching cosmic proportions.[26] There exist numerous eulogistic poems dedicated to Muhammad in various Islamic languages. Among them, the *Qasidat al-Burda* (Mantle Ode) written by al-Busiri (d. 1294 CE) counts as the most popular of the Arabic-language "prophetic praise poems" (*al-mada'ih al-nabawiyya*). The author wrote his ode as a token of thanks after he dreamed of the Prophet covering him with his mantle (*burda*), thereby curing him of paralysis.[27] This poem also came to serve as a talisman whose verses were at times transcribed in ink, dissolved in water, and imbibed by individuals seeking cure and protection.[28] As a powerful praise poem and prophylactic, over the centuries the *Burda* has been produced in many manuscript copies and on printed posters, some of which combine the poem with Muhammad's many names in order to encourage the Muslim faithful to invoke the Prophet—in repeated and diverse ways—so as to secure increased protection for body, soul, home, and belongings (fig. I.2).

In the *Burda* and in many other Islamic devotional poems, Muhammad is said to display a perfection of physical and spiritual form. As the paradigmatic "complete man" (*al-insan al-kamil*), Muhammad has both inner and outer beauty approximating that of God, as al-Busiri's exclaims: "He is one whose interior and exterior form were made perfect / Then the Creator of men chose him as a beloved friend."[29] Conjured as a close and protective companion (of both God and humankind), Muhammad also is depicted as carrying a divine flux. This "light of Muhammad" (*nur Muhammad*) is said to emanate from God, whence it transmigrated and engendered all of creation until the Prophet's final physical incarnation on earth.[30] According to al-Busiri and many other mystically inclined writers, effulgence shone forth at Muhammad's birth, lighting up the world from the east to the west, and when Muhammad embarked on his celestial ascension (*mi'raj*), it was he who illuminated the stars and the entire cosmos.

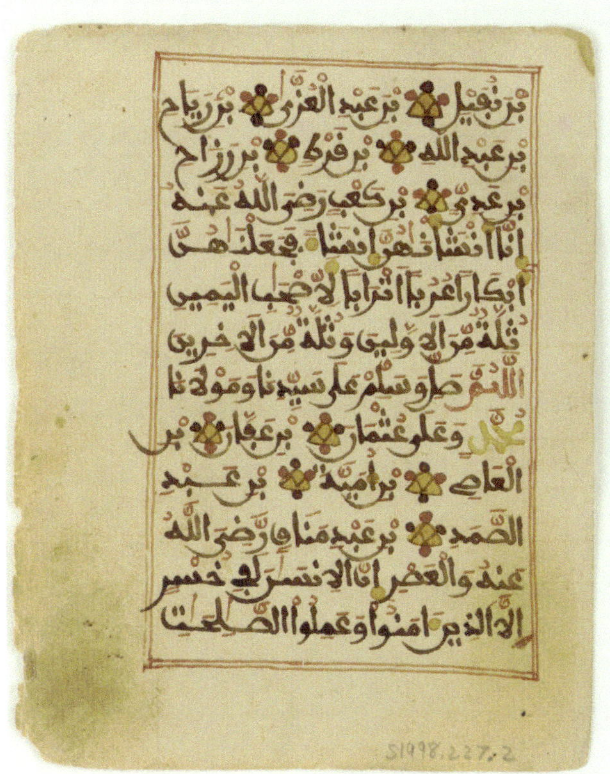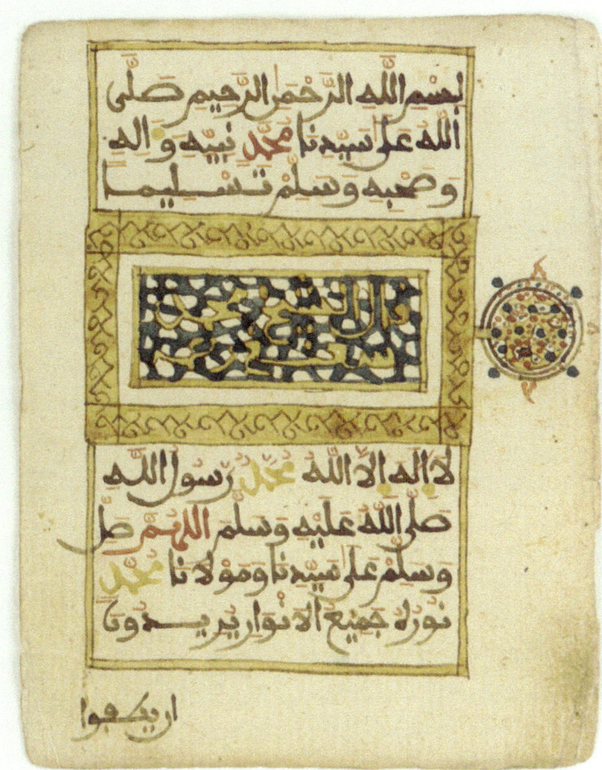

Such light allegories have suffused Islamic textual production, including Persian and Turkish eulogies, from the medieval period to today. For instance, the famous Persian mystical poet Nizami (d. 1209 CE) addresses Muhammad in his opening eulogy to *Makhzan al-Asrar* (Treasury of Secrets) with the exclamation "You, you are the light of the Great, have no shadow; you are yourself the shadow of the light of God."[31] The Persian poet also reminds his readers that Muhammad's "essence gives brightness to the sun."[32] Much like Nizami's versified praise of the Prophet as the ultimate luminary, the blind poet al-Darir, who was active during the late fourteenth century, lauds Muhammad as a "world of lights" in his Turkish-language vita.[33]

These imagistic tendencies in thought and rhetoric in turn influenced the appearance of Muslim prayer books and other manuscripts, which often include praises to Muhammad with his name written in gold ink (fig. I.3). This chrysography, or gold lettering, serves to visually single out the Prophet from the black or brown ink reserved for the rest of the transcription.[34] It also aims to capture the *nur Muhammad* as irradiated by the name, body, and being of the Prophet. In the end, this Sufi imagination of the Prophet via rhetorical symbolism and color coding renders him as visible yet immaterial, existent yet ineffable.

Over time, other mystical allegories coalesced to yield a more "metaphorical Muhammad." This suprahuman Muhammad is said to be a veiled secret, hidden from view and beyond comprehension. As an embodied unknown, he comes to surpass the writer's capacity to describe

I.3. Religious devotions to the Prophet Muhammad, whose name is transcribed in red and gold ink, prayer book, Western Africa, nineteenth century CE. Arthur M. Sackler Gallery, Smithsonian Institution, Washington, DC, S1998.227.1–2.

him, rendering language deficient—at times even useless. The Prophet's characteristics that transcend human limitations and comprehension include, among others, his ability to receive revelation and to survive the cracking open of his chest, and his rising into the domain of God.

Muhammad's celestial ascension, or *mi'raj*, holds pride of place for mystics and spiritualists, who often have interpreted it as a prophetic template for their own quests to reach awareness, love, perfection, unity, and even annihilation in the divine.[35] Indeed, as a "trailblazer into the secrets of God,"[36] Muhammad benefits from initiation into a sacred realm as well as from knowledge of the otherworld. In this manner, he provides a beautiful exemplum for the Sufi adept who seeks to perfect his soul by spiritually rising through various stations (*maqamat*) and states (*ahwal*) in a greater effort to reach proximity (*qurb*) with God.

Many mystics use the metaphorically loaded language of the *mi'raj* to describe their own gnostic journeys. Such is the case for the early Persian mystic Abu Yazid al-Bistami (d. ca. 874–78 CE), who speaks of his own spiritual and corporeal ascension,[37] as well as the medieval Andalusian Sufi master Ibn 'Arabi (d. 1240 CE), who reflects on his "ascent" within his own self.[38] Both mystics saw in the structure of the Prophet's ascension an extended allegory for the gnostic quest, in which the soul regenerates as it advances from one spiritual stage or state to another, exiting the mortal world to enter the eternal dimension.

To Ibn 'Arabi, God grants the "Muhammadan station" (*maqam Muhammadi*) and the knowledge of the "light of Muhammad" (*nur Muhammadi*) on the gnostic's arrival at the divine.[39] Thereupon, the Andalusian mystic states, he witnessed not God but his own soul, finally admitting, "My voyage was only in myself and only pointed to myself."[40] As they travel along a path similar to that of the Prophet's ascension, Ibn 'Arabi and other mystics attempt to demonstrate that the spiritualist can undertake a journey into the soul, a place where an already-present "inner Muhammad" can be accessed and unlocked. This internalization of the Prophet at the psychological level reveals one of many ways in which Muhammad and his miraculous ascent are homologized to the spiritual life and experiences of the Sufi.[41] For the mystically inclined faithful, both past and present, Muhammad is therefore "not just a model or a hero, but the object of their longing and love."[42] The imagined presence of the "Praised" and "Beloved" in essence issues from within the hearts and minds of the faithful as they strive for spiritual unity.

Feeling, thinking, speaking, writing, and visualizing count among the many creative techniques that devotees have cultivated to "paint" Muhammad as the ideal image of authority and beauty, refuge and perfection. To these many expressive strategies can be added that of the ritual, especially as performed during festivals commemorating the Prophet's birth (*mawlid*). Celebrated annually on 12 Rabi' I, Mawlid celebrations attest to the popularity of Muslim devotions, many of which revolve around the Prophet.[43] Today, Muhammad's birth is observed during Muslim community festivals across the globe—from the United

States to China.[44] However, it also has proved a subject of debate: while most religious scholars have considered celebrating Muhammad's birth a "praiseworthy innovation" (*bid'a hasana*) that increases piety, others interpret it as a heresy to be prohibited. It is for these reasons that in some contemporary Salafi spheres—most especially in Saudi Arabia and areas that were under the control of ISIS (Islamic State in Iraq and Syria)—festival celebrations of Muhammad's birth have been banned altogether.[45]

Despite occasional curbs, Mawlid festivals have thrived for many centuries. They include a number of practices that strengthen individuals' relationships with members of their community as well as their spiritual connections to the Prophet. Almsgiving and the sharing of food, nighttime vigils, and the recitation of poems come together to create a religious carnival. In Arabic-speaking countries, devotees often recite al-Busiri's *Burda*, whose verses describe Muhammad's birth as the end of the old world order, the flight of evil spirits (*jinns*) and Satan, and showers of meteors that echo the toppling of the pagan idols at the Ka'ba.[46] Moreover, in Ottoman and Turkish spheres, the Prophet's birth has been celebrated as the festival of the "Candle-Lit Birth" (*Mevlid Kandili*) since the sixteenth century;[47] festivities have included the nighttime illumination of religious buildings (with candles [*kandils*] and, more recently, electric lights), devotional gatherings, readings of poetry, musical performances, incense burning, and the offering of sweet drinks and food.

In Turkish spheres, the most popular poem for recitation has remained Süleyman Çelebi's (d. 1422 CE) *Mevlid-i şerif* (The Noble Birth), the verses of which were set to music in Ottoman times.[48] In this panegyric poem, Muhammad emerges as a radiant and sweet-smelling hero, bearing the "seal of prophethood" and performing miracles unlimited in their scope and number.[49] He also is described as the moon and sun of guidance: that is, as a theophanous entity sent by God to lead humankind to salvation. According to Süleyman Çelebi and like-minded individuals, this salvific path requires devotion to and love of the Prophet, who personifies divine mercy for all of humankind. In Turkish Sufi (especially Bektashi) settings, devotees also spiritually set alight their "inner Muhammad" by cultivating the symbolic meaning of the term *kandil*, which signifies both a wax candle and a nighttime festival. In one Turkish poem, for example, the pious exclaim, "On the candle nights, we become candles" (*kandil geceleri kandil oluruz*).[50] Here, then, individuals seek an annihilation of their own selves within the all-encompassing light of the Prophet, itself ignited by a community ritual.

Birth festivals are celebrated in many other parts of the world. On the Indian subcontinent, such commemorations often occur within, in the vicinity of, or under the sponsorship of Sufi groups and associations. Today, in the city of Thatta, located in the province of Sindh in Pakistan, the Sufi shrine of Hajji Baba hosts nighttime celebrations and prayers. Banners and other decorative items, including garlands and

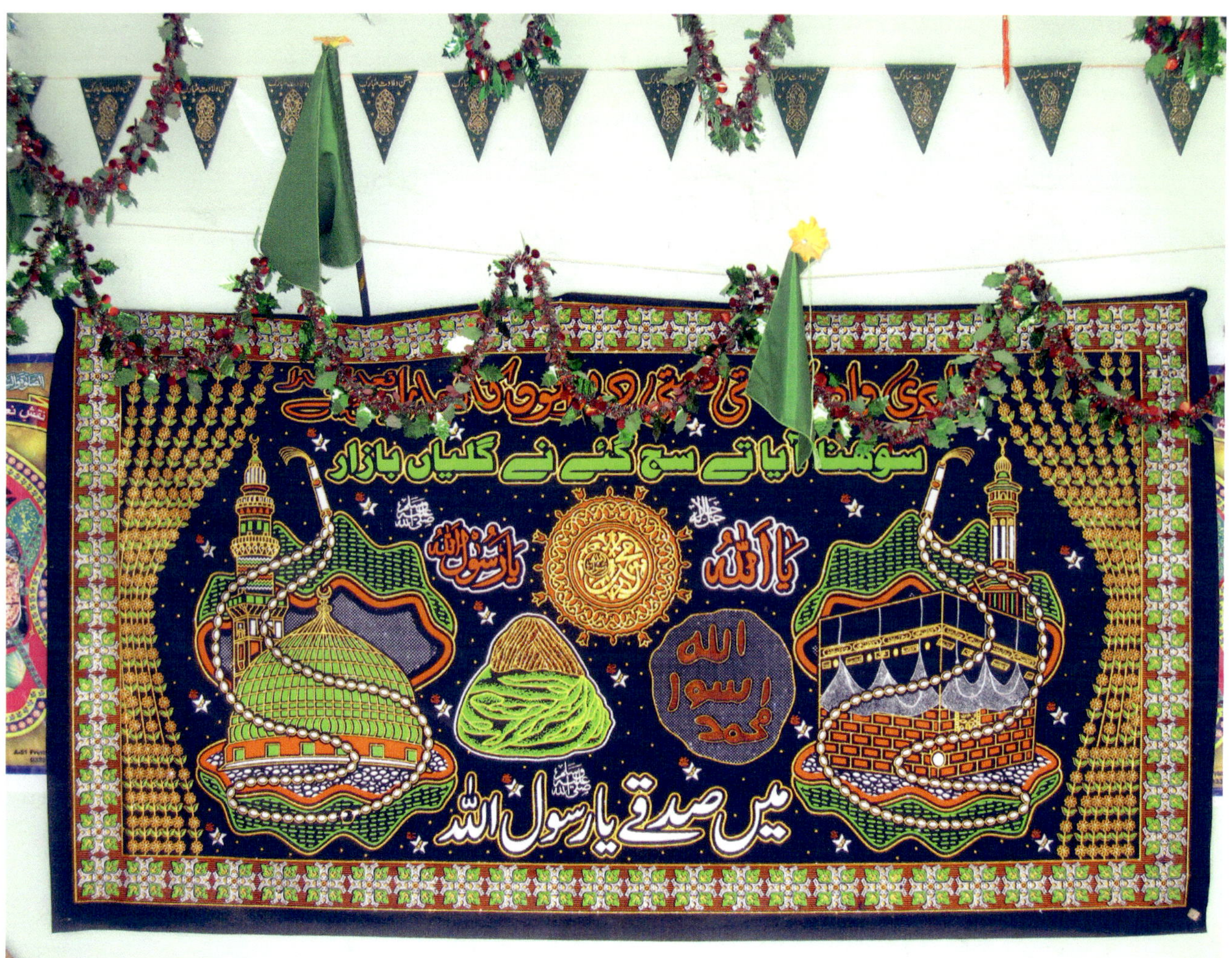

1.4. Banner depicting the Prophet Muhammad's relics, displayed in the compound of the Sufi shrine of Hajji Baba, Makli village, close to the city of Thatta, Sindh, Pakistan, February 2012 CE. Photograph courtesy of Jürgen Wasim Frembgen.

lights, ornament the walls of buildings and hang above the streets. A number of banners, which also are deployed during Sufi saints' annual death celebrations, depict the Prophet's two key geographic and architectural markers—the Ka'ba in Mecca and his tomb-mosque in Medina—as well as his object attributes and relics, particularly his two rosaries, signet ring impression (reading "Muhammad is the Messenger of God" [*Muhammad rasul Allah*]), and turban (fig. 1.4). Accompanied by calligraphic invocations, these types of representations found throughout the streets of Pakistan during Mawlid festivals recall Muhammad through the visual language of synecdoche, thereby energizing the many rhetorical metaphors nourished within Islamic devotional poetry.

Devotees across the world thus imagine the Prophet as partaking in a greater "exchange of merit" and "economy of salvation" as expressed within the context of Mawlid festivals.[51] In these cultic settings, Muhammad functions as the idealized heart of Muslim piety as well as the pinnacle of love.[52] He thus does not represent only prophecy and rulership; much more importantly, his imagination engenders a multisensory phenomenon, in which the believer's heart, ears, and eyes conjure his presence as lambent, boundless, and everlasting. From the

   THE PRAISEWORTHY ONE

earliest texts to medieval poems to contemporary religious festivals, the Prophet has thrived in rhetorical expression and ritual practice. Such creative activity has long featured visual dimensions, both engendering and echoing a wide range of representational strategies that were developed within Islamic figural arts.

From the first century of Islam to today, textual, oral, and ritual practices have yielded a rich array of images of Muhammad as the final envoy of God, creative light sent to the world, traveler and intercessor in the otherworld, and eternal presence in the hearts and minds of his followers. The visual arts have contributed to such devotional efforts in their own right: they have reflected, contributed to, and creatively expanded these many conceptual depictions by using the language of form and by appealing to pious viewers' optical perception. Indeed, much like writers and poets used the language of fact-centered narration or magical lyricism, artists employed their own iconographical lexicons and material resources in order to cultivate a range of positive emotions toward the Prophet, including respect, trust, and love.

Figural depictions of Muhammad emanated largely from Persian and Turkish lands from the thirteenth to the eighteenth century. While representational images may have been made prior to the medieval period, any evidence to this effect must have been destroyed during the Mongol sacking of the royal 'Abbasid library in Baghdad in 1258 CE. Although no material or visual evidence for the production of images of Muhammad in Islamic lands antedates 1200 CE, a series of Arabic-language texts narrates stories about depictions of the Prophet that were said to be in circulation during Muhammad's lifetime. These images of the Prophet, readers are told, were in the possession of a Byzantine emperor, an Iranian king, the patriarch of Alexandria, and a group of Christians living in the province of Syria.

The most popular among these "portrait stories" concerns Heraclius (r. 610–41 CE), the Christian Byzantine emperor to whom Muhammad sent letters and envoys. On one occasion, Heraclius welcomed the Muslim emissaries and brought out a box known as the "chest of witnessing" (*sanduq al-shahada*), which included several drawers or compartments containing pieces of silk with painted images of the prophets Adam, Noah, Abraham, and Muhammad. The "portrait of the Prophet" (*surat al-nabi*) was as luminous as the sun and more pleasing than any beautiful form. When the Prophet's dispatched companions looked at his portrait, "teardrops streamed like stars from their eyes, and a longing for the Prophet was renewed in their hearts."[53] In this version of the narrative—which was illustrated at least once in a manuscript painting (fig. I.5)—Muhammad's prophecy and Islam's ascendancy are foretold through a figurative image already in the possession of a pious Christian ruler and "near convert."[54] This sacred icon, it is further related, was utterly brilliant and gorgeous. For pious believers, gazing on it generated the emotions of longing and love—even prayerful physical poses. The

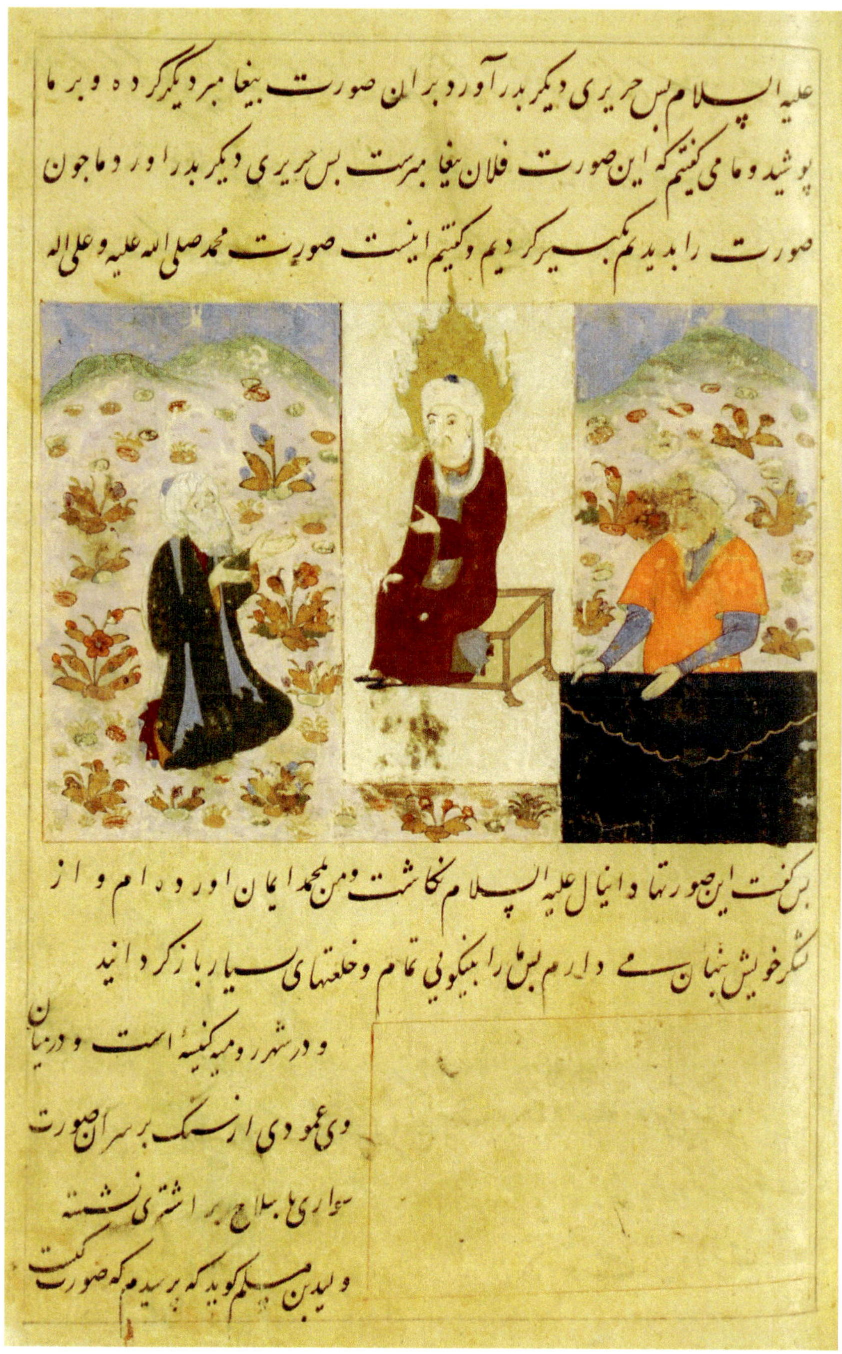

1.5. Heraclius presents a silk portrait of the enthroned Prophet to Abu Bakr, who lifts his hands in prayer, Tusi Salmani, *'Aja'ib al-Makhluqat* (Wonders of creation), Shiraz, early sixteenth century CE. Bibliothèque nationale de France, Paris, Suppl. Persan 332, folio 162r.

medieval Qur'an commentator Ibn Kathir (d. 1371 CE) states that these images representing Muhammad and the other prophets "according to the features and form they bore" prompted Muhammad's companions to stand in respect.[55]

This anecdote about Heraclius also is reported in al-Tusi's *'Aja'ibnama* (Book of Wonders), written in Persian and dedicated to Tughril b. Arslan (r. 1176–94 CE), the last ruler of the Great Seljuks. The author reports that the Byzantine emperor (Heraclius) secretly swore allegiance to Muhammad, either because he accepted the Prophet and Islam or because he simply believed in the last of the portraits in the "chest of witnessing" and thereby inadvertently embraced the Islamic faith.[56] In this twelfth-century variant of the narrative, a portable figurative image of Muhammad serves as a vehicle for foretelling the ultimate triumph of Islam. Additionally, it functions as a pictorial vehicle for converting a Christian ruler to the Muslim faith. Noteworthy here is a belief in the power of representational imagery—in both Christian and Muslim spheres—to convince individuals to adopt a faith and embrace its messengers.

In his *'Aja'ibnama*, al-Tusi also records two anecdotes related to images of the Prophet, stressing their pedagogical and protective potential. The first describes a portrait of Muhammad that was used by an Iranian king's diviner to foresee the victory of Islam. In this instance, a figurative image of the Prophet accompanies the practice of divination and therefore functions as a visual omen signaling Islam's supremacy. Building on this anecdote, al-Tusi's second story describes a copper statue of the Prophet in Constantinople, which was believed to prevent natural disasters (especially earthquakes). Interestingly, the author also states that apotropaic statues of Bilal, Muhammad's Ethiopian caller to prayer, and 'Ali, his son-in-law and cousin, were present in Constantinople.[57] In this instance, the anecdote of a figurative image of Muhammad painted on a flat (paper or silk) surface in the possession of Heraclius is expanded in at least two discernable ways: first, the visual representation becomes more fully embodied as a three-dimensional sculpture, thus joining Constantinople's other famous Greco-Roman and Byzantine statuary, and, second, a statue of 'Ali, the figurehead of Shi'i Islam, is said to have been regarded as similarly protective. Al-Tusi's descriptions of images of Muhammad thus are rhetorically sculpted in various ways, some of which may have had the potential to convey a sectarian message.

Another textual source of the tenth century narrates that an image of the Prophet was in the possession of al-Muqawqis, who served as the Byzantine or Sasanian provincial ruler of Egypt.[58] Muhammad sent a letter inviting him to the Islamic faith, much as he did for Heraclius. The Prophet also is said to have dispatched his companion Dihya al-Kalbi, who reported that al-Muqawqis had in his possession 313 pictures of the prophets and apostles (*suwar al-anbiya' wa'l-mursilin*), including one of Muhammad.[59] Even the staunch medieval Sunni theologian Ibn Taymiyya (d. 1328 CE) happily reports that al-Muqawqis had pictures of the prophets in his possession, among which were three images depicting Muhammad and his two companions (*sahaba*), Abu Bakr and 'Umar.[60] It appears that, for this Sunni author at least, an image of 'Ali was not deemed necessary to complete this pantheon of prophetic images.

The painting of the Prophet in the possession of al-Muqawqis proved unproblematic for a number of authors, including Ibn Taymiyya, insomuch as it attested to Muhammad's supreme position in a long line of divinely sent messengers. However, the Sunni theologian—who reviled a host of Islamic devotional practices, including grave visitation, the accumulation of relics, and worship at shrines—also turns to lambasting a group of Damascene Muslims who were said to have placed pictures of Muhammad and other saints in their mosques.[61] In Ibn Taymiyya's estimation, this practice derived from those of the "people of the book" (*ahl al-kitab*), particularly the Christian display of images and icons within churches. This specific account proves fascinating in two ways: it suggests, first, that some Muslims living in medieval Damascus may have placed images of Muhammad within mosques and other religious structures and, second, that Islamic representations of Muhammad in themselves were in some cases inspired by Christian religious paintings of Moses, Jesus, and other Abrahamic prophets.[62] Both of these possibilities are suggested by later Islamic depictions of the Prophet, which still today can be found within Iranian shrines.

Moving forward along the same vein, both the early Hadith compiler al-Tabarani (d. 971 CE) and medieval exegete Ibn Kathir (d. 1371 CE) relay a story about a Meccan man who traveled to Syria before Muhammad's emigration (*hijra*) to Medina in 622 CE. While in Syria, the Meccan met "people of the book"—that is, a group of Jews and/or Christians—who invited him into buildings where pictures of the prophets were preserved.[63] These included one of Muhammad, the last Messenger "after whom exists no other prophet" (*la nabi ba'dahu*).[64] This textual anecdote implies that Nestorian or Syriac Christians had in their possession an icon of Muhammad—and that they therefore recognized him as the seal of prophets. Just as importantly, the narrative shares features with a well-known story about the monk Bahira, who lived in Syria and recognized Muhammad's prophethood well before the beginnings of qur'anic revelations. Both of these Syrian recognition tales rhetorically depict members of the Jewish or Christian communities contemporary to Muhammad as proto- or would-be Muslims, whose acceptance of the Islamic faith arose thanks to two key visual signs: a figural image of Muhammad or a mark of prophecy imprinted on his body.

Islamic textual stories about images of the Prophet that circulated in Constantinople, Egypt, Iran, and Levantine lands during Muhammad's lifetime raise a number of important issues. First, these tales must be considered apocryphal insomuch as they follow and innovate on the same trope: that Muhammad was foreseen and possibly worshipped by Byzantine, Coptic, and Syriac Christians, Jews, Zoroastrians, and even Buddhists as far away as China.[65] These foretelling and recognition stories—as they promote the embracing of Islam among members of other faith communities living in the greater Middle East—attest to Muhammad's prophetic pedigree and supreme standing as God's last messenger. Moreover, tales about icons of Muhammad also could relay potentially sectarian messages, should their authors wish to mention a statue or images of the Prophet's family or companions. In that case, an icon-based discourse on prophetic superiority also could foster or further entrench a Sunni or Shi'i worldview. Finally, the attitudes that Muslim authors display toward such textual (rather than material) images of Muhammad is unequivocally positive—as long as the representations are not

placed inside mosques, in emulation of Christian image-based traditions of worship. The affirmation of the value of these conceptual images
emerges in great part due to the perceived power of the representational
mode. In these particular scenarios, images of Muhammad help attest
to the faith and sway to conversion; provide a positive omen concerning
Islam's ascendancy; and, as talismanic items, protect against disaster.

Muslim writers crafted iconic descriptions of Muhammad as part of
their supercessionary discourses. Such images, albeit rhetorical, shared
features with visual representations made by artists living (especially)
in Persian and Turkish lands from the medieval period onward. Like
textual images of the Prophet, Islamic depictions show Muhammad
both in a naturalistic manner—that is, in physical form and with visible facial features—and via a number of metaphors, chief among them
light allegories.[66] In addition to veristic and analogical portraiture, some
artists and cultural entrepreneurs have made use of synecdochic expression while others abstract the prophetic corpus to something entirely
other—such as a cosmic circle, scripted name, or sandal print.

These representational strategies disclose a general arc of evolution
from about 1200 CE to today. In the broadest sense, depictions of the
Prophet developed from naturalism to abstraction—that is, from figural
presence to physical absence. Medieval Persian paintings of Muhammad, who is depicted embodied in the flesh and bearing visible facial
characteristics, prove a vital challenge to certain contemporary claims
(emerging from both Islamic and non-Islamic spheres) that no images
of the Prophet exist and that they are putatively banned in Islam—a
disjuncture in practice, law, and belief to which we will return. In light
of the extant visual evidence, however, one may hypothesize that this
general move toward abstraction in the pictorial arts of Islam may be
due, in part, to long-held feelings of unease concerning figural imagery,
which increased during the modern period as images became more
widely available in the public sphere via the reprographic arts and mass
media. On the other hand, the embrace of pictorial allegories and even
abstraction within depictions of the Prophet, especially during and after
the fifteenth century, also must be understood as linked to the growth of
Islamic forms of mysticism, in which a clear preference for metaphorical figures of speech (rather than literal expression) dominate textual
sources, particularly Sufi poetry.

Some key questions thus arise: regardless of theoretical modeling,
methodological approach, personal presumption, or religiopolitical ideology, what story does the pictorial evidence itself tell? In other words,
what conclusions can be deduced from the extant corpus of Islamic
visual materials representing the Prophet Muhammad? And what clues
do these nontextual sources offer us that we might better track and
understand the diversity of Muslim life, thought, and practice over the
centuries? Unsurprisingly, no single answer to these questions exists.

Rather, some general patterns emerge, and this book attempts to pinpoint and investigate them.[67]

The earliest extant paintings of Muhammad date to the thirteenth and fourteenth centuries. No doubt influenced by pre-Islamic discourses on sacred rulership, artists active in Persian lands depicted Muhammad as both prophet and king within the manuscripts they illustrated. At times, these medieval manuscript paintings of the Prophet are tied to—and hence illustrative of—an accompanying narrative, while at others they appear to function rather autonomously, both expanding and transcending their textual milieus of presentation. In the latter case, prophetic images fulfill an iconic function and therefore are only secondarily related to a text.[68]

In their role as visual—rather than textual—icons, these early images of Muhammad often depict him enthroned and surmounted by angels providing him divine protection, scripture, light, and scent. Occupying a high office and granting audience to his entourage, Muhammad is presented in the flesh, his facial features entirely visible to the paintings' viewers. In other words, his prophetic attributes—a golden aureole, a fluttering ribbon, even a vase of flowers—remain external to his physical form. Combining regal and sacred motifs, painters crafted images of Muhammad according to a Persian ethos of sovereignty overlaid with the prophetic paradigm to emphasize his supreme standing as a divinely appointed monarch who bears revelation, dispenses justice, and secures salvation for the righteous in the faith.

During the fourteenth and fifteenth centuries, early images of Muhammad as a physically embodied prophet-king began to give way to larger pictorial cycles, in which narrativity and visuality came together in creative ways. Within illustrated manuscripts of the medieval period, painters depict the Messenger of Islam embarked on a quintessentially heroic quest: he is preordained and foretold, purified and selected, called to adventure and apotheosis, and triumphant in belief and deed from the time of his birth until his death. These patterns in the pictorial expression of biography and history served to increase Muhammad's prophetic preeminence through patterns of mythmaking, which in turn endowed him with superhuman dimensions and abilities.

Within the figural arts, painters deployed tactics of augmentation by developing new iconographical devices, chief among them the flaming aureole. Optimizing the potential of gold pigment as a visual marker of divine selection, artists depicted Muhammad as a human being emanating a clear sign of his sacred origins. At times, his radiance encircles only his own head or body; at others, it encompasses family members (the *ahl al-bayt*) and progeny (the imams), who in Shi'i thought are believed to preexist as light silhouettes in the domain of God. Linked to the growth of mysticism and sectarianism, these prophetic light metaphors in the painterly arts no doubt reflected—and further enhanced—Sufi and Shi'i modes of expression in Persianate lands.

Dreams of the Prophet are pervasive in Sufi cultures and other devotional contexts. Within a dreamscape often described as a "realm of likenesses" (*'alam al-mithal*), mystics communicate with their spiritual masters, perform group prayers, come together in fraternal gatherings (*majalis*), engage in social conversation (*suhbat*), ascend toward knowledge of and unity in God, and witness Muhammad. In this intermediary world, images of the Prophet are said to hover and crystallize, to have form but not substance. Perceptible yet immaterial, Muhammad is conceived by those who cultivate vision not merely as a perception of the eye but rather a deeper apprehension of the heart and mind. This inner vision is engendered by the imaginative faculty (*khayal*), and from it emerge many mental pictures of the Prophet as the ultimate Sufi master, otherworldly guide, and apocalyptical intercessor.

During the fifteenth and sixteenth centuries, a number of manuscript paintings essentially functioned as spiritual imaginations of the prophetic being and corpus. Emanating from Naqshbandi, Mevlevi, and Safavid Sufi milieus, such paintings pay tribute to the importance of pictorial expression within larger spiritual practices. They also highlight the ways in which the figural arts could be leveraged to generate images of Muhammad for initiates who wished to bring a visual conception of their primordial master (*shaykh*) into their hearts through methods such as facing (*tawajjuh*), observing (*muraqaba*), and creating a bond (*rabita*) with the object of their affection. As meditative devices, representations of the Prophet often show him in the flesh as well as carrying the flickers of divine disclosure; they also depict him in contexts of companionship, surrounded by his followers and seated in a Sufi *majlis*, or flying through the heavens as if a fully fleshed yet radiant expression of his devotees' spiritual imaginations. In such mystical environs, manuscript paintings of Muhammad challenge their viewers to grasp—but ultimately transcend—the realm of the perceptible, much as the Sufi poetical lexicon elevates the figurative mode above all else.

During the sixteenth century, practices of mysticism grew in tandem with sectarianism. In 1501 CE, the first Safavid ruler, Shah Isma'il I (r. 1501–24 CE), declared Shi'ism the official religion of Iran. From that moment on, various strategies were developed to differentiate the Safavid polity from its Muslim imperial competitors, most especially the Ottoman dynasty to the west. One of the major rhetorical and visual tactics employed to promote the superiority of Shi'i Islam consisted in praising the Safavid monarchs as offspring of the imams, themselves descendants of 'Ali. Safavid rulers thereby connected themselves to Muhammad through a carefully crafted pedigree; they also pictured themselves as carrying his prophetic mandate into the world. Within Shi'i contexts, 'Ali was extolled as Muhammad's partner in sacred origins and worldly authority. Not infrequently, they were deemed to share a soul and spirit, and to be equal in status and rulership. Going one step further, at times 'Ali's strength and standing are even described as angelic and godlike, allowing this figurehead of Shi'i Islam to symbolically surpass Muhammad's prophetic station and powers.

Images of Muhammad made in Iran during the sixteenth century mark a decisive turning point in the history of prophetic representation. It was at this time, and not earlier, that painters began to apply a white veil to the Prophet's face, thereby concealing it. At the same time, they extended the flaming aureole to 'Ali as well as the imams, all of whom are depicted wearing the *taj-i Haydari* (Haydar's crown), the turban wrapped around a rod worn by members of the Safawiyya Sufi order. These three iconographic innovations—the flaming aureole, Shi'i headgear, and, above all, the facial veil—cannot be explained solely as the result of an Islamic urge to avoid figural representation. Rather, it appears that Safavid artists wished to visually transform Muhammad into a veiled, luminous, and secret mystery in order to convey his supreme ontological status. Not halting there, they extended this pictorial strategy of concealment to 'Ali, often challenging viewers to distinguish one from the other. Through such purposeful couplings and conflations, Safavid painters showed Muhammad not as unique and incomparable; to the contrary, he shares his regency with 'Ali, who is shown taking a leading role in battles, salvation, and the establishment of a new world order. In the process, Muhammad moves to the margins of manuscript paintings, at times even disappearing from scenes of his own life story.

The Prophet has long been essential to claims to rightful rule, and from the sixteenth century to today such claims have at times (but not always) employed sectarian rhetoric. While Safavid painters attempted to Shi'ify images of Muhammad by depicting his progeny as his equals, Ottoman artists and cultural actors created their own set of prophetic images and liturgies in praise of Muhammad and his *sunna*. In Ottoman lands, Sunni forms of mysticism yielded a range of Prophet-centered devotions that were as pictorial and material as they were emotional and physical. While illustrated manuscripts continued to be made well into the nineteenth century, a new range of prophetic images and products also emerged. Among them, Muhammad's contact relics and personal effects, as well as textual icons (*hilye*s) describing his physical and moral characteristics, proved most innovative and popular among a princely and subroyal class of patrons. This skirting of figuration certainly reveals a desire to avoid mimetic literalism and instead embrace metaphor, synecdoche, and abstraction within the visual arts of Islam from the early modern period onward.[69] Just as significantly, these types of images and objects enabled the cultivation of a more multisensory Muhammad, who could be approached, activated, and internalized by devotees via thought, emotion, vision, touch, and even smell.

Within Ottoman illustrated manuscripts, artists depicted the Prophet as a holy enigma behind a white facial veil ablaze with a golden aureole. By no means a new iconographical device, the veil occasionally is not shared with 'Ali, who in some painted scenes does not partake in the *nur Muhammad* or altogether disappears from view. For his part,

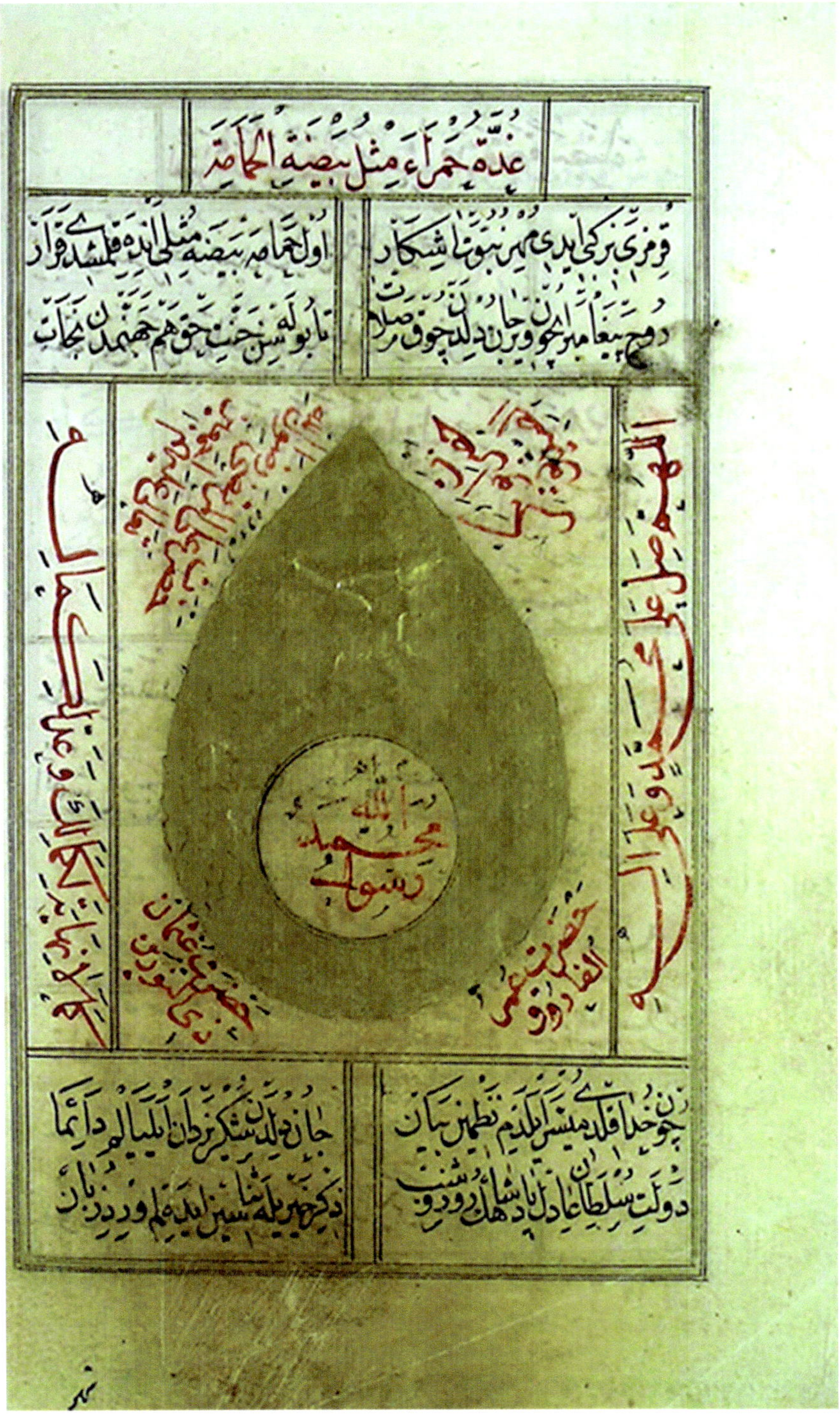

1.6. A depiction of Muhammad's "seal of prophecy" (*khatam al-nubuwwa*), the abraded gold pigment of which displays signs of devotional rubbing, compendium of devotional poems in Ottoman Turkish, Ottoman lands, eighteenth or nineteenth century CE. Süleymaniye Library, Istanbul, Nuruosmaniye 2872, folio 102v.

the Prophet's light may envelop his entire body or even supplant his head.

Muhammad's prophetic aura also multiplied through the material presence of his relics, both as artifactual objects and as depictions in various media, including paper, ceramics, textiles, and metalwork. Over the centuries, Muhammad's relics—chief among them his mantle, footprint, and sandal print—were amassed by the Ottoman sultans. Within Topkapı Palace in Istanbul, they served as centerpieces for devotions and festivities, during which they were rubbed, kissed, and washed in water—the liquid kept as potions believed to bear thaumaturgic properties. Still other prophetic marks, including depictions of Muhammad's seal of prophecy, were kissed and rubbed against the foreheads of devotees who wished to receive their blessings, among them protection from disasters and the curing of ills (fig. I.6).[70] Signs of wear on images of the Prophet's relics reveal the extent to which Muhammad—as depicted via nonfigural pictorial devices—could be palpated or even ingested as the ultimate good-luck charm.

From the seventeenth century onward, figural representations of the Prophet waned as the *hilye* came to dominate Ottoman religious art. *Hilyes* include a text describing Muhammad's physical traits and moral attributes, often laid out in a diagrammatic format. Some include seal and amuletic designs to magnify their perceived apotropaic powers, while others feature family trees or roses inscribed with the names of Muhammad's companions or the members of the House of Osman— both of which establish genealogies countering Safavid Shi'i discourses on prophethood and the imamate. Moreover, *hilyes* hanging on the walls of homes or carried in pockets suggest that Muhammad—as a prophetic force—could safeguard an individual's abode or escort him or her as the finest of chaperones. Within Ottoman devotional life, the Prophet thus acted as both refuge and vade mecum, as well as the supreme conveyor of blessing, love, cure, and protection.

Over the course of the nineteenth and twentieth centuries, a rich miscellany of images of Muhammad has thrived across the Islamic world. Some depictions show Muhammad in a veristic fashion while others cover his visage with a facial veil or an incandescent burst of gold. A number of images—almost exclusively made in Iran—draw on and adapt European prototypes, such as depictions of Jesus, Moses, and Muhammad clad in Oriental garb, including curled-toe sandals (fig. I.7). These images at times render the haloed Prophet in a prayerful pose as he strides, in an energetic frontal position, toward the pious viewer. In such images, he appears as if stepping from the sphere of the imagination into the sensual world of the living. Iranian artists surely understood the power of this type of composition and wished to guide their viewers' religious experience by incorporating qur'anic verses promising that belief in God, Muhammad, and holy scripture enables an improvement of one's condition, including the forgiveness of sins (Qur'an 47:1–3). Whether ecumenically treated or overlaid with sectarian motifs, such icons were—and, for some Muslim devotees, still are—intended to strengthen the viewer's faith. The cultivation of sight thus constitutes an important means of searching for, and ultimately securing, absolution and salvation.

Still other images produced in Arab lands, Turkey, the Indian subcontinent, Southeast Asia, China, Europe, and the United States tend to abstract the prophetic corpus into fire, silhouette, diagram, circle, name, or even animal proxy. In more recent years, new prophetic products have emerged thanks to techniques of mass reproduction and the

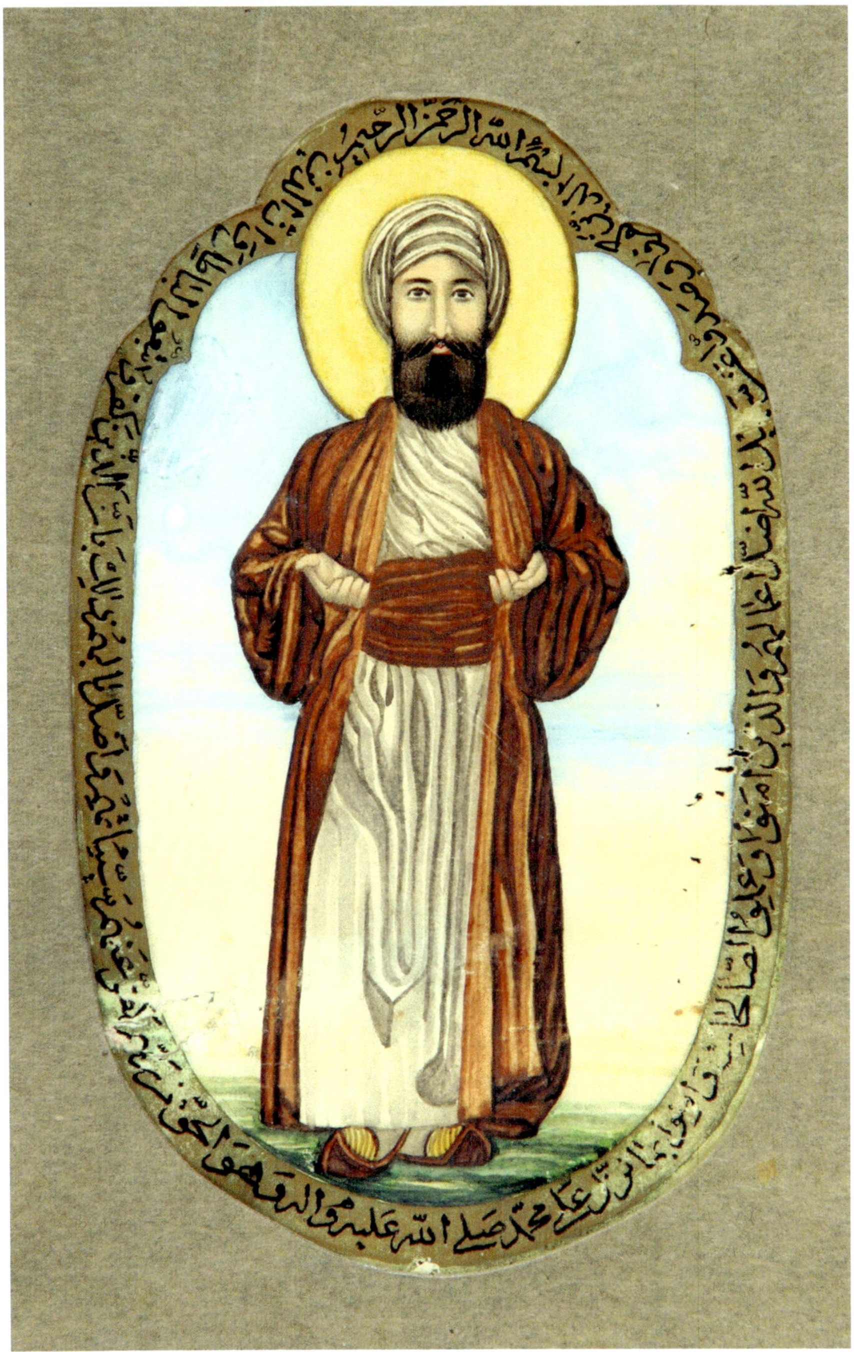

demands of consumer culture. In contemporary Turkey in particular, stores selling religious commodities thrive around Islamic shrines. The products sold there intersect with a long history of amuletic and talismanic arts, particularly the use of (otherwise pagan) protective blue beads that are believed to ward off the evil eye. Dangled from a car's rearview mirror or affixed to windows via a small suction cup, these Turkish protective beads are Islamized by the inscription of God's and Muhammad's names in Arabic script (fig. I.8).

Fulfilling similarly protective functions, laminated cards of Muhammad's relics and his *hilye*, along with pendants of his seal of prophecy and turban hats imprinted with his sandal print, cater to a growing

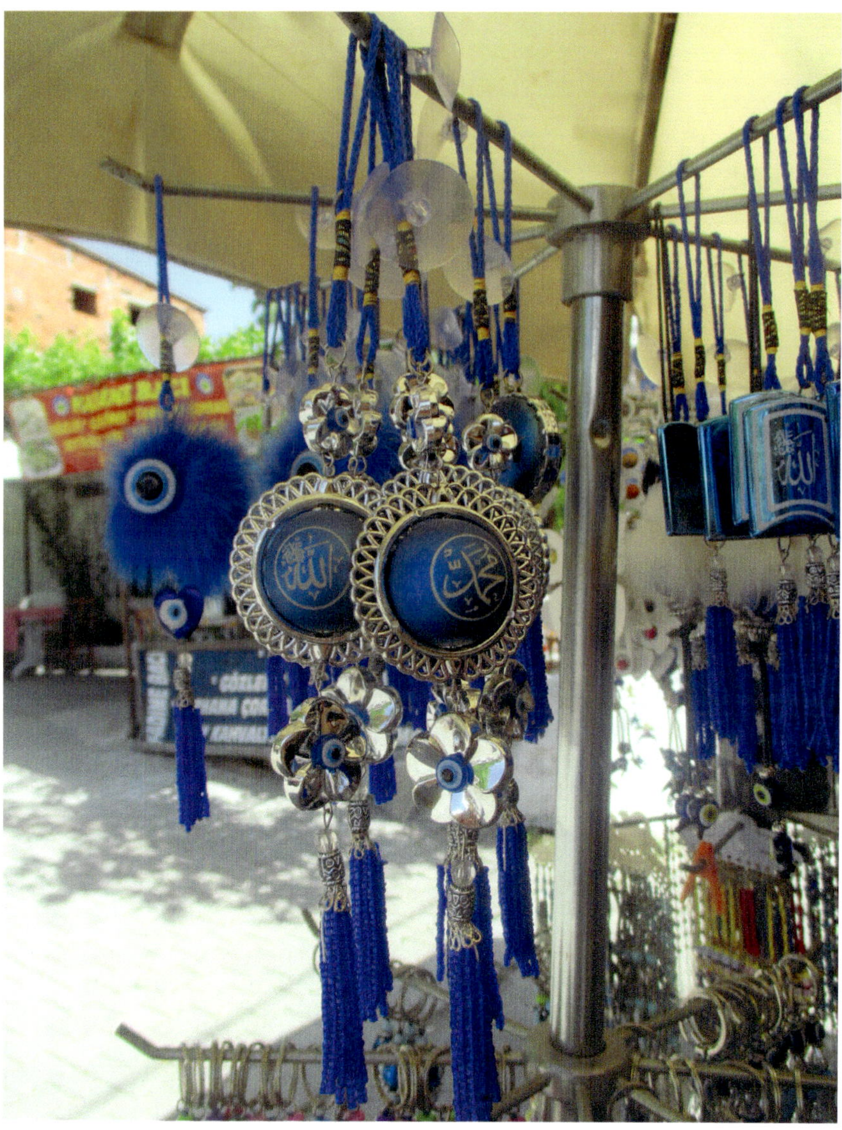

market for Islamic fashion, goods, and decor. While some consumers embrace a quietist form of Sunni mysticism, others purchase and wear prophetic products to construct a more emphatic "Jihadi look." In the latter case, individuals visually construct themselves as they self-avowedly carry forth Muhammad's *sunna* by waging war and seeking revenge on behalf of a sword-wielding, rather than peace-loving, Prophet.[71]

GOING BEYOND ISLAM'S
IMAGE PROBLEM

These allegorical and abstract modes of depicting the Prophet have come to dominate during the modern and contemporary periods. Additionally, the condemnation and suppression of figural representations has accelerated exponentially since the *Jyllands-Posten* Danish cartoon controversy of 2005–6 and the massacre of cartoonists at the Paris offices of the French satirical journal *Charlie Hebdo* by assassins claiming allegiance to ISIS.[72] Since these events, a dangerous dialectic of mutual provocation has emerged. In turn, this dialectic has created a "boomerang effect,"[73] in which a flurry of reactionary *fatwa*s against

THE PRAISEWORTHY ONE

visual representations of Muhammad are rejoined by equally flawed Euro-American discourses about Islamic iconoclasm. As Jytte Klausen rightfully observes: "Western media and cultural institutions have been colluding in enhancing the misrepresentation of Islam as a censorious faith and in contributing to a restriction on the opportunities available to both Muslim and non-Muslim readers and students to learn about the diversity of Islam."[74]

The narrow focus on Islam's so-called image problem has long been a driver of both scholarship in the field of art history and, particularly over the past two decades, political and religious ideology. Within contemporary international politics, satirical and representational imagery has been instrumentalized as never before. In such visually articulated conflicts, European and American cartoons of the Prophet Muhammad have served to strengthen a range of polemical stands as well as to sharpen otherwise blurred lines of conflict. For many Muslim faithful, however, such satirical images are puerile, lacking in creative and intellectual skill, and therefore best ignored; for others, such images clearly intend to agitate, affront, and disrespect; for still others, they qualify as hate speech and hence should be deemed illegal or blasphemous.

For their part, actors who, for one reason or another, wish to level criticism against Islam have found it expedient to strike against what is largely perceived as a medieval prohibition against the figurative arts, particularly images of Muhammad. Without a doubt, the discourse on Islamic iconoclasm has benefitted both Islamists and their secular opponents in their efforts to craft differential identities.[75] As Finbarr Barry Flood points out, both parties prove themselves to be two sides of the same coin insomuch as "the Danish cartoons (and those that they inspired) suggest themselves as correlates to the hammers of iconoclasts, swinging at the fracture lines of taboo and its objects in order to assert universalizing discourses about imaging as a sign of the modern."[76]

In this volatile mix, historical Islamic images of Muhammad time and again have been the proverbial lamb to slaughter. Boards at elite university presses have censored their illustration in academic studies due to security and financial concerns while news channels have chosen not to show satirical cartoons or Islamic images—as if these are one and the same thing—in order not to "offend Muslim sensitivities."[77] Moreover, mainstream newspapers and academic journals have taken up the issue of prophetic imagery in Islamic traditions but have decided to include "trigger warnings" cautioning readers that as they scroll down a web page or PDF file, their eyes will chance on one or several historical and/or contemporary Islamic illustrations of Muhammad.[78] Last but not least, after the *Charlie Hebdo* shooting in January 2015, one art museum in London—whose primary mission includes preserving historical works of art and presenting them to the public—refused to discuss with *The Guardian* an Islamic poster depicting Muhammad held within its collections, whose online entry and image are no longer to be found today.[79]

Across all of these dissimulative strategies—which encompass extraction and censorship, anxieties about security and sensitivity, and the inclusion of warning labels reminiscent of R-rated movies—one cannot help but detect a coded language born largely out of fear of revenge (physical, political, or pecuniary) exacted by members of local Muslim communities or the Islamic world at large. Here, the "boomerang" turns around only to sweep up and destroy art itself. Just as detrimentally, such jittery responses further solidify the notion that images do not exist or are banned in Islam—itself a premise that many Muslims worldwide recognize as overly simplistic, even erroneous. The discourse on Islamic iconoclasm thus proves to be, to a certain degree, a pernicious product of widely held misgivings that have entered the public arena during moments of horrific violence in the past two decades.

This said, anxieties about figural imagery have endured in Islamic religious and cultural spheres since the seventh century. Just as in Christian Byzantine and Protestant cultures, Islamic concerns about image making—particularly the artist's mimicking of divine creation, along with the viewer's potential worship of a manmade image or object—have come and gone. Often, diametrically opposed beliefs have coexisted in the same time and place. For example, from the early to medieval periods, some Muslim writers and jurists lambasted figural imagery, while others were either comfortable with or supportive of representations of living beings, including images of animals and humans carved into seals and chess pieces. Among them, pseudo-Jahiz (c. 900 CE) encouraged his readers to gaze on images of prophets and holy sites included in illustrated books (*kutub musawwara*) in order to open their hearts to spiritual subtleties (*riqqa*).[80] Such divergent opinions continued during the early modern period. For instance, one painter might be castigated for playing God in his shaping of human creatures, while another reminded that "portraiture (*tasvir*) is not without justification and therefore the portraitist's conscience need not be pricked by the thorn of despair."[81] In one seventeenth-century case recorded in writing, a self-avowedly pious man attempted to excise the eyes and cut the throats of painted beauties, thereby destroying an illustrated manuscript's integrity and value, only to be beaten, run out of town, and shouted down as an uncultured "philistine" and "monkey" by an angry mob.[82] Quite evidently, the fear and love of images—and thus their destruction and preservation—seem closely intertwined rather than mutually exclusive.

In the last century, messages about pictorial images of Muhammad have received equally mixed responses: while a 1926 *fatwa* issued in Cairo by al-Azhar banned a Turkish film about Muhammad, in the year 2000 a Sunni scholar considered a sculptural depiction of Muhammad in the US Supreme Court building not only permissible but laudable.[83] Moreover, after the Danish cartoon controversy of 2005–6, a Saudi *fatwa* stated, "Islam considers images of prophets disrespectful and caricatures of them blasphemous."[84] (It is important to note here

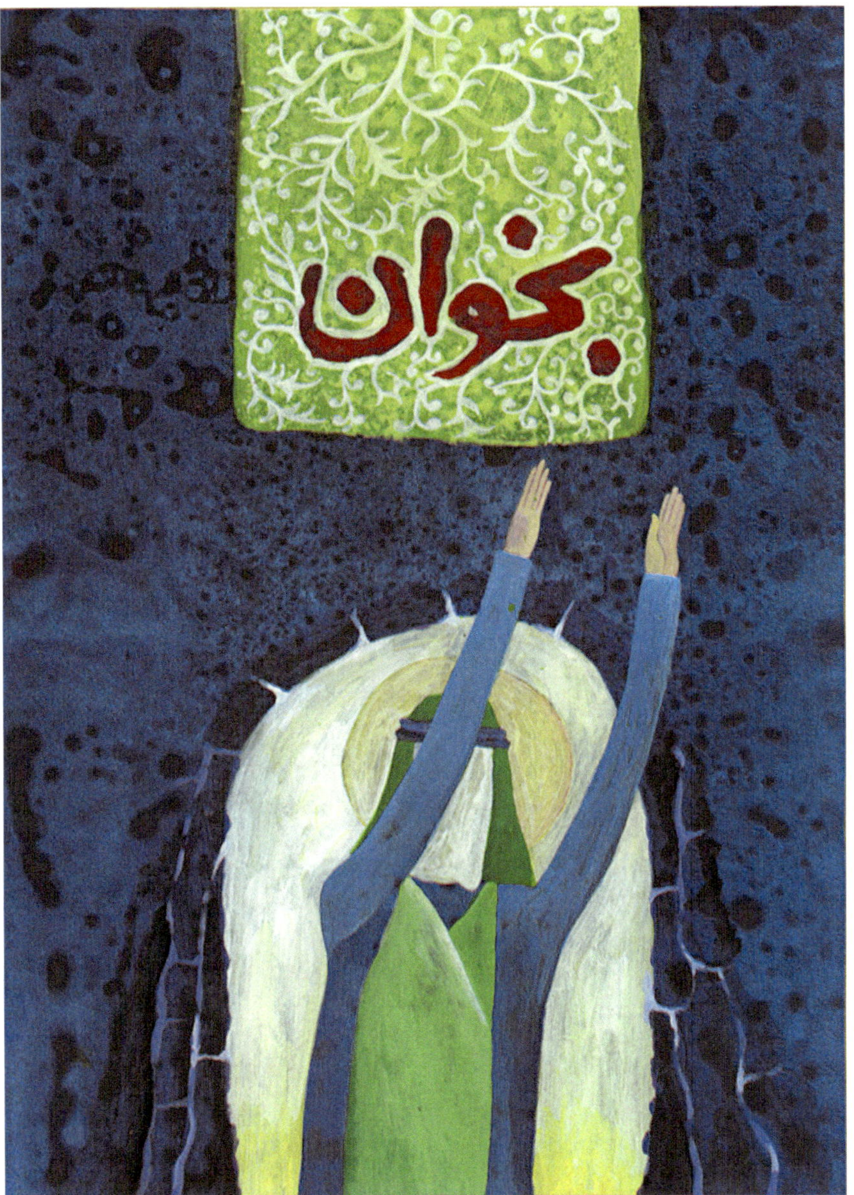

I.9. The Prophet, wearing a white facial veil and raising his arms in prayer, begins to receive qur'anic revelations with the command, "Read [in the Name of the Lord]," children's book on the life of Muhammad, Tehran, Iran, 2006 CE. Book in author's collection, p. 43.

the Saudi-Salafi position in 2006: images of the Prophet Muhammad are not forbidden wholesale; to the contrary, it is satirical imagery that must be deemed "disrespectful" and hence sacrilegious.) For its part, after the Danish cartoon controversy, Iran declared 2006 the Year of the Noble Prophet: thereafter, a large mural of Muhammad was painted on a public building,[85] a dozen illustrated children's books were published (fig. I.9), and a high-budget movie about the Prophet (directed by Majid Majidi) began production; on its release, in 2015, Sunni clerics from Egypt, India, and Saudi Arabia responded by issuing condemnations and *fatwa*s against it.[86] Within Shi'i spheres, approaches to depictions of Muhammad and other prophets seem to be more flexible today: for example, Ayatollah al-Sistani, the supreme Shi'i legal authority in Iraq, opines that representations of the Prophet are acceptable as long as they show due deference (*ta'zim*) and respect (*tabjil*).[87]

Such differing positions vis-à-vis the permissibility of representing Muhammad do not emerge due to a fear or aversion of the image qua image.[88] Much more critically, they adjudicate its modality, determine its tenor, and foresee its effects, with an eye toward ensuring its suppression or regulating its diffusion. Additionally, these divergent positions on prophetic images increasingly are embedded within a larger geopolitical fight between Saudi Arabia and Iran—and therefore have come to be interpreted along an axis that pits an Arab-Sunni versus an Iranian-Shi'i worldview. While such an ethnosectarian divide is oversimplified, it nevertheless carries some validity. Indeed, historically, images of the Prophet Muhammad have thrived mostly outside Arab lands, especially in the Turco-Persian world. In such geographical spheres, however, artists and devotees also have belonged to the Sunni faith community. Not infrequently, Sunni patrons and consumers have requested or purchased devotional imagery of Muhammad precisely to strengthen his prophetic legacy via the power of the visual mode. As a result, the sectarian divide—and, along with it, an ostensible Shi'i proclivity for images—can only go so far in explaining a much more complex, multifaceted landscape of religious belief, cultural practices, and visual products when it comes to depicting the Prophet of Islam.[89]

Grappling with such issues over the past century, scholars working in the fields of Islamic studies and art history have tackled Islam's supposed image problem—or, as some have termed it, its tendency toward iconoclasm and the "prohibition of images" (*Bilderverbot*). Fruitful discussions have emerged, although some academic analyses unfortunately have been inflected by an undergirding presumption that Islamic cultures either cautiously avoid images or actively seek to destroy them. This emphasis on Islamic aniconism or iconoclasm in turn has influenced terminology, methodology, and modes of argumentation. Just as critically, it also tends to cherry-pick data and skew outcomes. To give one particularly egregious example, in 1988 scholar Terry Allen argued that religious and narrative figural imagery does not exist in Islam. In order to prove his point, he explored images solely present on secular, portable objects that do not illustrate a text. He thus concluded that Islamic art is an art without narrative, and that it gives preeminence to emblematized cycles, inscriptions, geometry, and the arabesque. In his estimation, then, Islamic art does not have the "intellectual power and scope of antique art."[90] In order to reach this rather sanctimonious finding, Allen used a methodology that purposefully omits a discussion of Turco-Persian illustrated manuscripts and Islamic devotional arts. This glaring omission reveals the extent to which historical data can be selectively marshaled or ignored in order to promote the (foregone) conclusion that Islamic figural art comprises solely a nonreligious, nonnarrative tradition. It also showcases a long-standing disinterest in Muslim devotional imagery, a field of creative expression that only recently has drawn the attention of scholars of Islamic art.

Other scholars have made more judicious use of the scientific method, pursuing a deductive rather than inductive approach to extant pictorial material. Contra Terry Allen, Oleg Grabar sought to explore a "Muslim ethos"[91] toward images, arguing that the perceived divide is not religious/secular but public/private.[92] Grabar noted that, despite a number of image-averse statements in the Qur'an and Hadith,[93] there do not exist any internal edicts prohibiting or rejecting figural representations in Islamic traditions (unlike Catholicism, Islam has had no centralized authority, and therefore legal opinions are neither universal nor enforceable). At most, Grabar posited, one may detect a "prevailing mood" or an "expression of taste" within the visual arts.[94] While at times this mood or taste may shy away from the representational mode, at others aesthetic pleasure—not to mention devotional impulse—trumps philosophical and theological anxieties about figural likenesses.[95] Grabar concluded that many pictorial representations, including those of the Prophet Muhammad, have been made since 1300 CE, and he challenged his readers by posing a most productive question: "Under these circumstances, is it really correct to talk of an Islamic iconoclasm or even an avoidance of representations of living things?"[96]

Grabar's query calls attention to our shortcomings, blind spots, and presuppositions in exploring Islam's rich, varied, and at times contradictory relationship to figuration and the representational arts. To no small degree, our epistemological expectations about Islamic art have proven to be barriers in and of themselves.[97] Such obstacles nonetheless have been transcended in more recent years by scholars who have turned their attention to the depictive arts, especially portraiture. Among them, Priscilla Soucek has explored the intersections among figural representation, the science of physiognomy, and Neoplatonic texts exploring an individual's inner reality and beauty.[98] For his part, David Roxburgh has highlighted the divergent concepts of the portrait in Islamic lands; at times, such works function as the impressions of a presence, and at others they cycle back into abstraction.[99] Still other scholars, including Michael Barry, have tackled medieval portraiture through a Sufi lens, treating it as a rhetorical riddle and visual enigma.[100] Two recent book-length studies also have provided important insights into Islamic religious thought and practice, visual perception, and image making: namely, Jamal Elias's *Aisha's Cushion* (2012) and Houari Touati's edited volume of essays that explore human figuration and portraiture in Islamic art (2015).[101] Last but not least, a number of future studies—among them Finbarr Barry Flood's forthcoming book and a volume of essays on figural representation—promise to break new ground as well.[102]

Building on recent scholarship, this study of textual and visual images of the Prophet in Islamic traditions aims to define and explore Islamic religious figural art—a topic that remains to be given the attention it deserves. It draws on literature in Islamic studies and the history of art, among a number of cognate fields in the humanities. While it explores the various strategies that Muslim painters and artists eventually developed in order to depict Muhammad in nonfigural ways, it does not explain such abstracting tendencies simply as the outcome of Islam's so-called image problem or the result of a clearly articulated, timeless ban on representing the Prophet.

When it has come to representing the Prophet of Islam, anxiety and prohibition have not constituted the driving force behind Muslim artists' production and creativity. To narrowly focus on the question of Islamic aniconism or iconoclasm therefore detracts from the critical task of asking what impelled artists to depict Muhammad, which iconographic devices they adopted and why, and how Muslim viewers and devotees have responded to and used such images within their daily lives.

It is these key questions that propel this book as it sets out to understand an array of expressive traditions that, taken as a whole, comprise a small sliver of the rich and varied cultural and artistic heritage of Islamic civilization. In the end, this study aims to demonstrate the ways in which images of the Prophet function as heuristic by which to better gauge Muslim life, thought, and practice from the medieval period to today. Over the centuries, Muhammad has been imagined and depicted as sacred king, epic hero, visionary mystic, point of sectarian contestation, devotional object, protective and talismanic force, and even collectible item. These many manifestations of the prophetic corpus and spirit pay tribute to the remarkably flexible ways in which Muhammad has been seen as a praiseworthy model in the eyes of his followers, whose desires and needs have fluctuated with the flow of time.

NOTES

1. On the name "Muhammad" as an honorary epithet rather than a proper name, see Reynolds, *The Qur'an and Its Biblical Subtext*, 198.

2. On the *asma' al-nabi*, see al-Suyuti, *al-Riyad al-Aniqa fi Sharh Asma' Khayr al-Khaliqa*; al-Maliji, *Asma' al-Nabi fi'l-Qur'an wa'l-Sunna*; Siddiqi, *Ninety-Nine Names of Prophet Muhammad*; and Schimmel, *And Muhammad Is His Messenger*, 105–22.

3. Qur'an 3:144; 33:40; 47:2; and 48:29; Reynolds, *The Qur'an and Its Biblical Subtext*, 187; and Khalidi, *Images of Muhammad*, 24.

4. Khalidi, *Images of Muhammad*, 24.

5. On Muhammad's names in the Qur'an, see Watt, *Bell's Introduction to the Qur'an*, 25–29; and Khalidi, *Images of Muhammad*, 25.

6. On Jesus's foretelling of Muhammad as the Paraclete (intercessor, advocate, helper, and "celebrated one") in Qur'an 61:6, see, inter alia, Rubin, *The Eye of the Beholder*, 22–23; Reynolds, *The Qur'an and Its Biblical Subtext*, 188; Bevan Jones, "The Paraclete or Muhammad"; McAuliffe, "The Prediction and Prefiguration of Muhammad"; Guthrie and Bishop, "The Paraclete"; Watt, "His Name Is Ahmad"; al-Suyuti, *al-Riyad al-Aniqa fi Sharh Asma' Khayr al-Khaliqa*, 55; and al-Maliji, *Asma' al-Nabi fi'l-Qur'an wa'l-Sunna*, 11.

7. On the *asma' al-husna*, see al-Ghazzali, *The Ninety-Nine Beautiful Names of God*.

8. On Muhammad's metahistorical presence, see in particular Nagel, *Allahs Liebling*.

9. For this particular approach, see Zeitlin, *The Historical Muhammad*; Ibn Warraq, *The Quest for the Historical Muhammad*; Peters, "The Quest of the Historical Muhammad"; and Jeffery, "The Quest of the Historical Muhammad."

10. This method of analyzing the various receptions of the Prophet Muhammad in Islamic textual and devotional traditions is espoused in particular by Rubin in *The Eye of the Beholder* and Schimmel in *And Muhammad Is His Messenger*.

11. For a brief overview of the subject, see Hussain, "Images of Muhammad in Literature, Art, and Music."

12. The term "picturations" (*tasawwurat*) is borrowed from the medieval Muslim theologian and philosopher Fakhr al-Din al-Razi (d. 1209 CE). For a discussion of al-Razi's theory of sacred picturations, see Abrahamov, "Fakhr al-Din al-Razi on the Knowability of God's Essence and Attributes."

13. Hagen, "The Imagined and the Historical Muhammad."

14. On Muhammad as an exemplar and foil, see Waldman, *Prophecy and Power*, 79–135.

15. Schimmel, *And Muhammad Is His Messenger*, 26.

16. Gleave, "Muhammad and Personal Piety," 121.

17. On the Hadiths' narrative (or fictional) features and their various uses, see in particular Günther, "Fictional Narration and Imagination within an Authoritative Framework"; and Goldziher, "The Hadith as a Means of Edification and Entertainment."

18. Goldziher, "The Hadith as a Means of Edification and Entertainment," 145.

19. The phrase "memories of Muhammad" is borrowed from Safi, *Memories of Muhammad*.

20. On the "Prophet-image" as an expressive or experiential model, see Waugh, "The Popular Muhammad," 46.

21. Schimmel, *And Muhammad Is His Messenger*, 25.

22. Al-Yahsubi, *Kitab al-Shifa bi-Ta'rif Huquq al-Mustafa*; and al-Yahsubi, *Muhammad, Messenger of Allah*.

23. On Muhammad's miracles, see Schimmel, *And Muhammad Is His Messenger*, 67–80; Morabia, "Surnaturel prodiges prophétiques et incubation dans la ville de l'envoyé d'Allâh"; and Rubin, "Muhammad's Message in Mecca." On magical realism, see Williams, *Muhammad and the Supernatural*, 3.

24. Al-Yahsubi, *Muhammad, Messenger of Allah*, 165; also see a slight variant in al-Tabari, *Muhammad in Mecca*, 63–64: "Every stone and tree he passed would say, 'Peace be upon you, Messenger of God.'"

25. Asani and Abdel-Malek, *Celebrating Muhammad*, 13.

26. On poetry in devotion of the Prophet, see most especially de Vos, *Eloge du Prophète*; Schimmel, *As through a Veil*, 171–211; Schimmel, *Mystical Dimensions of Islam*, 213–28; and Asani and Abdel-Malek, *Celebrating Muhammad*. For modern Egyptian popular narrative ballads, folk songs, and eulogies that recount the life of the Prophet by drawing on and expanding themes found in *sira* literature, see Cachia, *Popular Narrative Ballads of Modern Egypt*; Abdel-Malek, *Muhammad in the Modern Egyptian Popular Ballad*; and Waugh, *The Munshidin of Egypt*.

27. The poem's full title is "Glistening Stars in Praise of the Best of Creatures" (*Al-Kawaqib al-Durriyya fi Madh Khayr al-Bariyya*). See Stetkevych, *The Mantle Odes*; and Jeffery, *A Reader on Islam*, 605.

28. On the *Burda* as a talisman, see Stetkevych, "From Text to Talisman."

29. Jeffery, *A Reader on Islam*, 610, line 41.

30. On the *nur Muhammad*, see Rubin, "Pre-existence and Light"; and Rubin, "More Light on Muhammad's Pre-existence," 294–95.

31. Nizami, *Makhzanol Asrar*, 106, line 249.

32. Nizami, *Makhzanol Asrar*, 104, line 214.

33. Darir, *Kitab-ı Siyer-i Nebi*, 1:35.

34. On the use of colored inks for the names of God and Muhammad in these types of prayer books, see Daub, *Formen und Funktionen des Layouts in arabischen Manuskripten anhand von Abschriften religiöser Texte*, 154–58.

35. Amir-Moezzi, *Le voyage initiatique en terre d'Islam*; Gruber and Colby, *The Prophet's Ascension*; Ranjabar, *Chand Mi'rajnama*; and Hanaway, "Some Accounts of the *Mi'raj* of the Prophet in Persian Literature," 558. On the mystic's self-annihilation in the Prophet Muhammad (*fana' fi'l-rasul*), see Hoffman, "Annihilation in the Messenger of God."

36. Waugh, "Following the Beloved," 64.

37. Sells, *Early Islamic Mysticism*, 242–50; and Nicholson, "An Early Arabic Version of the *Mi'raj* of Abu Yazid al-Bistami."

38. Morris, "The Spiritual Ascension: Ibn 'Arabi and the Mi'raj, Part I"; and Morris, "The Spiritual Ascension: Ibn 'Arabi and the Mi'raj, Part II."

39. Morris, "The Spiritual Ascension: Ibn 'Arabi and the Mi'raj: Part I," 71.

40. Morris, "The Spiritual Ascension: Ibn 'Arabi and the Mi'raj: Part I," 73.

41. Waugh, "Following the Beloved," 78.

42. Hoffman-Ladd, "Devotion to the Prophet and His Family in Egyptian Sufism," 620.

43. For a general discussion of the subject, see Padwick, *Muslim Devotions*.

44. On Mawlid festivals, see von Grunebaum, *Muhammadan Festivals*, 73–79; Kaptein, *Muhammad's Birth Festival*; Katz, *The Birth of the Prophet Muhammad*; Katz, "The Prophet Muhammad in Ritual"; Kleinmichel, *Die Geburt des Propheten Muhammad* (on Mawlid texts and festivities in Central Asia); Schimmel, *And Muhammad Is His Messenger*, 144–58; Gril, "La

commémoration de la naissance du Prophète"; and Chih, "La célébration de la naissance du Prophète (*al-Mawlid al-nabawî*)."

45. For a fifteenth-century *fatwa* in favor of Mawlid celebrations, see al-Suyuti, *Le mawlid*, and for a modern Egyptian one, see Schussman, "The Legitimacy and Nature of *Mawlid al-Nabi*." On the modern Wahhabi-Salafi opposition to Mawlid celebrations, and hence the "eclipse of the devotionalist model," see Katz, *The Birth of the Prophet Muhammad*, 169–207. In January 2015, ISIS banned Mawlid ceremonies in Iraq. See "ISIS Blocks Celebrations of Prophet Muhammad's Birthday," *Middle East Monitor*, January 3, 2015, https://www.middleeastmonitor.com/news/middle-east/16136-isis-blocks-celebrations-of-prophet-muhammads-birthday (accessed May 18, 2018).

46. Jeffery, *A Reader on Islam*, 611–12, especially line 71.

47. Zarcone, "*Mevlid Kandili*," 313; and D'Ohsson, *Tableau général de l'empire othoman*, 2:358–68.

48. Çelebi, *Mevlid-i şerif*; and Çağatay, "The Tradition of Mavlid Recitations in Islam, Particularly in Turkey."

49. Çelebi, *Mevlid-i şerif*, especially 34.

50. Zarcone, "*Mevlid Kandili*," 320.

51. Katz, *The Birth of the Prophet Muhammad*, 87–95.

52. On this "Muhammad cultus," see Waugh, "The Popular Muhammad," 215n3.

53. Thackston, *Album Prefaces and Other Documents on the History of Calligraphers and Painters*, 11; Roxburgh, *The Persian Album*, 274–76, 301–2; Roxburgh, *Prefacing the Image*, 170–74; Grabar and Natif, "The Story of the Portraits of the Prophet Muhammad," 20–22; Natif, "The Painter's Breath and Concepts of Idol Anxiety in Islamic Art," 44–45; and El-Cheikh, "Muhammad and Heraclius," 19.

54. The term "near convert" is borrowed from El-Cheikh, "Muhammad and Heraclius," 19. El-Cheikh also refers to Heraclius as an "Islamized legitimizing device" in these "chest of witnessing" narratives (21).

55. *Al-Maktaba al-Shamila*, viz. Ibn Kathir, *Sira*, 1:332 and viz. *Bidaya*, 6:72: *'ala na't wa'l-shakl al-ladhi kanu 'alayhi*.

56. Pancaroğlu, "Signs in the Horizons," 34, 37.

57. Pancaroğlu, "Signs in the Horizons," 34.

58. On the narrative of al-Muqawqis, see Grabar and Natif, "The Story of the Portraits of the Prophet Muhammad," 29.

59. *Al-Maktaba al-Shamila*, viz. Ibn Sam'un (d. 997 CE), *Amali Ibn Sam'un*, 1:71.

60. *Al-Maktaba al-Shamila*, viz. Ibn Taymiyya, *Minhaj*, ed. Salim, 7:120.

61. *Al-Maktaba al-Shamila*, viz. Ibn Taymiyya, *Iqtida'* (1369 AH), 1:318.

62. For a discussion of the diverging medieval legal opinions about the presence of figural representations (on robes, mats, and other visual materials) within mosques, see Touati, "Le régime des images figuratives dans la culture islamique médiévale," 5, 24, 27.

63. On a monastery in Busra containing these types of images, see Grabar and Natif, "The Story of the Portraits of the Prophet Muhammad," 22.

64. *Al-Maktaba al-Shamila*, viz. Ibn Kathir, *Tafsir* (1999), 3:487 (commentary on Qur'an 7:157); and al-Tabarani, *al-Mu'jam al-Awsat* (1983), 2:125.

65. For the textual description of an image depicting Muhammad on camelback owned by the Chinese, see Grabar and Natif, "The Story of the Portraits of the Prophet Muhammad," 23–24.

66. Other light devices functioning as stand-ins for Muhammad are found in Islamic architecture. For a discussion of a black disk in the Dome of the Rock, which may have functioned as a light and seal metaphor for Muhammad, see Flood, "Light in Stone," especially 357, in which Flood notes that this disk's "shape, its capacity to reflect light, and the star motif graven upon its surface were all intended to recall the physical manifestations of prophetic qualities."

67. For a preliminary investigation, see Boespflug, *Le Prophète de l'islam en images*.

68. Grabar, "Pictures or Commentaries," 104.

69. On the move from literal to spiritual depictions of the Prophet from the thirteenth to the seventeenth century, see Ali, "From the Literal to the Spiritual."

70. I wish to thank Emine Küçükbay for bringing this rubbed seal of prophecy to my attention.

71. Brockopp, "Muhammad the Peacemaker, Muhammad the Warrior," 39.

72. For a discussion of the *Charlie Hebdo* massacre and its relationship to images of Muhammad, see Gruber, "Images of the Prophet Muhammad."

73. Klausen, "Art History and the Contemporary Politics of Depicting Muhammad," 78.

74. Klausen, "Art History and the Contemporary Politics of Depicting Muhammad," 81.

75. Flood, "Inciting Modernity?," 62.

76. Flood, "Inciting Modernity?," 56.

77. Yale University Press extracted historical Islamic images from Jytte Klausen's *The Cartoons That Shook the World* (2009). For a further discussion, see chapter 6.

78. See the parenthetical caveats included in Gruber, "Prophetic Products," 260 (lower left corner); and John McManus, "Have Pictures of Muhammad Always Been Forbidden?," *BBC News*, January 15, 2015, http://www.bbc.com/news/magazine-30814555 (accessed May 18, 2018).

79. Emma Graham-Harrison, "V&A in Row over Self-Censorship after Muhammad Image Is Taken Down," *Guardian*, January 24, 2015, http://www.theguardian.com/world/2015/jan/24/victoria-and-albert-museum-muhammad-image-website (accessed May 18, 2018). Relatedly, Jytte Klausen notes that, after the Danish cartoon controversy and even more so today, "what to do with Islamic art is no longer a decision made by the curator alone. It is now a matter of international relations" (see her "Art History and the Contemporary Politics of Depicting Muhammad," 66).

80. Touati, "Le régime des images figuratives dans la culture islamique médiévale," 15.

81. See Dust Muhammad's preface to the album of calligraphies and paintings made for Bahram Mirza (1517–49 CE), brother of the ruler Safavid Shah Tahmasp (r. 1524–76 CE), transcribed and translated in Thackston, *Album Prefaces and Other Documents on the History of Calligraphers and Painters*, 12.

82. Dankoff, *Evliya Çelebi in Bitlis*, 294–95; and Flood, "Between Cult and Culture," 645.

83. For a *fatwa* in favor of the sculptural depiction of Muhammad in the US Supreme Court building, see al-Alwani, "Fatwa Concerning the United States Supreme Courtroom Frieze"; and for a scholarly study of the Supreme Court Muhammad, see Bjelajac, "Masonic Fraternalism and Muhammad among the Lawgivers in Adolph A. Weinman's Sculpture Frieze in the United States Supreme Court (1931–1935)."

84. For contemporary Iranian images of Muhammad, see Gruber, "Reclaiming the Prophet Muhammad in Iran," *Newsweek*, January 31, 2015, http://europe.newsweek.com/reclaiming-prophet-muhammad-iran-303526?rm=eu (republished and expanded in Gruber, "Images of the Prophet Muhammad," 40–45); and for Sunni clerical responses to Majidi's film, see "Imams Denounce Danish & Norwegian Newspapers in Cartoons Row," *Fatwa-Online*, January 28, 2006, http://www.fatwa-online.com/imams-denounce-danish-and-norwegian-newspapers-in-cartoons-row/ (accessed May 18, 2018).

85. For an in-depth discussion of the mural, see Gruber, "Images of Muhammad *In and Out of Modernity*."

86. "Sunni Clerics Call for a Ban on Iranian Prophet Muhammad Film," *Radio Free Europe*, July 29, 2016, http://www.rferl.org/content/sunni-scholars-call-for-ban-iranian-prophet-muhammad-film/27215186.html (accessed May 18, 2018).

87. Al-Sistani, "Question and Answer: Pictures," http://www.sistani.org/english/qa/01282/, http://www.sistani.org/arabic/qa/0384/ (accessed May 18, 2018).

88. For a discussion of the "Muslim aversion" to content rather than form in early Islamic coinage in particular, see King, "Islam, Iconoclasm, and the Declaration of Doctrine."

89. For a discussion of Sunni and Shi'i theological positions toward figural images, see Paret, "Das islamische Bilderverbot und die Schia"; Arnold, *Painting in Islam*, 3–13; Naef, *Y a-t-il une "question de l'image" en Islam?*, 13–32; and Hodgson, "Islâm and Image."

90. Allen, "Aniconism and Figural Representation in Islamic Art," 36.

91. Grabar, "Islam and Iconoclasm," 52.

92. Grabar, "Islamic Art: Art of a Culture or Art of a Faith?," 4.

93. For a compilation of statements about images in the Qur'an and Hadith, see in particular van Reenen, "The *Bilderverbot*, A New Survey"; 'Isa, *Painting in Islam*, an expanded study of his earlier article "Muslims and Taswir"; and Ghabin, "The Quranic Verses as a Source for Legitimacy or Illegitimacy of the Arts in Islam." Both 'Isa and Ghabin conclude that the Qur'an does not prohibit the figurative arts. Instead, the Qur'an and Hadith focus more strictly on eradicating pre-Islamic paganism and idolatry.

94. Grabar, "Islam and Iconoclasm," 45.

95. Rogers, "Approval and Disapproval of Images in Islam," 23.

96. Grabar, "Islam and Iconoclasm," 49.

97. As Oleg Grabar noted in the inaugural volume of the journal *Muqarnas* (1983), iconoclasm and ornament have tended to dominate scholarship in Islamic art; see Grabar, "Reflections on the Study of Islamic Art," 4.

98. Soucek, "The Theory and Practice of Portraiture in the Persian Tradition."

99. Roxburgh, "Concepts of the Portrait in the Islamic Lands, c. 1300–1600," 134.

100. Barry, *Figurative Art in Medieval Islam and the Riddle of Bihzâd of Herât*.

101. Elias, *Aisha's Cushion*; and Touati, *De la figuration humaine au portrait dans l'art islamique*.

102. Flood, *Image and Islam*; and Gruber, *The Image Debate*.

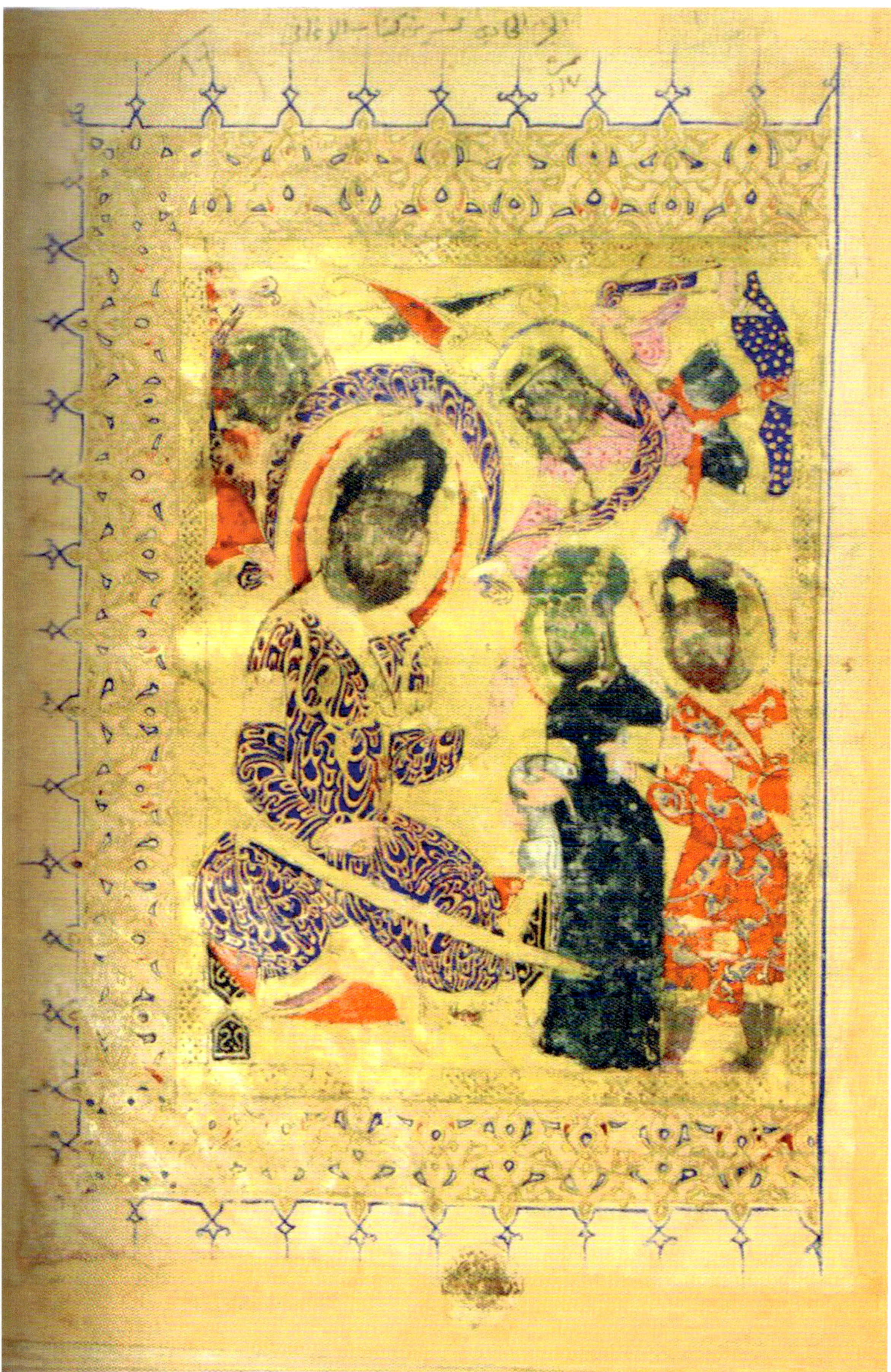

PAINTINGS OF THE ENTHRONED PROPHET-KING

Over the centuries, Muhammad-centered texts helped elaborate creative and powerful images of the Prophet. In the written record, Muhammad is described as radiating the proofs of prophecy, and in festivals, songs, and poems, he remains a touchstone for pious practice. During the medieval period, pictorial images of the Prophet emerged to complement an already mature and diverse corpus of texts. The earliest representations of Muhammad were included within manuscripts, uniting the experience of viewing with the habit of reading—such paintings echo the themes of the related texts while expanding the latter's parameters to convey a number of other messages. Thus artists, like writers, brought their own imaginative tools and tactics to the task of depicting the Prophet's sacred origins in the heavens and promoting his unequaled status as regnant on earth.

Without a doubt, images of Muhammad played a significant role in the construction of identity for members of the ruling political elite and participants in a variety of faith communities. Many paintings of Muhammad were produced after 1200 CE, and especially between 1300 and 1600 CE, a time of significant political and religious transition across the Islamic world. During this period, a number of powerful Turco-Persian dynasties emerged, claiming a sacred mandate to imperial rule that stemmed from their adherence to and support of the Islamic faith. In their symbolic formulations of rightful rulership, royal patrons and artists were clearly inspired by the model of the Prophet, who was portrayed in both texts and images as a divinely anointed monarch and an archetypical ruler worthy of emulation.

It is widely believed that Muhammad's prophetic rank and proximity to God endowed him with superhuman abilities, including the capacity to receive revelation, to perform miracles, to ascend to the heavens, and to speak with God directly, without intermediary. For these reasons, Muhammad also was imagined through a variety of symbolic abstractions—in particular, light analogies—that aimed to promote his preexistential nature as well as his ability to spread enlightenment to humankind through his unparalleled access to the divine. Through such metaphors, Muhammad is pictured as the ultimate source of spiritual and temporal authority. In faith and politics, he served as a point of reference within discourses of legitimacy and supremacy, and within more mystical milieus he was envisaged as an ideal conduit to God. These many conceptual images of Muhammad also display a distinctive visual shift during the medieval period, as painters and patrons turned to the expressive power of the pictorial mode to craft and communicate an image of a prophetic past according to a vision of the present.

Indeed, God and the angels send blessings upon the Prophet.

Qur'an 33:56

FACING, 1.1. An enthroned ruler (Badr al-Din Lu'lu' or the Prophet Muhammad) in audience, Abu'l-Faraj al-Isfahani, *Kitab al-Aghani* (Book of Songs), frontispiece to the eleventh volume, probably Mosul, 614 AH/1217–18 CE. Dar al-Kutub, Cairo, Adab 579, folio 2r.

Although a few paintings of Muhammad dating to the first half of the thirteenth century are extant, the production of his image(s) began in earnest around 1300 CE—that is, after the Mongol conquests of Eurasia and the sacking of the 'Abbasid library in Baghdad in 1258 CE. While it is impossible to know which (if any) depictions of the Prophet might have been included in the manuscript holdings of the famous library, illustrated books containing images of the prophets are mentioned by Muslim authors around 900 CE.[1] In addition, extant paintings of Muhammad appear by 1200 CE in illustrated manuscripts commissioned by the political elites who ruled immediately prior to and after the Mongol invasions. Having settled in Arab, Persian, and Turkic lands and largely embraced the Islamic faith, cultured patrons of the medieval period were some of the greatest sponsors of book arts, through which the biography of the Prophet and early Islamic history could be taught and passed down through generations of believers.

Manuscript paintings of Muhammad, especially those produced in Persian and Turkish spheres, were not intended merely as visual aids in the putatively objective narration of history. To the contrary, they lauded the Prophet as a repository of historic continuity, a means of salvation, and a pillar of traditionalism; such images were presented by and to ruling elites who sought to construct a corporate sense of superiority and legitimacy within new politicoreligious regimes. Thus, the earliest surviving images of the Prophet depict him according to visual models that essentially promote temporal authority and sacral rulership. Such paintings preserve and transform older conventions related to cosmic kingship, particularly iconographic patterns of divine sovereignty as found in Persian visual arts both before and after the advent of Islam.[2] Chief among these models is the recurring image of the enthroned monarch, appointed by God to rule on earth.

The earliest surviving paintings of the Prophet depict Muhammad as the prototypical ruler of the age, whose regal traits and posture could function as counterpoints to those of contemporary Muslim monarchs. A quintessential example of excellence and precedence,[3] the Prophet embodied a historic past in the service of the present. Throughout the centuries, dynastic founders and rulers symbolically recalled the exemplary order and justice that are said to have reigned under Muhammad's leadership:[4] while in Medina (622–32 CE), the Prophet established the first Islamic polity, an ideal community that later Persian sources describe through increasingly kingly language. For example, some texts refer to the Prophet as a "king" (*padishah*) and to his house-mosque in Medina as his "court" (*dargah*). Much like paintings produced after 1200 CE, these details reveal a shift toward courtly representations in which "prophetic simplicity has been somewhat eroded."[5] During the medieval period, a clear preference for regal symbols and patterns emerged, as artists combined religious with princely motifs and crafted innovative visual presentations of the Prophet's kingly prerogative and prestige.

　　THE PRAISEWORTHY ONE

To a large extent, medieval depictions of the Prophet as a divinely ordained monarch are invented traditions. Although novel in their emergence and motifs, they imply unbroken continuity with a remote, paradigmatic Islamic past, evoking the sanction of a prophetic precedent and refracting it via contemporary models and concerns. During this period of rapid political and societal change across the Islamic world, emergent ruling elites deployed a range of tactics to foster social cohesion, legitimize their rule, and inculcate beliefs. In other words, they invented traditions through various stratagems,[6] including claiming their rightful inheritance of the Prophet's tradition, of his *sunna*, through both rhetorical and visual means. The earliest surviving images of Muhammad thus must be understood as responses to novel situations by cultural actors who "find that they can be traditional only by being radical"[7] in their chosen strategies. In the medieval period, perhaps the most innovative—or radical—stratagems are Islamic paintings showing Muhammad as quintessential prophet and monarch.

The earliest surviving painting that possibly depicts the Prophet Muhammad is included in a twenty-volume illustrated copy of the *Kitab al-Aghani* (Book of Songs), an encyclopedia of poems composed in Persian by Abu'l-Faraj al-Isfahani (d. 965 CE). Dated 1215–19 CE, this monumental oeuvre took four years to complete; today, its six extant volumes are held in libraries in Cairo, Istanbul, and Copenhagen.[8] While the text is considered a landmark of Persian literature, the illustrated manuscripts were made in Mosul, located in Upper Mesopotamia (Jazira), before the Mongol conquest of 1258 CE.[9] The illustrated volumes of the *Kitab al-Aghani* thus belong to a broader corpus of medieval Arab painting, which includes illustrated copies of the *Maqamat* (Sessions) of al-Hariri and the *Kalila and Dimna* animal fables written in both Arabic and Persian.

Although manuscript illustration emanated from Arab lands during the 'Abbasid period, many of the depicted themes and motifs reveal a clear reliance on antecedent Persian pictorial models, among them princely scenes. Serving as a frontispiece to the eleventh volume of the *Kitab al-Aghani*, a full-page painting clearly falls within this royal paradigm: it represents an enthroned ruler flanked by two flying angels as he receives two individuals standing in respectful approach (fig. 1.1).[10] Like other frontispieces for illustrated manuscripts dedicated to rulers, princes, and elite patrons, the scene cleverly combines the two interrelated themes of angelic investiture and royal audience. Although such motifs are conspicuously august and dignified, the specific identities of the depicted figures—especially the large-scale seated ruler—remain unclear. Identification is made all the more difficult because the figures were subsequently subjected to defacement.

Writing in 1947, Bishr Farès argued that the painting must be interpreted as representing the Prophet Muhammad, enthroned in majesty, receiving the Christian bishop and prefect of Najran.[11] This encounter is said to have occurred in 631 CE and is known in Islamic sources as the Mubahala (day of cursing), on which Muhammad engaged in a disputation about the divinity of Jesus with Christian delegates. Farès's reading of the painting's iconographic details is supported by a textual gloss on its verso that specifically mentions the Prophet meeting with the Christians of Najran. Additionally, the episode of the Mubahala enjoyed some currency in Islamic book arts, as suggested by its inclusion in subsequent illustrated histories produced between 1300 and 1700 CE in both Persian and Turkish cultural spheres (figs. 4.6, 4.7).[12]

Rejecting Farès's proposed identification, however, a number of scholars have argued that this particular frontispiece—like those ornamenting the initial pages of other surviving volumes of the *Kitab al-Aghani*—must represent the manuscript's patron, the atabeg (regent) of Mosul, Badr al-Din Lu'lu'.[13] After 1210 CE, Badr al-Din Lu'lu' was virtual ruler of Mosul; subsequently, from 1233 until his death in 1269 CE, he reigned as sultan in the Jazira area. Because he is represented in a similar manner and with a robe bearing *tiraz* (epigraphic) inscriptions exalting his name in other frontispieces (fig. 1.2), Stern, Rice, and Hillenbrand prefer identifying the scene as the enthroned atabeg holding audience. According to this reading, the frontispiece aims to commemorate the manuscript's patron and his high office in a fairly generic princely mode rather than to specifically laud the Prophet's successful disputation against the Christians of Najran.[14]

Arguments can be made in support of both interpretations. On the one hand, the painting may indeed relate to its textual gloss, depicting a seated Muhammad in conversation with the Christians of Najran. In such a case, the Prophet is distinguished from Badr al-Din Lu'lu' in two key ways: first, via a *tiraz* inscription that does not provide the regent's full name and might instead spell *Muhammad*, and, second, by the inclusion of a sword, one of the Prophet's key object attributes. Textual sources record that Muhammad had nine swords, among them the famed Dhu'l-Fiqar, which were either passed down to him by his father or taken as booty following his many battles. Along with other weapons and objects, the sword is thus an important symbol and relic of the Prophet Muhammad.[15] On the other hand, the scene may depict Badr al-Din Lu'lu', wearing the typically Zengid fur-trimmed hat (*sarbush*)[16] and seated alongside two members of his court administration. Seljuk rulers also had an umbrella (*chatr*) among their regalia, which may be evoked by the cloth held by angels over the head of the seated protagonist.[17] The painting thus closely matches the depictions of the atabeg that initiate other volumes of the *Kitab al-Aghani*, forming a coherent set of frontispieces that, taken together, serve to promote and commemorate the regent's claims to sovereignty according to courtly paradigms.

The possibility of a double reading is significant in itself, as this would be the first instance in which a manuscript painting possibly

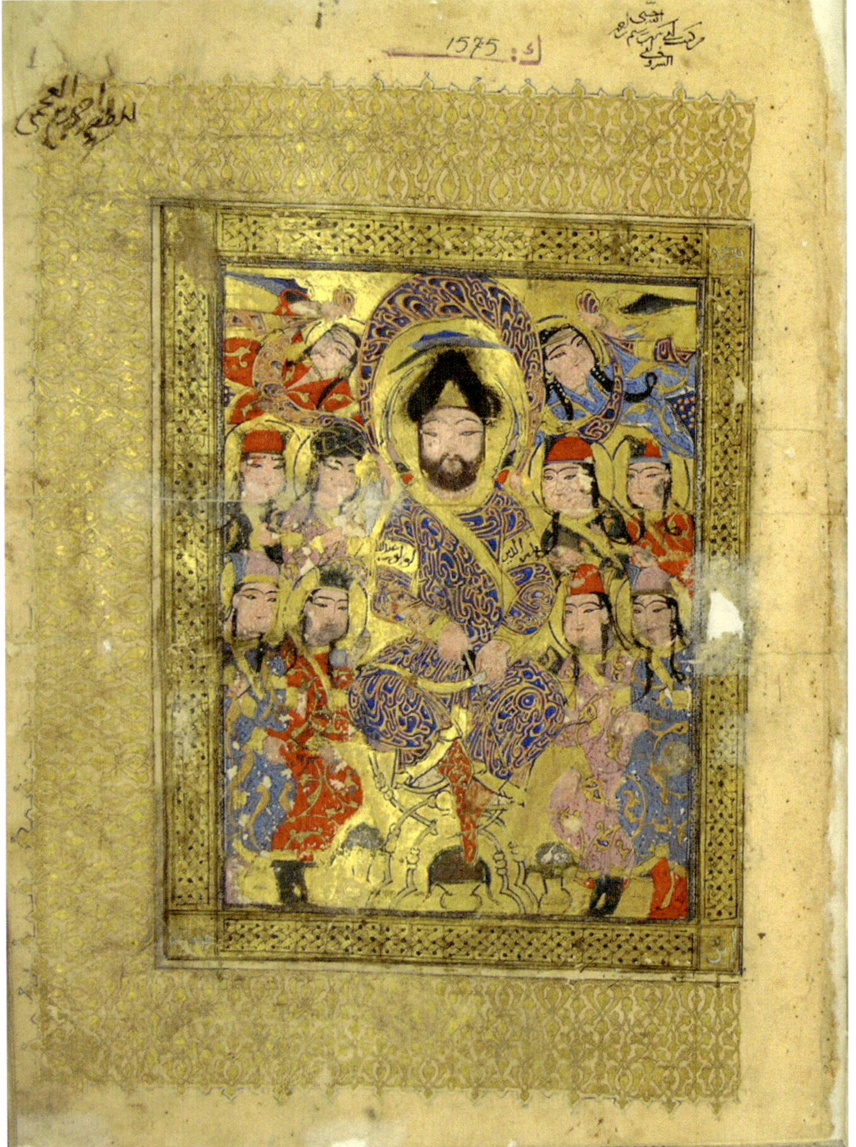

1.2. Badr al-Din Lu'lu' enthroned at court, Abu'l-Faraj al-Isfahani, *Kitab al-Aghani* (Book of Songs), frontispiece to the seventeenth volume, probably Mosul, 615 AH/1218–19 CE. Millet Yazma Eserler Kütüphanesi, Istanbul, Feyzullah Efendi 1566, folio 1r. Photograph courtesy of Scott Redford.

depicting Muhammad displays uncanny similarities to the representation of a contemporary ruler. Painterly parallels and iconographic correspondences between depictions of the Prophet and those of a regnant king are recurrent from the end of the thirteenth century onward, as is most clearly the case for the illustrated *Marzubannama* (Book of the Margrave) and *Shahnama* (Book of Kings) discussed later in this chapter. Through pictorial simile, the Prophet could be imagined via the courtly practices of the time as a quintessential *padishah* holding audience at his court in Medina. As Michael Cook notes in this regard, "what matters in this context is not how Muhammad actually was, but how he appeared to later generations."[18] Conversely, an elite patron such as Badr al-Din Lu'lu' could be imagined according to Muhammad's legacy as supreme leader of his community, thereby claiming inheritance of the prophetic *sunna* as well as divine sanction for his rule on earth. The rebounding of ideological readings catalyzed by such iconographic

1.3. A silver plate depicting a ruler seated on a bench surmounted by an angel holding a ribbon, Kushano-Sasanian, fourth century CE. Department of the Middle East, British Museum, London, no. 124093.

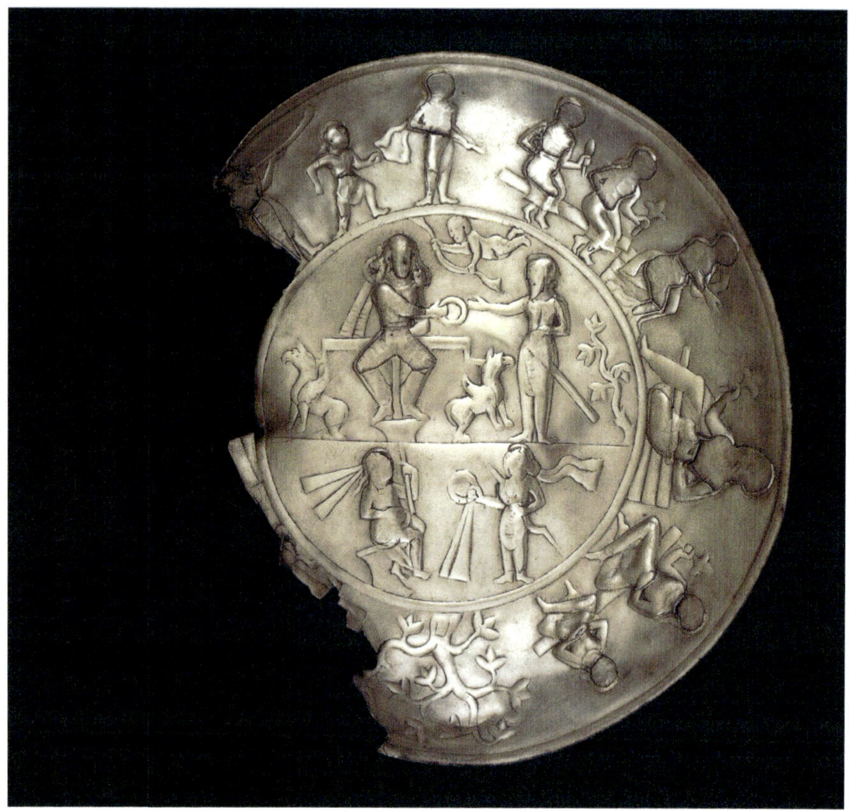

ambiguities should not be understood as mutually exclusive; on the contrary, such readings were productively coconstitutive, strengthening the status of each protagonist depicted within a manuscript, whether prophet or atabeg.

Debates over the identity of the royal sitter promise to continue. Rather than attempt to resolve the issue, at present it is more fruitful to explore the painting's key symbolic motifs: namely, the angels holding a long ribbon that creates a canopy—one could even say a secondary halo—around the head of the enthroned ruler shown in figure 1.1. Also noteworthy are the angels' wings, which intersect above the fluttering canopy to create a V-shaped design that crowns the double-haloed tableau.

The Islamic pictorial rendition of sacral kingship applied to images of the Prophet Muhammad and ruling monarchs frequently includes winged angels bearing banderols or ribbons, which are called *dastar*, meaning "purveyor of victory" in Persian.[19] This motif has a long history in pre-Islamic Persian visual culture, both in elite private spheres and in the public domain. For example, a number of Sasanian silver plates and bowls produced from the fourth to the seventh century depict investiture and banqueting scenes, in which a monarch sits enthroned while an angel or two flies above, holding a fluttering ribbon (fig. 1.3).[20] Additionally, royally sponsored Sasanian rock carvings feature similar motifs exhibited in public spaces. For instance, Taq-i Bustan, located near the Iranian city of Kermanshah, is a royal grotto that includes a

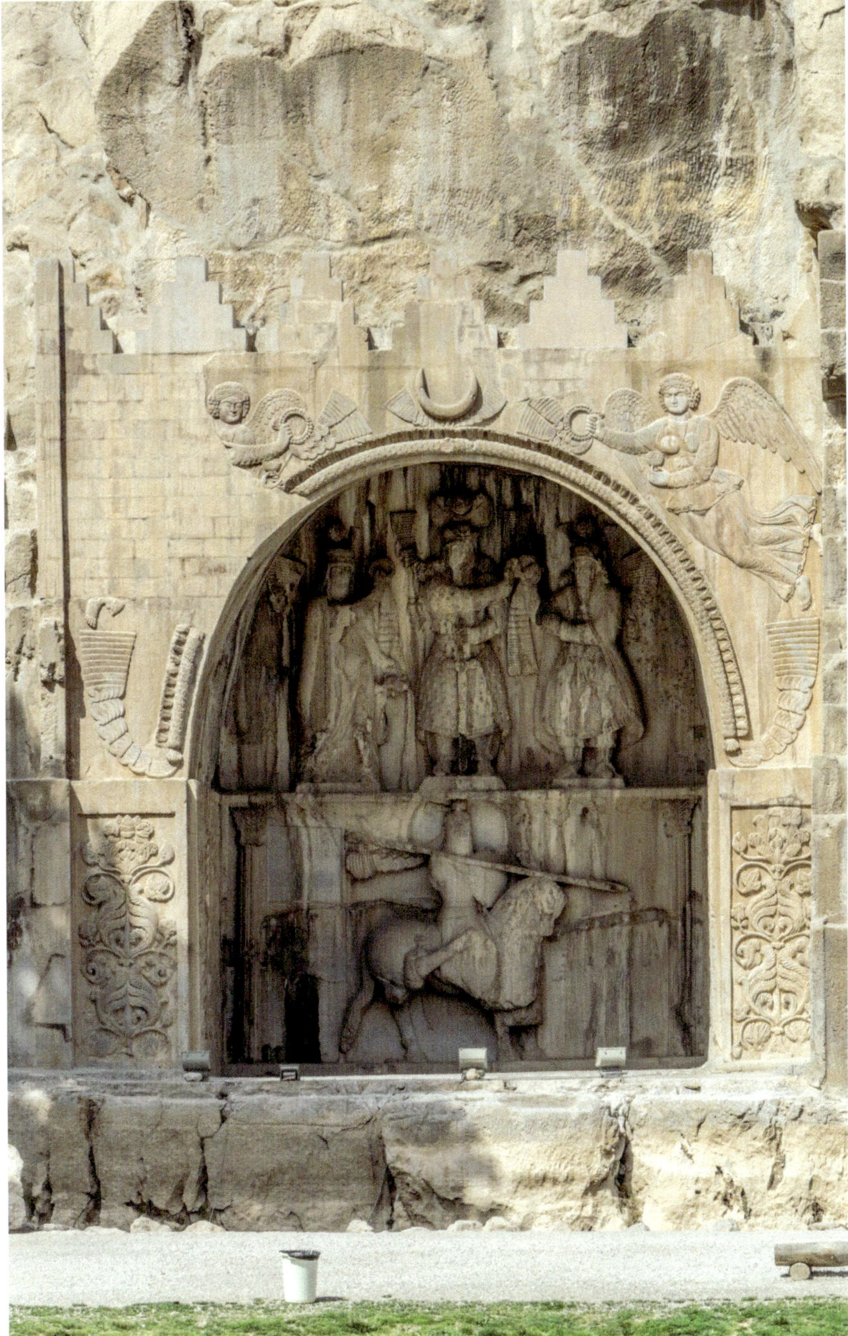

number of carved reliefs (fig. 1.4). The lower recessed horizontal panel shows the Sasanian King Khusraw II (r. 591–628 CE) as a royal equestrian, while the top register depicts his divine investiture. Above these two horizontal panels appear two flying entities, each holding a diadem and fluttering ribbons, twin symbols of Sasanian imperial accession and triumph.[21]

Although banderols and ribbons in Sasanian imperial iconography antedate the arrival of Islam in Iran, the term *dastar* was used in Persian literature for centuries, most especially in Firdawsi's (d. 1020 CE) *Shahnama* (Book of Kings), which was produced as an illustrated manuscript from the early fourteenth century onward. Thus, the ribbon retained its role as a symbol of divine triumph in both written and visual traditions in the Islamic period, during which time it was used to illustrate both prophetic and princely paradigms.

The earliest surviving Islamic paintings of enthroned rulers clearly follow in the tradition of the pre-Islamic Persian iconography of sacral kingship, which was in conversation with Roman pictorial conventions and developed in both private and public spheres in Iran before the advent of Islam. Iranian images of cosmic rulers evidently endured well after 1200 CE, and such images, whether of a king or a prophet, tend to depict an exalted protagonist who is invested with the right to temporal rule through God's angelic couriers bearing the *dastar*, a visible, material sign of the abstract concepts of sacred protection and divine triumph.

In the two enthronement scenes included in the *Kitab al-Aghani*, the ribbon that "purveys glory" takes the shape of a canopy that encircles the sitter's head, thus appearing as a halo that is both protective and decorative.[22] Moreover, in the painting that may depict the Prophet Muhammad (fig. 1.1), the angels' wings cross in a V-shape above this triple banderol-canopy-halo device. This is not the case with the depiction of Badr al-Din Lu'lu' (fig. 1.2), in which the angels' wings are angled to the upper corners of the painting rather than toward one another. The symbol of the paired wings crowning the halo may convey further political and religious messages, most especially if they are intended as prophetic crowning devices. Thus the double motifs of the ribbon and angels underscore the extent to which kingship and religion are indeed "twin brothers."[23]

Like the *dastar*, wings play an important role in pre-Islamic Persian iconographic traditions, in which they function as a divine and astral visual metaphor for immortality.[24] In Sasanian coins, a monarch may be depicted wearing a crown with one or two wings; the wings symbolize the gods of war and victory or divine glory and fortune (*farr* or *khawarnah*).[25] Additionally, pairs of wings are found in late Sasanian stuccowork as well as in seventh-century Islamic architectural mosaicwork. For example, the Dome of the Rock in Jerusalem (691 CE) includes pairs of wings combined with jeweled crowns, which may have served as shorthand symbols of Sasanian sovereignty, especially once the region came under Islamic control after the Arab sack of Ctesiphon in 637 CE.[26] Winged motifs—especially pairs of wings combined with crowns—were carried over from Sasanian royal traditions to early Islamic decorative programs, which promoted Islamic authority and hegemony through the strategic cooptation and depiction of older Persian regalia.

Pre-Islamic Persian symbols of divine appointment and protection—including the halo or solar disk, winged motifs (angels in particular), and imperial headgear—often appear in paintings of the Prophet Muhammad from the medieval period onward. While Islamic visual representations of the Prophet postdate Sasanian art by approximately six centuries, a number of older iconographic conventions appear to have survived in newly articulated ways. The Islamic reception and alteration of Sasanian regal iconography reveal a number of mechanisms through which signs of sacral rulership could be visually recast.

One particularly intriguing example is that of Persian coins produced after the Arab conquest of Iran, especially during the governorship of 'Abdallah ibn al-Zubayr, between 685 and 689 CE.[27] These so-called Arabo-Sasanian silver coins display pre-Islamic iconography combined with Islamic legends, including the portrait of a Sasanian monarch with a double-winged crown and Arabic-script inscriptions running along the edges reading "In the name of God" (*bismillah*) and "Muhammad is the messenger of God" (*Muhammad rasul Allah*) (fig. 1.5). At times, the Islamic proclamation of faith is included alongside other Muslim titles such as *amir al-mu'minin* (leader of the faithful) and *khalifat Allah* (deputy of God), thereby enabling the propagation of a "new Islamic imperial rule with reference to the Prophet and putative founder of the state" before the advent of aniconic coinage in Islamic lands.[28] Thus, on Arabo-Sasanian coins of the seventh century the figural representation of a Sasanian king, crowned with imperial regalia and cosmic symbols, is combined with a caption providing Muhammad's name and title. This coupling of image and text could insinuate a number of visual messages, one of which invites viewers to see within the Persian monarch a newly minted representation of the messenger of Islam. While such a conflation may have been accidental, it is nevertheless catalyzed by the close relationship between the coin's visual and textual components. That a figural image of Muhammad may have appeared in a numismatic context is further supported by the earliest Arab coins, whose inclusion of an image of a standing caliph may in fact have depicted the Prophet Muhammad rather than the Umayyad ruler 'Abd al-Malik (r. 685–705).[29]

Early Arabo-Sasanian coins reveal an Islamic engagement with older Persian artistic traditions that favor figural depictions of the Prophet Muhammad as found in medieval book arts. First, they provide tangible proof for the penetration of Sasanian visual culture into early Islamic expressive systems, wherein the Persian ethos of universal monarchy is received and overlaid with the prophetic paradigm.[30] Second, they speak to the continuation of Persian motifs and regalia emphasizing sacral kingship, particularly enthronement compositions and winged symbols. Extending the Persian ethos of kingship in rhetoric and representation, nascent Islamic political regimes—whether during the seventh century or under the rule of Badr al-Din Lu'lu'—responded to novel situations with amalgamations of historical references, which they ultimately transcended.[31] Thus, as an invented tradition, the earliest extant potential representation of the Prophet Muhammad, as found in the *Kitab al-Aghani* dated 1217–18 CE, did not appear ex nihilo. Rather, it represents a continuation of Persian artistic conventions of depicting sacred rulership, with both minor and major revisions.[32] As such, it is received tradition and radical invention, culmination and catalyst.

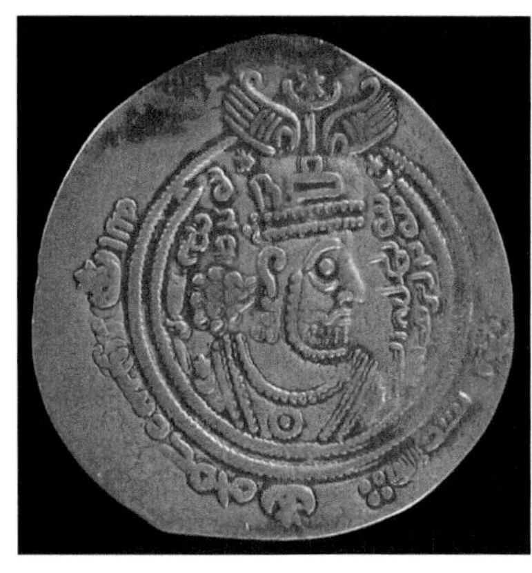

1.5. Arabo-Sasanian coin with the portrait of Khusraw II (r. 590–628 CE) and inscribed with the *bismallah* and "Muhammad is the Messenger of God," 67 AH/686–87 CE, Bishapur, Fars, Iran. Kelsey Museum of Archaeology, University of Michigan, Ann Arbor, 2009.01.0045 (obverse).

Paintings of Muhammad often appear as incipits to illustrated manuscripts, in which they both mirror and amplify introductory eulogies dedicated to God and his Prophet. In such cases, they serve as visual proclamations of the Islamic faith and confirmations of Muhammad's supreme status. Beyond functioning as symbolic entry points into a book, images of the Prophet might also provide a powerful close to an opus, acting essentially as pictorial capstones. When located at the end rather than the beginning of a work, prophetic images provide symbolic closure to a project or endeavor, their allegorical roles substantially altered as a result. Rather than lauding the initial launch of the faith and Muhammad's prophecy, they instead offer visual arguments in favor of conversion to the faith and promote its ultimate rewards. They thus help seal a book, catering to the hope of its author, patron, and reader to secure salvation at the end of time.

The Prophet Muhammad appears at the end of pre-Islamic tales that continued to circulate during Islamic times. One such tale was the story (*sira*) of 'Antara b. Shaddad, a hero of the pre-Islamic period (Jahiliyya) whose followers and descendants became Muslim. The *Sirat 'Antar* is among the longest and most popular works of Arabic epic fiction circulated in oral and written forms. Moreover, its novelistic tone parallels that of Ibn Ishaq's *Sirat al-Nabi* (Biography of the Prophet), a biographical account that also underwent a process of popular fictionalization.[33] During the Islamic period, Muhammad appears at the end of the *Sirat 'Antar*, permitting the narrator to exit the period of the Jahiliyya and to conclude his epic with the embracing of Islam among Arabs.[34] Just as significantly, at the close of the text the Prophet miraculously cures the handicapped daughter of King Habib, prompting the pagan king and his seventy thousand followers to convert to Islam.

Muhammad's recurring insertion at the end of epic tales yields what Bernhard Heller has termed "closing Muhammad legends,"[35] in which a prophetic miracle and cure initiate conversion to Islam as well as salvation through the faith. This "closing Muhammad formula" is also present in medieval Islamic romances, including 'Ayyuqi's epic tale of the two lovers Varqa and Gulshah, who (after numerous battles and missed opportunities) perish, are buried together, and finally are resurrected by the Prophet Muhammad after the Jews of Syria agree to convert to Islam.[36] Penned in Persian during the early eleventh century, 'Ayyuqi's text is dedicated to the Muslim ruler Mahmud of Ghazna (r. 999–1030 CE). The Ghaznavid sultan is best known for having conquered eastern Iranian lands and northwestern India, thereby establishing Islamic dominion over new territories. He also was the patron of the renowned poet Firdawsi, whose *Shahnama* influenced both the versified style and archaic lexicon of 'Ayyuqi's *Varqa and Gulshah*.[37] This romantic tale thus emerged at a particular cultural and political juncture, when Persian epic tales and Islamic hegemony in eastern lands were on the rise. The tale's "Muhammadan finale" thus served to

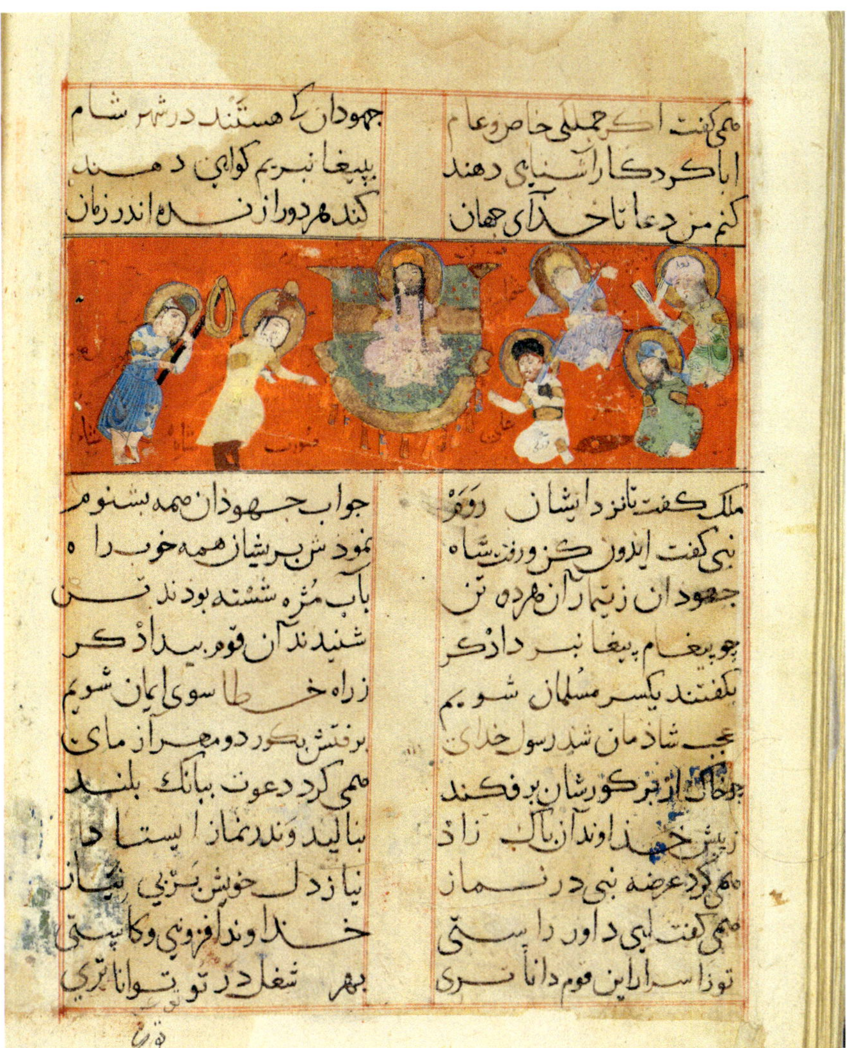

1.6. The Prophet Muhammad enthroned, with the *rashidun* seated on the right, and the king of Syria and his attendant on the left, 'Ayyuqi, *Varqa and Gulshah*, Konya, ca. 1200–1250 CE. Topkapı Palace Library, Istanbul, H. 481, folio 79v. Photograph by Hadiye Cangökçe.

1.7. Detail of figure 1.6.

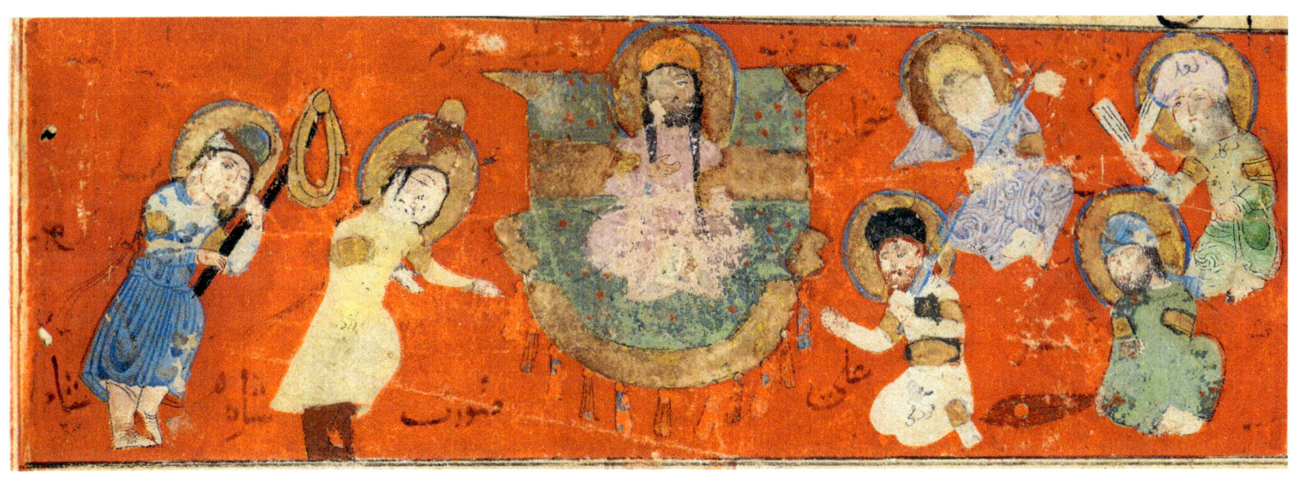

promote the supremacy of the Prophet and the salvific potential of Islam at this critical moment.

The appeal of 'Ayyuqi's *Varqa and Gulshah* grew during the medieval period, and by the first half of the thirteenth century the text was produced as an illustrated manuscript containing seventy-one lively and richly hued paintings. Made in Konya, the capital of the Seljuk sultanate (1077–1307 CE), it remains the most important example of medieval Anatolian book painting. It is also one of the earliest extant Islamic illustrated manuscripts and—most critically for the history of images of Muhammad—contains the oldest set of paintings that indubitably depict the Prophet.[38] Located on facing folios at the end of the manuscript, this pair of images thus creates a double-page finispiece for a medieval illustrated romance whose closing Muhammad legend appears designed for maximum effect.

The paintings glorify the Prophet as both earthly king and religious savior for a Sunni Turco-Persian elite ruling over a culturally and religiously heterogeneous area. As such, the images provide an enticing visual argument in support of Muslim authority and Sunni doctrine within the politicoreligious landscape of medieval Anatolia. Moreover, one of its paintings builds on the imagery of the enthroned prophet-king as found in the *Kitab al-Aghani*, inspiring similar depictions in Persian manuscripts through the later thirteenth and fourteenth centuries.

The first of the two paintings depicts the Prophet seated on a throne with the four rightly guided caliphs (*rashidun*) seated to the right and the king of Syria, with an attendant, standing to the left (fig. 1.6). The depiction accompanies the portion of 'Ayyuqi's text in which Muhammad arrives in Syria (Sham) and informs the king that he plans to request that God bring the deceased lovers Varqa and Gulshah back to life—on the condition that the Jews of Damascus accept his prophecy.[39] The image is seamlessly embedded into the text that it illustrates, but it nevertheless diverges from and expands on the written content in two discernable ways: first, within the text Muhammad is not described as enthroned, and, second, he is said to be accompanied by the *rashidun*, other companions, and his soldiers.[40] Thus, it is evident that the artist—a certain 'Abd al-Mu'min b. Muhammad[41]—chose to depict the Prophet as an enthroned monarch and to include only the four rightly guided caliphs. His decision reveals his desire both to depict Muhammad according to inherited kingly pictorial prototypes and to stress the continuance of the prophetic tradition as embodied by the *rashidun*.

A closer examination of the painting's contents reveals other important details (fig. 1.7). In the center, the Prophet is depicted seated cross-legged on a throne, whose backrest fans out and whose skirt is decorated with tassels. Muhammad has long black tresses—in accordance with earlier Arabic-language *shama'il* texts—while he raises his right hand in a gesture of dialogue directed to the king of Syria. Although the painting is slightly damaged, his facial features and beard are visible, and his head is surrounded by a gold halo rimmed with blue. To the right and left of the halo, a now damaged caption identifies the Prophet and closes with the prayer, "peace be upon him." Other captions populate the painting's bright red background. For example, on the bottom left appears an inscription identifying the "image of the king of Syria" (*surat-i Shah-i Sham*), while the *rashidun* are named on the right. In the upper right is Abu Bakr, holding an open book, flanked by 'Uthman, while in the lower right appears 'Umar, carrying a large brown mace, next to 'Ali, who wields his large double-pointed sword Dhu'l-Fiqar. Although 'Umar's and 'Ali's object attributes are correct, the captions for 'Uthman and Abu Bakr appear to be transposed, as the open book is traditionally associated with 'Uthman, who ordered the official recension of the Qur'an, and not Abu Bakr, who is best known as the confirmer (*al-Siddiq*) of Muhammad's prophetic mission and heavenly ascension.

This caption error notwithstanding, it is evident at an iconographical level that the Prophet's earthly authority is conveyed by the kingly attribute of the throne and his courtly entourage, the *rashidun*. Taken together, the two motifs depict Muhammad as a monarch. This convention must have appealed to an elite Seljuk patron interested in Turco-Persian regal motifs buttressed by a messaging system in support of his own inheritance of the prophetic *sunna*. That a contemporary ruler may have seen himself depicted in the prophetic exemplum is not out of the question. One possible way for viewer projection to occur is through the textual mode, especially via 'Ayyuqi's reference to the Prophet Muhammad as a king (*malak*).[42] The second is by pictorial means: although the author describes Muhammad at several turns as "luminous,"[43] here his facial features are visible (rather than veiled or obscured by a flaming aureole), while all individuals in the painting bear golden haloes. The central figure is indeed Muhammad, but he also could be viewed more generally as an earthly monarch dispensing royal justice and favor at court. Without a doubt, this potential double reading—of the Prophet as king, and a king as Prophet—is generated by the interpretative flexibility of the visual mode.

Within the city of Konya, where the *Varqa and Gulshah* manuscript was produced during the first half of the thirteenth century, visual articulations of Seljuk rulership were available in the public sphere via ceramics, metalware, and stone carvings.[44] For example, one stone relief depicting a princely figure, seated cross-legged and holding an orb in his hand, was placed on the city's walls (fig. 1.8).[45] Alongside other carved representations and designs, as well as a coin depicting an enthroned monarch surmounted by winged victories, these depictions suggest that Seljuk rulers, especially 'Ala al-Din Kayqubad (r. 1220–37 CE), were well versed in universal symbols of authority, on which were grafted angelic motifs and light symbols potentially derived from illuminationist mysticism.[46] Thus, the representation of the Prophet in the *Varqa and Gulshah* manuscript intersects with public art that aimed to promote Seljuk sacral rulership, virtue, and morality with visual strategies that aligned "court and cosmos."[47]

1.8. A seated Seljuk ruler, stone carving, Konya, thirteenth century CE. Ince Minareli Medrese Museum, Konya. Photograph courtesy of Suzan Yalman.

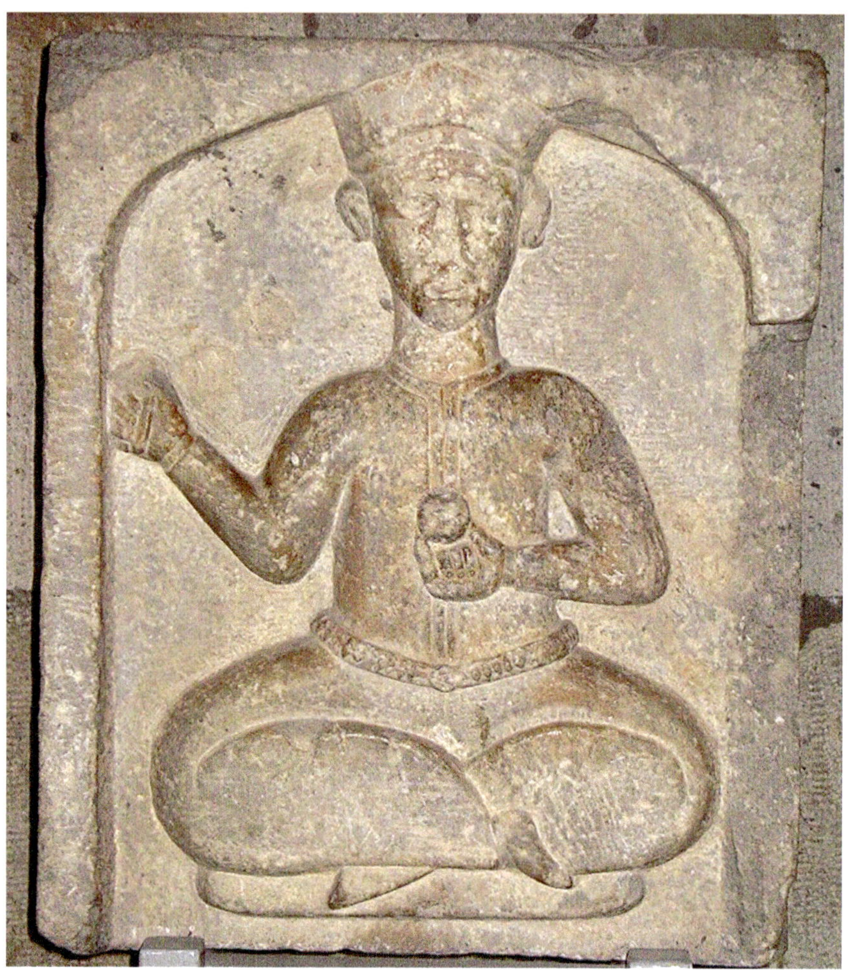

While the *Varqa and Gulshah* painting depicts the Prophet as an earthly monarch, it also encourages conversion from Judaism to Islam as necessary for resurrection and salvation. The image's salvific message is offered by Muhammad to the king of Syria in the form of the raised hand, a visual rendering of the Prophet's consent to the king's request that he "save us" or, literally, "give us a hand" (*mara dast gir*).[48] The Prophet's gesture therefore does not simply signify a dialogue. More tellingly, it pledges salvation through sign language, providing a symbolic bridge to the second image of Muhammad, located at the bottom of the facing folio.

This second painting provides the staging ground for the text's denouement (fig. 1.9).[49] Here, the Prophet Muhammad sits cross-legged—this time on the ground and not on a throne—as he is followed by the *rashidun*. In front of him stands the white-bearded king of Syria. The Prophet, *rashidun*, and king of Syria all face the lovers' tomb, a stepped pyramid out of which Varqa and Gulshah emerge in white cerements, raising their hands prayerfully toward the sky. The painting's background is an ethereal blue rather than bright red. No captions identify the figures; instead, a gold inscription across the top of the painting provides a simple descriptive statement identifying the scene as the resurrection of Varqa and Gulshah.

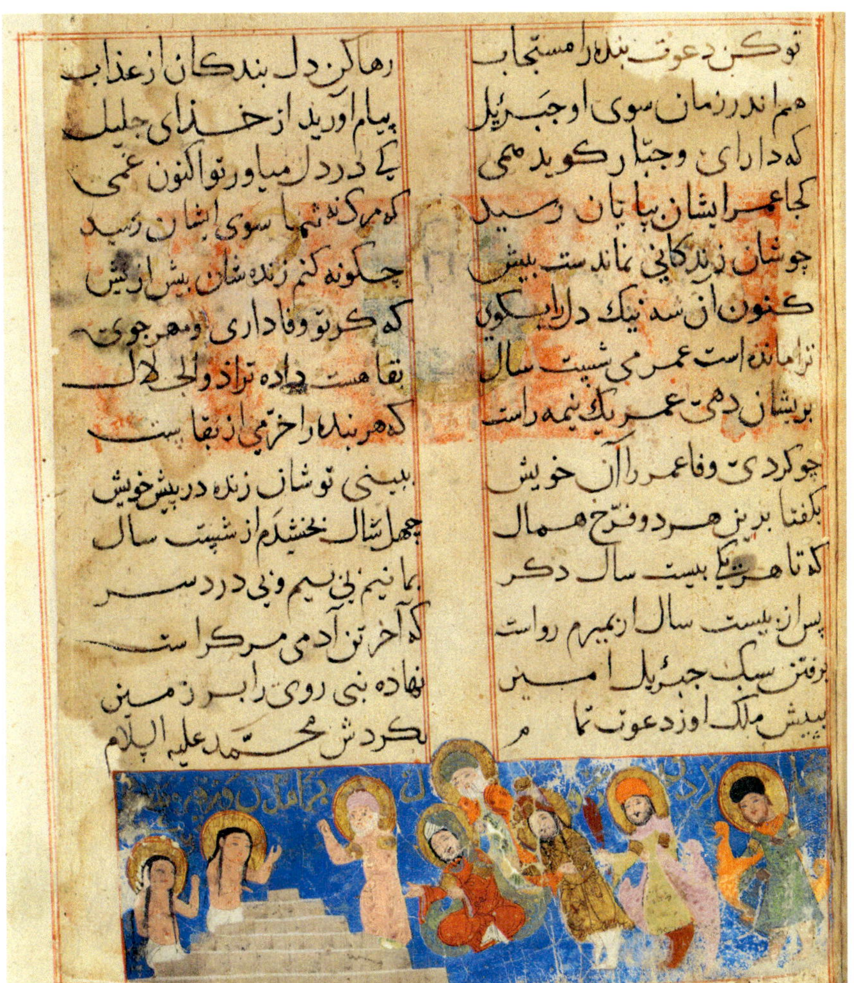

1.9. The Prophet Muhammad resurrecting Varqa and Gulshah from their tomb, ʿAyyuqi, *Varqa and Gulshah*, Konya, ca. 1200–1250 CE. Topkapı Palace Library, Istanbul, H. 481, folio 80r. Photograph by Hadiye Cangökçe.

1.10. Detail of figure 1.9.

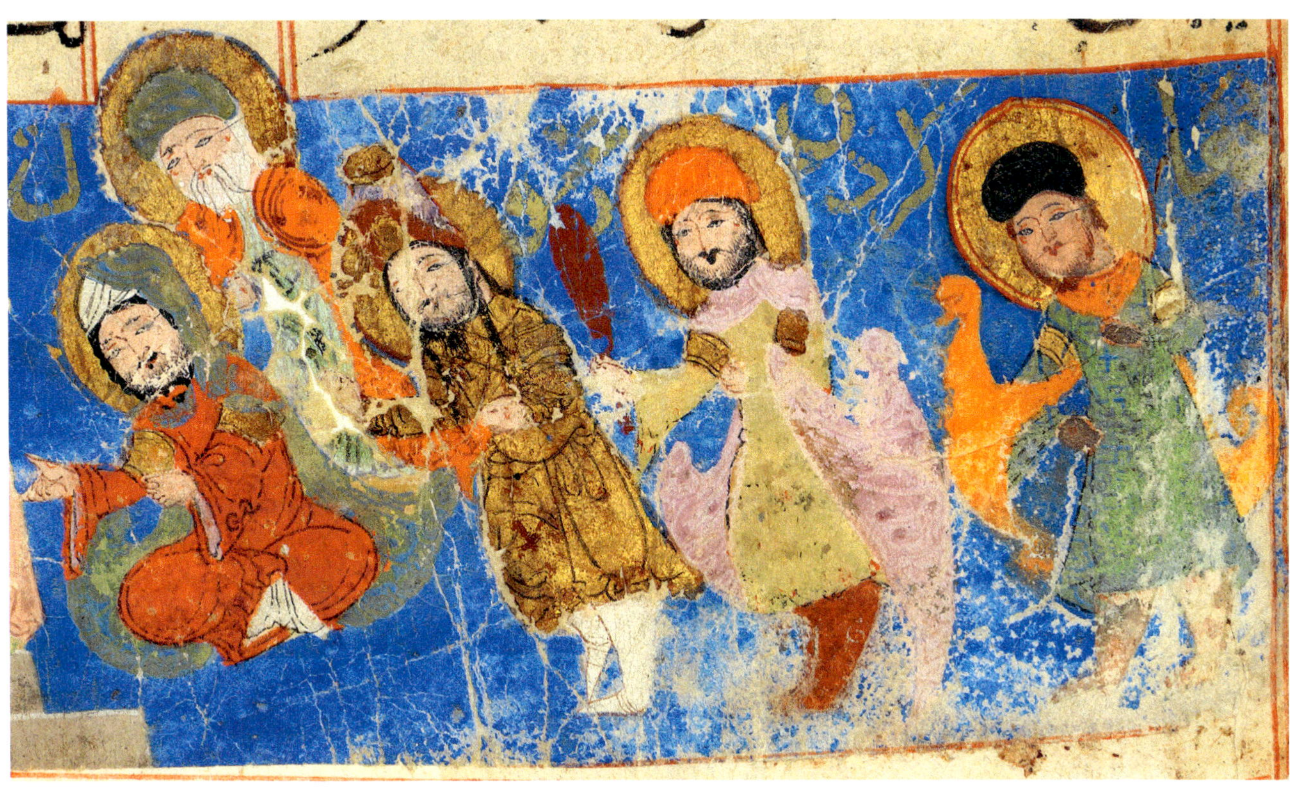

Much like the first painting of Muhammad, this second image both follows and diverges from 'Ayyuqi's text. Moreover, it serves as a finispiece to the manuscript, whose text concludes only fifteen verses later. The image illustrates the Prophet issuing a prayer (*namaz*), petition (*'arza*), and request (*niyaz*) to God that the two lovers be resurrected and saved.[50] In order for Muhammad's wish to be granted, the king of Syria must offer forty years of his own life in exchange; this transaction explains his aged appearance in the painting. God grants the Prophet's wish through the Angel Gabriel. As the verses located immediately before and after the painting relate, on the angel's departure Muhammad places his face to the ground while calling the lovers to life; subsequently all humans prostrate themselves.[51] The text concludes by lauding the Jews' conversion to Islam, the rewards for good action, and eternal life and joy in the union of love; its final verse offers peace and prayers to the Prophet Muhammad.

Once again, the painting simultaneously relies on and departs from 'Ayyuqi's script (fig. 1.10). While the text describes all humans as prostrate, the *rashidun* alone are depicted behind the Prophet, and they appear in a standing position rather than with their heads to the ground. Only Muhammad sits, the prerogative of communicating with God and securing resurrection through prayer being reserved for him alone. Additionally, although the heads of all depicted figures are encircled by gold halos, the Prophet is pictorially differentiated by the addition of a large green cloak that stretches from his white turban to his feet. This cloak is most certainly Muhammad's *burda*, a long piece of woolen cloth that he wrapped around his body during the day and used as a blanket at night.[52] In this instance, the *burda* must be understood as an iconographic indicator of the prayer that initiates the miracle.

Other medieval paintings depict Muhammad wearing an overcloak in similar circumstances of prayer and revelation. For example, in one Persian painting of the early fourteenth century, the Prophet wears a dark blue *burda* as he kneels on a carpet and raises his hands, asking God to grant him a vision of Jerusalem in order to prove the veracity of his celestial ascension (*mi'raj*), which convinces doubting Meccans to accept the Prophet's miracle and convert to Islam (fig. 1.11). As in other medieval paintings, the *burda* functions as a vestmental signifier of Muhammad's supreme status as a prophet capable of receiving divine response to his prayers. Within the *Varqa and Gulshah* illustrated manuscript, the Prophet's position, sitting on the ground while wearing the *burda*, thus forms a critical pendant to the facing painting, in which he sits in the regal mode of enthronement. Together, these terminal images depict Muhammad in his twin earthly and sacral roles as king and prophet.

In his romance, 'Ayyuqi stresses man's lack of control over his destiny and the inevitability of death,[53] folding the story into a larger Islamic eschatological narrative promising resurrection and salvation through

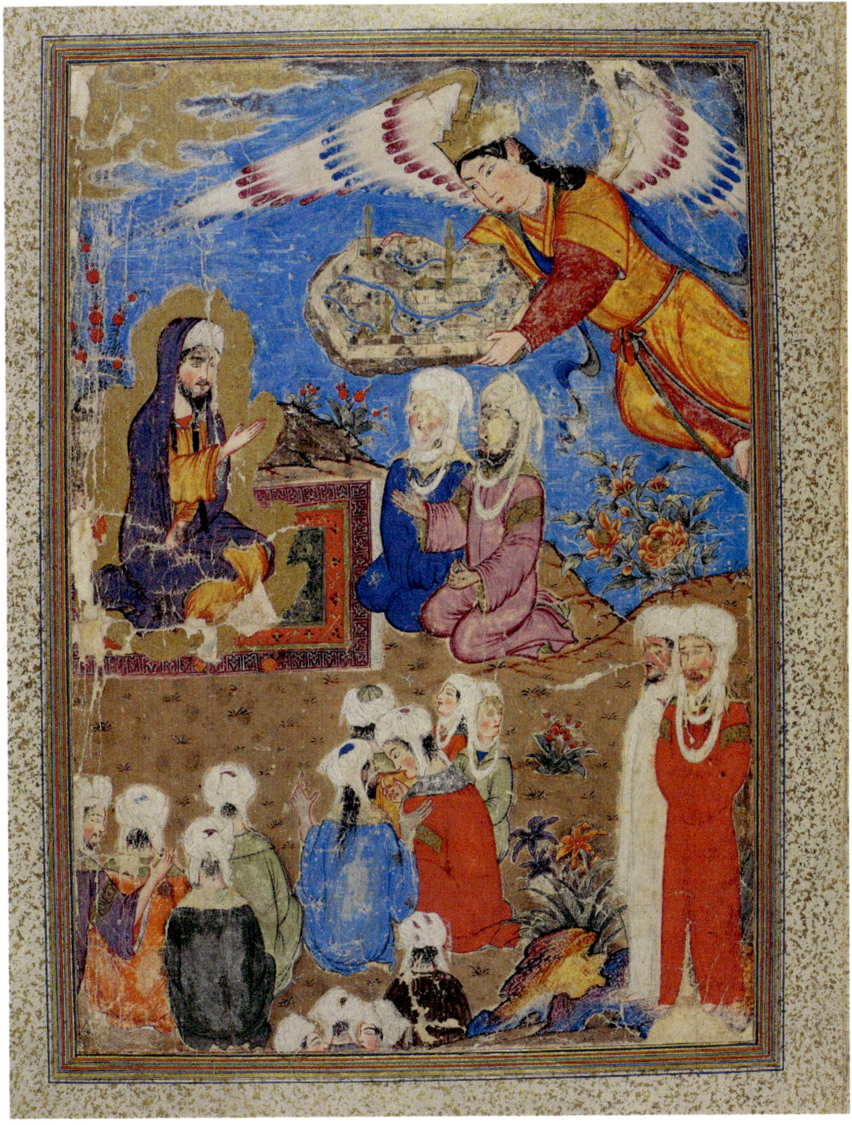

prophetic intercession. Part of the salvific process involves bartering (giving up years of one's life) and conversion to Islam, both of which are catalyzed miraculously by Muhammad as he piously requests and receives divine aid. In this triumphalist finale, the Prophet represents the realization and completion of the true faith, eternal life, and victory over death.

Within the *Varqa wa Gulshah* manuscript's painterly program, Muhammad also is depicted as the quintessential ruler-prophet, dispensing favors at court and securing the lovers' redemption. The two paintings promote the superiority of the Islamic faith through its custodians—which must have resonated with their elite Seljuk viewership—while fitting such emergent doctrinal messages within older artistic traditions of representing sacral kingship. Innovative yet conventional in their iconographic language, these two earliest surviving paintings herald Muhammad as both king and prophet, intercessor and redeemer for mankind.

The use of a double finispiece in the *Varqa and Gulshah* manuscript of around 1200–1250 CE was altered by the close of the thirteenth century. In later illustrated Persian books, the Prophet is typically depicted only once, at the beginning of the manuscript. In these texts, depictions of Muhammad tend to serve as eulogistic introductions rather than moralizing finales encouraging conversion and salvation. As frontispieces initiating a variety of tales and fables, they provide a pious visual threshold into praises of God and his messenger. Moreover, single images of the enthroned Prophet are accompanied, typically a few folios later, by a representation of a princely patron or ruling monarch. This kingly figure often is depicted in a similar manner, his relative rank nevertheless clearly differentiated from that of the Prophet. Thus, the double painting paradigm was in fact retained, its strategic location and visual analogies nevertheless reconfigured from around 1300 CE onward.

During the thirteenth century, illustrated manuscripts were produced in the city of Baghdad, first for high-ranking ‘Abbasid patrons and later, after the Mongol invasions, for members of the elite that thrived under Ilkhanid rule in Iran and Iraq (1258–1356 CE). Although the ‘Abbasid library was destroyed during Hülegü's sack of Baghdad in 1258 CE, the patronage and production of manuscripts was revived during the last decade of the thirteenth century. At this time, a number of illustrated manuscripts were produced, and these are especially important because they help fill the gap between pre- and post-Mongol painting traditions.[54] The subjects and motifs found within these manuscripts also provide a critical link in the history of Islamic book arts because they retain older pictorial conventions while concurrently initiating new ones, among them painterly dyads analogizing the Prophet Muhammad and an earthly ruler.

The earliest extant example of this pictorial convention can be found in an illustrated copy of Sa'd al-Din al-Varavini's *Marzubannama* (Book of the Margrave), made in Baghdad in 1299 CE. Belonging to a larger corpus of advice literature for princely patrons, this text comprises a collection of moralizing tales written in Persian.[55] The tales are not illustrated; instead, the manuscript includes only three paintings at its very beginning: these depict the Prophet Muhammad enthroned, the author al-Varavini composing his text, and an enthroned ruler, possibly Abu'l-Qasim Rabib al-Din (who served in 1210–25 CE as vizier in the atabeg court in Azerbaijan, where al-Varavini reworked his text).[56] The identification of the seated ruler is supported by the figure's placement within the text's preliminary section praising the vizier. Alternatively (but less likely), the enthroned ruler may have been the patron who commissioned the book's creation. The manuscript's prolegomenon thus extols prophetic, authorial, and regal excellence. Due to their visual similarities, the paintings of the Prophet Muhammad and the enthroned ruler are most closely associated and thus must be considered companion pieces.

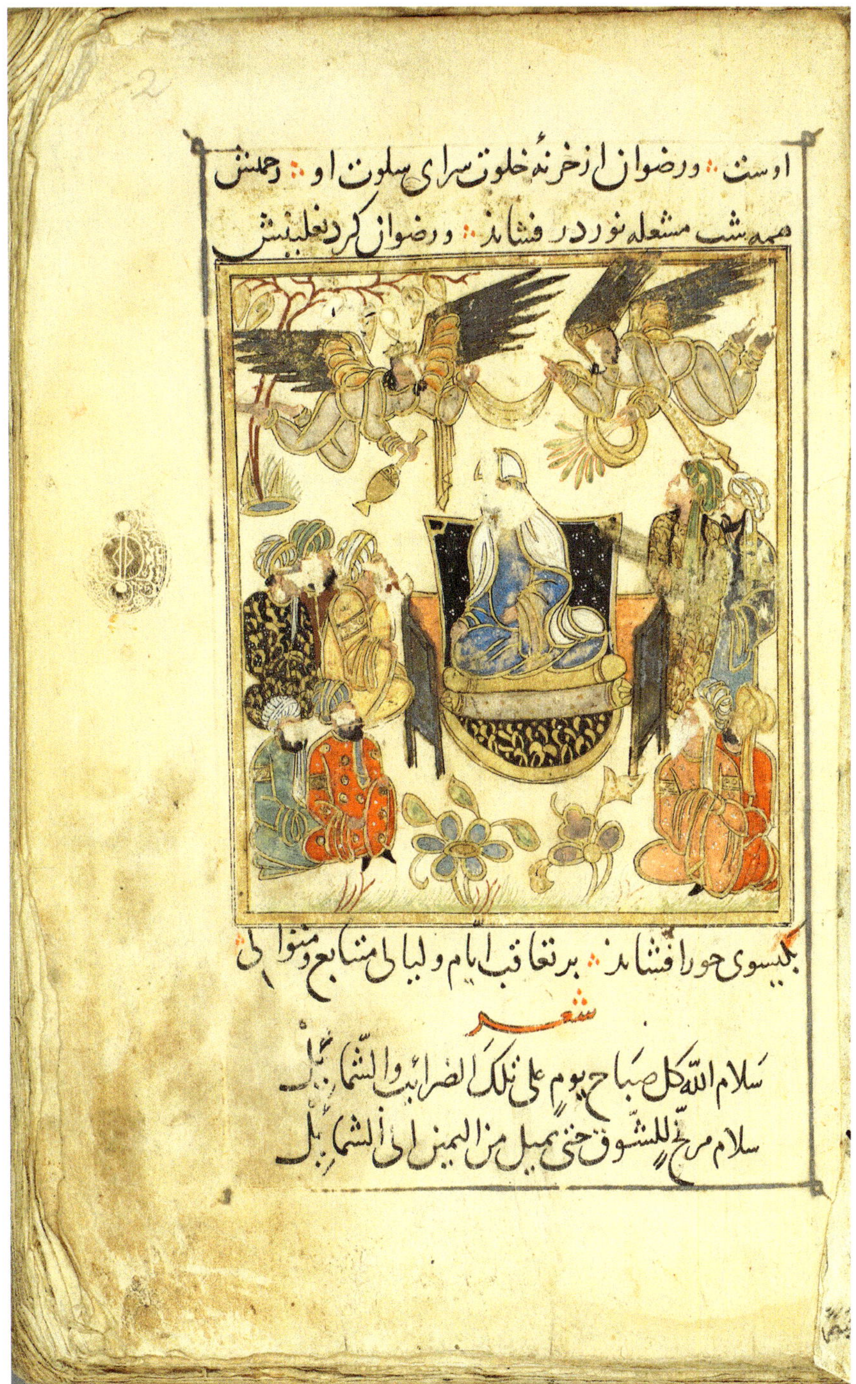

1.12. The Prophet Muhammad enthroned, Sa'd al-Din al-Varavini, *Marzubannama* (Tales of the Margrave), Baghdad, 698 AH/1299 CE. Archaeology Museum Library, Istanbul, Ms. 216, folio 2r.

Although this painting was later defaced, it originally depicted Muhammad with visible facial features (fig. 1.12).[57] He sits cross-legged and enthroned, wearing a white *burda* over his blue robe. Two angels, whose faces also have been scratched out, fly above him while holding a fluttering ribbon or piece of fabric. The angel on the right appears to pour rays of light on Muhammad, while the angel on the left seems to anoint him with a flask of heavenly liquid or scent. Other figures sit or stand around Muhammad; however, as is the case for the Prophet, their faces, and in particular their eyes, have been since damaged.

The Persian text accompanying the image describes the Prophet as emitting radiance much like a torch of light, and his two sandals as exuding the minty smell of the pennyroyal or black poley herb.[58] The angels imbue him with numinous brilliance and fragrant aroma, adding a layer to the Prophet's features otherwise not visible at first glance. The petaled flowers and leaves in the foreground, moreover, may represent two pennyroyal flowers and thus offer a more olfactory evocation of Muhammad's heavenly aroma, itself praised in al-Varavini's text as a "perfumed earth."[59]

Although the painting's composition and corresponding text suggest that the Prophet's inner essence, perfumed and radiant, can be an object of praise, it also venerates his more observable characteristics. Indeed, Muhammad's features are extolled in the two lines of Arabic poetry below the painting, which read:

> Peace of God every morning and day upon such characteristics and features
> Peace upon the mystic who, in longing, rocks from the right to the left

The Persian text and inserted Arabic poem in honor of the Prophet suggest that this painting is intended to depict the Prophet among his companions, who sit or stand in meditation of his noncorporeal attributes. The men's postures indicate that they are engaged in spiritual reflection and in active prayer. Indeed, they all seem to look up toward a vision of the Prophet, who is rendered sacrosanct by the angels hovering above. Swaying, seated, or raising their hands in prayer, the onlookers are engaged in visually rapturous praise of the Prophet, his physical characteristics, and his spiritual attributes. So while Muhammad appears to be represented corporeally and with his facial features (originally) visible, the painting also encourages the viewer to conjure up a vision of the Prophet through the metaphors of light and scent.

As discussed above, the angels holding a canopy-like *dastar* above the Prophet functioned as symbols for sacral investiture and royal triumph in Persian artistic traditions both before and after the advent of Islam. In medieval paintings of Muhammad, the angels' inclusion is strategic and purposeful, because they serve as external signs of the Prophet's heavenly origins and elevated status. In the *Marzubannama* painting in particular, the specific objects that the angels hold symbolize Muhammad's investiture and triumph (the *dastar*), his appointment and anointment by God (the flask), and his primordial radiance (the light rays). Also significant are the gestures the angels make directly above the Prophet's head: the angel on the right points its index finger while the angel on the left clasps its fist. In a variety of Islamic cultural traditions, the pointing of the index finger indicates the act of attesting to God's singularity and Muhammad's prophecy (*shahada*),[60] while the making of a fist symbolizes worldly authority and power.[61] The angels thus speak a form of sign language that serves to emphasize Muhammad's rule as both heavenly and earthly in nature. In other words, the

THE PRAISEWORTHY ONE

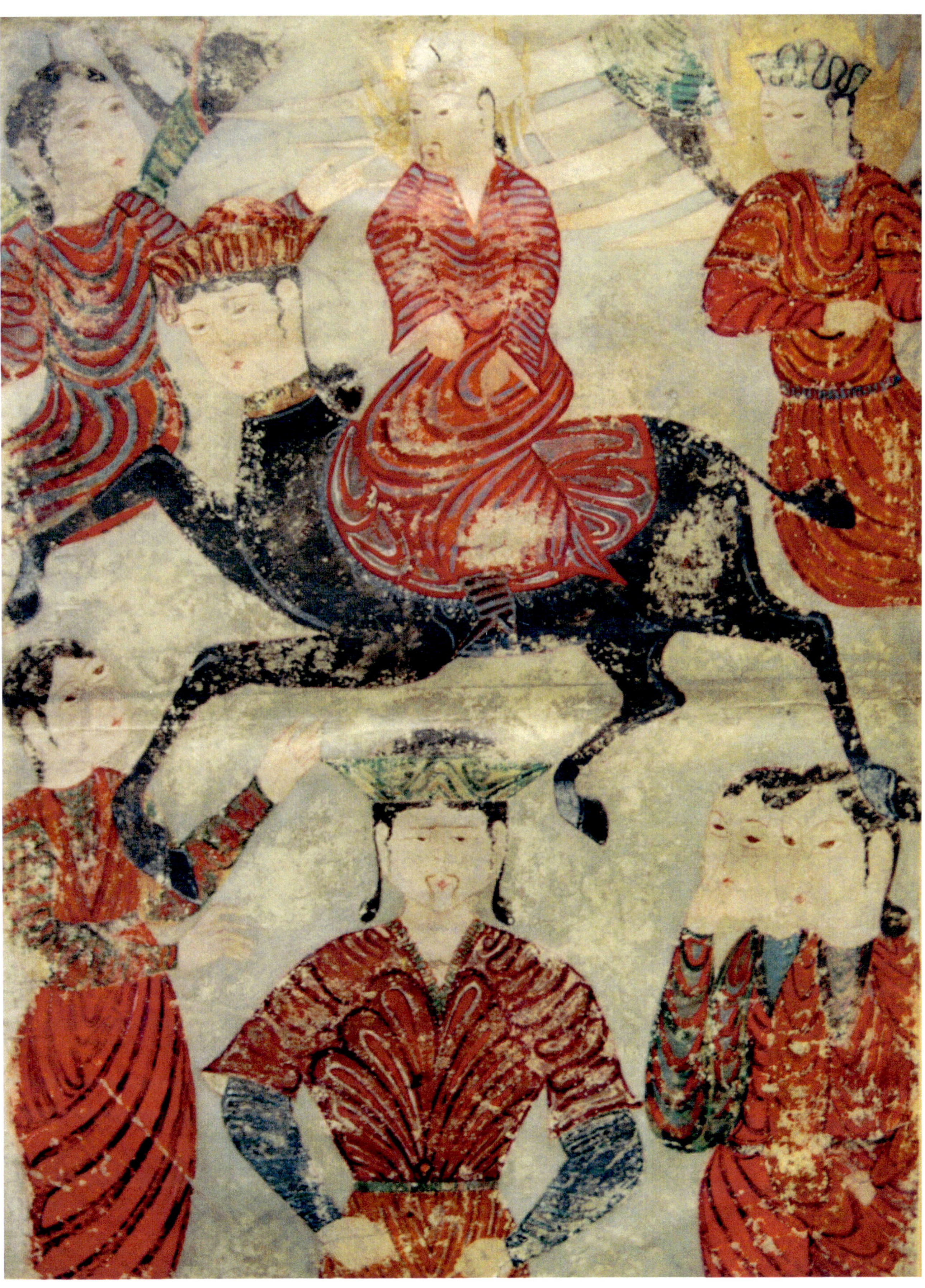

angelic gestures act as crowning devices that affirm Muhammad as the prophet-king of a single, all-encompassing God.

Gestural signs promoting worldly and otherworldly dominion are found in other Islamic paintings of Muhammad that intertwine the dual notions of prophecy and rulership. In one large-scale (40 x 30 cm) painting possibly made in Tabriz around 1400–1450 CE, the Prophet is depicted on the human-headed steed al-Buraq and accompanied by two angels as they fly above a crowned monarch flanked by his attendants (fig. 1.13).[62] In this image, which likely was used for storytelling, it is the Prophet who points his left index finger down at the ruler while his right hand makes a fist. His gestures suggest that his dominion (the fist) is harnessed by the witnessing and worshiping of a single God (the index finger) through his earthly representative, the monarch, to whom the Prophet conveys power. It is possible that the painting depicts a now-lost medieval oral narrative that promoted a ruling monarch's authority through the image of the Prophet's ascension to God. In such a case, the image may represent a ruler's dream of the Prophet, who in turn invests him with worldly authority.

The depiction of Muhammad in the *Marzubannama* gains further layers of meaning when viewed in relation to a painting that appears just five folios later in the same manuscript (fig. 1.14). In this scene, an enthroned ruler is depicted in the composition's center. He may represent al-Varavini's benefactor, a vizier active in the first decades of the thirteenth century, or the unnamed patron who commissioned the volume that was copied and illustrated in 1299 CE. Although the sitter's identity remains uncertain, he is clearly of high, perhaps even royal, standing. Much more significantly, the depiction of this royal audience shows undeniable parallels to the painting of the Prophet Muhammad located some folios earlier within the same codex: both rulers sit enthroned in an outdoor setting, and both are surrounded by followers and officials standing and sitting in poses of respect and praise.

Although the two paintings resemble one another in their formal structure, figural composition, and their inclusion of a floral landscape, they also diverge in a number of noticeable ways. For example, the kingly patron is shown wearing a golden crown and a robe crossed at the neck, while his attendants likewise wear contemporary garb as well as headgear and feathered caps typical of the time the manuscript was produced. Additionally, in the foreground, two courtiers sit on contemporaneous stools with pillows. From the crown to the vestments and furniture, these details reflect ceremonial fashions and effects current around 1300 CE. On the other hand, in the painting of the Prophet, details are intended to suggest a distant past: the Prophet's head is cloaked in a white *burda* rather than topped by a gold crown, his companions wear variously colored turbans rather than feathered caps, and they sit or stand on the ground without the aid of cushioned chairs. Evidently the painting's artist strove to represent the attire and etiquette current

    THE PRAISEWORTHY ONE

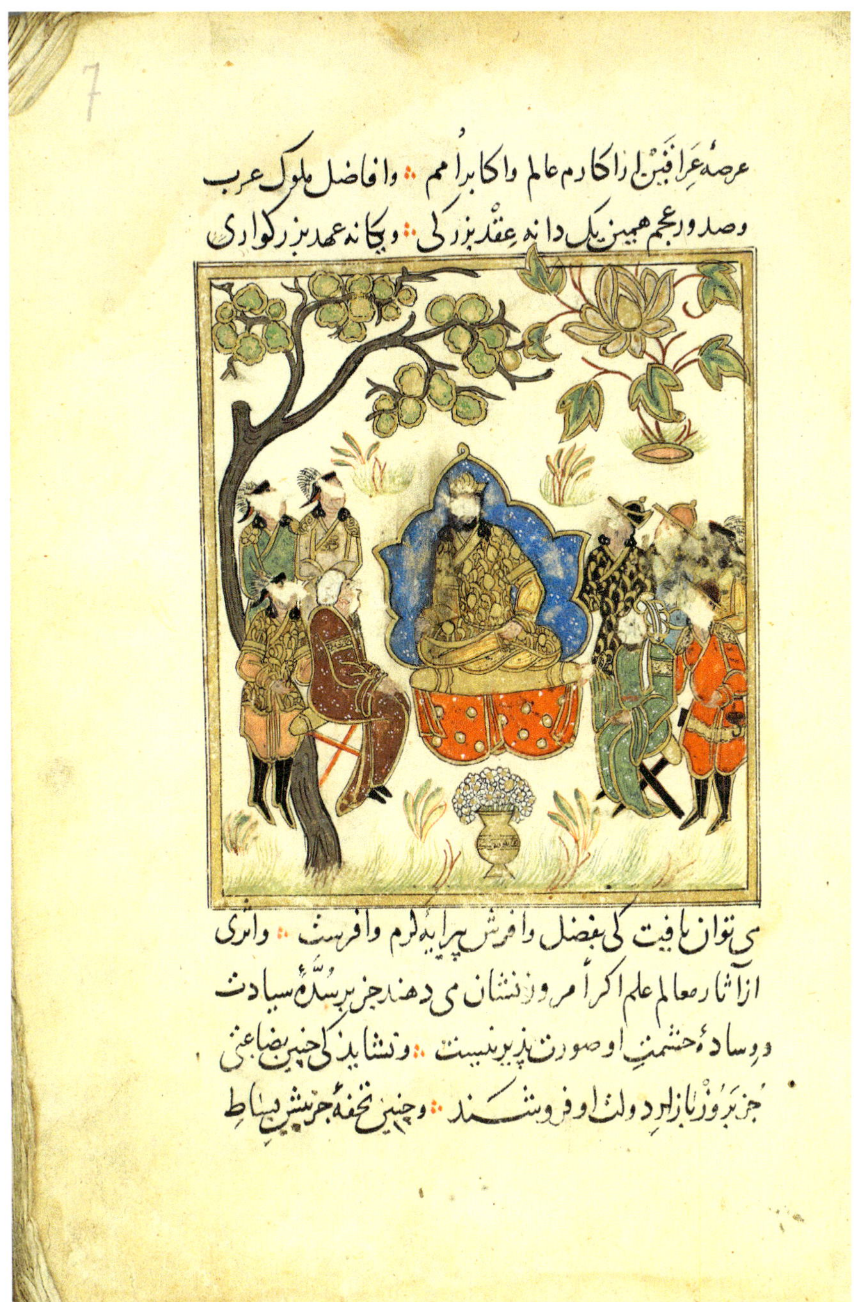

1.14. An enthroned ruler (possibly Abu'l-Qasim Rabib al-Din), Saʿd al-Din al-Varavini, *Marzubannama* (Tales of the Margrave), Baghdad, 698 AH/1299 CE. Archaeology Museum Library, Istanbul, Ms. 216, folio 7r.

during Muhammad's time while folding the scene within an enthronement paradigm.

Both prophetic and royal enthronement scenes continued to function as encomiastic frontispieces in illustrated manuscripts after 1300 CE. During the first half of the fourteenth century, members of the Ilkhanid ruling elite were quick to embrace Firdawsi's *Shahnama* as an epic history of the kings of Iran, which could be marshaled in support of their own claims to indigeneity and kingship. For example, verses of the *Shahnama* appear on a number of tiles at the Ilkhanid palace at Takht-i Sulayman; these excerpted verses allude to entire epic cycles, suggesting that *Shahnama* narratives were learned by heart and recited at court.[63]

The *Shahnama* tales also were produced as lavishly illustrated manuscripts, in both small and large formats. As Oleg Grabar and Sheila Blair have argued, these Ilkhanid illustrated manuscripts were significant to the creation of a protonational Iranian identity for Mongol princes and their entourages.[64] Moreover, their pictorial programs emphasize battle and enthronement scenes, thereby visually promoting the interlinked notions of military triumph and imperial majesty. Whether recited orally, molded into architectural tiles, or produced as illustrated manuscripts, Firdawsi's *Shahnama* functioned as an important narrative and pictorial vehicle through which a largely foreign ruling elite could lay claim to Persian heritage and princely authority.

Illustrated manuscripts of the *Shahnama* include numerous enthronement scenes, placed either at the beginning of a chapter recounting the reign of a particular monarch or within the narrative in order to depict events and encounters at court. A typical court scene in a *Shahnama* manuscript, made in Baghdad around 1300 CE, depicts the Iranian king Sam enthroned while granting audience to Queen Sindukht, who, as an envoy from the king of Kabul, is depicted bearing gifts in the lower right corner (fig. 1.15).[65] In this painting, Sam wears a gold robe and crown as he holds a scepter and sits on a large gold pillow. He turns toward the queen, who responds in a dialogic manner by raising her right hand. Below them are cushions and gifts, while a high-ranking member of the court (perhaps Sam's vizier) sits on a short bench in the lower left corner. In the upper horizontal area are four of the king's attendants, wearing feathered caps and holding animal-headed maces and bows, the latter intersecting directly above the monarch's head. Both Queen Sindukht and the seated minister wear robes lavishly embroidered with gold designs. The presence of gold in the many fabrics included in the painting echoes Ilkhanid gold-embroidered textiles, which were equated with imperial authority and legitimacy for Mongol rulers belonging to the so-called golden lineage (*altun uruq*) of Chengis Khan.[66]

Such enthronement scenes are recurrent in the so-called small illustrated *Shahnamas*. They are embedded within and illustrate the incipit or course of the text, serving both iconic and narrative functions. The iconography of kingly scenes can be traced to the very beginning of Firdawsi's text, which opens with praise of the Prophet Muhammad and his family, whom he likens to a "ship of salvation" (*safinat al-naja*). This pious preamble to the Book of Kings enabled Firdawsi to Islamicize—if only summarily and preliminarily—his epic text, which otherwise is entirely dedicated to recounting the lives and deeds of the rulers of pre-Islamic Iran. Within illustrated copies of the *Shahnama*, this laudatory section dedicated to the Prophet is at times provided with a painting that functions as a frontispiece.

The earliest surviving illustration of Firdawsi's "ship of salvation" encomium to Muhammad follows the enthronement paradigm (fig. 1.16).[67] In this Ilkhanid *Shahnama* of around 1300 CE, the depiction

   THE PRAISEWORTHY ONE

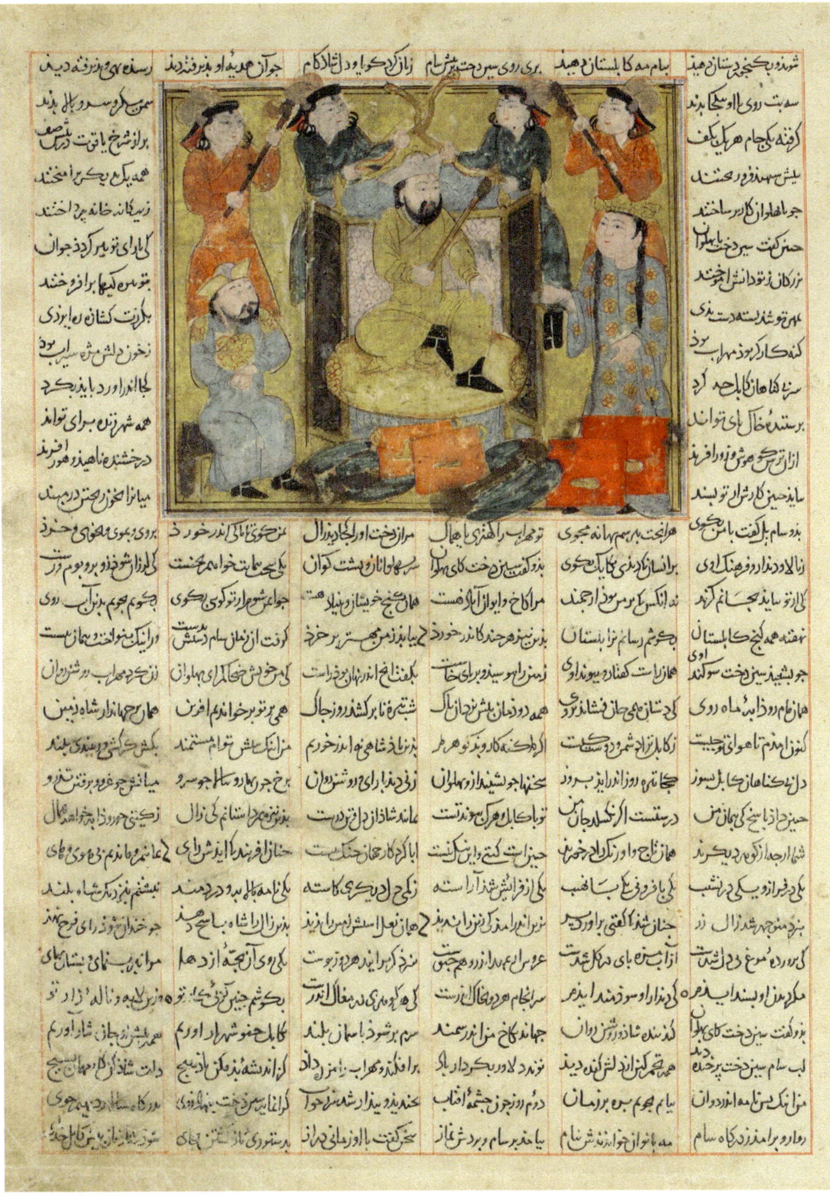

1.15. King Sam enthroned and granting audience to Queen Sindukht, Firdawsi, *Shahnama* (Book of Kings), probably Shiraz, early fourteenth century CE. Freer Gallery of Art, Smithsonian Institution, Washington, DC, F1929.33.

of Muhammad is reminiscent of other kingly representations within the same manuscript, including that of Sultan Mahmud of Ghazna, Firdawsi's patron, who is also praised and depicted on the folio's verso. Like Sam granting audience to Queen Sindukht (fig. 1.15), Sultan Mahmud is seated on a throne, surrounded by court members standing or seated on chairs. Neither monarch (Sultan Mahmud and King Sam), however, is accompanied by winged angels.

A series of enthronement scenes within the manuscript's pictorial cycle begins with a depiction of the Prophet, who is conceived within the regal paradigm. This composition thus does not correspond to later paintings of the ship of salvation, which depict the Prophet and the *rashidun* sitting in an actual ship—at times replacing the *rashidun* with the Shi'i imams to convey an overt sectarian message (figs. 4.1–4.3). In figure 1.16, the enthronement format is retained, yet Muhammad

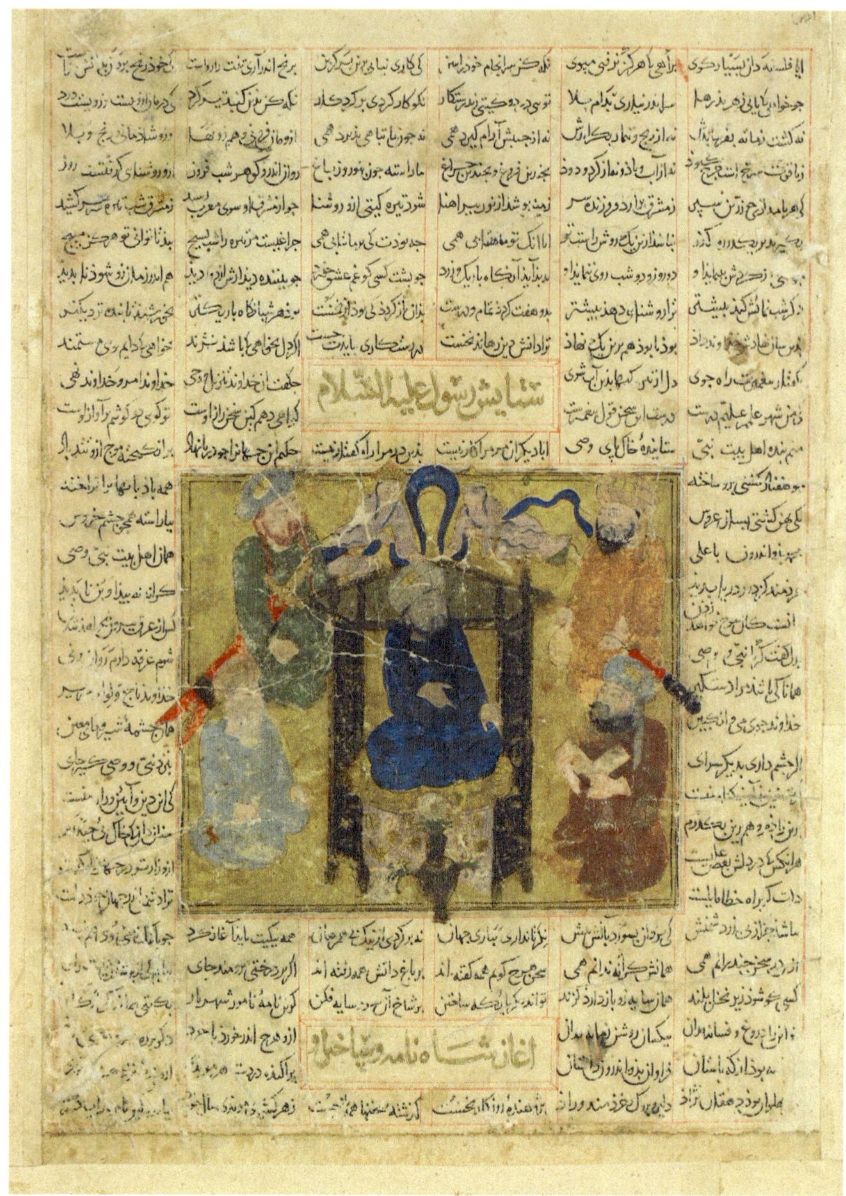

1.16. The Prophet Muhammad enthroned and surrounded by the *rashidun*, Firdawsi, *Shahnama* (Book of Kings), probably Shiraz, early fourteenth century CE. Freer Gallery of Art, Smithsonian Institution, Washington, DC, F1929.26r.

is distinguished from subsequent earthly rulers depicted within the same manuscript through subtle yet obvious iconographic shifts. First, over his long tresses he wears a white turban (not a crown); second, he is surmounted by two angels carrying a fluttering blue ribbon (not flanked by attendants crossing their bows); third, the four members of his entourage kneel directly on the ground (they do not sit on chairs or stand on foot); and, fourth, below Muhammad's feet appears a vase filled with pink flowers (there are no cushions or gifts). These visual details suggest that the Prophet is a worldly ruler of the past, acting under angelic protection, encircled by a community of believers, and eschewing worldly goods.

The painting illustrated in figure 1.16 occupies the largest portion of the introductory section entitled "Praise of the Prophet, peace be upon him" (*sitayash-i Rasul ʿalayhi al-salam*), located immediately prior to the chapter that opens the *Shahnama* proper. The textual eulogy describes the ship of salvation, in which the Prophet, his family, and his companions are likened to a boat that survives the waves at sea. The boat is a metaphor for the Islamic faith as well as the promise of salvation through proper belief. Many of Firdawsi's verses expressing the parable of the ship of salvation stress the importance of 'Ali, the Prophet's son-in-law, and the *ahl al-bayt*, the members of Muhammad's family. Most significantly, 'Ali is described as the Prophet's inheritor and legatee (*wasi*), his close companion and vicegerent (*wali*), and the lion (*haydar*) of God and the gate (*dar*) to Muhammad, who declares himself the "city of knowledge" (*shahr-i 'ilm*). Finally, the author warns that there is no person more miserable than he who bears animosity toward 'Ali, concluding: "If I shall go down with Muhammad and 'Ali, I sink in good company. Surely he will rescue me from ill, the Lord of the crown (*taj*), banner (*liwa*), and throne (*sarir*)."[68] In these verses, the "banner" refers to the Prophet's "banner of praise" (*liwa al-hamd*), under which Muhammad will intercede on behalf of believers during the Day of Judgment. Moreover, Muhammad's status as the possessor of the crown and throne echoes the princely attributes of earthly monarchs as described in the *Shahnama*. The painter thus follows Firdawsi's rhetorical tactic by adding a triumphal banner—that is, the ribbon-cum-canopy held by two angels—and throne, although he has replaced the kingly crown with the Prophet's turban (*'imama*).[69]

In the Ilkhanid painting, the textual encomium to the Prophet lacks four verses praising Abu Bakr, 'Umar, 'Uthman, and 'Ali, found in other written versions of the ship of salvation.[70] While the text omits or excises mention of the *rashidun* in order to deliver a more overtly pro-'Alid rendition of the parable, the painter nevertheless conceptualized the prophetic body as enframed and supported by the four founding figures of the prophetic *sunna*: 'Umar, holding a mace in the upper right; 'Uthman, holding an open Qur'an in the lower right; Abu Bakr, with a white beard in the lower left; and, in the upper left, 'Ali carrying his large double-pointed sword, Dhu'l-Fiqar, breaking through the painting's frame. Identifiable by their object attributes, the four rightly guided caliphs thus function as Muhammad's companions as they spatially encircle the Prophet and fill the painting's four corners.

As Raya Shani has argued, the artist's placement of 'Ali above Muhammad might visually suggest 'Ali's superiority vis-à-vis the Prophet, while the composition maintains a stance suggestive of the artist's and/or patron's Sunni faith combined with a particular veneration of the Prophet's family.[71] 'Ali's close connection to Muhammad is further proclaimed by the long tresses that only he and the Prophet bear. Alternatively, perhaps the painter drew on older pictorial prototypes in which Muhammad is enthroned and surrounded by the *rashidun*, as is the case for the two paintings included in 'Ayyuqi's *Varqa and Gulshah* (figs. 1.7 and 1.10).[72] In such a case, the inclusion of the *rashidun* could be as much a result of artistic tradition as of ideological messaging. Whether the painting was intended to advance a Sunni message or more passively follows inherited paradigms (or some combination thereof) cannot be ascertained with any degree of certainty. What is clear, however, is that, even within the ship of salvation parable in Firdawsi's *Shahnama*, the Prophet Muhammad remains pictorially conceptualized as a divinely appointed ruler surrounded by a courtly entourage—in this instance the four rightly guided caliphs.

Last but not least, there are no pillows or gifts strewn on the ground. Instead, below the Prophet's feet stands a vase in which a bouquet of pink roses bloom. These are reminiscent of the flowers and vase similarly placed below both Muhammad and a ruler at the beginning of al-Varavini's *Marzubannama* (figs. 1.12 and 1.14). In al-Varavini's text, the Prophet's aroma is likened to "perfumed earth" while his feet are said to emit the scent of the poley herb or pennyroyal flower. While in this case the representation of flowers may represent a link to the specific contents of the Book of the Margrave, Muhammad's floral aroma is not mentioned in the ship of salvation eulogy at the beginning of the *Shahnama*. In Firdawsi's prologue, the Prophet instead is imagined according to the four rivers of paradise, of which he is the "lord of the rivers of wine (*may*) and honey (*angabin*)" as well as the "source of milk (*shir*) and water (*ab*)." Through textual metaphors, Muhammad embodies paradise, the eternal abode of those who are saved by the Islamic faith, and the grace of God.

The painting's artist chose not to represent the rivers of paradise that form part of the Prophet's honorific epithets as found in Firdawsi's *Shahnama*. Instead, he included pink roses, a recurring motif in Islamic devotional texts that describe both Muhammad's skin color and his beautiful aroma.[73] In one of the earliest Arabic-language *shama'il* (characteristics) texts, for example, the hadith collector al-Tirmidhi (d. 892 CE) notes that Muhammad had a rose (or reddish-white) skin tone,[74] while medieval Persian poets such as Nizami (d. 1209 CE) directly address the Prophet, inquiring: "If you are a rose, send us perfume from your garden."[75] As a color, rose was understood to represent Muhammad's light of divinity combined with the blood-red of his humanity, while, as a transcendental odor, the rose scent paid tribute to his dispatch to humankind from the Garden of Eden. As a result, in the *Shahnama* enthronement scene illustrated in figure 1.16, the Prophet is shown under sacred protection and redolent of the scent of divine anointment. Through such angelic and floral metaphors at the top and bottom of the composition, the artist has effectively transformed the enthronement pattern into an allegorical scene praising the Prophet's investiture and triumph along with his supreme position as heavenly scented king sent from God to earth.

Over the course of the fourteenth century, similar experiments with enthronement scenes can be found within Persian book arts.[76] Beyond

THE PRAISEWORTHY ONE

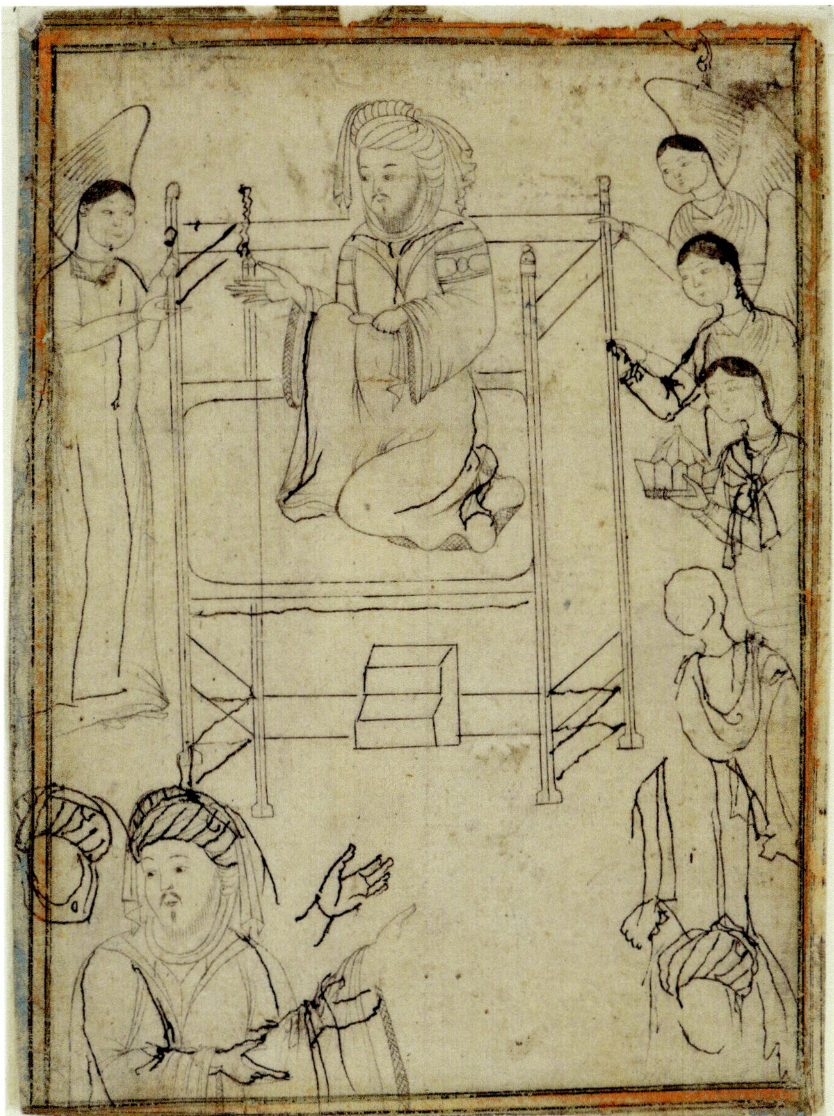

the finished painting as found in illustrated manuscripts, preparatory
sketches and single-page paintings preserved in albums reveal the various artistic methods and compositional possibilities which artists explored in depicting the Prophet Muhammad. For example, within the
so-called Diez albums, which preserve a variety of pictorial materials
dating from the thirteenth to the eighteenth century,[77] numerous premodern Persian images reveal the ways in which artists engaged with
the enthronement paradigm.[78] Most noticeably, some show experimentation with iconographic details and perspective, the latter enabling
charged interactions between the viewer and the depicted subject.

One fourteenth-century black-ink sketch of the Prophet enthroned
reveals the multiple maneuvers employed by an artist during the early
phases of the image-making process (fig. 1.17). Here Muhammad sits
with one knee raised, holding a handkerchief in one hand and pointing to the Angel Gabriel with the other. Standing on the left, Gabriel is
distinguished by his removal from a row of angels arranged vertically

along the sketch's right border. Moreover, his proximity to the Prophet is emphasized by the pointing of his index finger, which intersects with two diagonal strokes in darker black ink. This arrangement suggests that these two strokes, while functioning as perspectival lines for the throne's side panels, also act as lines of energy between Gabriel's hands and Muhammad's gaze and gesture. In this instance, the rendering of perspective serves to emphasize not only recession within a three-dimensional space but also an intimate and symbolically charged interaction between the Prophet and the angel of revelation. Finally, these two lines of energy reveal that the artist may have intended to provoke the viewer's eye into rebounding between the two depicted figures.

This sketch reveals further compositional methods used to emphasize Muhammad's importance and centrality. First, the angels and turbaned men are arranged in a manner suggestive of a circle. This frame focuses the viewer's eye on the Prophet and creates a halo-like form that spatially wreathes the Prophet. Acting as a central point, Muhammad is connected to other characters through multiple lines radiating outward: to the left, toward Gabriel; below, to the turbaned men; and to the right, toward the row of angels. The Prophet's link to the viewer is achieved through the two turbaned men below (one of whom bears facial features), who turn their heads and look out of the picture frame, as if to hail the onlooker to behold the enthroned hero.

To further accentuate this visual invitation, the artist explored several possible gestures, three of which reveal experimentation with the placement of the turbaned man's left hand, the palm of which is raised at different angles and heights immediately below Muhammad's throne. The highest and lowest hands are executed in dark black ink, suggesting that they are the preferred placement. As in other instances, the artist here refines the outline and internal details of a final painting within his preparatory sketch.[79] More intriguingly, in this trial run the artist appears to experiment with gestures and their placement to achieve an orbital effect around the Prophet. An enthroned monarch boasting an angelic entourage, Muhammad is here positioned as the "Center of a Compass"[80] as well as the focal point of his viewers' encircling gaze.

Beyond the artist's use of the enthronement paradigm and circular framing, the depicted objects also underline the importance of including symbolic attributes already during the sketch's inceptive phase. The throne is the largest and most central item in the composition, serving as a platform that physically separates the Prophet from members of his human and angelic court. The steps below further emphasize the throne's elevation, itself an apt metaphor for the Prophet's exaltation. Additionally, the Prophet wears a turban, although he is offered a crown by an angel standing on the left. By including both types of headgear, the artist depicts Muhammad as the seventh-century Arab leader of the community of faithful, who is recorded as wearing a turban despite his honorific title Possessor of the Crown (*sahib al-taj*).[81] The turban and

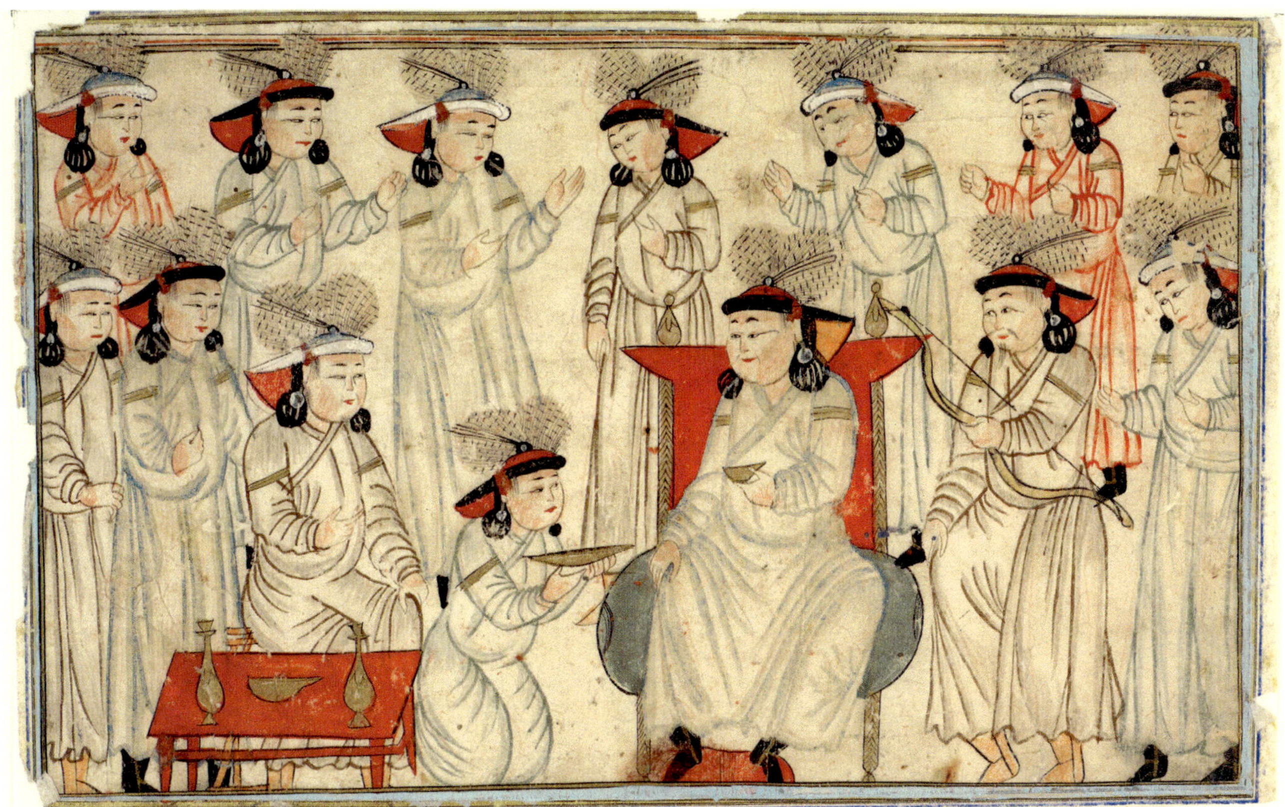

crown thus signal his dual role as spiritual and political leader—that is, his position as sacred ruler.

Instead of holding a weapon or other regalia, Muhammad lightly clasps a handkerchief in his left hand. A symbol of refinement retained in later Islamic depictions of earthly rulers,[82] the handkerchief is called a small ribbon (*dastarcha*) in Persian. A diminutive form of the ban-derol-canopy (*dastar*) found in coeval paintings of the Prophet, the handkerchief should be understood as the handheld symbol of impe-rial triumph.[83] Taken as a whole, this collection of objects—the throne, stepping stool, turban, crown, and handkerchief—relays Muhammad's supreme rank, his ascendancy in religious and worldly affairs, and his victory and immaculacy as God's elected messenger.

Fourteenth-century Persian drawings and paintings of enthroned rulers both echo and diverge from the sketch of the Prophet Muhammad in notable ways. As is the case for illustrated manuscripts that contain a set of images depicting both the Prophet and a ruler, compositional similarities show Muhammad according to a monarchical pattern while iconographic divergences stress his prophetic singularity. Numerous medieval Persian enthronement and audience scenes contained in the albums in which the sketch of the Prophet is included reveal this double practice of pictorial alignment and differentiation.[84] As a case in point, one watercolor painting shows an enthroned ruler holding a gold vessel and surrounded by men wearing similarly feathered headgear (fig. 1.18). On his left stands a man holding a bow (associated with the royal hunt),

1.18. An enthroned ruler, possibly Tabriz, ca. 1300–1325 CE. Staatsbibliothek zu Berlin—Preussischer Kulturbesitz, Orientabteilung, Diez A, fol. 71, p. 47.

and on his right kneels a court servant who ritually lifts a golden tray with both hands. Behind a low-lying table supporting several golden vessels sits another important personage, perhaps the ruler's minister or a master of ceremony.

This Ilkhanid enthronement scene from around 1300–1325 CE depicts a ruler in a court setting with attendants and dignitaries observing, assisting, or participating in a royal drinking ceremony. While it recalls the black-ink sketch of the Prophet in its use of the enthronement and audience format, it nevertheless diverges in both its composition and iconography. First, it is arranged in a landscape format with figures in two horizontal lines. Within this longitudinal layout, the enthroned ruler is slightly off-center in the bottom row and not substantially elevated above his entourage. Unlike the Prophet Muhammad, he is neither placed at the heart of an orbicular design nor depicted as larger or higher than the members of his court. Second, all his attendees are human—not angelic—and all wear caps ornamented with eagle or owl feathers, not white turbans. Although the enthroned protagonist does not sport a crown, the feathered cap remained closely associated with rulership within Mongol traditions and thus continued to be worn by Ilkhanid monarchs.[85] Such details suggest that the artist may have wished and/or was commissioned to record a real-life event that occurred at the Ilkhanid court during the early fourteenth century.

In this particular instance, the event appears to involve a drinking ceremony. The Mongols are well known for their rituals of libation, and Ilkhanid sources attest that drinks were offered when a ruler held an audience at his *ordu* (palace or camp) and when he acceded to the throne. During audiences and accessions, various drinks—including wine, clarified mare's milk (*kumis*), and honey mead—were selected by a master of ceremony and offered by a servant to honored guests according to rank.[86] In the Ilkhanid painting, the cupbearer offers the first drink to the enthroned ruler, the highest ranked member at court, while the master of ceremony choreographs the libation ritual from a table bearing the requisite golden vessels.

Additionally, the three potable substances of wine, milk, and honey presented at the Ilkhanid court find an intriguing parallel with the two, three, or four cups of similar liquids presented to the Prophet Muhammad during the so-called testing of the cups on the night of his celestial ascension, an episode that is depicted in detail within an Ilkhanid-period "Book of Ascension" (fig. 2.18). Much as the Prophet's ascent through the skies and his selection of the cup of milk fulfill initiatory purposes, the enthronement of a new Ilkhanid ruler and the imbibing of a liquid served as two key ritual components of accession ceremonies. In this painting, the cup that the ruler holds certainly alludes to his kingly investiture. However, through metaphorical allusion and interlinked storytelling, the Mongol enthronement libation ritual also held the potential to recall Muhammad's ritual passage into prophecy during his ascension to God. Thus, prophet and king not only are linked through enthronement paradigms but also engage in libations that both enact and bear witness to their divinely granted supremacy.

Despite such parallels, images of Muhammad remain distinguished from those of Ilkhanid monarchs through both pictorial composition and iconography. To give one final example, in another fourteenth-century Persian enthronement painting a ruler holds a jeweled ceremonial waistband, which symbolically cinches his body with worldly authority.[87] Thus, while contemporary rulers carry golden cups or gem-encrusted waistbands, they do not hold a handkerchief, which appears to remain a prophetic attribute and prerogative during the medieval period. In other words, while depictions of Ilkhanid rulers may cater to a documentary impulse, images of Muhammad appear more iconic in character, their visual indexes promoting his prophetic status rather than reflecting a specific courtly protocol.

It is important to remember that Muhammad had no palace in Medina. Indeed, "if we could speak of Muhammad having a court in our sense of the word, the mosque would have to be it."[88] To some extent, Muhammad's mosque-as-court helps explain the various visual parallels and divergences within medieval Persian depictions of the Prophet as king, in which motifs of religious sovereignty—such as angels, the flying *dastar*, a handheld handkerchief, and so on—give new meanings to enthronement and audience scenes, the latter a centuries-old mode of regal representation within the arts of the greater Middle East. In this regard, religious symbols can be considered a "voice-over" of older pictorial traditions, which themselves provide readymade patterns primed for reiteration.[89] Blending politics with faith, images of the enthroned Muhammad aim to display prophetic investiture by implementing new symbolic devices and compositional schemes within pictorial models commonly used to express worldly authority.

Depictions of the Prophet as a seated monarch surrounded by a courtly entourage did not end in the fifteenth century. Although Persian paintings depicting Muhammad as an active protagonist within his own life story became more popular at this time, the enthronement paradigm continued to be used by manuscript artists to pay homage to the Prophet at the beginning of illustrated books. But kingly audience scenes underwent further alterations and expansions. The resultant images highlight the fact that painterly practices emerge from the conjunction of artistic tradition and creative innovation, itself by no means an unprecedented phenomenon.

During the fifteenth century, several specific changes appear in paintings of the Prophet enthroned. Most important among them are, first, an increase in the number of individuals present at Muhammad's side; second, the inclusion of other narrative vignettes within the enthronement scene; and, third, the emergence of the Prophet's white facial veil and a large golden aureole encircling him and his companions. These three significant alterations in audience scenes could change the tenor, message, and interpretation of the depictions. For example, if an emphasis was placed on the Prophet's family and not just the *rashidun*, a greater devotional or perhaps sectarian reading of the image could unfold. Additionally, the inclusion of other tales within the painting may have served to locate Muhammad within a larger history of prophethood. And, finally, the emergence of the prophetic facial veil and flaming nimbus draw attention to Muhammad's divine beauty and light, which bewilder the mind and dazzle the eye of the viewer. Taken together, these three major changes in the iconography of enthronement scenes serve to emphasize Muhammad as God's prophet above and beyond his status as king—a major conceptual and pictorial shift that came to dominate Persian and Turkish manuscript paintings from the fifteenth century on.

The beginnings of this shift can be traced to a painting of the enthroned Prophet included at the beginning of an illustrated manuscript of Nasrallah Munshi's Persian translation of the popular animal fables *Kalila and Dimna*. While the Persian edition of the text was penned around 1145 CE, the date and provenance of the illustrated manuscript have been debated. Some scholars have attributed the manuscript to the patronage of the Timurid prince Baysunghur—and thus to the book atelier active in Herat between the 1410s and 1430s CE.[90] However, it seems more likely that the manuscript belongs to the courtly production of the Qara Qoyonlu (Black Sheep) Turkman governor of Shiraz and Baghdad, Pir Budaq (d. 1466).[91] A well-known patron of book arts, Pir Budaq supported artists from various cities, including Herat.[92] Thus, while a Timurid Herati style can be found within the manuscript's thirty paintings, it probably was made in Turkman Baghdad around 1460–65 CE.

The illustrated *Kalila and Dimna* manuscript opens with a series of three paintings before the tale of the two jackals begins in earnest. Serving as illustrations to the text's preliminary praises, the images include a frontispiece of a princely figure,[93] a depiction of the physician Barzuya before the Sasanian king Khusraw I Anushirvan (r. 531–79 CE), and a third and final painting showing Muhammad enthroned in an outdoor landscape (fig. 1.19).[94] The Prophet sits in what appears to be a wooden throne, whose side panels are ornamented with geometric latticework, and turns his head toward the Angel Gabriel. In response, Gabriel leans toward Muhammad; the figures exchange glances and gestures reminiscent of the earlier black-ink sketch of the enthroned Prophet (fig. 1.17).

While the composition's emphasis clearly centers on the intimate colloquy between Muhammad and Gabriel, its iconographic details and figural contents have expanded in a number of intriguing ways. First and foremost, a large flaming golden aureole encircles the Prophet and Gabriel, branching out on either side and encompassing the six figures on the right and left of the two central protagonists. In its size and shape,

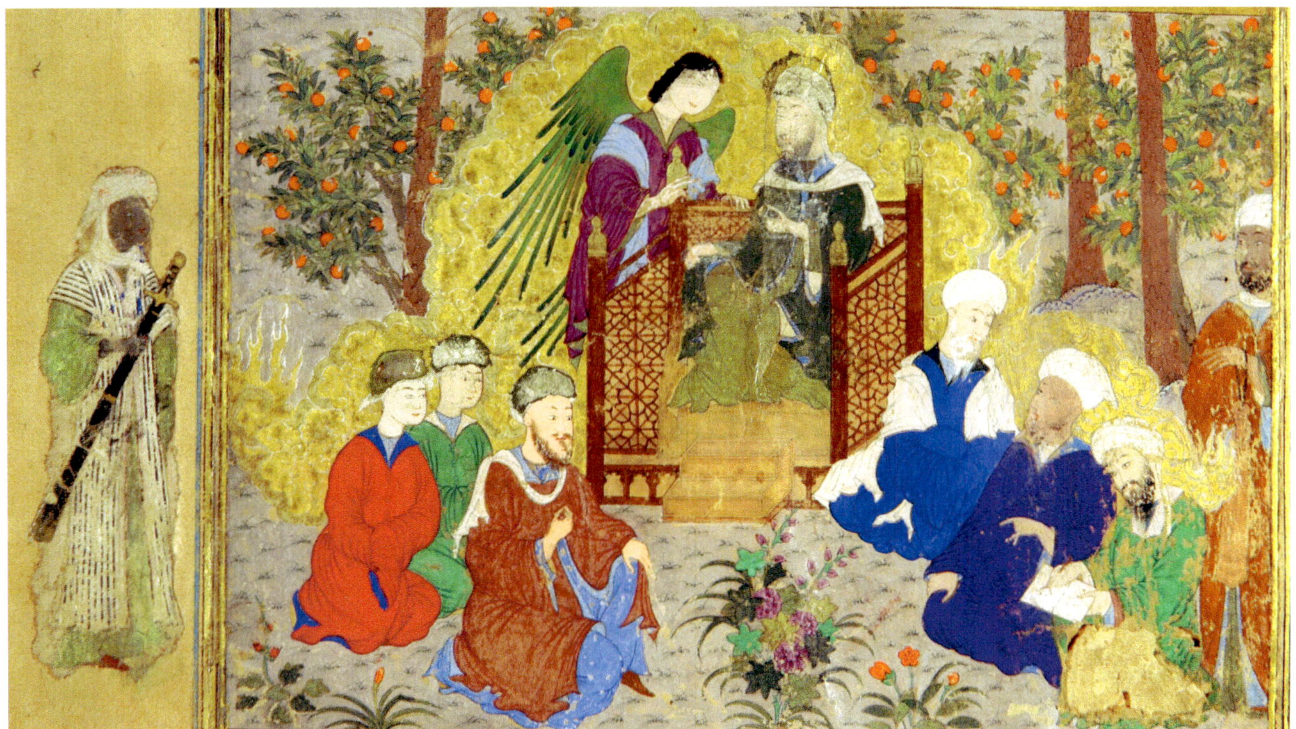

1.19. The Prophet Muhammad enthroned, his blazing aureole encompassing the four *rashidun*, Hasan, and Husayn, Nasrallah Munshi, *Kalila and Dimna*, Baghdad, ca. 1460–65 CE. Gulistan Palace Library, Tehran, ms. 2198, fol. 24r.

the aureole suggests unity and togetherness as well as sacred protection under an irradiating flux. Moreover, that it appears to emanate from Muhammad recalls the so-called light of Muhammad (*nur Muhammad*), also known as the light of prophethood (*nur al-nubuwwa*) and blaze of prophethood (*ghurrat al-nubuwwa*). The *nur Muhammad* is believed to be the primordial luminous substance created by God, which was transferred to Muhammad as a blessing for the entire Muslim community.[95] By means of the golden aureole, the painting analogizes the Prophet to a divine, generative, and all-encompassing radiance. Without a doubt, this symbolically charged iconographic device functions as a luminous metaphor for Muhammad while also serving as an indexical mark for God's presence on earth.

The pictorial development of the blazing aureole may be related to mystical devotions to the Prophet, which blossomed by the fifteenth century. At this time, Sufi texts compare the Prophet to a torch and light illuminating the darkness of the world.[96] For example, the writer al-Suyuti (d. 1505 CE) emphasizes the qur'anic terms illuminating torch (*siraj munir*) and light (*nur*), listing both among the many names of the Prophet (*asma' al-nabi*) in his work dedicated to the subject.[97] Mystical writers in particular saw a reflection of the prophetic presence in these two qur'anic expressions. For instance, al-Ghazali (d. 1111 CE) speaks of the *siraj munir* as a prophetic spirit and source of faith, while al-Sulami (d. 1021 CE) describes Muhammad's radiance as the light of guidance (*nur al-huda*) into true belief.[98] The painting echoes mystical descriptions of Muhammad as radiant light, adapting such allegorical expressions to older enthronement compositions in which the Prophet nevertheless remains represented with visible facial features. In other words, the paradigm of the Prophet as king here is overlaid with the pictorial analogy of the Prophet as flux, in some sense anticipating later works that render Muhammad wholly or partially as disembodied light (figs. 6.10 and 6.11).

In addition to the blazing aureole's link to mystical writing about the divine origins and luminous nature of the prophetic corpus, it appears that this iconographic device may also forward potentially sectarian claims. During the fifteenth century, Sunni and Shi'i communities in the Persian and Turkish world were not as firmly differentiated as they became after the battle of Chaldiran in 1514 CE. Indeed, members of the Prophet's family—including Imam 'Ali, the Prophet's son-in-law and one of the four rightly guided caliphs—were held in high esteem by Sunnis and Shi'is alike. Despite such commonalities, members of each faith community nevertheless elaborated ways to claim authority and legitimacy for themselves. Within Sunni spheres, emphasis is placed on the *rashidun* (including or omitting 'Ali), while in Shi'i spheres special devotion is afforded to 'Ali, Fatima, and their sons Hasan and Husayn. In Shi'i traditions, these four members of the Prophet's household, the so-called *ahl al-bayt*, are said to have existed in the divine realm as primordial silhouettes of light (*ashbah-i nur*) prior to their appearance in the flesh. Moreover, they are described as being made of, and partaking in, the *nur Muhammad*.[99] Thus, the metaphor of divine light is extended to members of the *ahl al-bayt* within Shi'i concepts of sacred immanence.

The artist who conceived the painting of the enthroned Prophet appears to engage, at least to a certain extent, with such sectarian discourses. The blazing aureole here acts as a spiritual device to highlight the supremacy of Muhammad and his companions: 'Uthman (holding a book), 'Umar, and Abu Bakr (with the white beard), seated on the right, and 'Ali, seated on the left. Although all four rightly guided caliphs are present in the scene, 'Ali has been separated from the three other *rashidun* and is accompanied by his young sons Hasan and Husayn, who kneel behind him. Outside of the aureole are two standing figures; these are perhaps Bilal, Muhammad's Abyssinian caller to prayer, and Qanbar, 'Ali's servant and sword-carrier. Like the warm embrace of an extended family, the flaming blaze encompasses Muhammad, Gabriel, the *rashidun*, and the *ahl al-bayt*. Most significantly, 'Ali, Hasan, and Husayn's simultaneous inclusion and separation (from the three *rashidun*) reveal that the artist purposefully bifurcated the painting in order to visually demonstrate a particular reverence for the figures at the core of Shi'i devotion. By including the Prophet's companions and the *ahl al-bayt*, the artist does not allow his painting to be interpreted as strictly Sunni or Shi'i. As a result, this fifteenth-century depiction highlights the process through which representations of Muhammad developed from the medieval to the early modern period, when faith systems were similarly in the process of crafting visual forms of expression based on both tradition and self-differentiation.

In this expanded enthronement scene, the aureole allows for a more mystical reading of the prophet-king as divine light. It also pays tribute to the *rashidun* while highlighting the set-apart members of the *ahl al-bayt*, allowing the viewer to engage in both nonsectarian and sectarian readings of the image. While the painting provides a testament to the growth of Sufi and Shi'i concerns, it also appears to follow Nasrallah Munshi's veneration of the Prophet in his foreword to *Kalila and Dimna*. Therein, he lauds God and Muhammad. He first describes God as "He Who illuminates the world with the lights of [His] knowledge" (*anvar-i hikmat* and *nur-i 'ilm*),[100] continuing with an elaborate homage to Muhammad, the seal of the prophets (*khatam al-nabiyyin*). Thereafter, he offers greetings and peace to Muhammad's companions (*sahaba*) and family (*al*).[101] These preliminary praises demonstrate that the Prophet's companions and family were frequently lauded conjointly rather than in isolation or contradistinction. In a similar manner, the painting's artist unifies the *rashidun* with the *ahl al-bayt* in his own visual encomium to God the "illuminator" and Muhammad the "seal of prophets."

In his foreword, Nasrallah Munshi also exhorts his readers to praise the Prophet and follow those who are in authority. Within the author's text and immediately above the painting appears a qur'anic verse urging the pious to honor Muhammad: "Indeed, God and His angels send blessings on the Prophet. Oh you who believe, send your blessings on him and salute him with respect."[102] Further, another verse from the Qur'an closes the author's encomium with the exhortation: "Oh you who believe, obey God, the messenger, and those charged with authority (*amr*) among you."[103] In this instance, the painting offers a pictorial exegesis to the qur'anic fiat excerpted by Nasrallah Munshi insofar as "those charged with authority" here include not only Muhammad's companions but also 'Ali, his sons Hasan and Husayn, and (by insinuation) their descendants, the imams. Adding a possibly sectarian twist to the author's textual praises, the painting's artist insinuates that authority—and not just reverence and devotion—are due to the Prophet's family.

Muhammad's "court" has thus expanded in two significant ways in this painting: it communicates a more mystical message about the Prophet's luminous being while simultaneously heralding the power and authority of both the *rashidun* and the *ahl al-bayt*. As such, it aids in tracking both Sufi and Shi'i concerns as these developed within depictions of Muhammad during the fifteenth century.

Beyond mystical and sectarian themes, at this time enthronement images of the Prophet also could promote Muhammad's foremost position as the seal of prophets within a long line of apostles sent to earth by God. In this regard, Muhammad's genealogy was significantly enhanced thanks to his placement within a venerable prophetic stemma.

His biography likewise could be augmented to include not only details from his life and times but also its prehistory, composed of numerous stories of the prophets who came before him. Collectively known as the *qisas al-anbiya'* (stories of the prophets), these tales circulated widely in both oral and written form by the fifteenth century. Within literary production, various versions of the *qisas al-anbiya'* were penned by medieval authors, most prominent among them al-Tha'labi (d. 1035 CE), al-Kisa'i (eleventh century CE), al-Nishapuri (eleventh century CE), Ibn Kathir (d. 1373 CE), and al-Rabghuzi (thirteenth and fourteenth centuries CE).[104] Written in Arabic, Persian, and Eastern Turkish, these prophetic tales enjoyed great popularity across the Islamic world, where they also thrived in practices of storytelling. Within oral spheres, the *qisas al-anbiya'* genre interacted with other tales, including narratives about the life of the Prophet Muhammad (*sirat al-nabi*) and the history of kings (*ta'rikh al-muluk*). As a result, histories of the prophets, Muhammad, and kings frequently were not separated according to a strict religious-profane dichotomy. To the contrary, they tended to intermingle freely in the flexible world of oral culture.

These multiple narrative genres also coexist in illustrated universal histories, which combine tales of the prophets and kings. While medieval Persian manuscripts typically depict these stories in discreet thematic and pictorial cycles, one single-folio painting highlights the manner in which kingly and prophetic tales could be represented in a complex and lively amalgam (fig. 1.20).[105] In this superb painting, most likely made around 1450 CE at the Turkman court in Shiraz, the Prophet Muhammad sits enthroned in the foreground while two other narrative vignettes fill the middle ground. These vignettes illustrate Moses slaying the giant 'Uj b. 'Anaq,[106] whose head protrudes through the painting's frame at the top, and the infant Christ in the lap of the Virgin Mary, who is accompanied by eight men sitting in rows behind her.[107] From Moses's triumphant miracle to the mother and child gathering in the upper left, this composite scene is populated with tales and images otherwise not found in representations of the Prophet enthroned.

As proposed by Basil Robinson, this unusual painting may depict an allegory of the Jewish, Christian, and Muslim religions.[108] This interpretation is supported by the inclusion of Moses, Jesus, and Muhammad, the prophetic messengers of the three major Abrahamic faiths. In such a case, then, it is possible that the painting served as a frontispiece or finispiece to a now-lost *qisas al-anbiya'* manuscript, as such tales were lavishly illustrated with paintings depicting the lives of the Abrahamic prophets, chief among them Moses, Jesus, and Muhammad.[109] The painting thus could be said to laud the triumvirate personifying the Abrahamic line while also supplying a visual summary of the lives of the text's most eminent protagonists.

Besides its allegorical function and synoptic effect, the painting also conveys the main message of all texts in the *qisas al-anbiya'* genre:

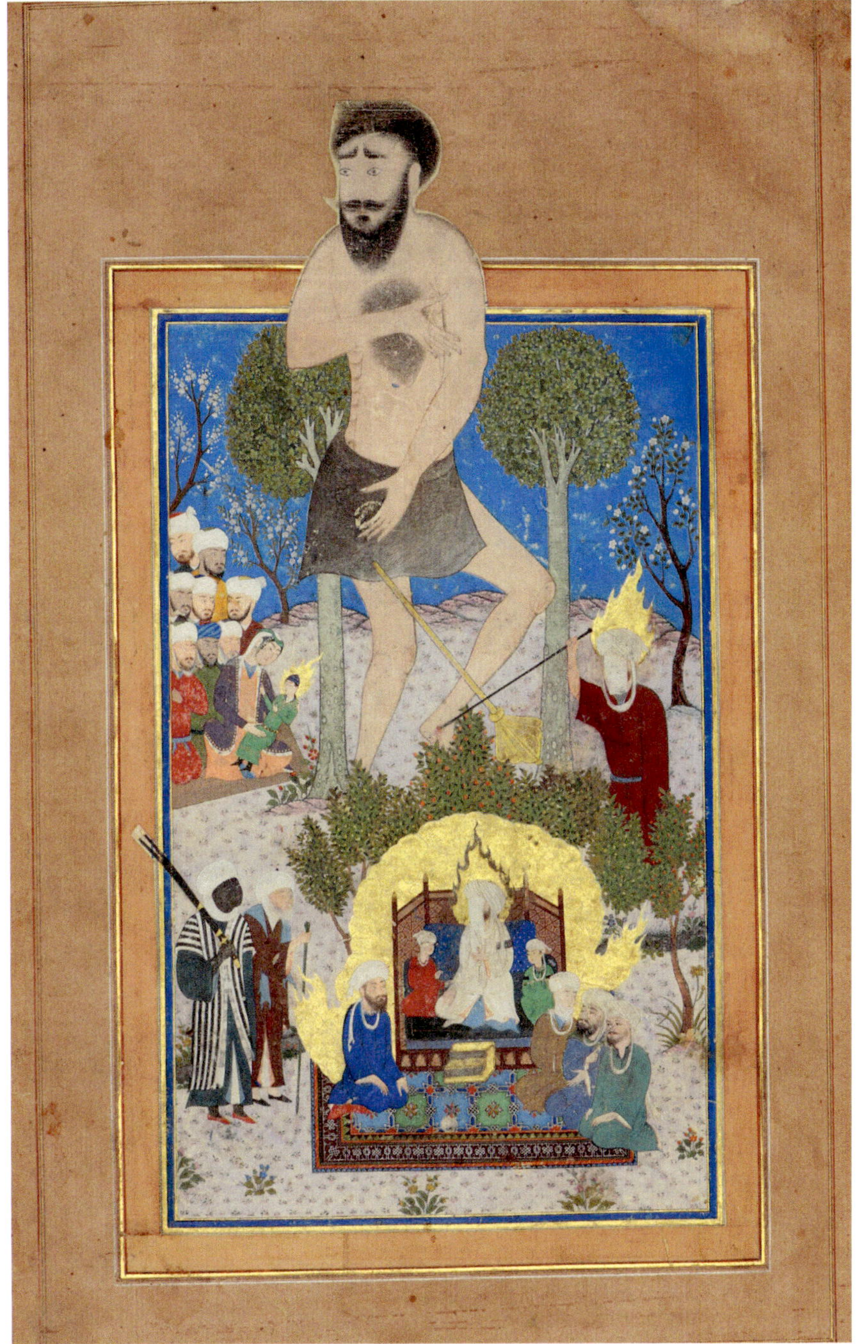

namely, that the prophetic past culminates in Muhammad, himself the
pinnacle of prophethood. In these stories of the prophets, Muhammad
is always the subject of the final chapter—and thus the symbolic seal
and formal culmination of a long line of delegates sent by God. So while
the painting may indeed provide an allegory of the Abrahamic faiths,
it also mobilizes the Judeo-Christian heritage in support of the finality
and supremacy of Islam and its messenger. The artist's placement of
Muhammad in the center foreground and within a throne encircled
by a blazing aureole serves to support his prophetic centrality, earthly
authority, and divine luminosity. Additionally, the vignettes depicting

Moses and Jesus are made to recede in space, acting as backdrops to the main act that unfolds front and center. So, while the painting may appear multiconfessional in its allegory of the Abrahamic faiths, it is far from ecumenical. On the contrary, it should be considered a visual argument for Muhammad's supreme rank, achieved here by the strategic cooptation of narrative scenes from the prophets' lives along with their insertion into a traditional enthronement scene. Here then, Muhammad accedes to the throne as primus inter pares.

Although a regnant legatee, Muhammad is also enmeshed in a series of miraculous tales associated with Moses and Jesus. Moses delivered a written law, spoke to God, and performed miracles, including the slaying of the giant 'Uj by striking him on the knee with his staff.[110] Moreover, in Sufi spheres, Moses is associated with divine light, which imprinted his face after God's revelations at Mount Sinai. A number of Islamic narratives inform us that he was so radiant that no man could look at him for forty days.[111] The painting's artist conveys Moses's miraculous deed and colloquy with God by depicting him with a white facial veil that barely contains the luminous imprint of the divine on his face, which bursts above his turban as a golden halo. Similarly, a miracle associated with Jesus appears depicted in the background: his ability to speak immediately after his birth, while in the cradle or when seated in Mary's lap.[112] As suggested by his gesturing index finger, the infant Christ appears to utter words or converse with his mother. Moreover, he bears a flaming halo indicative of his prophetic status, while the lack of a facial veil suggests that, unlike Moses and Muhammad, he has not yet received divine revelations or entered into a direct and intimate colloquy with God. The depictions of Moses and Jesus thus honor the miracles that exemplify their prophetic standing, while Moses's facial veil is intended to contain his blinding radiance in the aftermath of his encounter with God.

The narrative and iconographic devices used to depict Moses and Jesus enable the articulation of further symbolic messages about the Prophet Muhammad. By narrative association, the viewer is invited to interpret Muhammad's enthronement as a miracle. In this instance, however, the Prophet's miracle is not a supernatural action—such as his splitting of the moon or his heavenly ascension—but rather a state of being. Even more significantly, his status is not just that of a seated monarch but rather that of a sovereign flanked by Hasan and Husayn. No longer consigned to the ground (as in fig. 1.19), Muhammad's grandsons accompany him in cathedra. Although still young boys, they are elevated to the position and rank of the Prophet Muhammad, who is no longer alone or peerless in his kingly prerogative. Instead, Hasan and Husayn partake in Muhammad's rulership, miraculously sealing a long line of prophetic appointments.

The presence of Hasan and Husayn on the throne, encircled by a blazing aureole, supports the Shi'i belief that the light of God continued via Muhammad's descendants, the imams. Moreover, a number of Shi'i hadiths note that the prophethood (*nubuwwa*) of Muhammad was extended through the vicegerency (*walaya*) of the imamate—that is, that divinely decreed apostleship did not halt with the Prophet but rather continued through the imams, themselves considered primordial light silhouettes. While the prophecy of Muhammad came to an end with his death, a more "cosmic *walaya*," comprising the light of all the imams, remained alive as it percolated through the generations.[113] According to Shi'i belief systems, *walaya* is both the prolongation of *nubuwwa* as well as the element necessary to attain the completion of faith or religion (*kamal al-din fi'l-walaya*).[114] Accordingly, the miracle of prophetic sovereignty is not a stand-alone endeavor: it is inherited through the luminous substance sent by God and passed down via the prophetic bloodline. The painting captures this bitemporality by harking back to the light of God and the Abrahamic prophets and projecting forward to the Shi'i imams, who share in Muhammad's enthroned rulership. It also promotes a clear Shi'i interpretation of the Prophet's status as buttressed by his descendants, in the process insinuating that the last chapter of the "stories of the prophets" remains to be written.

Unlike this painting bearing Shi'i overtones, the vast majority of *qisas al-anbiya'* texts do not imply a sectarian stance. They do, however, describe Islam as the last of the Abrahamic faiths and members of the Muslim community as superior to all others. For example, one such narrative describes Muhammad's attainment of prophethood in the following words: "At that time the line of prophets had been broken. Commanding the enforcement of the good and prohibiting the bad had become extinct."[115] The Prophet thus resumes an interrupted line of prophecy, and, in his position as just and wise king, he enjoins good and forbids wrong.[116] Further, the text lists Muhammad's ascendancy and Islam's superiority among the many gifts granted by God. Among such gifts, God is said to have made Muhammad's followers the preeminent community per the qur'anic accolade "You are the noblest nation that has ever been raised up for mankind."[117] While this textual declaration encompasses the Islamic community writ large, the painting offers a more precise visual claim: that the "best of communities" is in fact the Shi'i community. The image thus presents a creative arena for sectarian messaging, above and beyond the text that it may have accompanied.

This last enthronement painting is remarkable in its sophistication. The Prophet Muhammad is shown as an ascendant messenger of God within a long line of miracle-working Judeo-Christian prophets. He is also a ruling sovereign, too brilliant to behold as he sits with a white facial veil and irradiates the golden light of God, which encircles members of his court, most especially 'Ali, Hasan, and Husayn. His two young grandsons do not sit on the floor; instead, they share in his kingship, just as they share in his bloodline. The painting stresses a past prophetic pedigree along with a future genealogical descent that is particularly central to Shi'i religious and political beliefs. These pictorial changes surely reflect new approaches to Muhammad's biography, anchoring it within other stories of the prophets as well as the growth of mystical devotions to the Prophet and Shi'i veneration of members of his family. Such Sufi-Shi'i trends emerged during the medieval period in a variety of spheres, in both doctrine and practice. Last, but certainly not least, by the fifteenth century mysticosectarian concerns also seeped into the pictorial arts, at which time painters saw fit to adopt and reconfigure the inherited enthronement paradigm to praise the Prophet according to the demands and expectations of an emergent elite clientele with increasing Sufi and/or Shi'i leanings.

From the thirteenth to fifteenth century, a number of illustrated manuscripts include depictions of Muhammad as an enthroned prophet-king. If placed at the beginning of an illustrated text, such paintings functioned as eulogistic frontispieces; if included at its end, as salvific finispieces. Unlike depictions that relate important moments in the Prophet's life (including his birth, revelations, miracles, celestial ascension, battles, and death) these images largely fulfill iconic rather than narrative functions. Even in paintings that include narrative scenes, the Prophet remains enthroned or sits cross-legged. Thus, these premodern images are rather static in their overall design, as Muhammad remains immobile within the parameters established by inherited enthronement and audience scenes.

The earliest surviving paintings of the Prophet Muhammad clearly follow the Persian iconography of sacral kingship, which was developed in both private and public spheres in Iran before the advent of Islam. Images of cosmic rulers endured well into the Islamic period. Whether included in manuscripts, coins, plates, or rock reliefs, such images of king and prophets tend to depict an exalted protagonist—seated or standing—who is invested with the right to temporal rule through God's angelic couriers. As such, early paintings of Muhammad show the Prophet imagined as a royal king bearing sacred qualities. Such attributes largely comprise nonphysical, external signs (ribbons, angels, flowers, etc.) that serve as visual indexes for his appointment, protection, and triumph under God. In these early Islamic paintings of Muhammad, he is shown as both a leader of his community and the last messenger of God. This conceptual composite of earthly and heavenly rule is refracted by inherited Persian artistic motifs that aim to bolster an imperial ideology of sacred governance for rulers whose right to sovereignty was doubly predicated on the Persian kingly paradigm and the Islamic prophetic example.

For many Muslim thinkers and writers, the generation of the Prophet and his immediate successors, the *rashidun*, epitomized an ideal and righteous rule in the history of humankind.[118] Thereafter, monarchs living in the lands of Islam turned to the prophetic exemplum, wishing to envision Muhammad as the paradigmatic sovereign within an Islamic context. For them, the Prophet served as the embodiment of a divinely decreed right to rule, in whose path they hoped to follow. Within Persian pictorial practices, Muhammad is shown as king—albeit with symbolic attributes that clearly elevate him to prophetic status—while kings are depicted as prophet-like. As a traditional repository of historic continuity, Muhammad was envisioned through texts and images whose rhetorical and visual strategies promoted his supreme rulership under God, a sacred sanction to which Muslim kings similarly laid claim over the centuries.

While some paintings of the enthroned Prophet emphasize Muhammad's angelic protection or primordial luminosity, others clearly address sectarian debates. During the fifteenth century in particular, increasing confessional differentiation can be tracked through historical and religious texts, ritual practices, and paintings of the Prophet enthroned. In such images, Muhammad is indeed a prophetic monarch, but he does not stand alone in his selection: he is either surrounded by the *ahl al-bayt* or shares his throne with his descendants. No longer the final culmination of the prophetic stemma, he is the momentary occupier of the institution of leadership, which is then passed down via his bloodline to the imams. In other words, he is a continuance and not an end—and he is placed at the very center of supercessionary sectarian discourses concerned with both politics and religion.

From the thirteenth to the fifteenth century, paintings of the Prophet enthroned are thus an invented tradition manifesting multiple iterations and following a variety of related visual typologies.[119] They present a sense of natural order that is rooted in the prophetic past, which is nonetheless constructed and invented time and again. As Craig Calhoun notes in this regard, "the continual reproduction of tradition necessarily involves many minor and some major revisions of it."[120] These improvisations are implemented by a variety of actors—including visual artists—and validated by group consensus. They also reflect contemporaneous religious, social, and political conditions, including the growth of mysticism and sectarianism across the Islamic world. Those promoting new worldviews often sought to legitimize their ideologies by recourse to the past, especially by recalling the prophetic exemplum; such newly emergent paintings of Muhammad demonstrate that "novelty is no less novel for being able to dress up easily as antiquity."[121] As ruler of a golden age, Muhammad was the quintessential prophet-king, a new yet traditional emblem of sacred authority as imagined within the realm of the painterly arts of premodern Islam.

1. Touati, "Le régime des images figuratives dans la culture islamique médiévale," 15.
2. For a general study of the subject, see L'Orange, *Studies on the Iconography of Cosmic Kingship*; for the Persian iconography of sacral kingship in particular, see, inter alia, Canepa, *The Two Eyes of the Earth*; Soudavar, *The Aura of Kings*; Baer, "The Ruler in Cosmic Setting"; and Choksy, "Sacral Kingship in Sasanian Iran."

3. Afsaruddin, "Where Earth and Heaven Meet," 197.

4. Meisami, "The Past in Service of the Present," 255.

5. Cook, "Did the Prophet Muhammad Keep Court?," 27.

6. On the invention of traditions through rhetorical stratagems, see Hobsbawm, *The Invention of Tradition*, 9–10.

7. Calhoun, "The Radicalism of Tradition," 911.

8. Ettinghausen, *Arab Painting*, 61. The volumes of this illustrated copy of the *Kitab al-Aghani* are held in the Millet Yazma Eserler Kütüphanesi in Istanbul (Feyzullah Efendi 1566), Dar al-Kutub in Cairo (Adab 579), and the Royal Library in Copenhagen (ms. no. 168). Also see the folio on loan at the David Collection, Copenhagen (inv. no. D 1/1990).

9. Farès attributes the Cairo volume to Baghdad in "Une miniature nouvelle de l'école de Bagdad."

10. Sayyid, *Dar al-Kutub al-Misriyya*, 102 (color image); Farès, "Une miniature nouvelle de l'école de Bagdad," plate III; and Farès, *L'art sacré chez un primitif musulman*, plates 4 and 5.

11. Farès, "Une miniature nouvelle de l'école de Bagdad"; and Farès, *L'art sacré chez un primitif musulman*, 661.

12. On Ilkhanid, Safavid, and Ottoman manuscript paintings of the *Mubahala*, see Gruber, "Questioning the 'Classical' in Persian Painting," 17–21.

13. See, in particular, Rice, "The Aghani Miniatures and Religious Painting in Islam," 130; Stern, "A New Volume of the Illustrated Aghani Manuscript"; and, most recently, Hillenbrand, "The Frontispiece Problem in the Early 13th-Century Kitab al-Aghani," 204–5.

14. On frontispieces showing rather generic depictions lauding a high office rather than a specific individual, see Hillenbrand, "The Schefer Hariri," 132; and on frontispieces as royal prototypes that convey a more general message about authority, see Ettinghausen, *Arab Painting*, 64; and Simpson, "In the Beginning," 241.

15. *Nasab Rasul Allah* (Genealogy of the Messenger of God), manuscript dated 1009 AH/1600–1601 CE, Doris Duke Collection of Islamic Art, Honolulu, Hawaii, acc. no. 10.3, folio 47; and Aydın, *Pavilion of the Sacred Relics*, 8.

16. Rice, "The Aghani Miniatures and Religious Painting in Islam," 133–34.

17. Redford, "Portable Palaces," 408. Additionally, Seljuk sultans were called the "possessor of the umbrella and bird" (*sahib al-qubba wa'l-tayr*). For a fourteenth-century tapestry depiction of the *chatr* held above an enthroned monarch, see Von Folsach, *For the Privileged Few*, 23, fig. 2.

18. Cook, "Did the Prophet Muhammad Keep Court?" 27.

19. Soudavar, *The Aura of Kings*, 13.

20. Harper, *Silver Vessels of the Sasanian Period*, 1:108–10, fig. 35; Harper, "Thrones and Enthronement Scenes in Sasanian Art"; and Grabar, *Sasanian Silver*, esp. plates 4 and 14.

21. Choksy, "Sacral Kingship in Sasanian Iran," 46; De Waele, "L'investiture et le triomphe dans la thématique de la sculpture rupestre sassanide"; and Berghe, "Les scènes d'investiture sur les reliefs rupestres de l'Iran ancien."

22. The canopy also recalls the personification of night (*Nux*) as depicted in Byzantine manuscript paintings.

23. Arjomand, *The Shadow of God and the Hidden Imam*, 93; and Curtis, "Royal and Religious Symbols on Early Sasanian Coins," 138.

24. Shenkar, *Intangible Spirits and Graven Images*, 178–79; Shenkar, "Royal Regalia and 'Divine Kingship' in Pre-Islamic Central Asia"; and Azarpay, "Crowns and Some Royal Insignia in Early Iran," 109, 114. Moreover, as noted in Azarpay, the highest deity of Zoroastrianism, Ahura Mazda, is frequently represented as a winged figure within a solar disk in Achaemenid and Hellenistic pictorial traditions.

25. Shenkar, *Intangible Spirits and Graven Images*, 131–40; and Curtis, "Royal and Religious Symbols on Early Sasanian Coins," 140.

26. Grabar, *The Shape of the Holy*, 71–104; and Grabar, "The Umayyad Dome of the Rock in Jerusalem," 48, plate 3, fig. 4.

27. On Arabo-Sassanian coins, see Gaube, *Arabosasanidische Numismatik*.

28. Heidemann, "The Representation of the Early Islamic Empire and its Religion on Coin Imagery," 38 and 44.

29. Hoyland, "Writing the Biography of the Prophet Muhammad," 593–96, fig. 2.

30. Arjomand, *The Shadow of God and the Hidden Imam*, 93.

31. Hobsbawm, *The Invention of Tradition*, 2; and Kubler, *The Shape of Time*, 64.

32. Calhoun, "The Radicalism of Tradition," 896.

33. Heath, *The Thirsty Sword*, 56.

34. Vermeulen, "L'Apparition du Prophète dans la *Sirat 'Antar*," 161.

35. Heller, *Die Bedeutung des arabischen 'Antar-Romans für die vergleichende Literaturkunde*, 34: "abschliessende Muhammad Legende."

36. For a summary of the tale, see Ateş, "Un vieux poème romanesque persan"; for a translation of the text in French, see Melikian-Chirvani, "Le roman de Varqe et Golshah"; and for a published Persian edition of the text, see ʿAyyuqi, *Varqa va Gulshah-i ʿAyyuqi*.

37. Khaleghi-Motlagh, "ʿAyyuqi," *Encyclopaedia Iranica*, http://www.iranicaonline.org/articles/ayyuqi-a-poet (accessed May 6, 2018).

38. For a description of the manuscript, its date, provenance, style, and contents, see Melikian-Chirvani, "Le roman de Varqe et Golshah"; and Pancaroğlu, "Resimli ve Tasvirli El Yazmaları," 575–79.

39. ʿAyyuqi, *Varqa va Gulshah-i ʿAyyuqi*, 120; and Melikian-Chirvani, "Le roman de Varqe et Golshah," 212, painting located between verses 2197 and 2198.

40. ʿAyyuqi, *Varqa va Gulshah-i ʿAyyuqi*, 119; and Melikian-Chirvani, "Le roman de Varqe et Golshah," 212, verses 2180–82. In ʿAyyuqi's text, the Prophet's followers include his companions (*sahiban*), friends (*yaran*), and soldiers (*sipah*). The term *yaran* in the plural indicates a group larger than the four rightly guided caliphs, who also are called in Persian the "four friends" (*char-yar*).

41. ʿAbd al-Muʾmin b. Muhammad moved to Konya from Khoy, Azerbaijan. See Pancaroğlu, "Resimli ve tasvirli el yazmaları," 576.

42. ʿAyyuqi, *Varqa va Gulshah-i ʿAyyuqi*, 121; and Melikian-Chirvani, "Le roman de Varqe et Golshah," 214, verse 2222.

43. In his text, ʿAyyuqi describes Muhammad as a sun (*shams*), the candle of Islam (*shamʿ al-Islam*), and the torch of mankind (*chirakh-i bashar*). See ʿAyyuqi, *Varqa va Gulshah-i ʿAyyuqi*, 119–20; and Melikian-Chirvani, "Le roman de Varqe et Golshah," 211, verse 2178; 212, verse 2179; and 212, verse 2194.

44. On Seljuk enthronement scenes in these various media, see Otto-Dorn, "Das seldschukische Thronbild"; Hillenbrand, "Images of Authority on Kashan Lustreware"; and Pancaroğlu, "A World unto Himself," 179–90. Pancaroğlu argues that Seljuk images of enthronements were intended to function as didactic praises to rulers, as visual enticements to monarchs to fulfill virtues associated with the ideals of rulership, and as aids to exhort the perfectibility of man, with the ruler as the apex of a process that is ultimately rewarded by cosmic status.

45. Yalman, "Building the Sultanate of Rum," 139, fig. 1.50.

46. Yalman, "Building the Sultanate of Rum," 140; and Yalman, "ʿAla al-Din Kayqubad Illuminated," 165, fig. 11.

47. On these symbolic intersections in Seljuk art, in particular within enthronement scenes, see Canby et al., *Court and Cosmos*, 76–77, 109–10.

48. ʿAyyuqi, *Varqa va Gulshah-i ʿAyyuqi*, 119; and Melikian-Chirvani, "Le roman de Varqe et Golshah," 212, verse 2187.

49. For a preliminary discussion of this painting, see Gruber, "Between Logos (*Kalima*) and Light (*Nur*)," 235–36 and fig. 3.

50. ʿAyyuqi, *Varqa va Gulshah-i ʿAyyuqi*, 120; and Melikian-Chirvani, "Le roman de Varqe et Golshah," 213, verse 2205–6.

51. ʿAyyuqi, *Varqa va Gulshah-i ʿAyyuqi*, 121; and Melikian-Chirvani, "Le roman de Varqe et Golshah," 214, verse 2221–24.

52. Dozy, *Dictionnaire détaillé des noms des vêtements chez les arabes*, 59.

53. Melikian-Chirvani, "Le roman de Varqe et Golshah," 35.

54. Simpson, "The Role of Baghdad in the Formation of Persian Painting," 115.

55. For an English translation (which omits the initial eulogies), see Levy, *The Tales of Marzuban*; and for the Persian edition, see al-Varavini, *Kitab-i Marzubannama*.

56. Simpson, "The Role of Baghdad in the Formation of Persian Painting," 103–5.

57. For a preliminary discussion of this painting, see Gruber, "Between Logos (*Kalima*) and Light (*Nur*)," 236–37 and fig. 4.

58. A member of the mint genus of herbs, the poley herb (*kaysu*), also known as pennyroyal or perennial mint (*Mentha pulegium*), has small blue or violet flowers with aromatic leaves that exude a minty aroma. Essential oil of the poley herb was used frequently in folk medicine, and today it is used in aromatherapy.

59. Al-Varavini, *Marzubannama*, Baghdad, 698 AH/1299 CE, Archaeology Museum Library, Istanbul, ms. 216, folio 1v; and al-Varavini, *Kitab-i Marzubannama*, 1.

60. Steingass, *A Comprehensive Persian-English Dictionary*, 114.

61. Eberhard and Boratav, *Typen Türkischer Volksmärchen*, 350–51.

62. Robinson, *Islamic Painting and the Arts of the Book*, 155–56, cat. no. III.103; and Gruber, "The Keir *Miʿraj*."

63. Masuya, "Ilkhanid Courtly Life," 102.

64. Grabar and Blair, *Epic Images and Contemporary History*, 25 and 52.

65. On the "small" illustrated *Shahnamas* of the Ilkhanid period, see Simpson, *The Illustration of an Epic*; and Simpson, "The Pattern of Early *Shahnama* Illustration."

66. Allsen, *Commodity and Exchange in the Mongol Empire*, 60–61.

67. See Simpson, *The Illustration of an Epic*, 56–83, plate 115; Soucek, "The Life of the Prophet," 194, fig. 1; and Shani, "Illustrations of the Parable of the Ship of Faith in Firdausi's Prologue to the *Shahnama*," 2–14, fig. 1.

68. English translation adapted from Warner and Warner, *The Sháhnáma of Firdausí*, 1:107; and Persian terms as found in the Ilkhanid *Shahnama* text illustrated in fig. 1.16.

69. On Muhammad's turban ('imama), see al-Tirmidhi, *Shama'il al-Nabi*, 56; and Hosein, "A Translation of the Ash-Shama'il of Tirmizi," 48.

70. See the four verses on the *rashidun* transcribed in Persian in Firdawsi, *Firdussi Liber regum qui inscribitur Schahname*, 6.

71. Shani, "Illustrations of the Parable of the Ship of Faith in Firdausi's Prologue to the *Shahnama*," 4–6, 12–13.

72. A possibility also noted in Soucek, "The Life of Prophet," 194.

73. See Gruber, "The Rose of the Prophet."

74. Hosein, "A Translation of Ash-Shama'il of Tirmizi," 283.

75. Nizami, *Makhzanol Asrar*, 109, verse 268.

76. Another enthronement scene also is included in an illustrated copy of Nizami's *Khusraw and Shirin* made in Tabriz in 1410 CE (Freer Gallery of Art, Smithsonian Institution, Washington DC, F1931.30, folio 6r). However, it was overpainted during the Safavid period with an overtly Shi'i composition. This painting and the manuscript of *Khusraw and Shirin* form the subject of a forthcoming study by Simon Rettig.

77. On the Diez albums in Berlin and Istanbul, see Roxburgh, "Heinrich Friedrich von Diez and his Eponymous Albums"; and on the Diez albums in Berlin, see İpşiroğlu, *Saray-Alben*; and Gonnella, Weis, and Rauch, *The Diez Albums*.

78. On enthronement scenes in the Diez albums, see İpşiroğlu, *Saray-Alben*, 12–13.

79. See Roxburgh, "Persian Drawing, ca. 1400–1450," 55.

80. On the Prophet Muhammad as the "Center of a Compass," see Ernst, "Muhammad as the Pole of Existence," 135.

81. Al-Suyuti notes that among the Arabs the turban is equivalent to the crown; see his *al-Riyad al-Aniqa fi Sharh Asma' Khayr al-Khaliqa*, 185–86.

82. See the depiction of the Ottoman sultan Mehmed II smelling a rose while holding a handkerchief in Rogers, "Mehmed the Conqueror," 91, fig. 35; and Raby, "Opening Gambits," 82, plate 2.

83. Soudavar, *The Aura of Kings*, 10.

84. For a discussion of these types of enthronement scenes in the Diez albums, see Kadoi, "The Mongols Enthroned"; İpşiroğlu, *Saray-Alben*, 10–11; and *Dschingis Khan und seine Erben*, 258–63.

85. Allsen, *Commodity and Exchange in the Mongol Empire*, 87.

86. Spuler, *History of the Mongols*, 100; and Tatar, "The Festive Beverages of the Khans," 457.

87. *Dschingis Khan und seine Erben*, 259, fig. 287 (Diez A, fol. 71, 47).

88. Cook, "Did the Prophet Muhammad Keep Court?" 25.

89. On the "voice-over" in art and received forms as "collecting equipment" ready for diversion, see Bourriaud, *Postproduction*, 7–11.

90. Binyon, Wilkinson, and Gray, *Persian Miniature Painting*, 65–66, cat. no. 44 [541B].

91. Robinson, "The Turkman School to 1503," 217.

92. Robinson, *Fifteenth-Century Persian Painting*, 23–24; and Stchoukine, "La peinture à Baghdad sous Sultan Pir Budaq Qara-Qoyunlu."

93. The princely figure could be the Ghaznavid sultan Bahramshah (r. 1117–52 CE), to whom Nasrallah Munshi dedicated his Persian translation, or Pir Budaq, for whom this illustrated copy may have been made.

94. A full reproduction of the folio with the painting and text is available in Robinson, "The Turkman School to 1503," 224, fig. 128; the painting (without text) is also published in Binyon, Wilkinson, and Gray, *Persian Miniature Painting*, plate 34-B.44 (c); and Fontana, *Iconografia dell'Ahl al-Bayt*, plate IX, fig. 15. For a related painting possibly by the same artist, also see Robinson, "The Turkman School to 1503," 225, fig. 229.

95. Rubin, "Pre-existence and Light," 94.

96. Schimmel, *And Muhammad Is His Messenger*, 123–43.

97. Al-Suyuti, *al-Riyad al-Aniqa fi Sharh Asma' Khayr al-Khaliqa*, 175 and 265. For these terms in the Qur'an, see Q 33:46 and Q 5:15.

98. Hermansen, "The Prophet Muhammed in Sufi Interpretations of the Light Verse," 224.

99. Rubin, "Pre-existence and Light," 99, 105, 113.

100. Nasrallah Munshi, *Tarjuma-yi Kalila va Dimna*, 2.

101. Nasrallah Munshi, *Tarjuma-yi Kalila va Dimna*, 2–3.

102. Nasrallah Munshi, *Tarjuma-yi Kalila va Dimna*, 3; and Q 33:56. On this qur'anic verse's use in practices of invoking blessings (*tasliya*) on the Prophet, see Meier, "Invoking Blessings on Muhammad in Prayers of Supplication and when Making Request"; and on its implications for

Islamic religious arts, see Blair, "Invoking the Prophet Muhammad through Word, Sound, and Image."

103. Nasrallah Munshi, *Tarjuma-yi Kalila va Dimna*, 4; and Q 4:59.

104. For two *qisas al-anbiya'* texts available in English translation, see al-Kisa'i, *Tales of the Prophets*; and al-Rabghuzi, *The Stories of the Prophets*.

105. Rogers, *Arts of Islam*, 175, cat. no. 207; Fontana, *Iconografia dell'Ahl al-Bayt*, plate VIII, fig. 13; and Robinson, *Fifteenth-Century Persian Painting*, 24–25, plate 2. Robinson also attributes the painting to the hand of the "Gulistan painter" because it resembles the illustrations included in the *Kalila and Dimna* manuscript produced in Herat around 1410–20 CE.

106. On Moses's slaying of the giant 'Uj b. 'Anaq when he entered the Promised Land, see Wheeler, "Moses," 255; and on the association of Moses's rod with supernatural feats, including the slaying of 'Uj, see Wheeler, *Moses in the Quran and Islamic Exegesis*, 61.

107. Per a *qisas al-anbiya'* text, the men may represent the children of Israel, to whom the infant Christ miraculously spoke while Mary carried him "on her breast." See al-Kisa'i, *Tales of the Prophets*, 330.

108. Robinson, *Fifteenth-Century Persian Painting*, 25.

109. On illustrated *qisas al-anbiya'* manuscripts, see Milstein, Rührdanz, and Schmitz, *Stories of the Prophets*; and Brosh and Milstein, *Biblical Stories in Islamic Painting*.

110. On Moses killing 'Uj with his staff (after the hoopoe pecked at the giant's brain) as related in a *qisas al-anbiya'* text, see al-Kisa'i, *Tales of the Prophets*, 253.

111. Brosh and Milstein, *Biblical Stories in Islamic Painting*, 35–39.

112. Milstein, Rührdanz, and Schmitz, *Stories of the Prophets*, 157–58.

113. Amir-Moezzi, *The Spirituality of Shi'i Islam*, 187.

114. Cited in Amir-Moezzi, "Notes à propos de la *walaya* imamite," 725.

115. Al-Rabghuzi, *The Stories of the Prophets*, 550.

116. On "enjoining good and forbidding wrong" (*al-amr bi'l-ma'ruf wa'l-nahy 'an al-munkar*) as an ideal form of just rule, see Cook, *Commanding Right and Forbidding Wrong in Islamic Thought*. The expression is based on a number of qur'anic verses (Q 3:104, 3:110, 7:157, and 9:71).

117. Al-Rabghuzi, *The Stories of the Prophets*, 552; and Q 3:110.

118. Cook, "Did the Prophet Muhammad Keep Court?" 27.

119. As David Roxburgh has noted, a number of drawings present a particular kind of "visual typology," in which types, sometimes recast, are used repeatedly. See Roxburgh, "Persian Drawing, ca. 1400–1450," 47 and 67.

120. Calhoun, "The Radicalism of Tradition," 896.

121. Hobsbawm, *The Invention of Tradition*, 5.

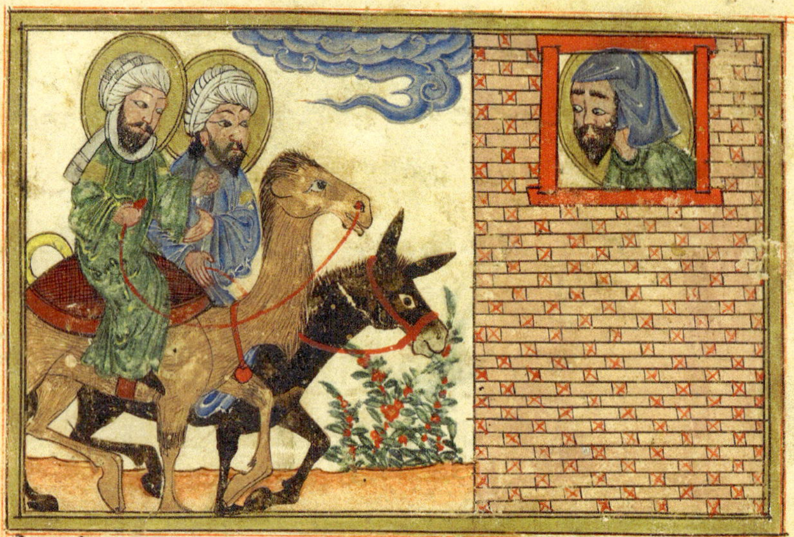

بالمسيح راكب الحمار ومحمد راكب البعير الذي بطونه موت بابل وكسرت اصنامها
وتزلزلت قصورها وازداد ملكها ۝ وفي كتاب اشعيا النبي من البشارة لمحمد عليه
السلم اقاويل كثيرة مزمون قريبه من واضح التأويل وعند ذلك يدعوهم الاصرار
على الباطل الا الافتراء بادعاء ما لم يعرف به الخلق من ان راكب البعير هو
موسى لا محمد عليه السلم ۝ وما الموسى واتباعه وبابل وهل طهرة له او لقومه بعده
ما ظهر لمحمد عليه السلم ولاصحابه فيها كلا لم يجاوز اهلها اسار اس ان رضوا من
الغنيمة بالاياب مع الياس ۝ ومما يوكد هذا الاستشهاد بقول الله الموتى في
السفر الخامس من التورية به الذي يعرف بالمثنى ۝ سوم اقيم لهم بنيا مثلك فراخوهم
واجعل كلمتي في فيه فيقول لهم كل شي آمره به وايما رجل لم يطع كلام من يتكلم
باسمي فأني انتقم منه فليت شعري هل خوف بني اسمي الاسوا الا اسمعيل فان قالوا
ان اخوتي من اسرائيل بمرا ولاذ العيص هل فيهم مثل الموتى بعد يستحق صفته
وتشابهه ۝ اليس يشهد لمحمد عليه السلم ما في هذا السفر ايضا ما هذه ترجمته ۝ جاء الله
من طور سينا واشرق لنا من ساعير واستعلن من رجل فاران ومعه ربوة الطاهرين

NARRATIVE IMAGES OF THE HEROIC PROPHET

From the fourteenth to the fifteenth century, a diverse array of narratives—most frequently treating biographical, historical, and apocalyptic themes—were augmented with cycles of paintings. Many such medieval and early modern illustrated texts include several sections, each accompanied by a series of illustrations, yielding a cumulative storytelling that takes both textual and visual form. With their images multiplied across chapters, illustrated manuscripts thus provide reels of information that produce almost cinematic effects.

In these painterly cycles, the Prophet can appear as if moving across a manuscript's pages, inviting readers to follow his tracks from the time of his birth until the moment of his death. Within Islamic book arts, Muhammad's life story was put on kinetic display, in the process showcasing Islamic practices of narration with increasingly imagistic tendencies. For writers, readers, and viewers alike, the making and viewing of images of the Prophet could serve to reinforce historical consciousness and knowledge, providing an immediate appeal through a reality effect engendered by the visual mode.[2] Indeed, as the Ilkhanid vizier Rashid al-Din notes above, the "signs" of Muhammad are marked on the "leaves of time," recorded "for all of us to see." These traces of the Prophet are made most visually manifest in painted manuscript folios.

Through the processes of historical recording, visual witnessing, and evoking emotional responses, images of Muhammad create symbolically charged tales that relate the life story and epic deeds of a divinely appointed protagonist. As a result, illustrated manuscripts that include images of the Prophet not only aid in constructing Muhammad's personhood but also generate paradigms of hero-hood. In many religious cultures, a hero must be commanding, compelling, and preordained; his heroic vocation is revealed through his external attributes as well as the particular features of his biography, which often follows a common three-part formula: earthly separation from the realm of God; initiation into hero-hood, prophethood, or sainthood; and eventual return to God.[3] As Joseph Campbell remarks in his seminal study of heroic paradigms, what such a figure in essence represents is the "benign, protecting power of destiny."[4]

Muhammad is by no means exempt from the hero formula. Already during his lifetime, his person and acts were lauded in almost mythic ways. In subsequent centuries, new narratives added a further aura of the miraculous and sacred to his biography. For example, some early histories of the Prophet simply provide the date of his birth, but later texts enhance the event with light metaphors and signs of the end of the existing world order. Taking such textual embellishments one step

The miracles of the Prophet are impressive, deeply affecting, and for all of us to see; the signs of its truth can be seen clearly and unmistakably in the leaves of time.[1]

Rashid al-Din (d. 1318 CE)

FACING, 2.1. Isaiah's vision of Jesus riding a donkey and Muhammad riding a camel, al-Biruni, *al-Athar al-Baqiyya 'an al-Qurun al-Khaliyya* (Chronology of Ancient Nations), Tabriz, 707 AH/1307–8 CE. University of Edinburgh Main Library, Ms. Arab 161, folio 10v.

further, images depicting Muhammad's birth commonly insert angelic actors, turning this human occurrence into a celestial event. Such textual and visual augmentations of Muhammad's biography transform historical narratives into tales of epic proportion, an evolution also discernable in pictorial representations from the medieval period onward.

Like other heroes, Muhammad's life is marked by major moments and enlivened by a myriad of metaphors. In addition to his momentous birth—a radiant and almost angelic arrival—other episodes and signs serve to bolster his position as God's final messenger. As foretold before his birth, Muhammad undergoes initiation into purity and is recognized as a prophet already during his childhood. As an adult, he is called to apostleship by God, enters seclusion, overcomes hardship and persecution, is forced into exile, and returns triumphant. As anointed prophet, he serves as a model leader of religious and political affairs, trustworthy arbiter of disputes, and reconsecrator of the Ka'ba. Along the way, he performs miracles and ascends through the skies to witness hell and heaven, where he communicates directly with God. Finally, after his death, he acts as chief intercessor for believers seeking salvation on the Day of Judgment. From Muhammad's emergence from the realm of the divine to his ultimate return to it, his time on earth is brief but decidedly heroic: he is protected and purified by God; he is called to spread, witness, and fight for the faith; he overcomes opponents and tribulations thanks to supernatural aid; and he builds a faith community on earth before making an apocalyptic return at the end of time. In short, Muhammad acts as master of the two worlds: the here and the hereafter.

In Islamic cultures, many historical and biographical narratives functioned as heroic cycles that were amplified by images of the Prophet. These texts were illustrated in Persian and Turkish cultural spheres most especially during the fourteenth and fifteenth centuries. Among them exists a series of universal histories, including al-Bal'ami's Persian translation of al-Tabari's *Ta'rikh al-Rusul wa'l-Muluk* (History of Messengers and Kings) of around 1300 CE, al-Biruni's *Al-Athar al-Baqiyya 'an al-Qurun al-Khaliyya* (Chronology of Ancient Nations) of 1307 CE, Rashid al-Din's *Jami' al-Tawarikh* (Compendium of Chronicles) of 1307–14 CE, and Hafiz-i Abru's *Majma' al-Tawarikh* (Quintessence of Chronicles) of about 1425 CE. Also noteworthy are three Ilkhanid and Timurid illustrated *Mi'rajnamas* (Books of Ascension), which today survive in both fragmentary and complete forms. These illustrated historical texts and books of ascension have been studied in the past, and such scholars as Priscilla Soucek and Robert Hillenbrand in particular have paid close attention to their pictorial representations of the Prophet.[5] Both Soucek's comparative study of several manuscripts and Hillenbrand's analysis of the pictorial cycle in Biruni's *Al-Athar al-Baqiyya* suggest that the episodes of Muhammad's biography selected for depiction served particular purposes: promoting Islam's superiority over other religions or forwarding a sectarian worldview, whether Sunni or Shi'i.

THE PRAISEWORTHY ONE

The illustrations thus provide insightful commentary on the ways in which images of the Prophet reflected, and possibly contributed to, inter- and intrafaith polemics.

The approach that this chapter adopts in studying paintings of Muhammad differs from previous scholarly endeavors. Rather than analyzing each manuscript on a case-by-case basis, or seeking to uncover primarily sectarian discourses, it aims to track an arc of iconographical development over the course of the fourteenth and fifteenth centuries. It thus moves freely between manuscripts in order to demonstrate that texts and images of the Prophet tend to construct a hero's life story, punctuated with tales of birth and infancy, a call to adventure, battles for the faith, ascendance to God, and acts of witness to the afterlife. These narrative patterns are constructed by interrelated images, whose pictorial development over time indicates that Muhammad became increasingly imagined via rhetorical tools and pictorial motifs supportive of his superhuman status. Through tactics of glorification and sacralization, the Prophet is shown as touched, guided, and shaped by a divine force throughout his valiant quest to secure and implement "true belief" (*iman*) in this world and the next.

Produced especially between 1300 and 1500 CE, these manuscript paintings provide a visual exegesis of history while creating a host of astutely crafted images and patterns that, despite their emergence from and debt to written narratives, promote Muhammad as a prophetic hero. Creative, expansive, and at times relatively autonomous from their accompanying texts, paintings offer important arenas in which visual metaphors intersect with narrative patterns in order to strengthen and magnify historical discourse. In many cultural traditions, great value is attached to narrativity, which provides a scaffold of sorts for cultural continuity, stabilizing the past and putting it to the service of the present.[6] Within premodern Islamic practices of crafting historical discourses about Muhammad, narrativity intersects with visuality in the artistic drive to create powerfully charismatic images of this hero-prophet of Islam.

Many Islamic textual and visual sources stress the Prophet's preexistential nature, impeccable character, and supreme status among humans and prophets. They describe Muhammad as foretold prior to his coming into the world and recognized as an apostle before his appointment to divinely ordained prophecy. Cosmic phenomena and portents also accompany his birth. Thereafter, in both childhood and adulthood, he must endure rites of purification and selection as well as a series of temptations and tribulations. Expressed through myriad motifs, the signs of Muhammad's predestined mission are couched as beatific and incontrovertible. What is more, they are unshackled from temporal and geographical limitations.

Celestial harbingers—including angels, clouds, and light rays—essentially serve as visions and proofs of Muhammad's prophecy. As visual devices, they bear witness to his special attributes and divine anointment. In Islamic traditions the two most important validations of God's presence among humankind are the Qur'an—a "clear book" (*kitab mubin*) that, in its written form, is concrete and tangible—and Muhammad, the ultimate embodiment and vehicle of God's "clear signs" (*bayyinat*). Via objecthood and personhood, the Qur'an and Muhammad conjointly epitomize sacred revelation and election on earth.

Much as qur'anic scripture signaled the descent and completion of a heavenly prototype considered existent since time immemorial, Muhammad was thought to have originated in a distant, numinous realm. Signs and visions of his future coming were discerned in events and texts throughout the centuries. For instance, early Muslim thinkers and writers turned to antecedent Jewish and Christian scriptures in an effort to uncover and decode presages of Muhammad's prophecy. In this particular practice of Muslim biblical scholarship, the Prophet is announced and identified as the last apostle sent by God.[7] The biblical annunciation of Muhammad was thought most evident in Isaiah 21:7, which describes a watchman's vision of chariots and horses as well as riders of camels and donkeys. For Muslim interpreters, this apocalyptic vision came to be understood as a twin prediction of Jesus, the donkey-rider, and Muhammad, the camel-rider.[8]

The biblical attestation of Muhammad's prophecy gained further traction in the Qur'an, most especially chapter 61 (*surat al-saff*), verse 6. In this declamatory verse, Jesus tells the children of Israel that a prophet will come after him: his name will be Ahmad, and he will carry "clear signs" (*bayyinat*) of prophecy, although he will be accused of practicing magic. For a number of exegetes, the name *Ahmad*—a superlative adjectival noun meaning "The Most Praised One" in Arabic—finds a parallel in the Paraclete, that is, "The Celebrated One" prefigured in the Bible (John 4:16 and 26; 15:26).[9] The Paraclete acts as a guide, witness, intercessor, and mediator, as well as an announcer of things to come. These manifold duties are also those of Muhammad, the final Messenger and herald of eschatological events.[10] Moreover, within the Hadith, Muhammad himself claims the name Ahmad as a form of prophetic self-attestation;[11] the name also is habitually listed among the many names of the Prophet (*asma' al-nabi*) in a variety of other texts.[12] Hence, the praise-name Ahmad serves to laud Muhammad's final position in the Abrahamic prophetic line as well as his preeminent position as the intercessor of his community on the Day of Judgment.[13]

Within written sources, Isaiah's apocalyptic vision of Muhammad and Jesus is discussed in the *Chronology of Ancient Nations*, an influential historical work composed by the medieval scholar and scientist al-Biruni (d. 1048 CE). In his treatment of the subject, al-Biruni is especially interested in computing the alphanumeric value of prophecies, including those found in the books of Daniel and Isaiah. Of Isaiah's vision, he states confidently that the "rider of the donkey" (*rakib al-himar*) is Jesus (*al-Masih*, or the Messiah), while the "rider of the camel" (*rakib al-ba'ir*)

    THE PRAISEWORTHY ONE

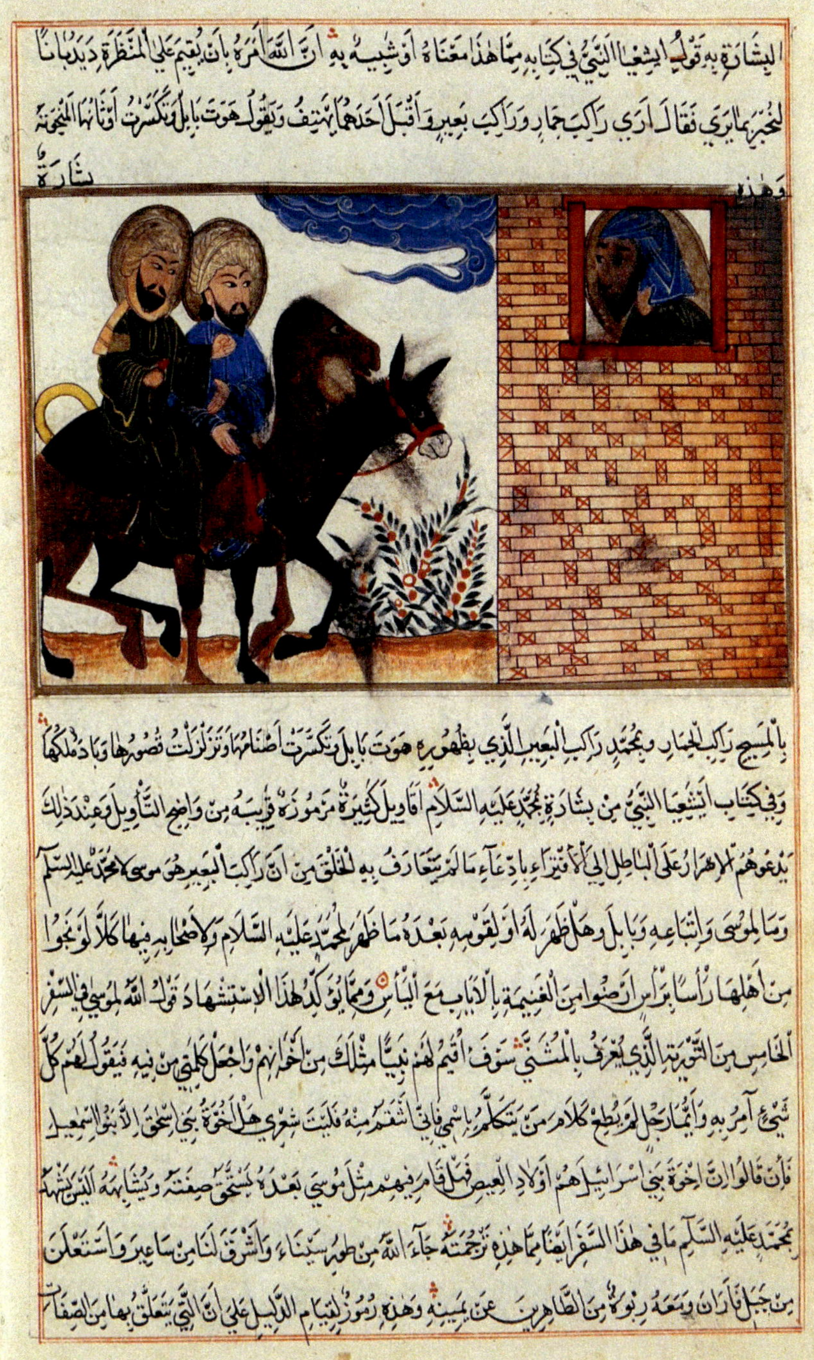

is none other than Muhammad—although some members of the Jewish community interpret the latter as Moses.[14] Additionally, al-Biruni informs his reader that the vision of Isaiah includes many hints (*aqawil kathira*) that are encoded (*marmuza*), rather than clear, statements; however, such enigmatic hints, he continues, easily lend themselves to an interpretation in favor of Muhammad's prophetic annunciation.[15]

During the Ilkhanid period, when al-Biruni's *Chronology of Ancient Nations* was produced as an illustrated manuscript (in 1307 CE), Isaiah's vision was a subject of pictorial depiction (fig. 2.1). Subsequent copies of the manuscript repeat this composition, as can be seen in a version produced in Ottoman lands around 1560 CE (fig. 2.2). Although separated by more than two hundred years, the two paintings are strikingly similar: in both, a watchman standing in a brick building observes two men riding beasts of burden, above whom a cloud swirls as if a felicitous celestial sign. In the foreground is a camel-rider represented in a larger scale, wearing a green cloak and a turban with an end piece (*shamla*) wrapped under his chin and resting on his left shoulder.[16] The camel, the color green, and the *shamla* function as Muhammad's attributes, enabling the viewer to properly identify the main protagonist, who is given prominence in the image's foreground. Behind the Prophet appears Jesus, riding a donkey and wearing a blue cloak and simple turban. Quite usefully, the Ilkhanid painting (fig. 2.1) includes a short, probably a posteriori inscription above the painting that identifies the scene as a "depiction of the Messiah [Jesus] and the Praised One [Muhammad]" (*surat al-masih wa'l-muhammad*).

Although Isaiah's vision is related to the fall of Babylon, the Ilkhanid painting has been interpreted as perhaps offering commentary on the recent fall of Baghdad to the Mongols—and the city's restitution under Islam thanks to the newly emergent Muslim ruling elites of Iran.[17] Indeed, in the past scholars have attributed this exegetic function of images to other illustrated manuscripts made during the Ilkhanid period.[18] However, this hypothesis is difficult to maintain in the case of the Ottoman painting (fig. 2.2), an almost exact replica of the Ilkhanid prototype. More significantly, beyond a possible yet tenuous reference to the fall of Baghdad, the painting's iconography constructs a visually legible transcript promoting Muhammad's divinely decreed election and his prophetic superiority through his juxtaposition with Jesus. As such, the image should instead be read as a visionary representation of the "glad tidings" (*bashara*)—a term used immediately above the Ottoman painting, as if it were the painting's caption—of the Prophet's ascendancy and finality, which may have echoed the particular religious discourses of the day.

The Prophet's superiority is achieved through a process of figural coupling. He stands before and partially obscures Jesus, much as the prophetic camel overshadows the Messiah's donkey. While his right hand holds the camel's rein, his left hand is prominently raised and shaped into a fist. This circular gesture is not only guided toward the watchman but also placed on full display for the viewer, whose eye is further drawn to the clenched fist by Jesus's upturned palm. As noted in the previous chapter, gestures count among the most important encrypted signs present in Islamic paintings—or, to borrow al-Biruni's fitting expression, signs that appear enigmatic (*marmuza*) but whose meanings are clear. Here, then, the round, globelike fist represents cosmic authority and worldly power, held aloft by the Prophet Muhammad, underpinned and upheld by his prophetic predecessor Jesus, and attested to by a third-party witness. The painting therefore offers a visual augury of Muhammad's divine sanction and earthly mandate.

As in Islamic texts, the image makes recourse to Christian precedent in order to promote Islam's superiority. It also relies on figural juxtaposition to articulate a point of comparison and differentiation for Muhammad, depicted as the companion and surpasser of Jesus, who in the Qur'an announces the former's preeminence as "The Most Praised One" (*Ahmad*). In both texts and images, Jesus acts as Muhammad's prophetic predecessor and foil, as well as a reference point to expedite a process of rhetorical and visual one-upmanship that ultimately grants Muhammad a clear competitive edge. As the embodiments of Christianity and Islam, respectively, Jesus and Muhammad epitomize the two faiths, partnered in mutual cooperation and opposition. They also form a binary paradigm within Muslim apologetics that aimed to counter anti-Islamic Christian narratives stating that Muhammad was not foreseen. Through the comparative and visionary mode, the painting thus offers corroborative evidence that authenticates Muhammad's heroic status and endorses Islam's ascendancy.

Much as Muhammad is twinned with Jesus, both the camel and donkey also carry messianic connotations. In this regard, Muslim sources state that the destruction of the idols at Babylon occurred only after the advent of Muhammad, the camel-riding redeemer of humankind after end times.[19] In addition, the camel acts as the proof of Muhammad's prophecy and his apocalyptic return, at which time this blessed "rider" and "possessor" of a camel is expected to reappear.[20] The conjoining of Jesus and Muhammad, along with their respective apocalyptic beasts, stresses Isaiah's vision as a glimpse into a faraway future—after time itself. As a result, the painting not only depicts a supercessionary discourse involving the prophetic protagonists of Christianity and Islam; just as critically, it discloses and imagines a visionary domain in which the depicted scene invites the painting's beholder into a kind of visual rapture.

The Prophet's entry into the terrestrial world ushered in a number of celestial signs and miraculous events. Much as he was foreseen by trustworthy witnesses and believed foretold in sacred books, the traces of Muhammad's divine origins were thought already imprinted on his father and mother, 'Abdullah and Amina, before his birth. Textual sources inform us, for example, that 'Abdullah's forehead emanated a light (*nur*). It was this light, rather than the man per se, that was of keenest interest to Amina.[21] On her pregnancy, 'Abdullah's light was transferred to her body, and she became so radiant that, according to Muhammad's biographer Ibn Ishaq (d. ca. 761–70 CE), she saw "a light come forth from her by which she could see the castles of Busra in Syria."[22] In this early account, it is evident that light symbolizes Muhammad's sacred preexistence within God's realm, his prophetic progenitors, and his own parents. Additionally, texts narrate that this effulgence—even while Muhammad was still in Amina's womb—was so powerful that it reached Busra, a Christian monastic center best known as home to the monk Bahira, who recognized Muhammad's signs of prophecy well before the beginnings of revelation. A complement to Isaiah's vision, this refulgent in utero light also enabled a Christian foreseeing of Muhammad's divinely decreed apostleship before his corporeal appearance on earth.

Christian and Islamic texts also describe the miracles that marked the conceptions and births of both Jesus and Muhammad.[23] For example, in his *Golden Legend*, a popular medieval religious work on the lives of Christian saints, Jacobus de Voragine (d. 1298 CE) enumerates several prodigies accompanying Christ's nativity. Among them were the collapse of the Roman Temple of Peace, the apparition to the magi of the star in the east (Matthew 2 and Luke 2), three suns that fused into one, and the ox and ass bowing to Jesus at the manger, where a multitude of angels appeared and sang.[24] Similar marvels heralded Muhammad's birth. For instance, Ibn Ishaq records a Jew in Yathrib calling out at the top of his voice: "Tonight has risen a star under which Ahmad is to be born!"[25] In this narrative, a member of the Jewish community living in what eventually would become the city of the Prophet (Medina) announces the coming of Muhammad the Paraclete through the cosmic sign of a rising star. Other Islamic narratives likewise describe shooting stars that pelted devils on Muhammad's birth. These devils were disallowed entry into three of the heavens on Jesus's nativity; on Muhammad's birth, Muslim writers stress, they were entirely disbarred from all seven heavens.[26] The stars pelting the devils were believed to provide a celestial sign of Muhammad's prophethood;[27] they also ushered in a final and complete triumph of good over evil, which had been achieved only partially by the Abrahamic prophets before the advent of Islam and its Messenger.

In other Islamic texts, a series of new order traditions herald Muhammad's birth. For example, according to the tenth-century Persian historian al-Bal'ami, when Muhammad was born, Persian Zoroastrian religious and palatial structures were annihilated alongside pagan statuettes of gods and goddesses; the idols in Mecca fell and broke, as did Persian fire-temples and the arch of the Palace of Ctesiphon, built by the Sassanian king Khusraw I (d. 579 CE).[28] It is not difficult to see reflected in this textual redaction al-Bal'ami's own geopolitical slant as well as his religious and cultural milieu in medieval Islamic Persia. However, the story also is reminiscent of apocryphal tales about Christ's nativity, most especially those trumpeting the collapse of the Temple of Peace. Thus, the destruction of Roman and Zoroastrian shrines to past religious and political power inaugurates the beginnings of sacred Christian and Muslim history, respectively. The starlit births of both Jesus and Muhammad thus are couched as triggering a total and absolute break with a putatively idolatrous and ignorant past.

The cosmic importance of the two figures' births is also elaborated through a variety of iconographical devices found within manuscript paintings. In both Western and Eastern Christian book art traditions, the representation of Jesus's nativity and the adoration of the magi were

     THE PRAISEWORTHY ONE

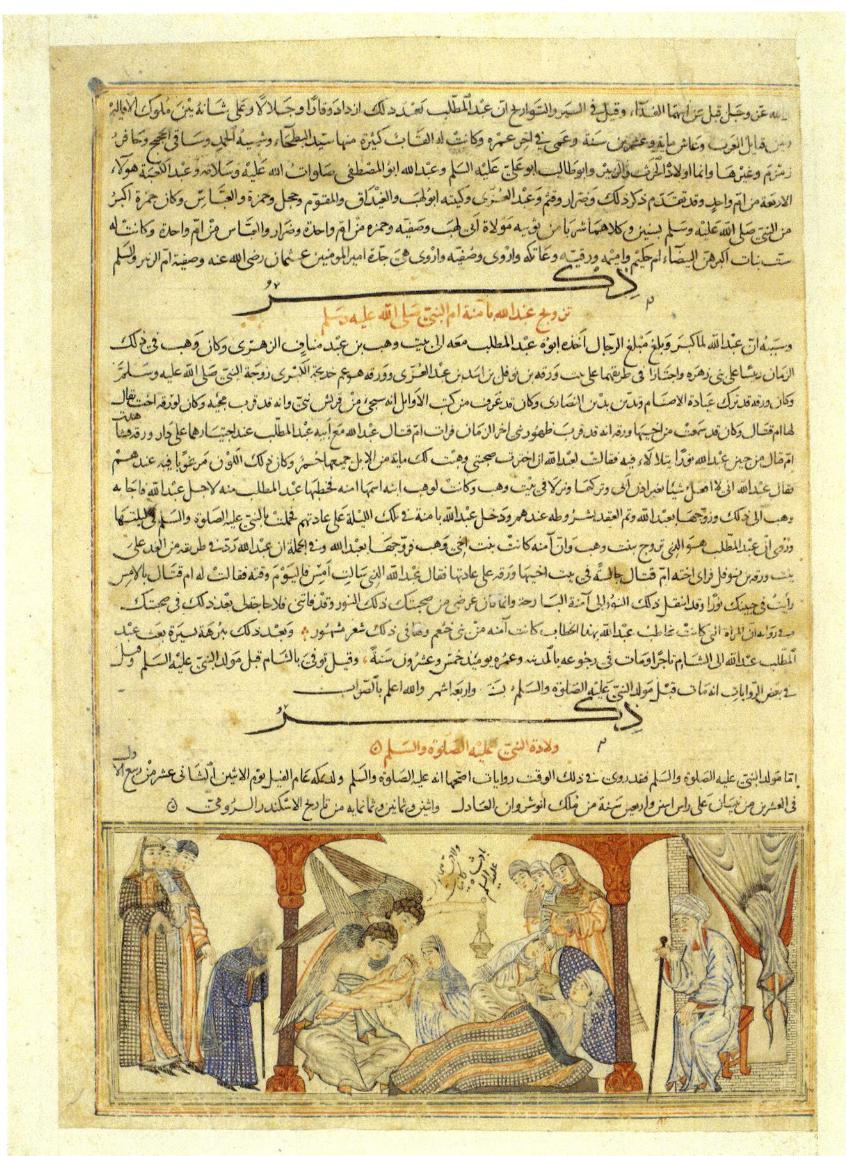

2.3. The Prophet Muhammad's birth, Rashid al-Din, *Jami' al-Tawarikh* (Compendium of Chronicles), Tabriz, 714 AH/1314–15 CE. University of Edinburgh Main Library, Ms. Arab 20, folio 42r.

standard subjects for iconographical treatment by 1300 CE,[29] at which time illustrated cycles of the life of Muhammad began to be produced in Ilkhanid Iran. In addition to a series of five paintings of the Prophet in al-Biruni's *Chronology of Ancient Nations*, the earliest and most extensive cycle of prophetic imagery appears in Rashid al-Din's *Compendium of Chronicles* of 1307–14 CE. This universal history includes a lengthy and detailed section narrating Muhammad's life, in which his birth, battles, and miracles accompany their related written descriptions. As in a graphic novel, the narration of the Prophet's biography in this medieval Persian illustrated manuscript is both effective and appealing because it enables the reader's constant visual shuttling between text and image.[30]

The painting depicting Muhammad's birth in the *Compendium of Chronicles* is the earliest surviving image of its kind in the Islamic pictorial record (fig. 2.3). While the illustration includes an abundance of visual details, the text that it accompanies is strikingly brief: in only two lines of text above the painting, the author Rashid al-Din records a statement by the Prophet's companions noting that Muhammad was born in Mecca during the year of the elephant. The equivalent dates are provided in accordance with the regnal years of the Sasanian monarch Khusraw I Anushirvan (r. 531–79 CE) and Alexander the Great (r. 336–23 BCE). No *hijri* year is provided; this omission may simply underscore the fact that the Islamic lunar calendar would only be established after Muhammad's emigration to Medina in 622 CE. The textual section on the Prophet's birth is here exceedingly succinct: it is devoid of particulars and explanations, and its only concern seems to be establishing the accurate year of Muhammad's birth per two of the major calendars in use at the time.

Despite (or perhaps due to) the brevity of the author's written account, the painting embellishes the narrative of Muhammad's birth by offering visual details that help fill in the gaps left by the text. In the central bay of the horizontal register, the Prophet's mother Amina is covered by a sheet as she reclines on a pillow. A midwife and other female servants tend to her with a golden chalice-shaped bowl and other dishes. A newborn Muhammad is swaddled in a cloth and held aloft by one of two angels, the second of which holds what appears to be a golden censer or lamp (above this angel a later inscription in Persian identifies the scene as the "royal birth of the Ruler of Mankind, peace be upon him"). In the right register sits an old man holding a walking stick; this figure is most likely Muhammad's grandfather, 'Abd al-Muttalib. Finally, on the left, a hunched lady leans on a cane beside three standing women, who may represent Muhammad's potential foster-mothers, including Halima.

As previous scholars have noted, this depiction of Muhammad's birth reveals the influence of Christian iconography on the formation on Ilkhanid figural compositions: the painting's tripartite structure echoes Christian triptychs, and the reclining mother, swaddled child, angels, and cluster(s) of three figures recall medieval European illustrations of Christ's nativity.[31] To no small extent, then, this painting reflects Mongol-Christian artistic exchange in Greater Armenia and the province of Azerbaijan between around 1250 and 1350 CE. At this time, the Ilkhanids established capital cities in Tabriz and Sultaniyya, northwestern Iran. During the first few decades of the fourteenth century, the book atelier in Tabriz—where manuscripts of Rashid al-Din's *Compendium of Chronicles* were produced and illustrated prior to being sent to Arab and Persian lands under Mongol control—was staffed with numerous scribes and painters, among them Christians from Byzantine lands (*Rum*), Georgia, and Armenia.[32] The Ilkhanid painting of Muhammad's birth thus exemplifies the ways in which diverse visual systems were adopted and adapted via the dynamic movement of peoples, goods, and art across Eurasia during the medieval period.

Christian pictorial traditions certainly contributed to the formation of Islamic religious painting under Ilkhanid patronage.[33] Armenian manuscript paintings played a particularly significant role, in no small

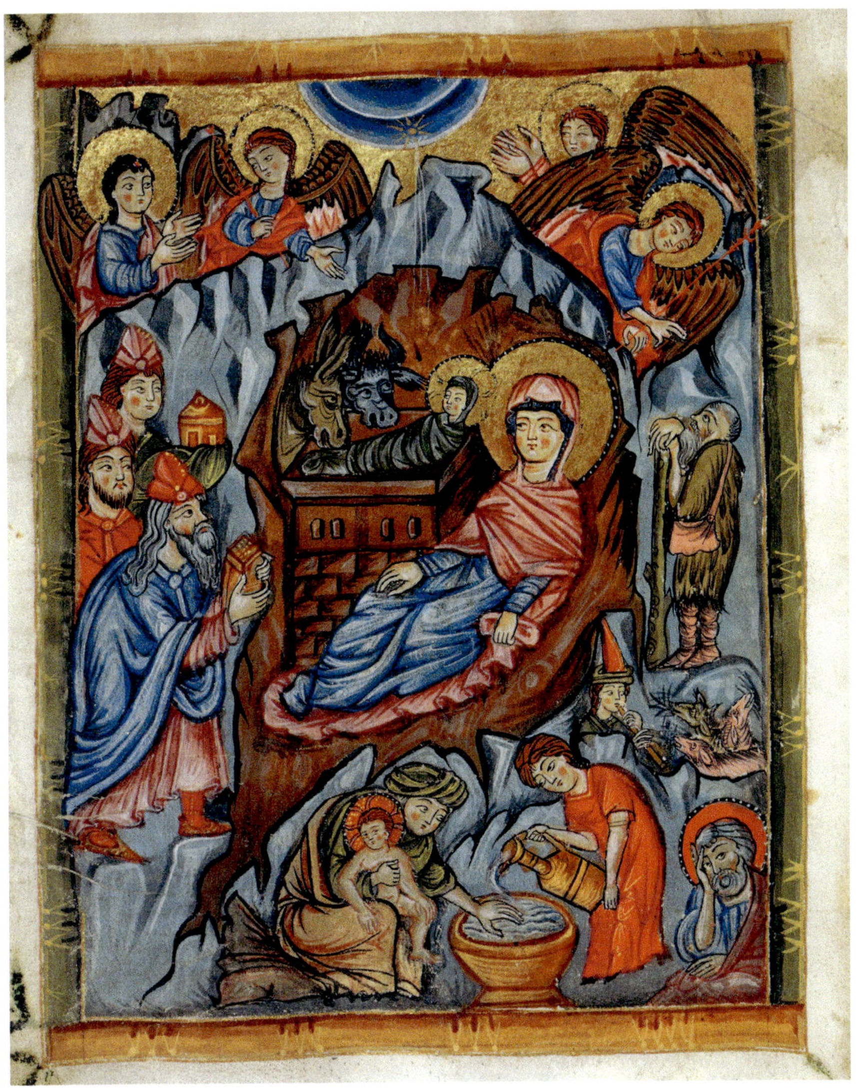

part because Armenian lands had come under Mongol rule. The town of
Gladzor, an important Armenian manuscript production center in the
Siunik area north of Tabriz, benefited from especially favorable conditions under the Ilkhanids, including the exemption of monasteries from
taxes. While some Armenian painters and scribes continued to produce
illustrated manuscripts in Gladzor and other monastic centers, others
sought Ilkhanid patronage in nearby Tabriz and Sultaniyya.[34] Thus,
Armenian artists produced illustrated manuscripts both in Christian
monasteries and in the Ilkhanid book atelier during the fourteenth
century. In Tabriz, these and other artists extended and creatively ad-
justed various Christian iconographical conventions and prototypes in
order to create, for the very first time in the history of Islamic book arts,
pictorial programs of religious themes and import.

By the early decades of the fourteenth century, Armenian manuscript depictions of Christ's birth had become relatively standardized,
as can be seen in an illustrated copy of the Gospels made in 1323 CE (fig.
2.4).[35] This manuscript was made by Toros Taronatsi, a scientist, poet,
scribe, and painter who worked in Gladzor, where he collaborated with

prominent intellectuals specializing in the interpretation of scripture.[36] In Taronatsi's depiction of the nativity, the Virgin Mary reclines below the swaddled Christ child, to whom the ox and ass bow in adoration. Above Jesus, a miraculous star emerges from the rounded blue firmament, its three white rays descending toward this "luminous child."[37] In the upper right and left corners of the painting, pairs of angels point to Jesus and make other prayerful gestures while engaging in dialogue. To Mary's left a shepherd receives news of the blessed birth; to her right the three magi approach with their gifts. Finally, in the lower right corner appears another pictorial vignette, in which the haloed Joseph sits pensively as two midwives bathe the newborn child, a second scene that is intended as a confirmation of Christ's sinless nature as well as a prefiguration of the rite of baptism.[38] In Taronatsi's painting, the star and bath offer a kind of pictorial exegesis doubly stressing the infant's sacred radiance and spiritual purity.

Although their formats and palettes diverge, the painting of Muhammad's birth appears in pictorial conversation with Taronatsi's near-contemporaneous depiction of Christ's nativity. The similarities can be seen especially in each painting's figural compositions: a reclining mother (Mary and Amina), a swaddled child (Jesus and Muhammad), an older man using a cane or support (Joseph and 'Abd al-Muttalib), clusters of three figures (magi, maid servants, and wet nurses), coupled angels, and a miraculous star or hanging lamp. The latter devices act as visual metaphors for both religious heroes' divine luminosity, revealing each painter's awareness of the power of iconography to emphasize the unseen but numinous attributes of both Jesus Christ and the Prophet Muhammad. At times, such visual glosses entirely transcend their attendant texts, as is the case for Muhammad's birth in Rashid al-Din's narrative, in which not a single mention of angelic beings or the "light of Muhammad" (*nur-i Muhammad*) is made. In this instance, the pictorial mode provides a nonverbal yet effusive disquisition of the Prophet's radiant, quasiangelic status.

Paintings of Muhammad's birth and life continued to be included in manuscripts made during the fifteenth century, particularly in illustrated copies of the *Majma' al-Tawarikh* (Quintessence of Chronicles) penned by Hafiz-i Abru (d. 1430 CE), the court historian of the Timurid ruler Shahrukh (r. 1405–47 CE). While based at the Timurid court in Herat, Hafiz-i Abru was officially responsible for writing universal and dynastic histories.[39] To no small extent, his *Quintessence of Chronicles* was intended as an updating of Rashid al-Din's *Compendium of Chronicles*. These Ilkhanid manuscripts served as both textual and visual templates for the historian and for artists tasked with producing an up-to-date illustrated universal history for the Timurid monarch.

Shahrukh's reasons for commissioning illustrated histories were many; for one, they enabled him to fashion himself as a historically conscious monarch and renewer of Islam.[40] Like his royal patron, Hafiz-i Abru was a strong proponent of history's capacity to inculcate moral behavior among individuals, especially rulers. In this regard, he wrote, "As for the ultimate point of history, it is to provide an example and an examination, an admonition and a warning, to know of the changes affecting dynasties, peoples, and faiths, so that one may follow the good and abstain from the sinful. . . . So in truth, the science of history is the knowledge of past people . . . and is a noble and honorable science, particularly for anyone seriously desirous of acquiring praise and a good name."[41] For ruler and writer alike, a sound knowledge of history was believed capable of inducing pious behavior and judicious action in handling the affairs of both religion and state (*din* and *dawlat*).

Within Islamic history, the sanction of precedent via the narration and illustration of Muhammad's biography enabled rulers such as Shahrukh to make claims to the prophetic legacy. Indeed, Hafiz-i

Abru draws a clear analogy between religion and rulership: to his mind, righteous government is the corollary of prophethood, and thus "religion and kingship are twins." He continues, "Neither is made perfect except through the other, for religion is like the base and kingship like the pillars: assuredly the base without the pillar is useless and the pillar without the base collapses. Thus religion without kingship is vain and kingship without religion has no foundation."[42] Divine kingship and justice count among the ruler's rights and duties; however, without the support of religion and the prophetic example, such regal prerogatives are bound to buckle and disintegrate.

Most likely energized by his belief in the educational and ethical lessons to be gleaned from history and religion, Shahrukh requested that Hafiz-i Abru's *Quintessence of Chronicles* be put to picture around 1425 CE.[43] In this Timurid illustrated manuscript, paintings of the Prophet's life follow the pattern established by its Ilkhanid precursor, the *Compendium of Histories*. However, both the Timurid text and images are often expanded to include more elaborate narratives and novel compositions, underscoring the extent to which the writing and illustrating of Muhammad's biography remained an active and ever-evolving craft, in which the Prophet's life story involved forms of fabulation, mythmaking, and allegorical expression—all of which were carefully cultivated to enhance his heroic cachet.

A scene of the Prophet Muhammad's birth is also included in Hafiz-i Abru's *Quintessence of Chronicles* (fig. 2.5). Like its Ilkhanid predecessor (fig. 2.3), the painting retains the horizontal format and includes three registers, here divided by a wall decorated with blue revetment tiles rather than by two red columns. To the right, 'Abd al-Muttalib sits on a chair as he holds a walking stick, and to the left an old woman hunches over. In the center of the composition, only a recumbent Amina and two angels holding Muhammad and a censer or lamp remain; the two clusters of three lady servants and three foster-mothers have been removed from the composition.

From a formal perspective, the Timurid painting appears more minimalist in its component parts. The synoptic effect is in large part due to the excision of nonessential figures, which may have been seen as detracting from the central subject matter: the birth of Muhammad. Moreover, unlike the Ilkhanid painting, whose colored washes are largely restricted to red, blue, and ocher, the Timurid scene includes large swathes of bright hues (including green and yellow). In the latter, a premium has been placed on bright coloration rather than gradated modeling, endowing the birth scene with a sense of vibrancy and immediacy.

Unlike the Ilkhanid manuscript, whose section on Muhammad's birth comprises only two lines of factual description, the Timurid text includes a much more elaborate entry highlighting a number of other significant details. For example, Hafiz-i Abru relates that when Amina was pregnant she received a revelation from heaven informing her that she was carrying a blessed creature, who is the "seal of [all] creatures"

    THE PRAISEWORTHY ONE

(*muhr-i khala'iq*) and who must be called Muhammad—"The Praise-worthy One." Further, Amina is recorded as stating that at the time of Muhammad's birth she saw a light emanating from her son that illuminated the entire world. Pavilions in the Levant were lit with his radiance, which rose to the heavens and stars. Hafiz-i Abru then moves on to a discussion of Muhammad's primordial light (*nur Muhammad*) and the signs of Islam's impending ascendancy at the time of his coming into the world. Such signs include the destruction of the idols at the Ka'ba in Mecca, the extinguishing of fire in all fire temples (*atashkadas*), the desiccation of the Lake of Saveh, and the smashing of the twelve parapets of the Arch of Nushirvan.[44] From prefiguring Islam's triumph over both Arab polytheism and Iranian Zoroastrianism to explaining the mysterious disappearance of a body of water and predicting the Muslim forces' military victory over the Sasanians at Ctesiphon in 637 CE, the birth of Muhammad takes on cosmic proportions, begetting a sacred and successful course for Islam in its Iranian geocultural milieu.

For some scholars, both this section's contents and its placement after the Sasanian dynasty in Ilkhanid and Timurid universal encyclopedias suggest that Muhammad's birth should be considered an appendix to Iran-centered—rather than Islam-centered—history.[45] Indeed, Hafiz-i Abru focuses his attention on the extinguishment of pre-Islamic Persian fire temples and the collapse of the palace of Ctesiphon, both of which function as architectural embodiments of religious and royal power in Iran before the advent of Islam. No mention of these quintessentially Iranian and Zoroastrian structures is to be found in Rashid al-Din's text. Hafiz-i Abru therefore must have augmented and tailored his narrative for Shahrukh and other Muslim members of the Timurid elite ruling over Persian lands. To craft his tale of Muhammad's birth and its portent signs, this creative compiler of history turned to oral tales and other written narratives on the subject. Among the textual sources that may have influenced him, Bal'ami's Persian-language history also enumerates the omens concerning the fall of the Persian Empire at Muhammad's birth. Bal'ami acknowledges such modifications, emphasizing the fact that "events in Arabia and Sasanian Persia were already interconnected before the rise of Islam."[46] Thus both Bal'ami and Hafiz-i Abru consider the two geocultural spheres to be part of the same trajectory that joined early Islamic history on the day of Muhammad's birth.

Although the Timurid painting of Muhammad's birth does not address the collapse of old world orders, it certainly pays visual tribute to the "light of Muhammad" (*nur Muhammad*) via a large flaming nimbus emanating from the newborn's head. The Timurid painter's accentuation of this metaphorical light provides a conspicuous and strategic modification of the Ilkhanid prototype, in which Muhammad's body does not exude any radiance whatsoever. Despite its novel inclusion in a birth scene, the notion of the *nur Muhammad* was not a new development during the fifteenth century. From early on, a number of exegetes, biographers, and mystical poets helped fashion the concept of

Muhammad as primordial light or luminous body derived from God's incandescent essence and emitted as creative substance into the world. This notion stipulates that God epiphanized himself as light, which then manifested itself as the light of Muhammad, from which the entire universe came to exist prior to the Prophet's later physical manifestation on earth. Within the history of Islamic pious imagination, the concept of the *nur Muhammad* highlights sustained attempts to reach beyond conceptual literalism in favor of imagining a more metaphorical Muhammad.

Already in the earliest Islamic textual sources, the analogy of light was harnessed as a rhetorical device to describe the Prophet's more sacred qualities. For example, in several places the Qur'an mentions a glowing light or lamp that writers understood as a metaphor for Muhammad. In a number of verses (e.g., 5:15, 33:46), it is stated that God sent a light and a book to his people to lead them out of darkness. Muslim exegetes interpreted these verses as evidence that God communicates with humans through his book (the Qur'an) and his Prophet, the latter an embodied light indicative of divine revelation. In addition, a number of the Prophet's Sayings (*Hadith*) further elaborate on the concept of the *nur Muhammad*. To give just one example, the famous Hadith compiler al-Bukhari (d. 256/870) records one of Muhammad's companions as having stated that: "Whenever he went in darkness, [the Prophet] had light shining around him like the moonlight."[47]

Still other verses in the Qur'an—most famous among them the "Light Verse" (24:35: *ayat al-nur)*—were interpreted by mystical thinkers as a metaphor for Muhammad as a torch (*misbah*) illuminating an eternal tabernacle (*mishkah*) shining from the east to the west.[48] Through Sufi hermeneutical practices, spiritually inclined exegetes made significant contributions to the idealization of the Prophet as divine light.[49] In such mysticointerpretative texts, Muhammad is often praised as the "light of faith" and the "light of guidance," both honorific epithets that equate light with prophetic guidance and Muhammad with embodied religion.[50] While the concept of the *nur Muhammad* developed in Arabic-language sources, it also pervaded medieval Persian Sufi texts, which tended to emphasize luminous forms of theophany.[51] Thus, a highly developed mystical lexicon that celebrated the Prophet through a plethora of light metaphors was well established by the Timurid period, at which time Sufi tendencies and concepts became increasingly manifest in the art and architecture of the greater Islamic world.

The Timurid painting of Muhammad's birth pays tribute to the evolution of the concept of Muhammad as sacred light. Indeed, the birth scene changed considerably within the span of just one century, from the Ilkhanid domestic scene populated with servants in wait to the later work in which a heavenly and radiant newborn lights up the sky-blue tiles in the background. Muhammad's entry into the human world is thus spiritual and heroic: he is born glowing with God's light, escorted by angelic regiments, and wrapped in a cerulean aura. His birth represents a sacramental and exalted encounter with worldly matter, in which the realms of the sacred and profane are shown as copresent.

In addition to his foretelling and luminous birth, Muhammad's childhood included a number of miraculous signs of his prophecy before his appointment to apostleship and the beginnings of revelation, both of which occurred in the maturity of adulthood. These infancy and coming-of-age stories stress his purity and superhuman strength as well as the signs of prophecy imprinted on his body, present in nature, and confirmed by celestial phenomena. As Ibn Ishaq relates in his biography, already as a newborn Muhammad caused a number of miracles, among them the overflowing of milk in his foster mother Halima's breasts as well as the gushing forth of milk in the udders of her she-camel and the sheep in her flock.[52] A "blessed creature" and a "gift from God," Muhammad proved a godsend to those who came into direct contact with his miracle-inducing, life-sustaining body.

The two most popular tales about Muhammad's childhood, which were illustrated in Islamic manuscripts from 1300 CE onward, were the splitting open of his chest and cleansing of his heart during his youth and his recognition as a future prophet by the Christian monk Bahira during his teenage years. The splitting open of the chest functions as physical evidence of Muhammad's spiritual cleansing and sinless nature, a necessary preparation for and significant precursor to his prophetic mission. The phenomenon attests to his singular capacity to survive a physical ordeal to which any ordinary human being would have succumbed. In addition, his recognition by Bahira as a divinely sent messenger echoes other narratives about Muhammad's predestination, which was thought to be encoded in antecedent Hebrew and Christian scriptures. In the latter instance, Muhammad's prophetic fate is observed and confirmed by a contemporary Christian holy man capable of reading signs in sacred books, in the sky, in nature, and on Muhammad's physical body. Taken together, the childhood episodes of the splitting of Muhammad's chest and his recognition as a prophet by Bahira deploy initiation and recognition tropes, both of which reinforce the formidable character and elevated status of the hero, who often traverses a long and arduous road of trials before reaching final triumph and apotheosis.[53]

The earliest ordeal that the young Muhammad faced was the so-called "splitting of the chest" (*shaqq al-sadr*).[54] Although the story varies in its details, its general narrative arc is as follows: when he was three years old, Muhammad played in the desert with his milk brother 'Abdallah under the watch of Halima. One day, three angels in the shape of men carried him off, split open his chest, and washed his heart in a golden washbasin containing water gathered from mountain snow, the Zamzam well, or the Kawthar pool. Once Muhammad's heart was cleansed and a black blood clot removed, the men placed his heart back into his chest cavity, which they fastened shut. The cauterization mark became widely known as Muhammad's "seal of prophecy" (*khatam al-nubuwwa*), although it is also described in Islamic textual sources as a mole-like protrusion located between his shoulder blades. It is this physically impressed proof of his sacred purity and prophetic call that Bahira recognized on Muhammad's body about a decade later.[55]

Biographers and historians disagree as to the number of occasions on which Muhammad's chest was split open: some argue that it only happened once, during his childhood; others believe that it happened twice, once when the Prophet was a young boy and once at the beginning of his celestial ascension; still others contend that the splitting of his chest happened three times: in childhood, at the beginning of his prophetic mission (*al-ba'th*), and just before his ascension. In all three cases, it is clear that the splitting of the chest functions as an initiation into prophethood and an invitation into the abode of God.[56] Through this radically invasive rite of purification, Muhammad's physical body thus transforms into an "angelic fabric" (*al-'amaliyya al-mala'ikiyya*)— and only in such a consecrated state of being can his prophetic mission and ascent to the celestial spheres occur.[57]

The splitting of Muhammad's chest and the washing of his heart occur before the launch of his prophetic appointment and vocation in adulthood. Despite the event being a momentous experience of his childhood, it was represented only rarely in Islamic book arts. The most significant depiction of this event appears in an illustrated manuscript copy of al-Bal'ami's Persian edition of al-Tabari's *Ta'rikh al-Rusul wa'l-Muluk* (History of Messengers and Kings), probably produced in Mosul around 1300 CE (fig. 2.6).[58] In this Persian manuscript painting, a very young Muhammad—without a robe, long hair plaits, or a beard—is held with his arms raised by three men, who, with surgical precision, open his chest to remove his heart and wash it in the gold vessel held below. On the left, a bare-breasted Halima runs toward the scene as she pulls her hair in a sign of distress. According to al-Bal'ami's account, which accompanies this scene, Muhammad informs Halima on her arrival:

> Three persons came with a golden basin and ewer. They opened my abdomen from the chest to the pelvis, and took out what was inside my abdomen and washed it in that gold basin. They put it back in and said to me: "You came pure (*pak*) into this world and now you are even purer." Then one of them inserted his hand into my chest and took out my heart, split it in two, removed a black blood [clot] (*khuni siyah*) from it, and threw it away. He said: "This [clot] belongs to Satan and it exists in everyone's body. However, we extracted it from yours." Then he put my heart back into place, where it was fastened with a seal (*muhr*). The third person arose and rubbed his hand over my abdomen and it was restored.[59]

Echoing the Christian concept of original sin, the illustration depicts the apex of this rite of passage, which seals Muhammad's utmost purity. While the black blood clot is not clearly visible in the painting, Islamic texts frequently analogize the blood clot(s) to evil, Satan, and ignorance, as well as the forbidden actions, shameful deeds, and filthy muck of polytheism (*shirk*) and unbelief (*kufr*) that were prevalent during pre-Islamic times (*Jahiliyya*).[60] A number of texts also note that once cleansed and thus free of impurities, the blood clot is filled with wisdom (*hikma*) and belief (*iman*) before being placed back into Muhammad's chest.[61] Thus, one or several black blood clots are likened to shortcomings and sins that had to be expunged from Muhammad's young body so that he could be sufficiently pure to take up prophetic office in his adult years. Put more simply, the splitting of the chest functions as a kind of Islamic baptism, in which this increasingly impeccable hero undergoes an expiation of sins before embarking on the path of monotheism—and hence salvation.

Like other prophets who came before him—in particular Jesus, who was baptized at the start of his public ministry, and Moses, who pleaded with God to expand his breast and ease his prophetic burden[62]—Muhammad was both literally and figuratively enlarged and immersed into his divinely decreed office. Unlike his predecessors, however, his chest was seared shut with a mark indicative of his exalted position as the final seal of all prophets. When his chest was slit open, he became pale but did not faint or die; his heroic strength enabled him to overcome what for a mere mortal would have resulted in death. Even as a toddler, then, Muhammad overcame corporeal mutilation to return stronger and purer.

Although the splitting of Muhammad's chest was popular in early Islamic sources and selected for depiction in the Ilkhanid-period illustrated copy of al-Bal'ami's history, it proved to be a problematic tale after the fourteenth century, when the concept of prophetic immunity from error and sin—known as 'isma—became more widely embraced as a doctrinal principle. At this time, a number of theologians tended to emphasize Muhammad's sinless and infallible nature. As a result, incidents highlighting his sins, mistakes, and weaknesses—chief among them his potential early worshiping of Arab pagan deities, the satanic interpolation and eventual abrogation of qur'anic verses, and the clot-like presence of sins and errors necessitating extraction from Muhammad's chest—were increasingly suppressed and denied.[63] The rise of the 'isma doctrine may thus explain to some extent why the splitting of the chest proved an extremely rare theme for representation.

As Harris Birkeland demonstrates, emphasis eventually was placed on the *positive* rather than *negative* aspect of this particular tale: that is, Muhammad's heart was filled with belief, wisdom, mercy, and compassion rather than purged of undesirable content.[64] The relative silencing of the negative aspect of the narrative—that is, the removal of evil and sins—permeates textual sources from the fourteenth century onward. This silence seems echoed in the Ilkhanid painting, in which the blood clot mentioned in al-Bal'ami's text seems omitted from the painted scene. Ongoing tensions and debates over the notion of prophetic 'isma thus can be detected in this illustrated manuscript, in which the tenth-century author al-Bal'ami and the later Ilkhanid artist appear to pursue divergent agendas. The manuscript's painter may have been exposed to predominant narratives stressing Muhammad's immunity from sin and so decided to highlight the positive expansion of the Prophet's breast over the negative extraction of the blood clot. The artist thus seems to advance a contemporary doctrinal position in favor of 'isma, in the process muffling some of the trickier details contained in the earlier text he was tasked to illustrate. As a result, this kind of pictorial omission reveals that a Muslim painter could stake a theological position by strategically ignoring textual details that by around 1300 CE ran contrary to an ascendant majority view espousing Muhammad's immaculacy.

While the depiction of the splitting of the chest could emerge from and contribute to an evolving Islamic doctrinal stance, it also may reflect contemporary Mongol customs, such as curative evisceration and brotherhood ceremonies. As Teresa Fitzherbert notes, the Mongols removed the organs of humans and animals in order to cure ills, and these types of extractive procedures may have rendered the splitting of the chest scene "less shocking and more meaningful to recent Mongol converts than to established Muslim communities."[65] For an Ilkhanid audience, Muhammad's physical ordeal thus could be perceived as therapeutic rather than injurious. Additionally, the Mongols made blood sacrifice offerings and used blood in *anda* ceremonies in which two contracting parties swore an oath with blood to establish kinship ties.[66] The Mongol practice of establishing blood brotherhoods and sisterhoods continued into the Islamic period, especially in Shi'i spheres, in which it became connected to the Feast of the Pond (*'Id al-Ghadir*). During this festival, on the eighteenth day of Dhu'l-Hijja, individuals became godchildren and godparents or expanded family bonds by sharing a shirt in mutual affection, thereby emerging as brothers and sisters in religion.[67] These contemporary *anda*-cum-Islamic rites of fraternization may have enabled the painting's viewers to interpret the splitting of Muhammad's chest as a ceremonial invitation to become the Prophet's blood siblings—expanded, purified, and united in the faith.

The splitting of Muhammad's chest marshals the narrative trope of the infant hero's early trial and preparation for prophetic office; it was not, however, the only miraculous event of his childhood years. Numerous narratives highlight another pivotal encounter, which was not as doctrinally disputable within (if not outside of) Islamic spheres. According to these accounts, the Christian monk Bahira met Muhammad when the latter was between eight and thirteen years of age.[68] Although the Bahira legend varies in its details, the major thrust of the story is the monk's recognition of the young Muhammad as a future prophet thanks to a miracle and the seal of prophecy on his body.[69] Authors such as Ibn Ishaq, al-Tabari (d. 923 CE), and others specify that this encounter occurred when Muhammad accompanied his uncle Abu Talib on a caravan trip. Once they reached Busra, Syria, they met the monk Bahira, who was well versed in scriptural traditions. According to some accounts, Bahira notices a cloud that moves to provide shade for Muhammad; in others, a tree droops and bends its branches to protect the latter from the sun. When he looked more closely at Muhammad's body, the Christian monk recognized the seal of prophecy as described in his "sacred books." In some accounts, Bahira also greets Muhammad with the Arab custom of swearing by the pagan gods al-Lat and al-'Uzza, whereupon the Prophet responds by invoking Allah alone. This particular exchange of greetings no doubt aims to depict Muhammad as a "proto-Muslim" who was protected from the "vileness of heathenism" even before the beginnings of qur'anic revelation.[70] Last but not least, a number of texts conclude with Bahira warning Abu Talib to protect Muhammad from Jews and/or Christian Byzantines—because "great things lie ahead" for this "Messenger of the Lord of the Worlds."[71] The Islamic Bahira narrative thus asserts multiple proofs of Muhammad's prophecy as well as refutes accusations that Muhammad had been a

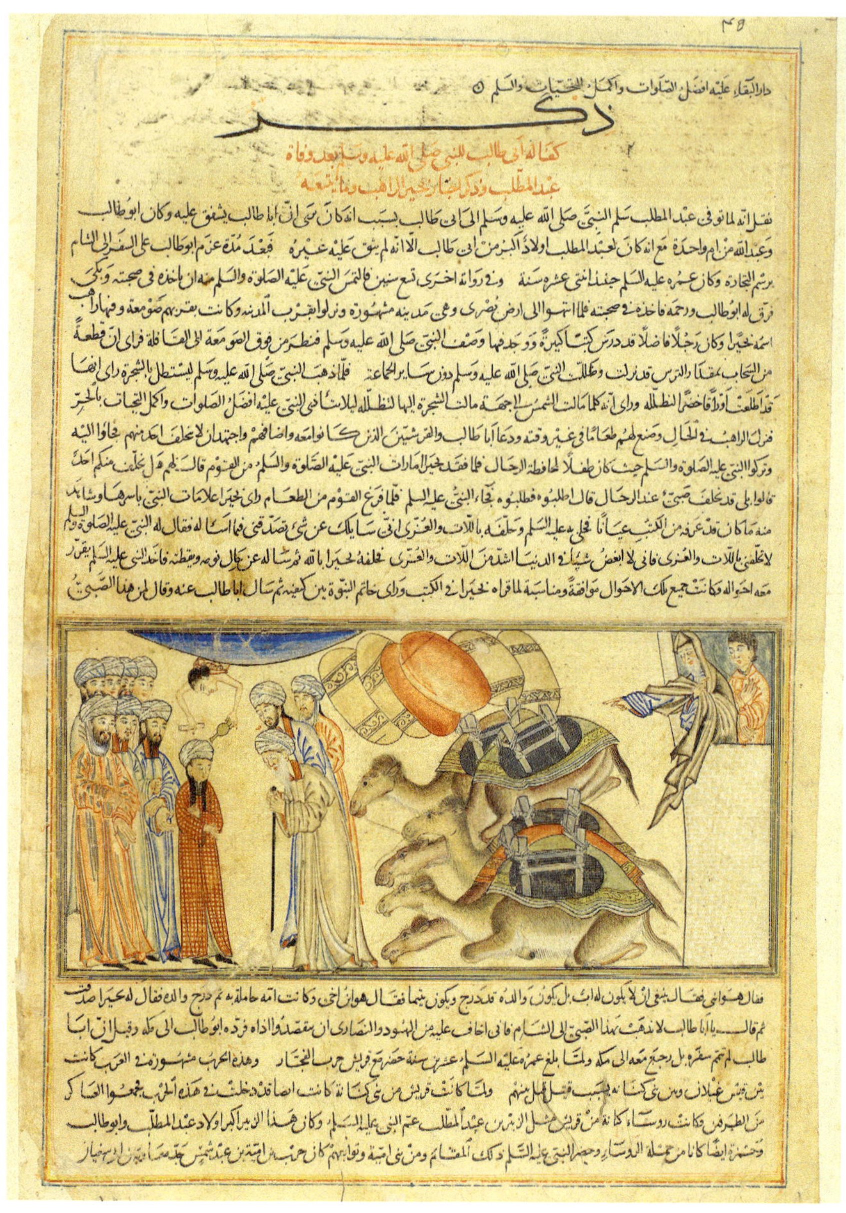

pagan idolater before his appointed mission. It also functions as a powerful discourse in favor of Islam within the interconfessional polemics of the greater Middle East, where both Jewish and Christian holy books retained validity and predictive value even though they were superseded by the Qur'an.[72]

Mirroring the tale's popularity within textual sources, Bahira's encounter with the young Muhammad has been a subject of depiction in Turco-Persian lands since 1300 CE. The earliest extant painting of the episode is included in Rashid al-Din's *Compendium of Chronicles* (fig. 2.7). In the composition, the Christian monk (accompanied by a young deacon) stands in his elevated cell to the right, holds his robe, and extends his right hand to point to Muhammad, who is standing on the left. All of the men and even the camels face the Prophet, bowing and genuflecting as they encircle him. The young Muhammad stands upright, wearing a checkered red tunic and a white turban. Above him, an

THE PRAISEWORTHY ONE

angel emerges from a distended blue sky as it reaches for Muhammad's head. This angel appears to anoint the Prophet with a golden perfume flask held in one hand and to transmit God's Logos through the rolled parchment held in the other.[73]

All movements—human, animal, and even cosmic—rotate around the Prophet, who serves as a centripetal force in the composition. The Ilkhanid painting stresses Muhammad's prophetic centrality by means of this circular arrangement. It also provides a visual amplification of the text's supercessionist rhetoric, which claims that Muhammad was foretold to humankind and that his predestination is recognizable to a Christian witness conversant in monotheistic scripture. Just as importantly, the depiction expands on and diverges from narratives that describe Muhammad's sacred selection through a shade miracle. Rather than depicting God's favor through the shade cast on him by a cloud or tree, the Ilkhanid artist here stresses God's sacred selection of Muhammad as his prophet through visual uranophany—that is, a bend in the celestial arc indicative of divine presence—as well as angelic anointment and scriptural revelation.[74]

Intriguingly, the bend in the firmament, swooping angel, perfume flask, and scroll are not mentioned in Islamic Bahira legends. Rashid al-Din's account, which brackets the painting, similarly remains moot about these pictorial details. Instead, the author provides an overview of the reports (*akhbar*) concerning the encounter between the Christian monk (here named Buhayr) and Muhammad. He informs his readers that Bahira was a virtuous man who had studied many books, in which he had found a description of the Prophet (*wasf al-nabi*). When Muhammad arrived in Busra, the monk immediately recognized his prophetic signs (*'alamat al-nabi*), among them the seal of prophethood between his shoulders as well as a cloud (*abr*) and tree (*darakht*) leaning toward him to shade him from the sun. Bahira then greeted the young man by swearing to al-Lat and al-'Uzza. In response, Muhammad asked Bahira to profess allegiance not to these pagan deities but instead to Allah. The monk obliged and then cautioned Abu Talib not to take Muhammad to Syria (*al-sham*), for fear that the Jews and Christians might harm him. The Prophet's uncle heeded the monk's advice and sent Muhammad back to Mecca.[75]

Rashid al-Din's synopsis includes the major narrative elements of the Bahira legend; however, like other antecedent accounts, it does not utter a word about a bent sky, angel, flask, or scroll, which are prominent iconographical devices in the text's attendant painting. Thus, in order to determine why the Ilkhanid painter inserted these novel motifs—and what symbolic function they may have played in constructing an Islamic visual language at the dawn of the fourteenth century—one must seek the source of these pictorial details elsewhere.

As noted previously, Armenian illustrated manuscripts served as visual inspiration for Ilkhanid paintings depicting the life of the Prophet, and at this time Christian artists worked in the book atelier in Tabriz.

2.8. Christ's baptism, gospel, copied and illustrated by Toros Taronatsi, 1323 CE. Matenadaran Library, Erevan, Armenia, Ms. 6289, folio 18r. Image courtesy of Scala/Art Resource, NY.

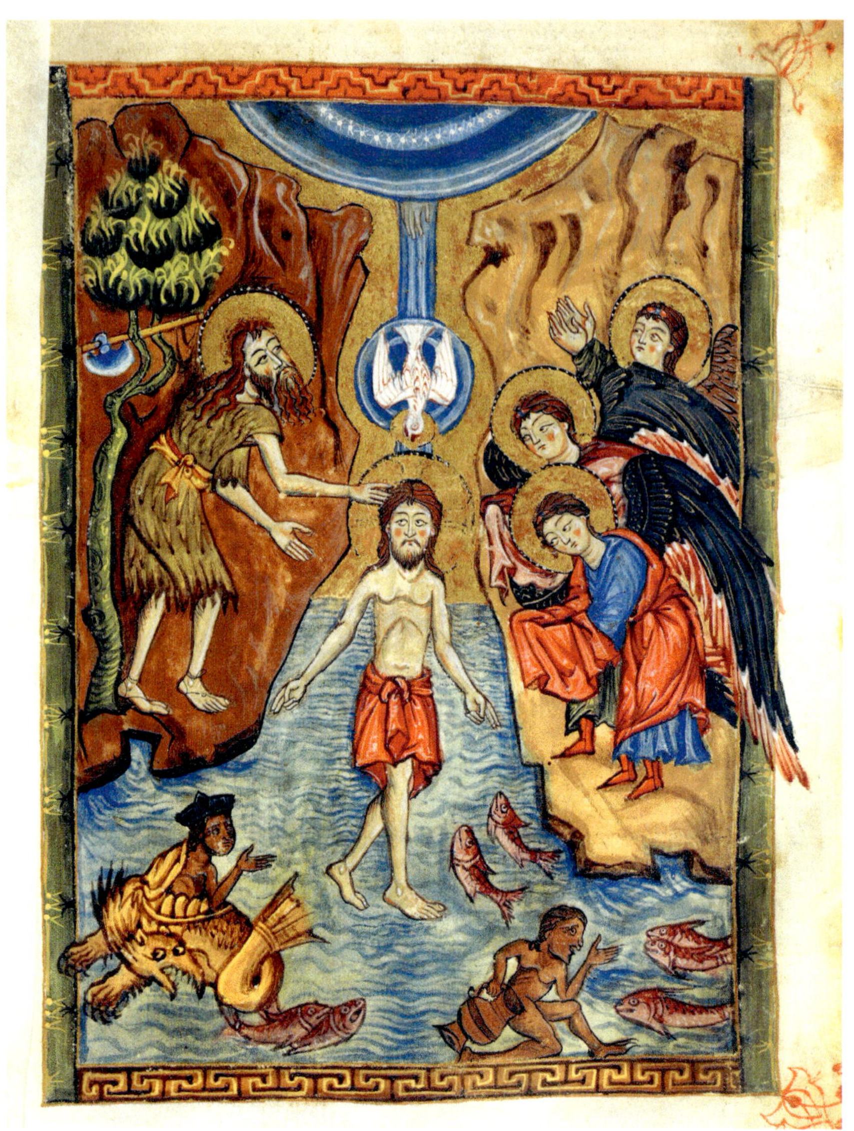

Such pictorial cross-pollinations can be detected in representations of Muhammad's birth that appear to be indebted to nativity scenes in illustrated Armenian Gospels (figs. 2.3–2.4). Similar parallels can be found between the Ilkhanid Bahira painting and Armenian depictions of Christ's baptism (fig. 2.8), in which the distended blue sky quickens the descent of a holy winged entity (whether angel or dove) carrying God's message (embodied through scroll and scent or the divine hand). These symbolic devices in medieval Christian and Islamic manuscript paintings visually promote their prophetic protagonists' proximity to and selection by God through celestial, angelic, olfactory, and scriptural proxies.

In medieval Christian scenes, Jesus is shown with John the Baptist and an angel holding a flask; this angel is at times labeled "the bearer of chrism," a fragrant oil used in church ceremonies. As Priscilla Soucek has noted, these pictorial similarities suggest that the Ilkhanid Bahira scene should be seen as reflecting Armenian rites of baptism, which included anointment with the oil of the Holy Spirit. Additionally, Soucek

THE PRAISEWORTHY ONE

contends that the figure of Bahira should be interpreted as a kind of chrism-bearing angel who affirms Muhammad's religious prestige, while the scroll functions as the youth's promise prior to the beginnings of his prophetic mission and qur'anic revelation.[76]

While Soucek rightly points to these pictorial overlaps, their potential meanings remain open to further investigation and interpretation. For instance, rather than a chrism-bearing angel, Bahira might essentially serve as a polemicized witness to and guarantor of the superiority of Islam over Christianity.[77] Moreover, while the scroll may point to Muhammad's promise as a future apostle, it also—more critically—serves as a visible confirmation of God granting the Qur'an to his chosen Messenger. The divine quality of qur'anic revelation was especially important within an Islamic setting because it aimed to counter Christian anti-Muslim polemical arguments that the Qur'an was coauthored by the "heretical" or "schismatic" monk Bahira and his young and naive pupil.[78] Thus, while Rashid al-Din remains silent about the matter, the painting emphatically restitutes the numinous quality of the Qur'an, quite possibly as a retort to contemporary Christian claims that it was merely a human, not divine, creation—a corruption of "true" Christian doctrine. Finally, the Ilkhanid depiction also dispels Christian allegations that Muhammad should be deemed a false prophet who founded his own religion due to Bahira's wayward tutelage. The artist represents the young hero as an exalted recipient of divine Logos, recognized and endorsed as the "Anointed One" (*al-Masih*).[79] Thus, while inspired by Christian religious iconography, the Ilkhanid painting stakes an unequivocal position in favor of Muhammad and Islam within a larger landscape of Bahira legends, themselves popular polemical tools for Christian-Muslim wrangling over religious authority and supremacy.

The Ilkhanid painting reveals an engagement with Christian iconography and narrative at a moment of great religious flux in Iran. At this time, Rashid al-Din, the author of the text, was a Jewish convert to Islam, while Sultan Öljeitü (r. 1304–16 CE), under whose aegis the *Compendium of Chronicles* was produced as an illustrated manuscript, was born a Christian (under the name Nicholas) and converted to Islam (under the name Muhammad Khudabanda ['Abdullah or Servant of God]).[80] Rashid al-Din and his royal patron lived during a period of Jewish, Christian, and Muslim cohabitation and contestation, and Muslim converts occupying the highest echelons of society used their expert knowledge of other (sometimes previous) faiths to position Muhammad as the rightful inheritor and final contributor to the line of Abrahamic prophets. Within this overarching context of conversion, Ilkhanid narratives describe Mongol rulers becoming luminous forms of the Prophet on their embrace of Islam.[81] Such is the case of Sultan Ghazan (r. 1295–1304 CE), who, according to Rashid al-Din, was "enlightened through the light of the religion of Muhammad streaming into his radiant inner being."[82] In addition, by adopting the title "Ruler of Islam" (*Padishah-i Islam*), Ghazan promoted his regal standing and

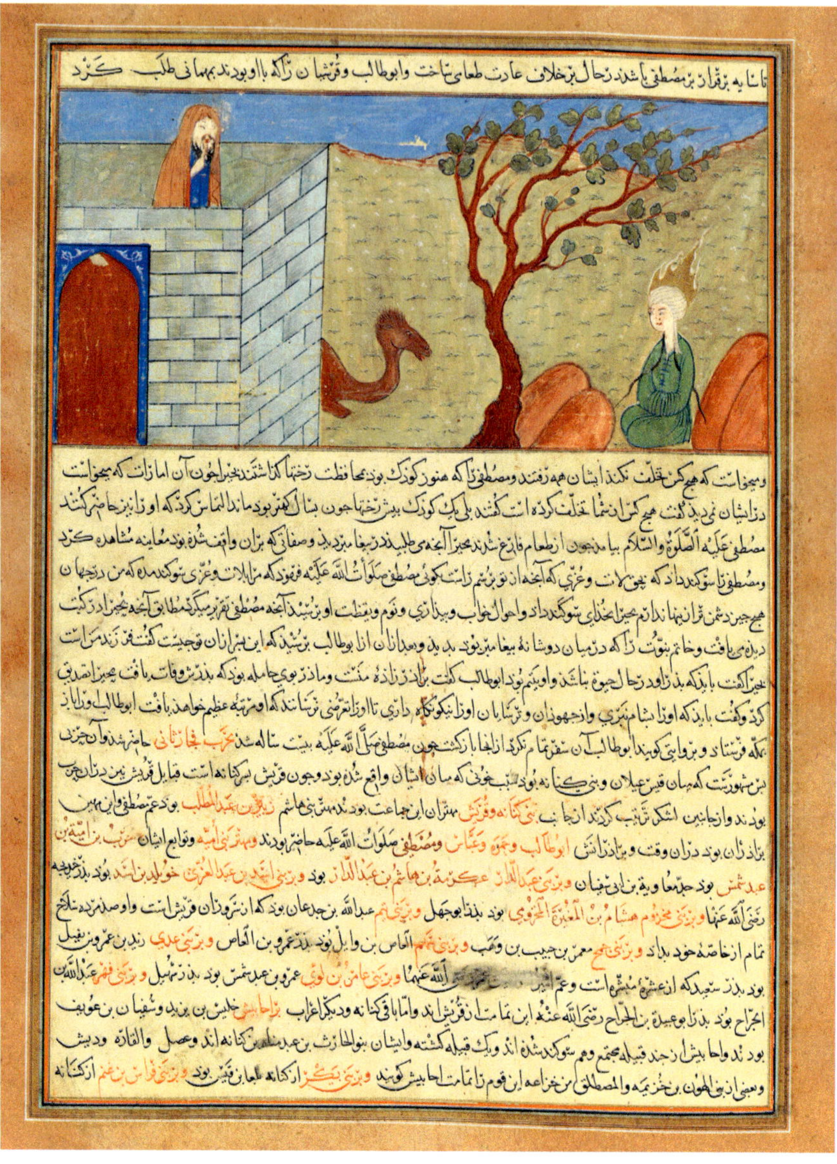

2.9. The Christian monk Bahira recognizes the young Muhammad as a prophet, Rashid al-Din, *Jami' al-Tawarikh* (Compendium of Chronicles), Tabriz, text dated 717 AH/1317 CE, paintings added ca. 1350–1400 CE. Topkapı Palace Library, Istanbul, H. 1654, folio 57r. Photograph by Hadiye Cangökçe.

religious affiliation, while semantically embodying the honorific moniker used for the Prophet Muhammad as well.[83]

As exemplified by the Ilkhanid painting of Bahira affirming Muhammad's prophetic status, the currency of Christian iconography and Islamic recognition narratives coalesced to generate a new tradition of religious figural art in Iran around 1300 CE. This composition's innovative iconographical devices thus should be understood as expressive validations of Islam's ascendancy in an elite milieu marked by interconfessional debate. This polemical context, however, began to fade during the second half of the fourteenth century, by which time the rulers of Iran were born—rather than converted—into Islam.

To a certain degree, the disputatious quality of the Bahira legend abated within Islamic painterly arts after around 1350 CE, as can be seen in a later illustration of the episode (fig. 2.9). Added between 1350 and 1400 CE to an earlier copy of the *Compendium of Chronicles* (copied in 1317 CE), this and other paintings in the manuscript fill an important

THE PRAISEWORTHY ONE

gap between Ilkhanid and Timurid styles of manuscript illustration.[84] As can be detected in the Timurid Bahira illustration, Christian baptismal iconography has been removed from the painted scene. Muhammad is no longer depicted as the recipient of angelic anointment and qur'anic revelation; rather, he bears a flaming halo, a visual index of his prophetic status that was believed to be preordained and existent well before his encounter with the Christian monk. Moreover, in the painting, Muhammad kneels below a tree whose inclined branches provide him with shade. This depiction closely follows and illustrates Rashid al-Din's narrative, which describes this particular shade miracle; unlike the Ilkhanid artist, the artist of this manuscript has developed a visual apparatus more faithful to its accompanying text. As a result, the later Bahira painting positively highlights Muhammad's prophetic recognition without pictorially engaging in Christian-Muslim debates over the young hero's status and mandate—debates that had largely lost their urgency and pertinence in eastern Islamic lands after 1350 CE.

In illustrated historical manuscripts of the fourteenth and fifteenth centuries, paintings of Muhammad's early life aimed to make manifestly evident that he was foreseen as a prophet, foretold as an apocalyptic messiah, born luminously into a new order, expanded, purified, and sealed into the faith, and recognized as an apostle endowed with God's physical imprimatur, aromatic anointment, and scriptural mandate well before adulthood, when his prophetic career began in earnest. At this innovative time for the pictorial arts in Persian lands, such paintings also function as gauges for religious polemics, especially during the Ilkhanid period. Additionally, they highlight an iconographical trajectory that was initially experimental and reliant on a Christian visual language, whose influence subsided once a pictorial system for prophetic representation became more firmly established. Like the narratives they accompany, these novel depictions of the hero-prophet nevertheless were couched as "historical" and "traditional,"[85] thereby enabling members of the newly converted Mongol elite to foster a corporate sense of religious superiority, especially because they did not already possess it by birth. Newly invented and yet rooted in a prophetic past, these images make claims to historic continuity and envision a sacred order for the Mongol-Muslim rulers of medieval Iran.

Muhammad's infancy stories foreground his prophetic path in adulthood, the pivotal moments of which are similarly illustrated in premodern historical texts. Like other heroes, he embarks on a sacred endeavor from the time of his divine appointment to his corporeal death on earth. Once tasked with apostleship, Muhammad must receive and spread God's revelations (see figures 3.9–10). This call to adventure comes as a sudden and unsuspected fiat, announced by an angelic assistant and guardian. In this and other cases, destiny summons the hero to a zone unknown yet filled with potential—and variously represented as a desert, lofty mountain, or secluded cave.[86]

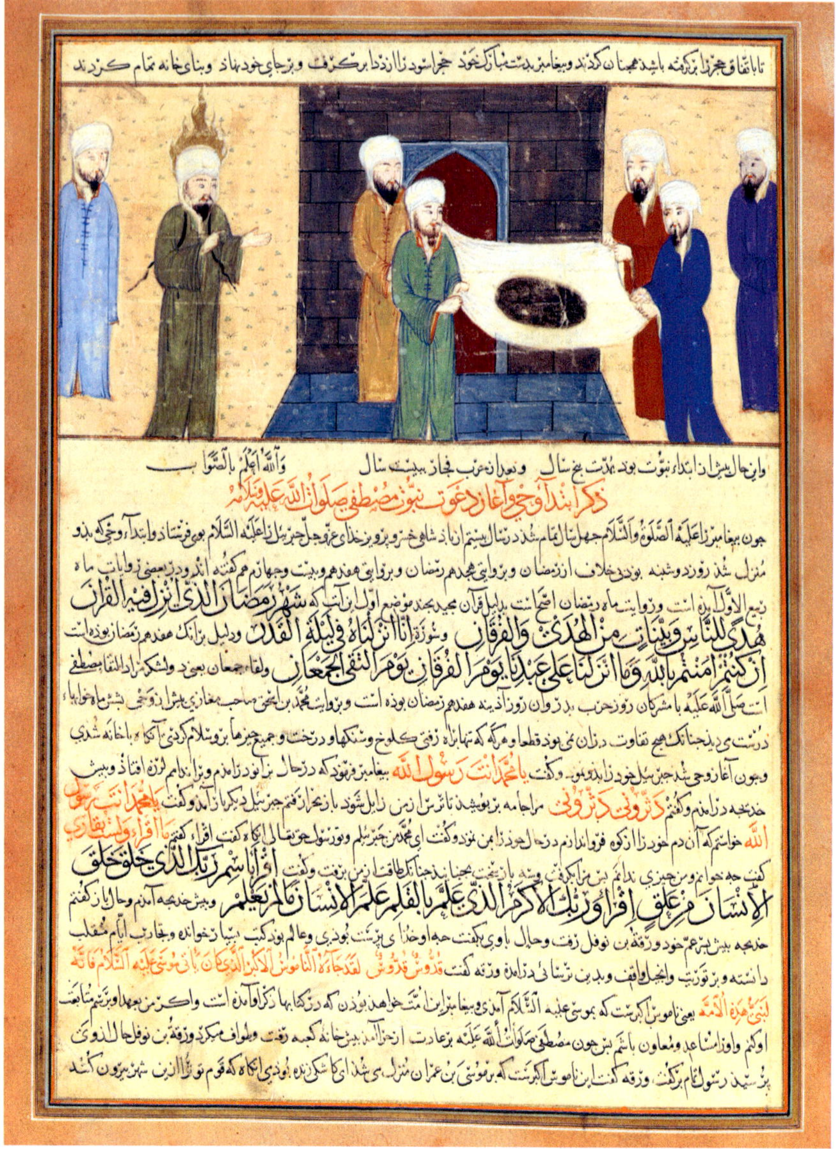

2.10. The Prophet Muhammad acts as an arbiter to enable competing tribes to collaborate and place the Black Stone back into the restored Ka'ba, Rashid al-Din, *Jami' al-Tawarikh* (Compendium of Chronicles), text dated 717 AH/1317 CE, paintings added ca. 1350–1400 CE. Topkapı Palace Library, Istanbul, H. 1654, folio 59r. Photograph by Hadiye Cangökçe.

Although often going into retreat, Muhammad nevertheless lived and functioned within a society in which he was impelled to withstand opposition and persecution, build and expand the faith community, face competitors and fend off false prophets, combat legions of enemies and detractors, and select his successor before his death.[87] Along the way, he found it necessary to provide ample evidence of his moral virtue, immutable credibility, and prophetic standing: via the seal impressed on his body, his acting as a trustworthy judge in the resolution of disputes (fig. 2.10), his performance of shade and milk miracles, his splitting of the moon in half, and his ascendance through the celestial spheres to converse with God and witness heaven and hell.

In Islamic textual and visual sources, Muhammad is depicted as the quintessential carrier of revelation, harnesser of supernatural forces, and overcomer of hardships. He also is praised as a steadfast and talented warrior for the faith, whose heroic exploits are often described as ordained by God and secured with the help of angelic recruits. Indeed,

   THE PRAISEWORTHY ONE

more than any single event—as momentous as it might be—Muhammad's military campaigns (*maghazi*) compose the most recurrent and cohesive sequence of images within historical manuscripts of the fourteenth and fifteenth centuries.

The pictorial cycles depicting the Prophet confronting his enemies, especially the Quraysh and Jewish tribes of Mecca and Medina, hold a prominent place in Ilkhanid and Timurid illustrated universal histories composed by al-Bal'ami, Rashid al-Din, and Hafiz-i Abru. These manuscripts' battle paintings include a range of iconographical devices that primarily supported the belief that Muhammad's victories were achieved due to divine intervention and angelic assistance.[88] Just as importantly, such illustrations offered opportunities to elaborate on the circumstances surrounding the revelation of the Qur'an, particularly the verses that helped formulate a set of rules governing just military engagement and proper conduct in war. Paintings of Muhammad's *maghazi* thus should be understood as visual "occasions of revelation" (*asbab al-nuzul*), as they offer pictorial elucidations of scripture and hence both echo and expand on the practice of qur'anic exegesis.[89] As such, these premodern battle images essentially provide illustrative explanations of the Prophet engaged in heroic acts, with divinely sent angels serving as troops as well as conduits for the Qur'an as revealed in martial contexts.

Muhammad was celebrated as a skillful military leader.[90] With the notable exception of his defeat at Uhud, the great majority of his battles led to success for the Muslim troops. Thanks to his offensive strategies and the unity of his followers, Muhammad was able to secure victories at Badr, against the Jewish tribes of Banu'l-Nadir and Banu Qaynuqa', and at the battles of the Trench (Khandaq) and the Fortress of Khaybar. His triumphs in war underscore his forces' organization and discipline and were praised as incontrovertible signs of God's favor. In addition to shedding light on early Muslim military operations, accounts of Muhammad's battle victories reveal the progressive emergence of war policy, particularly practices surrounding the treatment of prisoners and the distribution of booty. War spoils enriched the Muslim community with animals, goods, and resources, in the process drawing greater numbers of adherents to the Islamic faith. Among such harbingers of good fortune were also a number of qur'anic signs or *ayas*—verses revealed in battle, whose contents were interpreted as supportive of military endeavors and practices.

After 1300 CE, historians of both the Ilkhanid and Timurid courts "asserted Islamic principles by liberally sprinkling their narratives with quotations from the Qur'an."[91] These textual sources offer an ethical framework for imperial dominion in support of religion, both past and present. By the same token, when such qur'anic excerpts are woven into battle accounts, they also signal heavenly support for sacred forms of kingship (military or otherwise), with Islam serving not only as a new religious ideology but also as leverage for greater sociopolitical

2.11. The battle of Badr, al-Bal'ami, *Ta'rikh al-Rusul wa'l-Muluk* (History of Messengers and Kings), Mosul, ca. 1300 CE. Freer Gallery of Art, Smithsonian Institution, Washington, DC, F1957.16, folio 182r.

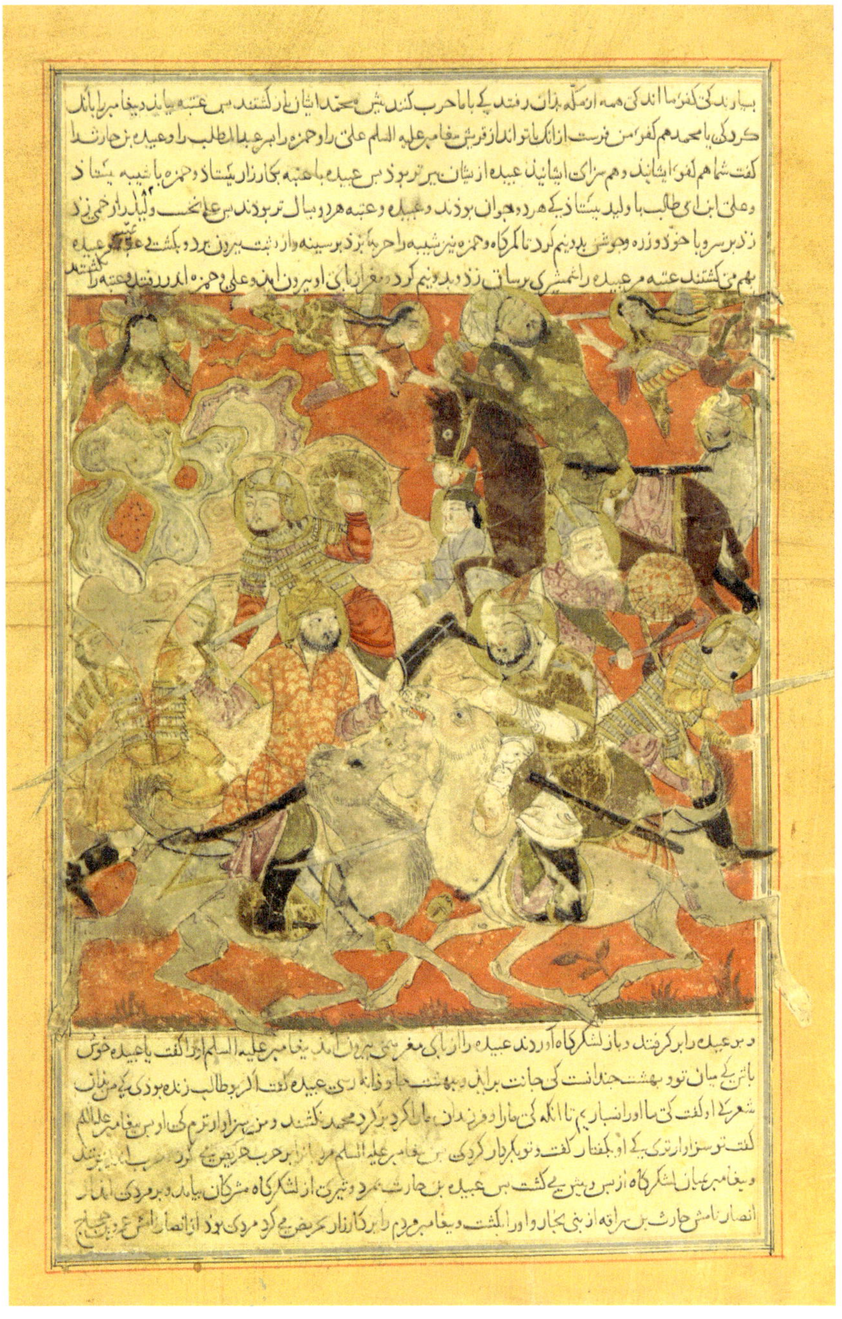

ascendance and integration.[92] As a matter of course, military campaigns therefore tend to be described as battles for the faith, with successes bolstering the legitimacy of a particular order, from Muhammad's first community of believers to later Muslim sovereigns claiming prophetic inheritance.

Muhammad's first major victory, against the Quraysh forces from Mecca, occurred at Badr in the second year of the *hijra* (624 CE). A key triumph for Muslim forces, the confrontation transformed Muhammad's series of occasional raids into a full-fledged war. The expedition, events, fighters, prisoners, and qur'anic verses revealed at the battle receive close attention in the early biographies of the Prophet—including Ibn Ishaq's *sira* and al-Waqidi's (d. 822 CE) *Kitab al-Maghazi* (Book

THE PRAISEWORTHY ONE

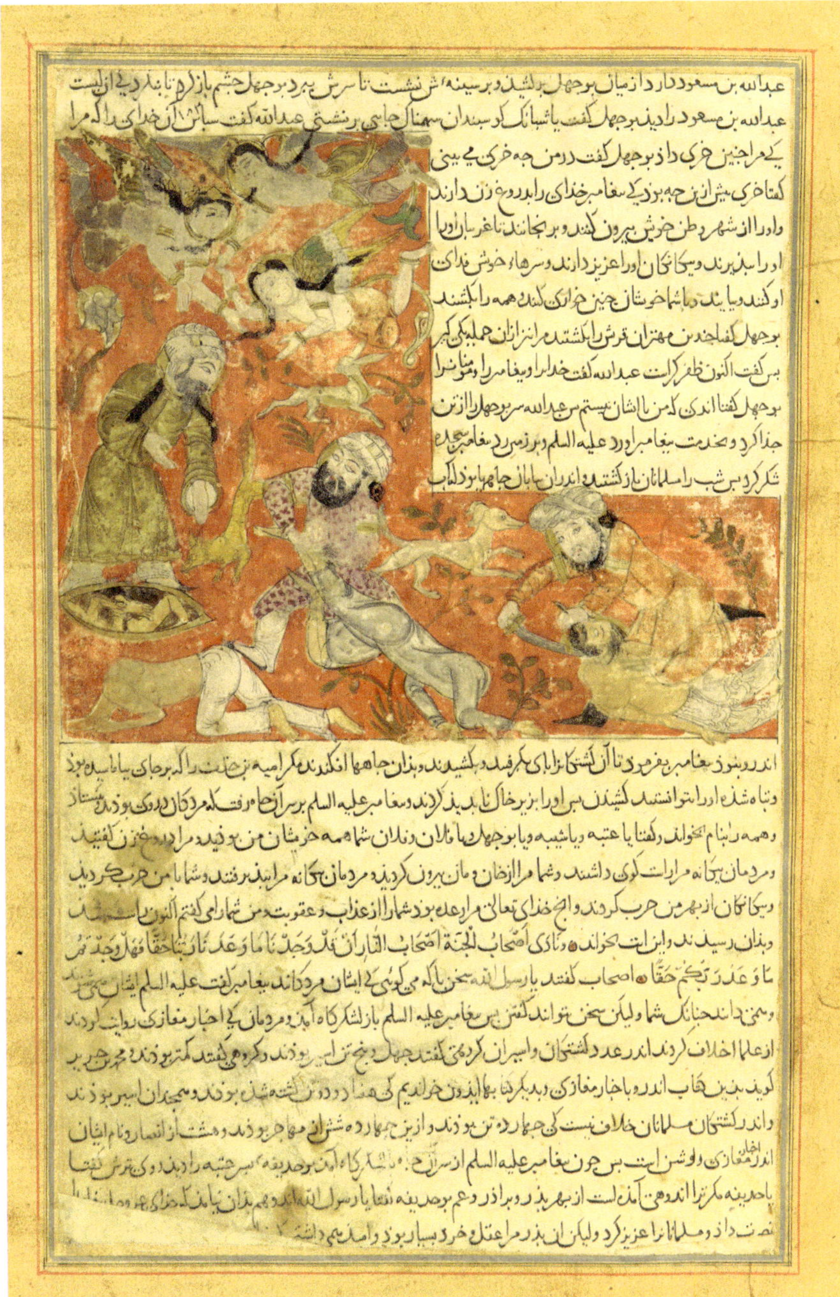

2.12. The Prophet Muhammad orders the disposal of corpses into a well while ʿAbdallah b. Masʿud decapitates Abu Jahl at the battle of Badr, al-Balʿami, *Taʾrikh al-Rusul waʾl-Muluk* (History of Messengers and Kings), Mosul, ca. 1300 CE. Freer Gallery of Art, Smithsonian Institution, Washington, DC, F1957.16, folio 184r.

of Raids), which is entirely devoted to Muhammad's expeditions and conquests.[93] The battle of Badr is also recorded in detail in universal histories of the medieval period, among them al-Balʿami's Persian translation of al-Tabari's *History of Messengers and Kings*.[94] In his account of Badr, al-Balʿami substantially expands the battle narrative by weaving in information gleaned from al-Waqidi's *Book of Raids* and various exegetical texts. Moreover, he expends substantial effort to attach qurʾanic verses to the battle of Badr and other historical anecdotes, in a literary practice that Elton Daniel terms "historical exegesis."[95]

The illustrated manuscript of al-Balʿami's text made around 1300 CE includes not one but two depictions of Badr.[96] The first shows the Prophet on horseback, his steed striding behind the large melee (fig.

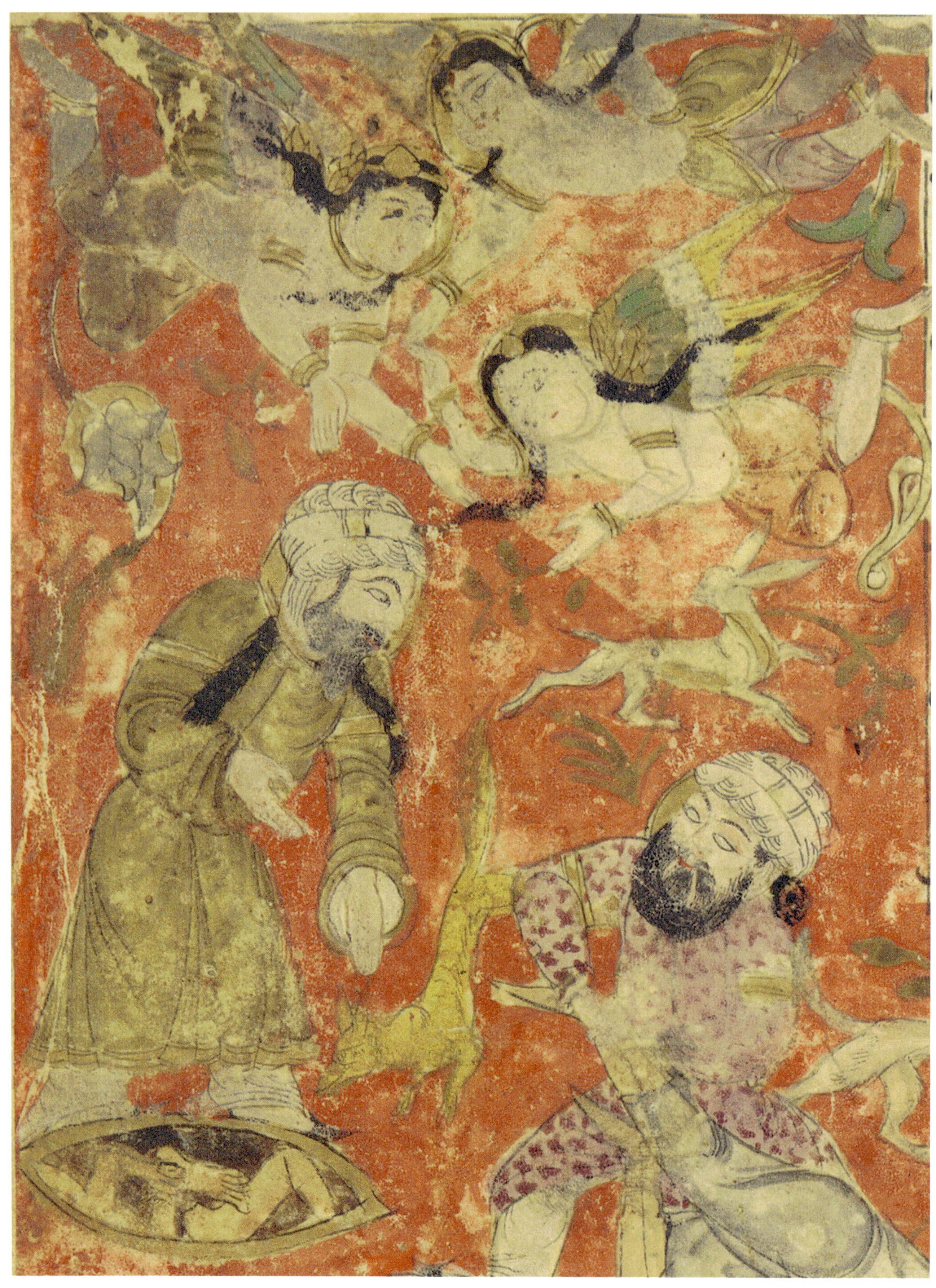

2.11).[97] In this painting, Muhammad is set apart in the upper right corner of the composition, looking up toward the sky—rather than at the dynamic scene below—as three angelic escorts fly above him.[98] The second painting represents the end of the confrontation, at which time Abu Jahl (Muhammad's lifelong enemy) is decapitated by 'Abdallah b. Mas'ud (fig. 2.12). Standing on the left, the Prophet points to a well as he orders the corpses of the enemies disposed. As in the previous example, in this painting of the decisive final moment of the battle of Badr, Muhammad is visually set aside from the scene's main action, and once again he appears surmounted by an angelic trio hovering in midair. In both paintings, Muhammad is thus clearly set apart and identifiable through his prophetic tresses, inspired disposition, authoritative posture, and angelic cohort. In other words, there is no mistaking him for any of the other protagonists caught in the fray.

The two paintings of Badr depict Muhammad as animated in ways more spiritual than martial. The angels descending on him appear to provide divine assistance or to communicate God's sacred mandate (fig. 2.13). A number of textual sources, including al-Bal'ami's attendant narrative, highlight the angels' presence at the battle of Badr for both reasons: to strengthen the Muslim troops and to reveal the Qur'an's eighth chapter, entitled "The Spoils" (*al-Anfal*). In their Badr narratives, Ibn Ishaq and al-Waqidi include separate subsections entirely dedicated to discussing—one might even say narrativizing—the verses of *al-Anfal*, with the primary purposes of explicating the angelic assistance that was offered to the Muslim troops, the legality and equitable distribution of war booty, and the proper treatment of prisoners of war.[99]

While he did not create a section dedicated strictly to discussing the revelation of *al-Anfal*, al-Bal'ami also peppered his Badr narrative with several verses from the Qur'an's eighth *sura*. Among them, the historian cites 8:7 as proof that God wished "to wipe the disbelievers out to the last"; 8:9, in which God states "I shall send a thousand angels following behind you for your aid"; and 8:11–12 to demonstrate that the Lord sent down water to purify the believers as well as angels "to strengthen the faithful." These qur'anic verses from *al-Anfal* are further reinforced by al-Bal'ami's citation of Qur'an 3:123–24, which makes direct reference to the battle by posing the rhetorical question, "For God had helped you during the battle of Badr at a time when you were helpless. . . . Is it not sufficient that your Lord should send for your help three thousand angels from the heavens?" These selected verses enlivening al-Bal'ami's account help to ensconce scriptural revelation within a particular historical event.[100] They also promote a particular retelling of the battle, which in Islamic history was seen as an unmistakable vindication of Muslim believers, whose triumph was both decreed by God and secured through angelic soldiers.

To a certain extent, al-Bal'ami's account should be understood as a historical form of qur'anic exegesis, as it provides a narrative tale explaining the particular contexts and reasons for scriptural revelation. Beyond their literary application, other qur'anic verses in his Badr narrative also bear legal implications. Such is the case with 8:1, which discusses booty and which exegetes cite to explain how war spoils are to be divided into equal shares. Similarly, 8:67–69—also part of *al-Anfal*, as revealed during the battle of Badr—prompted discussions on the legality of taking spoils and the preference for sparing (rather than slaughtering) prisoners of war.[101] The qur'anic verses traditionally associated with the battle of Badr, including those found in al-Bal'ami's account, therefore fulfill both narrative and legalistic functions by explaining the miraculous nature of the Muslims' victory and establishing rules of engagement during wartime.

Although the two paintings accompanying al-Bal'ami's text depict battle and execution scenes, they emphasize Muhammad's heroic stature through his pictorial disengagement from the warring jumble and his exclusive proximity to the angels. In both illustrations the Prophet appears largely preoccupied with receiving God's revelations and celestial support. As a consequence, both illustrations appear aligned to the exegetical practice of *asbab al-nuzul*—the explanation of occasions for revelation. Broadly speaking, both exegesis and painting serve to explain the unknown and to eliminate ambiguity, with the added bonus that the paintings offer depictions of a seeming reality.[102] As pictorial parables, the two Badr paintings appear to function as opportune occasions for depicting qur'anic revelation within a martial context. Moreover, through iconographic expansion and embellishment such paintings weave a visualized event around qur'anic verses, providing a clear *sabab*, or reason, for confrontation: a way to guarantee the veracity of God's revelation to the Prophet.[103]

Similar visual metaphors for God's symbolic propinquity to the Prophet appear in other battle paintings included in Rashid al-Din's *Compendium of Chronicles*. One depicts Muhammad besieging the fortress of the Banu'l-Nadir after they had broken a treaty with him and conspired to kill him (fig. 2.14). Here, the Prophet sits astride his mount, accompanied by his Muslim foot soldiers as he approaches the stronghold of the Jewish tribe. Above him, an angel—most likely Gabriel—descends energetically, holding a gold flask above the Prophet's turban and a gold cup or basin at the height of his waist. Emerging from the upper horizontal frame of the composition, a golden sun illuminates the scene with shooting rays of light, toward which the members of the Banu'l-Nadir, perched atop their fortress, raise their hands in gestures of supplication as they submit to the victorious Muslim forces.

Several elements in this painting are worthy of note. First, the Prophet riding on horseback toward a fortified city echoes medieval Christian depictions of Christ's entry into Jerusalem.[104] Second, the Angel Gabriel recalls Christian pictorial conventions of representing the Holy Spirit as God's hand or as a bird, synecdochal and metaphorical representations of the divine that also were used by Ilkhanid artists,

     THE PRAISEWORTHY ONE

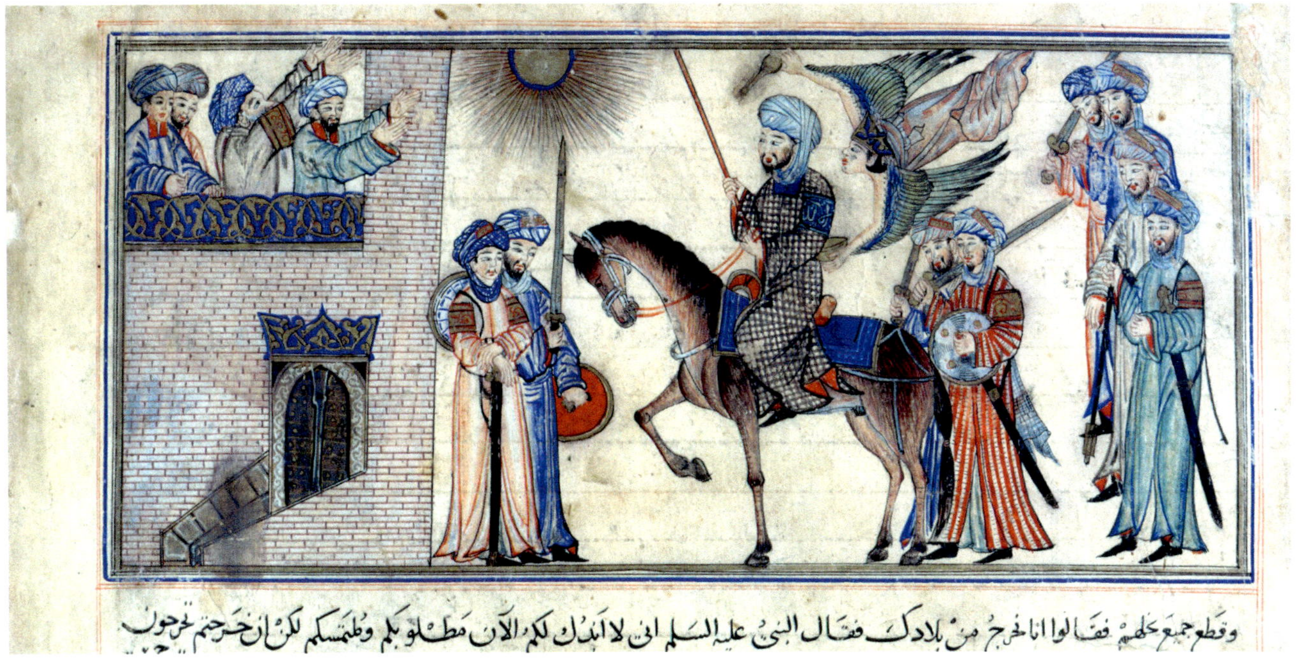

2.14. The Prophet Muhammad receiving the submission of the Banu'l-Nadir from their fortress, Rashid al-Din, *Jami' al-Tawarikh* (Compendium of Chronicles), Tabriz, 714 AH/1314–15 CE. Nasser D. Khalili Collection of Islamic Art, London, MSS 727, folio 8r.

as seen in the Bahira painting (fig. 2.7).[105] Moreover, God's selection of Muhammad again is by angelic descent and anointment—the former being all the more significant because the entirety of chapter 59 of the Qur'an (The Confrontation, or *al-Hashr*) is said to have been transmitted to the Prophet during his campaign against the Banu'l-Nadir. The consecrated nature of the military undertaking is further expanded by visual means through the inclusion of an incandescent gold sun, here perhaps understood as the symbol of God's immanent presence and the revelation of portions of the Qur'an—God's so-called "enlightened" or "luminous" book (*kitab munir*)[106]—to Muhammad on this particular occasion. That the besieged members of the Banu'l-Nadir turn to the sun in gestures of imploration supports this interpretation of God depicted as radiant light. Such a visualization of the divine is not entirely surprising: these types of battles were considered theophanies, in which God was believed to reveal himself in order to secure triumph for his elected community.[107]

Sira, maghazi, and exegetical texts inform us that it was during the expedition against the Banu'l-Nadir that the entire chapter of Confrontation was revealed to the Prophet. The first verses of *sura* 59 describe these Jewish "people of the book" (*ahl al-kitab*) being pushed out of their homes and forced into exile because they "had opposed God and His Apostle"; and "whosoever opposes God, then God is severe in retribution" (59:4). Muhammad's biographer, Ibn Ishaq, explains these verses by stressing that it was by God's permission and decree that Muhammad and the believers were successful in battle.[108] Other authors point to several verses in *surat al-hashr*, revealed on this occasion, to stress God's protection of the Muslim community (5:11), the legitimacy of expelling traitors from their abodes even if they are "people of the book" (59:2 and 11), and the rules governing the allotment of war booty (59:7).

Additionally, in his book dedicated to Muhammad's campaigns, al-Waqidi includes an entire section on the qur'anic verses revealed during the battle against the Banu'l-Nadir, in which he argues that the Jewish tribe incurred divine wrath because they resisted God and his Messenger.[109] For al-Bal'ami as well, such verses prove that God, through his Prophet, drove the Jewish tribe from their homes for refusing to believe.[110] Finally, in his treatise describing the "occasions for revelation," the qur'anic scholar al-Wahidi (d. 1075 CE) cites 59:1–6 to explain the Banu'l-Nadir's breach of their agreement with Muhammad and their plot to kill him. For al-Wahidi, the qur'anic verses justify Muhammad's decision to evict the Jewish tribe, seize their arms and armor, and cut down their palm trees.[111]

These texts collectively describe the actions of the Banu'l-Nadir as an affront committed against God, who in turn exacted retribution through the Prophet. As such, Muhammad's swift victory, his expulsion of the Jewish tribe, his confiscation of war booty, and his destruction of natural resources were seen as initiated and enabled by divine directive. The Ilkhanid painting illustrated in figure 2.14 similarly depicts the Prophet's triumph through the artist's insertion of a prominent and energetic angel in the battle scene. Here, the angelic being, especially if identified as Gabriel, fulfills several functions: it is a celestial sign of God's presence on earth, it anoints Muhammad as divinely decreed victor, and it transmits the entirety of *surat al-hashr*. Above all of the other details included in the composition, it is the angel that visually argues for Muhammad's battle against the Banu'l-Nadir as a blessed occasion for qur'anic revelation. Additionally, that the angel's flask appears to have been rubbed suggests that the painting's viewers may have perceived the depiction as containing latent powers of the divine, which could be transmitted through touch. The painting thus relates a religiously consecrated historic event by visually expanding it with symbolically charged actors and details, concurrently providing viewers with a pictorial arena in which to approach or even feel the realm of the sacred.

The viewers of this illustrated manuscript included the Ilkhanid ruling elites who, like other Muslim and non-Muslim dynasts, positioned themselves as world conquerors and champions of the faith. Influenced by Mongol concepts of rightful rulership, the Ilkhanids interpreted military successes as grants of sovereignty from an eternal heaven or supreme deity (*mönke tengri*), whose raw might (*güç*) is passed down to human actors through a heavenly mandate (*yarlïq*).[112] Such expressions of sacred kingship as ratified by martial victory were embedded into a preexisting and consonant Islamic framework, in which Arabic and Persian terms were commensurate with Mongolian ones. Thus, under the Ilkhanids and their Turco-Persian successors, the "eternal sky god" was synonymous to the one single God (*Allah* or *Khuda*), whose force (*quwwat*) is granted to his chosen people through a celestial decree (*firman*) and signs (*ayat*).[113]

   THE PRAISEWORTHY ONE

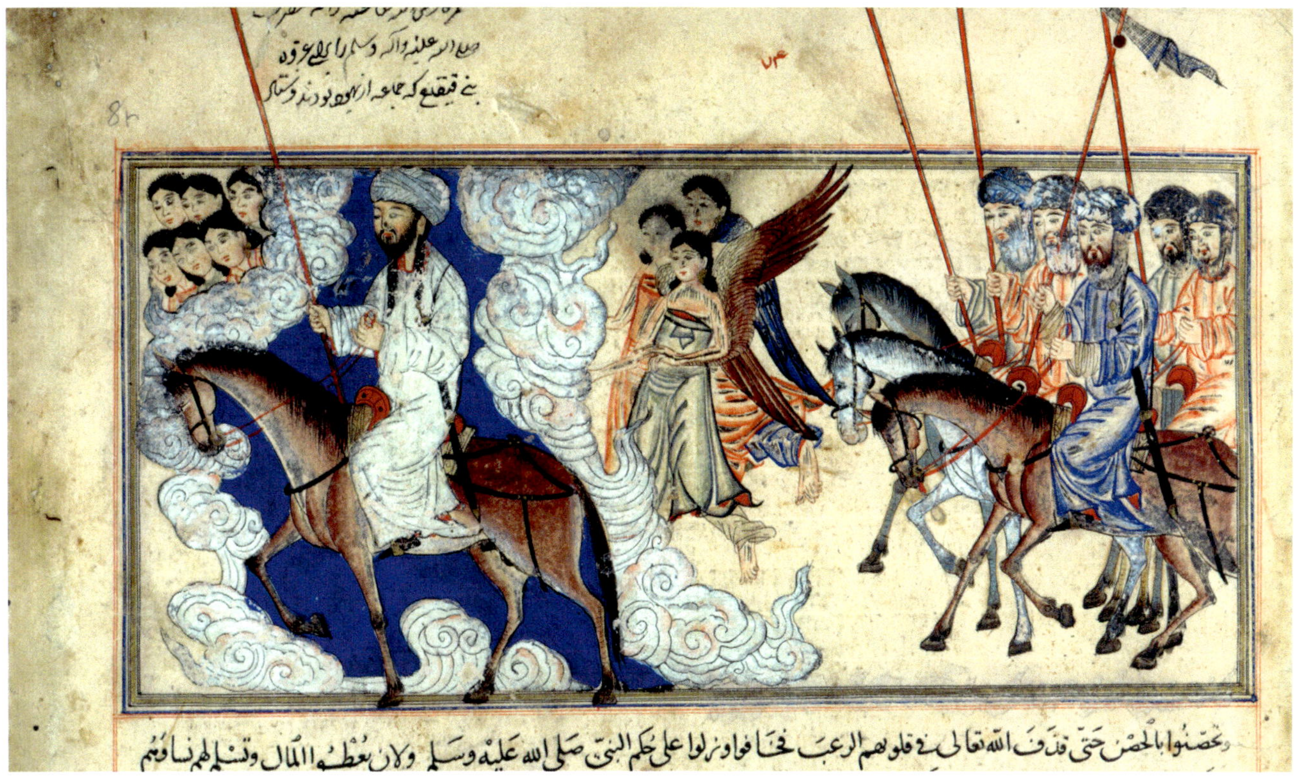

Such Mongol-Muslim expressions of divinely granted triumph carried over to the painterly arts, particularly scenes of Muhammad's war campaigns. On one hand, manuscript viewers could interpret such compositions as prophecies of their own military accomplishments, thereby boosting their political, religious, and cultural cachet. On the other, the particular iconographical devices found in battle paintings appear to echo and reinforce Ilkhanid expressions of triumph stipulating that a sky god or Allah displays omnipotence and endorsement through written decrees and angelic signs. Although the depicted angel may well have had Christian iconographic antecedents, its inclusion in paintings depicting Muhammad's battles also reflects and reasserts contemporary Mongol-Muslim concepts of heroic victory and good fortune.

Such symbolic correlations between martial success and divine support were strongly reaffirmed by Ilkhanid artists as they sought to expand their visual repertoire so as to convey God's presence in Muhammad's battles. The pictorial insinuation of divine and angelic assistance can be found in other paintings in Rashid al-Din's *Compendium of Chronicles*, particularly the depiction of Muhammad on his successful campaign against the Banu Qaynuqa', another Jewish tribe who lived in a redoubt close to Medina and who also broke their coalition agreement (fig. 2.15). Rather than representing the battle scene per se, the painting depicts the moment the Prophet and his troops decide to embark on their campaign—in other words, here Muhammad is not shown as a "shedder of blood" but rather as a "Commander-in-Chief."[114]

The composition is weighed heavily to the left, with the Prophet depicted as a heroic equestrian who is visually set apart from the cavalry,

2.15. The Prophet Muhammad, surrounded by legions of angels, sets out to fight the Banu Qaynuqa', Rashid al-Din, *Jami' al-Tawarikh* (Compendium of Chronicles), Tabriz, 714 AH/1314–15 CE. Nasser D. Khalili Collection of Islamic Art, London, MSS 727, folio 6r.

which follows at some distance behind. Muhammad strides forward with confidence in his divinely ordained mission. Additionally, he is encircled by thickly applied sky-blue paint forming a mandorla, with billows of white clouds curling around its perimeter. Interestingly, this pictorial motif is reminiscent of the *imago clipeata*, a framing device used in medieval Christian painting to suggest Jesus's presence in heaven.[115]

All around the billowing aperture appear legions of angels, God's soldiers (*ghaziyan*) sent as Muhammad's seraphic helpers during his expeditions and raids. A contemporaneous Ilkhanid text relates that Muhammad asked Gabriel about these angels when he encountered them in the heavens. He inquired: "O Gabriel, who are they?," and Gabriel answered: "They are the warriors' reinforcements. God sends them whenever He wants to help the warriors."[116] The angels surrounding Muhammad join his ranks as he embarks on his military campaign. At the same time, they provide a clear indication of God's intervention during an event that is once again construed not only as belonging to the realm of worldly matters but also, more importantly, as a religiously consecrated enterprise of superlative proportions.

While the angels serve to buttress Muhammad's mission, they once again pay tribute to the revelation of Holy Scripture. Some writers, like Ibn Ishaq, state that the fifty-sixth verse of the chapter of the Table (*surat al-ma'ida*, 5:56)—"Those who take God and His Prophet and the faithful as their friends are indeed men of God, who will surely be victorious"—was revealed during the Prophet's expedition against the Banu Qaynuqa'. Ibn Ishaq elaborates on this verse, clarifying that military victory is an act of God granted to the believers and friends of the Prophet, who compose "God's party."[117]

According to the *maghazi* historian al-Waqidi, a number of other verses were revealed during the campaign against the Banu Qaynuqa'. Among them is 3:183 (as well as 3:184), which praises Muhammad as belonging to a long line of messengers who come bearing "clear signs" or "manifest proofs" (*bayyinat*) of their prophecy, as well as "enlightened scripture" (*al-kitab al-munir*). The second qur'anic revelation consists in 2:103, which warns that those who do not listen to God will suffer consequences. A third is 8:58, which stipulates that a treaty must be rescinded if treachery is committed, "for God does not like those who are treacherous." Al-Waqidi cites this particular verse as the impetus for Muhammad's decision to march out against the "traitorous" Banu Qaynuqa'.[118] Finally, al-Bal'ami also points to 8:41, which stipulates the division of war spoils, of which one-fifth is set aside for God and the Prophet, with the rest allotted to relatives, orphans, the poor, and wayfarers.[119] The author's interest here clearly lies in explicating the legal regulations and ramifications governing the distribution of war booty, as set forth during this martial occasion for revelation.

It is most likely that the Ilkhanid painting illustrated in figure 2.15 depicts the genesis of the campaign against the Jewish tribe through the revelation of parts of the Qur'an, in particular 8:58. These verses are

germane to a close iconographical scrutiny of the painting. The Ilkhanid artist used the motif of parted clouds as well as a sky-blue color to
suggest God's celestial presence and all-encompassing protection of
the Prophet. In this instance, Muhammad is enclosed by the opening
of the sky and surrounded by God's angels as twin marks of the "clear
signs" of his prophecy. Likewise, the mention of an "enlightened book"
points to the qur'anic verses that were gradually revealed by God to the
Prophet. Such verses inscribe Muhammad's *maghazi* into a consecrated
chronicle of early Islamic history, in which God is imagined, rhetorically as well as visually, as the supreme activator and actor in human
acts—including war.

This pictorial conceptualization of military action as divinely mandated finds intriguing echoes in a number of Ilkhanid texts concurrent
with Rashid al-Din's illustrated manuscript. Of particular interest are
the letters penned by the Muslim sultans Ghazan (r. 1294–1303 CE) and
Öljeitü (r. 1304–16 CE) to their European counterparts, with whom they
wished to establish a military alliance in order to combat their shared
enemy, the Mamluks. For example, in his letter to Pope Boniface VIII
(1294–1303 CE), Sultan Ghazan prays to the sky (*tengri*) to prepare his
and the pope's troops.[120] Similarly, in his letter to Philip IV of France
(r. 1285–1314 CE), Öljeitü states that he and his forces are protected and
granted inspiration by the sky (*tengri*), which possesses all power and
acts as a witness and arbiter of good fortune. In this document, the
Mongolian term *tengri*, as used by the Ilkhanids, clearly signifies "God,"
an interpretation supported by the document's Italian translation of the
term as *Dio*.[121] In his letters, Öljeitü also included a three-part incipit
formula reading, "In the might the everlasting sky / In the support/belief
(*iman*) of the Prophet Muhammad / Under the protection of the Flame
of Great Fortune."[122]

Just as this initial triad praising God, Muhammad, and fortune was
typical of Ilkhanid expressions of power at the time that Rashid al-Din's
text was illustrated under the aegis of Sultan Öljeitü, so, too, were other
Mongolian and Islamic expressions of royal power. Among them were
Ghazan's and Öljeitü's emphasis on their Chingizid pedigree, along with
their adoption of the Muslim regal title "Emperor of Islam" (*Padshah-i
Islam*). Within their expansionist ideology, and especially in their campaigns against the Mamluks, these Ilkhanid rulers claimed a heavenly
mandate for world dominion, to which the enemy would fully submit—
or face total destruction.[123] They also called on Muhammad's charisma
as a military leader and his prophetic legacy. As Anne Broadbridge
aptly summarizes, the Ilkhanids used a range of strategies to express
their supremacy within the Muslim world, including appropriating "for
themselves Muhammad's claims to be a model Muslim ruler."[124]

During the early years of the fourteenth century, Mongolian-Muslim expressions of power equated the sky with God, under whose mandate the Prophet Muhammad acted in order to secure good fortune and
a triumphant legacy—which was in turn claimed by the Ilkhanid ruling

elites. This conceptual triad combining (a nonanthropomorphic blue sky with) God, Muhammad, and good fortune is artfully encompassed and reasserted in Ilkhanid paintings depicting the Prophet's successful campaigns, especially those at Badr and against the Banu'l-Nadir and Banu Qayquna'. In these paintings, Muhammad is either accompanied by angels or framed by a sky-blue mandorla; he also is set apart and anointed as God's heroic Messenger. Most crucially, he wages war armed with qur'anic revelation. In the depiction of his battle against the Banu'l-Nadir in particular (fig. 2.14), a swooping angel appears to function as a celestial metaphor for the descent (*tanzil*) of qur'anic chapters and verses, excerpts that are woven into *maghazi* tales to create a smooth narrative of the Prophet's military expeditions as sacred occasions for revelation.[125]

These Ilkhanid paintings of the Prophet's campaigns highlight the intersections among annalistic writing, scriptural exegesis, and pictorial imagination, in which the impulse to portray moral claims to authority and truth hinges on representing facts of a distinctly historical order. Per Hayden White, this kind of "imaginative identification" provides wholeness and closure in history as well as the construction of moral meaning in the present.[126] The Ilkhanids were keen to relay such meanings and narratives through their self-fashioning activities, among them the painterly arts. Within illustrated manuscripts, paintings of the hero-prophet victorious in battle thus symbolically sealed victories in the faith. Just as importantly, such images enabled the artful crafting of a distinctly Mongolian-Muslim vision of the ever-triumphant workings of God, his Messenger, and good fortune.

ASCENDING TO GOD

At first glance, the painting of the Prophet setting out to combat the Banu Qaynuqa' does not resemble an obvious battle scene. Although Muhammad is accompanied by troops on horseback, he appears as if airborne, surrounded by angels and clouds against a bright blue background. The Ilkhanid artist responsible for the composition illustrated in figure 2.15 decided to completely shed the trope of a military battle, instead depicting a kind of apotheosis. This imagining of a prophetic or sacred flight into the skies is typical of heroic motifs found in other world cultures and religions.[127] Within Islamic traditions in particular, this visual trope also forecasts a highly popular and frequently illustrated event in Muhammad's life: his celestial ascension, or *mi'raj*.

Recounted in numerous Islamic biographical, historical, and ascension texts, Muhammad's heavenly ascent holds pride of place as the most remarkable miracle of his prophetic career. Performed during his adult years, it consists of his nighttime travel (*isra'*) to Jerusalem, followed by his ascension (*mi'raj*) through the heavens. His journey is populated by a host of characters, including al-Buraq (his flying, human-headed steed), the Angel Gabriel, a variety of angels of different shapes and sizes, and Abrahamic prophets of the past. In addition, texts enrich the story with engaging descriptions of the marvels of the celestial spheres, its fauna

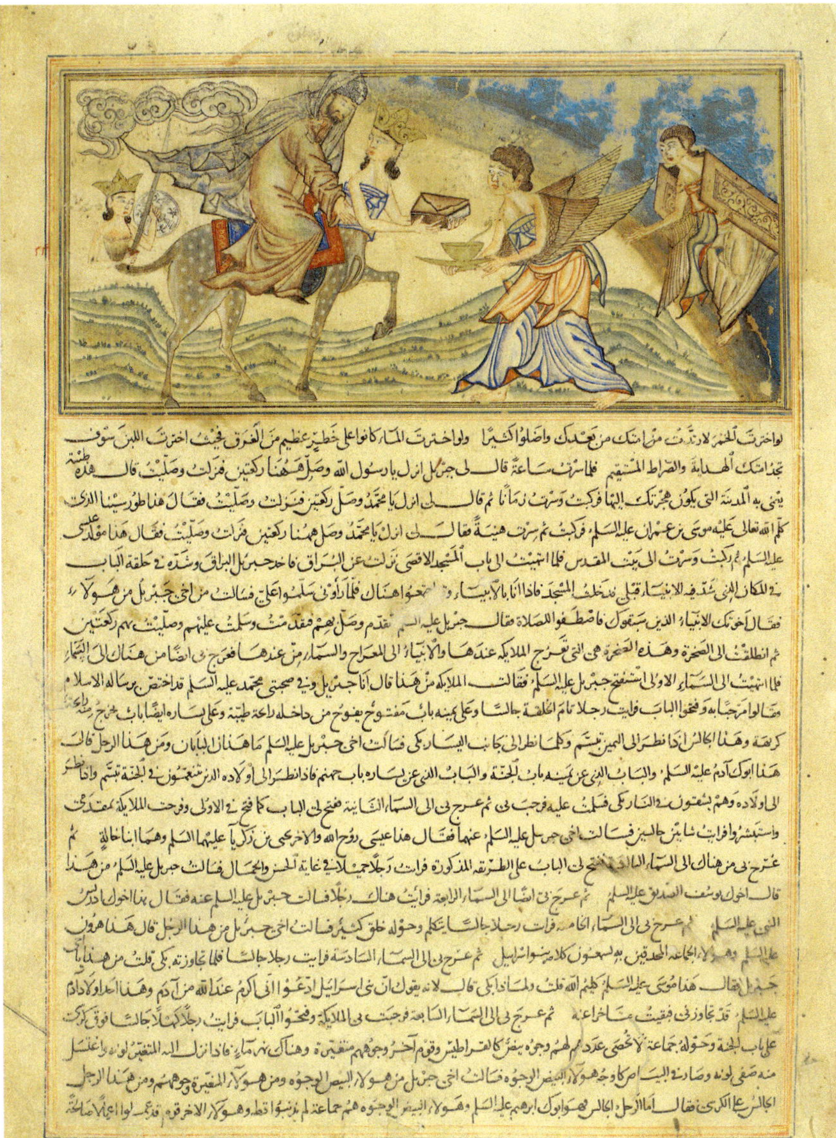

2.16. The Prophet Muhammad's ascension on Buraq, Rashid al-Din, *Jami' al-Tawarikh* (Compendium of Chronicles), Tabriz, 714 AH/1314–15 CE. University of Edinburgh Main Library, Ms. Arab 20, folio 55r.

and flora, Muhammad's encounter with God, the delights of heaven, and the torments of hell. Passed down through the centuries in the form of oral tales and written narratives, stories of Muhammad's *mi'raj* have inspired and awed audiences since the first century of Islam. They also have been used to teach the basic tenets of the Islamic faith, to enable the implementation of proper social and religious etiquette, and to draw their audiences toward Islam in both its Sunni and Shi'i iterations.[128]

During and after the medieval period, ascent narratives prompted patrons and artists to take advantage of the painterly mode in envisioning the exuberance of the celestial world, its inhabitants, and its marvels. A number of paintings produced most especially in Persian and Turkish lands between 1300 and 1600 CE reveal the extent to which such tales catalyzed imaginative visions of Muhammad's supreme miracle. During the Ilkhanid and Timurid periods in particular, the ascension story began to garner greater attention and autonomy. Although it was but one of many events in Muhammad's biography, the *mi'raj* was extracted from biographies and world histories to become the central subject of freestanding illustrated Books of Ascension (*Mi'rajnamas*). In these visually poignant picture books, the bioapocalyptic tale of the Prophet's *mi'raj* transcended purely linguistic description to convey more fully the extraordinary wonders of otherworldly spheres.

The earliest extant ascension painting appears in Rashid al-Din's *Compendium of Chronicles* (fig. 2.16),[129] which also includes Muhammad's birth, his recognition by Bahira, and his many battles. Unlike the multiple battle scenes, however, the ascension is depicted in only one painting in this manuscript's narrative cycle. In order to relay a number of details and messages within the small space allotted, the painter seems to have opted for a synoptic pictorial strategy, combining several episodes of the *mi'raj* narrative into a single image, in which Muhammad sits atop Buraq—who holds a closed codex and whose tail terminates in a gladiatorial angel—as he approaches two angels, one of whom offers a golden cup while the other emerges from a door in the arc of the firmament. The event is shown as occurring on earthly ground rather than in the celestial spheres: Buraq treads gently across fertile terrain while the heavens, although in close sight, remain to be entered. The depiction thus shows the Prophet during his horizontal, earthly night journey (*isra'*) from Mecca to Jerusalem, prior to his ascension (*mi'raj*) from Jerusalem to the heavens.

A number of Islamic ascension narratives describe the various trials that Muhammad underwent during his *isra'* in order to confirm his proper faith and prophetic status prior to entering the celestial spheres. The two most important among these tests are the so-called "lure of the tempting voices" and the "trial of the cups." The first obstruction comprises a number of voices, sometimes up to four in number, that try to attract Muhammad's attention and veer him off course. These voices either represent other faiths, such as Judaism, Christianity, and Zoroastrianism, or the temptations of earthly wealth and power. In all *mi'raj* narratives, Muhammad consistently ignores these siren-like diversions, steadily proceeding toward God.[130] He also successfully passes a second trial, in which one or more angels offer him two, three, or four cups containing milk, water, honey, and/or wine. Regardless of the number of cups and whether they are offered on earth or in the heavens, Muhammad always selects the cup of milk, the most primordial and uncorrupted substance a newborn ingests. The Prophet's correct selection of the cup of milk serves to establish his pure character as well as his and his community's placement on the path to paradise and salvation.[131]

These two tests appear in the Ilkhanid *mi'raj* painting: one angel holds a golden vessel, suggestive of Muhammad's correct selection of the cup of milk, and Buraq's tail terminates in a warrior angel that possibly embodies worldly desires and thus the incorrect path. The Prophet ignores the lure of evil hovering behind him as he approaches the looming firmament. Another detail included in the depiction is also noteworthy: the closed codex held aloft by Buraq's human arms and hands. Placed

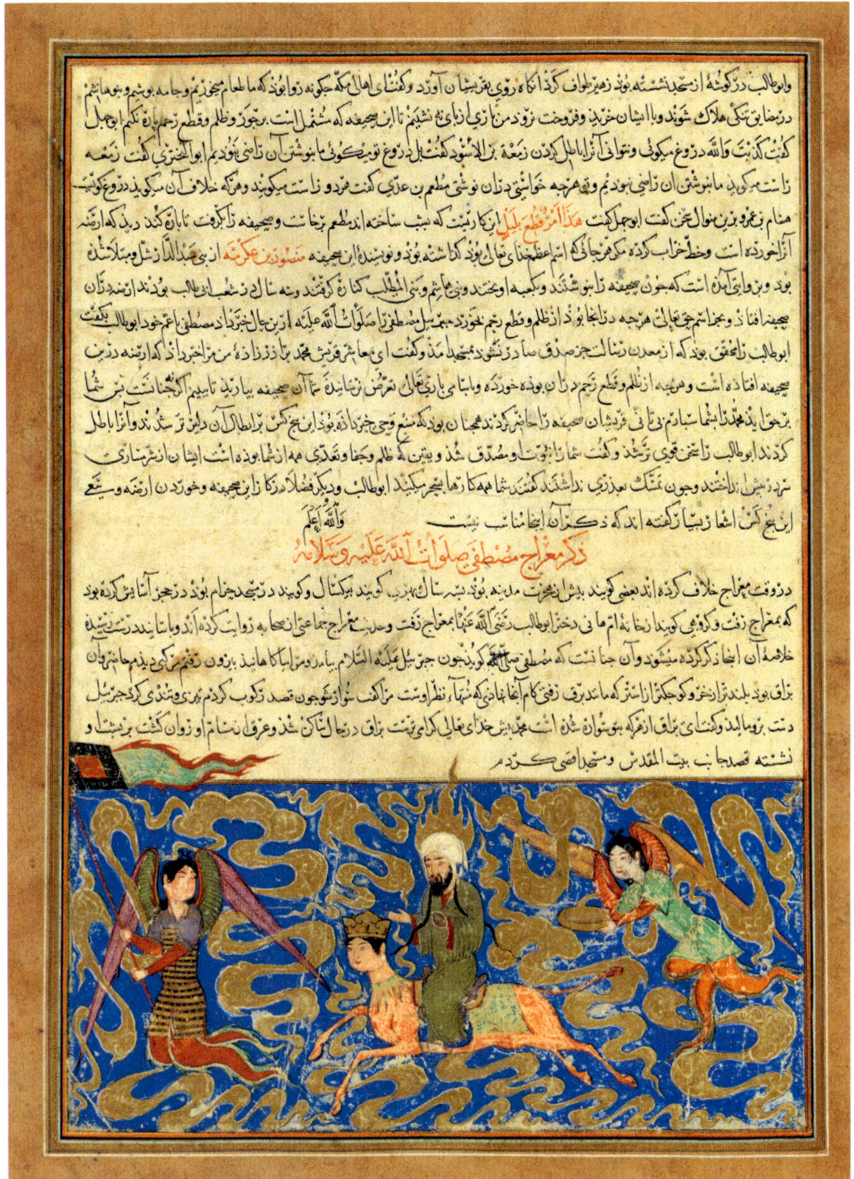

2.17. The Prophet Muhammad's ascension on Buraq, Rashid al-Din, *Jami' al-Tawarikh* (Compendium of Chronicles), Tabriz, text dated 717 AH/1317 CE, paintings added ca. 1350–1400 CE. Topkapı Palace Library, Istanbul, H. 1654, folio 69r. Photograph by Hadiye Cangökçe.

at the very center of the composition, it grabs the viewer's attention. As previous scholars have noted, this book, encased in an envelope binding, is most certainly the Qur'an.[132] In this particular instance, the Qur'an may represent the "straight path" (*al-sirat al-mustaqim*) toward God and the sacred realms as well as the revelation of Holy Scripture—in whole or in part—to the Prophet during the night of his ascension. The *mi'raj* painting included in Rashid al-Din's *Compendium of Chronicles* thus provides a visual amalgam that attests to the righteousness of the prophetic path and Muhammad's supreme status, in the process offering a compelling pictorial argument in support of embracing Islam and its Messenger.

The Prophet's ascent proved a popular theme in Iran during the fourteenth and fifteenth centuries. While the earliest surviving painting in the *Compendium of Chronicles* of 1306–7 CE depicts the *isra'* and its earthly trials, a subsequent copy of Rashid al-Din's text, penned in

2.18. The Prophet Muhammad sits with other prophets in Jerusalem as he undergoes the test of the cups, anonymous, *Mi'rajnama* (Book of Ascension), Tabriz, ca. 1317–30 CE. Topkapı Palace Library, Istanbul, H. 2154, folio 62r. Photograph by Hadiye Cangökçe.

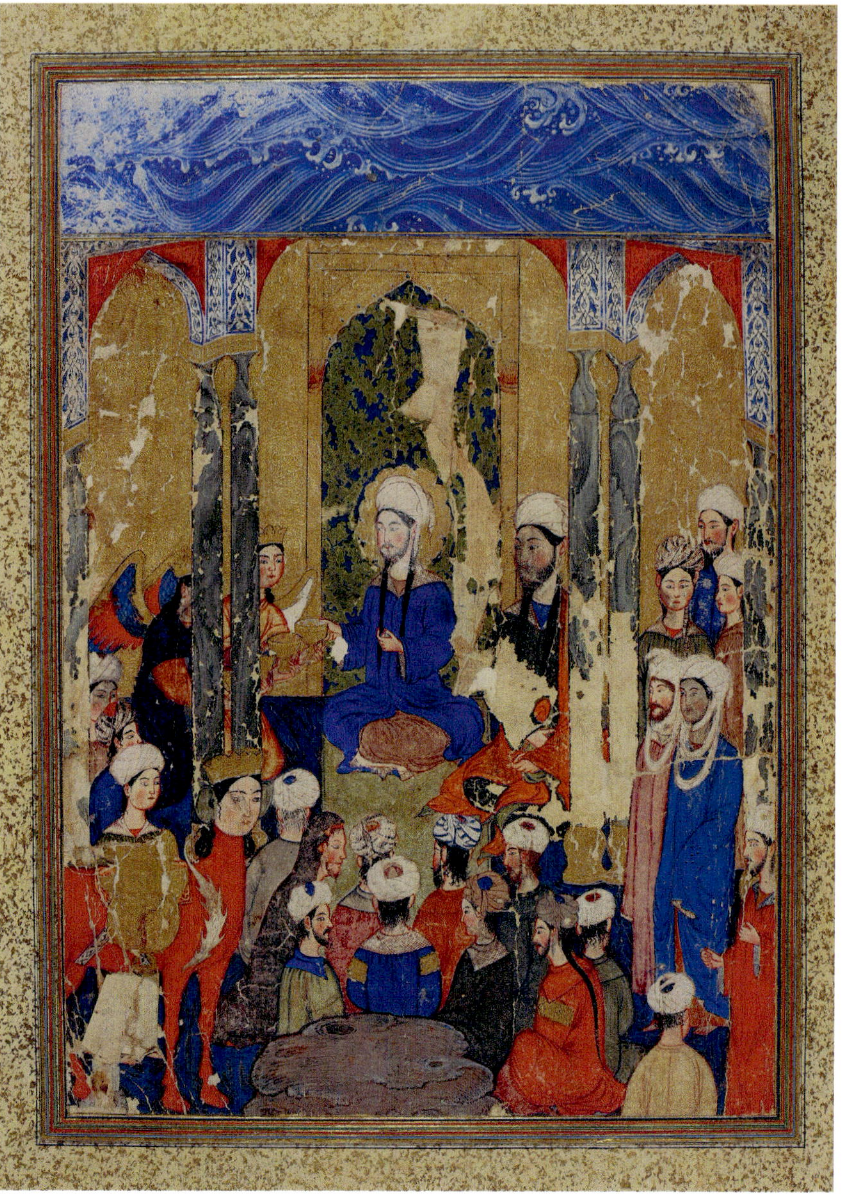

1317 CE, includes illustrations added around 1350–1400 CE. In the later copy, a single image of Muhammad's ascension, located at the very beginning of the narrative (fig. 2.17), functions almost like a frontispiece. The depiction illustrates the Prophet's flight through the celestial spheres—that is, the *mi'raj* proper. Here, Muhammad follows the Angel Gabriel, who brandishes a flaming banner and is flanked by another angel extending a platter of offerings. The three protagonists fly through a lapis blue sky, encircled by golden swirls, which become all the more energetic and dazzling as they gird the Prophet and join at the tip of his flaming halo. This painting of Muhammad wreathed in radiant light and angelic companions represents his *mi'raj* as transcending narrative details, creating a distinctly iconic effect. This visual trope eventually became the quintessential pictorial formula for single-page ascension paintings produced in Iran during the sixteenth century, a topic further discussed in chapter 4.

THE PRAISEWORTHY ONE

In the Ilkhanid period, *mi'raj* texts and images made appearances in illustrated biographical and historical manuscripts; they also catalyzed a new genre of picture books commonly known as Books of Ascension (*Mi'rajnama*s). The earliest among these is attributed to the patronage of the Ilkhanid ruler Abu Sa'id (r. 1316–35 CE) and thus datable to the first few decades of the fourteenth century.[133] Unfortunately, this illustrated *Mi'rajnama* survives only in fragmentary condition: its original text has been entirely lost, and only ten of its large-scale paintings remain.[134] While related evidence suggests that this particular *Mi'rajnama* may have been used to promote conversion to Islam and/or a specifically Sunni Muslim worldview among members of Abu Sa'id's entourage, its paintings address an array of themes and concerns, chief among them Muhammad's supreme rank and the proper performance of Muslim prayer practices. As such, the paintings in the Ilkhanid illustrated *Mi'rajnama* offer *tableaux vivants* of the faith.

The ten extant paintings depict Muhammad's arrival in Jerusalem, ascension through the skies, encounter with various angels, visit to heaven, and return to Mecca. In this illustrated version, the test of the cups occurs after the Prophet arrives in Jerusalem (fig. 2.18). Having entered the holy city, Muhammad sits at the top center of an enclosed space—most likely the Dome of the Rock, with the rocky outcrop preserving his footprint, located in the middle of the painting's foreground—where he serves as prayer leader for a large group of prophets who have gathered for the occasion. Behind two columns and above the red-bodied and green-eared Buraq kneel two angels who offer four golden cups to Muhammad. The painting thus effectively combines two key episodes of selection and initiation: Muhammad's recognition as the last of the Abrahamic prophets and the confirmation of his pure disposition through the cup trial.

Throughout the centuries, the test of the cups proved a recurrent motif in ascension tales and images. However, its depiction in early fourteenth-century Persian paintings (as in figures 2.16 and 2.18) may have held a particularly charged significance for an Ilkhanid princely audience. At this time, the ruling elites of Iran were still in the process of converting to Islam and retained certain Mongolian traditions. Ilkhanid conversion narratives thus frequently include topoi that highlight "wrong alternatives" in contradistinction to the "right choice" made by the Muslim convert.[135] Muhammad's temptation by the voices representing other religions and his testing by the cups align readily with such conversion tales, in which both tests serve to assure the righteousness and elevated position of the Prophet and the Muslim community—itself a promise of divinely appointed superiority germane to the particular religious context of Ilkhanid Iran.

In addition, the test of the cups may have echoed royal practices at the Ilkhanid court, in which diverse drinks were used during accession ceremonies. For example, Abu Sa'id—to whom the patronage of the illustrated *Mi'rajnama* is attributed—was offered a drinking cup on his

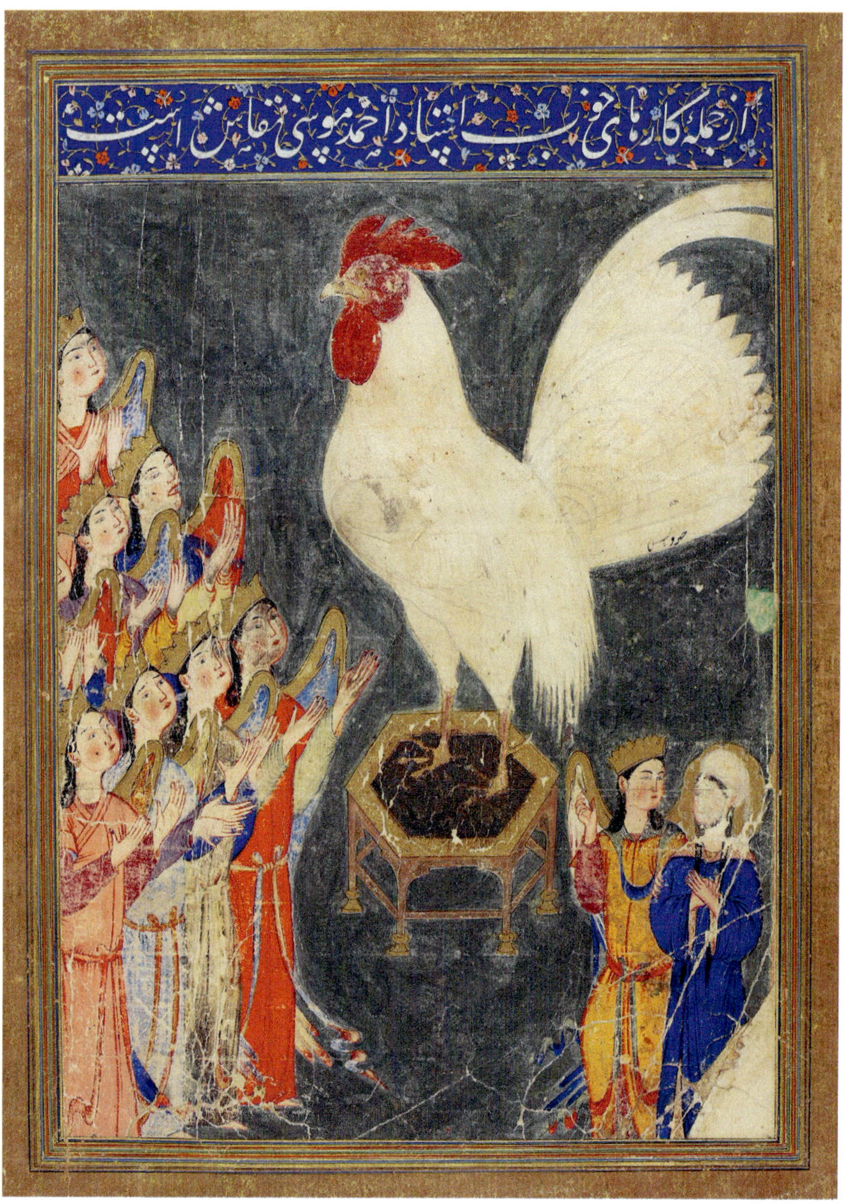

2.19. The Prophet Muhammad, Angel Gabriel, and other angels pray at the foot of the celestial rooster angel, anonymous, *Mi'rajnama* (Book of Ascension), Tabriz, ca. 1317–30 CE. Topkapı Palace Library, Istanbul, H. 2154, folio 61v. Photograph by Hadiye Cangökçe.

accession to the throne in 1317 CE.[136] During Ilkhanid audiences and receptions, several drinks were offered to those in attendance, including wine, clarified mare's milk (*qara qumis*), and honey mead (*bal*).[137] Mongolian traditions included milk sacrifices to idols, as well.[138] Intriguingly, the three liquid substances of wine, milk, and honey—with milk serving as the foremost religious offering—are clearly echoed in the test of the cups episode present in *mi'raj* narratives. The use of libations thus cuts across both Ilkhanid political and religious practices and Islamic ascension tales, enabling multiple discourses about ascendancy and power to be deftly articulated and intertwined through the cup motif.

The Ilkhanid illustrated *Mi'rajnama* also includes a number of minor and major angels, one of which is shaped like a rooster (fig. 2.19).[139] This white celestial rooster angel functions both as a zoomorphic symbol for the five daily prayers on earth and as a channel for the perpetual remembrance and praise of God in the heavens. The painting depicts

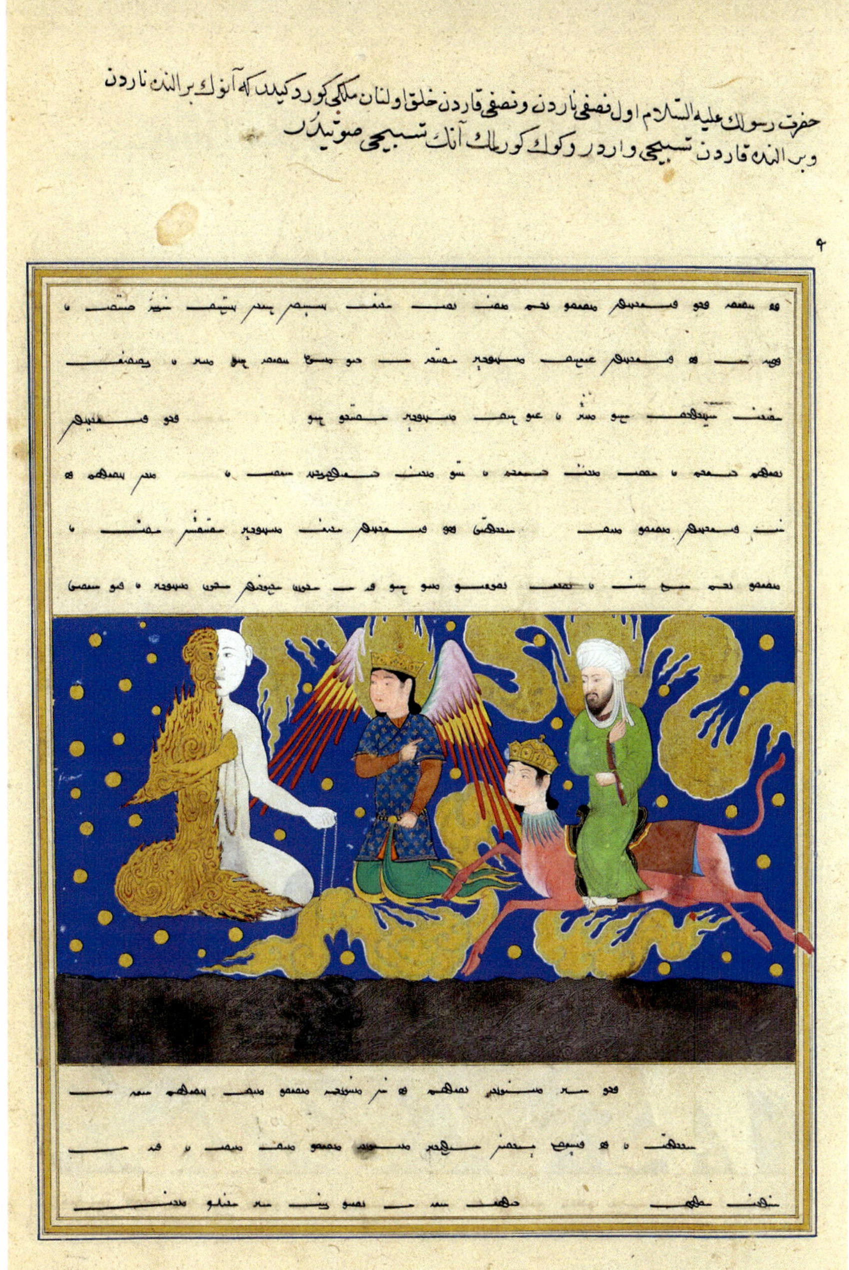

2.20. The Prophet Muhammad encounters the angel of half-fire and half-snow, anonymous, *Mi'rajnama* (Book of Ascension), Herat or Samarqand, ca. 1450–60 CE. David Collection, Copenhagen, 13/2012 verso. Photograph by Pernille Klemp.

the celestial rooster standing on a dais while a choir of angels lifts their arms in a prayerful position known as the "raising of the two hands" (*raf' al-yadayn*). As the Angel Gabriel points to the rooster angel, he touches the Prophet's upper arm. In turn, Muhammad displays proper piety through another prayer position, known as the "grasping" (*qabd*) of the two hands at the chest level. Both the raising and the clutching of the hands are traditionally accepted gestures used in Islamic communal prayer practices,[140] and the representation of such pious postures within the Ilkhanid *Mi'rajnama* may well have enabled the manuscript's readers—especially an elite audience still new to or undergoing conversion to Islam—to better learn the proper physical practice of the faith.

While Muhammad and the angels might act as visual exemplars in physically enacted forms of devotion within the Ilkhanid *Mi'rajnama*, its rooster angel embodies prayer itself. In addition to this zoomorphic creature, other composite angels are described and illustrated in subsequent books of ascension, especially two illustrated copies produced in Herat and possibly Samarqand around 1430–60 CE.[141] These Timurid manuscripts include lavish pictorial cycles of Muhammad's ascension, in which the Prophet is shown encountering the rooster angel, several polycephalous angels, and the angel of half-fire and half-snow (fig. 2.20).[142] While the rooster and polycephalous angels act as stand-ins for prayer, the Timurid text describes the angel of half-fire and half-snow as holding a rosary (*tasbih*) in each hand and having a voice so thunderous that men can hear its prayers on earth.[143] As the perfect union of opposite elements, in which fire does not melt snow and snow does not extinguish fire, this particular angel represents the ideal equilibrium between the angelic realms and the world's elemental forces. Put simply, it is the Islamic angelic equivalent of the Chinese concept of yin and yang.

Although the image appears to be loyal to the text—indeed, the angel is depicted with its right side made of fire and its left side of snow, holding a rosary in each hand—the angel's position and facial traits link it to the iconography of Buddhist artistic traditions in Central Asia and China. Many Buddhist murals and book paintings depict the Buddha or monks sitting in the lotus position, with their arms and hands engaged in various symbolic gestures (mudras). Perhaps this Islamic painting reveals more than a simple, fortuitous confluence of pan-Asian forms. Indeed, the artist's selection of the lotus position and mudras appears purposeful and strategic: both elements represent spiritual equanimity and physical balance and therefore are appropriate to representations of both the Buddha and the angel of half-fire and half-snow. This conceptual conjunction would not have been lost on a viewer conversant in Islamic and Buddhist scriptural traditions during this period of heightened cross-Asian cultural dialogue.

Premodern illustrated Turco-Persian books of ascension also narrate and depict Muhammad's encounters with prophets and God as well as his visits to heaven and hell. In a number of cases, their conclusions—and hence key moral lessons and portents—diverge in a number of revealing ways. For example, some narratives describe Muhammad's return to Mecca after his nighttime journey to Jerusalem and ascension to the heavens. Once he is back in the city, his enemies, chief among them Abu Jahl, dismiss his miraculous journey as a fanciful fabrication. Moreover, some of the Prophet's followers apostatize from Islam while others gain guidance and strength through this "searching test."[144] However, on establishing the veracity of his *mi'raj* through a number of verifiable proofs—including predicting the arrival of a caravan in Mecca and/or accurately describing the city of Jerusalem, which he had never visited previously—the Prophet earned his followers' support and garnered converts to his cause and thus his faith. This conversion conclusion was particularly well suited to efforts to lure further adherents to Islam in medieval Iran, which to a certain extent may explain its depiction in the Ilkhanid *Mi'rajnama* (see fig. 1.11).

This ending may not have been as relevant during the Timurid period, at which time Iran and Central Asia fell under the expanding fold of Dar al-Islam. The conclusions of the two Timurid books of ascension—which were both made during the middle decades of the fifteenth century—thus posit divergent possibilities for the tale's ending. Rather than concluding the *mi'raj* tale with Muhammad's return to Mecca and the conversion of pagan Arabs, the later texts either end with a theological description of hell and its tortures or describe the Prophet flying on Gabriel's wing to Mount Qaf, at the end of the known world.[145] Once there, he visits the cities of Jabalsa and Jabalqa, which are inhabited by the "people of Moses." These Jews speak with Muhammad and then believe in him, an act of conversion to Islam that grants them remission from hell and the rewards of paradise. According to Wheeler Thackston, this conversion narrative may reflect Timurid missionary initiatives to better convert the "heathen Mongolized Turks of Moghulistan," who were only nominally Muslim.[146] Alternatively, according to Maria Subtelny, the Timurid text may preserve an earlier Persian narrative of the conversion of Jews in Iran and Central Asia.[147] The two lavishly illustrated *Mi'rajnama*s considered here must have invited their readers and viewers to be all the more righteous in their faith through such comparative and superlative statements. Regardless of their intended audiences—members of the Jewish faith, Turks of dubitable Muslim suasion, or elite Muslims of true conviction—these books of ascension provide an allegory of the faith described in sequence, with the purpose of moralizing according to a particular socioreligious system.[148]

Neither Timurid illustrated *Mi'rajnama* depicts Muhammad's return to Mecca or his visit to Mount Qaf, thus subduing the tale's missionary tone through carefully crafted pictorial programs. Instead, their painting cycles end with Muhammad's visit to heaven and hell (figs. 2.21–22).[149] In heaven, the Prophet witnesses saved souls resting and playing in the delights of nature and coupledom, while in the infernal realms he sees the denizens of hell tortured in horrific ways for a host of sins, including lying, backbiting, cheating, and stealing the wealth of orphans, among others. With their final emphasis on listing and illustrating a dozen sins that result in chthonic tortures, both Timurid illustrated books of ascension emphasize proper behavior within a larger social contract. These manuscripts act more like picture books advertising moral conduct than as manuals for conversion to Islam, thereby catering to an elite Muslim audience wishing to cultivate piety among both its older and younger members.

The two Timurid *Mi'rajnama*s also must be understood as belonging to a larger corpus of premodern Islamic advice texts that include the "mirror for princes" genre.[150] In addition, had the manuscripts functioned as graphic novels for a juvenile audience, they also could have formed a kind of medieval child-enrichment literature, whose goal was the cultivation of a pious younger generation (itself a tradition that is flourishing in the Islamic world today, as discussed in chapter 6). These

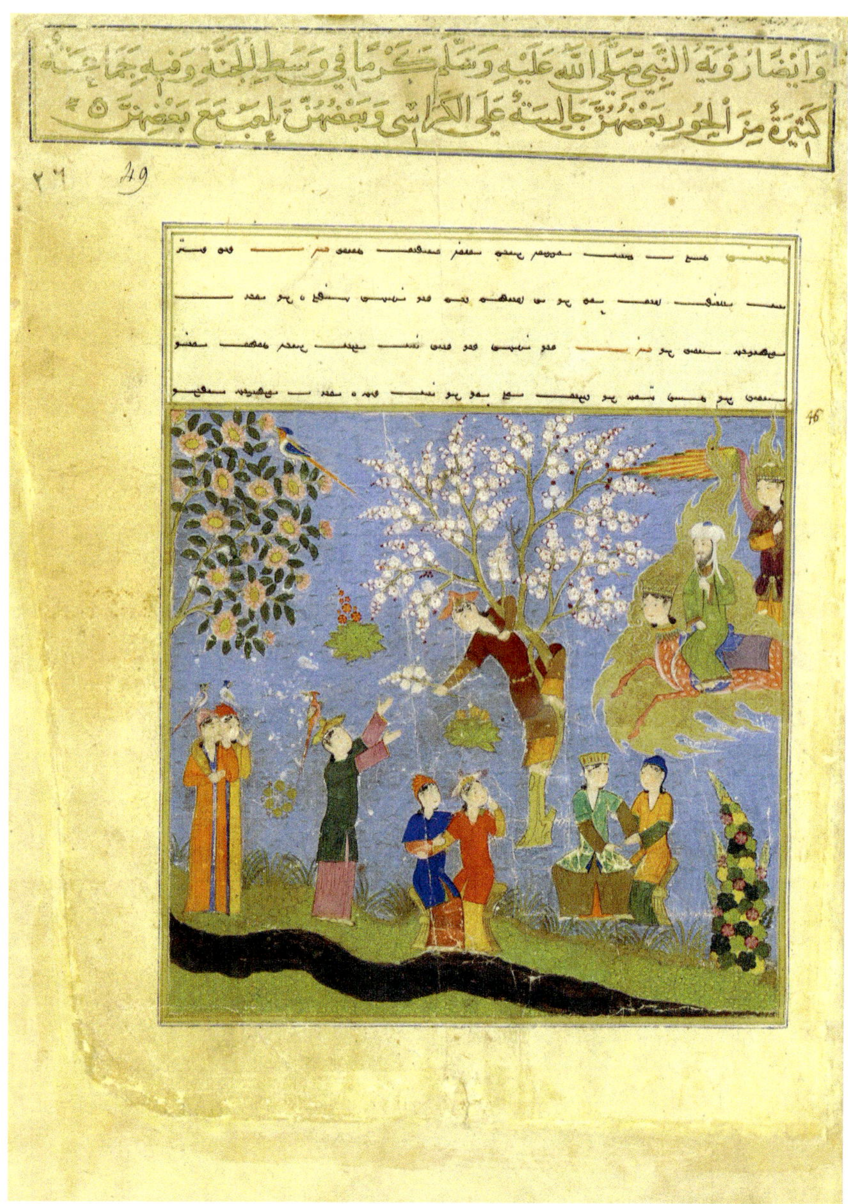

books' pedagogical potential must have been manifold: they presented the Prophet's chief miracle in fantastic detail; enumerated previous Abrahamic prophets; described the heavenly spheres and angels; explained God's selection of the Muslim *umma* as the best of communities; taught proper behavior that would result in salvation; and warned of sins resulting in damnation to hellfire. These narrative illustrations of Muhammad's life thus engage in the proverbial tactic of the "carrot and stick" by combining positive reinforcement with negative admonition via the prophetic *sira* and its creative interweaving with moral expectations of the day.

In these Ilkhanid and Timurid paintings of Muhammad's *mi'raj*, the Prophet is depicted as the "rider of Buraq" and "possessor of the ascension,"[151] as well as an apocalyptic wayfarer, inviter to the Islamic faith, and instructor in social and religious ethics. His apotheosis is not a resurrection, and his departure is not death. Rather, his celestial journey

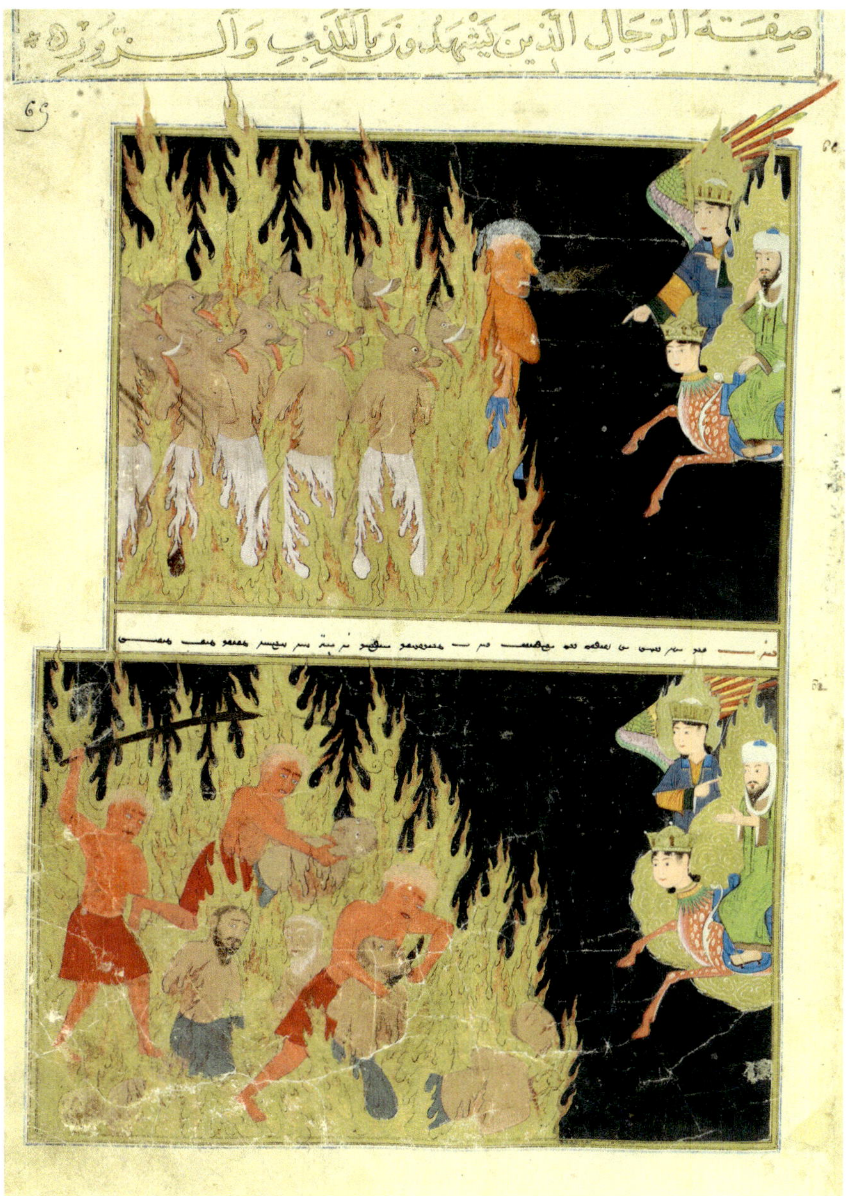

2.22. The Prophet Muhammad witnesses the tortures of hell, anonymous, *Mi'rajnama* (Book of Ascension), Herat, ca. 1436–37 CE. Bibliothèque nationale de France, Paris, Suppl. Turc 190, folio 65r.

is one of ascending into faith and morality and returning to earthly terrain stronger and more enlightened than before. While the Ilkhanid *Mi'rajnama* may have been used to enable conversion to Islam among the Mongol ruling elites of Iran, the two Timurid books of ascension could have taught the basic tenets of the faith along with acceptable codes of conduct to a younger, and already Muslim, circle of princely readers. Without a doubt, the Islamic *mi'raj* parable—regardless of its manifold textual and visual details and presentations—describes Muhammad's heroic experience of the beyond. Just as significantly, it served to foster cohesive group identity and moral behavior among both adults and children.

The fourteenth and fifteenth centuries witnessed the rise of Muslim world empires in eastern Islamic lands. While the Ilkhanids were of Mongol extraction and the Timurids also claimed Chingizid origins,

HEROIC ACCRUALS

these Turco-Persian dynasties embraced Islam and became some of the greatest patrons of art and architecture, including book arts. Illustrated historical manuscripts made in Iran and Central Asia between around 1300 and 1500 CE include universal encyclopedias and books of ascension that contain the earliest extant pictorial cycles depicting the Prophet Muhammad and the events of his life. These paintings reveal some of the earliest sustained efforts to construct a vision of the Islamic past for elite audiences who wished to proselytize Islam or to reaffirm their adherence to the Muslim faith through the prophetic paradigm. As the quintessential leader in religion, war, and statecraft, Muhammad provided an exemplum worthy of adulation and emulation for these dynastic households ruling in the name of Islam.

In a number of manuscript paintings, the Prophet bears all the marks of a heroic protagonist. On the one hand, such marks are inspired by textual sources while, on the other, they quite frequently prove the outcome of creative interpolation by artists who drew on their own imaginations and artistic prototypes to create a new visual lexicon for Islamic religious painting. In these early paintings, prior to his coming into the world, Muhammad is foreseen in a creative yet competitive conjoining with Jesus, while his luminous birth is envisioned as an angelic, quasicelestial event. During his childhood, the Prophet is shown purified of evil blemishes and recognized as an apostle by a Christian holy man. Once embarked on his prophetic mission, Muhammad engages in a number of military campaigns, whose successes are depicted as occasions for revelations and victories by God, while his celestial ascension enables him to witness heaven and hell and to converse directly with God. From his foretelling and birth to his battles and ascent, Muhammad is invariably depicted with God on his side, in large part through symbolic details such as light metaphors, angelic assistants, bent celestial arcs, olfactory anointment, and scriptural revelation. Such visual motifs in effect boost the prophetic premium, allowing Muhammad to accrue prestige and power in the eyes of his beholders.

Through such textual and visual patterns, it becomes clear that the writing and illustrating of history is never a neutral or straightforward endeavor. As a form of communication about the past that always reflects the present, the telling of history is essentially a narrative construal. It tends to "marinate" in symbolic references while not infrequently adopting practices of fabulation.[152] Undoubtedly, the crafting of fabulae—mythic stories and legendary tales—enables a view of history that is often superhuman, accentuating the life and deeds of heroic figures such as Muhammad. As Hayden White notes in this regard, "the value attached to narrativity in the representation of real events arises out of a desire to have real events display the coherence, integrity, fullness, and closure of an image of life that is and can only be imaginary."[153] While it would be foolish to state that the life and deeds of the Prophet are imaginary, certain elements of his biography nevertheless were clearly subjected to metaphorical thought and strategic fabulation. Such practices of augmentation and mythmaking are prevalent in the textual and visual presentation of heroes, including those who, like Muhammad, were nonetheless born in the full light of history.

1. Quoted in Rashid al-Din, *Geschichte Gazan Hans*, 79; and Spuler, *History of the Mongols*, 145.

2. On narrative structure, fictions, and signs of reality, see Barthes, "The Reality Effect."

3. Campbell, *The Hero with a Thousand Faces*, 23.

4. Campbell, *The Hero with a Thousand Faces*, 59.

5. See, inter alia, Soucek, "The Life of the Prophet"; Soucek, "An Illustrated Manuscript of al-Biruni's *Chronology of Ancient Nations*"; Fitzherbert, "'Bal'ami's Tabari'"; Hillenbrand, "Images of Muhammad in al-Biruni's *Chronology of Ancient Nations*"; Blair, *A Compendium of Chronicles*; Inal, "Miniatures in Historical Manuscripts from the Time of Shahrukh in the Topkapi Palace Museum"; Gruber, *The Ilkhanid Book of Ascension*; Gruber, *The Timurid Book of Ascension*; and Sims, "The *Nahj al-Faradis* of Sultan Abu Sa'id ibn Sultan Muhammad ibn Miranshah."

6. Bruner, "Past and Present as Narrative Constructions," 37.

7. McAuliffe, "The Prediction and Prefiguration of Muhammad," 116–17.

8. Rubin, *The Eye of the Beholder*, 36; and Bashear, "Riding Beasts on Divine Missions," 42. For Muhammad's epithet "rider of the camel" (*rakib al-jamal* and *rakib al-ba'ir*), see al-Suyuti, *al-Riyad al-Aniqa fi Sharh Asma' Khayr al-Khaliqa*, 162.

9. Rubin, *The Eye of the Beholder*, 22–23; Wansbrough, "Emblems of Prophethood," 63–64; and al-Yahsubi, *Muhammad, Messenger of Allah*, 122. Also see al-Zamakhshari's interpretation of "Ahmad" as the Prophet Muhammad in Gätje, *The Qur'an and Its Exegesis*, 69.

10. Barrett, "The Holy Spirit in the Fourth Gospel," 11 and 14.

11. Rubin, *The Eye of the Beholder*, 39.

12. For a general discussion of the *asma' al-nabi*, see Schimmel, *And Muhammad Is His Messenger*, 105–22, 257–59; and Andrae, *Die Person Muhammeds in Lehre und Glauben seiner Gemeinde*, 272–76.

13. Al-Maliji, *Asma' al-Nabi fi'l-Qur'an wa'l-Sunna*, 11; and al-Suyuti, *al-Riyad al-Aniqa fi Sharh Asma' Khayr al-Khaliqa*, 55.

14. Jesus is commonly referred to as "*al-Masih*" (the Anointed One) in the Qur'an; see Reynolds, *The Qur'an and Its Biblical Subtext*, 196.

15. Al-Biruni, *The Chronology of Ancient Nations*, 22; and al-Biruni, *al-Athar al-Baqiyya 'an al-Qurun al-Khaliyya*, 25.

16. On the *shamla*, see Hosain, "A Translation of the Ash-Shama'il of Tirmizi," 48.

17. Soucek, "An Illustrated Manuscript of al-Biruni's *Chronology of Ancient Nations*," 107–8; and Hillenbrand, "Images of Muhammad in al-Biruni's *Chronology of Ancient Nations*," 132, in which Hillenbrand states that the painting appears to emit a "sigh of relief that Islam is back in the saddle again."

18. A similar argument for the Great Mongol *Shahnama* is forwarded in Grabar and Blair, *Epic Images and Contemporary History*, 52.

19. Bashear, "Riding Beasts on Divine Missions," 43.

20. Bashear, "Riding Beasts on Divine Missions," 39.

21. Rashid al-Din, *Jami' al-Tawarikh (Iran wa Islam)*, 931–32.

22. Ibn Ishaq, *The Life of Muhammad*, 69.

23. McAuliffe, "The Prediction and Prefiguration of Muhammad," 126–27.

24. De Voragine, *The Golden Legend*, 1:37–43.

25. Ibn Ishaq, *The Life of Muhammad*, 70.

26. Leites, "*Sira* and the Question of Tradition," 57.

27. Leites, "*Sira* and the Question of Tradition," 59 (*dalalatan li-nubuwwatihi*); and al-Tabari, *Muhammad in Mecca*, 66.

28. Al-Bal'ami, *Tarikh-i Bal'ami*, 734, where Ctesiphon is referred to as the "arch (*ivan*) of Nushirvan."

29. See Cornell, *The Iconography of the Nativity of Christ*.

30. For a comparison of comic books and Persian manuscript painting and a discussion of a viewer's "shuttling" between text and image, see Roxburgh, "Micrographia," 19.

31. Arnold, *Painting in Islam*, 99, plate 23; Talbot Rice, *Illustrations to the "World History*," 9, 97, plate 29; and Hillenbrand, "The Arts of the Book in Ilkhanid Iran," 149–50.

32. Inal, "Some Artistic Relationships between the Far and Near East as Reflected in the Miniatures of the *Gami' at-Tawarih*," 113; and for the most recent English translation of Rashid

al-Din's endowment deed for his book atelier (the *Rab'-i Rashidi*), see Ruggles, *Islamic Art and Visual Culture*, 35–38.

33. For an exploration of such exchanges, see Soucek, "Armenian and Islamic Manuscript Painting"; Blair, "The Religious Art of the Ilkhanids," 115; Blair, "Patterns of Patronage and Production in Ilkhanid Iran," 53; and, as these concern Ilkhanid illustrated copies of the *Shahnama* (Book of Kings), see especially Simpson, "Manuscripts and Mongols."

34. Taylor, "Armenian Illumination under Georgian, Turkish, and Mongol Rule," 94.

35. Painting reproduced in Mazaéva and Tamrazyan, *La miniature arménienne*, 210, plate 146.

36. Korkhmazian, *Toros Taronatsi*; Mathews and Taylor, *The Armenian Gospels of Gladzor*; Mathews and Sanjian, *Armenian Gospel Iconography*, 61; Korkhmazian and Hacopian, "L'enluminure de l'Arménie Majeure," 38–39; Korkhmazian and Hacopian, "Greater Armenia," 12; and Taylor, "Armenian Illumination under Georgian, Turkish, and Mongol Rule," 91.

37. Réau, "La nativité et l'adoration des images," 227.

38. Réau, "La nativité et l'adoration des images," 223–24.

39. Woods, "The Rise of Timurid Historiography," 96–99.

40. Subtelny and Khalidov, "The Curriculum of Islamic Higher Learning in Timurid Iran in the Light of the Sunni Revival under Shah-Rukh."

41. Quoted in Melville, "The Mongol and Timurid Periods," 200.

42. Cited in Lambton, "Early Timurid Theories of State," 6.

43. For a discussion of the manuscript paintings and their eventual dispersal, see Ghiasian, "The 'Historical Style' of Painting for Shahrukh and Its Revival in the Dispersed Manuscript of *Majma' al-Tawarikh*."

44. According to Persian historical texts, the Lake of Saveh dried up on the night of the birth of Muhammad. A recent investigation in the area between Tehran and Saveh has revealed evidence for the existence of this lake in the Zarand Plain. See Okhravi and Djamali, "The Missing Ancient Lake of Saveh."

45. Morgan, "Persian Historians and the Mongols," 119–20.

46. Daniel, "Bal'ami's Account of Early Islamic History," 168.

47. Quoted in Rubin, "Pre-existence and Light," 62, citing al-Bukhari's *Sahih* IV:229.

48. Schimmel, *And Muhammad Is His Messenger*, 123–43; Böwering, "The Light Verse"; and Hermansen, "The Prophet Muḥammed in Sufi Interpretations of the Light Verse."

49. Nwyia, *Exégèse coranique et language mystique*, 95–97.

50. Hermansen, "The Prophet Muhammed in Sufi Interpretations of the Light Verse," 224. On Muhammad as "embodied religion" (*din mushakhkhas*), see Rasheed, "The Development of Na'tia Poetry in Persian Literature," 61.

51. Corbin, *The Man of Light in Iranian Sufism*.

52. Ibn Ishaq, *The Life of Muhammad*, 70–71. In adulthood, Muhammad also milks a goat for his army at camp so that three hundred men have enough to drink. Similarly, the barren sheep of Umm Ma'bad become engorged with milk at his touch. On these and other milk miracles, see al-Yahsubi, *Muhammad, Messenger of Allah*, 175 and 195; and Hauglid, "On the Early Life of Abraham," 101.

53. Campbell, *The Hero with a Thousand Faces*, 81.

54. For an overview of narratives about the splitting of the Prophet's chest, see Birkeland, *The Legend of the Opening of Muhammad's Breast*; and for its narrative and pictorial adaptations in European illustrated manuscripts of Dante's *Divine Comedy*, see Coffey, "Encountering the Body of Muhammad."

55. On the seal of prophethood as a symbol of the beginning of Muhammad's prophetic call or affair (*'amr*), see Rubin, *The Eye of the Beholder*, 64.

56. On the splitting of the chest as a form of *Berufungserlebnis* or initiatory experience, see Schimmel, *And Muhammad Is His Messenger*, 161.

57. Ibn Dihya, *al-Ibtihaj fi Ahadith al-Mi'raj*, 56–66.

58. Fitzherbert, "'Bal'ami's Tabari,'" 1:1; and Fitzherbert, "Religious Diversity under Ilkhanid Rule c. 1300 as Reflected in the Freer Bal'ami," 404–5. Fitzherbert argues that the manuscript was produced in Jazira, around 1300 CE, rather than in Fars, around 1330–50 CE, as originally presupposed. More precisely, she proposes that it was made for Sultan Ghazan's governor in Mosul, the known bibliophile Fakhr al-Din 'Isa. Additionally, the painting of the splitting of the chest is discussed and illustrated in Fitzherbert, "'Bal'ami's Tabari,'" 2:160–63, plate 24; Fitzherbert, "Religious Diversity under Ilkhanid Rule c. 1300 as Reflected in the Freer Bal'ami," 400–1, fig. 93; and Soucek, "The Life of the Prophet," 198, fig. 2.

59. Al-Bal'ami, *Ta'rikh al-Rusul wa'l-Muluk* (History of Messengers and Kings), Mosul, ca. 1300 CE, Freer Gallery of Art, Smithsonian Institution, Washington, DC, F1957.16, folio 138r (author's translation); al-Bal'ami, *Tarikh-i Bal'ami*, 739–40; al-Tabari, *La chronique de Tabari*, 410–11; and Fitzherbert, "'Bal'ami's Tabari,'" 160–63, with a partial translation.

60. Al-Tabari, *Muhammad in Mecca*, 63; Ibn Dihya, *al-Ibtihaj fi Ahadith al-Mi'raj*, 57 and 65; and Rubin, *The Eye of the Beholder*, 66.

61.   'Abd al-Mun'im, *Al-Sahih min Qissat al-Isra' wa'l-Mi'raj*, 43 and 46.

62.   On the expansion of Moses's breast, see Qur'an 20:25–26: "[Moses] said: 'O my Lord, enlarge my breast and make my mission easy'"; and on the qur'anic verse most likely to have inspired narratives of the splitting of Muhammad's chest, see Qur'an 94:1: "Have we not cut open your breast and removed from you your burden?"

63.   Andrae, *Die Person Muhammeds in Lehre und Glauben seiner Gemeinde*, 128–33; Rubin, *The Eye of the Beholder*, 67; Armstrong, *Muhammad*, 108–33; and Ahmed, "Ibn Taymiyyah and the Satanic Verses," 69–74.

64.   Birkeland, *The Legend of the Opening of Muhammad's Breast*, 53.

65.   Fitzherbert, "Religious Diversity under Ilkhanid Rule c. 1300 as Reflected in the Freer Bal'ami," 401.

66.   Meserve, "The Uses of Blood in Traditional Inner Asian Societies," 36 and 44.

67.   Massé, *Croyances et coutumes persanes*, 1:137–39.

68.   According to Stephen Gero, the Islamic Bahira legend echoes Christian flight into Egypt narratives of a holy child; see his "The Legend of the Monk Bahira, the Cult of the Cross, and Iconoclasm," 48.

69.   The legend was popular in eastern Christian apocalyptic and polemical literature, in which it was used to describe Islam as a Christian heresy, Muhammad as a false prophet, and the Qur'an as authored by Muhammad and Bahira rather than revealed by God. On the Christian Sergius Bahira legends, see Roggema, *The Legend of Sergius Bahira*, 37–60; and Szilágyi, "Muhammad and the Monk."

70.   Ibn Ishaq, *The Life of Muhammad*, 81.

71.   Al-Tabari, *Muhammad in Mecca*, 45–46.

72.   McAuliffe, "Connecting Moses and Muhammad," 334.

73.   Talbot Rice, *The Illustrations to the "World History" of Rashid al-Din*, 99.

74.   On medieval Christian depictions of the bent sky as a metaphor for theophany, see Boespflug, "Un étrange spectacle," 15.

75.   Rashid al-Din, *Jami' al-Tawarikh*, Tabriz, 707 AH/1306–7 CE, University of Edinburgh Main Library, Ms. Arab 20, folio 43v (author's English translation); also see the published edition, which contains slight variants in language and details, in Rashid al-Din, *Jami' al-Tawarikh*, 939–42.

76.   Soucek, "Armenian and Islamic Manuscript Painting," 126–29, figs. 47–48.

77.   Abel, "Bahira," 922.

78.   Roggema, *The Legend of Sergius Bahira*, 54; and Szilágyi, "Muhammad and the Monk," 174 and 183.

79.   *Al-Masih* (Messiah or Anointed One) is often listed among the many names of the Prophet; see al-Suyuti, *al-Riyad al-Aniqa fi Sharh Asma' Khayr al-Khaliqa*, 244.

80.   Boyle, "Rashid al-Din," 19–20; Blair, "Patterns of Patronage and Production in Ilkhanid Iran," 39–40; and Pfeiffer, "Conversion Versions," 37.

81.   For the most recent discussion of this topic, see Brack, "Mediating Sacred Kingship," 195–275.

82.   Spuler, *History of the Mongols*, 144.

83.   Melville, "Padshah-i Islam."

84.   Inal, "Some Miniatures of the *Jami' al-Tavarikh* in Istanbul," 173–74. This later copy of the *Compendium of Chronicles* also includes illustrations of the birth of the Prophet and the beginnings of revelation; on these scenes, see Inal, "Miniatures in Historical Manuscripts from the Time of Shahrukh in the Topkapi Palace Museum," 111 (H. 1654, folios 55v and 154r).

85.   Hobsbawm, *The Invention of Tradition*, 7–14.

86.   Campbell, *The Hero with a Thousand Faces*, 48.

87.   For a discussion of Persian manuscript paintings depicting Muhammad's appointment of 'Ali as his successor during his Farewell Pilgrimage, see Gruber, "Questioning the 'Classical' in Persian Painting," 17–21.

88.   Hillenbrand, "Muhammad as Warrior Prophet."

89.   On the "occasions of revelation" (*asbab al-nuzul*) within exegetical practices, particularly to construct explanatory narratives or establish qur'anic chronology or law, see Rippin, "The Function of *Asbab al-Nuzul* in Qur'anic Exegesis"; and Wansbrough, *Quranic Studies*, 141–42 and 177–83.

90.   Armstrong, *Muhammad*, 164–210.

91.   Melville, "Between Tabriz and Herat," 36.

92.   Khazanov, "Muhammad and Jenghiz Khan Compared," 464 and 471.

93.   Al-Waqidi, *The Life of Muhammad*, 11–85; and Ibn Ishaq, *The Life of Muhammad*, 289–360.

94.   Al-Tabari, *La chronique de Tabarî*, 527–51.

95.   Daniel, "Bal'ami's Account of Early Islamic History," 166–67.

96.   For a synoptic discussion of both paintings, see Soucek, "The Life of the Prophet," 195–96, figs. 5–6.

97.   For a comparative illustration of the battle of Badr in a copy of Rashid al-Din's *Compendium of Chronicles*, with a text dated 714 AH/1314 CE and paintings added around 1350–1400 CE, see Inal, "Some Artistic Relationships between the Far and Near East as Reflected in the Miniatures of the *Gami' at-Tawarih*," 122, fig. 10 (Topkapı Palace Library, Istanbul, H. 1653, folio 165v).

98.   Teresa Fitzherbert notes that Muhammad is not described as on horseback and in battle in the text. Instead, in this painting he appears as if a royal hunter, perhaps in emulation of the Christian warrior-saint paradigm, especially St. George, the patron saint of Mosul. See Fitzherbert, "'Bal'ami's Tabari,'" 401–3.

99.   Ibn Ishaq, *The Life of Muhammad*, 321–27; and al-Waqidi, *The Life of Muhammad*, 66–69.

100.   Al-Tabari, *La chronique de Tabarî*, 532 (Q 8:7); 537 (Q 8:11); and 539 (Q 8:9 and Q 3:123–24).

101.   On Q 8:1, see al-Tabari, *La chronique de Tabarî*, 543; and al-Wahidi, *al-Wahidi's Asbab al-Nuzul*, 113. On Q 8:67–69, see al-Wahidi, *al-Wahidi's Asbab al-Nuzul*, 116–18.

102.   On the "explication of the unknown" (*ta'yin al-mubham*) in *asbab al-nuzul* works, see Rippin, "The Function of *Asbab al-Nuzul* in Qur'anic Exegesis," 6; and Rippin, "Al-Zarkashi and al-Suyuti on the Function of the 'Occasion of Revelation' Material," 256.

103.   Rippin, "Al-Zarkashi and al-Suyuti on the Function of the 'Occasion of Revelation' Material," 258.

104.   Soucek, "Armenian and Islamic Manuscript Painting," 126–29, figs. 49–50.

105.   Hillenbrand, "The Arts of the Book in Ilkhanid Iran," 145.

106.   For a discussion of the term *kitab munir* as denoting the Qur'an, see Ayoub, *The Qur'an and Its Interpreters*, 396.

107.   Armstrong, *Muhammad*, 177.

108.   Ibn Ishaq, *The Life of Muhammad*, 438.

109.   Al-Waqidi, *The Life of Muhammad*, 186.

110.   Al-Tabari, *La chronique de Tabarî*, 581.

111.   Al-Wahidi, *Al-Wahidi's Asbab al-Nuzul*, 223–24.

112.   Allsen, "Changing Forms of Legitimation in Mongol Iran," 223; Beffa, "Le concept de *tänggäri*," 216 and 220; Baumann, "By the Power of Eternal Heaven"; and Mostaert and Woodman Cleaves, *Les lettres de 1289 et 1305 des ilkhan Argun et Öljeitü à Philippe le Bel*, 55–58.

113.   Kotwicz, "Formules initiales des documents mongols aux XIII-e et XIV-e ss," 136–38; and Roux, "Tängri," 79.

114.   Hillenbrand, "Muhammad as Warrior Prophet," 75.

115.   Kessler, *Spiritual Seeing*, 128–29.

116.   *Mi'rajnama*, Iran, 685 AH/1286 CE, Süleymaniye Library, Istanbul, Ayasofya 3441, folio 24r. The term used here for "reinforcements" is *madad*, a word typically used in the military expression "army reinforcements" (*madad al-jaysh*).

117.   Ibn Ishaq, *The Life of Muhammad*, 363–64.

118.   Al-Waqidi, *Muhammed in Medina*, 95; and al-Waqidi, *The Life of Muhammad*, 88.

119.   Al-Tabari, *La chronique de Tabarî*, 555.

120.   Mostaert and Woodman Cleaves, "Trois documents mongols des Archives Secrètes Vaticanes," 470–71.

121.   Mostaert and Woodman Cleaves, *Les lettres de 1289 et 1305 des ilkhan Argun et Öljeitü à Philippe le Bel*, 55–58 (line 22); and Broadbridge, *Kingship and Ideology in the Islamic and Mongol Worlds*, 95.

122.   Woodman Cleaves, "The Mongolian Documents in the Musée de Téhéran," 7 and 26; and Kotwicz, "Formules initiales des documents mongols aux XIII-e et XIV-e ss," 134 and 138.

123.   Amitai, "Mongol Imperial Ideology and the Ilkhanid War against the Mamluks," 64.

124.   Broadbridge, *Kingship and Ideology in the Islamic and Mongol Worlds*, 98.

125.   On narrative flow and the circumstances of *tanzil* in *asbab al-nuzul* literature, see Wansbrough, *Quranic Studies*, 140–41.

126.   White, "The Value of Narrativity in the Representation of Reality, 18–23.

127.   On the heroic apotheosis, see Campbell, *The Hero with a Thousand Faces*, 127–47.

128.   For a survey of Islamic *mi'raj* narratives, see in particular Widengren, *Muhammad, the Apostle of God, and His Ascension*; Amir-Moezzi, *Le voyage initiatique en terre d'Islam*; Gruber and Colby, *The Prophet's Ascension*; and Colby, *Narrating Muhammad's Night Journey*.

129.   For a further discussion of this painting, see Gruber, "Signs of the Hour," 40–45, fig. 1; Talbot Rice, *The Illustrations to the "World History" of Rashid al-Din*, 111, fig. 36; and Arnold, *Painting in Islam*, 119, plate LIII.

130.   On the tempting voices, see Colby, *Narrating Muhammad's Night Journey*, 102–3, 133–36; and Gruber, *The Ilkhanid Book of Ascension*, 15, 22, 40–41.

131.   On the test of the cups, see Colby, *Narrating Muhammad's Night Journey*, 81–82, 135–36; and Gruber, *The Ilkhanid Book of Ascension*, 11, 26–28, 44–45.

132.   Blair, "Calligraphers, Illuminators, and Painters in the Ilkhanid Scriptorium," 175; and Talbot Rice, *The Illustrations to the "World History" of Rashid al-Din*, 111.

133.   On the Ilkhanid illustrated *Mi'rajnama*, see especially Ettinghausen, "Persian Ascension Miniatures of the Fourteenth Century"; Gruber, *The Ilkhanid Book of Ascension*; and Gruber, "The Ilkhanid *Mi'rajnama* of ca. 1317–35 as an Illustrated Sunni Prayer Manual."

134.   For a list, identification, and reproduction of all paintings, see Gruber, *The Ilkhanid Book of Ascension*, 26, plates 3–12.

135.   Pfeiffer, "Conversion Versions," 39. For a further discussion of Ilkhanid rulers converting to Islam, see Pfeiffer, "Reflections on a 'Double Rapprochement'"; Melville, "Padshah-i Islam"; Amitai-Press, "Sufis and Shamans"; and Brack, "Mediating Sacred Kingship," 133–94.

136.   Abu Sa'id's accession to the throne in 1317 CE was marked by a ceremony that included seven princes, four of whom held the corners of the felt on which he was lifted up, two of whom held his arms, and the last of whom offered him a cup. Howorth, *History of the Mongols*, 586.

137.   Spuler, *History of the Mongols*, 100.

138.   Spuler, *History of the Mongols*, 72.

139.   For a more detailed discussion of this painting, see Gruber, *The Ilkhanid Book of Ascension*, 28; and Gruber, "The Ilkhanid *Mi'rajnama* of ca. 1317–35 as an Illustrated Sunni Prayer Manual," 35–37.

140.   On these prayer positions of the hands, see Dutton, "'Amal v. Hadith in Islamic Law."

141.   On the two Timurid illustrated *Mi'rajnamas*, see in particular Gruber, *The Timurid Book of Ascension*; Séguy, *The Miraculous Journey of Mahomet*; Masuya, "The *Mi'radj-nama* Reconsidered"; and Sims, "The *Nahj al-Faradis* of Sultan Abu Sa'id ibn Sultan Muhammad ibn Miranshah."

142.   For a further discussion of this painting, see Gruber, *The Timurid Book of Ascension*, 314–16; and Sims, "The *Nahj al-Faradis* of Sultan Abu Sa'id ibn Sultan Muhammad ibn Miranshah," 101, 120–21, plate 2.

143.   Pavet de Courteille, *Mirâdj-Nâmeh*, 6; and Thackston, "The Paris Mi'rajnama," 269. The Arabic caption in gold ink above the painting specifies that one rosary is made of snow and the other of fire.

144.   Ibn Ishaq, *The Life of Muhammad*, 181.

145.   On the conclusion of the Timurid illustrated *Mi'rajnama* of ca. 1436 CE, see Thackston, "The Paris Mi'rajnama," 284–85; and on the ending of the Timurid *Mi'rajnama* of ca. 1450–60 CE, see Eckmann, *Nehcü'l-Feradis*, 49–50.

146.   See Thackston, "The Paris Mi'rajnama," 264.

147.   Subtelny, "The Jews at the Edge of the World in a Timurid-Era *Mi'raj-nama*."

148.   White, "The Value of Narrativity in the Representation of Reality," 14.

149.   Gruber, "Signs of the Hour," 45–49; and Gruber, *The Timurid Book of Ascension*, 308–9.

150.   For a general discussion of early to medieval Persian advice literature, see De Fouchécour, *Moralia*.

151.   Al-Suyuti, *al-Riyad al-Aniqa fi Sharh Asma' Khayr al-Khaliqa*, 161 (*rakib al-buraq*) and 196 (*sahib al-mi'raj*).

152.   Bruner, "Past and Present as Narrative Constructions," 31–32.

153.   White, "The Value of Narrativity in the Representation of Reality," 24.

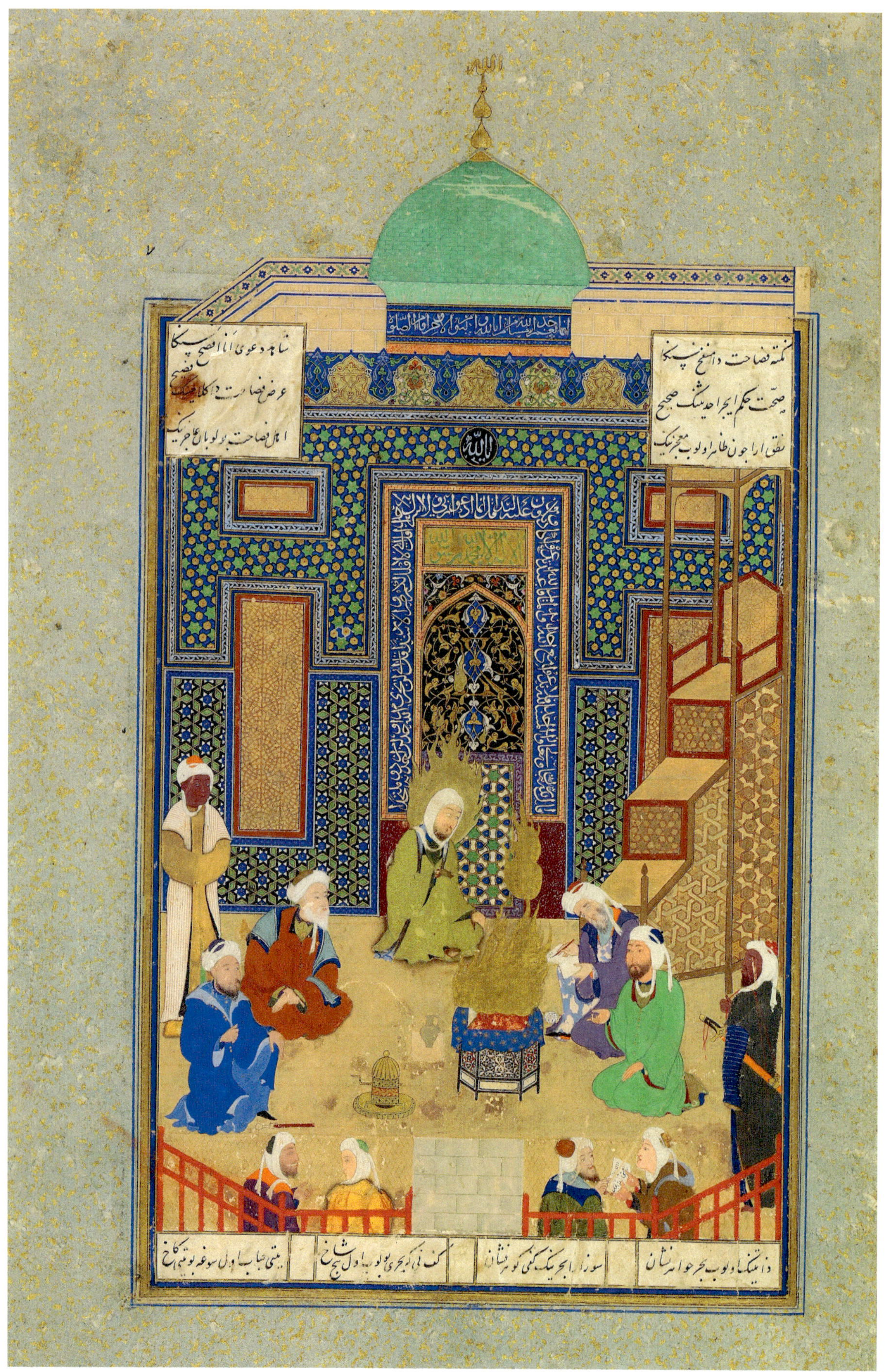

Between the thirteenth and fifteenth centuries, artists cultivated images of the Prophet-king and Prophet as hero in their manuscript paintings. However, by the late fifteenth century and over the course of the sixteenth century, depictions of Muhammad began to stress his more spiritual aspects. In this regard, painters followed greater cultural, social, and religious trends across the Islamic world, especially in Persianate lands. Among the most notable of these developments was the growth of Sufism, the mystical branch of Islam composed of various orders or *tariqas*.

Influential Sufi treatises were already penned during the medieval period by a number of mystics, including al-Qushayri (d. 1072 CE) and Ibn ʿArabi (d. 1240 CE), whose Arabic-language expositions were intended to provide an overview of Sufi doctrine as well as guidance to devotees seeking to perfect their spiritual states. Sufism soon spread to Iran and Central Asia through Persian and Turkish practitioners and writers, including al-Hujwiri (d. 1077 CE) and Ahmad Yasavi (d. 1166 CE). In eastern Islamic lands, medieval Sufi mystics frequently were lauded for their ability to convert both ruling elites and the general populace to the Islamic faith.

Despite their adherence to various branches of mysticism, Sufis are united in their dedication to discovering the mystery of God in the world and seeking divine unity (*tawhid*) through the annihilation of the self (*fana'*). Following a spiritual path that is framed as a quest, an aspirant uses prayer and other pious practices to achieve a particular state (*hal*) or station (*maqam*) of spiritual purity, which in turn is believed to lead to spiritual knowledge or gnosis (*maʿrifa*). In other words, the Sufi is essentially a wayfarer who has embarked toward spiritual knowledge and union with God. His methods include various forms of worship—such as reciting (*tilawa*) the Qur'an, devotional prayers (*duʿas*), and pious forms of recollection (*dhikr*), performed either in silence or aloud—as well as sustained mental contemplation, undertaken in seclusion or in the company of members of his mystical brotherhood.[2]

Through a myriad of practices, treatises, and poems, Sufis developed an expressive lexicon that is notable for its highly metaphoric imagery and allegorical tropes, chief among these the spiritual ascent (*miʿraj*) and dream vision (*ruʾya*). The mystic's description of the flight of his soul toward the divine was largely inspired by the Prophet Muhammad's own heavenly ascension and colloquy with God. The *miʿraj* motif thus pervades Sufi texts and paintings, especially in Persian literary and artistic production of the premodern period. Similarly, the dream played

It was God's wish that prophethood and apostleship should end with Muhammad. Nonetheless, though the period of prophethood has receded and ended, what has happened to godliness? Godliness is ongoing and those with godly attributes are permanent.[1]

Jalal al-Din Rumi (d. 1273)

FACING, 3.1. The Prophet Muhammad seated in a mosque space and surrounded by his companions and followers, Nava'i, *Hayrat al-Abrar* (Remarkable Deeds of Pious Men), Herat, 890 AH/1485 CE. Bodleian Library, Oxford University, Ms. Elliott 287, folio 7r.

a key role in mystical thought and practice because it was considered a particularly powerful aperture into the realm of the unseen, through which direct disclosures from God could be communicated to a spiritual seer. In other words, the dream acted as a lively zone of interaction in which a variety of images could appear to, and be activated by, the mind and heart of the mystic. As an intermediary space of being, it offered a symbolic means of transcending the physical world, and a conduit to the realm of the sacred.

Like the visionary mode, paintings of dreams made in Turco-Persian lands between circa 1485 and 1600 CE essentially offered a method for telepathic contact between the living and the dead, between devotees and Muhammad. At this time, such images reflect a number of growing trends, among them the importance of dream visions of the Prophet among Sufis, especially the Naqshbandis, Mevlevis, and followers of the Safavid ruling order. Early modern Sufi visionary paintings often echo Islamic notions of the dream world—known as the "realm of likenesses" (*'alam al-mithal*)—and could enable a Sunni or Shi'i mystical worldview as well. Regardless of their sectarian readings and applications, such images essentially challenge Sufi adepts to transcend temporal and spatial limitations by couching the *picture* as *picturation*—that is, as an embracing yet transcending of the pictorial mode in order to secure a spiritual vision of the Prophet Muhammad as the quintessential spiritual father and apocalyptic guide.

Within Sufi thought and practice, the dream was not considered merely a private occurrence. Rather, it was experienced by an individual who often communicated his experience to one or several listeners. A Sufi master or disciple might describe his vision to a close companion or raise it as a topic of discussion at a gathering (*majlis*) of members of his brotherhood. In this and other cases, the dream is considered an event that bears public resonance.[3] Within this more communal setting, it could communicate an array of messages that aimed to strengthen a mystic's spiritual authority while concurrently promoting his *tariqa's* religious worldview and devotional practices.

The dream typically catered to the needs and desires of an individual mystic. Within his social group of cospiritualists, a Sufi typically spoke of his dreams in order to announce his special access to divine knowledge, to impart advice to wayfarers similarly embarked on the Sufi path, and to provide compelling evidence for his supreme spiritual status and state. Furthermore, if a Sufi disciple (*murid*) had a dream of his master (*pir*), he could achieve proximity to his predecessors while also reaffirming his position and pedigree via his *tariqa's* accepted genealogy. Last, but certainly not least, through dreams the Sufi visionary could promote himself as especially amenable to receiving divine disclosure.

To no small extent, the Sufi's spiritual inspiration (*ilham*), couched as a dream vision, follows the symbolic pattern of the Prophet Muhammad's revelation (*wahy*) of the Qur'an by God through the Angel

Gabriel. Both initiatory events act as sacred invitations communicated to recipients, whether Messenger or mystic. Qur'anic revelation is a miracle (*mu'jiza*) of the Prophet, while the dream vision is a marvel (*karama*) of the spiritually elect. By aligning themselves with Muhammad through the revelatory nature of dreams, Sufis presented themselves as spiritual heirs to the prophets (*wurrath al-anbiya'*). As a result, dream visions helped Sufi practitioners partake in "post-prophetic heirship,"[4] extending Muhammad's call to spiritual guidance across generations of believers.

The symbolic parallels between Muhammad's call to divine revelation and the mystic's quest for spiritual inspiration were enhanced in other ways as well, especially through the use of highly figurative language. In the poetic lexicon of Sufi Islam, the dream is described as a vision (*ru'ya*), often achieved in a state of sleep (*fi'l-manam* or *fi'l-nawm*). For these reasons, the Persian word *khwab* is used interchangeably, for both *dream* and *sleep*. The dream is conceptualized as a nocturnal visionary activity: in the darkness of night and in a state of drowsiness or sleep, the mystic is able to "see" images as he enters a "realm of likenesses." In this intermediary spiritual zone, which encompasses form but not substance, the dreamer's power of imagination surpasses sense perception.[5] Consequently, the dream is not considered an optical vision but rather a subtle discernment or "inner seeing" (*mushahada*) that is achieved by the "inner eye" (*'ayn basira*) or by the heart (*ru'ya fi'l-qalb*). The dream is thus closely aligned to the dreamer's imaginative faculty, which to some mystics proves that our concept of the senses should not be limited to five.[6]

In addition to transcending the limitations of sense perception, the dream gained further metaphoric meaning in the Islamic imagination. For example, Sufis often analogized the dream vision to a kind of unveiling (*mukashafa*) that signaled their clairvoyance of things spiritual or emphasized their exceptional ability to access the realm of the divine. This entrance into a higher plane of being was described as a process of discovery (*kashf*) as well as an opening (*fath* or *futuh*). With regards to the latter, the aperture allegory might express the aspirant's entrance into a new spiritual domain—that is, a traversing of the veils that separate him from the realm of God—or the ripping open of his own heart. As a twinned allegory, the dream as voyage and as rupture doubly describes the wayfarer's momentum en route to spiritual breakthrough.

By such explorations, a dreamer can reach a liminal place, which is often described as an isthmus (*barzakh*) that appears to be hanging (*mu'allaq*) in midair[7]—an intermediate, pendent world located between concrete reality and mental abstraction. Like the dream, the *barzakh* is a locus of incorporeal archetypes that become sensibly intelligible thanks to the imaginative faculty.[8] In other words, it is a special zone of mental activity that gives the impression that the human senses can perceive otherwise formless, nonmaterial images. It is also considered an arena of interaction between the living and the dead, especially if the mystic happens to have a vision of his deceased spiritual master or the Prophet Muhammad. Having passed on, these high-ranking spiritual and religious guides are recognized as not existentially real; however, in the "realm of likenesses" that is the dream world, they are "enrobed with a special sphere of existence of their own."[9] In this case, the dream as *barzakh* functions as a suspended spiritual interface in which the living and the dead can communicate and coexist.

At other times, mystics may describe this in-between dream world as flooded with colorless light but lacking form and images. In this case, the dream is no longer merely an inner witnessing, an imaginative exploration, or place of liminality. Much more importantly, it is a locus of illumination, a light-based metaphor suggestive of the aspirant's impending spiritual enlightenment. Sufis speak of this special light in a number of ways. For some, it is an emblem of the essence of total unity to which the dreamer's soul becomes increasingly attuned in this higher plane of existence.[10] For others, the dream is stippled with flickers of light (*lawa'ih*) as well as flame-like phenomena. For the Persian mystic Jami (d. 1492 CE) in particular, these flashes of light symbolize spiritual insights and verities—hence he entitled his treatise on Sufism *Lawa'ih* (Flashes of Light). For others still, the dream is like a ladder composed of lights, each lifting the seer from heaven to heaven until he reaches the light of theophany (*nur-i tajalli*).[11] In mystical texts, the apex of a spiritual dream is therefore described as a sea or ocean of light, flashes of light, or an effusion (*fayd*) of divine grace, in which the Sufi finds himself submerged and enlightened in the presence of a formless God and other figures, including the Prophet Muhammad and deceased spiritual guides.[12]

While the Qur'an promises that believers will "see" the Lord on Judgment Day,[13] a mystic could experience a beatific vision of God during his lifetime via the contemplation and exclamation of his greatest name (Allah) or through an inner witnessing of a sea of light or flashes of lights. Although dreams of God are recorded in Islamic textual sources, they nevertheless are much less numerous than visions of the Prophet Muhammad.[14] The reasons for the preponderance of dreams of the Prophet are many; such visions could legitimize religious arguments, advance political policies, or elevate the status of particular persons.

Muhammad considered the dream an allotment of his own prophecy. Thus, dreamers could symbolically partake in the revelatory experience, boosting their status among members of their entourage by means of the prophetic paradigm. Secondly, dreams of the Prophet were considered real based on Muhammad's declaration: "Whoever has seen me in a dream has seen me truly, for Satan cannot imitate my shape."[15] Based on this prophetic statement, a dream of Muhammad is considered a sound or veridical vision (*ru'ya saliha* or *ru'ya haqq*) that cannot lead to evil.[16]

After the Prophet's death, it was considered imperative that dream apparitions capture his physical likeness. No doubt the emphasis on corporeal similitude was precipitated by the famous dream interpreter Ibn Sirin (eighth century CE), who stipulated that a true vision of Muhammad can occur only if the dreamer sees the Prophet in his real shape (*fi suratihi*).[17] His statement stresses the paramount importance of dreaming of Muhammad in his physical state rather than via abstraction and allegory,[18] an emphasis that is likewise central to pictorial images depicting Sufis' visions of the Prophet. Whether in the mind's eye or on the painted page, such prophetic picturations substantiate the argument that the dreamer cannot be misled by a sound vision of Muhammad in his putatively true form.

While dreams of the Prophet may at times (but not always) tend toward the veristic, they nevertheless fulfill a wide array of allegorical purposes. In the broadest sense possible, they relate to the Hadith insomuch as both sayings and visions of the Prophet can be accessed by successive generations of believers.[19] A significant difference between the two exists, however: Hadith are essentially verbal relics penned in ink and thus devoid of shape and sentience; visions, on the other hand, insinuate the presence of human form and thereby suggest the continued presence of the Prophet in a "world of likenesses," itself available to a pious individual in a state of sleep or to a mystic in a psychically perfected condition.

In dreamscapes, Muhammad is an active agent. He functions as an interlocutor, both speaking and responding to the dreamer. He is a teacher, ancestral figure, and exemplary man, a model for ritual behavior, a clarifier of theological questions, and an arbiter of legal disputes—he may even serve as a book critic or ghostwriter.[20] Finally, he also can promise future life changes: if the dreamer has debts, these will be forgiven; if he is sick, he will get well; if he wages war, he will win; and so on.[21] In his visionary manifestation, Muhammad thus appears to remain alive, accessible, and active in the present world.

For a Sufi practitioner wishing to be recognized as a "friend of God" (*wali Allah*), visions of Muhammad are a requirement. They signal a close bond and personal intimacy between the mystic and the Messenger, in the process giving the visionary a kind of prophetic imprimatur through which he might enhance his standing or impart knowledge to members of his brotherhood. Additionally, visions can occur throughout a mystic's lifetime, from the beginning of his spiritual quest until his death. For example, while mystics typically entered their orders thanks to the guidance of a spiritual master or *shaykh*, in a number of instances they are said to have been initiated into a particular *tariqa* by the Prophet himself. Such is the case of the Timurid mystic Abu Yazid Purani (d. 1457 CE), who is reported to have been initiated into the Naqshbandi order by Muhammad.[22] Purani also is said to have taken some of his intellectual problems directly to the Prophet.[23]

From serving as the most perfect spiritual master to appointing a *shaykh* as his spiritual successor on earth to explaining mystical doctrine, Muhammad fulfilled both initiatory and practical purposes in the prophetic dreams of Muslim mystics. Although many such accounts exist, perhaps the most extensive record is *Kashf al-Asrar* (Unveiling of Secrets), written by the medieval Persian mystic and visionary diarist Ruzbihan Baqli (d. 1209 CE). His text records his many encounters with the Prophet, whom he claims to have seen more than a thousand times.[24] In some instances, Muhammad appears in a variety of human forms, while in others he takes the shape of an ocean of pure light, the moon, or a red rose. These metaphors aim to convey Muhammad's radiant majesty—what Ruzbihan calls his "light of manifestation" and "light of pre-eternal essence"[25]—as well as his cosmic beauty and heavenly scent.[26] Not mutually exclusive, such visionary images of Muhammad as human, light, and flower offer an aggregate of three prophetic paradigms, themselves depicted in Persian and Turkish paintings from the thirteenth century onward.

In a number of Ruzbihan's dreams, the Prophet appears encircled by other important figures, most especially his companions (*sahaba*).[27] In one vision, for example, his companions, prophets, and Sufi masters gather before Muhammad, who has risen from his grave. Ruzbihan reports that in this particular vision the Prophet's face shone like a red rose, his tresses were pungent like musk, and he wore a patched cloak in the manner of a Sufi;[28] most noteworthy in this instance is that Muhammad is pictured as the ideal mystic, whose supreme status is certified by a surrounding group of high-ranking individuals. In this and other mystical visions, the Prophet appears as if he were the first and highest spiritual master, whose presence takes on greater import when he is surrounded by his companions. As a consequence, mystical visions of Muhammad effectively echo and sustain the confraternal milieus and social gatherings found within a number of *tariqas* across the Islamic world. Such visionary dreams depict Muhammad not as a sacred king or warrior-hero but rather as the supreme *shaykh* encircled by his disciples, teaching them the tenets of the faith while leading them on the path toward spiritual enlightenment and salvation in the afterlife.

MUHAMMAD AT THE *MAJLIS*

Dreams of Muhammad within the context of Sufi gatherings seem to have been quite common in Persian mystical practice. While Ruzbihan and other authors recorded their visionary experiences in treatises and diaries, late Timurid, Safavid, Ottoman, and Mughal artists attempted to convey prophetic dreams through the painterly arts as well. These visual records echo and sustain a number of patterns found within textual sources, expanding them in intriguing ways through the expressive potential of pictorial language. In some sense, paintings could be argued to offer more accurate *re-presentations* of—and thus continued access to—the dream world, as such visions are essentially described as visual experiences of forms emanating from the "realm of likenesses."

THE PRAISEWORTHY ONE

The practices of producing and perceiving *amthal*—forms, similitudes, likenesses, and images—undoubtedly align the enterprises of both the visionary mystic and maker of paintings.

The earliest surviving painting that depicts a visionary appearance of the Prophet seated among his companions was made in the Timurid capital of Herat in 1485 CE (fig. 3.1).[29] The illustration is included at the beginning of *Hayrat al-Abrar* (Remarkable Deeds of Pious Men), the first book of the *Khamsa* (Quintet) composed by the late Timurid states-man and writer, Mir ‘Ali Shir Nava’i (1441–1501 CE). The text is written in Chaghatay Turkish, in emulation of Nizami’s much beloved Persian-language *Khamsa*, while the illustrated manuscript copy of the text was made for Badi‘ al-Zaman, the son of the last Timurid ruler, Sultan Husayn Bayqara (r. 1469–1506 CE).[30] With paintings likely executed by leading court painters, the manuscript is a princely product that pays tribute to its patron’s literary interests. Moreover, it highlights the prac-tices of the Naqshbandi order, the foremost Sufi *tariqa* to which mem-bers of the Timurid Herati political and cultural elite, including Nava’i himself, adhered during the last quarter of the fifteenth century. Most important among Naqshbandi practices at the time were social gath-erings, devotional recollection, and contemplative image-based forms of communication that sought to unite living and deceased spiritual masters—supreme among them the Prophet Muhammad—with their disciples and descendants.

Emerging from Central Asia, the Naqshbandi Sufi order became firmly established in Herat around 1460 CE.[31] Soon thereafter the *tariqa* became the preferred confraternity for those in the upper echelons of society, who were initiated into the brotherhood by the spiritual master Sa‘d al-Din Kashgari. Among the *shaykh*’s most prominent followers was the Persian poet-theologian Jami (d. 1492 CE), who initiated Nava’i into the order. While Jami is best known for his mystical poetry, equally important are his biography of Sufi saints, *Nafahat al-Uns* (Breaths of Intimacy), and his treatise on Sufi doctrine, *Lawa’ih* (Flashes of Light). In *Nafahat al-Uns*, Jami records the dream of a mystic who saw the Prophet attending a Sufi gathering.[32] This dream is reminiscent of other mystical visions of the Prophet and parallels the late Timurid depiction of Muhammad seated among his companions. In the latter case, the mo-tif of the Sufi gathering, or *majlis*, finds a fitting match in the painting, or *majlis-sazi*, the Persian term designating a group portrait.[33]

In the late Timurid painting, the Prophet wears a green robe as he sits cross-legged, his right hand gently resting on his raised knee (fig. 3.2). His central position is further emphasized by the flaming gold nimbus framing his radiant face; moreover, his headgear is dissimilar to that of his companions: it appears to be a long white cloth loosely hanging around his head and over his two shoulders, a style of pro-phetic headgear recorded in early Arabic texts.[34] Much like the flaming halo, Muhammad’s head cover serves to emphasize his higher status by visually differentiating him from members of his entourage. From a

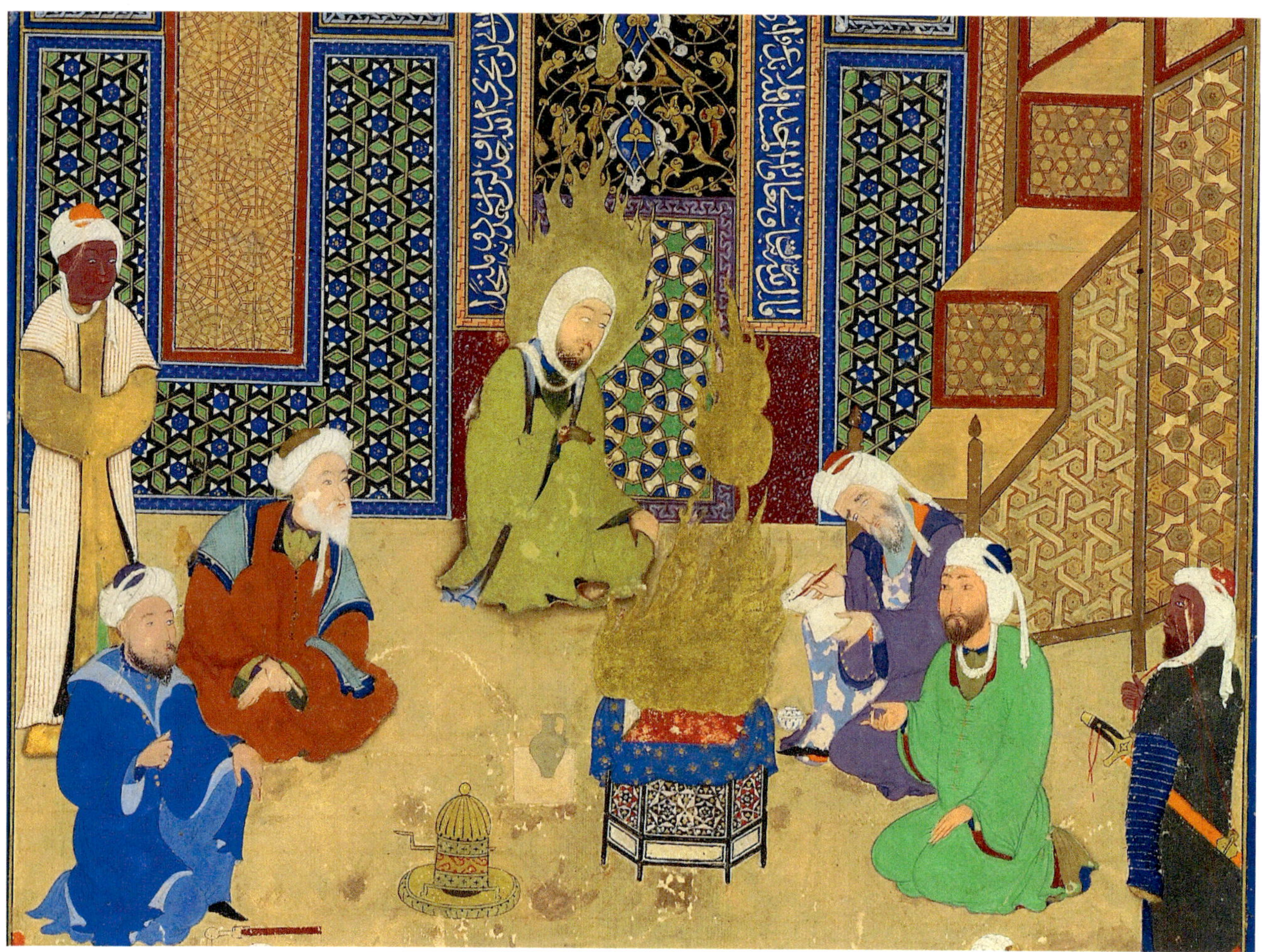

purely iconographical point of view, the painting depicts the Prophet as centrally important as well as touched by a sacred flux.

Notwithstanding his supreme rank, Muhammad's position is socially defined by his inclusion in a *majlis*-like setting. Diagonally to his right and left sit four figures, most likely his companions. These include, on the left, Abu Bakr, with a white beard, and ʿUmar, with a mace on the ground, and, on the right, ʿUthman, symbolically transcribing the Qurʾan, and ʿAli, dressed in a green robe that emphasizes his kinship to the Prophet.[35] In the left corner stands Bilal, the emancipated Ethiopian slave and close companion of Muhammad, whose melodious voice called members of the early Muslim community to prayer. Bilal is the compositional parallel of a figure who holds a sword, standing in the lower right corner. While the sword is an attribute of ʿAli, it is also associated with Salman the Persian (Salman al-Farsi), another close companion of the Prophet. As is the case with the representation of Bilal, the man's skin tone suggests a non-Arab ethnicity, supporting his identification as Salman the Persian. Not only is Salman revered in an Islamic Persian setting, he also is considered the third person in the chain connecting Naqshbandi Sufis with the Prophet Muhammad via Abu Bakr.[36] These seven figures—Muhammad, the four *sahaba*, Bilal, and Salman—therefore represent Muhammad's core circle of

THE PRAISEWORTHY ONE

companions while also symbolically serving as embodiments of the Naqshbandi genealogical line.

These seven important individuals are surrounded by other objects, motifs, inscriptions, and figures that aid in understanding the possible meanings of the painting as well as the cultural and religious contexts in which it was produced. Centrally placed and most noticeable among the objects is an inlaid *kursi*, or bookstand, over which a blue fabric with gold designs has been draped. On this fabric appears an open book, its white folios releasing golden flames that fan upward, toward the Prophet's equally radiant halo. To the left of the *kursi* are two other objects on the ground below Muhammad: a small gray flask, perhaps intended to contain perfume or essential oil, and a metal censer on a tray. These three objects are highly suggestive: the flaming book may be the Qur'an, with the light of God emanating from within, or perhaps a book of prayers that could help a Sufi induce a vision of Muhammad and his companions. The flask and censer may point to Muhammad's nonphysical attributes, in particular his heavenly scent, described in Persian Sufi poetry—especially in Nizami's *Khamsa*—as similar to sandalwood, musk, ambergris, and rose.[37] These objects thus either reflect the prophetic presence or are intended to induce it symbolically.

Other motifs and inscriptions in the composition frame and delimit the work's possible interpretations. The gathering occurs within the interior of a lavishly decorated mosque, whose turquoise-tiled dome is capped with a gold finial bearing the name of God (Allah) at its apex. The building's identification as a mosque is further supported by the white inscription on the dome's lapis-blue drum, which partially transcribes a qur'anic verse (9:18), stating that only those who believe in God and the Last Day, and who perform prayer and a number of other religious duties, can visit the mosques of God (*masajid Allah*) and thus hope to be counted among the divinely guided. Further qur'anic verses (72:18–22) are transcribed in white around the *mihrab*, before which the Prophet Muhammad sits. These verses continue along the same lines, noting that all mosques (*masajid*) are for God, who alone must be invoked by devotees in their search for guidance and refuge. Shorter epigraphic inscriptions within the building include the *shahada*, executed in green on a horizontal gold register within the *mihrab*, and a roundel above summoning God with the vocative expression "*Ya Allah*." In sum, these qur'anic, creedal, and vocative inscriptions indicate that this prophetic gathering occurs in a mosque, whose structure, furnishings, and decorative motifs largely reflect contemporary Timurid architecture.

While the painting seems to depict a gathering of Muhammad and his followers, its inclusion within a Sufi poetic text suggests that it bears greater mystical implications. Indeed, the image does not belong to a narrative text in prose form; rather, it is included in Nava'i's *Hayrat al-Abrar*, a versified treatise that provides biographical information about the great spiritual masters along with a discussion of the principal tenets of Sufism. A Naqshbandi mystic himself, Nava'i was interested in

Islamic hagiography in general and the genealogy (*silsila*) of the Naqsh-bandi order in particular. Located at the beginning of Nava'i's text, the painting is thus intended to depict the very first spiritual master of the Naqshbandi line, the Prophet Muhammad himself, sitting within a mosque space and *majlis* setting, both of which reflect Timurid structures and Sufi practices of the period.

The painting of the Prophet appears in the section of Nava'i's text in which the author provides a summary of Muhammad's life, focusing on the signs of his prophecy, his revelations, and his heavenly ascension. In a highly poetic fashion, the author highlights Muhammad's position as the first master in the Naqshbandi *silsila* as well as his role as a model wayfarer on the Sufi path. The verses that appear at both the top and bottom of the depiction directly address the reader-viewer in the second person singular, asking him to witness (*shahid*) without saying a word (*söz*), as those who speak are weak. Nava'i then suggests to the silent witness that he will see an ocean (*bahr*) scattering a gem (*jawhar*) and promises, "When your essence (*dhat*) has perished, the sea will give a sign (*nishan*) of that jewel." In these verses girdling the image, it is evident that Nava'i invites devotees to remain silent—perhaps to engage in the Naqshbandi tradition of silent rather than vocal recollection (*dhikr*) of God and the Prophet—in order to truly "see" Muhammad. By overcoming the self and finding annihilation (*fana'*) in deep and closed-lipped contemplation, the mystic can witness a sign, or *nishan*, of his Prophet. This sign is a prophetic vision, and the vision here is reified through pictorial representation.

As a visual sign and spiritual vision, the painting functions as a record, potentially even a catalyst, of transcendent reality according to a Naqshbandi Sufi worldview. In this specific scenario, it is quite possible that the four extraneous figures sitting at the bottom of the painting, close to the red balustrade, represent contemporary Sufis engaged in a generative yet taciturn *dhikr* that produces a spiritually "real" vision of the Prophet and his companions within their midst. In the lower left corner, two mystics appear to discuss this remarkable occurrence, while, in the right corner, a man points his index finger to a white bifolio, presented by his companion, which is inscribed with a minute (and barely legible) transcription of the qur'anic verses (92:1–2) exclaiming, "I call the night to witness when it covers over, and the day when it shines bright (*tajalla*)." Like Nava'i's poetic text, the inscription issues a call to witnessing. However, in this specific instance, it is also suggestive of the Naqshbandi Sufi practice of nighttime prayers and dream visions, by which the Prophet Muhammad can become copresent with pious devotees via the epiphanic manifestation (*tajalli*) of his spiritual being (*ruhaniyya*).

The painting thus should be considered the pictorial record of a mystical vision of the Prophet set in a late Timurid Naqshbandi elite milieu, both paralleling and enhancing Sufi practices of spiritual seeing. It is well known that the Naqshbandis cultivated a variety of visualizing

   THE PRAISEWORTHY ONE

practices. The order's eponymous *shaykh*, Baha al-Din Naqshband (d. 1389 CE), received his honorific epithet *naqsh-band* to commemorate the "binding image" by which he imagined and impressed an image of the divine presence on his heart.[38] He and subsequent practitioners of the Naqshbandi Sufi order also engaged in the spiritual affixing of images of their deceased masters, so that their presence would be deeply imprinted on their followers' hearts. This practice of a disciple fastening a visual sign of his spiritual guide to his heart came to be known as the *rabita*—link or bond—between master and pupil, making both individuals spiritually present through the creation of covenantal images. Such images are considered especially important for the novice, who is encouraged to maintain a constant awareness of the physical form of his master while embarked on the Sufi path.[39] In some instances, Naqshbandi disciples are specifically instructed to picture the form of their masters' spiritual beings (*ruhaniyya*) "between the two eyebrows,"[40] suggesting that such images were not only imprinted in the heart but were produced in the mind and eyes as well. Naqshbandi *rabita* practices thereby underscore the various benefits of producing mental pictures and ocular visions for the Sufi wayfarer in his search for spiritual knowledge and unity.

In addition to enabling the pupil to absorb his living *shaykh*'s spiritual qualities, *rabita* also helped connect a Sufi with deceased spiritual guides. This practice was known as *tawajjuh*, the master "facing" his pupil, and *muraqaba*, the mystic's imaginative "observation" of his spiritual master, the Prophet Muhammad, and God.[41] Whether *shaykh* or Prophet, these ancestors serve as spiritual mediators who come to disciples from the world of the unseen. As intermediaries, they are often likened to mirrors reflecting the Prophet's form or divine effulgence (*fayd*), shaped as a column of pure light.[42] In Naqshbandi practices, *rabita* images were cultivated to help mystics exit the material world and gain entrance to a higher existential plane known as the *'alam al-mithal*, or "realm of images."

The late fifteenth-century Timurid painting of Muhammad surrounded by his companions and several observing figures takes on greater significance within the framework of Sufi dream visions of the Prophet. It also gains shades of meaning within the visualizing techniques of *rabita* and *tawajjuh*, key features of the Naqshandi Sufi worldview espoused by members of the Herati cultural and ruling elite, including the poet-*shaykh* Jami, the author-politician Nava'i, and the ruler Sultan Husayn Bayqara, all of whom were spiritual adherents and/or generous patrons of the order.[43] Furthermore, that the text framing the painting was composed by Nava'i, that it describes the great Sufi masters (including Muhammad, who is first and supreme), and that it poetically invites devotees to witness the Prophet all circumscribe the image's range of possible meanings. The image's iconographic language similarly praises the Prophet's sacred effulgence while positing his physical—and thus observable—reality within a social gathering of companions and devotees, all of whom are assembled in a decidedly

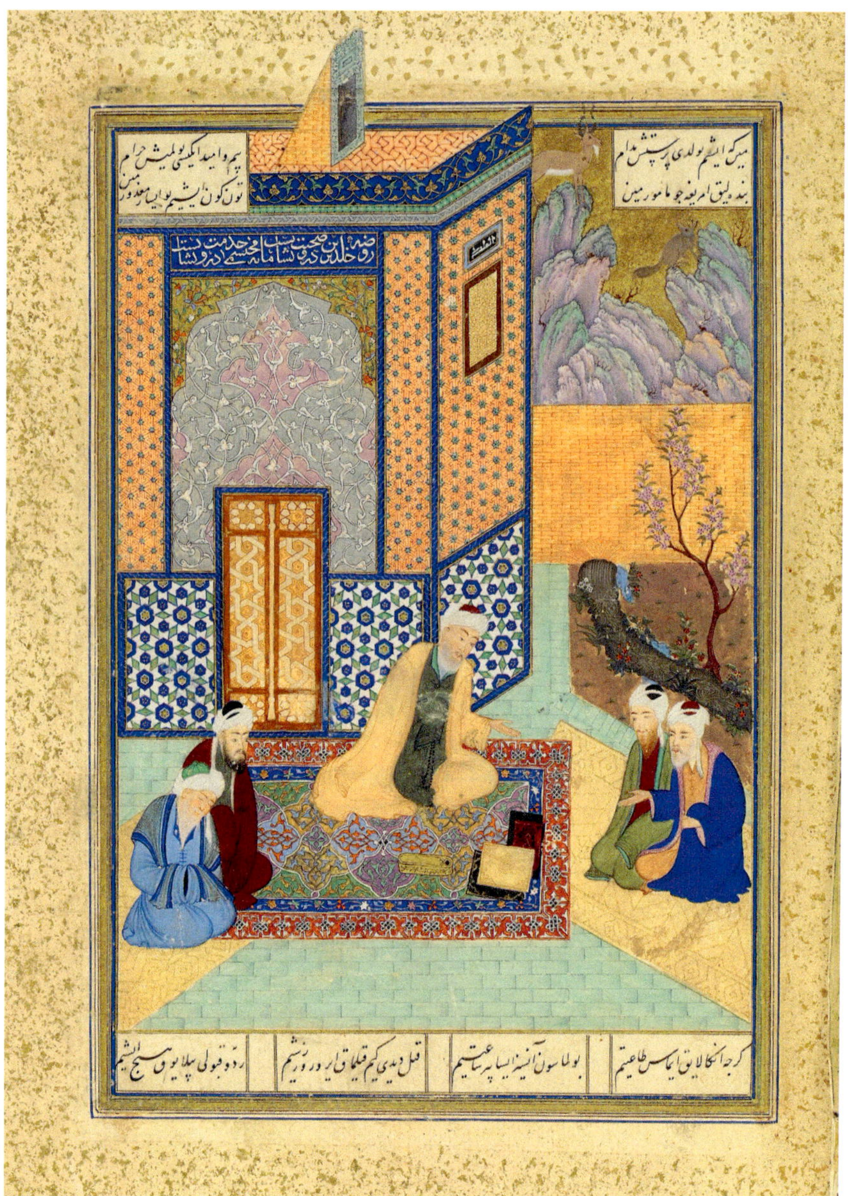

Timurid mosque setting—which was perhaps intended to represent Herat's main congregational mosque, to which the Naqshbandi chamber was attached.[44] From text to context and finally image, the painting depicts Muhammad as a preceptor who lives spiritually among his followers, who is accessible in form through communal dream-events (*waqayiʿ*), and who remains perpetually engaged in posthumous guidance and initiatory activity.[45]

The painting also depicts the Prophet as a spiritual guide by following and slightly altering the iconographic template that the Timurid artist(s) used to represent a Sufi *shaykh* within the very same manuscript. The pictorial paradigm of the "Sufi master" can be seen some folios later, in the chapter devoted to Khwaja ʿAbdallah Ansari (d. 1089 CE) (fig. 3.3). Here, the medieval Sufi traditionalist is rendered in a manner that recalls the earlier composition depicting Muhammad among his companions.[46] Like the Prophet, Ansari is centrally located among four

　　　THE PRAISEWORTHY ONE

disciples as he turns to the right, while a companion gesticulates in return, as if in conversation. Ansari also sits before a lavishly decorated building, covered with tilework and inscribed with an epigraphic band. These visual and formal parallels invite the reader-viewer to imagine Muhammad as primordial spiritual guide—and Ansari as the Prophet revived and reincorporated. Under the Timurids, Ansari was indeed described as a kind of neo-Muhammad: he was called the "champion of the Sunna" (*nasir al-sunna*) as well as the embodiment of the Hadith.[47]

Despite such similarities, several motifs in both paintings make clear that the prophetic paradigm must be distinguished from the Sufi model. Most noticeably, Muhammad bears a flaming halo while he sits before a radiant text, most likely the Qur'an. The holy book's numinous character—as God's Logos, unwritten and eternal—is symbolically emphasized by its golden blaze. Conversely, the open books at Ansari's feet are material codices—a collection of folios housed within bindings—that must be transcribed using a stylus, itself stored in a metal pen box lying at the *shaykh*'s feet. These books are most likely Ansari's two Arabic-language texts, *Munajat* (Supplications) and *Kitab al-'Arba'in* (Forty Hadith), both of which were highly popular during the late Timurid period.[48]

Another evident difference between the paintings is their settings. Muhammad is seated within a mosque, before a *mihrab* and next to a *minbar*. Although displaying Timurid architectural vocabulary, and possibly inspired by the decorative features of the congregational mosque of Herat, the image nevertheless insinuates that the Prophet is seated in his house-mosque in Medina. Ansari, however, remains outdoors: the Sufi *shaykh* sits on a colorful carpet while other members of the gathering kneel on brick-covered ground. Some plants and a flowering tree grow on the banks of a river that runs through a tall brick wall separating the architectural enclosure from the rocky terrain and animal world represented in the background. These many details suggest that the setting is the shrine of 'Abdallah Ansari, located in Gazurgah, just outside Herat. Ansari's tomb complex was developed into a major center for pilgrimage by the Timurid rulers, who saw in the local Sufi master a perfect synthesis of Sunni Islam and expressive modes of spirituality. While Shahrukh built an enclosure (*hazira*) around the shrine, Sultan Husayn Bayqara—who claimed descent from Ansari—built a funerary memorial for male members of his family.[49] Last, but certainly not least, under the Timurids, preachers at the Ansari shrine gave sessions of advice (*majalis-i nasihat*),[50] expanding the *majlis* scenario from the prophetic circle, Sufi assembly, and literary-artistic gathering to include sermonizing lessons on ethics and morality.[51]

The homiletic character of the image depicting Ansari is further emphasized by the epigraphic band on the portal. The inscription records an aphorism penned by Ansari, in which he offers the advice that: "Conversation (*suhbat*) with dervishes is a paradisiacal garden; [but] to be in the service (*khidmat*) of dervishes is the very stuff of veneration (*muhtashami*)."[52] While the saying encourages devotees to obey and follow spiritual masters, its emphasis on the notion of *suhbat*—participation in social conversation in the companionship of a Sufi master—is of particular note within a late Timurid religious setting. Indeed, alongside silent *dhikr*, the practice of *suhbat* is central to Naqshbandi Sufism. Literally meaning "society," *suhbat* also signifies the intimate spiritual relationship between a *shaykh* and his disciple, an initiatory form of friendship that is highly spiritual and especially transformative for the Sufi pupil.[53] This kind of *suhbat* relationship would have been cultivated between the author Nava'i and his living Naqshbandi *shaykh*; additionally, a similar relationship could be established between Nava'i and Ansari through the telepathic processes of *rabita* and *tawajjuh*.

Nava'i's proximity to the Sufi master could be increased by his possible inclusion among Ansari's disciples in the painting, in some sense predicting the Timurid poet-courtier's eventual retirement to the Ansari shrine.[54] If, as proposed by Maria Subtelny, the prematurely white-bearded man with closed eyes sitting in a prayer position can be identified as Nava'i,[55] then here he is shown as having spiritually transported himself to the time of Ansari, joining the ranks of the master's followers. Moreover, his inclusion in a group of four companions visually recalls the *sahaba* of the previous painting of the Prophet, while his appearance may have been purposefully aged so that he might resemble more closely the white-bearded Abu Bakr, who also sits on the left side of the painting depicting the Prophet Muhammad in *majlis*.

The striking visual alignments between Nava'i and Abu Bakr, and between Ansari and Muhammad, seem no mere coincidence. Such pictorial tropes appear tactically ambiguous, enabling a variety of messages to be extrapolated from the paintings or embedded into them. The slippages of meaning would have been detected by a contemporary Timurid viewer, trained and able to solve a variety of similar visual riddles.[56] In browsing through the manuscript's folios and looking at its paintings, Badi' al-Zaman, Sultan Husayn Bayqara, and/or Nava'i could envision the spiritual presence and heritage of the Prophet as alive, passed down through the Sufi masters, and thriving under their current custodianship.

In a Timurid Naqshbandi milieu, Sufi practitioners also placed particular emphasis on Abu Bakr, through whom they traced their lineage to Muhammad via the so-called golden chain (*silsilat al-dhahab*).[57] The Bakri lineage was combined with the genealogies of Sufi saints, including Bayazid Bistami (d. 784 CE), in a prophetic-spiritual amalgam very much reminiscent of the two paintings of Muhammad and Ansari. In symbolic dialogue, these images envisage Timurid authority by combining the sobriety of Sunni Islam with a markedly spiritual orientation. From mystical Prophet to Muhammadan Sufi, these two *majlis* paintings offer a coupled vision of Timurid Sunni-Sufi Islam in figural form.

The late Timurid painting of the Prophet seated among his companions eschews an overly wrought visionary mode to create the kind of realism that, in Islamic spirituality, is believed to accompany dreams of Muhammad. To a certain extent, such a lifelike rendering must be based on the Prophet's declaration that whoever sees him in a dream has seen him in reality. In visionary experiences and paintings of Muhammad and his companions, the Prophet's depiction must suggest presence and truth. To a certain extent, this "reality effect" aids in proving that a prophetic dream is a perceptible and intelligible event.[58] In Sufi milieus in particular, the dream is believed to enable an aspirant to reach the "Muhammadan reality" (*al-haqiqa al-Muhammadiyya*), wherein the Prophet is deemed copresent with his devotees as both perfect man (*al-insan al-kamil*) and most holy effusion (*al-fayd al-aqdas*).[59] No mere fiction or imagination, the mystic's prophetic dream—much like a Sufi *majlis*—brings persons and realms together as one all-encompassing visionary reality.

There exist other early modern Persian images that depict mystics' visionary encounters with the Prophet Muhammad, which emanate from Naqshbandi Sufi milieus. For example, three decades after the production of the Nava'i manuscript, a copy of Sa'di's *Bustan* (Fruit Orchard) was transcribed in Herat in 1514 CE. The *Bustan* manuscript subsequently arrived in Bukhara, where it was provided with paintings around 1530–35 CE. Among its folios is a depiction of the Prophet Muhammad ascending on Buraq, surrounded by legions of angels flying above three men kneeling in meditation within an enclosed mosque-like space (fig. 3.4).[60] The upper portion of the composition clearly recalls earlier paintings of the *mi'raj* (see fig. 2.17). In this instance, however, the ascension motif has been excerpted and inserted into a representation of a mystical vision of the Prophet by a triumvirate of contemplative Sufis.

While the Nava'i manuscript text was transcribed in Timurid Herat, the illustration of the mystical vision of Muhammad's celestial ascension dates to the period of Shaybanid rule in western Central Asia (1500–1598 CE). The Shaybanid elite comprised Muslim Uzbeks who traced their origins through the Timurids back to the Mongols. During the early decades of the sixteenth century, Shaybanid rulers were keen on perpetuating the Timurid cultural and artistic legacy within Transoxiana. They did so in a number of ways, including through the transference of individuals and objects from Herat to Bukhara. In one well-recorded episode, the Shaybanid ruler 'Ubaydallah (r. 1512–39 CE) captured calligraphers, artists, and manuscripts during a series of raids on Herat between 1512 and 1536 CE. These artists and their successors extended the Timurid artistic legacy in Bukhara by painting in the Herati style and, in subsequent decades, by emulating Timurid models.[61] 'Ubaydallah so aspired to preserve and continue Timurid high culture that, in the words of the contemporaneous historian Mirza Muhammad Haydar Dughlat (d. 1551 CE), "Bukhara has become such a center of arts and sciences that it recalls Herat in the days of Mirza Sultan Husayn."[62] For these reasons, the Shaybanid painting of about 1530 CE

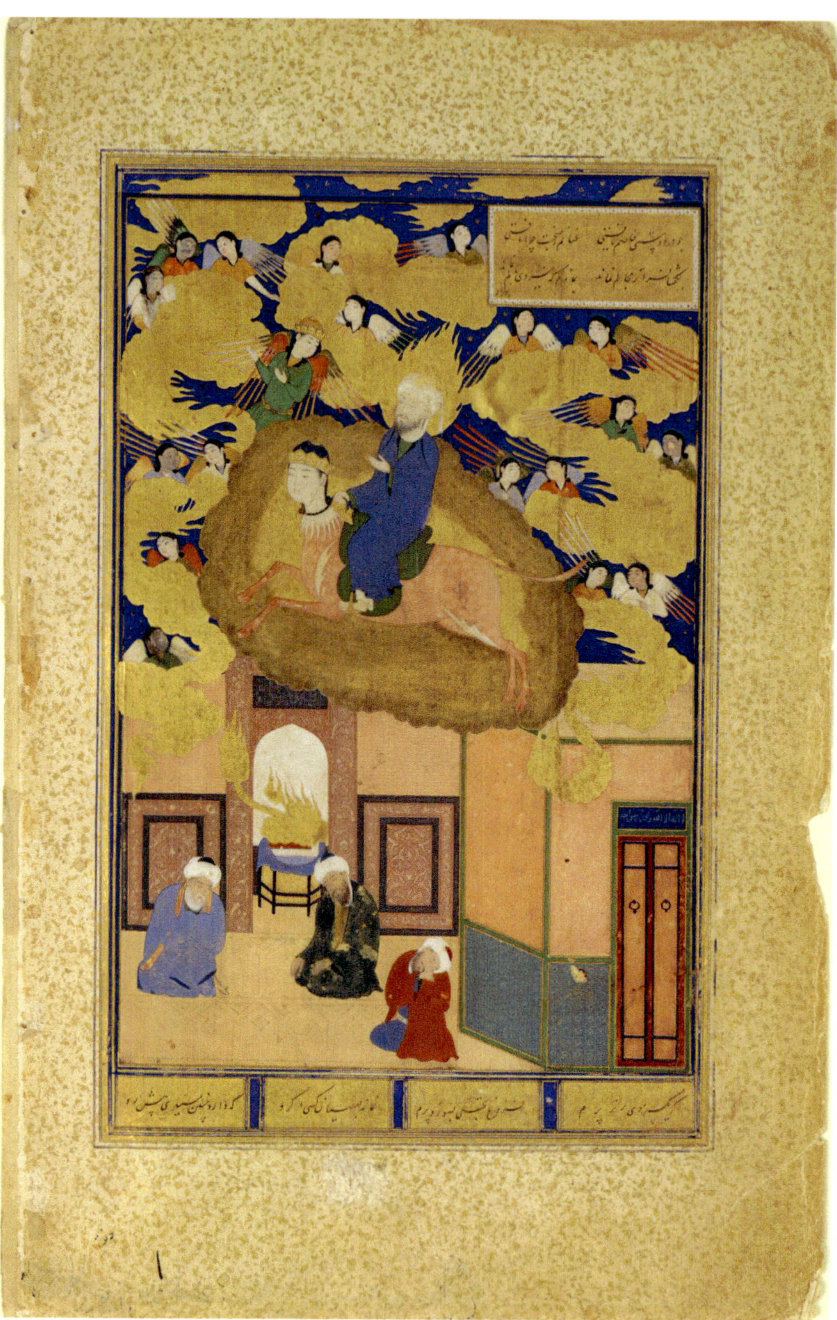

recalls earlier painterly styles and models, including Timurid paintings depicting the prophetic *miʻraj* and the mystical *majlis*, which it strategically combines into a single scene.

In addition to its Timurid artistic themes and origins, the Shaybanid painting's production in the city of Bukhara around 1530 CE bears significance. By this time, Bukhara was famed as the birthplace of Baha al-Din Naqshband, who was born in 1317 CE in a nearby village. After his death in 1388 CE, his tomb became a site of pilgrimage for Sufi devotees across Central Asia. Over the course of the fifteenth century, Bukhara witnessed the increasing strength of the Naqshbandi order in the realm of cultural and political life. Brotherhood members, including artisans,

     THE PRAISEWORTHY ONE

merchants, poets, scholars, nobility, and rulers, met regularly for meals, sermons, and evening prayers.[63] Armed with influence, wealth, and royal favor, members of the Naqshbandiyya also became architectural patrons. Through their efforts, a large complex—including a shrine, mosque, and Sufi lodge—was built in Bukhara during the 1540s CE to honor the *tariqa*'s eponymous founder, Baha al-Din Naqshband. The complex also included a domed chamber known as a *dhikr-khana*, or recollection room, for Naqshbandi mystics to engage in communal ritual remembrance of their spiritual masters, the Prophet Muhammad, and God.[64] As reflected in Muhammad's placement in the painting, formal seating arrangements in Shaybanid *majlis* sessions similarly reflected the participants' standing, with the seat of honor placed in the center.[65]

Within this cultural-religious context, the Shaybanid painting may well represent a group of three Naqshbandi Sufis gathered in a Bukharan *dhikr-khana*, where they are granted a vision of the Prophet through the practice of communal recollection and contemplation. A number of literary tropes in Saʿdi's *Bustan*, iconographic motifs in the painting, and Naqshbandi visionary practices all support this interpretation. Saʿdi's encomium lauds the Prophet as primordial flux and object of praise, while the painting shows Muhammad's luminous appearance, as if begotten by golden flames bursting from a book—perhaps the Qurʾan or a collection of prayers—placed on a bookstand within a *mihrab*'s recess. Within the prayer room, three men sit or kneel, their eyes closed as if intently focused on generating a dream vision of the Prophet. Lastly, the white-bearded mystic also holds a rosary in a hand hidden in the long sleeve of his Sufi's cloak. The rosary here suggests the performance of repeated prayers, a practice considered essential to the visual and spiritual stimulation of the dual Naqshbandi practices of *rabita* and *tawajjuh*.

This *miʿraj-majlis* painting is located in the opening eulogy dedicated to the Prophet in Saʿdi's *Bustan*. It therefore functions as a panegyrical frontispiece of the manuscript. Like other Persian mystical poets before and after him, Saʿdi included a number of *naʿts*, or praises, to God and Muhammad in his encomium. In these poetic prolegomena, one of the three or four *naʿts* often is dedicated to describing the Prophet's celestial ascension. Using allegorical vocabulary, the *miʿraj* verses offer a parallel to the Sufi's path, his spiritual states, and his quest to secure divine knowledge and unity.

In his praise of Muhammad's *miʿraj*, Saʿdi pays tribute to the Prophet's many names (*asmaʾ al-nabi*) and his primordial light (*nur Muhammad*). While the *asmaʾ al-nabi* attempt to express the all-encompassing totality of Muhammad's many qualities and attributes, the *nur Muhammad* aims to conceptualize the Prophet as a primordial, generative, and enlightening substance that flows through time, touching the hearts of the spiritually receptive along the way. As Saʿdi says of the Prophet, "all lights are of his light but rays."[66] The author further describes Muhammad as "well-favored, full-bodied, fragrant, and gloriously marked" as well as "the root of existence" (*asl-i wujud*), from whom the entirety of the created world is merely a branch (*far'*).[67] Finally, Sa'di encourages his readers to issue a prayer (*du'a*) for Muhammad, bemoaning in the conclusion to his eulogy that he is too imperfect to provide a proper description of the "prophet of humankind" (*nabi al-wara*).[68]

The image accompanying Sa'di's praise of Muhammad and lament for his own verbal limitations seems, to a certain degree, to solve the impossibility of expressing the ineffable. By harnessing the power of the visual mode, the depiction builds on the allegorical imagery in the author's text while simultaneously transcending the restrictions of both written and spoken language. The upper portion of the painting directly addresses Sa'di's ascension eulogy by depicting the Prophet's *mi'raj*; however, its iconographic details make certain metaphorical concepts that relate to the prophetic paradigm more immediate and perceptible. Among them is the notion of the *nur Muhammad*, here visually materialized in various ways: the flaming aureole that encircles the Prophet's face, the two-toned gold mandorla that frames his full body and that of Buraq, and the ribboned clouds that swirl around the angels who hover in the night sky, itself stippled with small, shimmering gold stars (fig. 3.5). These pictorial devices create a wholly incandescent scene, whose brilliance appears to radiate, washing over the registers of poetic verses in gold pigment.

Beyond the artist's skillful pictorial rendition of the *nur Muhammad*, which recalls its allegorical description as radiant genesis in Sa'di's eulogy, the image of the Prophet Muhammad is not strictly bound to an abstracted mode of visual expression. To the contrary, it is quite literal in its depiction of the Prophet's physical body. For instance, his bare feet and toes are visible on Buraq's stirrup, while one hand holds the flying beast's reins and the other is raised gently, gesturing toward the Angel Gabriel. Similarly, Muhammad's face benefits from the same attention to detail: his soft beard and black tresses frame his jaw, while beneath arched brows his eyes look up to Gabriel. His facial features suggest a man of strength and poise, at once energetic and pensive.

Despite his radiant surroundings, the Prophet is depicted in an emphatically realistic manner, with details suggestive of a physical body. Within the context of this painting, the visual articulation of Muhammad's corporeality may be due, at least in part, to the fact that his presence is shown as if emanating from a vision produced by three mystics in vigil (fig. 3.6). In their nighttime prayers, these devotees appear to witness Muhammad in a dream vision. As noted previously, visions of the Prophet are, almost without exception, considered literal dreams (and not allegorical imaginings) in Islamic traditions. In this case, the naturalistic mode of representation helps forward the argument that the dream is not a mere fabrication of the mind but rather a manifest occurrence. For these reasons, the artist may have wished to show prophetic verisimilitude as observed by the Sufi dreamers in their hearts, minds, or, per the Naqshbandi idiom, "between the two eyebrows." In short, the

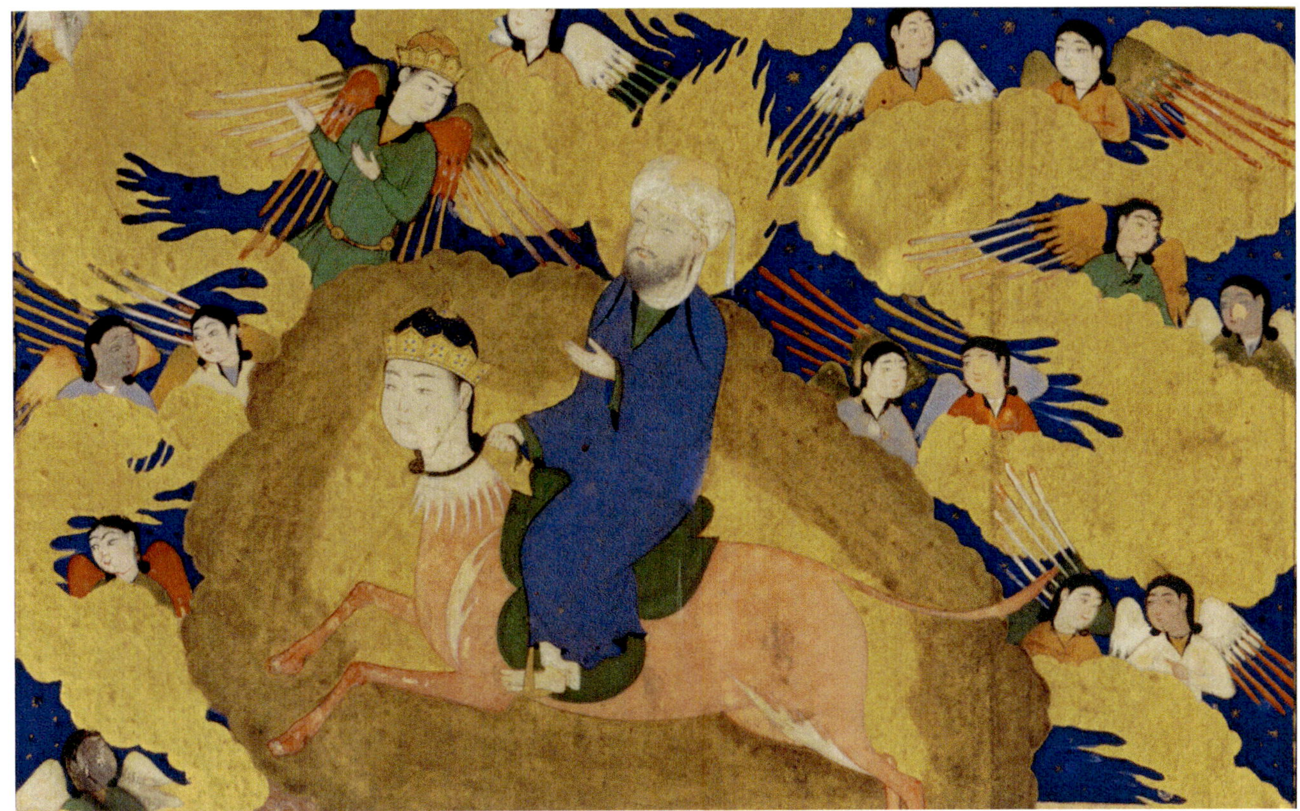

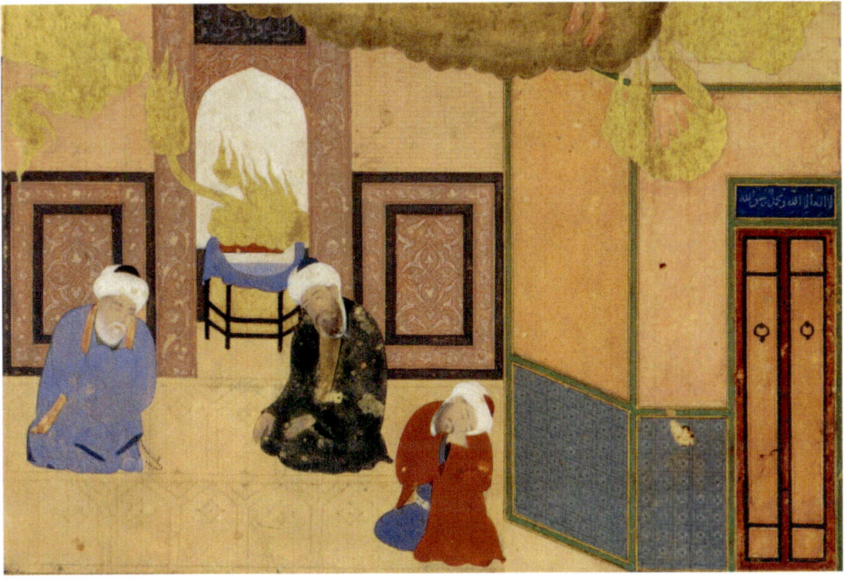

conjunction of the literal and symbolic pictorial modes here suggests a perceptibly real yet wholly visionary event.

Depicted in a Bukharan mystical milieu, the three kneeling men likely represent Naqshbandi mystics engaged in a contemplative vision of the Prophet Muhammad. The most important visionary practices of the Naqshbandiyya include *rabita* and *tawajjuh*, by which a disciple can envision his master or the Prophet, who in return may show himself spiritually to his followers. Both imagistic efforts help form a bond of love between *pir* and *murid*, wherein the master either is likened to a mirror reflecting the light of the Prophet or, as the last link on the Sufi *silsila*, is filled with and conveys the *nur Muhammad* to his community of followers.[69] The Sufi master is thus the deputy and stand-in of the Prophet Muhammad, the carrier of his spiritual energy in physical form.

While the two paintings of Muhammad and Ansari in the Nava'i manuscript suggest Prophet as *shaykh* and *shaykh* as Prophet (figs. 3.1 and 3.3), the Bukharan painting instead stresses a supernatural vision of Muhammad as produced through mystical contemplation and communal prayer. The image of the Prophet can be brought about through the twin processes of *rabita* and *tawajjuh*, which stress the cultivation of sight as a mental activity and form of spiritual training. It also can be achieved through silent recollection. In Naqshbandi Sufi traditions, silent recollection—termed "hidden recollection" (*dhikr khafi*) and "recollection of the heart" (*al-dhikr al-qalbi*)—is preferred to recollection uttered aloud, called "vocal recollection" (*dhikr-i jahri*) and "recollection by the tongue" (*dhikr al-lisan*). According to Naqshbandi traditions, silent *dhikr* is considered sober and rigorous, unlike other Sufi *dhikr* practices, including vocal prayers, music, and dance. Moreover, silent recollection is considered part of the Sunna, as it is believed to have been taught to Abu Bakr by Muhammad while both hid in a cave during their flight from Mecca to Medina.[70] With its Bakri origins stipulated in Naqshbandi doctrine, silent *dhikr* was thus construed as an orthodox— even prophetic—mode of pious conduct.

As revealed to Baha al-Din Naqshband, silent *dhikr* consisted of reciting either the *tahlil* ("There is no god but God") or the complete *shahada* ("There is no god but God and Muhammad is the Messenger of God") in a closed-mouth fashion.[71] At other times, devotees silently repeat the name of Allah, which is considered supreme among God's many "beautiful names" (*al-asma' al-husna*).[72] According to the medieval mystical theologian al-Ghazali (d. 1111 CE), the name Allah is the greatest name, as it contains all of the divine attributes as well as the essence of God. He further notes that the devotee should repeat the name Allah in order to "eliminate what is faulty in himself and try to increase what is good in himself,"[73] so that he might become a perfect human being. Similarly, for the renowned mystic and philosopher Ibn 'Arabi (d. 1240 CE), Allah is the all-inclusive name indicative of God's absolute singularity, and the devotee must persevere in reciting the *tahlil* in order to reach divine knowledge.[74] This process of perfecting one's state of being is at the heart of the mystic's quest, which in Naqshbandi milieus in particular is articulated as both negation and affirmation: that is, eliminating the bad ("there is no god but God") and increasing the good ("and Muhammad is His Prophet").[75]

The *shahada* and other creedal formulas also are included in the Bukharan painting, as two inscriptions in the intermediary zone between the cogitating mystics and the Prophet Muhammad. Above the building's entrance door, on the far right, the complete *shahada* is inscribed within a blue horizontal frieze. As the proclamation of the faith, it praises both God and the Prophet. Moreover, the *shahada* within the painting also provides a powerful threshold into belief, much as its epigraphic rendition serves as an initiatory entryway into the practice of prayer. The second inscription, located in the *mihrab* above the flaming book, continues by declaring that "God is Alone and has no equal." Much like the *shahada*'s first clause, this text includes both affirmation and negation. Collectively, the painting's inscriptions glorify Islam as a monotheistic faith, herald the supremacy and singularity of God, and attest to the divinely decreed apostleship of the Prophet Muhammad. What is more, they visually convey the otherwise inaudible practice of silent *dhikr* as performed by Naqshbandi Sufis.

In the painting, the three mystics also appear engaged in silent recollection, their eyes shut or their heads resting on their knees. In Sufi traditions in general, it is recommended that prayer be performed with eyes to the ground,[76] while in Naqshbandi practices in particular, both *dhikr* and *rabita* practices were carried out with one's eyes shut, so that the imaginative faculty (*khayal*) could be activated fully.[77] Moreover, it is believed that the state of sleep allows one to witness realities inaccessible in a state of wakefulness. In the painting, the three mystics appear drowsy, with closed eyes, or asleep, suggesting that they embody the three states of transfixion that allow visionary experiences to occur. In this instance, the vision of the Prophet may be catalyzed by the Naqshbandi collective recitation of the *khatm*, or closing prayer, which frequently invokes Muhammad through recitations counted with pebbles or clay beads, such as those on the rosary held by the white-bearded mystic sitting on the left.[78] This ascension-cum-meditation painting thus encompasses a range of Naqshbandi visionary and prayer practices, including *rabita* and *tawajjuh* as well as silent *dhikr* and *khatm* prayers. As such, it may have functioned as a pictorial memorial of a particular visionary *majlis* in Shaybanid Bukhara or as a visual stimulant of prophetic visions for future generations of viewers leafing through the illustrated manuscript.

Also noteworthy in the painting is the fact that there are only three meditating mystics, whereas the *majlis* painting in the Nava'i manuscript represents all four *rashidun* alongside other important companions of the Prophet. In this instance, the three individuals most likely stand in for Abu Bakr, 'Umar, and 'Uthman, with Abu Bakr as the bearded man sitting on the left and holding prayer beads. Although all four *rashidun* are associated with the Prophet and praised individually in Sa'di's encomium, it appears that the artist has purposefully omitted 'Ali. After the battle of Chaldiran (1514 CE) and certainly by the 1530s CE, the figure of 'Ali had become increasingly subject to sectarian dispute. At this time, the Shaybanids' western enemies—the Safavids (r. 1501–1722 CE)—claimed descent from the Prophet and his son-in-law and thus portrayed themselves as both *sayyids* and 'Alids.

The potential excision of 'Ali from the painting can be understood as a Shaybanid act of iconoclasm that symbolically eradicates the figurehead of the Safavid polity. 'Ali is altogether omitted while the white-bearded Abu Bakr is emphasized, an iconographic act of negation and affirmation that emphasizes a Bakri pedigree over 'Alid lineage. So, while the painting indeed speaks to contemplative visions of the Prophet within Sufi milieus, it also may bear witness to the unfolding of sectarian contention within the visual arts during the early modern period. In this self-proclaimed Sunni painting, a mystical vision of the Prophet may be found but only if 'Ali is removed from the picture.

One last detail of central importance to the composition is the flaming book on a stand within a *mihrab*. While a flaming book also is included in the Nava'i painting, it is Muhammad who is placed before the niche, symbolically aligned with the codex and present at the gathering. In the Shaybanid painting, however, Muhammad is depicted ascending on Buraq. This two-part composition makes a clear distinction between the worldly realm, below, and the celestial domain, above. The object that appears to connect the two worlds is the codex, whose golden flames fan out like branches that metaphorically beget a heavenly vision of the Prophet.

Not confined to painterly spheres alone, this motif of the "begetting book" can be found in Naqshbandi reports of mystical visions of Muhammad. For example, in his Sufi hagiographical work *Rashahat-i 'Ayn al-Hayat* (Dewdrops from the Elixir of Life), the Naqshbandi mystic 'Ali b. Husayn Kashifi Safi (d. 1532–33 CE) describes a number of instances in which Sufis witnessed the Prophet by reading books of devotions.[79] On one occasion, a mystic named Ruji sat with his companions while they read from a book of prayers that was believed to cause one to see the Prophet. Once the book of prayers was read and other invocations to the Prophet offered, Ruji fell asleep and had a vision of Muhammad sitting near a wall with individuals seated around him. The Prophet then read a document and handed it to Ruji, as if it were an affidavit or certificate.[80] This and other Naqshbandi reports indicate that dreams of Muhammad could be generated through three mutually constitutive practices: reading prayer books, uttering invocations, and falling asleep. Quite significantly, this triad of visionary practices is emphasized within the Shaybanid painting via the flaming book, the rosary, and the slumbering devotees.

The book's flames further enable the viewer to conceptualize the prophetic dream as a kind of radiant flash that inaugurates a theophanous manifestation. Mystics speak to this subject with relative frequency. For example, in his epistle on Sufism, al-Qushayri includes an entire chapter dedicated to glimmers (*lawa'ih*), dawnings (*tawali'*), and flashes (*lawami'*). In this section, he relates that Sufi initiates must strive "to ascend with their hearts" in order to reach the "rays of the suns of divine knowledge."[81] Similarly, for Ruzbihan Baqli, visions of the Prophet are like oceans of light, overpowering in their majesty and awe.[82] And, finally, for Jami, the towering figure of Naqshbandi mysticism, the symbol of the flicker was so important that he entitled his treatise on Sufism simply *Lawa'ih* (Flashes of Light). In these various texts, the radiant flicker is equivalent to the unveiling of God and the descent of divine grace. For some Sufis, these glimmers pass, leaving no trace; for others, vestiges remain.[83] Within the Sufi flicker-dream pattern, the Shaybanid painting thus can be understood as a permanent and visible trace of a mystical vision of the Prophet, experienced as a spiritual yet visible reality begotten by flashes of light.

Although placed on a bookstand, the flaming book in both the Timurid and Shaybanid paintings is suggestive of a brazier, a container that produces heat through the burning of wood or coal, or a censer that emits a perfume of plants and essential oils. Beyond its conceptual link to the *nur Muhammad*, the brazier hints at the Prophet's heavenly scent by insinuating an olfactory presence. Engaging the viewer in a synesthetic experience by which optical perception stimulates the olfactory sense, the artist suggests that Muhammad is induced here through flames of light as well as natural aromatics, including musk, ambergris, and camphor, all three prominent scent-symbols of the prophetic corpus as found in Persian Sufi poetry. The brazier is also a fitting motif for the Naqshbandi notion that visions of Muhammad are induced through the prayerful process of "incubation" (*istikhara*), by which this supreme spiritual master is summoned to initiate a Sufi novice into the *tariqa* or to help him perfect his spiritual state as he ascends, seeking proximity and unity with God, much as the Prophet did on the night of his celestial ascent.[84]

Emerging from a decidedly Sunni-Sufi milieu, the painting essentially functions as an external visualization of an internal practice of pious imagination. To a certain degree, the picture is intended as picturation: it is not a depiction of perceived reality but rather an inducement to a prophetic dream. The work artfully highlights one of the paradoxes of the pictorial mode, in which and through which the believing viewer is challenged to overcome optical perception in order to secure a vision of the heart. For Sufis, a vision of the Prophet was real but not material, his appearance merely a representation of his spirit in human form. According to al-Ghazali, a vision of Muhammad offers a symbolic representation (*mithal*) of his sacred spirit in absolute truth (*tahqiq*).[85] Like the vision, the painted image also must be seen as a symbolic analogue for the world of the unseen, a topic that Jami himself addresses. In discussing representation, Jami states that Sufis understand "form" (*sura*) to signify the means whereby unseen realities (*haqa'iq ghaybiyya*), which are disengaged (*mujarrad*) from and transcend physical realities, can be conceived and understood.[86] The visual mode once again dares viewers to reach beyond the material image to discover its true essence—that is, its *ma'na*, or inner meaning.

Implemented but ultimately transcended, the pictorial mode invites its observing devotees to spiritually envision a Muhammadan reality (*haqiqa muhammadiyya*), the ultimate source of divine grace and light, truth and authenticity. This prophetic reality is both manifestation and effusion, passed from master to pupil. The vision seeks to activate the devotee's "inner Muhammad"[87] through Naqshbandi pious imagistic practices including dream, prayer, sleep, *rabita*, *tawajjuh*, and, last but certainly not least, picture. Through these multiple visionary modes, the mystical seer of the prophetic dream and its painterly representation can witness and be touched by Muhammad, himself the trailblazer into the secrets of divinity and the archetypal spiritual initiate capable of achieving union with God.[88]

During the second half of the sixteenth century, visionary representations of the Prophet continued to be incorporated into manuscripts made in Persian and Turkish cultural spheres. In a number of cases, paintings of Muhammad appear at the beginning of illustrated biographies of Sufi masters, no doubt as pictorial praise for his position as first and supreme spiritualist in a long line of enlightened saints. While sectarian concerns are not especially apparent in some of the Persian images, in others an emerging pro-Shi'i narrative became more pronounced after the Safavid-Ottoman battle of Chaldiran (1514 CE). Similarly, an emergent pro-Sunni position can be detected in the Shaybanid painting of the 1530s CE from which 'Ali appears to have been excised, leaving only three *rashidun*-like figures to benefit from a vision of the Prophet and his *mi'raj*. While this image forwards a Sunni religious worldview through the process of subtraction, later sixteenth-century Safavid paintings forwarding a pro-Shi'i message engage instead with the principle of addition. In Safavid visionary images, new casts of characters—from 'Ali, Hasan, and Husayn to later Shi'i Sufi *shaykhs*—access or enter the visionary realm. These iconographic alterations reveal the extent to which prophetic dreams, coupled with their pictorial representations, could legitimize a particular Sufi group or promote a sectarian viewpoint, with both Sunni and Shi'i actors wishing to affirm religio-political identities during the early modern period.

Books on the lives of Sufi masters belong broadly to the literary genre known as *tazkira*. Encompassing biographical anthologies and literary memoirs, these written records of the lives of mystics were especially popular from the medieval period onward. Most important among such works is Farid al-Din 'Attar's (d. 1221 CE) *Tazkirat al-Awliya'* (Biographies of the Saints), a text in Persian prose describing the great Muslim mystics, whose special marvels (*karamat*) symbolically recall Muhammad's prophetic miracles (*mu'jizat*).[89] During the sixteenth century, a variety of other Sufi *tazkiras* were composed, including those by Kamal al-Din Husayn Gazurgahi (flourished ca. 1500 CE), a close companion of Sultan Husayn Bayqara and a student of the Naqshbandi mystic and poet Jami. The Timurid ruler appointed Gazurgahi as *shaykh* at the shrine of 'Abdallah Ansari near Herat, where he also served as overseer of its endowed property.[90] By 1504 CE Gazurgahi completed his *Majalis al-'Ushshaq* (Assemblies of the Beloved), a biography of the lives of famous Sufis, including Ibrahim b. Adham, al-Hallaj, Sana'i,

San'an, 'Attar, and Jami. From one biographical sketch to the next, Gazurgahi's *tazkira* aims to demonstrate the virtues of the Sufi path. Moreover, he extols the mystical practice of confraternal gatherings (*majalis*) throughout his text, an emphasis similarly echoed in the title of his *tazkira*.

While one copy of Gazurgahi's *Assemblies of the Beloved* was produced with paintings in Herat in 1502 CE, the great majority of illustrated manuscripts were made during the second half of the sixteenth century in the Iranian city of Shiraz. Some copies were intended for a Safavid audience while others were meant for export to Istanbul, where such works were enthusiastically sought by an Ottoman elite clientele.[91] These manuscripts of Gazurgahi's Sufi *tazkira* typically include cycles of paintings that depict court scenes, episodes of urban life, and Sufi marvels and gatherings. Either placed at the very beginning of a manuscript or interwoven into the tales of mystics who experience prophetic visions, paintings of Muhammad create a pictorial chain, or *silsila*, across generations of enlightened saints. Through both text and image, illustrated manuscripts of Gazurgahi's *Assemblies of the Beloved* depict Muhammad as a mystical initiate along the Sufi path.[92]

Paintings of the second half of the sixteenth century follow patterns established more than a century earlier. For example, one luxurious copy of Gazurgahi's *tazkira*, made in Shiraz in 1581 CE, launches its narrative cycle with a painting of the Prophet seated among his companions in an interior space, with a white veil covering his facial features and a gold aureole flaming toward the text block above (fig. 3.7).[93] He sits cross-legged, his arms crossed at his waist, and his hands camouflaged by the long sleeves of his Sufi's robe. Sitting and kneeling in a circle around him are men engaged in conversation and gesticulating toward a closed book on a stand. To Muhammad's right sits a man in an orange robe; one young man stands on each side of the painting's middle ground. In its overall composition, the painting recalls the *majlis* setting in the late Timurid copy of Nava'i's *Khamsa* (fig. 3.1). However, in this illustration the book is not alight in a blaze of gold, and the interior space is not a mosque outfitted with a *mihrab* and *minbar*. Instead, Muhammad and his companions appear to gather in a humble prayer room accessible by the three wooden doors in the painting's background.

The painting accompanies the section of Gazurgahi's text that describes the Angel Gabriel's revelations to the Prophet. The author informs the reader that, at first, Muhammad was so fearful of these angelic transmissions that he would perspire and nearly faint. To comfort him, and to make the experience less overwhelming, the Angel Gabriel appeared to him at least twice in the form of Dihya al-Kalbi, his young and unusually handsome companion.[94] Citing the qur'anic verse "and thus [God] revealed to His servant what He revealed" (53:10) immediately above the painting, Gazurgahi continues his narrative by describing Muhammad's spiritual ecstasy and Gabriel's departure, following which he sought solace either in solitude or in the company of his wife

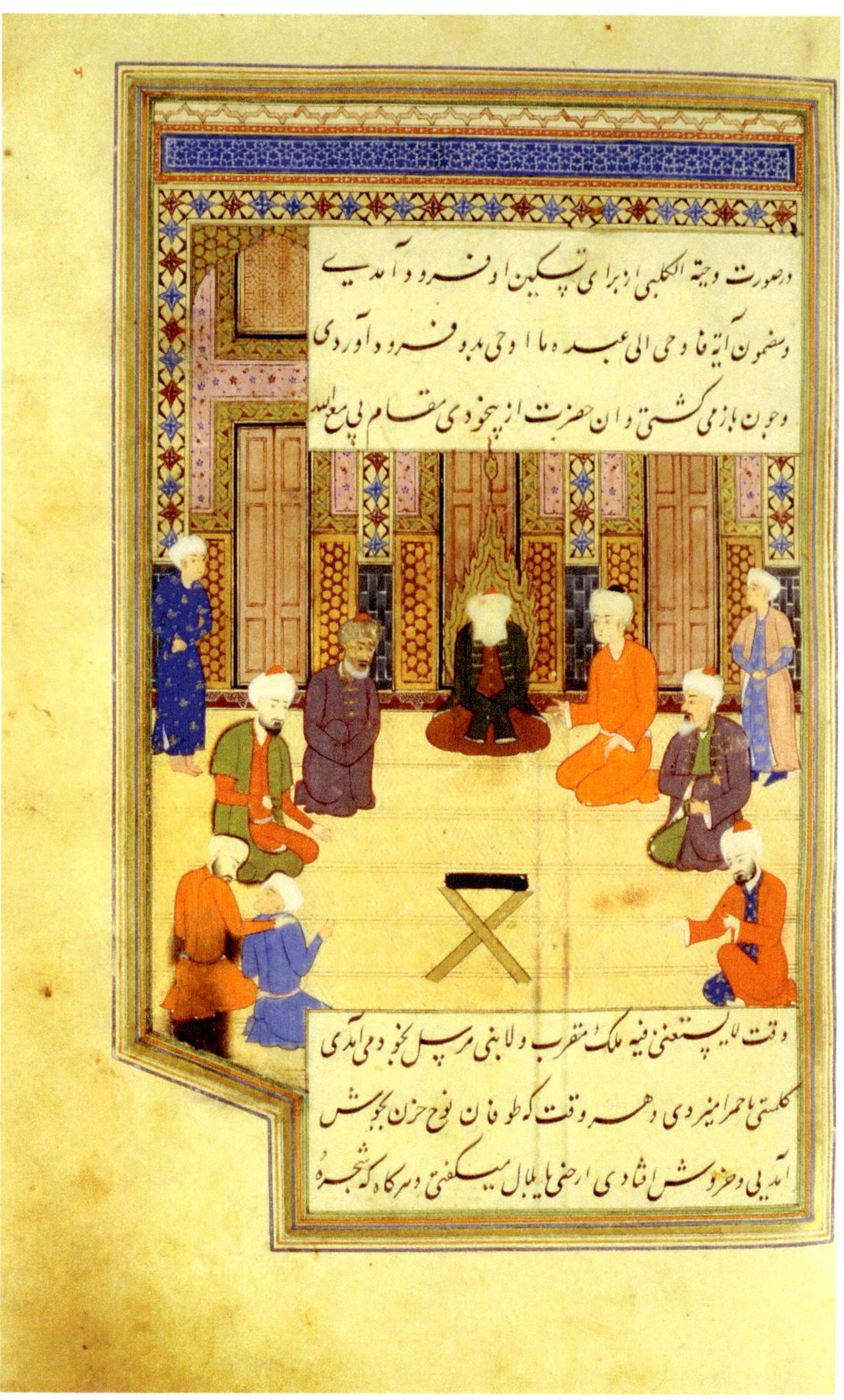

ʿAʾisha, Bilal, or his followers. Finally, Gazurgahi's text pays tribute to the
Prophet's scriptural revelations (*wahy*) and Muhammad "losing himself" (*bi-khudi*) in sacred rapture.

This section of Gazurgahi's text also is illustrated in a near-contemporary copy of the *Assemblies of the Beloved* (fig. 3.8).[95] The author's narrative remains the same: it cites the same qurʾanic verse and describes
the Prophet "losing himself" in the spiritual ecstasy of *wahy*. The painting accompanying the text has been composed differently: here, the
Prophet Muhammad sits at the head of a long carpet, his hands raised in
prayer as he looks toward a handsome young man, no doubt the Angel

   THE PRAISEWORTHY ONE

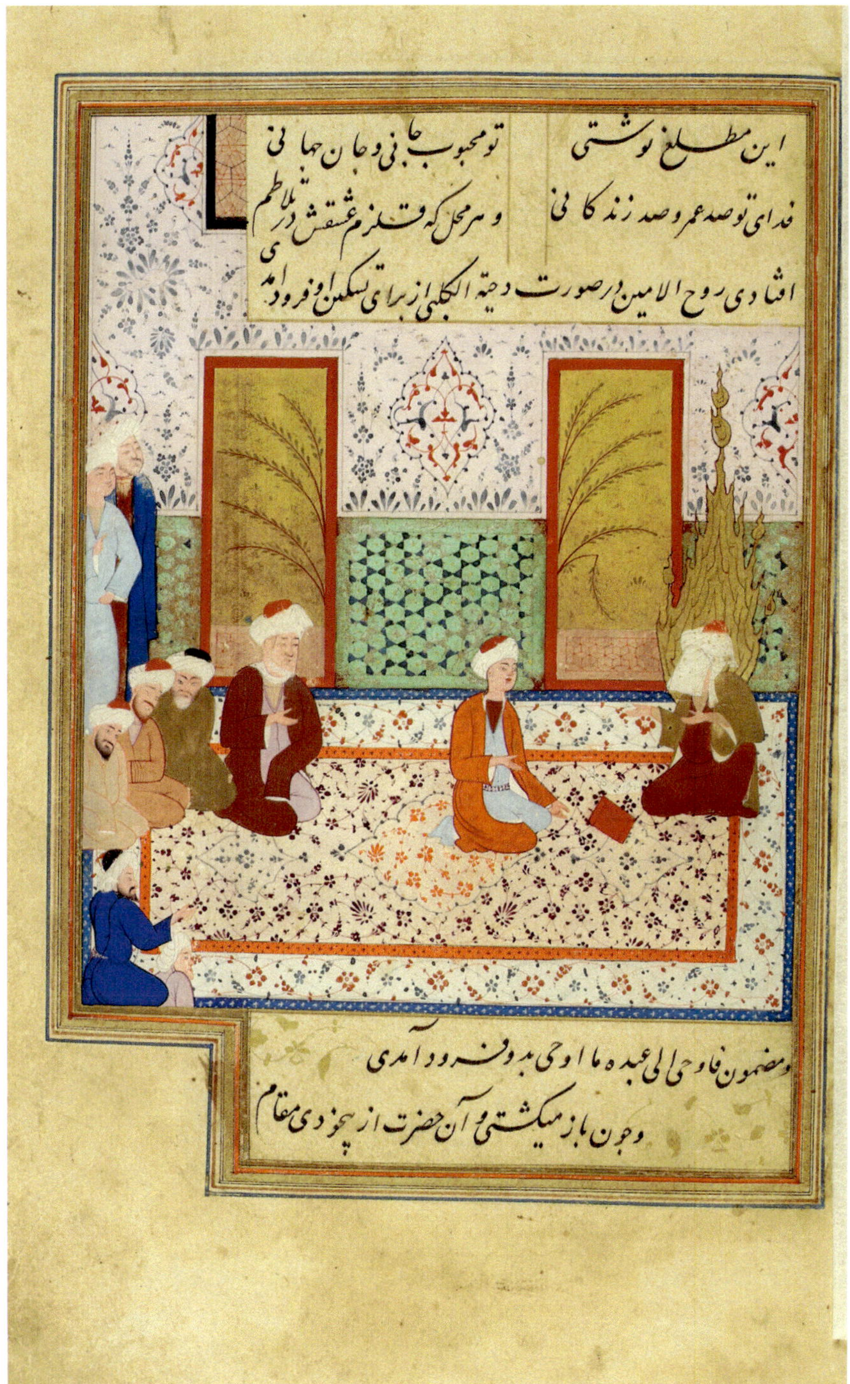

3.8. The Angel Gabriel, in the form of Dihya al-Kalbi, before the Prophet Muhammad, Gazurgahi, *Majalis al-'Ushshaq* (Assemblies of the beloved), Shiraz, ca. 1575–1600 CE. Bibliothèque nationale de France, Paris, Suppl. Persan 1559, folio 26r.

Gabriel in the form of Dihya al-Kalbi. On the carpet between them is a closed book bound in brown leather, most likely the Qur'an. At the other end of the carpet stand and sit a number of other individuals, one of whom wears a Sufi robe with a noticeably long sleeve. All congregate in a room whose wall is decorated with hexagonal tile dadoes and blue-and-white frescoes depicting flowers and plants.

These two paintings that depict the beginning stages of Muhammad receiving revelations via the Angel Gabriel are striking in a number of ways. First, their iconography diverges substantially from earlier Persian illustrations of the episode, as found in Rashid al-Din's *Compendium of*

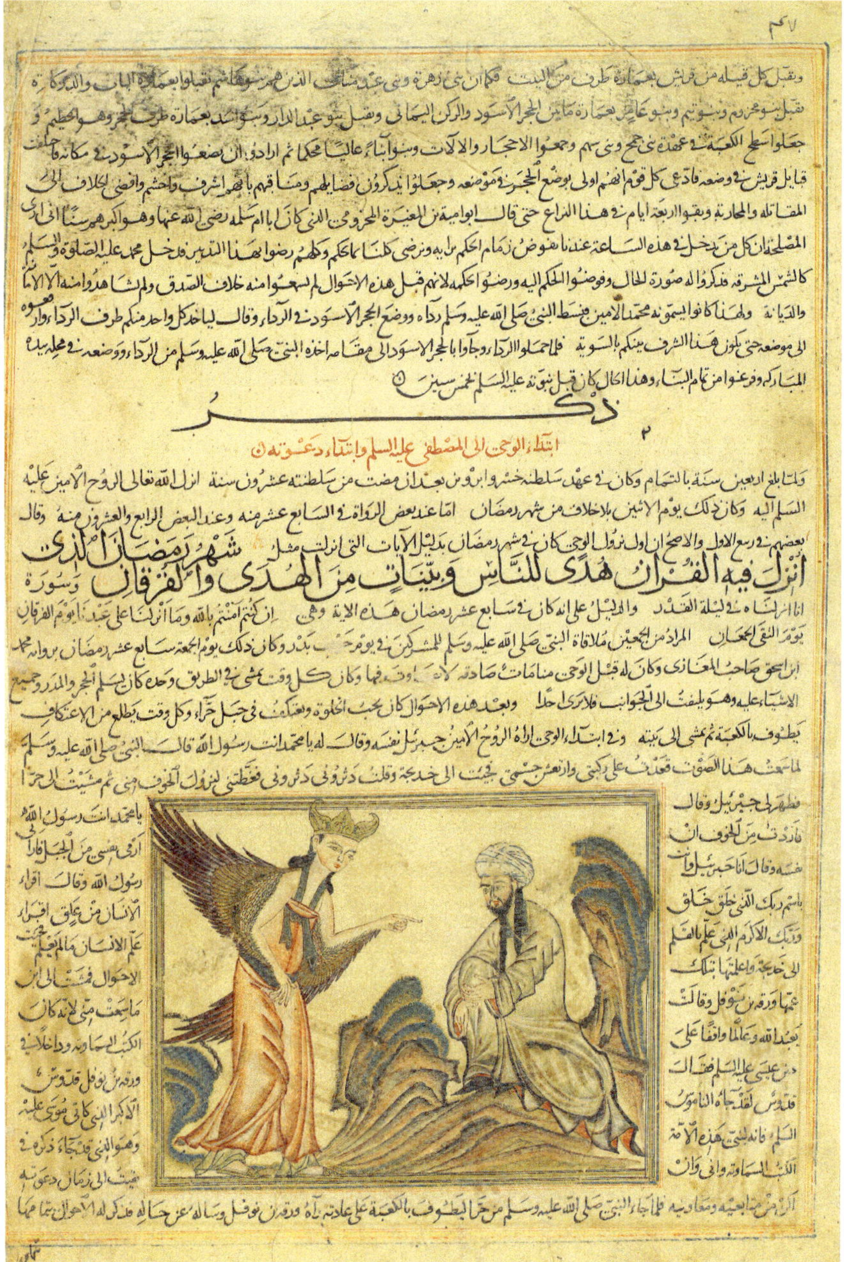

Chronicles of 1307–14 CE and Hafiz-i Abru's *Quintessence of Chronicles* of about 1425 CE. Both Ilkhanid and Timurid universal histories include a chapter on the beginning of revelation and the launch of Muhammad's apostleship, accompanied by a painting that shows the Prophet seated alone in a rocky landscape as a winged Gabriel approaches from the left, commanding him to recite in the name of the Lord (figs. 3.9–3.10). While iconographic differences between the two paintings exist—for example, in the Ilkhanid painting Gabriel's wings grow along his arms rather than his shoulders, and in the Timurid painting both Gabriel and Muhammad bear golden halos—their compositions are remarkably similar. In both instances, the Prophet is secluded outdoors in a rocky landscape as Gabriel approaches. Both historical texts attempt to relay a relatively straightforward narrative, while the artists of both

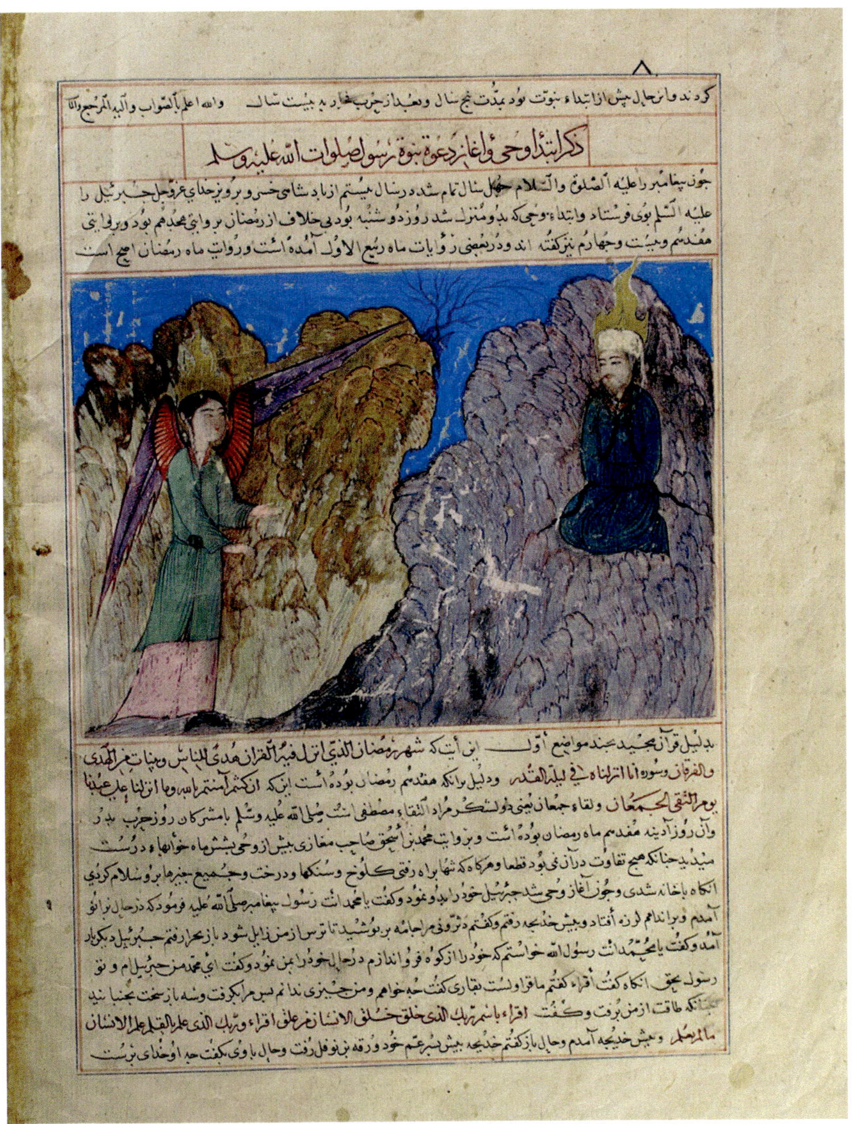

3.10. The Prophet Muhammad begins to receive revelations from the Angel Gabriel, Hafiz-i Abru, *Majma' al-Tawarikh* (Collection of Chronicles), Herat, ca. 1425 CE. Metropolitan Museum of Art, New York, 57.51.37.3.

illustrations sought clarity in their renderings of this pivotal moment in Muhammad's prophetic career.

Conversely, the text and paintings of Muhammad receiving revelations from Gabriel found in later illustrated copies of Gazurgahi's *Assemblies of the Beloved* (figs. 3.7–3.8) convolute this episode in striking ways. In his Sufi *tazkira*, the author prefers to describe Gabriel appearing to the Prophet in the handsome, young form of Dihya al-Kalbi. Moreover, to describe Muhammad's experience during *wahy*, Gazurgahi employs the term *bi-khudi*, an expression drawn directly from the Persian Sufi lexicon. Meaning "selflessness" or "the state of being egoless," *bi-khudi* describes the Sufi's spiritual ecstasy, when he achieves self-annihilation (*fana'*) in his love of and unity with God. Thus, Gazurgahi applies a Persian mystical term to describe the prophetic experience of revelation as both transcendental and all-encompassing. Through the power of rhetoric, Muhammad is presented as the paradigmatic, egoless mystic.

Beyond Sufi terminology, the Prophet is depicted as the quintessential spiritual master within the illustrated manuscripts of Gazurgahi's

Assemblies of the Beloved. He does not sit alone outdoors to receive Gabriel; instead, he is shown in an interior space, most likely a prayer room, surrounded by his companions. Gabriel is young and handsome and, in one case, is engaged face-to-face with Muhammad, as if he were in an intimate master-pupil relationship. Not winged and angelic, Gabriel appears to take the shape of a young novice, receiving wisdom from a *shaykh* rather than transmitting the Logos of God to the Prophet. In some sense, the interaction has been inverted: Muhammad now appears in an instructional role, guiding his followers—Dihya al-Kalbi among them—into spiritual knowledge. Within a mystical *majlis* framework, Muhammad is depicted as the ultimate *pir*, whose young and handsome *murid* is invited to cultivate his angelic self. The Prophet's revelation is thereby reconfigured both textually and visually, in the process aligning the *wahy* episode with Sufi devotional patterns. The painting thus may have allowed a Sufi viewership to imagine itself achieving divinely inspired selflessness through a prophetic encounter.

As the first of the great spiritual masters in a chain of Sufi biographies, the Prophet Muhammad makes additional pictorial appearances in the form of dream visions. For example, in his *tazkira*, Gazurgahi includes a biographical sketch of the Sufi mystic Mawlana Muhammad Tabadkhani. The author informs his readers of the *shaykh*'s various activities, including those in taverns and in ritual dances (*sama'*), themes that are illustrated in sixteenth-century manuscript copies of the text.[96] Additionally, we are told that this dervish secretly loved Dihya al-Kalbi. One cold day, in a prophetic vision, Tabadkhani sees Muhammad at his companion's house; inside the home is a fire, around which children play. Tabadkhani asks the Prophet if he would allow Dihya al-Kalbi to wash him at the time of his death, to which Muhammad responds in the affirmative—while also advising Tabadkhani that he who is in love must keep his passion a secret so that he may die a witness to the faith (*shahid*). Tabadkhani's dream thus demonstrates his ardent desire to be purified by the Angel Gabriel as well as his unusual propinquity to the Prophet, who emerges from the realm of the unseen to grant him his final wish.

Late sixteenth-century copies of Gazurgahi's *Assemblies of the Beloved* at times include a depiction of Tabadkhani's dream (fig. 3.11). Unfortunately, the details of such paintings are difficult to identify with any degree of certainty.[97] For example, in figure 3.11, who are the two seated individuals with flaming nimbi in lieu of facial features: Muhammad and 'Ali, Muhammad and Dihya al-Kalbi, Muhammad and Tabadkhani, or perhaps 'Ali and Husayn? Who are the companions, children, and woman who stand and sit with them? Is the food being cooked in the background an aspect of Tabadkhani's dream, in which Muhammad is described as present in a well-warmed house with playing children, or is this a meal prepared by contemporary mystics, perhaps to celebrate 'Ashura? The impossibility of precisely determining the image's protagonists and setting—past, present, or somewhere suspended in the

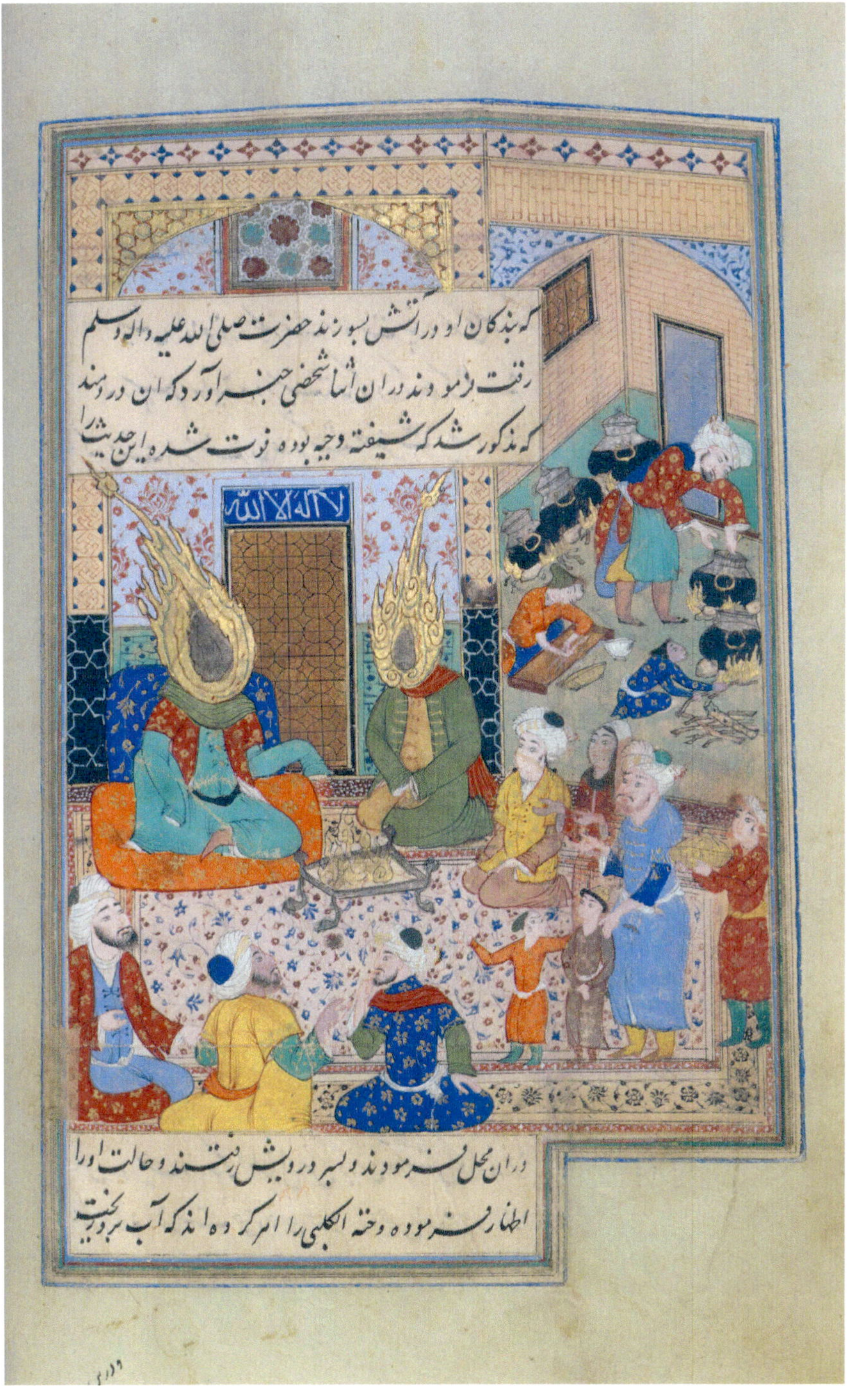

3.11. Tabadkhani's dream of the Prophet Muhammad, Gazurgahi, *Majalis al-'Ushshaq* (Assemblies of the Beloved), Shiraz, ca. 1575–1600 CE. Museum of Islamic Art, Staatliche Museen zu Berlin, I.1986.229, folio 147r.

dream world—presents the viewer with an interpretive challenge. Like a dream vision, the painting seems to obfuscate, even collapse, prophetic history with contemporary circumstances, even those as mundane as food cooking in large pots. Further, the platter of gold flames that appears between the two holy personages is especially enigmatic. Perhaps it is intended as a signifier of the dream world, itself a locus of light, heat, and vapor.

While Tabadkhani's dream depicts him as a seraphic witness to the faith, other mystics' visions helped them promote the spiritual authority of their own *tariqa*s. For example, through the mechanism of the prophetic dream, Mevlevi mystics also entered into communication with Muhammad to receive inspiration and direction. The Mevlevi order is named after the famous Persian mystical poet Jalal al-Din Rumi (d. 1273 CE), known as Mawlana or Mevlana, meaning "Our Master." Rumi settled in the Anatolian city of Konya, where his follower Hüsamettin (Husam) Çelebi (d. 1294 CE) established a mystical order in his honor around his tomb. Now a museum, the Mevlana shrine complex benefited from royal Ottoman patronage over the centuries and included the saint's tomb, a mosque, a dervish lodge, kitchens, and an assembly hall for the ritual of *sama'*, the whirling form of *dhikr* for which the Mevlevi Sufis remain famous today. Combining dance and music (typically produced with the *nay*, or reed flute), these so-called whirling dervishes differ from the Naqshbandis, who preferred a more sober, silent form of *dhikr*. Additionally, in Mevlevi milieus, a third essential text was added to the reading of the Qur'an and prayers: Rumi's *Masnavi* (Rhyming Couplets), a collection of approximately twenty-five thousand verses of Persian mystical poetry teaching Sufis to become one with God through spiritual love and the imaginative spirit.

During the sixteenth century, the Mevlevi order was popular among Ottoman royal ranks. It appears that Sultan Murad III (r. 1574–95 CE) was especially keen on the Sufi order. In 1590 CE, he entrusted Derviş Mahmud Mesnevi of Konya with the task of translating Shams al-Din Ahmad Aflaki's (d. 1360 CE) biography of Mevlevi mystics, *Manaqib al-'Arifin* (The Feats of the Knowers of God), translated from the original Persian into an abridged Ottoman Turkish version. The Turkish text was almost immediately made as an illustrated manuscript, several copies of which survive in international collections.[98] Produced in the Ottoman book ateliers of Baghdad during the 1590s CE, this illustrated Sufi *tazkira* of the Mevlevi saints is artistically linked to a number of other texts that feature pictorial cycles, including *Qisas al-Anbiya'* (Stories of the Prophets), Shi'i martyrologies, and Ottoman sultanic genealogies.[99]

One late sixteenth-century copy of the text includes twenty-nine paintings, two of which depict visions of Muhammad witnessed by Rumi and his successor, Husam Çelebi (d. 1284 CE).[100] According to Aflaki, in one of his dreams, Husam Çelebi saw Muhammad and Bilal: Bilal was holding the Qur'an, and the Prophet grasped the *Masnavi* close to his chest. Muhammad then read its verses and praised its virtues as he shook his head with pride. On hearing of the dream, Rumi informed his Sufi pupil that the *Masnavi*, like the Qur'an, is a "spiritual beloved who has no peer in beauty and perfection."[101] He added, "it requires great faith, persevering love, and upright sincerity and a sound heart to penetrate the deep light-filled secrets of the *Masnavi* . . . and the clear proofs of the mysterious treasures and subtleties of mystical realities which it contains."[102] In this dream episode, the *Masnavi* is equated with the Qur'an, gaining quasiscriptural status.

Even more daring in Husam Çelebi's dream vision is the fact that the Qur'an is placed in Bilal's hands while the *Masnavi* is held close to

   THE PRAISEWORTHY ONE

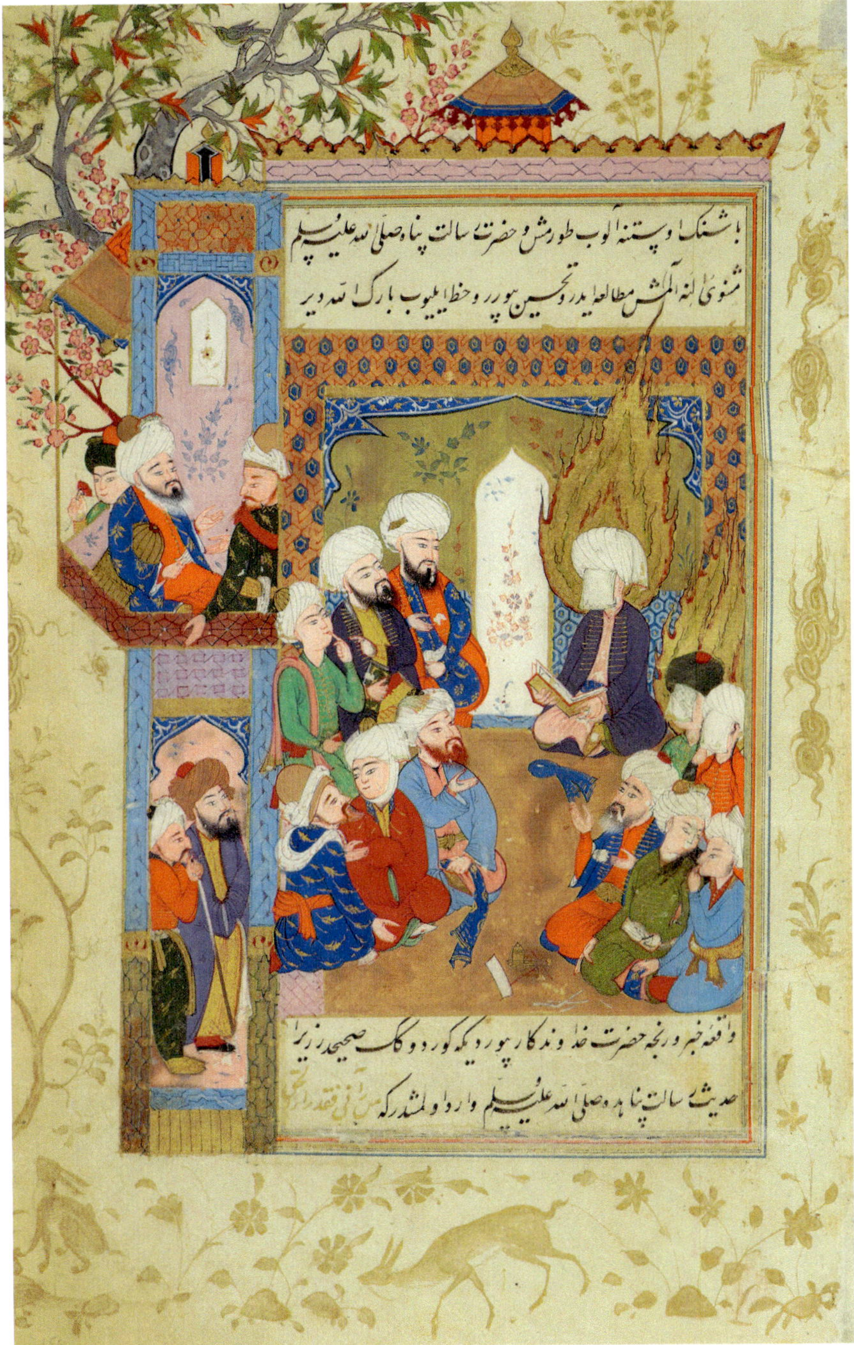

3.12. Husam Çelebi's dream of the Prophet Muhammad reading Rumi's *Masnavi* (Rhyming Couplets), Ottoman Turkish translation and abridgement of Aflaki, *Manaqib al-'Arifin* (The Feats of the Knowers of God), Baghdad, 1590s CE. The Morgan Library, New York, MS M.466, folio 156r.

Muhammad's chest. The removal of the qur'anic text from the Prophet's grasp insinuates that Rumi's collection of verses should be considered superior to the Qur'an. In Islamic theology, the Qur'an is considered God's hidden mystery (*al-sirr al-maknun*) made accessible to humankind. Moreover, a well-known *Hadith Qudsi* (holy saying) records God as stating: "I was a Hidden Treasure. I wanted to be known, so I made creation."[103] The Qur'an often is interpreted as the earthly self-disclosure of God as a "hidden treasure," whose material manifestation echoes and leads its readers or listeners to an eternal divine prototype. In this dream episode, however, the secrets (*asrar*), subtleties (*lata'if*), and realities (*haqa'iq*) of divinity are made manifest not via the holy scripture of

Islam but rather through Rumi's *Masnavi*, itself a wellspring of spiritual enlightenement according to Mevlevi thought. Though its closest companion is the Qur'an, the *Masnavi* is described in this particular dream vision as as a compendium of sacred verses that, per Rumi, has "no peer in beauty and perfection."

In the image depicting Husam Çelebi's dream vision of the Prophet, Muhammad is shown within the context of a social gathering (fig. 3.12). He is differentiated from his entourage by his white facial veil and flaming nimbus, which likewise are applied to two other figures, possibly Hasan and Husayn, who are seated to his left. Many other figures surround him, suggesting a *majlis* composed of a spiritual master teaching a group of his pupils. Moreover, Muhammad kneels before a *mihrab*-like recess within what appears to be a prayer room, gently holding open a book clad in a luminescent gold binding. Were it not for the details included in Aflaki's description of Husam Çelebi's dream, which this painting illustrates, the viewer would be tempted to identify the open codex as the Qur'an or perhaps a miscellany of prayers. However, the Ottoman Turkish text immediately above the painting clearly states that Muhammad took the *Masnavi* in hand, consulted it, praised it, and asked for God's blessings on it. Thus, the text glorifies Rumi's poetic oeuvre by means of Muhammad's blessing, while the image enables the copresence of the Prophet and the *Masnavi*, which, albeit separated by six centuries, are spiritually conjoined within the dream world of the Mevlevi mystic.

In this late sixteenth-century Ottoman painting, Husam Çelebi's dream of the Prophet holding the *Masnavi* does not appear in a dreamlike manner. Much as the painting appears rather realistic in its motifs and composition, the accompanying text below the depiction also stresses that Husam Çelebi's vision was an "event" (*vaqi'a*) that Rumi declared sound or reliable (*sahih*), a statement that he based on the Prophet's Hadith: "Whoever sees [e.g., has a dream vision of] me, then he has seen me in reality (*fi'l-haqq*)." Within the text, the Hadith's pivotal importance is highlighted with eye-catching gold ink, while its truth lies once again in the notion that dreams of Muhammad are literal events whose spiritual reality must be accepted. By extension, the image must also offer a reliable rendering of the dream event by avoiding pictorial metaphors that might suggest the realm of fantasy. In both text and image, the promotion of what is imagined as observable reality serves as a compelling argument in favor of the reality of the prophetic encounter.

Spiritual seeing and the use of images as a means to access truth and reality are also of central importance to the tale of Husam Çelebi's dream of Muhammad. Once conveyed to Rumi, the Mevlevi *shaykh* confirms the veracity of the prophetic vision while also using it as an occasion to wax poetic about the special virtues of the eye and of vision. With confidence and ebullience, Rumi professes to Husam Çelebi, "By God, it is just as your blessed eye beheld. For God forbid that your eye would ever report what it had not seen. And every eye which confides in this visionary eye (*dida-yi didar-dida*) will become one of the people of vision (*ahl-i dida*) so that invisible matters are seen by it."[104] Rumi further argues that only "men of God" can benefit from a vision of Muhammad: "Blessed [is] the soul which is allotted the good fortune of beholding this invisible fair one and enjoys the favor-bestowing gaze of men of God."[105] These "people of vision" and "men of God" are no doubt Mevlevi Sufis who are fortunate enough to experience prophetic dreams, in which immaterial substances and invisible persons became accessible to those fortunate enough to possess and cultivate the visionary eye. This inner, spiritual eye of the mystic grants him direct access to the dream domain, the "world of representations" in which the Prophet Muhammad exists as a spiritually real, visible form.

The painting of Husam Çelebi's prophetic dream also suggests the visionary domain. On the one hand, the Prophet seems immediately present—rather than in some faraway realm—as he sits indoors, surrounded by members of his entourage, in a setting reminiscent of the Sufi *majlis*. On the other, the vision proper must be separated visually from the nondream world, which in this example is insinuated by the balcony and tree in the composition's upper left corner. On the balcony sit several men: the older man with a Mevlevi turban might be Rumi, while the younger individual smelling a pink rose could be Husam Çelebi, contemplating his prophetic vision through the aroma of the pink "rose of Muhammad" (*gul-i Muhammad*).[106] In the painting, both figural depiction and rose scent invite the viewer to gaze on and synesthetically experience the Prophet.

While Husam Çelebi reminisces via the rose, Rumi appears to witness the dream vision as if it were a real event unfolding before his eyes. Despite their proximity to the dream, both master and pupil are kept out of the interior space in which the Prophet sits in congregation. The architecture of the painting thus physically separates the real world from the dream realm. Like a vision, the painting enables the viewer to see and contemplate but not penetrate. Dream and image thus act as thresholds between the real and the imagined worlds as well as contact zones between the realm of the sensible and the intelligible. In this and other cases, representational images without a doubt share much in common with the *'alam al-mithal*.

The painting of Husam Çelebi's dream raises one final issue: that of pictorial allusions and their symbolic implications in late sixteenth-century Ottoman manuscript production. As noted previously, the Prophet sits on a *minbar*, and to his left appear two other individuals, possibly Hasan and Husayn. They bear white facial veils and flaming halos, attributes that link them visually to Muhammad and thus symbolically extol their prophetic pedigree. The inclusion of Hasan and Husayn, along with the overall composition of the painting in Aflaki's *tazkira*, is not, however, particular to this illustrated biography. A number of other manuscripts made in Baghdad include similar illustrations, especially Turkish-language copies of Fuzuli's (d. 1556 CE) *Hadiqat al-Su'ada'*

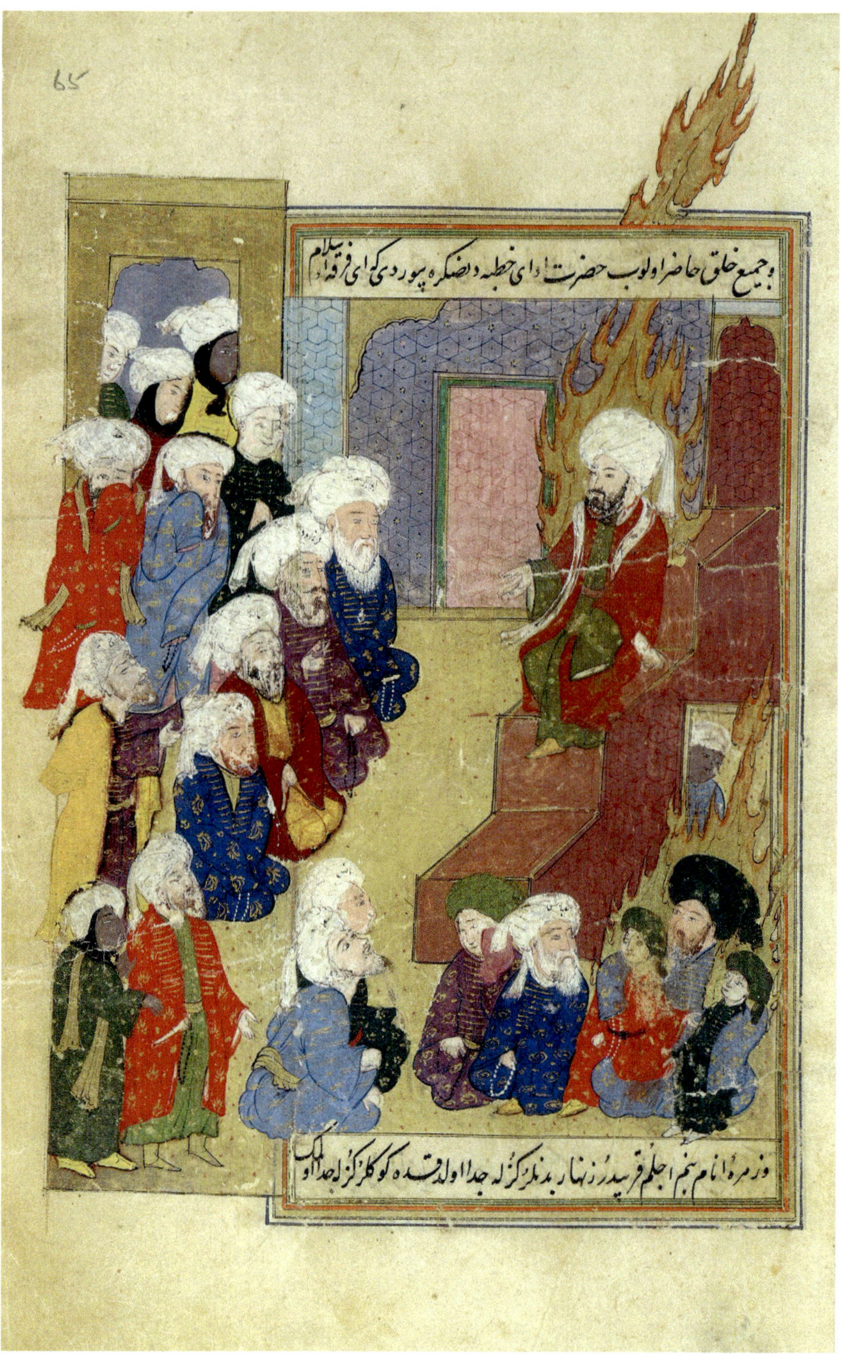

(Garden of the Blessed) and Lami'i Çelebi's (d. 1532–33 CE) *Maqtal Al al-Rasul* (The Murder of the Prophet's Family).[107] Both texts recount the lives and suffering of members of the Prophet's family and thus were intended to appeal particularly, though not exclusively, to a clientele of Shi'i inclination living in both eastern Ottoman and western Safavid realms.

In illustrated manuscripts of these two texts, Muhammad is depicted seated on a *minbar* delivering a sermon, accompanied by 'Ali, Hasan, and Husayn. In some instances, the Prophet is shown unveiled (fig. 3.13),[108] while in others he is depicted with a white facial veil (fig. 3.14). The presence or absence of the facial veil notwithstanding, almost all

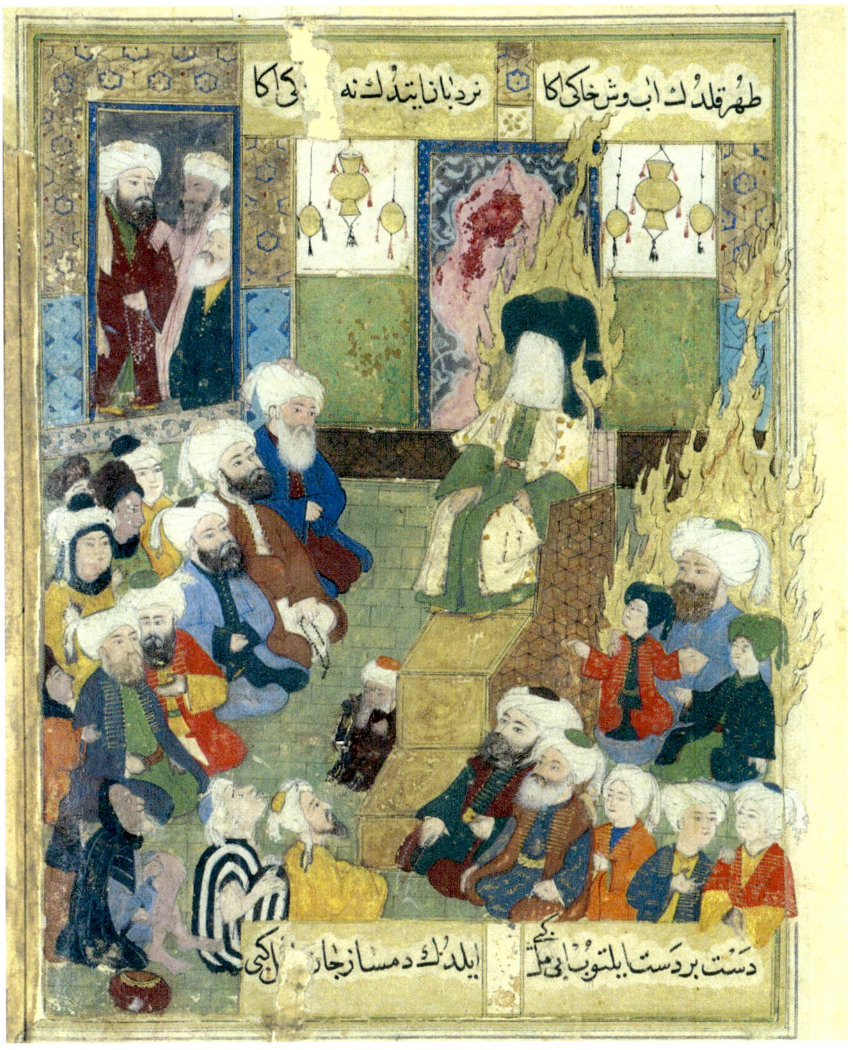

3.14. The Prophet Muhammad delivers a sermon while seated on a *minbar*, Lami'i Çelebi, *Maqtal Al al-Rasul* (The Murder of the Prophet's Family), probably Baghdad, late sixteenth century CE. The Metropolitan Museum of Art, New York, 55.121.40.

paintings include three figures who also partake in the flaming aureole: 'Ali with his two sons Hasan and Husayn seated on his lap. The depiction of all three protagonists reflects the emphasis on the *ahl al-bayt* while also visually sustaining the Shi'i agenda found within Fuzuli's and Lami'i Çelebi's texts. While the incorporation of these members of the Prophet's household may not come as a surprise within such texts, what is more intriguing in this instance is, first, that this pictorial composition migrated from Shi'i-inflected texts to Aflaki's Mevlevi *tazkira*; second, that the depiction of Muhammad delivering a sermon was transformed into a dream vision of the Prophet reading Rumi's *Masnavi*; and, third, that one of the members of the *ahl al-bayt* has been removed, leaving only two individuals to partake in the prophetic attributes of the facial veil and flaming aureole.

During the late sixteenth century, paintings often migrated between illustrated texts. Their compositional details were not blindly copied from one manuscript to the next; rather, and quite tellingly, their motifs could be altered depending on literary content and religious context. This process of pictorial borrowing and editing is made especially evident by comparing the painting in Aflaki's *tazkira* to those typically found in Fuzuli's and Lami'i Çelebi's narratives. In juxtaposing such images, two major alterations can be detected in the Aflaki painting. The first is the addition of an outside space and balcony, in which Rumi and Husam Çelebi sit while contemplating and discussing the prophetic dream represented within an interior space to the right. These architectural and figural additions aid in the depiction of a dream vision together with its explication—that is, of a visionary realm and the real world. The second alteration visible in the Aflaki painting is the absence of one member of the *ahl al-bayt* from the dream vision scene. The absent figure might be 'Ali—at this time considered the figurehead of the Safavid rulers—or perhaps Husayn, the "prince of martyrs" (*shahid al-shuhada'*) central to both tales of the battle of Karbala and larger Shi'i narratives of redemptive suffering. Evidently the triumvirate of 'Ali, Hasan, and Husayn, as found within illustrated texts of a Shi'i bent, was not deemed appropriate for the depiction of a dream vision narrated according to an Ottoman Sunni-Sufi worldview.

As these examples clearly demonstrate, dream images played a significant role in the expressive traditions of various early modern mystical communities, especially the Naqshbandis and Mevlevis. The appearance of Muhammad in the visions of mystics could add a prophetic imprimatur to their respective doctrines and endeavors, from promoting silent *dhikr* to exalting the supreme position of Rumi's *Masnavi*. Moreover, paintings of prophetic dreams were not exempt from intraconfessional pressures, and artists were not silent when the time came to stake a position in the faith. They, too, engaged in sectarian polemics through pictorial stratagems, which could catalyze Sunni or Shi'i discourses at a time when the Ottoman and Safavid political split was crystallizing. That these Naqshbandi and Mevlevi paintings of prophetic dreams depict only three *rashidun* or only two members of the *ahl al-bayt* hints at the formation of a Sunni identity by subtraction, rather than addition, within Persian and Turkish artistic traditions of the fifteenth and sixteenth centuries. Thus, when Muhammad appears among dreaming or cogitating mystics, he is shown according to a variety of Sufi belief systems as well as embedded within the greater politicoreligious landscape of the early modern Islamic world.

Like Timurid and Ottoman painters, Persian artists produced dream images that catered to various mysticosectarian agendas. While paintings stemming from Sunni-Sufi milieus tend to display figural excision, those promoting a Shi'i Sufi worldview typically employ addition. During the sixteenth century, Safavid images tended to depict Muhammad accompanied by new protagonists and in different contexts, expanding the interpretive purview of the prophetic dream according to Shi'i religious imagination. In general, these types of visions of Muhammad could serve as visual confirmations of Safavid claims to prophetic heirship through the *tariqa*'s eponymous founder, Shaykh Safi al-Din Ardabili (d. 1334 CE). For this reason and others, Shaykh Safi al-Din is included in paintings of prophetic visions, either as the visionary agent or as a companion to the Prophet in dreams experienced by mystics of the Safawiyya order. In still other cases, Imam ʿAli, members of the *ahl al-bayt*, and the imams are included as well; this is especially the case for Safavid paintings of the last judgment, a topic that became more prominent as the *hijri* millennium (1591 CE) drew closer.

As founder of the Safawiyya order in Ardabil, Shaykh Safi al-Din served as the Safavids' genealogical and spiritual forefather. Consequently, a number of Safavid chronicles pay close attention to his life and deeds. The emphasis on his status as a descendant of Imam ʿAli and as a practitioner of Twelver Shiʿism, however, did not occur until during and after the reign of Shah Tahmasp (r. 1514–76 CE). The imagination of Safi al-Din as both ʿAlid and *sayyid* unfolded in multiple ways, including through the editing of older histories as well as the penning of new ones from the mid-sixteenth century onward. The most evident Safavid attempt to "Shiʿify" Safi al-Din occurred in 1533 CE when Shah Tahmasp ordered a revised edition of the biography of the Sufi *shaykh*, which was originally written by Ibn Bazzaz in 1358 CE under the title *Safvat al-Safa* (Quintessence of Purity). In the 1533 text of the *Safvat al-Safa*, Safi al-Din's lineage does not stop with Firuzshah Zarrin-Kulah, as in the 1358 edition. Instead, it is traced further back, to Imam ʿAli via Musa al-Kazim, the seventh imam. Moreover, Safi al-Din's religious affiliation is clearly shown to be Twelver Shiʿi rather than (more likely) Sunni.[109] One method by which to claim the Sufi *shaykh*'s adherence to Shiʿism consisted in removing declarations of his affection for the Prophet's companions (*sahaba*), as found in the 1358 edition, and replacing them with pronouncements of his love and following of the imams only, as found in the 1533 edition.[110] In comparing both editions of the *Quintessence of Purity*, moreover, it is clear that Safi al-Din's genealogy (*nasab*) was reframed as ʿAlid and his religious affiliation *(madhhab)* specified as Twelver Shiʿi during the first half of the sixteenth century so that the Sufi *shaykh*'s image could be properly tailored to Shah Tahmasp's politicoreligious agenda.

The *Safvat al-Safa* and other Safavid chronicles also pay special attention to Safi al-Din's miracles, including his many dreams. As Sholeh Quinn has demonstrated, the *shaykh*'s visions tend to include various celestial signs that were interpreted as confirming his supreme authority as a spiritual guide. They also were thought to prefigure the greatness of the Safavid dynastic line, whose ruling monarchs were deemed similarly anointed by divine sanction.[111] We are told that Safi al-Din had visions of the sun or rays of light in his dreams. One night, for example, he fell asleep in the congregational mosque of Ardabil and dreamed of a sun that illuminated the whole world. When he looked at it, the sun was his own face. When he asked his disciple Zahid to interpret the dream, Zahid responded that the sun stands for the *nur-i vilayat*[112]—an expression that can be translated as the "light of sainthood" or the "light of [ʿAli's] vicegerency." In yet another dream, Safi al-Din sees the sun covering his head and face. He asks his mother for an interpretation, to which she replies, "You will be a *shaykh* from whose teachings and guidance the entire world will be enlightened (*rushan*) and luminous (*nurani*)."[113] The *shaykh*'s dreams of the radiant sun thus served to confirm his status as a descendant of Muhammad, whose own light passed down to 'Ali. This light also augured the global spread of his illuminated teaching and anointed him as a rightful vicegerent of God. Safavid historians posited that his light was hereditary and so later passed on to the Safavid rulers, who were described as the "rising of the sun of kingship" (*tulu'-i aftab-i shahi*).[114] Such dreams and their interpretations thus draw a direct line from the Safavid monarchs to 'Ali and Muhammad through their spiritual founder, Safi al-Din, himself considered the carrier and perpetuator of divine light.

In the *Quintessence of Purity*, other dreams by Safi al-Din make use of light metaphors, among them the candle (*sham'*). While the candle could refer to a religious figure—including the Prophet Muhammad—it also could prefigure a particular political leader and his descendants. For example, in the sole surviving illustrated manuscript copy of the text, produced in the city of Shiraz in 1582 CE, Safi al-Din has a vision of the unfortunate fate of the Chupanids, who briefly ruled over western Eurasia from 1335 to 1357 CE (fig. 3.15).[115] In the painting's lower register, the Sufi *shaykh* is shown recumbent next to a flowering tree and rivulet, with two disciples asleep in the lower right corner. One arm is folded under his turban, as if to provide support for his head, heavy with slumber, while the other is gently placed on his chest. The dream that Safi al-Din witnesses (*khwab didan*) unfolds in the upper register, in which the *shaykh*, against a light pink landscape, approaches a circle of seven burning candles with a water jug. Although the iconography in the painting's upper portion is not especially surreal, the two-part horizontal paneling structurally distinguishes the earthly realm from the dream world.

Further information about the painting's content and message can be glossed from the accompanying text, in which Safi al-Din is recorded as stating, "Tonight I saw a desert and there were many candles (*sham'ha*) in it. They were all Chupanids and their offspring. I had water in my hand. I extinguished each one of the candles with a handful of water. I put out all except one that I left." The text continues by providing the author's explication of the dream, which notes that "time passed and it came to be that from Chupan's descendants only one branch remained who became rulers."[116] In this particular dream, Safi al-Din not only foresees the demise of the Chupanid rulers but, even more significantly, serves as the agent who extinguishes this dynasty.[117] Safi al-Din's premonitory dream may have been attributed to him posthumously by writers catering to Safavid dynastic interests.[118] Consequently, his dream vision—as both narrative and image—showcases the success of the Safawiyya order's religious and political ascendancy,

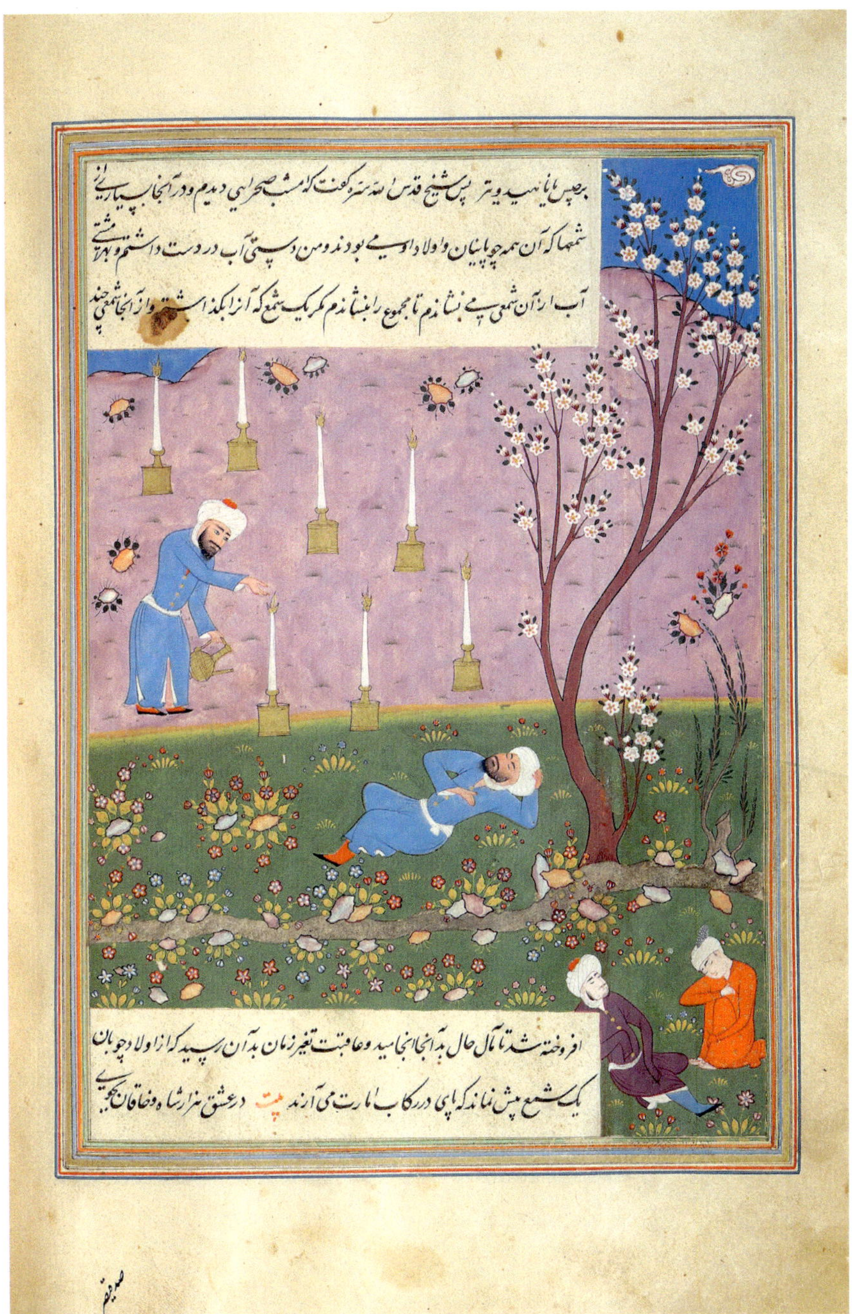

with its spiritual founding father symbolically limiting Chupanid rule to a brief interregnum.

While the candle could symbolize a dynastic line and its aborted power, in Safi al-Din's other dreams it serves as an object-analogy for the light of prophethood, vicegerency, and sainthood. It thus expresses religious rather than political authority. A single-page painting illustrating an unidentified text, possibly a copy of Ibn Bazzaz's *Quintessence of Purity* made in Shiraz during the last decades of the sixteenth century, depicts such a dream (fig. 3.16). Once again, the image is divided into two registers; in this case, however, the division is vertical rather than horizontal. The real world, in which Safi al-Din sleeps and dreams, is to the right, while the dream realm, in which the Prophet Muhammad sits on a *minbar* above four lit candles, appears on the left. The *shaykh* clearly slumbers in an indoor space, his body tucked in a gold-patterned red cover and his head supported by two oblong pillows. To his right and left, respectively, are a platter of pomegranates and a lit candle. Within the vertical dreamscape at left, the Prophet is depicted with a white facial veil and a large flaming nimbus as he gestures back to Safi al-Din with both hands. Even without reading the attendant text, the painting of the *shaykh*'s prophetic dream suggests that, although they inhabit two different spaces, both Muhammad and Safi al-Din are copresent and interact within the conjoint "world of likenesses" that is both pictorial image and dream realm.

The coincident character of both worlds appears to require no written interpretation, and in fact the surviving text on this single-page folio does not explore the symbolic interaction that is so carefully articulated within the painting. Instead, the narrative that accompanies the image relates that one night "they"—a respectful third-person plural pronoun most likely referring to Safi al-Din—had a vision while in a state between sleep and wakefulness. In the vision, Safi al-Din sees himself in the congregational mosque of Ardabil, where he notices a candle (*sham'*) placed on a *minbar*. That candle, the reader is explicitly told, is the Prophet Muhammad. Then, Safi al-Din sees that the whole courtyard is filled with candles, which are the prophets (*anbiya*) and saints (*awliya*). The text concludes by stating that "the dreamer the [*sic*] candle that was the Prophet." Although the rest of the narrative is unfortunately not available, it is possible to imagine that the dreamer (Safi al-Din) spoke with the Prophet-as-candle and perhaps inquired about the candles overtaking the courtyard of the Ardabil mosque. The painting suggests that Muhammad responded to the query, gesturing back to the dreaming *shaykh* and offering him the good news that he and his spiritual successors (of the Safawiyya order) are indeed the *awliya*. Through the dream vision, Muhammad, as seal of prophets and supreme spiritual master, here appears to initiate Safi al-Din into prophetic heirship.

Both the visual and textual elements of this painted episode recall other dreams experienced by Safi al-Din and by initiates of the Safawiyya order. As noted previously, while in the congregational mosque of Ardabil the *shaykh* also dreamed of a sun that symbolized his *nur-i vilayat*. In another case, a man named Pirah 'Izz al-Din, who initially had refused the spiritual guidance of Safi al-Din, had a dream vision of the Prophet while in the Ardabil mosque. In the vision, Muhammad appears seated on a chair, surrounded by a large group of prophets and saints as well as a man whose face is covered by a veil (*burqa'*). Pirah 'Izz al-Din asks the Prophet to show him a guide, to which Muhammad responds by giving his own name, followed by those of spiritual masters, while pointing to the person seated next to him. Pirah 'Izz al-din asks the Prophet about the man's identity. By way of response, Muhammad pulls aside the man's facial veil to reveal Safi al-Din, telling Pirah 'Izz

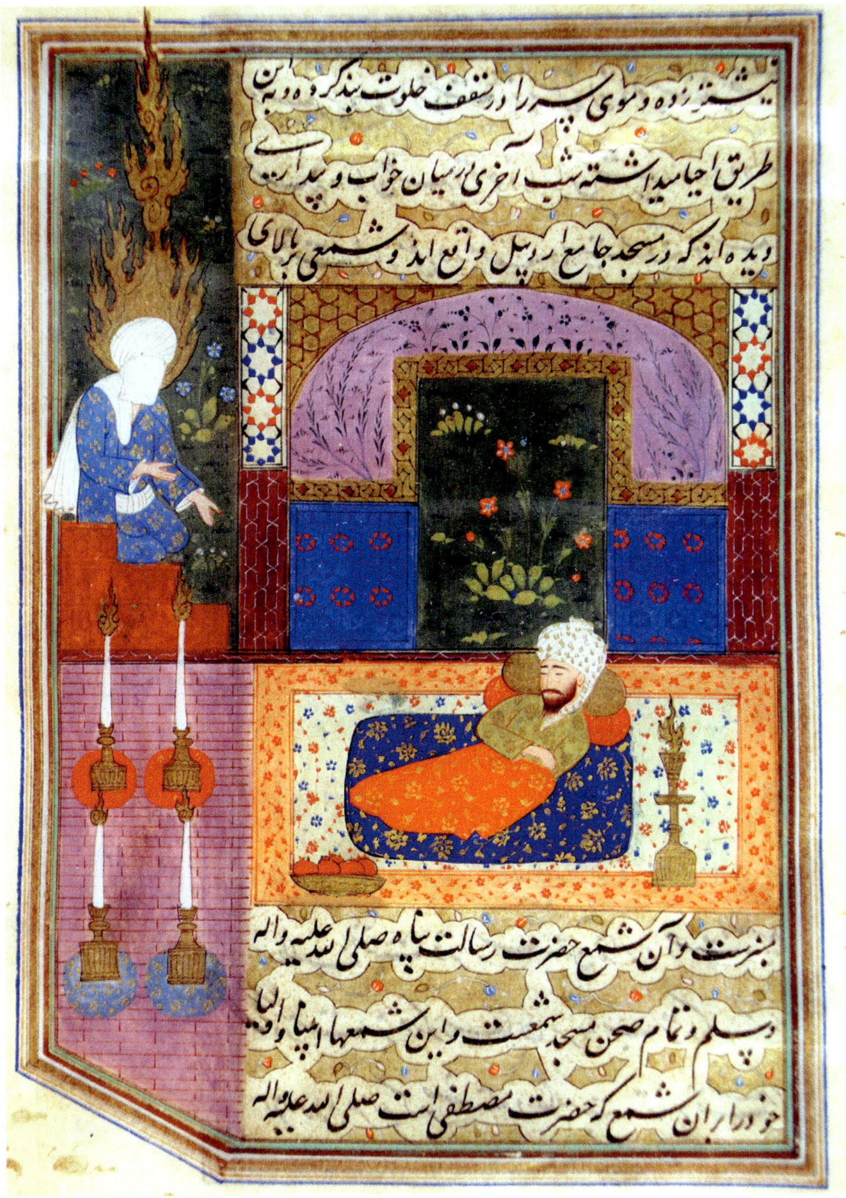

3.16. A mystic (probably Shaykh Safi al-Din) has a dream vision of the Prophet Muhammad, unidentified text (perhaps Ibn Bazzaz's *Safvat al-Safa*), possibly Shiraz, late sixteenth century CE. National Museum, Delhi, 61.572.

al-Din not to worry, as the *shaykh* would forgive him (for not believing in his spiritual leadership) on the Prophet's behalf. Muhammad then asks Safi al-Din to initiate Pirah ʿIzz al-Din into the Sufi *tariqa*. At this moment, Pirah ʿIzz al-Din awakes from his dream, goes to Safi al-Din, and recounts his vision; thereupon, the *shaykh* initiates him into the Safawiyya order.[119] The nonbelieving subject is here convinced to join the *tariqa* by means of a prophetic dream, in which Muhammad quite literally removes the veil on the identity of his living spiritual descendant, Shaykh Safi al-Din of Ardabil.

These prophetic visions take center stage in chapter 19 of Ibn Bazzaz's *Quintessence of Purity*, which is dedicated entirely to dreams of the Prophet. In these dreams, oftentimes Muhammad guides individuals to the community (*umma*) of Safi al-Din.[120] Moreover, Muhammad is typically depicted as chief spiritual initiator as well as convertor to the proper faith. For example, in one instance, a certain man named

Sayyid Mushrif al-Din has a vision of the Prophet, and, when he looks at Muhammad's face, he sees the visage of Safi al-Din. On awakening, he asks to be initiated into the Safawiyya order by Safi al-Din.[121] In another case, a Christian man named Ibrahim has a dream in which the Prophet helps him convert to Islam. When he asks Muhammad for guidance concerning the laws and manners of the right spiritual path, the Prophet responds by telling him to follow his pious offspring and his vicegerent-saint (*khalifa*), Safi al-Din.[122] Once awake, Ibrahim seeks out Safi al-Din, who guides him to the faith. As can be seen from these textual passages, in one case, the Sufi *shaykh* initiates a disciple into the Safawiyya order, while in another he converts a nonbeliever to the proper (Shi'i Sufi) faith through the intercession and imprimatur of a prophetic dream.

Taken as a whole, visions of Muhammad as described in the *Quintessence of Purity* aim to depict Safi al-Din as supreme authority and guide for the mystic who has embarked on a journey toward divine knowledge and salvation. They also couch the state of *wali*-hood as a triad of descent, vicegerency, and saintliness as well as a form of "esoteric prophecy" (*nubuvvat batiniyya*) particular to the founding father of the Safawiyya order.[123] Furthermore, in Safavid textual sources the Prophet and the *shaykh* are conceptually aligned in other ways: Muhammad is the repository of prophethood (*nubuvvat*) while Safi al-Din is the possessor of vicegerency and sainthood (*valayat*); Muhammad receives revelation (*wahy*) while Safi al-Din experiences divine inspiration (*ilham*); and Muhammad is able to perform miracles (*mu'jizat*) while Safi al-Din likewise is capable of producing marvels (*karamat*).[124] The Sufi master is likened to the Prophet through these parallels in personhood and performance; he also is rendered Muhammad-like by analogical statements, including Ibn Bazzaz's rhyming maxim "The *shaykh* is among his people as the Prophet is among his community" (*al-shaykh fi qawmihi ka'l-nabi fi ummatihi*).[125] Within the framework of Sufi Shi'i prophetology, both Muhammad and Safi al-Din were often conjoined rhetorically because both served as supreme spiritual guides and embodiments of religious purity.

In Safavid texts and images, Safi al-Din is also linked to Imam 'Ali, the figurehead of Shi'i Islam, as well as the Hidden Imam, who arises as Mahdi and leads his community to salvation after the end of time.[126] These many symbolic overlaps among the Sufi *shaykh*, the Prophet Muhammad, Imam 'Ali, and the Mahdi are a hallmark of dream visions, apocalyptic tales, and messianic discourses in early modern Iran. Such obfuscations also are found in a painting included in the chapter on dreams within a unique illustrated manuscript of Ibn Bazzaz's *Quintessence of Purity* made in 1582 CE (fig. 3.17).[127] In this complex visual amalgam, the viewer is confronted with several turbaned figures—two of whom are veiled, bear flaming halos, and are seated on beasts (Buraq and a camel), while three others stand behind Buraq or before the camel;

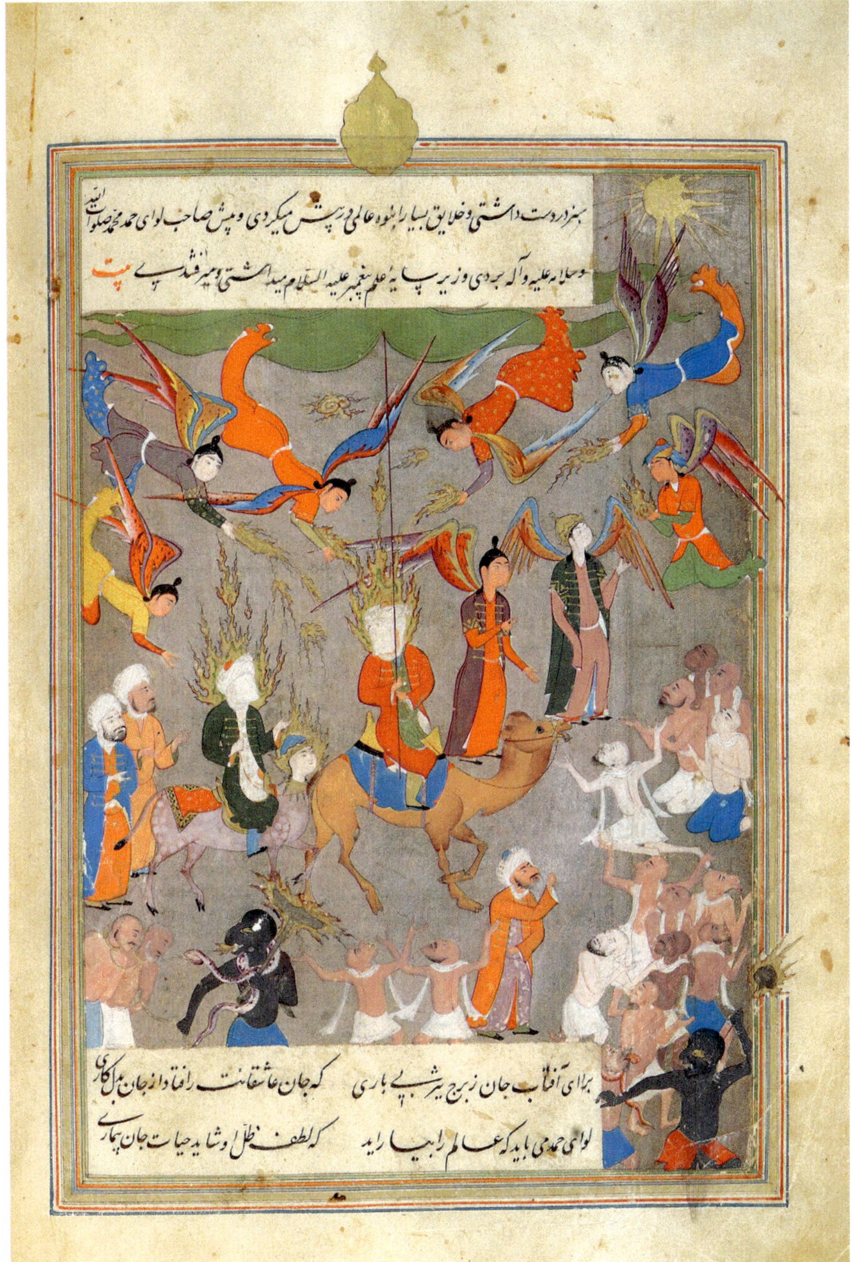

3.17. Pirah 'Ali Pirniqi's apocalyptic vision of the Prophet Muhammad and Shaykh Safi al-Din, Ibn Bazzaz, *Safvat al-Safa* (Quintessence of Purity), Shiraz, 990 AH/1582 CE. Aga Khan Museum, Toronto, Ms. 264, folio 115v.

they approach shackled prisoners who are tormented by demons and beg the protagonists' help and forgiveness. Above this populated scene, a semicircle of flying angels pour rays of golden light onto the veiled camel rider, whose large green banner punctures the text frame above. These many pictorial elements suggest an apocalyptic vision of the last judgment or a tale related to the Prophet's ascension.

Although not entirely conclusive, the painting's accompanying text provides help in identifying the figures. In this illustrated section of Ibn Bazzaz's text, a certain Pirah Siraj reports that his father, Pirah 'Ali Pirniqi, had a dream of Safi al-Din. In the dream, the Sufi *shaykh* was seen holding a green staff (*'asa-yi sabz*) in his hand as he led a large group of people to the "possessor of the banner" (*sahib-i liwa*), Muhammad

Mustafa, so that they could be under his protection, or shadow (*sayah*). Then follow verses of poetry (located at the bottom of the painting) that petition the Prophet, nicknamed the "sun of life" (*aftab-i jan*), to rise and comfort the souls of his followers. The verses also describe Muhammad's "banner of praise" (*liwa al-hamd*) as a necessary ornament for the world and a shade for the souls of those who are ill.[128] Thus, the text surrounding the painting suggests that the depiction represents Pirah 'Ali Pirniqi's dream of Safi al-Din, who in the vision carries a green staff as he leads a number of individuals to the Prophet Muhammad, twice mentioned in conjunction with the banner of praise that is raised on the day of resurrection. It is at this time that the Prophet intercedes on behalf of members of his community, whose deeds are weighed and fates sealed. In light of such textual details, the painting seems to depict a visionary dream of Safi al-Din within a last judgment context, the motifs and messages of which accord with the overarching narrative of Ibn Bazzaz's biography of the Sufi *shaykh*.

Although the written narrative provides some aid in interpreting the painting, the text and image display several noticeable inconsistencies. For one, although the text makes no mention of Buraq, Muhammad can be identified as the rider of this human-headed flying steed, a key part of his prophetic equipage.[129] Additionally, the text's mention of the "banner of praise" pays tribute to the Prophet in his role as intercessor (*shafi*) on the day of judgment. However, in the painting the banner is held not by Muhammad but by the camel rider, who in this instance must be identified as Safi al-Din. There are a number of reasons for this identification: first, the *shaykh* is the central protagonist in Pirah 'Ali Pirniqi's dream vision; second, although the text describes Safi al-Din's green staff, here he holds a comparable green signpost; and, third, a number of other depictions of Safi al-Din within the same manuscript depict him wearing a green robe with a red cloak, as can be seen in a painting of the *shaykh* on horseback (fig. 3.18). Without a doubt, the camel rider holding the banner of praise is the Sufi *shaykh* rather than the Prophet Muhammad or Imam 'Ali, both of whom are otherwise frequently coupled with the green banner in Safavid paintings depicting the last judgment, imams in paradise, and deceased souls brought together for the day of gathering (figs. 3.19–3.20).[130] However, in the *Quintessence of Purity* scene, the banner of praise belongs to Safi al-Din, thereby suggesting that the *shaykh*—and not Muhammad—has the power to intercede on behalf of his community of believers. In the apocalyptic dream painting, Safi al-Din appears utterly prophet-like in his eschatological position and responsibilities.

The representation of Shaykh Safi al-Din in figure 3.17 is unusual in other ways as well. In the manuscript's other paintings, the *shaykh* neither bears a facial veil and flaming nimbus nor rides a camel. In general, within Safavid pictorial practices the veil and aureole are attributes reserved for Muhammad, 'Ali, and (at times) the imams, who partake in the light of Muhammad or are considered ontologically preexistent

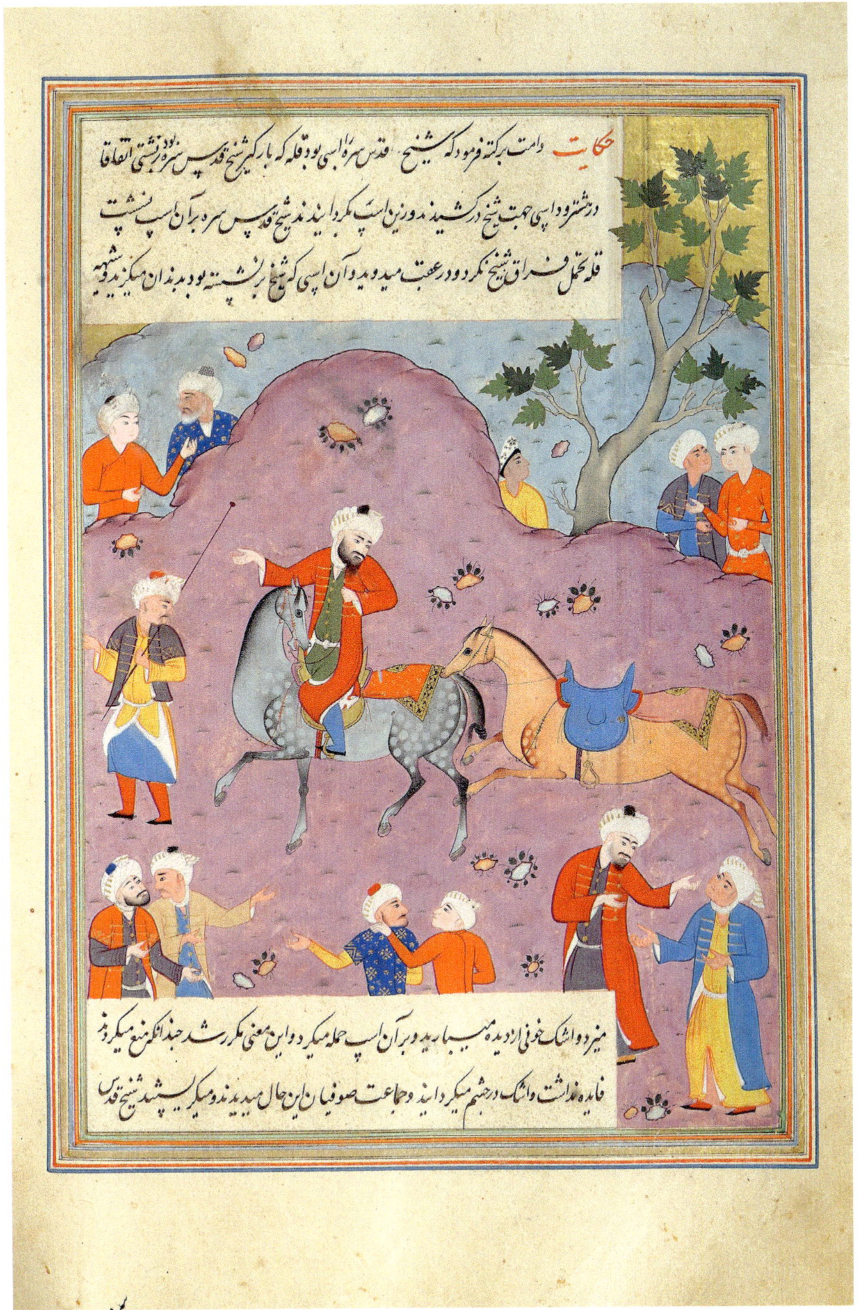

3.18. Shaykh Safi al-Din on horseback as one of his favorite horses attacks the mount, Ibn Bazzaz, *Safvat al-Safa* (Quintessence of Purity), Shiraz, 990 AH/1582 CE. Aga Khan Museum, Toronto, Ms. 264, folio 268v.

as silhouettes of light. Safi al-Din is almost never depicted according to such conventions. That said, Ibn Bazzaz's *Quintessence of Purity* describes mystics who had visions of the *shaykh* wearing a facial veil. In one instance, Safi al-Din's veil is removed from his face to reveal his spiritual leadership to Pirah ʿIzz al-Din. In another dream narrative, the veil serves to contain Safi al-Din's divine luminescence. As Ibn Bazzaz reports, the *shaykh* was so surrounded by light that no one was able to look at his blessed face directly.[131] It thus becomes clear that the facial veil and radiant nimbus are attributes of Safi al-Din when he is witnessed not in reality but in a dream vision. As such, the veil and aureole serve as proof, sent from the "world of the unseen," of the *shaykh* partaking in the light of prophecy, revelation, and guardianship. Just

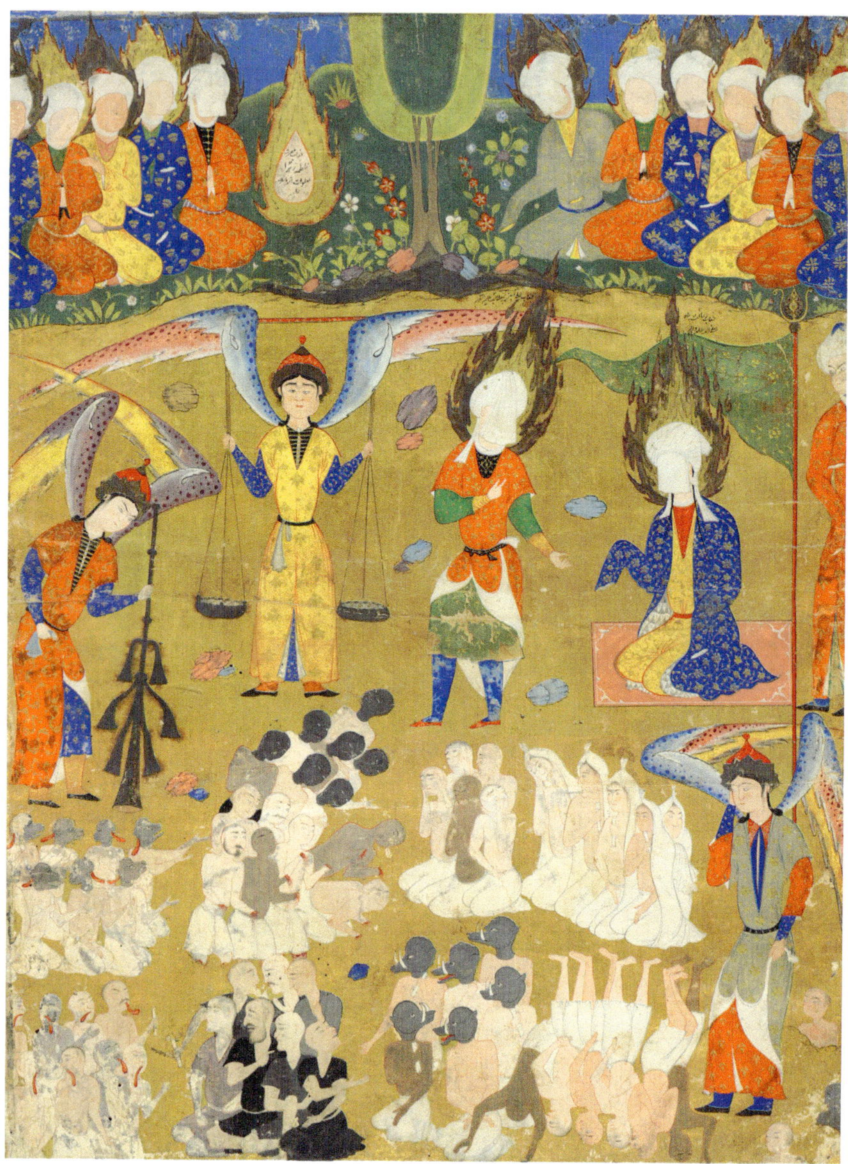

as importantly, both iconographic details could enable Persian painters and viewers to visually equate the Sufi *shaykh* to both the Prophet
Muhammad and Imam ʿAli, thereby elevating Safi al-Din to an utmost
rank in the hierarchical chain of saintliness according to Safavid Shiʿi
creed and pictorial systems.

Beyond the facial veil and flaming nimbus, Safi al-Din's position,
size, and beast of burden bear further symbolic implications. First, the
shaykh is placed at the very center of the composition, serving as a pivot
around which figures converge and events unfold. Second, his stature is
also noticeably oversized: in comparison to the other figures depicted
in the scene, he appears to be of superhuman dimensions. He even
dwarfs the Prophet Muhammad, who is seated behind him on a rather
diminutive Buraq. Through central positioning and relative size, Safi
al-Din becomes the focal point of both painting and devotion. Finally,
the fact that he is depicted riding a camel bears unmistakable prophetic
and messianic connotations. As discussed in chapter 2, the camel was

   THE PRAISEWORTHY ONE

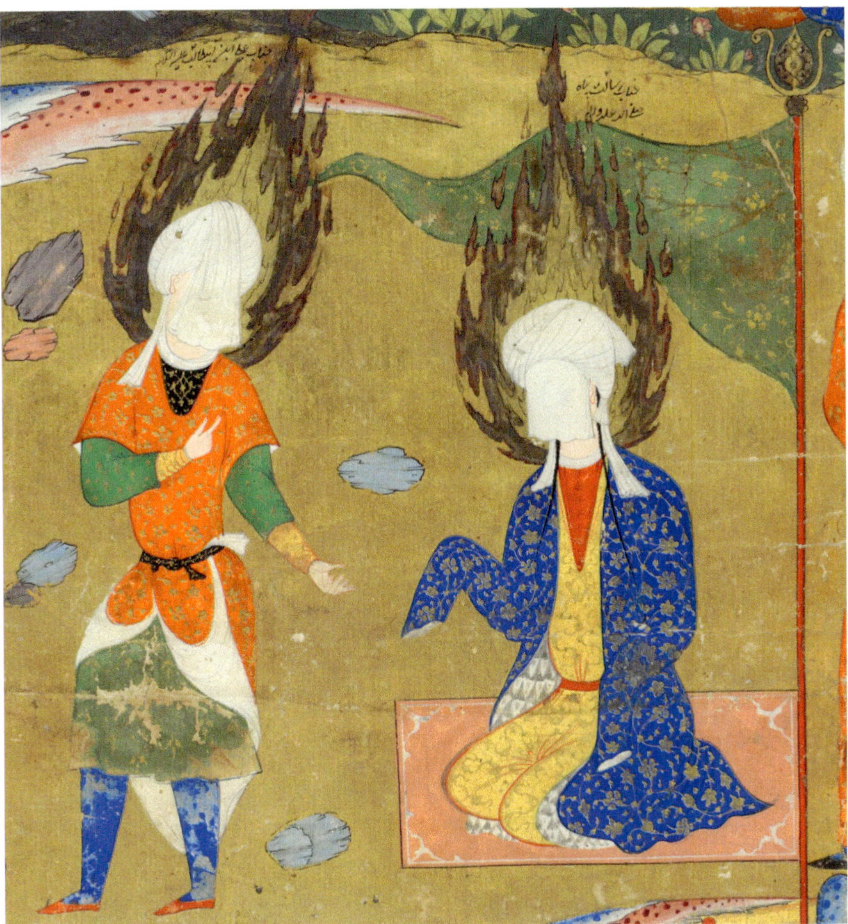

3.20. Detail of figure 3.19 showing Muhammad (right) and 'Ali (left), with identifying captions inscribed above their flaming nimbi, interceding on behalf of sinners during the last judgment.

associated with Muhammad (and the donkey with Jesus), as can be seen in the depiction of Isaiah's vision (figs. 2.1–2.2). Moreover, in Islamic apocalyptic literature, the Prophet is described as arriving at the end of time as the awaited "camel rider" (*rakib al-jamal*).[132] The camel functions as a proof of Muhammad's prophecy as well as an annunciation of his arrival on the day of judgment, at which time he fulfills his role as intercessor for his community. In the painting, conversely, the announced and awaited camel rider capable of intercession is not Muhammad but Safi al-Din, whose facial veil and flaming aureole similarly grant him the aura of prophethood.

Through pictorial stratagems, the Sufi *shaykh*'s presence is enlarged and his status ennobled within the context of an apocalyptic dream. Such visions of, and flights into, the afterworld were by no means a new motif, however. Within Islamic literary and artistic traditions, the Prophet's *mi'raj* functioned as a powerful apocalyptic tale that could support sectarian claims: if presented to a Sunni audience, it could promote the first three *rashidun*, while in Shi'i milieus it could laud 'Ali's supreme celestial position.

After the declaration of Shi'ism as the official religion of Savafid Iran in 1501 CE, Persian paintings of the *mi'raj* often included pictorial details stressing Shi'i supremacy. Chief among these is the inclusion of Imam 'Ali as a leonine angel, whom Muhammad witnessed in the

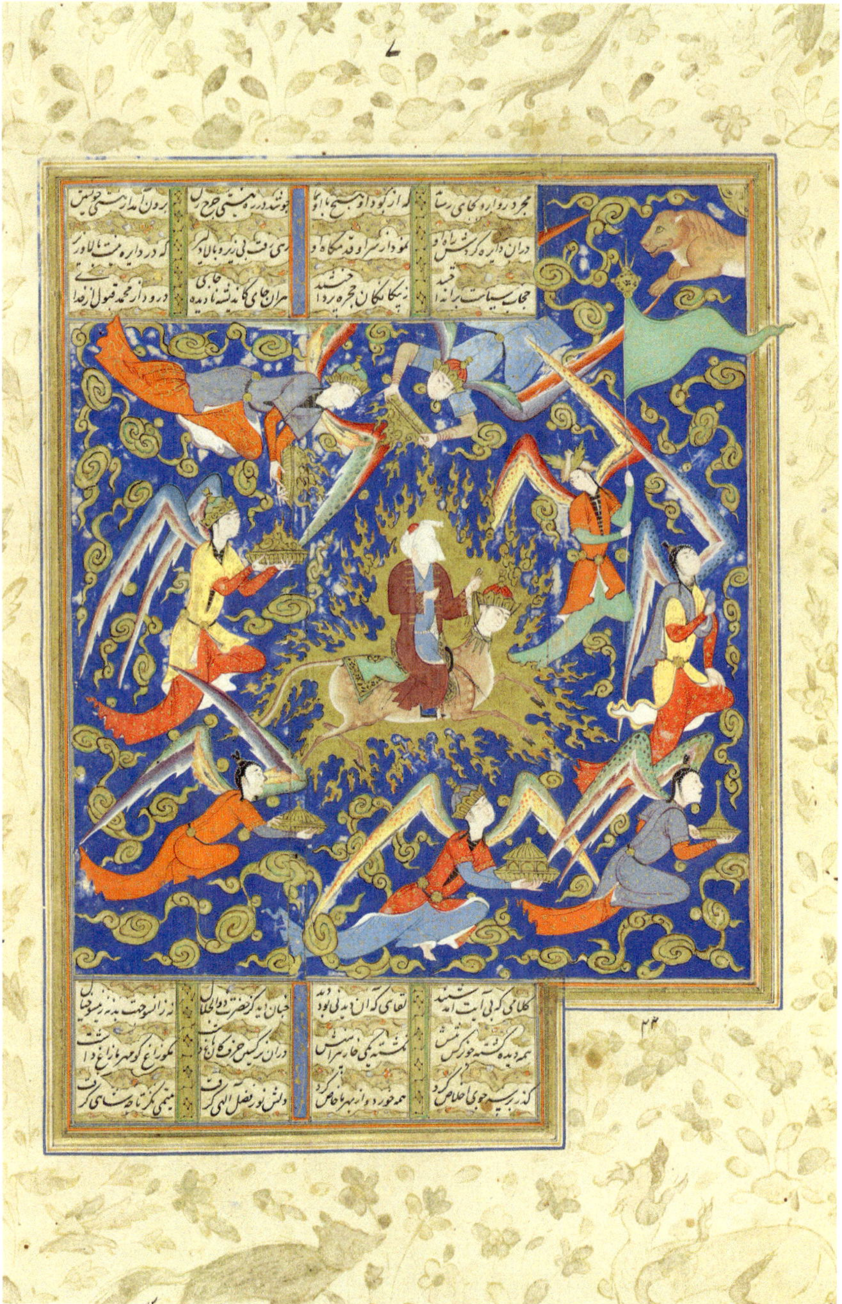

utmost heaven and from whom he was granted his own authority (fig. 3.21).[133] While the lion is not included in the painting of the apocalyptic dream of Safi al-Din in Ibn Bazzaz's *Quintessence of Purity*, other Safavid *miʿraj* pictorial elements have been adopted and adapted for the illustrated Safavid *tazkira*. For example, Muhammad rides Buraq, but now he is placed off center in the composition; the green banner is held aloft by Safi al-Din and not the Angel Gabriel; and a circling group of angels pour rays of light on Safi al-Din rather than on the Prophet Muhammad. Without a doubt, the artist(s) who composed the painting of the apocalyptic vision of the Sufi *shaykh* drew on, and strategically altered, ascension motifs that were prevalent in Iran during the second half of the sixteenth century.

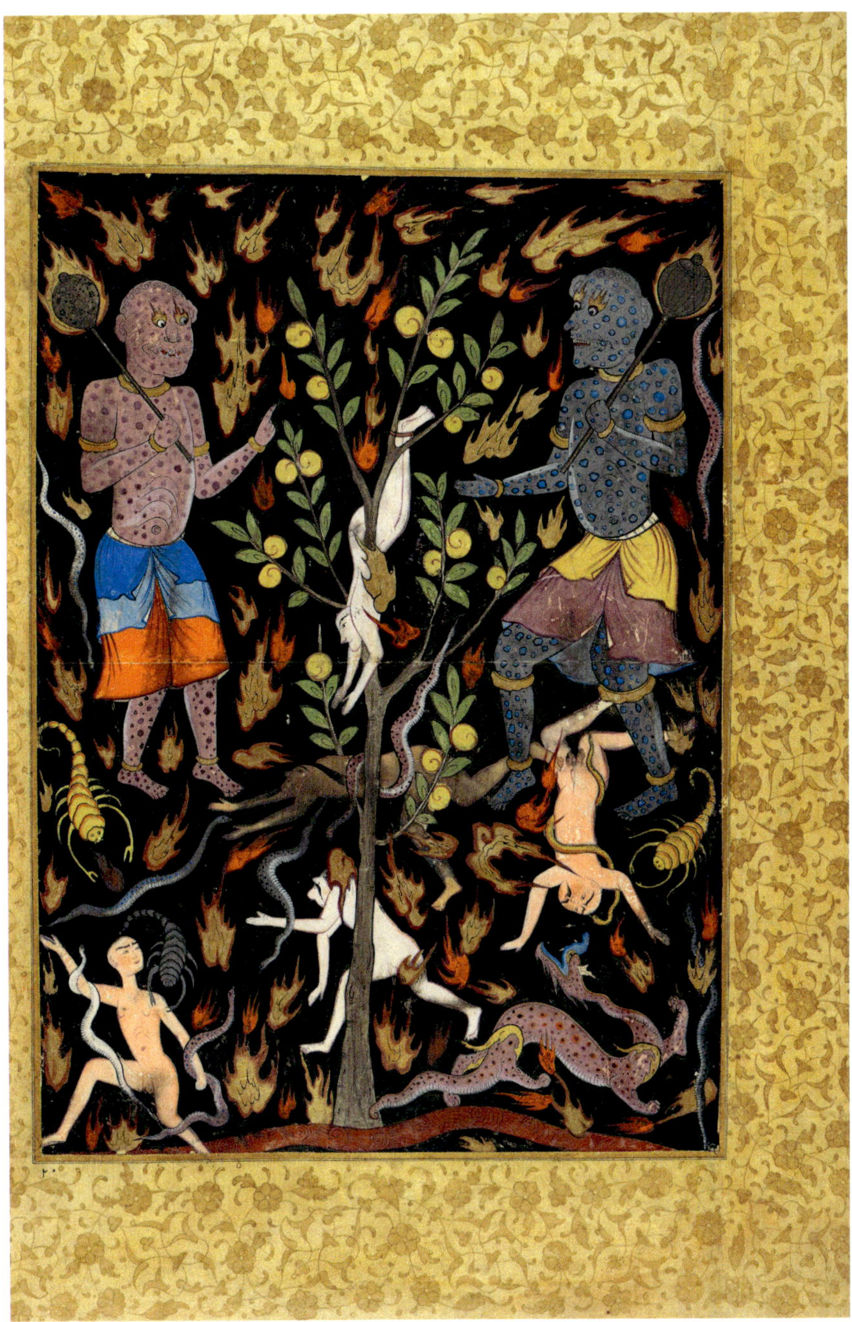

In Sufi circles, the Prophet's ascent acted as a symbolic foil for the mystic's spiritual journey. It is therefore not entirely surprising to find it discussed within Ibn Bazzaz's *Quintessence of Purity*. This biography records that Safi al-Din was asked whether Muhammad's ascension was physical or spiritual. The *shaykh* responded to the inquiry by stating that Muhammad performed his *mi'raj* with his blessed body, itself a radiant (*nurani*) entity that casts no shadow.[134] Safi al-Din is also recorded as stating that, on his return from the ascension, the Prophet saw a group of women in hell, where demons were cutting their flesh with fiery scissors. The *shaykh* informs his listeners that these women bore children out of wedlock. He then boldly declares that any group or nation (*qawmi*) that claims spiritual guidance (*irshad*) will be punished seventy times harsher than this."[135] This comparative caveat, deftly extrapolated from the *mi'raj* narrative, insinuates that spiritual leadership, authority, and guidance belong to Safi al-Din; other claimants and their followers will be doomed to hell, where they will be severely punished.

In Ibn Bazzaz's biography, the Sufi *shaykh* claims knowledge of the afterworld through the ascension trope in order to demonstrate that his *tariqa* provides the path to salvation. The painting in turn mobilizes varied motifs by depicting Safi al-Din as the awaited camel rider, accompanied by the Prophet and angels, with three other mystics (possibly Pirah Siraj, Pirah 'Ali Pirniqi, and Pirah 'Abdallah) on foot. All protagonists appear to approach and intercede for the assembled souls, some of whom are beaten by demons or ensnared by snakes. Along with their darkened skin tones, signifying inner decay, their tortures indicate that they are bound for hell.[136] To the dream, apocalyptic, and ascension motifs is thus added the chthonic theme, which is also included in Safavid illustrated manuscripts, in particular illustrated *Falnama*s (Books of Omens) produced during the second half of the sixteenth century (fig. 3.22).[137] Intended for prognostication and anticipating the millennium, *Falnama* paintings are accompanied by good or bad omens. If the viewer chances on the image of hell illustrated in figure 3.22, the augury asks why he foolishly prepares himself for hellfire by following the devil, urging him to repent by lighting candles at mosques and shrines as well as to engage in acts of charity.[138] By borrowing from the iconography of hell within Persian omen books, the painting of Safi al-Din in *apocalypsis* within Ibn Bazzaz's illustrated biography invites its viewership to follow the prophetic path toward salvation, which here is pictured as that of the Sufi *shaykh* and his visionary followers.

PICTURING A
PROPHETIC LEGACY

Between about 1485 and 1600 CE, a number of paintings depicting mystical dreams of the Prophet were produced in Turco-Persian cultural spheres. While such images reflect a clear growth in Sufism and sectarianism during the early modern period, they also provide powerful testament to practices of picture making. Whether emanating from the visionary world of the mystic or from the artist's painted page, dream images act as arenas for spiritual seeing as well as thresholds into a world of likenesses. In this *'alam al-mithal*, the presence of the Prophet is considered a literal analogue and hence real. For these reasons, images of prophetic dreams shirk complete abstraction and instead show Muhammad as an ontological reality—as a *haqiqa muhammadiyya*—even if this reality remains immaterial or representational. Whether in the dream world or in figural arts, such images suspend the viewer between form and substance, enabling him to establish a bond of affection with the Prophet by visiting and seeing, even if briefly, a special place of in-between.

In the end, paintings of prophetic dreams act as visual externalizations of internal experiences. While their outward forms invite literalism, they nevertheless suggest—and perhaps are intended to catalyze—

inner visions for dreamers in their attempts to establish contact with the spiritual realm and its exalted occupants. Whether in dreams or in paintings, Muhammad is shown as eternally living in the spirit through both telepathic communications and visual representations. Both realms of likenesses offer glad tidings (*mubashshirat*),[139] one of which heralds the dream as an allotment of Muhammad's prophecy. Such glad tidings are believed to continue through visions experienced by generations of believers. Thus, by gazing on Muhammad, both musing mystics and viewers of images are invited to partake in and extend the prophetic legacy.

1. Aflaki, *The Feats of the Knowers of God*, 540.

2. For an overview of Sufi Islam, see Schimmel, *Mystical Dimensions of Islam*; and Nicholson, *The Mystics of Islam*.

3. Katz, "Dreams and Their Interpretations in Sufi Thought and Practice," 182; and Bashir, "Narrating Sight," 233.

4. Ohlander, "Behind the Veil of the Unseen," 207.

5. On the "realm of likenesses" in Sufi thought and writing, see Rahman, "Dream, Imagination, and 'Alam al-Mithal."

6. On the premise that the imaginative faculty (*khayal*) is a sixth sense, see, in particular, Suhrawardi, *The Philosophy of Illumination*, 136–38.

7. On the theme of suspension, see Corbin, "The Visionary Dream in Islamic Spirituality," 407.

8. Katz, "Dreams and Their Interpretations in Sufi Thought and Practice," 187.

9. Green, "The Religious and Cultural Roles of Dreams and Visions in Islam," 295.

10. Katz, "Dreams and Their Interpretations in Sufi Thought and Practice," 189.

11. Corbin, "The Visionary Dream in Islamic Spirituality," 397–98, per the Shi'i mystic Shams al-Din Lahiji (d. 1506 CE).

12. See Corbin, "The Visionary Dream in Islamic Spirituality," 395, for the Persian *shaykh* Najm al-Din Kubra's (d. 1221 CE) discussion of the "person of light" (*shakhs min nur*).

13. Q 75:22–23: "Some faces that day will be radiant, looking (*nazaratun*) at their Lord." For an overview of the debates over the modality of "seeing" God, see Gimaret, "Ru'yat Allah"; and Lory, *Le rêve et ses interpretations en Islam*, 139–45, 196–203.

14. On dreams of God, see Schimmel, *Die Träume des Kalifen*, 159–72.

15. Al-Bukhari, *Sahih*, vol. 9, 104 (book 87, numbers 122 and 123). Both sayings use the term *sleep* (*manam*) in lieu of *vision* (*ru'ya*).

16. Lory, "La vision du Prophète en rêve dans l'onirocritique musulmane," 189.

17. Ibn Sirin's statement appears alongside the veridical dream Hadith in al-Bukhari, *Sahih*, vol. 9, 104 (book 87, number 122); and Ibn Sirin, *Le grand livre de l'interprétation des rêves*, 87.

18. In this case, the Prophet's body could symbolize the whole faith community or reflect the power of the ruler. Lory, *Le rêve et ses interpretations en Islam*, 154.

19. Kinberg, "Literal Dreams and Prophetic Hadiths in Classical Islam," 282.

20. On dreams of Muhammad as a book critic and ghostwriter, see Schimmel, *Die Träume des Kalifen*, 258.

21. Ibn Sirin, *Le grand livre de l'interprétation des rêves*, 87.

22. Ter Haar, "The Importance of the Spiritual Guide in the Naqshbandi Order," 314, citing Jami's biography of Sufi saints entitled *Nafahat al-Uns* (Breaths of Intimacy).

23. Forbes Manz, *Power, Politics, and Religion in Timurid Iran*, 187n34.

24. Baqli, *The Unveiling of Secrets*, 19.

25. Baqli, *The Unveiling of Secrets*, 21, 29.

26. Baqli, *The Unveiling of Secrets*, 61, 75. On the symbol of the rose in the *Kashf al-Asrar*, see Ernst, *Ruzbihan Baqli*, 66–67.

27. Baqli, *The Unveiling of Secrets*, 11, 31, 81.

28. Baqli, *The Unveiling of Secrets*, 127.

29. Information about the manuscript and reproductions of this particular painting can be found in Robinson, *A Descriptive Catalogue of the Persian Paintings in the Bodleian Library*, 65–67; Stchoukine, *Les peintures des manuscrits tîmûrides*, plate 72 (the painting is here attributed to Bihzad); and Arnold, *Painting in Islam*, plate XXII.

30. The manuscript is now held in two collections in Great Britain. Four of the five books are held in the Bodleian Library, Oxford (MSS Elliott 287, 408, 317, and 339), and one is preserved in the John Rylands Library, Manchester (Turk. MSS M3; see Robinson, *Persian Painting in the*

John Rylands Library, 116–17). For further information about Badiʿ al-Zaman, see Maria Subtelny, "Badiʿ-al-Zaman," *Encyclopaedia Iranica*, http://www.iranicaonline.org/articles/badi-al-zaman-b (accessed May 10, 2018).

31. The Naqshbandi order spread to Herat with Khwaja ʿUbaydallah Ahrar, the spiritual guide of the Timurid Sultan Abu Saʿid (r. 1424–69 CE). See Algar, "The Naqshbandi Order," 138.

32. This is the dream of the Kubrawi Sufi, Saʿd al-Din, as given in Green, "The Religious and Cultural Roles of Dreams and Visions in Islam," 310.

33. Porter, *Peinture et arts du livre*, 1068–109. A *majlis-sazi* is frequently used to depict banqueting scenes, battles, and hunts in Persian painterly traditions.

34. The ends of Muhammad's turban were loosely wrapped over his shoulders; see al-Tirmidhi, *Shamaʾil al-Nabi*, 56; and Hosein, "A Translation of the Ash-Shamaʾil of Tirmizi," 48.

35. Conversely, Thomas Arnold identifies the scribe not as ʿUthman but as Muhammad's secretary, Zayd b. Thabit, and ʿAli as the dark-faced man carrying a sword in the lower right corner. See Arnold, *Painting in Islam*, 97.

36. See the genealogical table of the Naqshbandi Sufi order in Weismann, *The Nashbandiyya*, 23,

37. On the Prophet's scent as sandalwood, musk, and ambergris, see Nizami, *The Haft Paykar*, 6–10; and on his rose scent, see Nizami, *Makhzanol Asrar*, 109, verse 268.

38. Algar, "The Naqshbandi Order," 137. While "binding image" is the preferred interpretation of Baha al-Din's *laqab*, the term *naqshband* may also indicate that Baha al-Din was a weaver or tracer of designs in metalwork—hence the popularity of the order among artists and artisans.

39. Algar, "Devotional Practices of the Khalidi Naqshbandis of Ottoman Turkey," 213; Ter Haar, "The Importance of the Spiritual Guide in the Naqshbandi Order," 312; and Bashir, "Narrating Sight," 243.

40. Algar, "Devotional Practices of the Khalidi Naqshbandis of Ottoman Turkey," 217.

41. Algar, "Devotional Practices of the Khalidi Naqshbandis of Ottoman Turkey," 213–15.

42. Algar, "Devotional Practices of the Khalidi Naqshbandis of Ottoman Turkey," 217–18; and Weismann, *The Naqshbandiyya*, 29.

43. Under Nava'i's auspices, the Naqshbandi order was granted rich endowments, and its influence reached the ruler, Sultan Husayn Bayqara. Weismann, *The Naqshbandiyya*, 33.

44. Algar, "The Naqshbandi Order," 140.

45. On dreams as events or episodes (*waqayiʿ*), see Ohlander, "Behind the Veil of the Unseen," 202, 205; and Katz, "Dreams and Their Interpretations in Sufi Thought and Practice," 188. On Muhammad's posthumous initiatic activity, see Algar, "The Naqshbandi Order," 131.

46. The painting is reproduced in Gray, *The Arts of the Book in Central Asia*, 185, fig. 107; and Subtelny, "The Cult of ʿAbdallah Ansari under the Timurids," 395.

47. Subtelny, "The Cult of ʿAbdallah Ansari under the Timurids," 383–84. Ansari's honorific title, "champion of the Sunna" (*nasir al-sunna*), is given by Jami in his *Nafahat al-Uns*.

48. Subtelny, "The Cult of ʿAbdallah Ansari under the Timurids," 400–401.

49. On the Ansari shrine as a *hazira*-compound, see Golombek, *The Timurid Shrine at Gazur Gah*, 109–21; and Subtelny, "The Cult of ʿAbdallah Ansari under the Timurids," 389–91.

50. Subtelny, "The Cult of ʿAbdallah Ansari under the Timurids," 382.

51. On Timurid literary-artistic circles or soirées (*majalis*)—in which members of the Timurid court, such as Sultan Husayn Bayqara and Nava'i, would engage in word games and riddles—see Subtelny, "Scenes from the Literary Life of Timurid Herat."

52. English translation provided in Subtelny, "The Cult of ʿAbdallah Ansari under the Timurids," 394–96.

53. Ter Haar, "The Importance of the Spiritual Guide in the Naqshbandi Order," 315; Algar, "Devotional Practices of the Khalidi Naqshbandis of Ottoman Turkey," 213–14; Chodkiewicz, "Quelques aspects des techniques spirituelles dans la *tariqa* Naqshbandiyya," 79; and Schimmel, *Mystical Dimensions of Islam*, 366.

54. Nava'i retired to the honorary post of sweeper at the Ansari shrine in 1499 CE, fourteen years after the production of the manuscript. Subtelny, "The Cult of ʿAbdallah Ansari under the Timurids," 396.

55. Subtelny, "The Cult of ʿAbdallah Ansari under the Timurids," 396.

56. Kia, "Sufi Orthopraxis," 4.

57. Le Gall, "Forgotten Naqshbandis and the Culture of Pre-modern Sufi Brotherhoods," 109; Algar, "The Naqshbandi Order," 128–30; and Weismann, *The Naqshbandiyya*, 23.

58. On tactics of realism, see Barthes, "The Reality Effect."

59. Chittick, "The Perfect Man as the Prototype of the Self in the Sufism of Jami," 137n1.

60. For a preliminary discussion of the painting, see Gruber, "Between Logos (*Kalima*) and Light (*Nur*)," 11–12, fig. 6; and Ekhtiar et al., *Masterpieces from the Department of Islamic Art in the Metropolitan Museum of Art*, 199–200, fig. 136B.

61. On the Shaybanid school of painting, see, inter alia, Ashrafi-Aini, "The School of Bukhara to c. 1550"; Schmitz, "Bukhara VI"; and Bahari, "The Sixteenth Century School of Bukhara Painting and the Arts of the Book."

62. Cited in Ashrafi-Aini, "The School of Bukhara to c. 1550," 263n24; and Subtelny, "Art and Politics in Early 16th Century Central Asia," 148.

63. Yusupova, "Evolution of Architecture of the Sufi Complexes of Bukhara," 127–28.

64. Yusupova, "Evolution of Architecture of the Sufi Complexes of Bukhara," 130.

65. Subtelny, "Art and Politics in Early 16th Century Central Asia," 142.

66. Sa'di, *Morals Pointed and Tales Adorned*, 7, line 73; and Khaza'ili, *Sharh-i Bustan*, 13.

67. Sa'di, *Morals Pointed and Tales Adorned*, 7, line 75, and 8, lines 95–96; and Khaza'ili, *Sharh-i Bustan*, 18.

68. Sa'di, *Morals Pointed and Tales Adorned*, 7, lines 85–86, and 8, lines 101–2; and Khaza'ili, *Sharh-i Bustan*, 16.

69. Weismann, *The Naqshbandiyya*, 29; and Chodkiewicz, "Quelques aspects des techniques spirituelles dans la *tariqa* Naqshbandiyya," 74.

70. Le Gall, "Forgotten Naqshbandis and the Culture of Pre-modern Sufi Brotherhoods," 93, 108; Algar, "The Naqshbandi Order," 129; and Weismann, *The Naqshbandiyya*, 24.

71. Algar, "The Naqshbandi Order," 129; and Bashir, "Narrating Sight," 243.

72. Anawati, "Le nom suprême de Dieu."

73. Al-Ghazali, *The Name & the Named*, 45–47.

74. Ibn 'Arabi, *On the Mysteries of Bearing Witness to the Oneness of God and Prophethood of Muhammad*, 40–41, 53–55.

75. Algar, "Devotional Practices of the Khalidi Naqshbandis of Ottoman Turkey," 219. On Ibn 'Arabi's view of negation and affirmation in the *tahlil*, see his *On the Mysteries of Bearing Witness to the Oneness of God and Prophethood of Muhammad*, 53.

76. Ibn 'Arabi, *On the Mysteries of Bearing Witness to the Oneness of God and Prophethood of Muhammad*, 180, in which he recommends, "When you pray, do not lift your eyes to heaven. You do not know whether God will return your sight to you or not."

77. Algar, "Devotional Practices of the Khalidi Naqshbandis of Ottoman Turkey," 220.

78. On Naqshbandi *khatm* recitations, see Algar, "Devotional Practices of the Khalidi Naqshbandis of Ottoman Turkey," 222.

79. For an analysis of the *Rashahat*, see Bashir, "Narrating Sight," 234–46.

80. Bashir, "Narrating Sight," 241–42.

81. Al-Qushayri, *Epistle on Sufism*, 99.

82. Baqli, *The Unveiling of Secrets*, 33, 60, 120, 122.

83. Al-Qushayri, *Epistle on Sufism*, 100.

84. On *istikhara* in Sufi and Naqshbandi practices, see Ohlander, "Behind the Veil of the Unseen," 204; Algar, "Devotional Practices of the Khalidi Naqshbandis of Ottoman Turkey," 214; and Schimmel, *Die Träume des Kalifen*, 41.

85. Lory, "La vision du Prophète en rêve dans l'onirocritique musulmane," 193.

86. Chittick, "The Perfect Man as the Prototype of the Self in the Sufism of Jami," 145.

87. Waugh, "Following the Beloved," 78.

88. On the seer's sacralization through visions, see Katz, *Dreams, Sufism and Sainthood*, 224; and on Muhammad as a Sufi trailblazer, see Waugh, "Following the Beloved," 64, 72–73.

89. For a study of Sufi marvels (*karamat*), their various manifestations, and their implications for Islamic theology, see Gramlich, *Die Wunder der Freunde Gottes*.

90. Shiro, "Gazorgahi, Mir Kamal-al-Din Hosa."

91. Uluç, *Turkman Governors, Shiraz Artisans, and Ottoman Collectors*, 184; and Uluç, "The *Majalis al-'Ushshaq*."

92. On Muhammad as a mystical initiate, see Waugh, "Following the Beloved," 73.

93. Blochet, *Catalogue des manuscrits persans*, vol. 1, 270, cat. no. 427.

94. On the Angel Gabriel appearing to the Prophet in the form of Dihya al-Kalbi, see al-Bukhari, *Sahih*, book 1, no. 0321.

95. Blochet, *Catalogue des manuscrits persans*, vol. 1, 270, cat. no. 426.

96. See, for example, the Museum of Islamic Art, Berlin, I.1986.229, folio 147v (von Gladiss, *Die Freunde Gottes*, 48, entry no. 53); and Bodleian Library, University of Oxford, MS Ouseley Add. 24, folio 119r, showing Tabadkhani and other mystics in ecstatic dance (Robinson, *A Descriptive Catalogue of the Persian Paintings in the Bodleian Library*, 97–102; and Arnold, *Painting in Islam*, plate XLVIIIa).

97. For example, in Von Gladiss, *Die Freunde Gottes*, 82, plate 26, the painting's narrative is described: "two prophets, possibly 'Ali and Husayn, with flaming nimbi, take part in an 'Ashura ceremony in a convent [dervish lodge]." This copy of the *Assemblies of the Beloved* includes a total of four paintings of the Prophet Muhammad: two of his ascension (folios 4r and 23v), a *majlis* scene (folio 22r), and the dream of Tabadkhani (folio 147v).

98. For an English translation of the original Persian text, see Aflaki, *The Feats of the Knowers of God*; for three Ottoman illustrated manuscripts of Aflaki's text, see Milstein, *Miniature Painting in Ottoman Baghdad*, 96–99; and for an analysis of the depiction of emotions in its paintings, see Elias, "Mevlevi Sufis and the Representation of Emotion in the Arts of the Ottoman World," 187–94.

99. On late sixteenth-century illustrated manuscripts made in Baghdad, see Milstein, *Miniature Painting in Ottoman Baghdad*, 27–34; and Taner, "'Caught in a Whirlwind.'"

100. Aflaki, *Manaqib al-ʿArifin* (The Feats of the Knowers of God), Baghdad, 1590s CE, the Morgan Library, New York City, MS M.466, folios 96r and 156r. The second dream, which is not discussed here, depicts Rumi's vision of the Prophet revealing the secrets of the reed flute to ʿAli. In this vision, the reed flute's melody is described as similar to faith in that it "consists entirely of ecstatic delight and passion." Aflaki, *The Feats of the Knowers of God*, 333. Thus, through this particular dream, the Mevlevis legitimized the use of the reed flute within their *samaʿ* practices as following prophetic practice.

101. Aflaki, *The Feats of the Knowers of God*, 535.

102. Aflaki, *The Feats of the Knowers of God*, 536.

103. On this *Hadith Qudsi*, see Eschraghi, "'I Was a Hidden Treasure'," in which Mulla Sadra's (d. 1640 CE) commentary on the *Kuntu Kanzan* Hadith is provided.

104. Aflaki, *The Feats of the Knowers of God*, 535.

105. Aflaki, *The Feats of the Knowers of God*, further citing Qur'an 38:29.

106. On the use of the pink rose motif to describe the Prophet Muhammad allegorically in Islamic textual sources and Ottoman artistic traditions in particular, see chapter 5 and Gruber, "The Rose of the Prophet."

107. For a selection of illustrated manuscripts of Fuzuli's *Hadiqat al-Suʿada*, see Milstein, *Miniature Painting in Ottoman Baghdad*, 100–105; and Taner, "Caught in a Whirlwind," 116–63. Fuzuli's text is based on Husayn Waʿiz Kashifi's (d. 1504–5 CE) earlier Persian-language *Rawdat al-Shuhada* (Garden of Martyrs), which also commemorates the martyrs of Karbala. On the question of Kashifi's Sunni, Naqshbandi, and Shiʿi religious affiliations and the composition of his *Garden of Martyrs* during the late Timurid period, see Amanat, *"Meadows of the Martyrs"*; and on an illustrated copy of the text, see Milstein, *Miniature Painting in Ottoman Baghdad*, 106, cat. no. 33. Kashifi's *Garden of Martyrs* was seminal to the development of mourning recitations (*rawda-khwani*), mourning verses (*nawha*), and passion plays (*taʿziya*) associated with Shiʿi Muharram commemorations.

108. Figure 13 is listed (but not illustrated) in Milstein, *Miniature Painting in Ottoman Baghdad*, 102, cat. no. 18.

109. For Safi al-Din's full genealogy back to Imam ʿAli, see Quinn and Melville, "Safavid Historiography," 237; and Ibn Bazzaz, *Safvat al-Safa*, 70.

110. Mazzaoui, "A 'New' Edition of the *Safvat al-safa*," 309.

111. Quinn, "The Dreams of Shaykh Safi al-Din and Safavid Historical Writing," 128, 130; Quinn, *Historical Writing during the Reign of Shah ʿAbbas*, 149–54; and Ahmadi, "The Role of Dreams in the Political Affairs of the Safavid Dynasty."

112. Cited in Quinn, "The Dreams of Shaykh Safi al-Din and Safavid Historical Writing," 133–34; on the sun as a symbol of *vilayat*, also see Ahmadi, "The Role of Dreams in the Political Affairs of the Safavid Dynasty," 181.

113. Ibn Bazzaz, *Safvat al-Safa*, 86.

114. Cited in Quinn, "The Dreams of Shaykh Safi al-Din and Safavid Historical Writing," 138.

115. On the Chupanid dynasty, see Melville and Zaryab, "Chobanids"; and for a discussion of the painting, see Erkmen, "The Visualization of Shaykh Safi al-Din Ishaq Ardabili," 64, fig. 14.

116. Ibn Bazzaz, *Safvat al-Safa*, 375.

117. During Safi al-Din's lifetime, the Safawiyya order benefited from Ilkhanid patronage, which in part explains the text's aversion to the Chupanids. For example, the Ilkhanids endowed the shrine complex at Ardabil with land and exempted it from taxation. See Potter, "Sufis and Sultans in Post-Mongol Iran," 90.

118. For Safi al-Din's other dream of the Chupanids, see Ahmadi, "The Role of Dreams in the Political Affairs of the Safavid Dynasty," 182–83.

119. Ibn Bazzaz, *Safvat al-Safa*, 254–57. In this passage, the term for facial veil is *burqaʿ*, which suggests that either Muhammad's eyes are visible or, more metaphorically, that the Prophet helps "resolve or unveil every difficulty" (*burqaʿ-kusha'i har mushkil*). For this Persian expression, see Steingass, *A Comprehensive Persian-English Dictionary*, 176.

120. Ibn Bazzaz, *Safvat al-Safa*, 254–91. In its title, chapter 19 also includes the famous Hadith, "Whoever sees me in a dream has seen me [in reality] because Satan cannot impersonate me."

121. Ibn Bazzaz, *Safvat al-Safa*, 258–59.

122. Ibn Bazzaz, *Safvat al-Safa*, 263–64.

123. On the expression "esoteric prophecy," see Corbin, "The Visionary Dream in Islamic Spirituality," 385.

124. Nikitine, "Essai d'analyse du *Safvat-us-safa*," 388.

125. Nikitine, "Essai d'analyse du *Safvat-us-safa*," 390.

126. Nasr, "The Sufi Master as Exemplified in Persian Sufi Literature," 40.

127. For a discussion of the painting, see Erkmen, "The Visualization of Shaykh Safi al-Din Ishaq Ardabili," 51–56, fig. 5.

THE PRAISEWORTHY ONE

128. Ibn Bazzaz, *Safvat al-Safa*, 279. The slight textual variation provided here is based on the verses found at the bottom of the painting.

129. For a detailed description of Buraq, see Gruber, "Al-Buraq"; and Arnold, *Painting in Islam*, 117–22, plate LIII. On the other hand, in her "The Visualization of Shaykh Safi al-Din Ishaq Ardabili," Erkmen identifies the camel rider as Muhammad and the Buraq rider as ʿAli (55). This alternative reading of the image points to the creative confusion (even conflation) of the protagonists' identities the Safavid artist may have intended.

130. For a detailed discussion of the last judgment painting illustrated in figure 3.19, see Gruber, "Curse Signs."

131. Ibn Bazzaz, *Safvat al-Safa*, 99.

132. Bashear, "Riding Beasts on Divine Missions," 44.

133. Gruber, "When *Nubuvvat* Encounters *Valayat*"; and Shani, "The Lion Image in Safavid *Miʿraj* Paintings."

134. Ibn Bazzaz, *Safvat al-Safa*, 470–71.

135. Ibn Bazzaz, *Safvat al-Safa*, 571.

136. On the black face as a sign of damnation in Islamic theology, see Lange, "'On That Day When Faces Will Be White or Black.'"

137. Farhad with Bağcı, *Falnama*, 192–93, cat. no. 56.

138. Farhad with Bağcı, *Falnama*, 192.

139. Katz, "Dreams and Their Interpretations in Sufi Thought and Practice," 184; and Lory, "La vision du Prophète en rêve dans l'onirocritique musulmane," 189.

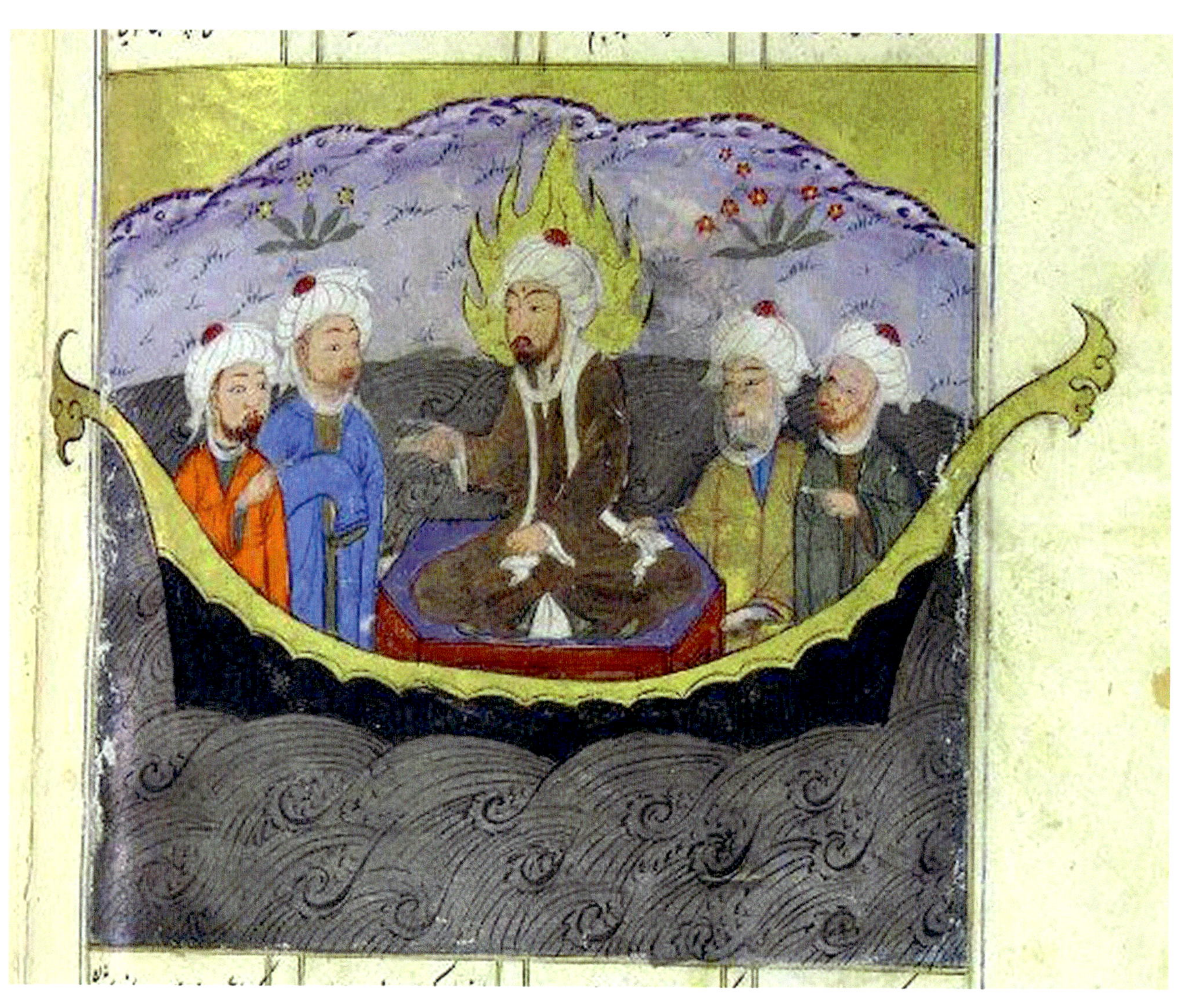

SAFAVID PAINTINGS AND A "SHI'I" MUHAMMAD

4

In Islamic book arts, the Prophet is depicted as a sacred king ruling under angelic protection, a radiant and miracle-working hero, an apocalyptic wayfarer into the celestial realms of God, and a spiritual reality within the visions of mystics. From one manuscript painting to the next, these images of Muhammad reflect and reinforce a number of historically and religiously significant discourses, especially those advanced by patrons who laid claim to the prophetic tradition according to their own beliefs, traditions, and views on history—both past and unfolding.

From the sixteenth century onward, other concerns can be detected in the figural arts, including the looming millennial mark of the *hijri* calendar as well as various elite groups' attempts at self-definition and claims to authority on a global scale. Early modern Muslim empires, including the Safavids, Ottomans, and Mughals, employed various tactics of differentiation. Because these world polities comprised ethnically mixed, polyglot communities, strategies of self-identification tended to bypass language and race. Instead, they frequently aimed to construct articulations of religious doctrine and a perceived orthodoxy crafted along sectarian lines. Thus, over the course of the sixteenth century, the Ottomans in western Eurasia increasingly envisioned themselves as Sunni rulers who followed the prophetic paradigm at the same time as the Safavid rulers of Iran saw themselves as the guardians of Shi'ism, which they promoted as the one and only true faith.

At this time, sectarian overtones were by no means new to depictions of the Prophet. From about 1300 CE onward, paintings of Muhammad enthroned and surrounded by his companions or members of his family could promote partisan positions both openly and by insinuation. However, Sunni-Shi'i rivalries became more explicitly vocalized and more deeply entrenched in cultural production over the course of the sixteenth century, especially after Shah Isma'il I (r. 1501–24 CE) declared Shi'ism the official religion of Iran on his accession to the throne in 1501 CE.[1] The battle of Chaldiran (1514 CE) further exacerbated Ottoman-Safavid rhetorical antagonism, which reached its apex during the reigns of Sultan Süleiman (r. 1520–66) and Shah Tahmasp I (r. 1524–76 CE). As Ottoman and Safavid elites argued over contested territory and resources, they simultaneously struggled over power and influence more broadly. Cloaked in the sacred language of religion, such wrangling accelerated other discourses concerned with promoting each dynastic household's God-given authority—and thus its divine mandate to rule in Islamic lands.

There is no god but God, Muhammad is His Messenger, and 'Ali is the Vicegerent of God.

Shi'i walaya

FACING, 4.1. The ship of salvation, Firdawsi, *Shahnama* (Book of Kings), possibly Bukhara, ca. 1480–90 CE. Malik Library, Tehran, ms. 5986, folio 13v. Photograph courtesy of Said Khoddari.

Over the course of the sixteenth century, Ottomans and Safavids claimed rightful inheritance of the Prophet's sacred mandate to oversee both worldly and otherworldly affairs. While Ottoman princely patrons were keen to collect Muhammad's relics and to commission a variety of devotional arts (see chapter 5), the Safavids lavished much of their attention on book arts, especially illustrated manuscripts containing historical and biographical accounts. During the so-called Safavid century, both old and new narratives were illustrated in Iran. In addition to well-loved Persian classics—Firdawsi's *Shahnama* (Book of Kings), Nizami's *Khamsa* (Quintet), and various *Qisas al-Anbiya'* (Stories of the Prophets)—a number of more recently penned texts were enlivened with pictures. Dynastic and universal histories proved quite popular, particularly Mirkhwand's (d. 1498 CE) *Rawdat al-Safa* (Garden of Purity) and Khwandamir's (d. 1534 CE) *Habib al-Siyar* (The Friend of Biographies).[2] These histories tend to emphasize Persian contributions to world and Islamic history, while biographies of the Prophet—such as Astarabadi's *Athar al-Muzaffar* (Traces of the Victorious), composed in 1516 CE—and of the imams, such as Varamini's *Ahsan al-Kibar* (The Best of Great Men), composed around 1300 CE and illustrated in 1525 CE, display a distinctly Sufi approach to, and Shi'i interpretation of, the life and deeds of the Prophet Muhammad, his family, and his descendants.[3] Last but not least, as the *hijri* millennium mark approached, illustrated *Falnama*s (Books of Omens) with dramatic eschatological imagery were produced in both Persian and Ottoman lands (figs. 3.19 and 3.22).[4]

Within Safavid realms, illustrated histories, biographies, and books of divination both reflected and strengthened political and religious agendas espoused by the ruling elites via their patronage of book arts. Such discourses and worldviews about Safavid power and Shi'i ascendancy also were promoted among the general public through tales and performative practices, including storytelling with pictures.[5] Cutting across socioeconomic classes from the princely to the popular, Persian pictorial arts underwent a series of noticeable changes, to no small degree in order to assist various viewers in envisioning a distinctly Safavid and sectarian worldview. Much like texts and sermons, illustrated manuscripts and paintings thus contributed to the development of what was deemed a theologically admissible form of Sufism and a doctrinally sound articulation of Imami Shi'ism.

Figural imagery functioned as an important arena for the crafting of several intersecting symbolic discourses germane to the greater Safavid project of visually asserting power and authority, which the ruling monarchs believed they inherited through the imams, stretching back to the Prophet. At this time, paintings representing Muhammad thus inhabited a charged zone of contestation marked most especially by Safavid-Ottoman vying over the prophetic legacy. Rulers, writers, and artists deployed a range of rhetorical and visual devices that essentially

        THE PRAISEWORTHY ONE

aimed to amplify the charisma of contemporary rulers. Through word and image production, Muhammad was rendered as the paradigmatic ruler in religion and state, and, in a reciprocal manner, contemporary monarchs were depicted as carrying the mantle of sacred rulership in the lands of Islam long after the Prophet's death.

Iconographic changes in prophetic representation marked Safavid figural practices over the course of the sixteenth century. The most noticeable changes include the addition of a veil typically executed in white pigment, which obscures Muhammad's facial features. A delicately thin yet ineluctably present veneer, the Prophet's facial veil does not serve simply to transform his figure into a subject that is concealed from view. Even in legal contexts, premodern jurists, such as the Hanbali scholar Ibn Qudama (d. 1223 CE), did not issue bans against the use of figural imagery. Rather, they encouraged artists to adopt nonrealistic devices to avoid the representation of facial features.[6] When it came to depictions of Muhammad, the facial veil and flaming nimbus count among the most prominent of such devices.

Much more capacious as a carrier of meaning, the veil in particular serves to contain Muhammad's sacred brilliance and to camouflage key markers of his personal identity, in the process catalyzing various discourses about the Prophet's luminous nature as well as causing potential confusion among viewers who might not be able to distinguish him from other figures represented in painted scenes.[7] Such confusion is frequently exacerbated by the insertion of a tall red baton into Muhammad's turban, transforming it into the *taj-i Haydari* (Haydar's crown) worn by members of the Safawiyya Sufi order.[8] On the one hand, the baton's facets symbolized the twelve imams and thus helped develop a Shi'i discourse in support of the imamate; on the other, its association with Safavid monarchs made its addition to the Prophet's apparel anachronistic and, more importantly, suggestive of a conflation of prophetic and royal identities.

At the same time that the Prophet became veiled and crowned with the *taj-i Haydari* within Safavid paintings, his flaming nimbus was enlarged and used to mark other characters. Indeed, artists began to apply all three of these highly charged visual devices—the facial veil, Safavid crown, and irradiant flux of God—to depictions of Muhammad's son-in-law and cousin, 'Ali, as well as to other members of the Prophet's household and his descendants, the imams. This iconographic triad served to allegorically unite Muhammad with his family and offspring, granting them the same concealed, royal, divine status. Thus, the Prophet is shown rarely as a stand-alone protagonist but instead with 'Ali—with whom he forms a visual duo in which the two men are at times indistinguishable from one another—or girdled by his family and progeny. In the ever-growing companionship of others, including mystics and monarchs, Muhammad is surrounded by a miscellany of symbols, many of which exalt the authority of the Safavid politicoreligious apparatus and present its rulers as the embodiments of the hidden imam and shadows of God on earth.[9]

Sixteenth-century Persian paintings of Muhammad express a form of Shi'ism that laid claim to a prophetic pedigree and thus an orthodox character. Within these dynamic efforts to delineate doctrine, Safavid discursive strategies employed insinuation and suggestion as well as secrecy and mystery. These tactics were augmented by the painterly arts, in which depictions of Muhammad and his entourage served to create parables of belief; confirmations of the primordial origins, miraculous powers, and authority of 'Ali and the imams; the promotion of a new world order under the Safavids; and the promise of salvation in the true belief: Shi'i Islam. The major pictorial stratagems of facial veiling, mysticosectarian headgear, multiplied flaming aureoles, and figural association and obfuscation all served to heighten these key discourses within Safavid book arts, which inherited older traditions of Islamic iconography that were adopted and adapted at will.[10] Within such paintings, images of the Prophet generate an array of calculated ambiguities and uncertainties, including the enduring question of whether it is possible to speak of a "Shi'i" Muhammad.

During the sixteenth century, older texts and pictorial tropes continued in Persian book arts at the same time as new trajectories began. Among the favored narratives for illustration was Firdawsi's *Shahnama* (Book of Kings), the epic history of the kings of Iran. This text's status as a historical—rather than mythical—work may have precluded the penning of dynastic histories and court chronicles that are a staple of Ottoman and Mughal production. In addition to the *Shahnama*'s paramount importance in Persian literature and culture, in Safavid Iran, as Charles Melville notes, "history books may not have been perceived as an effective way to project a state ideology that became increasingly engaged in religious and spiritual debate."[11] Although past and contemporary histories indeed did not provide the most opportune vehicle for the picturing of mystical and sectarian concerns, through their inventive pictorial programs they nevertheless could, in some cases, provide faith-based allegories and thus partake in the active construction of a Safavid Shi'i worldview.

The *Shahnama* provides a case in point. The text's prologue is the only section in which Firdawsi expresses his praise of God and Muhammad, thus inscribing the Persian epic tales within a Muslim religious ambit. The author's prolegomenon includes the famous parable of the ship of salvation, whose illustration in the early fourteenth century depicted the Prophet Muhammad enthroned in an outdoor setting surrounded by the first four rightly guided caliphs beneath angels spreading victory ribbons (fig. 1.16). A relatively rare subject for illustration, the ship of salvation provides an allegory of the Islamic faith and its ultimate rewards, much like the *Navis Ecclesiae* (Ship of the Church) carrying Jesus and his disciples symbolized the Christian church's salvific powers in medieval European devotional thought and artistic practice.[12] Within Firdawsi's analogy, moreover, the ship's safe journey is ensured not only by Muhammad but also by his kin, most especially 'Ali.

In their role as laudatory and religiously inflected frontispieces, paintings of the ship of salvation are included in *Shahnama* manuscripts illustrated prior to 1500 CE. The compositions diverge from each other and their accompanying text in a number of ways. For example, figure 1.16 depicts Muhammad enthroned outdoors rather than aboard a stately vessel at sea, thus folding the parable into inherited visual paradigms that favor enthronement scenes.[13] Even when the paintings follow Firdawsi's verses more closely, depicting the Prophet in a boat, they tend to show him surrounded by the four *rashidun* rather than by his family, relatives, or descendants.

A painting belonging to a group of illustrated *Shahnama*s most likely made in Transoxiana between 1450 and 1500 CE reveals the iconographical uncertainties with which artists grappled in creating images of the sailing Prophet as allegories for salvation through the Islamic faith (fig. 4.1).[14] According to Basil Robinson, this manuscript painting displays a provincial Timurid style that he considers "second-rate Bukhara work."[15] While its place and date of production remain open to conjecture, the work nevertheless falls within a larger Turco-Persian cultural milieu that bridges the Ilkhanid and Safavid periods and thus provides important evidence for the development of book painting and prophetic iconography over the course of the fifteenth century. The painting of the ship of salvation from the so-called Transoxiana group highlights precisely this state of pictorial in-betweenness by showing Muhammad sitting cross-legged on a squat throne platform while sailing with the *rashidun* in a black vessel. The Prophet's throne appears to levitate above the ship, yielding a composition that clearly combines earlier enthronement scenes with later depictions of the vessel. The visual result is unsteady, to say the least.

This fifteenth-century painting also depicts Muhammad in conversation with the four rightly guided caliphs. While Abu Bakr can be recognized by his white beard, the three other *rashidun* are not clearly identifiable, as their key attributes are not included in the composition. Abu Bakr, cloaked in yellow, appears most intimately linked to the Prophet as he grasps his throne and robe. Two other companions point their index fingers toward Muhammad in a gesture that indicates and bears witness to the Prophet's central status as God's Messenger. The remaining member of the *rashidun*, to whom the Prophet appears to signal with an open palm, is cloaked in a blue robe with an overlong sleeve covering his hand. This robe, which is suggestive of a Sufi's garb, may serve to identify 'Ali, who during and after the fifteenth century increasingly came to be imagined as the founding father of Sunni and

Shi'i mystical orders, such as the Naqshbandiyya and the Safawiyya respectively.

While the Prophet retains his supreme status as an enthroned and centrally located protagonist, for whom the prerogative of the flaming halo is reserved, in this interim painting he appears connected to and conversing with 'Ali, who is depicted as favored among his peers. As a result, this and similar paintings of the ship of salvation indicate the artist's decision to emphasize 'Ali, a key figure in Firdawsi's praiseful prologue, while also carefully tempering sectarian readings by depicting 'Ali as part of the *rashidun* rather than rooting him within the familial collective of the *ahl al-bayt* and their descendants, the imams.[16] Paying (partial) tribute to the *Shahnama* verses while folding them into the pictorial paradigm of the enthroned Prophet flanked by his four companions, this ship of salvation painting reveals the ways in which sectarian readings of painted images were nuanced before 1500 CE.

Persian manuscript paintings made under the aegis of Safavid royal patrons after the turn of the sixteenth century became more overtly pointed in their pro-Shi'i content and messages. While the dynasty's founder Shah Isma'il I aligned himself with Imam 'Ali, the Prophet, and God through his mysticomessianic poetry,[17] his successor Shah Tahmasp oversaw the alignment of his and his forefathers' pedigree with the Prophet's family line while attempting to render Imami Shi'i doctrine internally cohesive and externally differentiated from Sunni Islam. During Shah Tahmasp's rule, a growing number of texts and images placed an increasing emphasis on the Safavids' illustrious 'Alid genealogy and the supreme authority of the imams, both of which proved key in promoting Safavid Shi'ism as the only true orthodox faith capable of securing salvation. Under royal patronage, this double emphasis on 'Ali and the imamate rebounded within the field of manuscript production, in which painted images both echoed and sustained a Safavid elite vision of power and authority, which in turn artfully reasserted and expanded the prophetic paradigm.

During the 1520s and 1530s CE, Shah Tahmasp sponsored a luxurious copy of Firdawsi's *Shahnama*, to which some of Iran's most talented artists—among them Sultan Muhammad, Mir Musavvir, Aqa Mirak, and Mirza 'Ali—contributed many magnificent paintings.[18] Although the manuscript's folios are now dispersed, among the known paintings is its frontispiece depicting the ship of salvation (fig. 4.2).[19] Attributed to the painter Mirza 'Ali, this illustration of Firdawsi's parable fully embraces the author's marine metaphor. Instead of depicting Muhammad enthroned in a verdant, sunlit landscape, the painter shows the tale's protagonists sailing across dark seas. The number of individuals and vessels has multiplied, and the event is set at nighttime, with only a sliver of the glistening moon illuminating the scene from the upper-right corner. The painting is bracketed at the top and bottom with Firdawsi's verses, and an orange sail playfully pierces the frame and into the lavishly gold-flecked margins.

     THE PRAISEWORTHY ONE

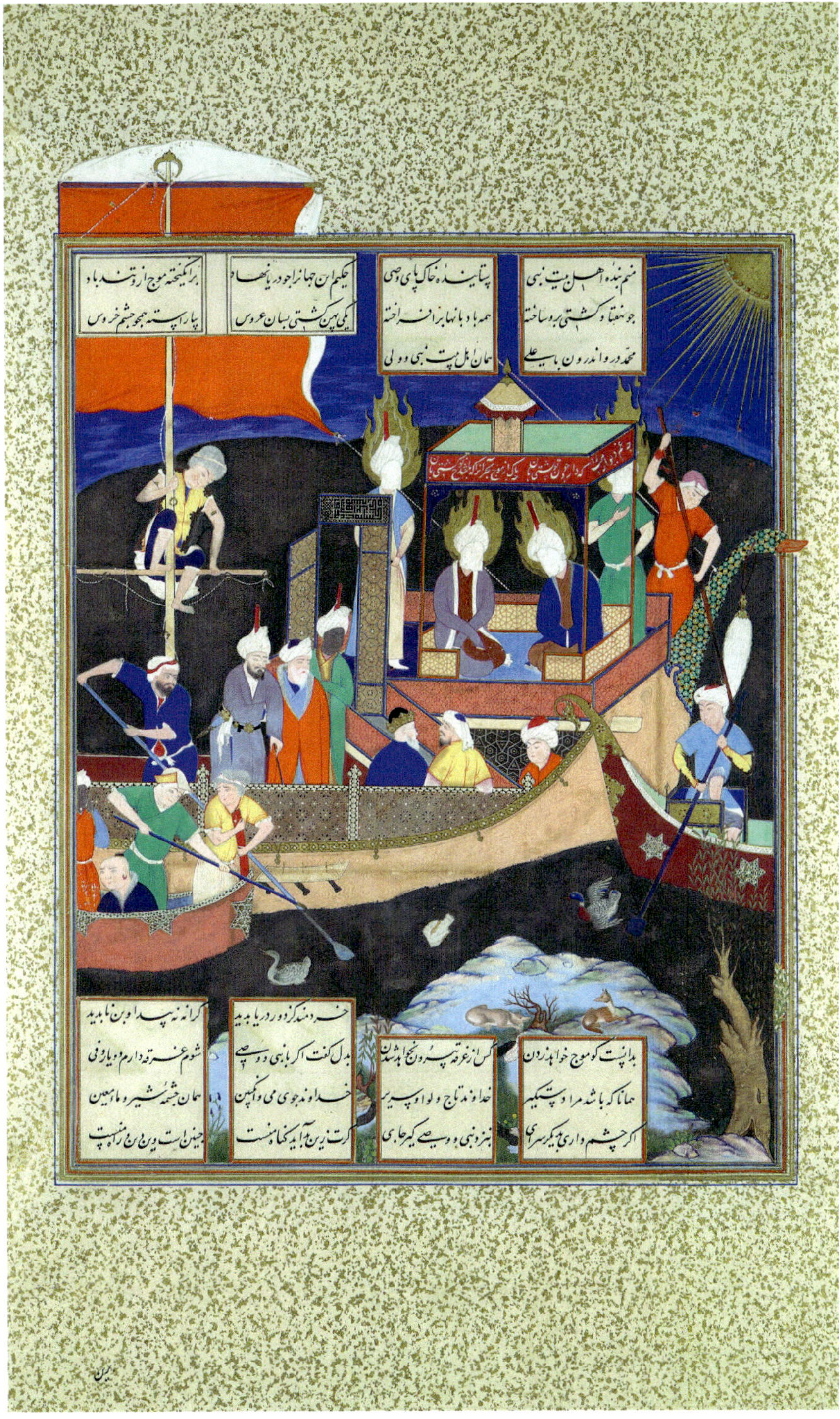

4.2. The ship of salvation, Firdawsi, *Shahnama* (Book of Kings), Tabriz, ca. 1525–35 CE. Metropolitan Museum of Art, New York, 1970.301.1.

In his prolegomenon, Firdawsi describes the flotilla as composed of seventy gallant ships and one stately vessel carrying Muhammad, 'Ali, and all their kin.[20] The painting takes a cue from the author's verses by depicting several ships, whose largest and most luxurious vessel—with a prow shaped like a duck's head—is reserved for its chief protagonists, here shown as Muhammad and 'Ali (kneeling below a canopy) together with Hasan and Husayn (standing to the right and left). While the identities of the scene's other individuals remain unclear,[21] these four most important characters are clearly set apart by means of an ornamented

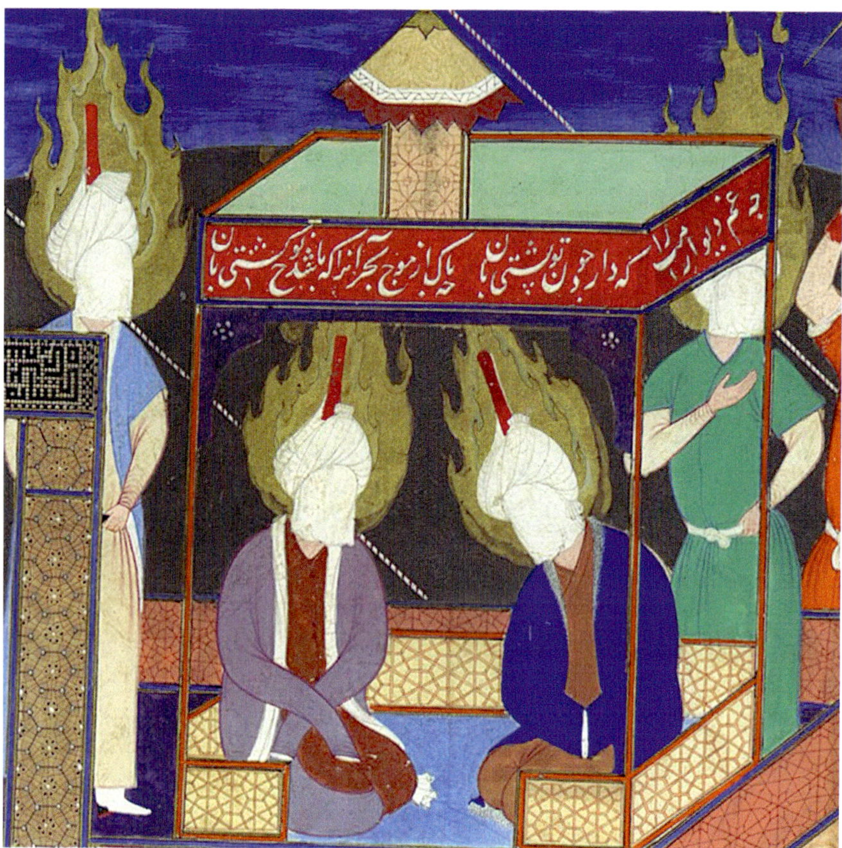

gateway and throne-like enclosure. They also are closely connected to each other through three special attributes: flaming halos, white facial veils, and the *taj-i Haydari* (fig. 4.3).

This triad of iconographical devices applied to Muhammad, his son-in-law, and his two grandsons offers a prime example of the major pictorial innovations in paintings of the Prophet created by artists working in the Safavid royal book atelier in Tabriz during the first few decades of the sixteenth century. Benefiting from princely patronage and thus interacting with a learned elite, painters were familiar with state-sponsored narratives about religion and authority. In turn, they became active contributors to Persian Shi'i discourses stressing the superiority of the *ahl al-bayt*, the imams, and the Safavid monarchs as the rightful inheritors to prophetic rule. Such alignments between contemporary rulers and Muhammad's household and descendants were openly asserted via both text and image production. Within painterly traditions, visual language achieved its full symbolic potential by depicting these four protagonists as anachronistically sporting the *taj-i Haydari*, the key object attribute of Safavid imperial sovereignty. To no small degree, retrofitting members of the *ahl al-bayt* in Sufi-Shi'i headgear served to visually align the prophetic family with ruling members of the Safawiyya order. Through the metaphor of a turban, past and present leaders of the Muslim community thus appear as if part of the same regal collective.

Beyond this striking iconographic manipulation, Safavid painters also made the strategic decision to depict Muhammad, his family

    THE PRAISEWORTHY ONE

members, and his descendants as veiled and luminous beings. While the flaming aureole did not originate with their era, in earlier paintings it tended to be reserved for the Prophet, distinguishing him from his companions and followers (as can be seen in fig. 4.1). During the Safavid period, however, the "light of Muhammad" (*nur Muhammad*) came to be extended to members of his family. As a consequence, 'Ali is often shown touched by the flux of the divine, as are Fatima, Hasan, Husayn, and the imams.

The flaming aureoles illuminating the heads of the four protagonists in the ship of salvation scene from Shah Tahmasp's *Shahnama* likely were inspired by a number of factors, including Firdawsi's accompanying verses, which describe Muhammad's kin with the following words: "These are the moons, the Prophet is the sun; with them in union is the way to run."[22] Through this poetic allegory, the author describes Muhammad and his family as a luminous cosmos—embodiments of celestial radiance—through whom salvation must be sought and secured. It should be noted, however, that these verses did not inspire earlier painters to apply the nimbus to figures other than the Prophet Muhammad. Thus, the reasons for this new pictorial development must be sought in the painting's contemporary religious and political context, especially as it intersects with Shi'i discourses lauding Muhammad and the imams as eternally effulgent beings.

A number of Shi'i texts describe the imams as pure and impeccable beings emerging from the preexistential world of shadows or particles, in which they exist as light silhouettes (*ashbah nur*), spirits of light (*arwah min nur*), or shadows of light (*azillat nur*).[23] Moreover, ascension narratives penned by Shi'i authors relate that Muhammad saw the imams' names inscribed on the throne of God or else witnessed their presence at the throne as flaming nimbi.[24] One Hadith in particular records Muhammad glancing at the feet of the throne, stating, "I saw twelve lights each containing an inscription in green indicating the names of my legatees, from the first, 'Ali b. Abi Talib to the last, the Mahdi of my community."[25] Ascension tales likewise record God speaking to the Prophet the following words: "Muhammad, I created you, Fatima, Hasan and Husayn as figures of light out of my light. . . . Those who accept your authority become close companions in my eyes, and those who struggle against it become unbelievers."[26] From the Hadith to ascension tales, Shi'i texts sought to praise the imams' preexistence as light sources emanating from the heavenly spheres; they also projected their postexistence in paradise, the eternal abode promised for the righteously faithful.

The Safavid artist responsible for the ship of salvation scene in figure 4.2 seems to have been cognizant of the light metaphors used for Muhammad and the *ahl al-bayt* as they developed within Shi'i milieus over the centuries. Here, the painter applies the flaming aureole in an egalitarian manner, suggesting that Muhammad's, 'Ali's, Hasan's, and Husayn's luminous essences are homologous and equally distributed.

Moreover, the viewer is hard pressed to distinguish between Muhammad and 'Ali, lambent, veiled corulers sitting under the baldachin of their shared throne while the radiant Hasan and Husayn stand in wait on either side. Emitting a similar radiant flux, veiled from view, and donning kingly headgear, Muhammad and 'Ali indeed each appear as the other's doppelgänger in sacred rulership.

Like the flaming aureoles, the white facial veil that covers all four protagonists causes the viewer to contemplate a series of multiplied likenesses. While previous scholars have argued that the addition of a facial veil to representations of the Prophet and other holy figures was due to a Safavid form of pietism,[27] a diverse body of evidence indicates that much more is at stake than a putatively image-adverse form of religious devotion. To the contrary, figural representations were widespread at this time, and within the representational arts the facial veil appears to have emerged from several factors as well as catered to specific politicoreligious demands. Indeed, the rhetoric of concealment and the elaboration of veil metaphors contributed to Shi'i expressive traditions over the centuries. By the sixteenth century these two discourses—dissimulation and occultation—intersected with painterly practices to catalyze, for the very first time in Islamic artistic traditions, the systematic application of veils to the faces of the Prophet, 'Ali, the *ahl al-bayt*, and the imams. Put more simply, facial veiling became a common iconographical device within Persian pictorial arts only after 1500 CE, for a range of reasons that transcend the otherwise opaque and ill-defined notion of pietism.

In both Sunni and Shi'i spheres, the Prophet Muhammad often was described as "wrapped up" in a mantle while in a state of devotion. Using the qur'anic terms *al-muzzammil* (Q 73:1) and *al-muddaththir* (Q 74:1) as honorific epithets for the Prophet, Muslim writers described Muhammad as metaphorically "enwrapped" and "enveloped" in divine revelation and prophecy.[28] Some exegetes offered a further explanation of the prophetic corpus based on these two qur'anic terms in order to stress that Muhammad's inner, eternal being (*al-haqiqa al-muhammadiyya*) was covered by a human form.[29] Through the rhetorical analogy of cloaking, written sources imagine the Prophet as fleshed yet shrouded.

Textual metaphors describing Muhammad as enveloped in a sacramental encounter with God appear in a number of Islamic texts regardless of doctrinal orientation. Within Shi'i traditions, however, this particular discursive strategy was augmented and applied to 'Ali. For example, already during the ninth and tenth centuries, the early Shi'i exegete Furat al-Kufi reports a Hadith in which Muhammad states that 'Ali is the "most radiant imam (*al-imam al-azhar*). . . . No curtain (*sitr*) hides God from him, no veil (*hijab*) lies between God and him. For 'Ali is the curtain and the veil (*huwa'l-hijab wa'l-sitr*)."[30] Other Shi'i texts report 'Ali declaring himself the "mystery of the unknown" and the "mystery of mysteries" as well as the one who is "manifest" even though he remains "concealed" and "hidden."[31] Within Imami Shi'ism in particular, 'Ali often is described as emanating from divine light, much like

THE PRAISEWORTHY ONE

the *nur Muhammad*, while his physical appearance acts as an embodied manifestation (*mazhar*) of God.[32] As a result, 'Ali is couched as a theophanic entity combining human and sacred qualities,[33] outwardly manifest yet concealing a world of mysteries in his position as the ultimate "curtain" that allows for absolute and inseverable unity with God.

As a duo, the "enwrapped" Muhammad and the "veiled" 'Ali form a sacred core in Shi'i devotional thought. By the sixteenth century in Iran, the articulation of both leading personas took on a distinctive pictorial turn under the Safavids, as can be seen in the ship of salvation painting, in which Muhammad and 'Ali are indistinguishable and share a single throne inscribed with a verse likening the ship to Noah's ark—and thus salvation.[34] With their radiant auras, veiled visages, and Safavid turban-crowns, the Prophet and his son-in-law are shown partaking in the same sacred source—God's irradiant light and concealed being—as well as sharing responsibility over earthly dominion. This prerogative is then passed down to Hasan and Husayn, who are likewise blessed with luminosity and mystery as they prepare to secure their own divinely decreed mandate.

The sectarian message embedded within and carried throughout the painting's iconography would not have been lost on artist, patron, or elite viewers of either Shi'i or Sunni leaning. Indeed, within contestations over power and authority the image formed a subject of interpretative reframing after Shah Tahmasp gifted this royal Safavid *Shahnama* to Sultan Selim II (r. 1566–74 CE) on the Ottoman ruler's accession to the throne in 1568 CE. In subsequent centuries, the illustrated manuscript formed part of the Ottoman royal library, where it was provided with glosses in Ottoman Turkish during the early nineteenth century. The later Ottoman Turkish commentary on the Safavid ship of salvation painting clearly privileges the Prophet Muhammad as the sole source of the law despite the fact that the image depicts Muhammad and 'Ali as equals in religion and rulership. In his study of these textual glosses, Ünver Rüstem notes that, by bringing 'Ali into the Sunni fold, the Ottoman interpretation of the painting aims to minimize his personal cult, "stressing instead his place within a long caliphal tradition at whose helm now stood the Ottomans."[35] Thus, via this and other manuscripts on the move, both Shi'i and Sunni differential positions could be articulated or suppressed via a range of pictorial and textual expressions.

The verses and paintings accompanying the ship of salvation in Firdawsi's prologue to the *Shahnama* seem to have caused rivalry especially during the sixteenth century, at which time the Safavid-Ottoman divide crystallized through an array of rhetorical and visual strategies. Another example of this phenomenon can be found in a second Safavid painting of the parable, belonging to a *Shahnama* manuscript most likely made in Tabriz and dated 1536 CE (fig. 4.4).[36] This illustrated codex is contemporary with Shah Tahmasp's royal commission and may well have been produced for a member of the royal entourage. Among its forty-eight paintings, the ship of salvation appears only after three

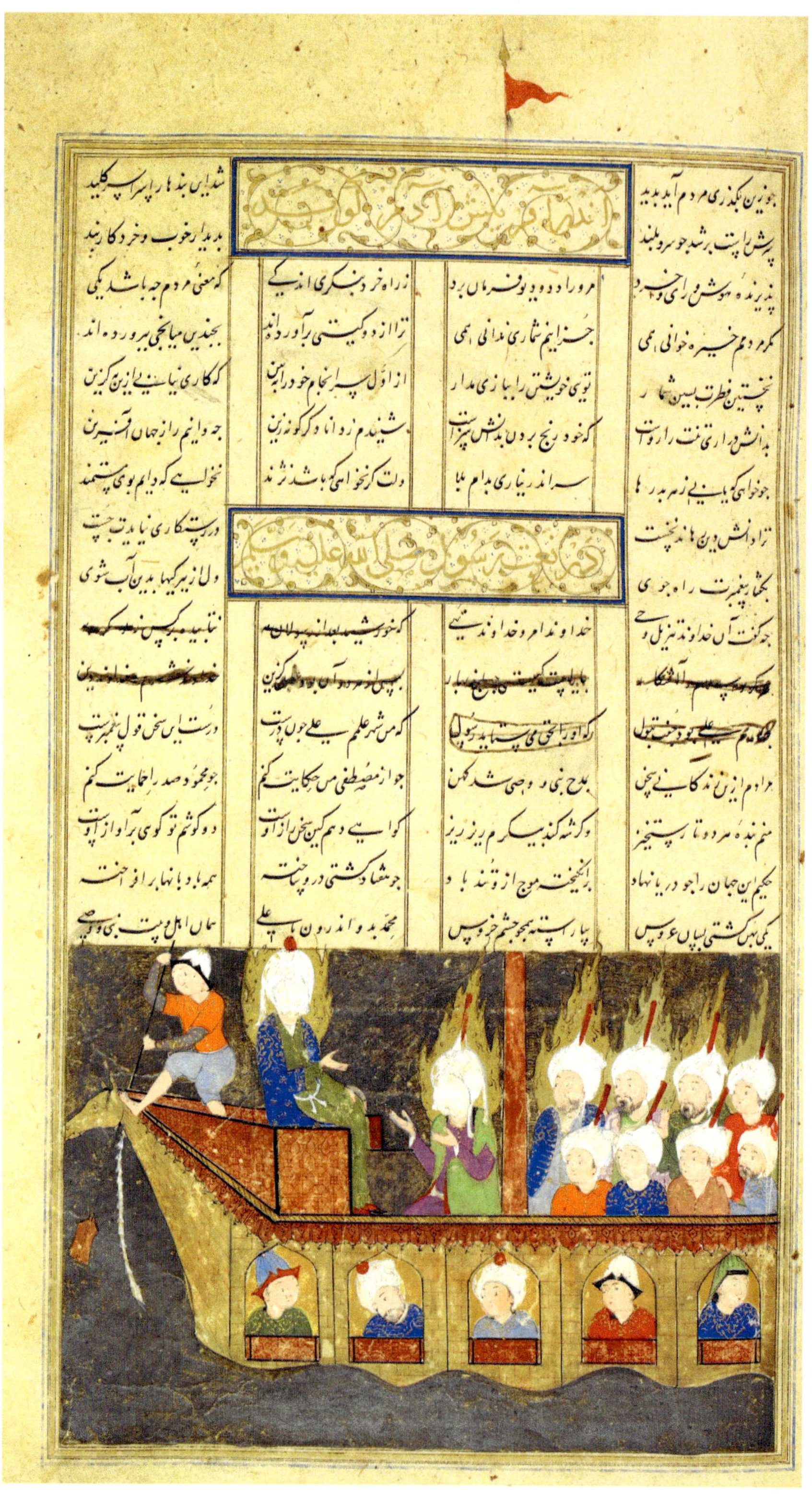

paintings that depict feasting courtiers, a prince on a balcony, and a
prince with his retinue.[37] Intended as visual eulogies and mementos of
its high-ranking Safavid patron, these three opening images set the tone
for the painting of Muhammad sailing at sea as included in the chapter
"on praising the Prophet" (*dar naʿt-i rasul*).

Immediately above the painting, a number of Firdawsi's verses praising the *rashidun* have been conspicuously crossed out with black ink. Gone are the plaudits of Abu Bakr, who shines like the sun; 'Umar, who spreads Islam into the world; 'Uthman, who is the model of piety; and 'Ali, who is the spouse of Fatima, praised by the Prophet. These verses (rather sloppily) excised, only 'Ali remains intact as the gate to the city of knowledge, on whom two further praises have been added in the margins of Firdawsi's text. Evidently, a reader of this manuscript deemed it necessary to copyedit the author's praiseful prologue, in the process censuring all mentions of the *rashidun* except a stand-alone verse glorifying 'Ali. In a very real sense, this intrusive act constitutes a literary *damnatio memoriae*.

Such textual censures are in turn echoed by this second Safavid painting of the ship of salvation, which depicts the scene in a manner that is both similar to and divergent from its depiction in Shah Tahmasp's *Shahnama* (fig. 4.2). Besides its rendering in a horizontal rather than vertical format, and its iconographic simplification through the removal of several elements, the vessel also hosts a greater number of protagonists, who are arranged according to a different spatial configuration. In this instance, Muhammad and 'Ali no longer sit on the same throne while flanked by Hasan and Husayn. Instead, in the painting shown in figure 4.4, the Prophet sits alone on an enclosed pedestal, which comes to a triangular point at the ship's horse-headed prow, where an attendant steers the vessel with a paddle and the help of his bare foot. Although set apart from and raised above the crowds, Muhammad remains nevertheless closely paired with 'Ali. The imam sits below, his back pressed against what appears to be a dividing wall, as he raises both palms in a responsive gesture toward the Prophet, who himself addresses his kneeling interlocutor. Behind 'Ali and past the vertical divide sit eight unveiled protagonists with flaming halos and wearing the *taj-i Haydari*; faces that exude no radiance and wear no royal headgear look out from windows in the ship's hull.

The eight individuals bearing these special attributes are most likely the imams, those descendants of Muhammad and 'Ali through whom the Safavids laid claim to power and authority. Their importance in the painting is due to two key factors. First, they function as a kind of embodied pedigree, offering the viewer a royal Safavid genealogy stretching back to the Prophet via Musa al-Kazim and Imam 'Ali. It was around 1533 CE and under Shah Tashmap—during whose reign this painting was produced only three years later, in 1536 CE—that the genealogy (*nasab*) of the Safavid royal household and its eponymous founder, Shaykh Safi al-Din, was revised in order to stress the dynasty's 'Alid origins.[38] This particular depiction minimizes the figures of Hasan and Husayn and instead elevates the imamate above all else, a visual emphasis that clearly falls in line with Tahmasp's religiopolitical agenda during the 1530s.

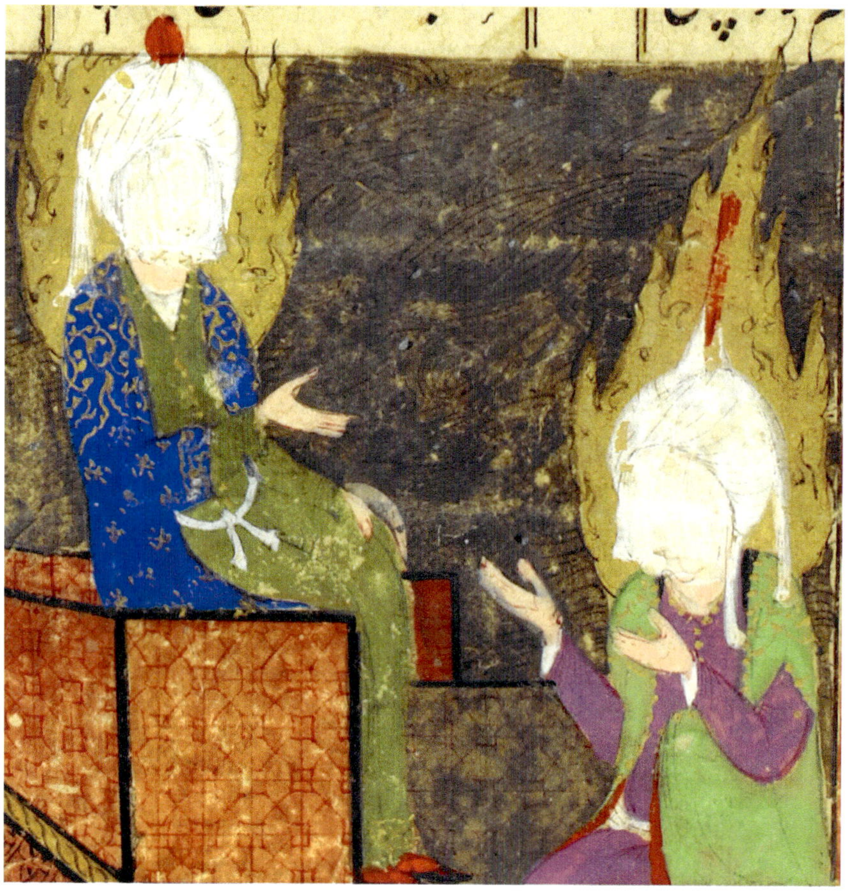

Second, through his discriminating use of the flaming aureole, the Safavid artist offers a forceful pictorial statement in which the imams are depicted sharing in the same sacred light source as Muhammad and 'Ali. The image thus belongs to, and further promotes, longstanding Shi'i narratives describing God's *nur* as passing down from the Prophet to his offspring, eventually enlightening the Safavid rulers, as well. Although such declarations about divine light diminished by Shah Tahmasp's time, his predecessor Shah Isma'il I had claimed that he embodied the arrival of the "light of God" (*nur-i khuda*) on earth.[39] As the painter makes clear through his application of the Safavid *taj-i Haydari*, the radiant imams and 'Ali should be considered earlier manifestations of the Safavid monarchs. Here, the light of God becomes contained and passed down through the generations in tandem with this semiotically charged headgear. Not just an anachronistic detail, therefore, the *taj-i Haydari* should be understood as the vessel for God's light, which grants regal and religious authority to the Shi'i imams and ruling members of the Safavid household.

While the imams and 'Ali wear the Safavid crown-helmet, the Prophet has on a turban wrapped around a squat conical cap rather than a tall rod (fig. 4.5). The artist thus draws a distinction between Muhammad and 'Ali, in which the turban is juxtaposed with the *taj-i Haydari*, the latter clearly marking 'Ali as the paramount progenitor of the imamate and Safavid line. Both are nevertheless closely affiliated through the use of the white facial veil, which is not applied to the visages of the imams and other individuals aboard the ship. Indeed, the two facial veils—whose delicate folds drape over pale faces lacking any discernible features—are solely reserved for the Prophet and his son-in-law. The facial veil in this painting (and others) thus should not be interpreted as a putative ban on depicting the Prophet and other saintly figures. To the contrary, and much more significantly, it should be understood as a Safavid painterly attempt to envision Muhammad and ʿAli as coequals via two key visual signs—flaming gold aureoles and white facial veils—that indicate their shared numinous origins and radiant mystery, which emanates from the realm of God, above and beyond the high status afforded to the imams themselves.

As masters of the earth and seas, Muhammad and ʿAli are coupled in kingship and faith, and both are luminous and veiled human beings. The facial veil in particular carries further connotations when examined in light of royal practices of accession and audience in Islamic lands. Over the centuries, a number of Muslim rulers made use of symbolic veils and curtains to promote their divine mandate, resplendent origins, and inviolable character, with moments of revelation staged as highly charged events. For example, as surveyed by Gülru Necipoğlu, textual sources record that the ʿAbbasid caliph sat on an elevated throne and was "veiled behind a curtain that would be periodically lifted to reveal him in splendor. Adorned with the insignia of the Prophet's sword, staff, and holy mantle, he projected a sacred image as the Prophet's legitimate successor."[40] The ruler was imagined to embody Muhammad, veiled in the light of prophecy while girdled by his key object attributes. Similarly, ceremonial veiling and unveiling, as well as the use of grilled windows designed to dissimulate the ruler's presence, were elements of ʿAbbasid, Fatimid, and Ottoman palatial traditions, as well.[41] Not to be outdone by their Ottoman neighbors, the Safavids and Mughals also employed veil metaphors within their own kingly practices. For example, Safavid coronation narratives, including that of Amir Mahmud, describe Shah Ismaʿil I's accession to the throne with the following words: "Praise be to God that from the fortune (*dawlat*) of the Safavid King, the witness of the Prophet's religion has emerged from behind the veil (*amad az pardah*)."[42] While Shah Ismaʿil's coming to power was described as a becoming visible, the Mughal emperor Shah Jahan (r. 1628–58 CE) also cultivated dramatic moments for his epiphany. For example, we are told that he would put a veil on his face and then remove it before his courtiers, who would exclaim in amazement: "Light has shined forth!"[43] Over the centuries, Muslim monarchs embraced veil and light metaphors to stress their mysterious and radiant natures, a conceptual apparatus promoting sacred forms of kingship, to which the Safavid dynasts made their own contributions, among them the facial veil, the flaming aureole, and *taj-i Haydari*.

As the most significant innovation of Safavid pictorial arts, the depiction of the facial veil expressed Islamic narratives about the

impenetrable yet transcendental mysteries of sacred rulership. Moreover, it also must have intersected with—and further solidified—sectarian discourses on esotericism and occultism, chief among them the Shiʻi
doctrine of concealment (*kitman*) and dissimulation (*taqiyya*). As Maria
Dakake notes, the Shiʻi rhetoric of secrecy is essentially a discursive
strategy that serves to reinforce and mystify the authority of existing
elites by creating internal boundaries and hierarchies.[44] This form of
esoteric knowledge and encoding stresses the existential hiddenness of
God, the imams, and other infallible leaders that is real yet intangible,
both visible and unseen—or, to borrow Dakake's fitting expression,
a kind of "hiding in plain sight." Like Shiʻi rhetorical strategies that
provide explanations of the inner truths of religion and scripture,[45] the
facial veil displays yet conceals the mysterious character of sacred beings, including that of the Prophet Muhammad and ʻAli. Within Safavid
paintings that clearly construct a Shiʻi message through the strategic
use of iconographic devices, the facial veil thus must be understood as a
visual strategy that makes manifest esoteric notions of religious truth.[46]

Manuscript paintings of the ship of salvation produced during the
reign of Shah Tahmasp highlight the evolution of Safavid royal and
religious ideology in Iran during the first half of the sixteenth century.
The most notable innovations within Safavid depictions of Firdawsi's
laudatory prologue to his *Shahnama* include the replacement of the four
companions of the Prophet (the *sahaba*) with ʻAli, flanked by Hasan and
Husayn or accompanied by the imams. Additionally, the application of
the *taj-i Haydari* to ʻAlid protagonists—which at times may include or
exclude Muhammad—pictorially argues for the Safavid dynasts' *sayyid*
and/or ʻAlid pedigree, itself a genealogical emphasis echoed in Shah
Tahmasp's explicit directive to revise the lineage of the dynasty's eponymous founder, Shaykh Safi al-Din. In turn, within Safavid paintings, the
Prophet, ʻAli, and his descendants bearing the royal crown-turban are
depicted as if primordial Safavid rulers, present and visible yet veiled and
luminous at the same time. Moreover, the flaming aureole and facial veil
at times make the Prophet and ʻAli indistinguishable from one another.
They also show the protagonists as coequals, sharing kingship, the light
of God, and God's veiled mystery. Taken altogether, these three major
iconographic innovations craft a distinctly Shiʻi salvific worldview, in
which secrecy and dissimulation offer—much as the paintings do—a
depiction of conspicuous concealment and "hiding in plain sight."

ATTESTATION AND
INVESTITURE

While innovative visual devices could relay both overt and furtive Shiʻi
messages within figural representations of the Safavid period, narratives and themes that were of particular importance to Shiʻi faith
communities had been depicted in Ilkhanid book arts since the early
fourteenth century. In addition to the ship of salvation parable in the
Shahnama, several episodes in the life of Muhammad encouraged sectarian readings of his biography. Most important among these episodes
were the Prophet's disputation with the Christians of Najran on the

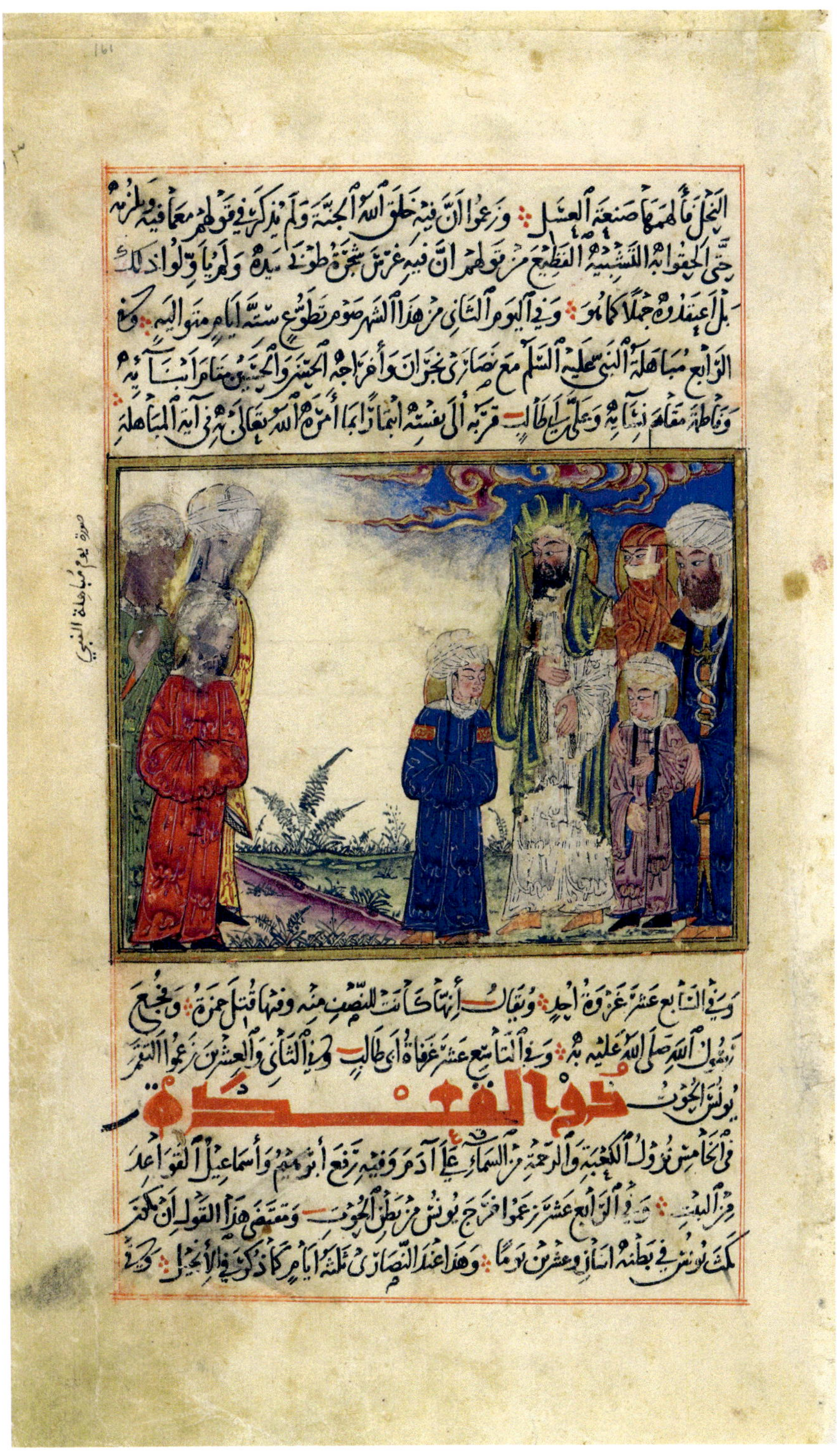

Day of Cursing (*Mubahala*) and his halt at the Pond of Khumm (*Ghadir Khumm*) during his farewell pilgrimage. According to authors and exegetes of Shi'i persuasion, the Mubahala and Muhammad's speech at Ghadir Khumm provided incontrovertible proof of the preeminence of the *ahl al-bayt* and 'Ali's appointment as Muhammad's rightful successor. Taken together, these two episodes served as confirmation narratives that promoted members of the Prophet's household as the embodiment of true belief. In addition, they also praised 'Ali's supreme status as

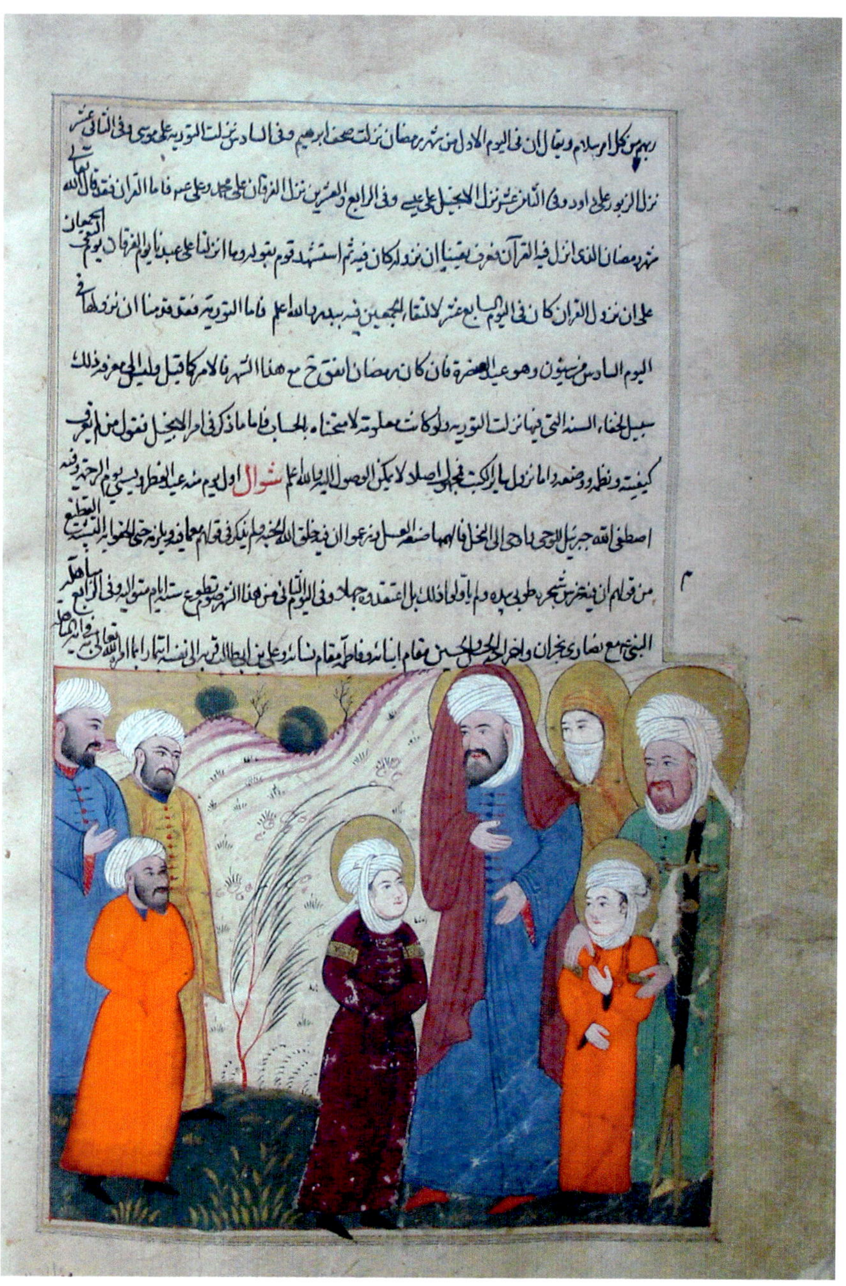

Muhammad's soul mate through his continuation of the divine mission after the Prophet's death.

Two hundred years prior to the Safavid century, the early fourteenth century witnessed a burst of artistic and architectural activity under the patronage of the Ilkhanid sultan Öljeïtu (r. 1304–16 CE). Born a Nestorian Christian with the name Nicholas, Öljeïtu converted to Sunni Islam then Shi'i Islam (1309 CE) and possibly back to Sunni Islam before his death in 1316 CE. The ruler's interest in and embrace of Shi'i Islam via his relationship with the influential Twelver Shi'i theologian al-Hilli (d. 1325 CE) is recorded in textual sources. Such sources highlight Öljeïtu's devotion to the holy family and his interest in the nobility of the 'Alid lineage, which echoed his Chingizid belief that authority was acquired through genealogical descent from a glorious ancestor.[47] As Judith

Pfeiffer notes in this regard, "the parallel between the legitimization of the Ilkhan through Ghingizid descent and the legitimacy of Shi'i claims to the caliphate through their relation to the Prophet is skillfully used [by al-Hilli] to convince Öljeïtu of the superiority of Shi'i over Sunni Islam."[48] For Öljeïtu, noble descent from Chengiz Khan aligned with the Shi'i notion that legitimacy lies within Muhammad's progeniture, who partake in, embody, and thus extend the prophetic mandate.

It is within illustrated manuscripts produced during the reign of Öljeïtu that the Mubahala and Ghadir Khumm are first depicted and given prominence. These images are included in the copy of al-Biruni's *Al-Athar al-Baqiyya 'an al-Qurun al-Khaliyya* (Chronology of Ancient Nations) made in 1307 CE.[49] The manuscript's pictorial program shows a clear bias in favor of the Shi'i cause and thus may offer an early indication of Sultan Öljeïtu's conversion to the faith two years later.[50] The emphasis on a Shi'i interpretation of Muhammad's biography is not due to its textual narration of the events at the Mubahala and Ghadir Khumm in al-Biruni's text alone. Just as significantly, the two paintings of these scenes are in the full-folio format and located at the end of the section, thereby providing large-scale visual capstones to the text and image cycle devoted to explicating the events of Muhammad's life.

These terminal scenes, along with all of the others included in the manuscript, were recreated in at least two later copies: an Ottoman manuscript of around 1560 CE (which will not be discussed here)[51] and a Safavid copy made in or near Isfahan during the year 1647–48 CE.[52] The Ilkhanid painting of the Mubahala depicts the Prophet wrapped in his green *burda*, accompanied by a huddled group of four figures who confront three figures on the left, which were defaced subsequently (fig. 4.6). The later Safavid painting follows its earlier prototype, although the figural forms and colors are flattened, a pink hill in the background makes the picture plane appear shallower, and the three figures on the left have been either restituted or left intact (fig. 4.7).[53]

The Mubahala essentially comprised a dispute on Christology and prophetology between Muhammad and a group of fourteen Christians from Najran. According to Ibn Ishaq, three of these Christian men spoke with Muhammad about Jesus's miracles, the signs of his prophecy, and his Crucifixion, with the Prophet emerging triumphant from the theological dispute.[54] In Sunni spheres, the narrative was largely understood as a confirmation of the doctrinal superiority of the Islamic faith. While it fulfilled a similar purpose in Shi'i spheres, the narrative was amplified to include the "people of the cloak" (*ahl al-kisa'*), whose purity provided the ultimate vindication of Muhammad's stance. For example, al-Biruni, the author of the illustrated text, reveals a penchant for this interpretation of the episode by stating that Muhammad was accompanied by 'Ali, Fatima, Hasan, and Husayn, and that he appointed 'Ali his intimate friend (*wali*) on the occasion in compliance with the order of God as found in the Qur'an.[55] The Ilkhanid painting thus closely follows the textual narrative by depicting the Prophet Muhammad accompanied by the *ahl al-bayt* as the five family members successfully dispute three Christians from Najran.

Although al-Biruni does not specify the passage in the Qur'an, he undoubtedly is referring to 3:61: "Tell those who dispute this with you even after the knowledge has reached you: 'Come let us gather our sons and your sons, our women and your women, our souls and your souls, and pray and solicit God to curse those who lie.'" Although al-Biruni does not elaborate on this verse, a number of Shi'i exegetes, including Shaykh al-Mufid (d. 1022 CE), Tabarsi (d. 1153 CE), and al-Majlisi (d. 1698 CE), interpret its contents as referring specifically to the *ahl al-bayt*. For these writers, the expression "our women" denotes Fatima, "our sons" points to Hasan and Husayn, and "our souls" refers to Muhammad and 'Ali conjointly or simply to 'Ali, who is considered the complete manifestation of the Prophet's soul (*nafs*).[56]

Shaykh al-Mufid expounds further on the topic, noting that during the Mubahala 'Ali was of the same station as the Prophet, at which time 'Ali revealed "his equality with the Prophet in terms of perfection and protection (*isma*) from sin. Indeed God made him ['Ali] and his wife and his two sons a proof for His prophet and evidence for His religion."[57] Within the context of a theological debate with Christian emissaries, the presence of 'Ali is interpreted by Shi'i writers and exegetes as an evidentiary sign for the veracity of the Muslim faith as well as indisputable confirmation of his equality (*musawa*) with the Prophet, whose own soul he is seen as embodying.[58] Thus, 'Ali is conjoined spiritually to the Prophet, and the legitimacy of Islam is vindicated by a sacramental solidarity among the five members of the *ahl al-bayt* who were present during the Mubahala.[59]

Shi'i sources also describe a number of cosmic phenomena pointing to the preeminence of Muhammad and his family on the Day of Cursing; among them are stars shining and lightning flashing above the *ahl al-bayt*. While these marvels frightened the Christian opponents, Arab Muslim followers who were present at the event are said to have described the Prophet's family as a collective theophany surrounded by a dazzling aureole of divine glory.[60] Like the *burda* that enwraps the Prophet during pivotal moments of piety and revelation, in the Ilkhanid painting (fig. 4.6) the swirling, almost thunderous clouds and bright blue sky above Muhammad and the *ahl al-bayt* visually highlight their divine selection—and thus their superiority over the Christians, who are relegated to the painting's otherwise empty left margin. Last but not least, clad in a blue robe and shown holding his emblematic double-pointed sword, Dhu'l-Fiqar, 'Ali resembles Muhammad in his facial features, long tresses, and similar size, a strategy of pictorial equivalence through which the Ilkhanid artist seems to insinuate 'Ali's spiritual conjoining with both the soul and body of the Prophet.

The later Safavid rendition of the Mubahala omits the cloud swirls, but the depiction of the three Christian emissaries remains intact (fig. 4.7), an act of painterly preservation that may be a testament to peaceful

Christian-Muslim cohabitation in the Persian imperial city of Isfahan during the seventeenth century. At an unknown date, however, the Ilkhanid painting (fig. 4.6) suffered an iconoclastic act, in which the Christian protagonists were defaced, possibly with several flicks of a wet thumb. This disfiguration was carried out against the visual representation of those who dared to question the authority of the Prophet—and, by extension, that of his family. Thus, this kind of "iconoclash"—to borrow Bruno Latour's portmanteau term—also is an "ideoclasm," a destruction of visualized ideologies, in this case a potential Christian challenge to the Islamic faith as personified by the Prophet and his nuclear family.[61] Such an iconoclastic act thus aims to destroy not figural representations per se but rather perceived religious enemies. Moreover, it does not merely target an image; much more importantly, it ensures the preservation and integrity of the representation of Muhammad and the *ahl al-bayt*, thereby emphasizing and reenergizing a pictorial form of Muslim devotion that is personified by the leading figureheads of Shi'i Islam.[62] The painting thus bears witness to several moments of sectarian expression, at the time of its manufacture and during its later reception.

Textual narratives and visual representations of the Mubahala provided powerful attestations to the ascendancy of Shi'ism within the context of a Christian-Muslim theological dispute. More central to Muslim intrafaith contestations, however, were the events at Ghadir Khumm. Textual sources inform us that, immediately prior to his death, Muhammad embarked on a pilgrimage, stopping at the Pond of Khumm to deliver a speech. In his biography of the Prophet, Ibn Ishaq states that at this time Muhammad taught men *hajj* rites and delivered a speech in which he glorified God, abolished usury, prohibited intercalation, and declared Rajab, Jumada, and Sha'ban sacred months.[63] Shi'i sources offer additional details about the circumstances and content of Muhammad's speech, at which time it is believed that 'Ali was invested with authority and therefore was to be considered a living extension of the Prophet and his mission.

For example, in his *Kitab al-Irshad* (Book of Guidance) Shaykh al-Mufid states that Muhammad stopped at Ghadir Khumm not to gather water but because God revealed to him that he should appoint 'Ali his successor. He goes on to describe the two men standing above a group of individuals, to whom the Prophet announces his impending death and his legacy: the Qur'an and his family's offspring. The Prophet then raises 'Ali's two arms and proclaims: "Whoever I am the master (*mawla*) of, this man, 'Ali, is his master."[64] Al-Biruni expands the narrative even further: he relates that Muhammad gave orders for saddles and riding equipment to be gathered into one heap, which he ascended with the support of 'Ali's arm. Then, the Prophet is reported to have declared: "To every man whose friend I am, also, 'Ali is a friend. O, God, befriend him who befriends 'Ali, and oppose him who opposes 'Ali, help him who helps 'Ali, and desert him who deserts 'Ali. Let truth go about with him wherever he goes."[65]

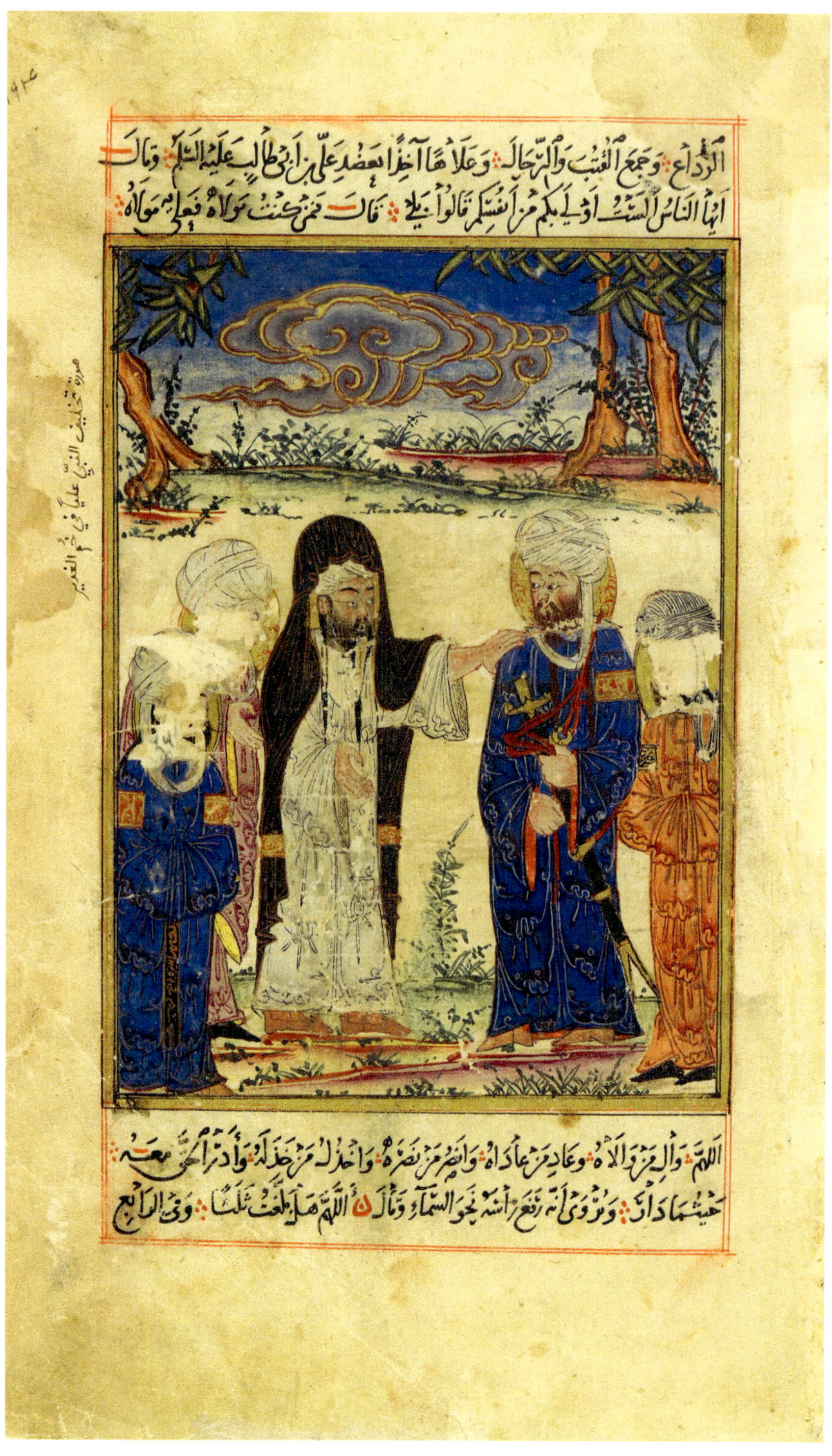

For Shaykh al-Mufid, al-Biruni, and others, the events at Ghadir Khumm offer incontrovertible proof of 'Ali's exalted merit and rank—that is, his God-revealed trusteeship, publicly affirmed and commanded by the Prophet himself. These authors also note that at this moment God declared to Muhammad: "I have completed your religion,"[66] a verse indicating that the transmission (*tabligh*) of the prophetic message does not die with Muhammad but rather continues to propagate via 'Ali and his descendants, all of whom partake in and extend Muhammad's

THE PRAISEWORTHY ONE

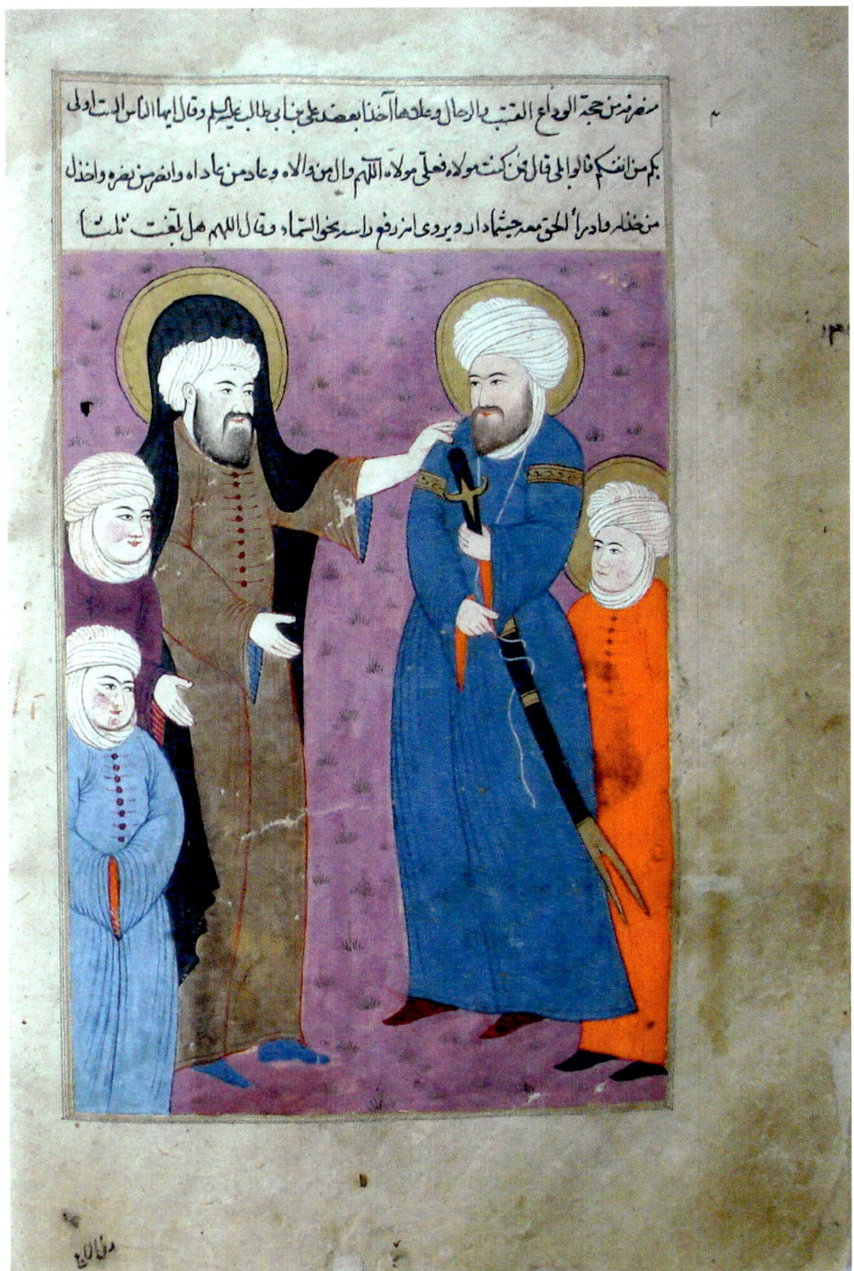

4.9. The Pond of Khumm (*Ghadir Khumm*), al-Biruni, *al-Athar al-Baqiyya 'an al-Qurun al-Khaliyya* (Chronology of Ancient Nations), probably Isfahan, 1057 AH/1647–48 CE. Sepahsalar Madrasa, Tehran, ms. 1517, folio 287r.

prophecy (*nubuwwa*) through their vicegerency (*walaya*). In this way, the prophetic message remains dynamic as it cascades down generations of leaders in the faith.

As the pivotal moment establishing 'Ali's divinely mandated selection as Muhammad's successor, the story of Ghadir Khumm has played a prominent role in Shi'i-inclined biographies of the Prophet and Shi'i commemorative holidays from the earliest centuries to today. It also has been depicted in both the Ilkhanid and Safavid illustrated copies of al-Biruni's *Chronology of Ancient Nations*. The earlier painting includes the thunderous cloud—a celestial indication of God's selection and protection—hovering above Muhammad and 'Ali, who stand in the middle of the composition (fig. 4.8). Although the later composition repeats the same grouping of five figures and a similar color scheme for their robes, the landscape has all but disappeared, with a background washed in pink and small tufts of grass pushing the protagonists to the front of the picture plane (fig. 4.9).[67] This perspectival flattening and the increased opacity of the pigment yield a composition whose look and character appear more iconic than narrative.

A caption was inscribed in the left margin of the Ilkhanid painting (fig. 4.8) sometime after its creation, reading: "A depiction (*surat*) of the Prophet's selection of 'Ali as his successor at the pond of Ghumm." The use of the verb *takhlif* (to select as successor) reveals the annotator's Shi'i position. Here, an overtly sectarian interpretation of the painting articulates support for 'Ali's appointment as the successor to the Messenger of God (*khalifat rasul Allah*). Such a conclusion is easily drawn from the painting's iconography, which emphasizes Muhammad and 'Ali, the latter holding Dhu'l-Fiqar as he is designated *khalifa* by the touch of the Prophet's hand on his shoulder. This symbolic gesture visually joins the protagonists, whose position in the narrative of Ghadir Khumm is emphasized by their large size and central placement in the composition.

Defacement of the painting's imagery followed. At some later date, a viewer intruded forcefully into the pigments, scraping away the faces of the three other figures present. Two male figures bear the remains of black beards, and a third, standing next to Muhammad, appears to have a white beard. These remaining iconographic details clearly indicate that Muhammad and 'Ali's three companions are adult males, who therefore must be identified as the three *rashidun*: 'Uthman, 'Umar, and Abu Bakr, the latter usually depicted with a white beard. Their inclusion in the depiction is not surprising, as Shi'i sources describe their presence at Ghadir Khumm. However, such texts paint these characters in a noticeably pejorative light. For instance, we are told that Abu Bakr and 'Umar demanded to know whether 'Ali's appointment was an order of God, and only after Muhammad responded in the affirmative did they accept the necessity of paying homage to 'Ali.[68] This episode highlights their reluctance to recognize 'Ali as Muhammad's rightful heir.

Reviled in a number of Shi'i textual sources as the "three cursed ones" (*mala'in thalatha*),[69] the Prophet's first three companions often were the targets of sectarian hostility. An abundance of accounts denounce them as usurpers, going so far as to brand them apostates for having rejected the authority of 'Ali. As a result, the doctrine known as *takfir al-sahaba*, in which the companions were excoriated as unbelievers, emerged. Beyond vilifying them as non-Muslims and therefore banishing them from the faith community, Shi'i sources especially denigrate Abu Bakr and 'Umar through a number of derogatory names and epithets, including *jibt* and *taghut* (both meaning false idol), Munkar and Nakir (the denied and the denier, as well as the angels who test the faith of the deceased in their graves), and 'Uff and Tuff (dirt in the ears and dirt under the nails). At times, they were denied names altogether and simply called "so-and-so" (*fulan*).[70]

     THE PRAISEWORTHY ONE

While prevalent, such curses nevertheless did exist in tandem with more moderate attitudes toward the *sahaba* within Shiʻi spheres, as evidenced by the Ilkhanid painting of Ghadir Khumm, which originally displayed respect for the *sahaba* as a visual support and framing for ʻAli's preferential treatment. However, just as Shiʻi texts censured the companions for their effrontery at Ghadir Khumm, painted images similarly offered an opportunity for visual castigations impelled by a sectarian animus. Although most likely not part of its function as originally intended by both artist and patron, the Ilkhanid painting extended an invitation to viewers to interact with it in a variety of visual and tactile ways. As a consequence, a later individual (or several) saw it fit to commit a highly intrusive act of *damnatio memoriae*, in the process purging the three *rashidun* from representational visibility—and hence symbolic existence.

Cursing the *sahaba* was a trademark of the Safavid period, and thus it is possible that this act of iconoclasm occurred during the sixteenth or seventeenth century, at which time the Ilkhanid manuscript appears to have been consulted in order to produce a copy. The institutionalization and spread of Shiʻi cursing practices in Iran accelerated after 1511 CE, when al-Karaki (d. 1534 CE), chief jurist under Shah Tahmasp, penned his treatise entitled *Nafahat al-Lahut fi Laʻn al-Jibt waʼl-Taghut* (Breath of Divinity in Cursing Witchcraft and Idolatry).[71] Al-Karaki's manifesto lauds the merits of cursing Sunni opponents, among whom he singles out the three *rashidun* as well as any individual perceived as unjust toward ʻAli and the *ahl al-bayt*. Vilifying these Sunni enemies, he argues, is not only permitted but required, as expressing "hatred of God's enemies forms an integral part of one's faith (*iman*)."[72] Ergo, for al-Karaki this expression of hatred is a virtuous act and a "most beloved form of devotion" (*ahabb al-ʻibadat*).[73]

The potentially Safavid-period mutilation of the *sahaba* in the Ilkhanid painting likewise should be understood as a "most beloved form of devotion" according to a Shiʻi religiopolitical worldview. The agent of the iconoclastic curse essentially performs a mode of character assassination. This symbolic act of destruction is physically enacted against the faith's oppositional icons, its false idols. What is more, the extirpation of the three *rashidun*'s facial features renders them unidentifiable, effectively reducing them to a triumvirate of disfigured and nameless so-and-sos.

In both rhetorical and pictorial practices, violent acts of iconoclasm often are highly ritualistic and thus spiritually resonant. As Fabio Rambelli and Eric Reinders note in this regard, "the destruction of sacred objects can also represent acts of piety, sacrifice, communication, provocation, or renovation," while "the iconoclast's attempt to destroy the icons is still an acknowledgment of their power, an affirmation qua negation."[74] Acts of disfiguration therefore comprise a form of cursing and humiliation even as they acknowledge the power, even sanctity, of the targeted image. In the case of the Ilkhanid painting of Ghadir Khumm, the remaining icon—that is, the image spared symbolic disfiguration—comprises only Muhammad and 'Ali. Here, the sacred pair is kept in a pristine state, thereby demonstrating that the love of an image (iconophilia) can coexist with, and even be an affirmative outgrowth of, the hatred or fear of an image (iconophobia). Thus, within early modern Persian painterly traditions and sectarian practices, iconoclasm can serve to reaffirm both creation and destruction as equally necessary in their maintenance and purification of a putatively correct sacred order, in this instance an order visually enshrined and embodied solely by the Prophet and his son-in-law.

Unlike its Ilkhanid prototype, the Safavid painting of Ghadir Khumm (fig. 4.9) has not been expurgated through an iconoclastic act. Instead, an entirely new cast of characters has been inserted. In lieu of the three disfigured *rashidun*, three young, beardless boys stand alongside Muhammad and 'Ali, whose importance and interrelation are emphasized by their centrality, size, and gestural connection. The young boys who accompany the duo are most likely 'Ali's sons, Hasan and Husayn, and perhaps Zayn al-'Abidin, who thereby visually continues the line of the imamate through which the Safavid dynasts claimed rightful rulership. In addition, golden halos are no longer uniformly applied. While they illuminate Muhammad and all four caliphs in the Ilkhanid painting, in the Safavid rendition they are strictly reserved for the Prophet, 'Ali, and the young Husayn, who stands next to 'Ali and wears a robe of bright red, symbolizing his martyrdom at the battle of Karbala (680 CE). The two figures on the left likewise differ from their Ilkhanid prototypes: these are no longer haloed, vandalized adults but rather two youths witnessing the critical moment of 'Ali's investiture. Thus, the principal figural elements in this Safavid composition of Ghadir Khumm display a major iconographic revision of the Ilkhanid original, a process that allowed a Shi'i ideological discourse to be extrapolated from, and woven back into, the painting.

The Safavid painting depicts the story of Ghadir Khumm as a familial or even genealogical event, emphasizing Muhammad and 'Ali's intimate relationship, 'Ali's equal status with the Prophet and divine right to rule, and Husayn's sharing in the light of God through his sacrifice on behalf of the Shi'i community. The rendering of the event appears to emphasize a blood brotherhood in a gathering of leaders, as is the case with the Ilkhanid painting. Not only does this fraternity in the faith reflect Safavid Shi'i ideology, it also seems to pay tribute to holidays and rituals prevalent in seventeenth-century Isfahan. Among the most important feast days celebrated in the imperial capital was 'Id al-Ghadir (Feast of the pond), which was celebrated annually on the eighteenth day of Dhu'l-Hijja. This feast is described in Safavid texts as well as in travelogues penned by European visitors to Isfahan. In their travel diaries, for example, Pietro Della Valle (d. 1652 CE) and Adam Olearius (d. 1671 CE) describe 'Id al-Ghadir as not merely a Shi'i festival but predominantly a ritual of brotherhood, in which men and women become brothers and sisters in religion. During this feast of fraternity, individuals adopted children, reconciled with their enemies, and created long-lasting kinship ties through reciprocal affection with friends and relatives.[75] In light of sectarian discourses and fraternal festivities of the same period, the Safavid painting of Ghadir Khumm appeals to an acculturated viewership who also envisioned the event as a celebration of intimacy and fellowship.

Ghadir Khumm was a subject of repeated representation during the sixteenth and seventeenth centuries in Iran, no doubt because it could be marshaled in support of the Safavid dynasts' own claims to rightful rulership via the 'Alid paradigm. A number of similar paintings exist in other illustrated manuscripts made especially between 1540 and 1575 CE, including biographies of the Prophet and at least one illustrated *Falnama* (Book of Omens). In these portable, large-scale manuscripts catering to both royal and nonroyal patrons, illustrations of Ghadir Khumm visually herald 'Ali's unmatched propinquity to the Prophet and his ontological status as Muhammad's alter ego.

A number of Shi'i-slanted biographies of the Prophet were written and illustrated during the Safavid period. Among the most popular for illustration was Nizam al-Din Astarabadi's *Athar al-Muzaffar* (Traces of the Victorious), written as a Persian-language poem in 1516 CE. The author begins his historical text with a number of eulogies in praise of God as well as an ode (*qasida*) in honor of Muhammad and his family, Iranian rulers, and his patron, Khwajah Sayf al-Din Muzaffar Bitikchi, a member of the Safavid court who was involved in ministerial affairs and served as an officer in Astarabad, a stronghold of Shi'ism and his family of provincial notables.[76] In addition to this series of laudatory remarks, Astarabadi includes a preamble lauding the light of Muhammad, describing it as vested in the imams, who were themselves the ancestors of the Safavid kings. The book's front matter thus establishes an overtly pro-Shi'i and pro-Safavid framework for the greater portion of the text, which is otherwise dedicated entirely to the history of Muhammad's life.[77] This authorial incipit that Shi'ifies the prophetic *sira* is not an unusual feature for biographies of the Prophet penned during the Safavid period.

Sectarian messaging also is embedded in the paintings of four illustrated copies of the *Exploits of the Victorious* that were produced in northeastern Iran (Gurgan and Khurasan) between 1560 and 1580 CE.[78] While the patron of these Safavid provincial manuscripts remains unknown, it appears that his (or her) goal was to promote a text written by a local author working under regional patronage—in this case members of the Bitikchi family—while also teaching the life of the Prophet through the staunch Shi'i viewpoint that characterized the region during the sixteenth century. In this group of illustrated Shi'i Safavid *siras*, paintings depict Muhammad and 'Ali in close tandem, at times even physically fusing into one another. In addition, 'Ali often is hardly distinguishable

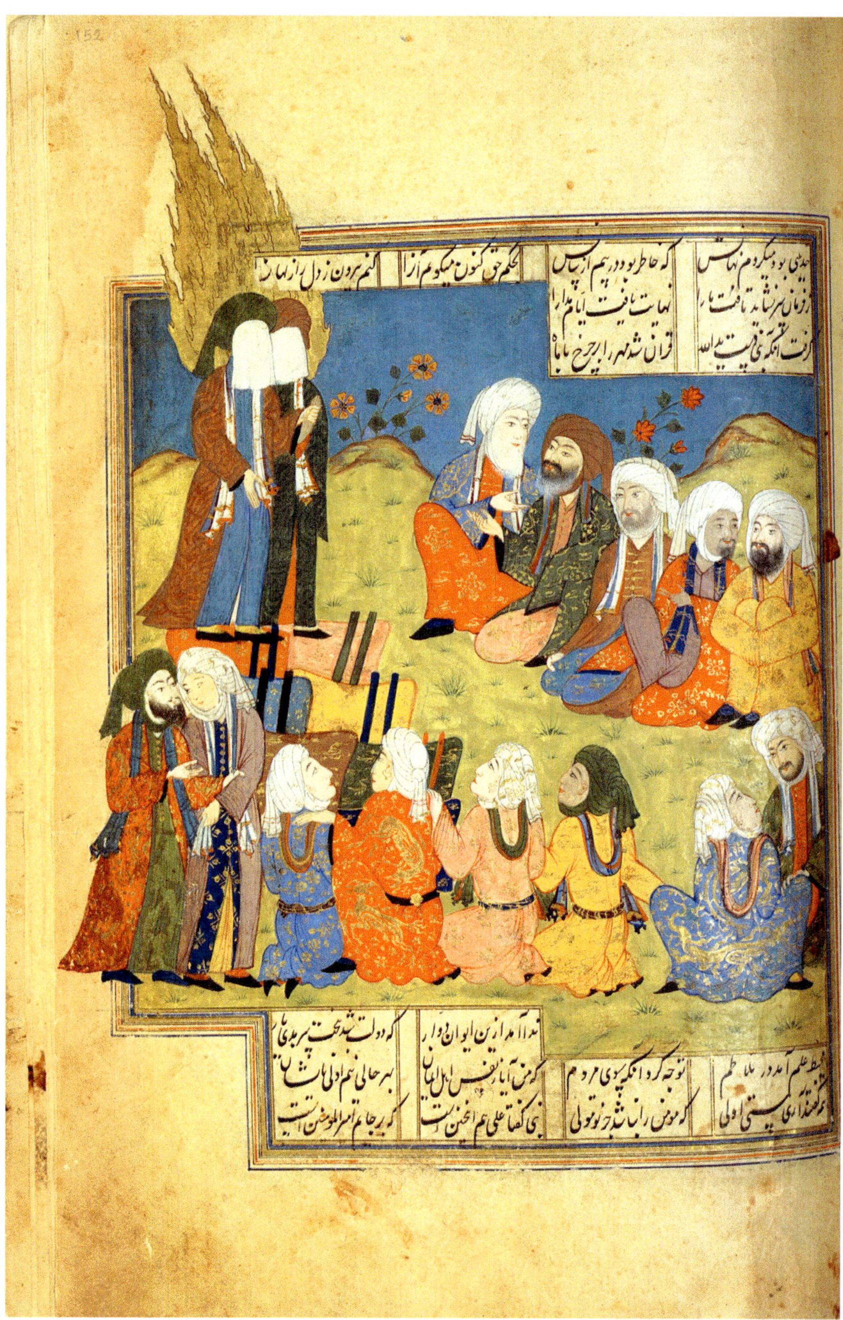

from the Prophet, as both are represented with similar white facial veils and flaming gold nimbi. The iconographic rapprochement between the Prophet and the imam thus emerges as the most important pictorial innovation stressing the duo's physical and spiritual inseparability.

In one copy of Astarabadi's Shi'i biography of the Prophet, dated 1567 CE, the pivotal events at Ghadir Khumm take pride of place among the three extant paintings in the manuscript (fig. 4.10).[79] The composition shows Muhammad and 'Ali standing atop a pile of camel saddles and surrounded by figures engaged in conversation seated in a circular formation that gives depth to the painting while also emphasizing the two protagonists' elevated position. Here, however, it is nearly impossible to distinguish the Prophet from 'Ali; they are of the same size, both

   THE PRAISEWORTHY ONE

wear white facial veils, and they share the same gold nimbus. Moreover, Muhammad is not represented with his characteristic tresses, which often serve to distinguish him from others among a group of similarly veiled and radiant heroes. Despite such ambiguity, Muhammad nevertheless can be identified as the man wearing the green turban who holds the hand of ʿAli in an authoritative gesture of display and nomination.

Neither the *rashidun* nor the *ahl al-bayt* flank the two protagonists in this painting of the event at Ghadir Khumm. Instead, the Prophet and his *wali* form a unified figural set. The visual emphasis on the duo and their elevated status certainly echoes Shiʿi biographies of the Prophet, which extol the pair's absolute equality (*musawa*) at Ghadir Khumm and during the Mubahala.[80] Authors such as Shaykh al-Mufid likewise contend that the events at Ghadir Khumm provide proof of ʿAli's outstanding merit and his exalted rank, thus demonstrating "that he was the best of the creatures of God, the noblest of His creation."[81] In conversation with and expanding on these written discourses, the Safavid painter transformed the two protagonists' equality and rank into iconographic form through their commensurate size, shared flaming nimbus, and linked hands (fig. 4.11).[82] This pictorial rendition of the concept of *musawa* compels the viewer to envisage Muhammad and ʿAli as cosubstantial in essence, copresent in physicality, and coequal in rulership—in other words, as a consecrated "two of a kind" rising above all others.

During the sixteenth century the event at Ghadir Khumm also appears to have been considered a propitious "sign" (*nishan*) and so was included in at least one illustrated *Falnama* (Book of Omens) possibly made in Tabriz or Qazvin around 1540–50 CE (fig. 4.12).[83] The painting shares similarities with the depiction included in Astarabadi's illustrated *sira*, including the mound of camel saddles and the group of companions sitting and standing in contemplation and conversation. However, perched atop the columnar saddle-throne appears one sitting body with two heads rather than two standing men holding hands. Again, it is almost impossible to identify which head belongs to the Prophet and which to ʿAli, as both are veiled and share the same flaming halo. If Muhammad is to be identified by the green turban, then it is his head that extends from ʿAli's body—and not vice versa. Moreover, like conjoined twins, this bicephalous entity unites two individual souls into a single body. No longer is ʿAli depicted as Muhammad's close companion or mirror image; instead, he is shown as the Prophet's alter ego. Thus, in this painting the figurative concept of absolute equality has been harmonized and reconciled through the visual metaphor of the two-headed body.[84] Here, Muhammad and ʿAli are envisioned as quintessential soul mates, joined at the neck and conjugated as one.

The painting includes two other notable details. First, in its upper left corner, a bearded man in the rocky background appears to hurl a rock toward the enthroned duo. This individual may represent one of the assailants who tried to ambush and assassinate Muhammad the night

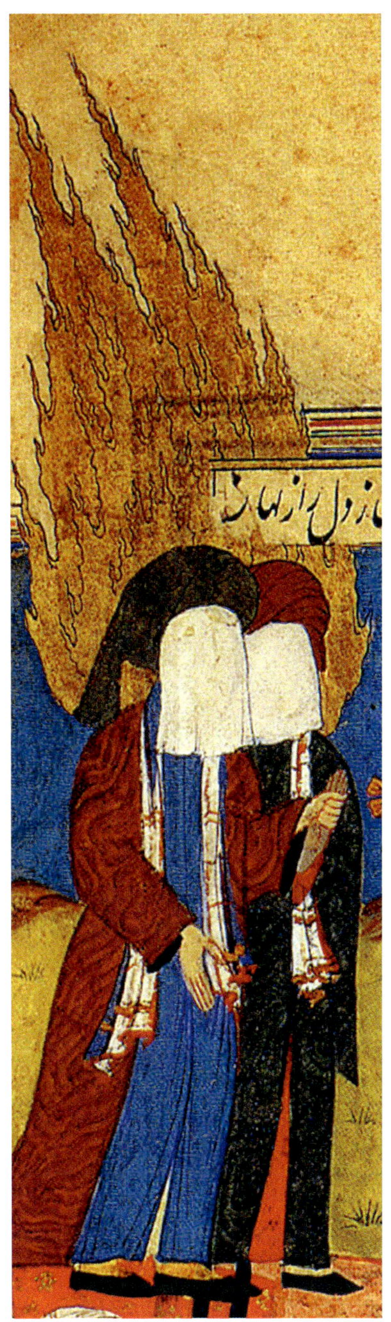

4.11. Detail of figure 4.10, showing the indistinguishably veiled and radiant Muhammad and ʿAli holding hands.

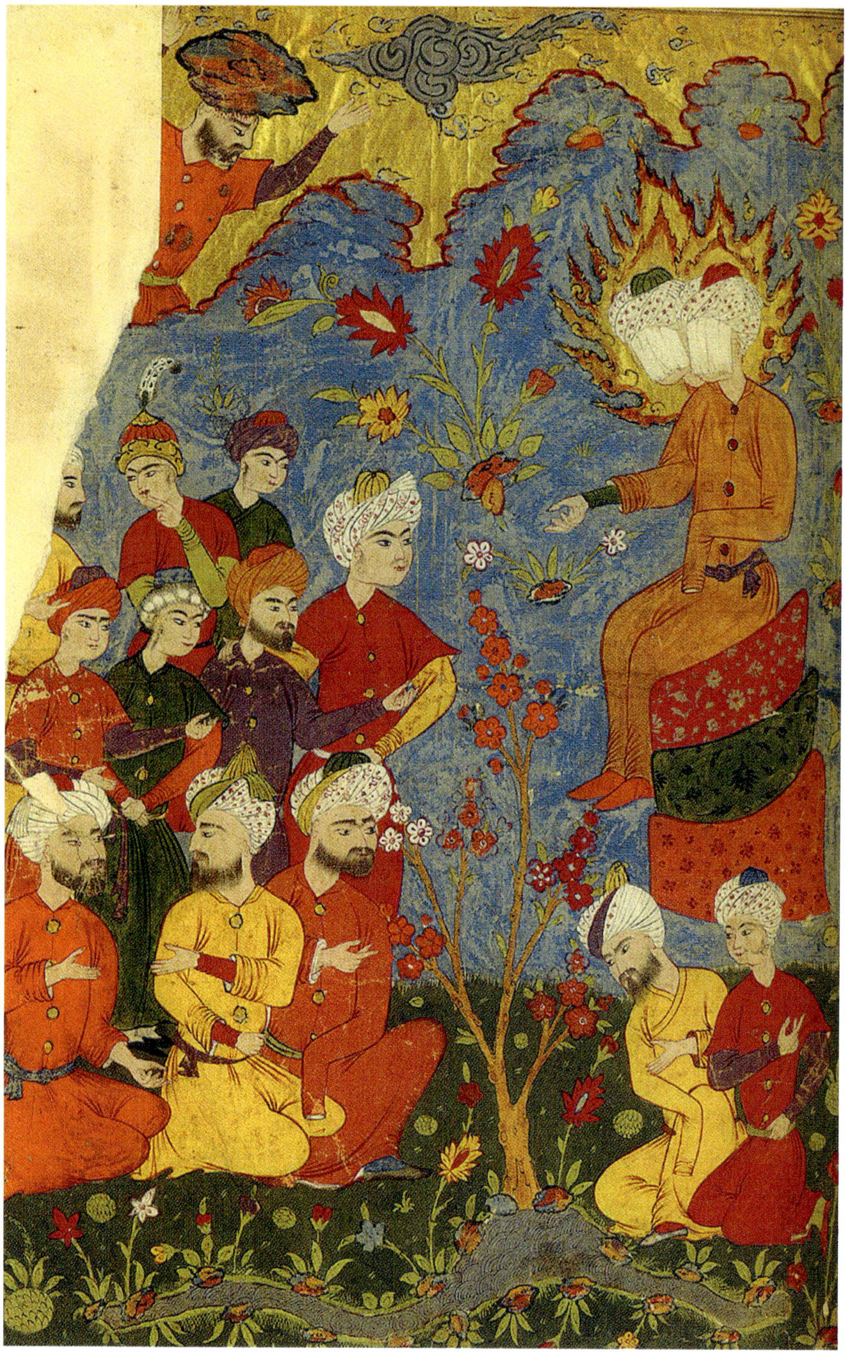

after his stop at Ghadir Khumm. Muhammad foiled the conspiracy and identified fourteen of its plotters, among them Abu Bakr, 'Umar, and 'Uthman. The assailant at the top of the painting therefore may represent the corporate embodiment of Muhammad and 'Ali's enemies, in particular 'Umar, who is said to have had in his possession a document drafted at that time repudiating 'Ali's claims to succession.[85] Second, the group of men witnessing the enthroned Muhammad-cum-'Ali totals twelve in number. While this number is certainly suggestive, its accompanying textual augury specifically mentions 'Ali's appointment as Muhammad's legatee (*wasi*) and the twelve imams.[86] As a consequence, it is possible that the artist altered the Ghadir Khumm narrative—even

THE PRAISEWORTHY ONE

as it was conveyed in Shiʻi textual sources—to further emphasize its sectarian dimensions by placing the two chief protagonists within the entourage of the imamate, itself standing in evident contradistinction to the treasonous enemies of the "true" faith, who are left to fade into the backdrop of history.

The painting of Ghadir Khumm as included in the illustrated *Book of Omens* was not necessarily made for an individual with "relatively heterodox views," as has been previously suggested.[87] While unique in its rendering of Muhammad and ʻAli as conjoined twins, it nonetheless reiterates and crystallizes a number of widespread Shiʻi discourses that intimately align the Prophet with his son-in-law. Simultaneously, the painting also reflects an increasing regularization of a Safavid Shiʻi worldview via the inserted cast of twelve characters now present at Ghadir Khumm. This cohort of twelve imams echoes the evolving doctrine of Twelver Shiʻism during the reign of Shah Tahmasp, at which time an emphasis on hereditary guardianship, genealogical descent via the imamate, and antithetical positioning contra the first three *rashidun* and Sunni adversaries was mobilized to reinforce an emergent Safavid rhetoric on imperial authority and religious supremacy.[88]

Paintings of the Mubahala and Ghadir Khumm provide a kind of litmus test for the development of Safavid religious and political ideology. As evidentiary narratives put to picture, these images provide overt visual confirmation of the supreme status of ʻAli, the *ahl al-bayt*, and the imams. In Mubahala scenes, the Prophet's three first companions are execrated and excised, as well as replaced by members of Muhammad's family, who serve as the ultimate proof of the "correct" faith. An even greater emphasis on the superiority of ʻAli can be found in Safavid illustrations of the events at Ghadir Khumm, in which the Imam's *walaya* is confirmed through his selection by and proximity to the Prophet. In at least one painting of this story, ʻAli's closeness to Muhammad is highlighted by a depiction of the pair as two sacred souls united in one body in absolute equality and harmony. This fusion of the Prophet and his son-in-law yields a hybrid entity, in which ʻAli is shown as copresent with Muhammad and hence his living legatee, whose authority is passed down through the imams to the Safavid rulers. As a result, these paintings of attestation and investiture creatively contributed to the construction of a Shiʻi worldview, in which Muhammad no longer stands alone or unique in his prophetic prerogative. Instead, he appears encircled by his family and descendants at the same time that his luminously veiled appearance becomes aligned—even alloyed—with that of ʻAli, the sprouting figurehead of the Safavid polity.

This emphasis on ʻAli's contributions to Muhammad's glorious life and deeds multiplied in Persian book arts over the course of the sixteenth century. In addition to his presence during moments of attestation and investiture, he also accompanies the Prophet on numerous military campaigns, playing a key role during the successes at the battles of Badr and Khaybar in particular. As discussed in chapter 2, Muhammad's *maghazi* often were framed as divine triumphs, granted by God due to the intercession of angels who not infrequently joined the ranks of Muslim soldiers while also transmitting qur'anic revelation. Moreover, within Shi'i spheres, textual sources emphasize that a number of the Prophet's military victories were secured thanks to the assistance of 'Ali, whose valor and strength are praised. For instance, Shaykh al-Mufid proudly affirms that "no rival escaped from him ['Ali] in battle, no one could escape his blow" and that "despite the length of time which he fought against his enemies, he acquired no ugly wound nor was anyone able to do him harm."[89] In this and other sources, 'Ali's physical endurance is described as miraculous and a sign of God's selection crucial to the Prophet's successes on the battlefield.

During the early modern period, Safavid artists augmented narratives lauding 'Ali as the quintessential warrior of the faith by creating paintings of battle scenes. Although such images clearly draw on Ilkhanid and Timurid prototypes, their novel approaches to narrative content and figural imagery helped promote a number of ideological concerns germane to the Safavid claim to the prophetic *sira*. In this regard, there exist several noteworthy iconographic developments within Persian battle scenes of the sixteenth century. First, 'Ali is depicted as a highly energetic central protagonist in battle scenes in which he previously either played a supporting role or was not depicted at all. Second, 'Ali often is shown benefiting from the assistance of angels, a trope that previously had been reserved for the Prophet. Finally, in Safavid paintings this angelically supported and superhuman 'Ali tends to marginalize Muhammad from his own military exploits, in some cases to such an extent that the Prophet altogether disappears from the painted page. In sum, 'Ali tends to displace Muhammad as the consummate hero of military campaigns supported by soldier angels.

The battle of Badr (624 CE) counts among the most important early triumphs for the Muslim forces. Early and medieval Sunni-sympathetic texts describe the battle as an occasion for the revelation of qur'anic verses that explicate the distribution of war spoils. While 'Ali is indeed present at the battle, his exploits are described as modest and his valor equivalent to that of Abu Bakr.[90] By the early fourteenth century, Persian manuscript paintings of Badr present the Prophet Muhammad as the hero of the campaign—a prophet-soldier aided by angels bearing divine scent, light, and scripture (figs. 2.11–2.15). 'Ali, on the other hand, remains difficult to identify within a painted group scene of the battle of Badr made during the Ilkhanid period (fig. 4.13).[91] He may be the individual wearing a white robe and carrying a sword accompanying the horse-rider clad in a green robe, the latter identifiable as the Prophet Muhammad.

This pivotal confrontation takes a noticeably different turn in Shi'i contexts. In both texts and images, it is 'Ali—and not Muhammad—who shines as the divinely supported slayer of the Muslim community's

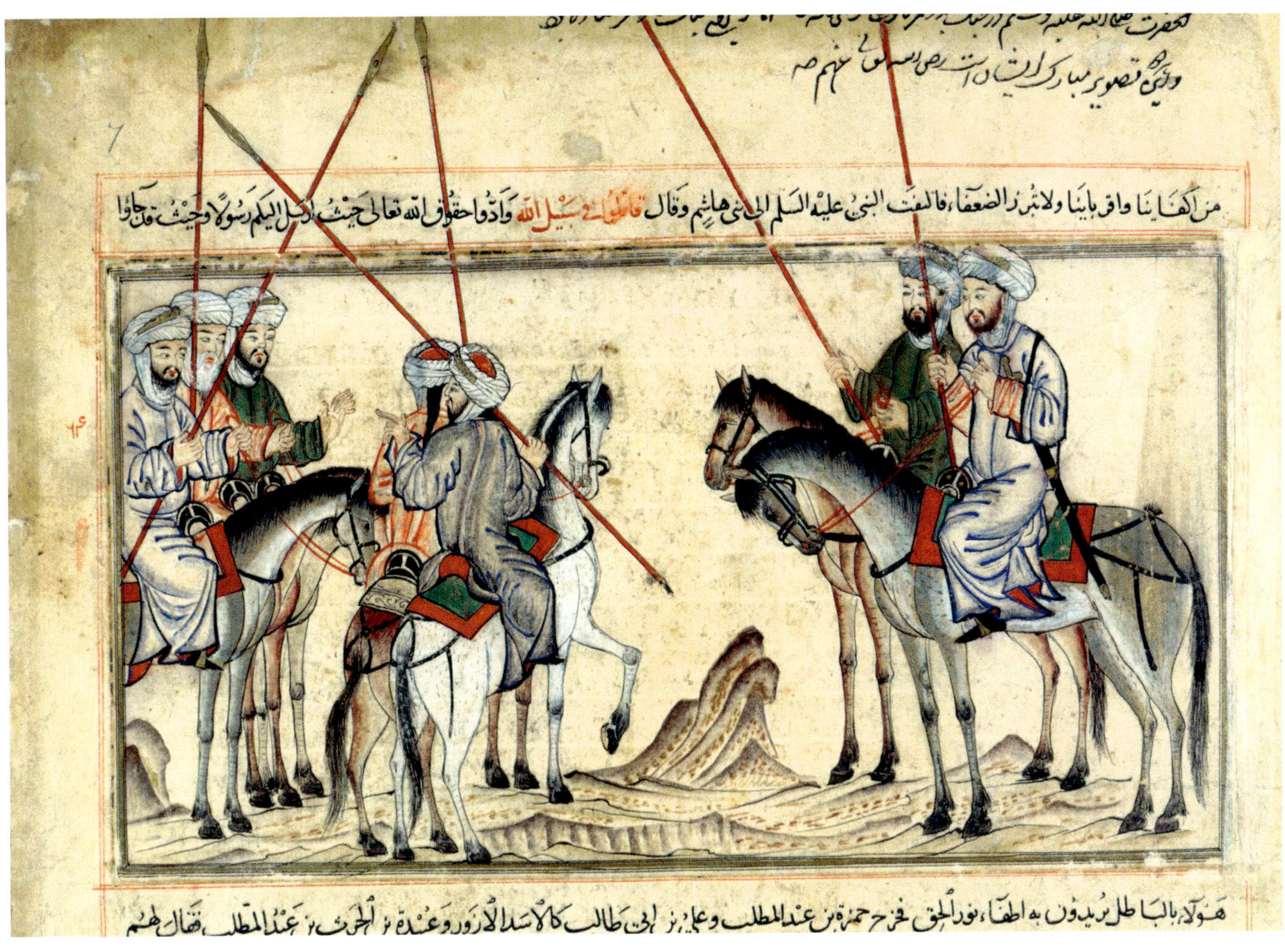

4.13. The battle of Badr, Rashid al-Din, *Jami' al-Tawarikh* (Compendium of Chronicles), Tabriz, 714 AH/1314–15 CE. Nasser D. Khalili Collection of Islamic Art, London, MSS 727, folio 5r.

enemies. For instance, in his *Book of Guidance*, Shaykh al-Mufid depicts 'Ali as a paradigmatic hero, whose bravura secured the victory at Badr. By the author's own account, 'Ali engaged in single combat against Hamza as well as 'Ubayda b. al-Harith and also killed al-Walid and Nawfal. Moreover, 'Ali is said to have slayed more than half of the seventy Meccan warriors who fought against the Muslim forces (with the other half either killed by the Prophet and his followers or decimated by three thousand angels).[92] As the battle's principal protagonist in this and other Shi'i accounts, 'Ali is shown outperforming Muhammad and all other Muslim soldiers, and his strength is likened to that of three thousand angels. Clearly, his is a battlefield fortitude of supernatural proportions imagined as surpassing the Prophet's own.

Representations of the battle of Badr are included in several Safavid historical manuscripts of the sixteenth century. In these illustrated books, depictions of the episode echo and amplify pro-'Alid motifs found in both earlier and contemporary texts. For example, Astarabadi's *sira* of the Prophet includes a chapter dedicated to the battle, which is lavishly illustrated in a copy dated 1567 CE (fig. 4.14).[93] As Karin Rührdanz has noted, this composition is indeed daring in its insertion of armed angels that not only swoop down from the sky but also ride on horseback at a full gallop in the painting's lower right corner. She also states that the text demands that 'Ali be identified as the main actor in

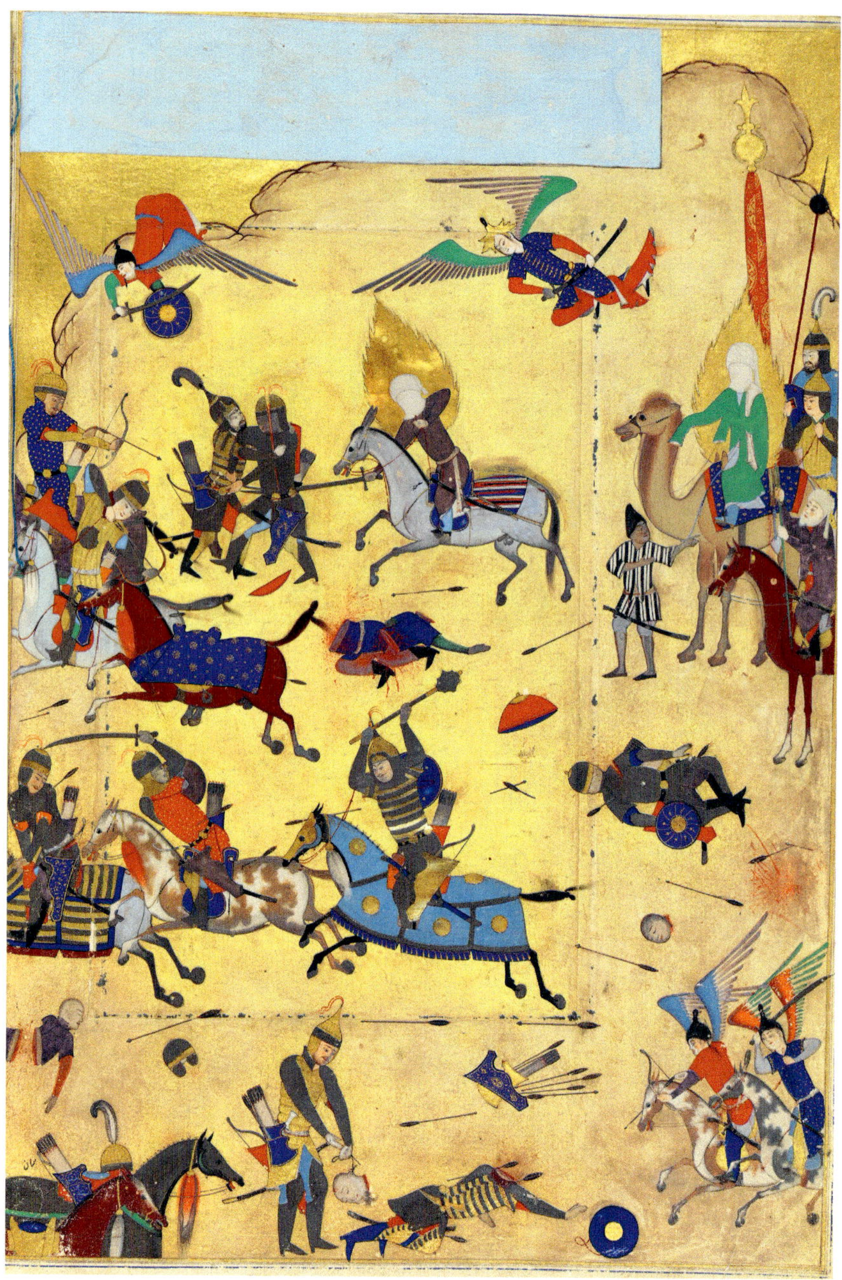

the top center of the composition.[94] Rührdanz is correct on both counts: the angels on horseback are not found in Ilkhanid and Timurid depictions of Badr and thus constitute a novel motif in the history of Persian painting, and the central protagonist on horseback must be identified as ʿAli for a number reasons, including, most prominently, his wielding of the double-pointed sword Dhu'l-Fiqar, which slices his opponent (probably Nawfal) in half.

However, this manuscript painting of Badr is not as astonishing as one might imagine. To the contrary, its angelic motifs appear in both Sunni and Shiʿi texts over the centuries. The presence of warrior angels in the Safavid image builds on Islamic texts that describe the triumph at Badr as part of God's plan to strengthen Muslim forces by sending legions of angels to their aid. This military success, like so many others,

THE PRAISEWORTHY ONE

was described in the Qur'an (8:45) as a blessing from God, and the Muslim soldiers are reminded that "it was not you who killed them, but God did so" (Q 8:17).[95] These clashes provide occasions for theophany, at which time God's appearance in the form of angels ensures victory, itself a sign of salvation (*furqan*).[96] As a result, the Safavid painting's depiction of angels—fully armed and engaged in combat—aims to portray the battle of Badr as the ultimate *furqan* for the Muslim community.

The inclusion of angels in the Safavid depiction must have carried sectarian connotations, as well. Like Shaykh al-Mufid's narrative, Shi'i texts stress 'Ali's key contribution to the battle, equating his strength to that of three thousand angels. In the painting, the Safavid artist therefore strives to show angels not only contributing to the success at Badr but also acting as the attendants of 'Ali and not Muhammad. The two angels swooping down from the sky no longer come to the Prophet, offering him divine scripture and scent, as they do in Persian paintings of the fourteenth and fifteenth centuries. To the contrary, in this sixteenth-century depiction the angels flank 'Ali, the veiled and radiant protagonist executing Nawfal in the center of the composition. As Shaykh al-Mufid notes regarding this event, "Ali gave the final blow and then went to the Prophet, who praised 'Ali's feat with the following words: 'God is Great! Praise be to God who has answered my prayer concerning him ['Ali].'"[97]

In this Shi'i text and the Safavid painting, the Prophet is literally marginalized from the event, appearing as if he were not participating in the battle. Instead, he sits on camelback with his robe's long sleeves covering his hands, effectively hindering physical participation in battle. Acting as a passive observer rather than an active participant in warfare, Muhammad sits on the sidelines, petitioning God to help 'Ali secure victory. In the Safavid pictorial rendering of the battle of Badr, Muhammad's prophetic prestige and prerogative have been ceded to 'Ali, who is depicted as a triumphant warrior-leader thanks to both his own superhuman strength and the legions of angels sent by God.

Other Safavid book paintings that depict the Prophet's *maghazi* put forth a similar set of messages by visually emphasizing 'Ali as a military hero of stupefying strength while minimizing Muhammad's presence in and contributions to battle. In this regard, the battle at the oasis of Khaybar is even more significant than the battle of Badr. The battle of Khaybar took place in 629 CE, when the Muslim army staged a decisive raid against the Jewish Banu'l-Nadir tribe, whose members took refuge in the Fort of Qamus. Islamic sources state that the attack was ordered by Muhammad after the tribe had failed to avert—and even incited— several attacks against Muslim forces. Like Badr, Khaybar proved a major victory for the Prophet and his followers, yielding substantial booty that helped sustain subsequent campaigns.

Regardless of their sectarian inclinations, Islamic chronicles stress the pivotal role played by 'Ali in securing the victory at Khaybar, describing his strength as miraculous and his victory as granted by God.

For instance, Ibn Ishaq states that Muhammad first sent Abu Bakr and 'Umar to take the fort, but both failed. Thereupon he selected 'Ali, gave him his banner, and cured his ophthalmia by applying saliva to his eyeball while declaring to his followers: "God will conquer it [the fort] by his means." As 'Ali approached the redoubt, a Jewish soldier named Marhab struck him, causing him to drop his shield. To compensate for the loss, 'Ali picked up a door of the fortress and held it in his hand during the offensive, "until God gave victory, throwing it away when all was over." According to witnesses cited by Ibn Ishaq, the door was so heavy that even eight men were not able to turn it over.[98] Thus, in even the earliest of sources, 'Ali emerges as the Herculean hero of Khaybar, whose victory is effectuated by the will and advent of God in battle.

Ibn Ishaq's account planted the seeds for a further elaboration of 'Ali's special status and characteristics, which can be found in later historical sources written in Persian. Within medieval Iranian spheres, al-Bal'ami's Persian translation of al-Tabari's history, penned in 963 CE, provides an expanded chapter on the battle of Khaybar, in which the author notes that it was 'Ali—and not Muhammad—who killed Marhab, slicing him in two.[99] He also reports that 'Ali ripped off the fortress door by its handle thanks to the assistance of the Angel Gabriel.[100] That these particular details are not included in al-Tabari's original text suggests al-Bal'ami's discreet but palpable sectarian take on the battle.[101] It also reveals an increasingly favorable disposition toward 'Ali within the arena of war.

The hero's military achievements and angelic strength are further amplified in overtly pro-Shi'i texts from the medieval period onward. For example, Shaykh al-Mufid, al-Bal'ami's near-contemporary, also describes the campaign at Khaybar. However, in his *Book of Guidance* he adds an entirely separate chapter dedicated to praising 'Ali's prodigious strength during the battle, stating that 'Ali's removal of the fortress door took the strength of twenty, fifty, or even seventy men—and other Shi'i texts increase this number to five hundred.[102] Moving forward in this vein, Shaykh al-Mufid continues, "God sets 'Ali apart by his signs, and strength is one of them. . . . This is an example of the special strength with which God endowed him. Through it the normal (human) qualities were transcended and it became a miraculous sign."[103] In other words, in Shi'i textual sources the battle of Khaybar was understood as an occasion for God to reveal himself through the miracle of 'Ali's fortitude, itself an indication of the hero's divine selection. Muhammad, on the other hand, appears largely incidental to the exploits of his valiant counterpart.

As a blessed sign, the battle of Khaybar also formed the subject of representation in at least two Safavid *Falnama*s (Books of Omens). Made during the mid-sixteenth century and linked to the patronage of Shah Tahmasp, these luxuriously illustrated augury books also depict a number of other Islamic, Shi'i, and Persian tales and motifs. Some of 'Ali's greatest miracles—removing the door, storming the fortress,

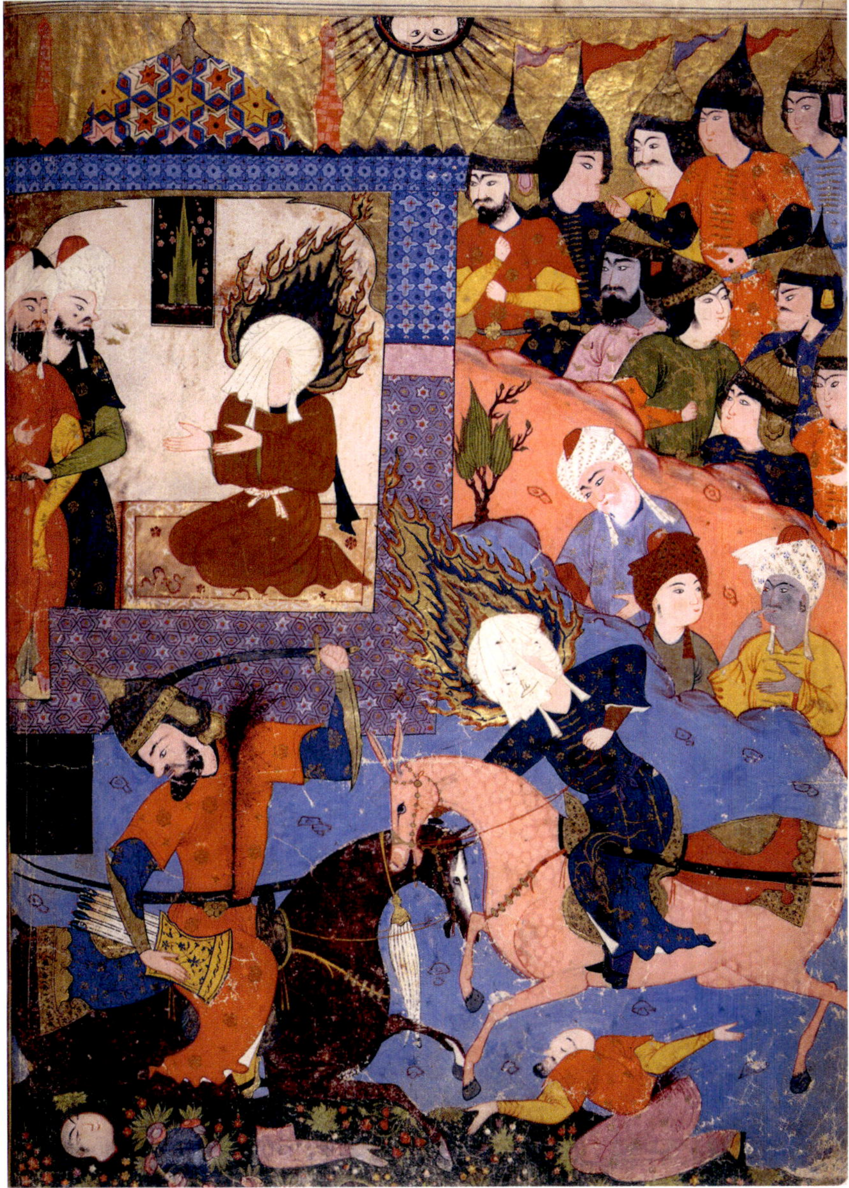

4.15. The battle at Khaybar, attributed to Jaʿfar al-Sadiq, *Falnama* (Book of Omens), Tabriz or Qazvin, ca. 1540–50 CE. Sächsische Landesbibliothek, Dresden, E445, folio 3v. Image courtesy of SLUB Dresden/Digital Collections/Mscr.Dresd.Eb.445.

and leading the way to success at Khaybar—were considered especially good omens for augury-seekers who might happen on the battle's illustration. This type of auspicious depiction included within a Safavid *Book of Omens* shows Imam ʿAli on horseback as his sword halves his opponent, Marhab (fig. 4.15).[104] The protagonist's high-powered feat in the painting's foreground is set ablaze by the golden halo bursting forth from his head. Like the Prophet, who kneels in prayer in a domed building behind the confrontation, ʿAli is touched by radiant light. Unlike Muhammad, however, ʿAli is dynamic and engaged in the battle as well as clearly identified (and perhaps invoked) through his personal name inscribed in gold ink on his facial veil. Thus, while both protagonists partake in the same veiled mystery and radiant flux, there is no mistaking ʿAli for the Prophet—and it is ʿAli who emerges centrally triumphant while Muhammad remains relegated to the back, petitioning God to grant him victory through his son-in-law.

In addition to the Prophet's prayerful pose, which appears undermined by his physical inertia as well as constricted by a small domed edifice, several other motifs stand out in this Safavid depiction of the battle of Khaybar. First, three turbaned individuals count among a group of soldiers wearing helmets on the painting's right side. One of the men bears a white beard, and this visual attribute may serve to identify Abu Bakr. Close to him stands a young man with darker skin who bites his finger in amazement; this individual may be Qanbar, 'Ali's loyal companion and servant. Last, but not least, among the troops stands a man with dark gray skin and a black beard; this may be 'Umar. Like Abu Bakr, 'Umar failed to take the fortress prior to 'Ali's successful sortie. It is possible that the Safavid painter rendered 'Umar with a blackened face as an indication of his damnation to hell for offenses including his injustices against and disloyalty to 'Ali.[105] In this manner, the gray skin motif, as applied to 'Umar in particular, may function as a sectarian curse in pictorial form, joining other forms of Shi'i maledictions against past and present Sunni adversaries that were prevalent in Iran during the sixteenth century.[106]

Also prominent in this painting is the sun depicted with (upside down) facial features and rays of light bursting from the top center of the painting. Although the sun does not play an important role in the battle of Khaybar, it is nonetheless associated with 'Ali's miracles, among which was his angelic fortitude at the Fort of Qamus. Shi'i writers who were interested in 'Ali's miracles, such as Shaykh al-Mufid, report that 'Ali commanded the sun to return to its earlier position on two occasions: once at noontime, when Muhammad fell asleep on his thigh, hindering his ability to move and perform prayer, and then again when 'Ali and his followers were crossing the Euphrates River. Both times, 'Ali's sending back of the sun (*radd al-shams*) caused a loud screech, similar to a saw cutting through wood or a violent vibration.[107] In addition, Shi'i narratives record the sun speaking to 'Ali, specifying that this miracle provided clear evidence that 'Ali was the unquestioned legatee (*wasi*) of Muhammad. Still other writers, including the Safavid theologian al-Majlisi, record sun miracles for both Muhammad and 'Ali, revealing the extent to which the miracles and functions of the Prophet and his son-in-law were interchangeable.[108] Such is the case with the painting of the battle of Khaybar, which pictorially praises 'Ali, the sunlit and miracle-working warrior-*wasi*.

Another Safavid *Book of Omens* painting of the battle of Khaybar takes the visual narrative one step further by incorporating a number of other motifs (fig. 4.16).[109] In this depiction, the Prophet straddles his white horse below the banner that he granted to 'Ali on the occasion of his raiding of the fortress. Muhammad's identification is made possible thanks to a small inscription to the left of his facial veil, which provides his honorific title "His Excellency the Refuge of Prophecy" (*janab-i rasalat-panah*). Without this added caption, and without knowledge of the narrative, the painting's viewer easily could confuse Muhammad

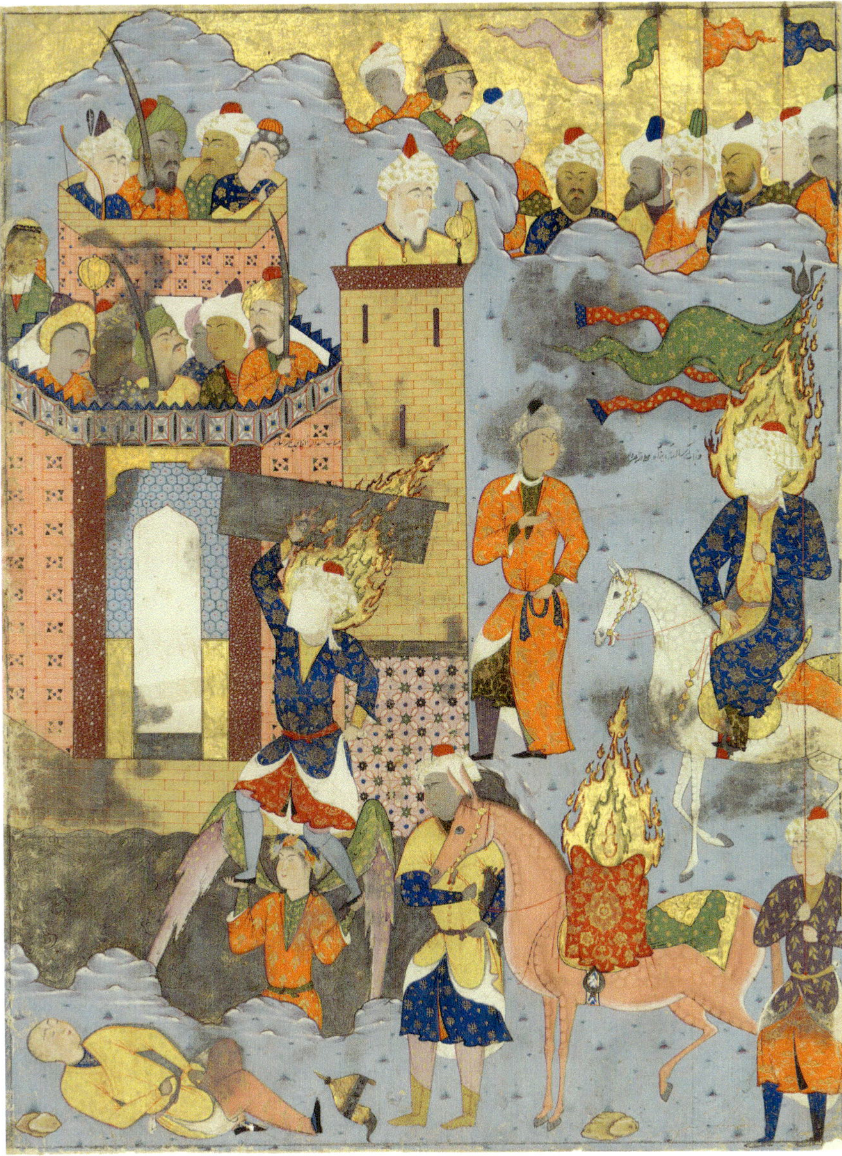

with 'Ali—both are marked by identical flaming aureoles, patterned turbans, white facial veils, and blue robes embroidered with golden flowers.[110] Moreover, it would stand to reason to identify 'Ali as the Prophet, as the valiant conqueror of the Qamus fortress does not ride a horse or walk on the ground but rather is lifted into the air by Gabriel, the transmitter of God's Logos, who almost without exception serves as Muhammad's angelic guide and companion. Instead, in this depiction it is 'Ali, not Muhammad, who rises triumphantly from Gabriel's palms, as if he were launched on a symbolic ascension out of the dark waters below.

As he leaps from his horse, 'Ali has a radiance so enduring that Duldul's saddle remains ablaze, marking the sacred spot that his body occupied an instant earlier. Above the hero, a Jewish man stands perched above the fort's tower, holding what appears to be an astrolabe in his hand. Although it has been conjectured that he is announcing the battle hour to the Jewish soldiers,[111] it is more likely that this individual is the Jewish soothsayer who witnessed 'Ali and then swore by his name, an act that Muslim historians considered a good omen. For instance, Ibn Ishaq describes the episode, stating that a "Jew looked at him ['Ali] from the top of the fort and asked who he was, and when he told him he said, 'You have won, by what was revealed to Moses!'"[112] The wise Jew thus announces 'Ali's victory as a felicitous sign from God, a narrative and pictorial motif that is germane to the overarching thrust of the illustrated *Book of Omens* genre and Safavid divinatory practices in general.[113] Moreover, it aligns well with the textual augury that accompanies this painting of the Muslim conquest at Khaybar, which informs the reader that all of his wishes and desires will come true and that "you have become successful in all your desires, and the closed door opened to you, and your difficulties relieved."[114] Thus, the events at Khaybar bestow glad tidings—foretelling that doors will be pried open and burdens removed—while 'Ali, not Muhammad, embodies the most auspicious sign of all.

Last but not least, below the Jewish augur and above the large black door carried by 'Ali appears a second small inscription identifying the conquering hero as "His Excellency the Victorious Lion of God" (*janab-i Asadullah al-ghalib*). As is the case with the caption identifying Muhammad, 'Ali is named via one of his honorific titles. In this instance, however, his sobriquet *lion of God* holds particular importance as some narrative sources, especially those of Shi'i leaning, inform us that it was during the battle of Khaybar that 'Ali truly earned his leonine epithet. For example, in his *Book of Guidance*, Shaykh al-Mufid records an exchange between Marhab and 'Ali, in which Marhab declares himself a carrier of arms as well as a tested hero, to which 'Ali responds:

> I am he whom my mother called a lion.
> Like a lion of the forests, fierce in strength,
> With my sword I will make you weigh the weight of an ear torn off.[115]

Through both bestial and martial metaphors, 'Ali's fierceness and strength are equated to those of a lion, the roaring king of the animal world. The allegory also anticipates Safavid depictions of 'Ali as a celestial lion-angel, which the Prophet encounters during his ascension through the heavens (fig. 3.21).[116]

In addition to their importance within practices of divination, depictions of 'Ali confronting Marhab and storming the Qamus fortress appear in Safavid histories, as well. The 1567 CE copy of Astarabadi's *Traces of the Victorious* discussed previously includes scenes that depict the Prophet Muhammad's life and exploits, among them the events at Khaybar (fig. 4.17). Produced on the heels of the illustrated *Books of Omens*, the painting employs motifs found in Safavid depictions of this momentous confrontation. 'Ali's white facial veil and golden aureole, as well as the equestrian combat at the base of the redoubt and the slicing in half of Marhab, are motifs common to renditions of the episode.

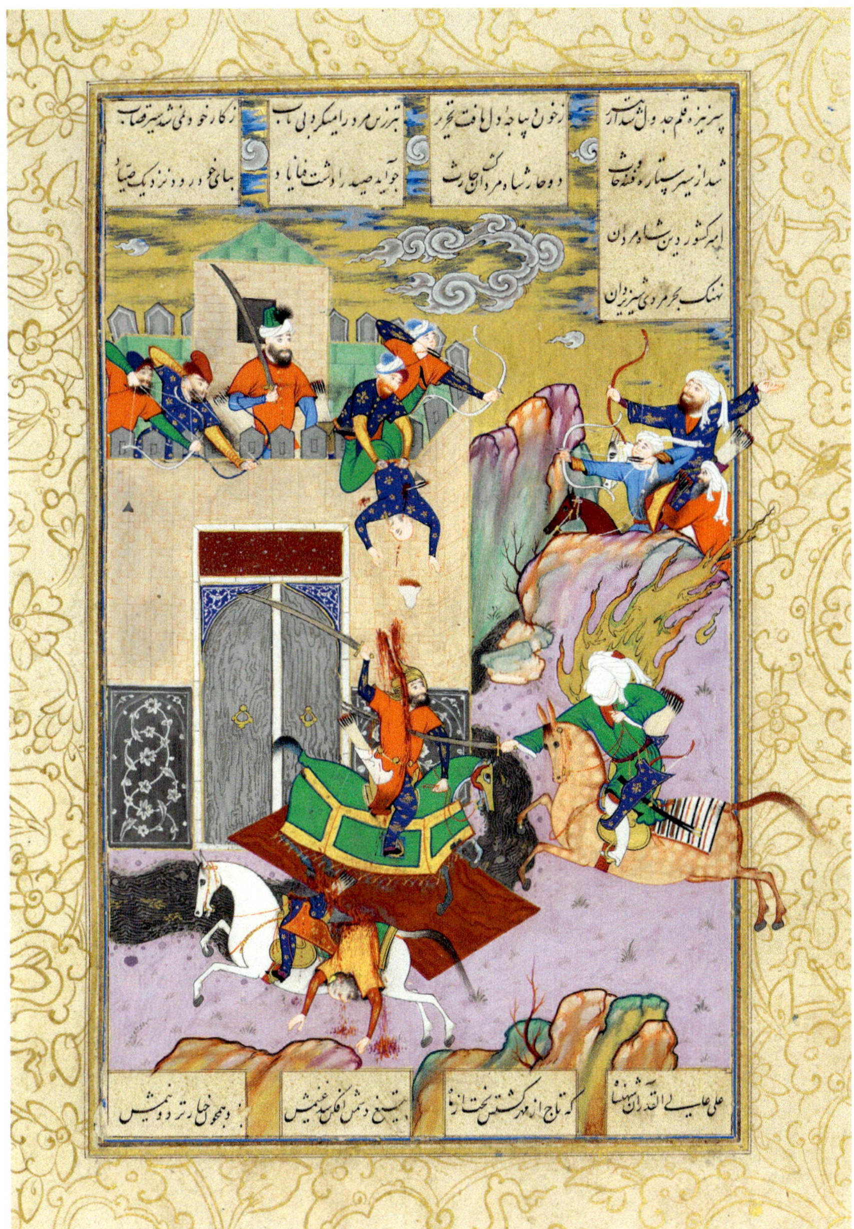

4.17. The battle at Khaybar, Astarabadi, *Athar al-Muzaffar* (The Exploits of the Victorious), Iran (possibly Qazvin), 974 AH/1567 CE. Topkapı Palace Library, Istanbul, H. 1233, folio 158v. Photograph by Hadiye Cangökçe.

Departing from other illustrations, however, this scene is overtly sanguine: the artist has emphasized the blood gushing out of Marhab's helmet and body; the bloodied person cut in half at the waist, whose torso falls to the ground; and the Jewish man shot with an arrow and impaled against the wall of the fortress, his hat tumbling from his head. The scene emphasizes 'Ali's ability to secure total military triumph, regardless of the means to that end. Here, the pattern of angelic assistance (or even ascension) is cast aside in favor of a portrayal centered on blood, itself a key rhetorical device within the painting's accompanying Persian verses.

Besides the image's graphic rendering of the military confrontation, another element should catch the viewer's attention by its absence. Indeed, as much as the eye may travel the painting and observe its most minute details, it will fail to detect Muhammad. Gone is the Prophet from the battle of Khaybar, one of his most important early victories. His absence is conspicuous, to say the least: after all, in Ilkhanid and Timurid battle paintings, he acts as the chief protagonist, triumphing and receiving revelation, while in other Safavid representations of Khaybar he prays for or watches 'Ali's success, even if from the background or the outer edges of the main action. However, in figure 4.18, Muhammad is neither recessed nor marginalized: he has altogether vanished, leaving his son-in-law, veiled and aglow, to dominate the scene alone.

PARTNERS IN IDOL BREAKING

Safavid illustrations of Badr and Khaybar display a panoply of iconographical strategies and settings that, much like Shi'i texts, aim to render 'Ali as an equal to or even a supplanter of the Prophet. Capable of performing miracles of fortitude and supported by angelic reinforcements, 'Ali is rendered increasingly prophet-like in his demeanor and feats within Safavid war paintings. Beyond these two battles, one final victory remained to be achieved that would confirm Muhammad as the ultimate leader of the new faith community: the smashing of the pagan idols at the Ka'ba. The destruction of these object-signs of Arabian polytheism ushered in a new world order under the Islamic faith, symbolically obliterating the so-called Age of Ignorance (*Jahiliyya*).

In his *sira*, Ibn Ishaq states that Muhammad purged the Ka'ba of 360 idols, some of which were strengthened with lead. While smashing these statuettes to smithereens with his stick, the Prophet is said to have proclaimed aloud, "The truth (*al-haqq*) has come, and falsehood (*al-batil*) has passed away" (Q 17:82). The icons of Jesus and Mary were preserved, but the Prophet ordered all idols of Arabian pagan deities gathered and burned. Thereafter, he stood at the door of the Ka'ba, declaring, "There is no god but God Alone. He has no associate. He has made good on His promise and helped His servant."[117] As in many other Islamic textual sources, Ibn Ishaq's account of the retaking of Mecca and Muhammad's reconsecration of the Ka'ba establishes this last success as the beginnings of the true faith and the arrival of God's light on earth.

While narrated as a historical event, this episode features details that are highly metaphorical insomuch as they describe the triumph of monotheism over polytheism, the latter reified as three-dimensional statues. In this regard, the conservation of the images of Mary (a holy woman) and Jesus (an Abrahamic prophet) reveals that Muhammad's pivotal act of iconoclasm did not annihilate images indiscriminately. Much more significantly, it targeted the Arabian heathenism, idolatry, and ignorance that the idols represented.[118]

In some *Hadith*s and many Shi'i textual and visual sources, the Prophet's destruction of the idols at the Ka'ba—a watershed moment for the decisive implementation of the true faith in Mecca, whence it would spread to lands both east and west—necessitated the assistance of his son-in-law.[119] For instance, Shaykh al-Mufid's account of the episode

THE PRAISEWORTHY ONE

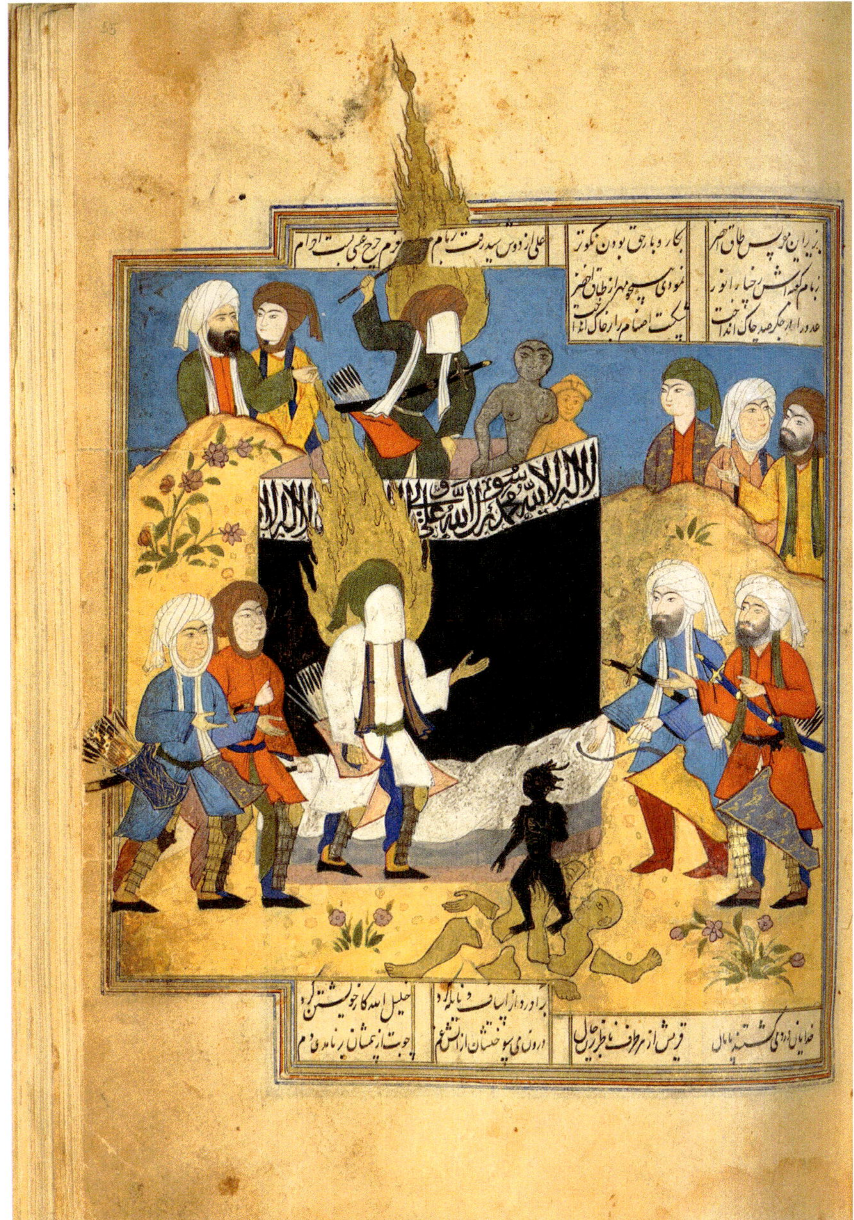

4.18. The breaking of the idols at the Ka'ba, Astarabadi, *Athar al-Muzaffar* (The Exploits of the Victorious), Iran (possibly Qazvin), 974/1567 CE. Chester Beatty Library, Dublin, Per. 235, folio 55r. © The Trustees of the Chester Beatty Library, Dublin.

records Muhammad and his family entering the sacred precinct, whereupon the Prophet saw the pagan idols. He asked 'Ali to bring him stones, which he threw at the idols while proclaiming, "The truth (*al-haqq*) has come, and falsehood (*al-batil*) has passed away," a verse included in most textual narratives regardless of their sectarian agendas. The idols thus fell to the ground and were broken. This seminal act, as Shaykh al-Mufid concludes, provides clear evidence for 'Ali's unmatched and divinely granted merit.[120]

In Shi'i medieval and postmedieval textual sources, the breaking of the idols at the Ka'ba is a collaborative act by Muhammad and 'Ali. By the sixteenth century, however, Persian prose and verse texts, as well as manuscript paintings, eclipse this teamwork model to instead endow 'Ali with primary agency for eradicating idolatry and inaugurating the

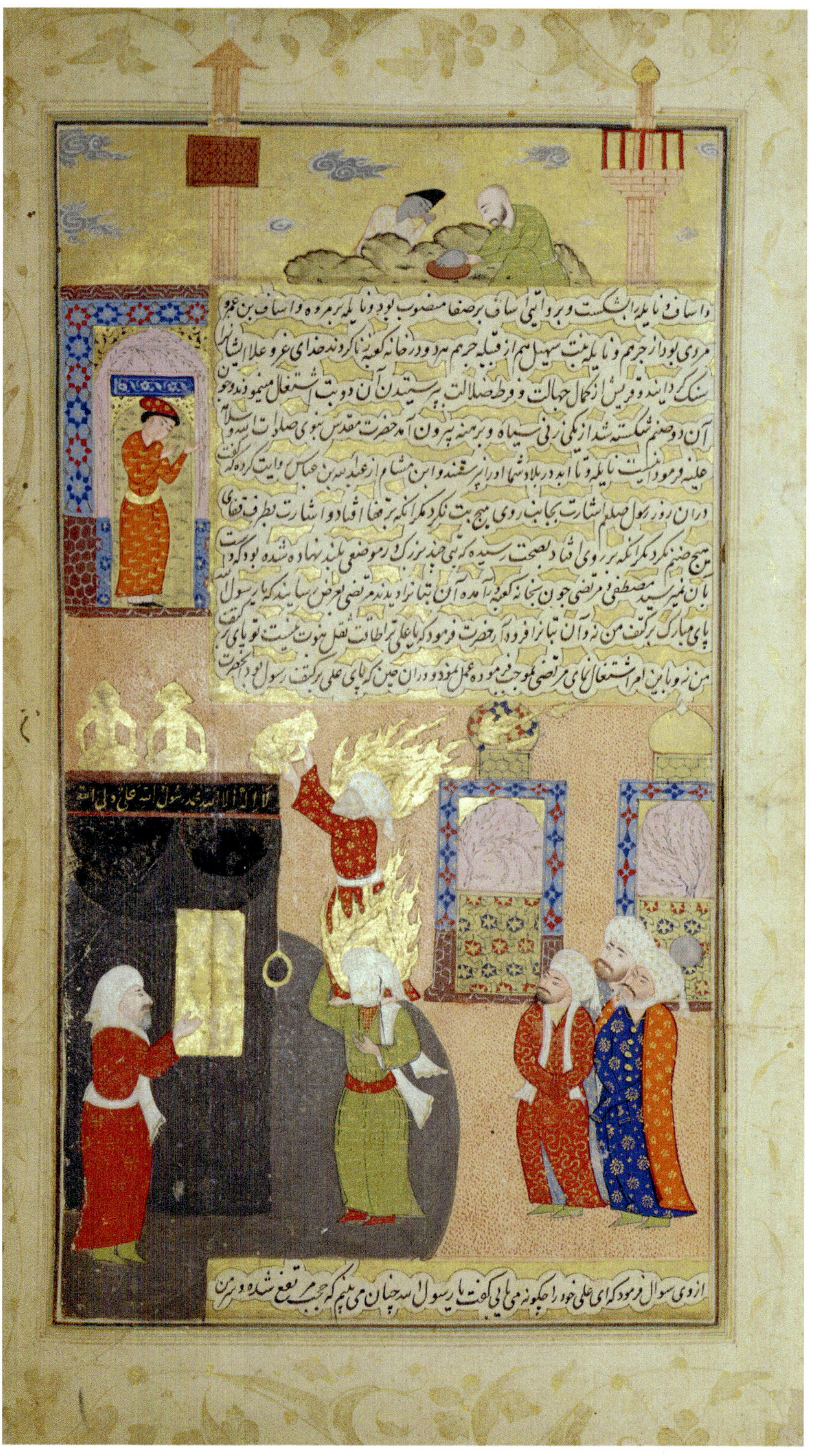

one true faith. For instance, in the 1567 CE copy of the *Traces of the Victorious*, the Safavid author Astarabadi poetically describes 'Ali's climbing to the top of the Ka'ba and his breaking of the idols. The episode is accompanied by a dynamic painting depicting 'Ali (carrying his sword Dhu'l-Fiqar) on the verge of hurling his mace at two seated idols, one of which appears to be made of silver (fig. 4.18).[121] On the ground,

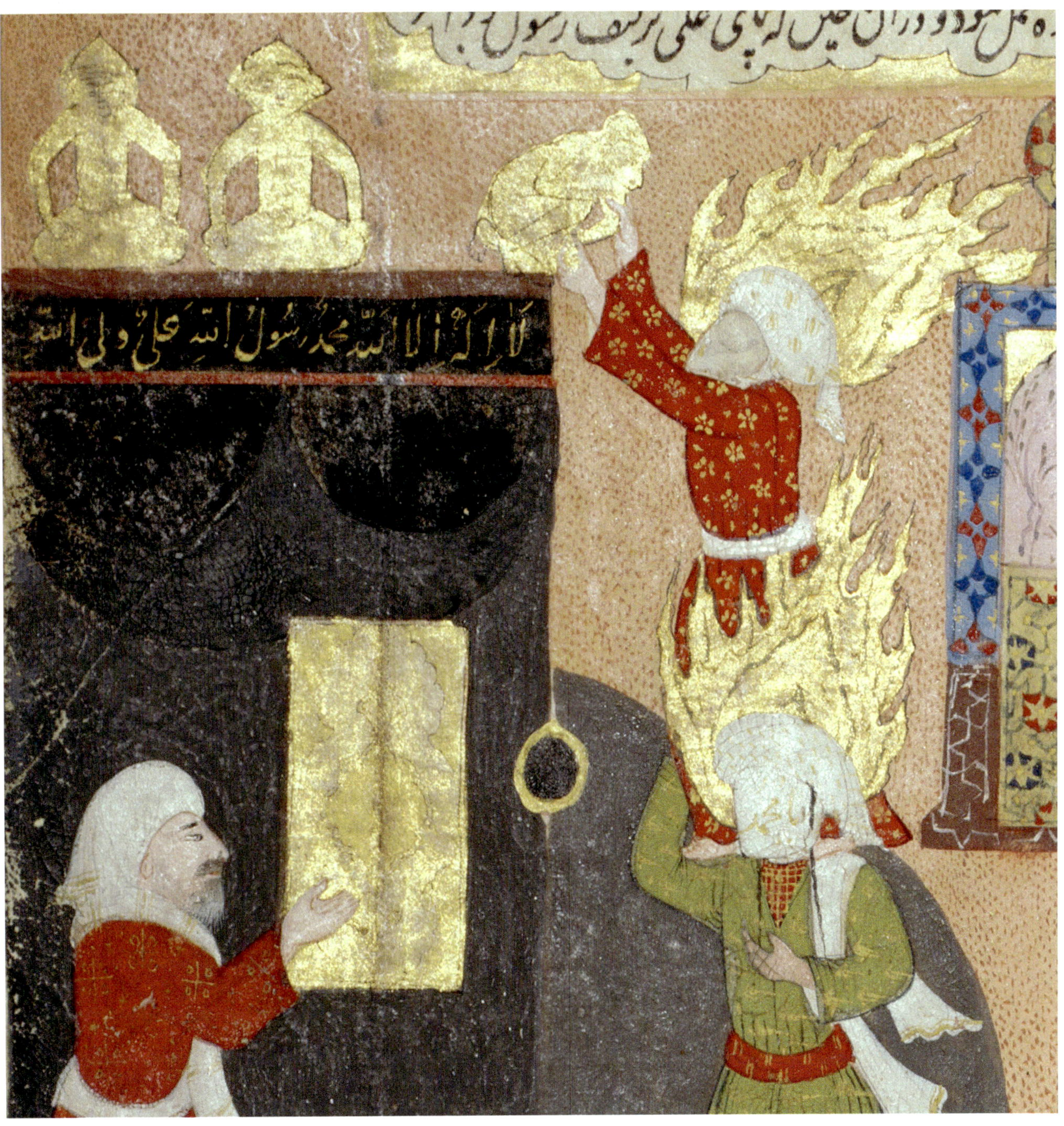

another smashed idol—perhaps of stone and representing the pagan god Hubal[122]—releases a black demon from its inner core.[123] For his part, the Prophet no longer acts as the primary mover in this radical act; instead, he stands, as if a mere observer, gesticulating at the foot of the Ka'ba while the action unfolds and Muslim followers and members of the Quraysh tribe look on.

Other Safavid paintings represent the breaking of the idols by depicting 'Ali on Muhammad's shoulders as he reaches for idols on the roof of the Ka'ba. Among these works, a painting included in a late sixteenth-century illustrated copy of Mirkhwand's world history *Rawdat al-Safa*

4.20. Detail of figure 4.19, showing 'Ali stepping on Muhammad's shoulders as he removes a monkey-shaped idol from the roof of the Ka'ba.

(Garden of Purity) shows both veiled and haloed protagonists forming a human ladder next to the Ka'ba's black stone (*al-hajar al-aswad*) (fig. 4.19).[124] The Safavid author relates that the Prophet wanted to destroy all of the idols in Mecca; however, he could not reach those on the roof of the Ka'ba and so ordered 'Ali onto his shoulders. Muhammad then lifted him, and 'Ali successfully completed the task. The painting follows the overall narrative of its accompanying text by depicting 'Ali standing on the shoulders of the Prophet while a number of individuals in the sacred precinct look on prayerfully, raising their hands in the air. Among them, three men—most likely Abu Bakr, 'Uthman, and 'Umar—do not stand in a devotional position as they observe the event from the lower right corner. These three cursed ones are hence excluded from Muhammad and 'Ali's intimate physical bond as well as from the achievement of the major turning point of early Islamic history.

On closer inspection, several other details are worthy of note (fig. 4.20). First, Muhammad is identifiable by his green robe, black tresses, and the pious "*Ya Muhammad!*" invocation inscribed in gold ink on his white facial veil. While this veil has remained intact, that of 'Ali has sustained evident damage. 'Ali's facial veil likely also was originally painted white and overlaid with a vocative inscription of his name, a motif seen in Persian drawings and paintings of the Timurid and Safavid periods (fig. 4.15).[125] The damage could be due to deliberate defacement or to repeated devotional rubbing and kissing of the veil. Because the pro-Shi'i inscription on the Ka'ba—a topic to which we will return shortly—remains intact, the damage here is most likely the result of viewers' physical expression of affection. As evidenced by other Islamic and medieval European paintings, devotees cultivated close physical relationships with images, and one form of devotion was kissing and rubbing.[126] Over time, these haptic acts, performed with lips and/or fingers, resulted in unintended damage,[127] revealing that at times iconophilic practices can be as destructive to images as iconoclastic ones. Thus, in the Safavid painting, the object of the viewer's devotion—and, ironically, thereby the defaced object—is 'Ali and not Muhammad, whose facial veil remains pristine.

Beyond the physical dimension of piously viewing images according to a mode of engagement that betrays sectarian sentiments, the Safavid painting also includes an inscription that is usually delivered by oral means. The epigraphic band ornaments the upper part of the embroidered *kiswa*, the black fabric that drapes over the Ka'ba during pilgrimage season, and reads, "There is no god but God, Muhammad is His Messenger, and 'Ali is the vicegerent (*wali*) of God." Also included in figure 4.18 and other Safavid paintings that depict the breaking of the idols, this declaration is essentially a Shi'ified version of the *shahada*. It is referred to either as the *walaya* (proclamation of allegiance [to 'Ali]) or as the "third *shahada*" (*al-shahada al-thalitha*), which symbolically completes the monotheistic creed by inserting a mention of 'Ali and his rightful rule as its third and last clause. In addition to ritual practices of public cursing in mosques as well as the delivery of the Friday sermon and the minting of coins in the name of the twelve imams, the *walaya* was ordered as an addition to the call to prayer (*adhan*) by Shah Isma'il I on his accession to the throne.[128] As Liyakat Takim notes, the *walaya* fulfilled a liturgical role and functioned as a public avowal of the religious affiliation of the Safavid state.[129] In turn, this pillar of Shi'i identity was asserted through both oral and pictorial production, enabling listeners and viewers to come to the conclusion that without 'Ali—without the *wali* of God—the "true" religion remains incomplete at best.[130] Thus, the Safavid painting depicts finished business: the end of the *Jahiliyya* and its idols along with the genesis and completion of the one true faith—that is, Shi'i Islam—at the hands of 'Ali.

As it tracked the development of Safavid manuscript paintings of the Prophet, this chapter began with a discussion of images of Muhammad and then embarked on an exploration of depictions of 'Ali. While this slip may seem accidental, it is telling in many ways. Perhaps most significantly, it reveals that it is nearly impossible to speak of Safavid depictions of the Prophet without speaking of those of 'Ali. In some instances, images of 'Ali surpass those of Muhammad to such an extent that the Prophet no longer forms the primary subject matter of his own biography. Instead Muhammad cedes the standard and prerogative of leadership to his lion-hearted son-in-law, the heroic progenitor of the Safavid new world order.

In these sixteenth-century paintings of the ship of salvation, investiture and attestation, military campaigns, and idol breaking, Muhammad no longer stands alone as a cosmic ruler and receiver of divine light and revelation. His special attributes become shared, primarily with 'Ali and in some cases with the imams, whose *taj-i Haydari* visually aligns their authority with that of the ruling members of the Safavid household. As visual groupings and pictorial genealogies, such depictions ensconce Muhammad within a larger familial setting as well as at the head of generations of rightful legatees. No longer is he unique, separate, and incomparable; to the contrary, his radiant aura and veiled mystery, as well as his authority as a warrior-prophet and ruler in worldly and otherworldly affairs, carry over to 'Ali, pass down through the imamate, and eventually are vested in the ruling monarchs of the Safavid Shi'i polity. As such, the *nur Muhammad* and facial veil must be understood as visual articulations of the sinlessness and infallibility extended to sacred kings who rule as the shadows of God on earth.[131]

Like occasions of idol breaking, Safavid paintings ushered in a new world order for the painterly arts of Iran, including depictions of the Prophet. This new order involved allegorical visual expressions that advanced the notion that Muhammad's luminous being—indexed by a flaming aureole—was cosubstantial with those of 'Ali and the imams, who were themselves considered preexistential light silhouettes. Additionally, the facial veil engaged a larger Shi'i discourse concerned with concealment and occlusion, discursive strategies that, at the pictorial level, provided hints and insinuations about the mysterious, hidden nature of the prophetic corpus, one of which was depicted as coextensive, even fused, with 'Ali's own body, being, and soul.

Much like rhetorical double entendres and allegories, Safavid paintings of the Prophet involve ambiguity and dissimulation—in other words, they act like open-ended questions inviting their acculturated, literate viewership to seek out otherwise clear messages hiding in plain sight. These sectarian tinctures in the figural arts of the sixteenth century both emanated from and contributed to an emergent Safavid "theocrative armature."[132] In these "Shi'i" paintings of the Prophet, Muhammad exits the solitary confinement of his prophetic mission to join family members, progeny, and monarchs similarly vested with the mandate of sacred rulership.

NOTES

1. Quinn, "Coronation Narratives in Safavid Chronicles"; Quinn and Melville, "Safavid Historiography," 241; Babayan, *Mystics, Monarchs, and Messiahs*, 143; and Babayan, "The Safavid Synthesis."

2. For an overview, see Melville, "The Illustration of History in Safavid Manuscript Painting," 168–80; and for a Safavid illustrated example of the dynastic history of Shah Isma'il I, see Wood, "The *Tarikh-i Jahanara* in the Chester Beatty Library." Mirkhwand's *Garden of Purity* is available in English translation; for the section covering the life of the Prophet, see Mirkhwand, *The Rauzat-us-Safa or Garden of Purity*, vol. 1, part II.

3. On these illustrated biographies of the Prophet and imams, see especially Rührdanz, "The Illustrated Manuscripts of *Athar al-Muzaffar*"; and Stchoukine, "Qasim ibn 'Ali et ses peintures dans les *Ahsan al-Kibar*."

4. Farhad with Bağcı, *Falnama*.

5. Although illustrated storytelling flourished in Iran during the nineteenth century, evidence exists for its practice already during the Safavid period. See Chelkowski, "Narrative Painting and Painting Recitation in Qajar Iran"; and Membré, *Relazione di Persia*, 59. In the latter, a travelogue written after his 1539–42 CE trip to the court of Shah Tahmasp, Michele Membré notes that "there are many Persian popular preachers seated on a carpet on the ground. They have a number of large paintings with figures. These preachers carry in their hands small sticks with which they show figure after figure. They predict the future and tell stories based on these figures, for which people give them money."

6. On Ibn Qudama encouraging the use of nonrealistic representational strategies, see Touati, "Le régime des images figuratives dans la culture islamique médiévale," 21.

7. For a preliminary discussion of the Prophet's facial veil as purposefully causing elision and confusion, see Gruber, "When *Nubuvvat* Encounters *Valayat*," 55–61.

8. On the *taj-i Haydari*, see Moin, *The Millennial Sovereign*, 81, 80, 124.

9. Arjomand, *The Shadow of God and the Hidden Imam*, 85–100; and Moin, *The Millennial Sovereign*, 88–91.

10. In his "The Genesis of Safawid Religious Painting," Rogers asserts that religious painting that aims to inculcate the spirit of pious emulation and devotion began with the Safavids (169). However, as discussed in this book's previous chapters, earlier Ilkhanid and Timurid paintings prove beyond a doubt that religious painting was developed well before 1500 CE.

11. Melville, "The Illustration of History in Safavid Manuscript Painting," 185.

12. See Peterson, "Das Schiff als Symbol der Kirche"; and, for a French manuscript painting of around 1425–30 CE depicting the *Navis Ecclesiae* with Jesus Christ and his disciples miraculously surviving a shipwreck, see Flatman, *Ships and Shipping in Medieval Manuscripts*, 94, fig. 89.

13. Warner and Warner, *The Sháhnáma of Firdausí*, 107.

14. Robinson also describes these manuscript paintings as rather incompetent imitations of the contemporary Herati style. See his "Two Illustrated Manuscripts in the Malek Library," fig. 7; and Shani, "Illustrations of the Parable of the Ship of Faith in Firdausi's Prologue to the *Shahnama*," fig. 5.

   THE PRAISEWORTHY ONE

15. Robinson, "Two Illustrated Manuscripts in the Malek Library," 94; and Robinson, *Fifteenth-Century Persian Painting*, 53.

16. A similar interpretation is offered for other paintings of the ship of salvation in Shani, "Illustrations of the Parable of the Ship of Faith in Firdausi's Prologue to the *Shahnama*," 27.

17. Minorsky, "The Poetry of Shah Isma'il I."

18. Dickson and Welch, *The Houghton Shahnameh*; and Hillenbrand, "The Iconography of the *Shah-nama-yi Shahi*."

19. Shani, "Illustrations of the Parable of the Ship of Faith in Firdausi's Prologue to the *Shahnama*," 28–30, fig. 6; Ekhtiar et al., *Masterpieces from the Department of Islamic Art in the Metropolitan Museum of Art*, 202–8, especially 204, fig. 138A; and Fontana, *Iconografia dell'Ahl al-Bayt*, 35, fig. 37.

20. Warner and Warner, *The Sháhnáma of Firdausí*, 107.

21. Dickson and Welch have suggested that the elderly man with a white beard in a red coat may be the author Firdawsi. Dickson and Welch, *The Houghton Shahnameh*, vol. 2, no. 6; and Ekhtiar et al., *Masterpieces from the Department of Islamic Art in the Metropolitan Museum of Art*, 203.

22. Warner and Warner, *The Sháhnáma of Firdausí*, 106.

23. Amir-Moezzi, "The Pre-existence of the Imam," 140–41; and Asatryan, "An Early Shi'i Cosmology," 6–8.

24. Amir-Moezzi, "The Imam in Heaven," 180.

25. Amir-Moezzi, "The Imam in Heaven," 180.

26. Colby, "The Early Imami Shi'i Narratives and Contestation over Intimate Colloquy Scenes in Muhammad's *Mi'raj*," 145–46, citing Furat al-Kufi.

27. Rogers, "The Genesis of Safawid Religious Painting," 188n34.

28. Rubin, "The Shrouded Messenger"; and al-Suyuti, *al-Riyad al-Aniqa fi Sharh Asma' Khayr al-Khaliqa*, 237–38.

29. Cited in Rubin, "The Shrouded Messenger," 99.

30. Amir-Moezzi, "Some Remarks on the Divinity of the Imam," 118; and Amir-Moezzi, "'Ali et le Coran," 694.

31. Amir-Moezzi, "Some Remarks on the Divinity of the Imam," 126, 128.

32. Amir-Moezzi, "Some Remarks on the Divinity of the Imam," 106–7.

33. Amir-Moezzi, "'Ali et le Coran," 694, and 696 on 'Ali's human (*nasut*) and divine (*lahut*) natures.

34. Written by the Persian poet Sa'di, the couplet inscribed on the canopy above Muhammad and 'Ali reads: "Muhammad is here to fortify our inner state. Why heed the waves when Noah is piloting our Ship of State?" (cited in Shani, "Illustrations of the Parable of the Ship of Faith in Firdausi's Prologue to the *Shahnama*," 28; and Ekhtiar et al., *Masterpieces from the Department of Islamic Art in the Metropolitan Museum of Art*, 203). This verse is linked to the Shi'i Hadith attributed to Muhammad: "My *ahl al-bayt* may be compared to Noah's Ark; whoever rides in it is saved, and whoever hangs onto it succeeds and whoever fails to reach it is thrust into hell" (cited in Shani, "Illustrations of the Parable of the Ship of Faith in Firdausi's Prologue to the *Shahnama*," 27–28).

35. Rüstem, "The Afterlife of a Royal Gift," 16, figs. 2–3.

36. See Shani, "Illustrations of the Parable of the Ship of Faith in Firdausi's Prologue to the *Shahnama*," 29, fig. 7.

37. Titley, *Miniatures from Persian Manuscripts*, 43, folios 2v–3r and 10r.

38. This topic is discussed in greater detail in chapter 3; also see Quinn and Melville, "Safavid Historiography," 232–36.

39. Minorsky, "The Poetry of Shah Isma'il I," 1032a, 1043a (no. 22), 1039a, and 1048a (no. 249); and Gruber, "When *Nubuvvat* Encounters *Valayat*," 57.

40. Necipoğlu, "An Outline of Shifting Paradigms in the Palatial Architecture of the Pre-modern Islamic World," 6.

41. Necipoğlu, "An Outline of Shifting Paradigms in the Palatial Architecture of the Pre-modern Islamic World," 12, 17.

42. Quinn, "Coronation Narratives in Safavid Chronicles," 317; Quinn and Melville, "Safavid Historiography," 243; and Amir Mahmud, *Iran dar Ruzgar-i Shah Isma'il va Shah Tahmasb Safavi*, 126, for the Persian expression "*amad az pardah*."

43. Cited in Necipoğlu, "Framing the Gaze in Ottoman, Safavid, and Mughal Palaces," 313n57.

44. Dakake, "Hiding in Plain Sight," 336.

45. Dakake, "Hiding in Plain Sight," 343.

46. Dakake, "Hiding in Plain Sight," 352.

47. Broadbridge, *Kingship and Ideology in the Islamic and Mongol Worlds*, 94.

48. Pfeiffer, "Conversion Versions," 45.

49. Hillenbrand, "Images of Muhammad in al-Biruni's *Chronology of Ancient Nations*"; Soucek, "An Illustrated Manuscript of al-Biruni's *Chronology of Nations*"; and Soucek, "The Life of the Prophet," 198, 205–6.

50. Hillenbrand, "Images of Muhammad in al-Biruni's *Chronology of Ancient Nations*," 135.

51. For a discussion of the Ottoman illustrated copy and its painting of Ghadir Khumm, see Gruber, "Questioning the 'Classical' in Persian Painting," 18–19, fig. 4.

52. Madadpur et al., "Fihrist-i Mawzu'i va Tahlili-i Kutub-i Tasviri dar Majmu'a-yi nusakh-i khatti-yi Kitabkhana-yi Madrasa-yi 'Ali-yi Shahid-i Mutahhari (Sipahsalar-i Sabiq)." The Safavid copy, now held in the library of the Sepahsalar Madrasa in Tehran (ms. no. 1517), includes a colophon on folio 314r signed by Muhammad Mu'min Gulpayagani and is dated 1057 AH/1647–48 CE. As the calligrapher's *nisba*—"of [the town of] Gulpayagan"—suggests, the manuscript is most likely a Safavid product of the province of Isfahan. Furthermore, the paintings leave little doubt that the artist who illustrated its text had direct access to the Ilkhanid original, which must have been held in the palace collections in the capital city of Isfahan by the reign of Shah 'Abbas II (1642–66 CE) at the latest. A handwritten note on the Ilkhanid manuscript's first page supports this hypothesis: the note states that R. M. Binning, a civil servant active in the East India Company, acquired the Ilkhanid manuscript in Isfahan on July 4, 1851.

53. For the Ilkhanid painting of the Mubahala, see Hillenbrand, "Images of Muhammad in al-Biruni's *Chronology of Ancient Nations*," 133, plate 14; and Soucek, "An Illustrated Manuscript of al-Biruni's *Chronology of Nations*," 151–55, fig. 24. For the Ilkhanid and Ottoman paintings of the Mubahala, see Fontana, *Iconografia dell'Ahl al-Bayt*, 16, figs. 5–6.

54. Ibn Ishaq, *The Life of Muhammad*, 270–77.

55. Al-Biruni, *The Chronology of Ancient Nations*, 332.

56. Reza'i and Bozorgi, "A Study of the Verse of Mubahalah," 77; and Strothmann, "Die Mubahala in Tradition und Liturgie," 22.

57. Shaykh al-Mufid, *Kitab al-Irshad*, 119.

58. Laoust, "Le role de 'Ali dans la sira chiite," 25.

59. Massignon, "La Mubahala de Médine et l'Hyperdulie de Fatima," 553.

60. Massignon, "La Mubahala de Médine et l'Hyperdulie de Fatima," 557.

61. Latour, "What Is Iconoclash?," 14.

62. On iconoclastic acts as occasions to reinvigorate a cult, see Rambelli and Reinders, "What Does Iconoclasm Create?," 20.

63. Ibn Ishaq, *The Life of Muhammad*, 649–52.

64. Shaykh al-Mufid, *Kitab al-Irshad*, 119–27, esp. 124.

65. Al-Biruni, *The Chronology of Ancient Nations*, 333.

66. Laoust, "Le role de 'Ali dans la sira chiite," 26.

67. For the Ilkhanid painting of Ghadir Khumm, see Hillenbrand, "Images of Muhammad in al-Biruni's *Chronology of Ancient Nations*," 134, plate 13; Soucek, "An Illustrated Manuscript of al-Biruni's *Chronology of Nations*," 154–55, fig. 25; for the Ilkhanid and Ottoman paintings of Ghadir Khumm, see Fontana, *Iconografia dell'Ahl al-Bayt*, 16, figs. 7–8; and for a preliminary discussion of the Ilkhanid and Safavid depictions of Ghadir Khumm, see Gruber, "Questioning the 'Classical' in Persian Painting," 17–21.

68. Kohlberg, "Some Imami Shi'i Views on the *Sahaba*," 153; and Shaykh al-Mufid, *Kitab al-Irshad*, 125, in which he relates that 'Umar refused to acknowledge 'Ali's command over the faithful.

69. Calmard, "Les rituels shiites et le pouvoir," 122.

70. Kohlberg, "Some Imami Shi'i Views on the *Sahaba*," 146–48, 164, 167.

71. For a detailed discussion of al-Karaki's treatise, see Gruber, "Curse Signs."

72. Al-Karaki, *Nafahat al-Lahut*, 26.

73. Al-Karaki, *Nafahat al-Lahut*, 21.

74. Rambelli and Reinders, "What Does Iconoclasm Create?," 24, 31.

75. Massé, *Croyances et coutumes persanes*, 1:137–38.

76. Aubin, "Revolution chiite et conservatisme," 16.

77. Arberry, Minovi, and Blochet, *The Chester Beatty Library: A Catalogue of the Persian Manuscripts and Miniatures*, 3:13–15; and Schmitz and Desai, *Mughal and Persian Paintings and Illustrated Manuscripts in the Raza Library, Rampur*, 208 (cat. no. IV.29).

78. Rührdanz, "The Illustrated Manuscripts of *Athar al-Muzaffar*."

79. Wright, *Islam: Faith, Art, and Culture*, 61, fig. 34; and Rührdanz, "The Illustrated Manuscripts of *Athar al-Muzaffar*," 206, fig. 5. Several other paintings seem to have been included in the original manuscript; however, these have been removed and are now held in various international collections.

80. Laoust, "Le role de 'Ali dans la sira chiite," 25, citing Shaykh al-Mufid's *Kitab al-Irshad*.

81. Shaykh al-Mufid, *Kitab al-Irshad*, 126.

82. Muhammad and 'Ali are described as holding hands in Shi'i narratives of the Mubahala; see Shaykh al-Mufid, *Kitab al-Irshad*, 117.

83. Farhad with Bağcı, *Falnama*, 60, 62, 67, and fig. 5.4; and Rührdanz, "Die Miniaturen des Dresdener 'Falnameh,'" 21, 39, and fig. 9.

84. On 'Ali as the alternate form of Muhammad's soul (*nafs*), see Laoust, "Le role de 'Ali dans la sira chiite," 25; and on the two-bodied figural representation as potentially "allegorical," see Rührdanz, "Die Miniaturen des Dresdener 'Falnameh,'" 21.

85. Kohlberg, "Some Imami Shi'i Views on the *Sahaba*," 153–55.

86. Rührdanz, "Die Miniaturen des Dresdener 'Falnameh,'" 21 (folio 42r).

87. Farhad with Bağcı, *Falnama*, 67.

88. On this triad (i.e., the cult of the imams, hereditary guardianship, and anti-Sunni rhetoric) during Shah Tahmasp's time, see Aubin, "La politique religieuse des safavides," 237–38.

89. Shaykh al-Mufid, *Kitab al-Irshad*, 231.

90. Laoust, "Le role de 'Ali dans la sira chiite," 10.

91. Hillenbrand, "Muhammad as Warrior Prophet," 72, plate 2.

92. Shaykh al-Mufid, *Kitab al-Irshad*, 45–46; and Laoust, "Le role de 'Ali dans la sira chiite," 10.

93. Rührdanz, "The Illustrated Manuscripts of *Athar al-Muzaffar*," 204, fig. 2.

94. Rührdanz, "The Illustrated Manuscripts of *Athar al-Muzaffar*," 202.

95. Armstrong, *Muhammad*, 176–77.

96. Armstrong, *Muhammad*, 178; and Watt, *Muhammad*, 125.

97. Shaykh al-Mufid, *Kitab al-Irshad*, 51.

98. Ibn Ishaq, *The Life of Muhammad*, 514.

99. Earlier texts do not emphasize 'Ali's performance at Khaybar and also describe Muhammad (rather than 'Ali) as giving the decisive blow to Marhab. See al-Waqidi, *The Life of Muhammad*, 323.

100. Al-Tabari, *La chronique de Tabarî*, 603.

101. Daniel, "Bal'ami's Account of Early Islamic History," 175.

102. Shaykh al-Mufid, *Kitab al-Irshad*, 86–87; and Laoust, "Le role de 'Ali dans la sira chiite," 17.

103. Shaykh al-Mufid, *Kitab al-Irshad*, 252.

104. Rührdanz, "Die Miniaturen des Dresdener 'Falnameh,'" 3–4 (fol. 3b, page 96).

105. Lange, "'On That Day When Faces Will Be White or Black' (Q 3:106)."

106. On Safavid ritual cursing, see Calmard, "Les rituels shiites et le pouvoir"; Stanfield-Johnson, *Ritual Cursing in Iran*; and Stanfield-Johnson, "The Tabarra'iyan and the Early Safavids."

107. Shaykh al-Mufid, *Kitab al-Irshad*, 261–62; and Capezonne, "Un Miracolo di 'Ali ibn Abi Talib."

108. Capezonne, "Un Miracolo di 'Ali ibn Abi Talib," 103; and al-Majlisi, *Bihar al-Anvar*, 41:166–91.

109. Wright, *Islam: Faith, Art, and Culture*, 26, fig. 8; and Farhad with Bağcı, *Falnama*, 120–21, cat. no. 23. For other depictions of the battle at Khaybar, see, inter alia, Wright, *Islam: Faith, Art, and Culture*, 25, fig. 7 (the 1567 CE illustrated copy of Astarabadi's *Traces of the Victorious*, Chester Beatty Library, Dublin, Per 235, folio 132r); and Milstein, Rührdanz, and Schmitz, *Stories of the Prophets*, 199–201, plate XVII (an illustrated copy of al-Nishapuri's *Stories of the Prophets*, New York Public Library, Spencer Collection, Persian Ms. 46, folio 166r).

110. As similarly noted in Farhad with Bağcı, *Falnama,* 120. In addition, Shaykh al-Mufid cites a panegyric composed on the occasion, in which Muhammad names 'Ali his "brother." Shaykh al-Mufid, *Kitab al-Irshad*, 86.

111. Farhad with Bağcı, *Falnama*, 120.

112. Ibn Ishaq, *The Life of Muhammad*, 514.

113. On Safavid divinatory practices, see Babayan, "The Cosmological Order of Things in Early Modern Safavid Iran."

114. Farhad with Bağcı, *Falnama*, 261 (translation by Wheeler Thackston).

115. Shaykh al-Mufid, *Kitab al-Irshad*, 85.

116. On ascension paintings that depict Muhammad's encounter with 'Ali in the shape of an angelic lion, see Gruber, "When *Nubuvvat* Encounters *Valayat*," 61–64; and Shani, "The Lion Image in Safavid Mi'raj Paintings." On calligraphic representations of 'Ali as a lion, see Shani, "Calligraphic Lions Symbolising the Esoteric Dimensions of 'Ali's Nature."

117. Ibn Ishaq, *The Life of Muhammad*, 554.

118. There exist numerous scholarly studies on this type of Islamic iconoclasm. For the most recent discussion of the topic, see Elias, *Aisha's Cushion*, especially chapters 3–4. The topic is also explored in Flood, *Image and Islam*; and Gruber, *The Image Debate*.

119. For a *Hadith* describing Muhammad and 'Ali destroying the idols at the Ka'ba, see van Reenen, "The *Bilderverbot*, A New Survey," 39.

120. Shaykh al-Mufid, *Kitab al-Irshad*, 94–95.

121. Wright, *Islam: Faith, Art, and Culture*, 182, fig. 135. In his *Kitab al-Asnam* (Book of idols) the early Muslim author Ibn al-Kalbi (d. 206/821–22) describes pagan idols as either raised stones (*ansab*) or figural (*tamathil*) representations. Pre-Islamic figural idols, he further states,

were made either of wood, gold, or silver. See Ibn al-Kalbi, *Les idoles de Hicham Ibn al-Kalbi*, 44 (viz. *sanam*); and Ibn al-Kalbi, *The Book of Idols*, 46.

122. In his Persian history, al-Bal'ami states that Muhammad destroyed an idol of Hubal, which was made of stone. He then requested that the smashed idol of Hubal be placed at the entrance door of the *haram* so that all who entered the sacred precinct would smash it underfoot (see al-Tabari, *La chronique de Tabarî*, 619). Moreover, in his *Kitab al-Asnam*, Ibn al-Kalbi specifies that the idol of Hubal was made of red agate, shaped like a man, and outfitted with a gold hand (see his *The Book of Idols*, 23).

123. A number of Islamic narratives describe the releasing of black demons on the destruction of the pagan idols they inhabit; see Hawting, "The Literary Context of the Traditional Accounts of Pre-Islamic Arab Idolatry," 37–38.

124. For comparable Safavid paintings of the breaking of the idols that depict 'Ali on Muhammad's shoulders, see Wright, *Islam: Faith, Art, and Culture*, 28–29, fig. 9 (a 1595 CE copy of Mirkhwand's *Garden of Purity*); Schmitz and Desai, *Mughal and Persian Paintings and Illustrated Manuscripts in the Raza Library, Rampur*, 207–9, plate 320 (a 1567 CE copy of Astarabadi's *Traces of the Victorious*); and Arnold, *Painting in Islam*, 96, plate XXI. On Safavid illustrated copies of Mirkhwand's *Garden of Purity*, see Melville, "The Illustration of History in Safavid Manuscript Painting," 168–71.

125. On "*Ya Muhammad!*" invocations inscribed above and below Muhammad's facial veil, see Gruber, "Between Logos (*Kalima*) and Light (*Nur*)," 240–47.

126. Rudy, "Kissing Images, Unfurling Rolls, Measuring Wounds, Sewing Badges and Carrying Talismans," 2.

127. Rudy, "Kissing Images, Unfurling Rolls, Measuring Wounds, Sewing Badges and Carrying Talismans," 21–30, fig. 18; and Bartholeyns et al, "Des raisons de détruire une image," 7.

128. Takim, "From *Bid'a* to *Sunna*," 169; and Quinn, "Coronation Narratives in Safavid Chronicles," 315, citing Khwandamir's *The Friend of Biographies*.

129. Takim, "From *Bid'a* to *Sunna*," 177.

130. Or per Amir-Moezzi, without a *wali*, there can be no religion at all. See his "Notes à propos de la *walaya* imamite," 727.

131. Arjomand, *The Shadow of God and the Hidden Imam*, 44–45.

132. On the "theocratic armature" of Shah Tahmasp, see Aubin, "Revolution chiite et conservatisme," 239.

دیم اول الصوندوغك یر مشرق میدر مغرب میدر تنا میدر روم مدر
قیغی اقلیم در آنی سکا بلدورم دیدی مینه خاتون ایدر اوغلی

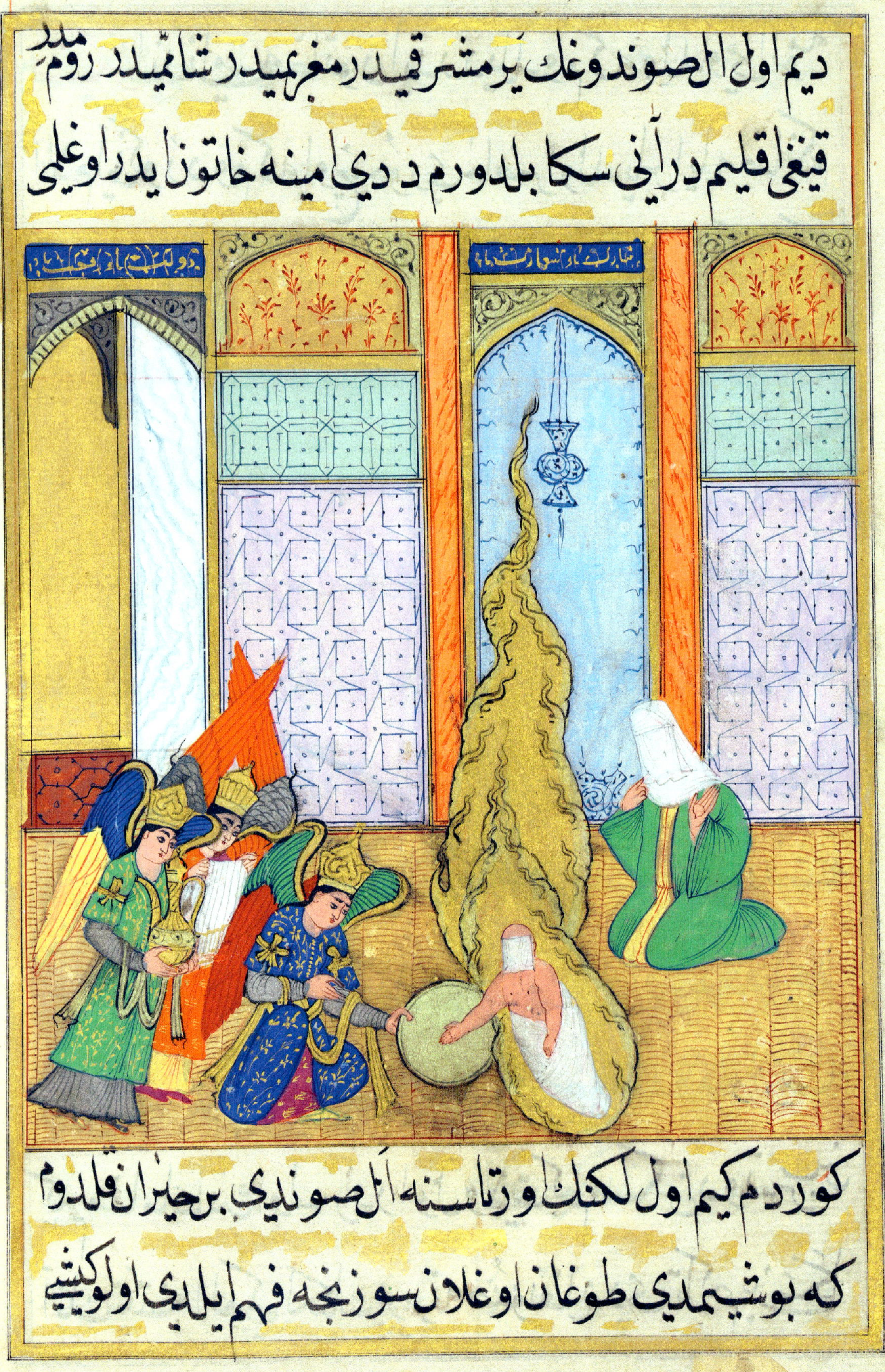

کوردم کیم اول لگنك و رتاسنه الصوندیدی بر حیراز قلدوم
که بوشیمدی طوغان اوغلان سوزنجه فهم ایلدی اولوکیشی

5

OTTOMAN PROPHET-CENTERED DEVOTIONS

The Safavids were not alone in laying claim to the Prophet's heritage and mandate. From the sixteenth to the nineteenth century, members of the Ottoman court and other elite individuals also cultivated the literary and visual arts in their own quest to teach Muhammad's biography, commemorate his spiritual being, and collect the blessed traces of his physical body. This creative output in Ottoman realms reflected learning and devotional practices related to the Prophet as well as the dynasty's bid for imperial dominion in the greater Islamic world—especially contra the Shi'i Safavids to the east.

Much as in Iran, book arts flourished in Ottoman realms during the last quarter of the sixteenth century and well into the seventeenth century. Illustrated texts included histories, biographies, genealogies, and apocalypses; a number were centuries old, but others were more recently penned. Some also included depictions of Muhammad's life and deeds, thereby extending the development of prophetic iconography into new creative domains.

In Ottoman lands, illustrated manuscripts, especially those made between 1580 and 1600 CE, formalize a new typology for representing Muhammad, one that consistently includes the facial veil and gold nimbus. At times, the flaming nimbus entirely replaces the Prophet's head, face, and facial features. On the one hand, the flames—much like the facial veil—reflect an increasing tendency toward abstracting the prophetic corpus in early modern Islamic pictorial arts. On the other, it also hyperbolizes the *nur Muhammad*, from which Ottoman monarchs (much like Safavid rulers) claimed emanation and descent. Through such visual strategies, Ottoman manuscript paintings elevated Muhammad's status into an even more luminous realm while concurrently promoting a golden aura and pedigree for the ruling House of Osman, which traced its origins to Muhammad, the last prophet, and to Adam, the first human.

After Sultan Selim I's (r. 1512–20) victory over the Mamluks in 1517 CE, Ottoman rulers increasingly presented themselves as the protectors and legatees of the Prophet's *sunna*. In their role as caliphs ruling over the Levant, North Africa, and the Hijaz, they controlled large swathes of Islamic territory. They oversaw and restored sacred sites in Jerusalem, Cairo, and Damascus, ensuring a steady flow of the Prophet's relics from these and other cities to Istanbul from the sixteenth century onward. Moreover, Ottoman rulers also adopted the title "custodian of the two noble sanctuaries" (*khadim al-haramayn al-sharifayn*). As the illustrious protectors of Mecca and Medina, they ensured safe pilgrimage

How can I describe your characteristics
How can I explain your beauties?[1]

Hakani (d. 1606 CE)

FACING, 5.1. The Prophet Muhammad's luminous birth, al-Darir, *Siyer-i Nebi* (Biography of the Prophet), Istanbul, 1003 AH/1595–96 CE. Topkapı Palace Library, Istanbul, H. 1221, folio 223v. Photograph by Hadiye Cangökçe.

routes, renovated and expanded historical buildings, and gifted a variety of objects (such as lamps, oils, and perfumes) to both the Ka'ba's sacred enclosure and the Prophet's mosque-house-tomb. Benefiting from—as well as embodying—the sultans' benevolence and wealth, the two holy cities associated with the Prophet's life thus were carefully integrated into Ottoman imperial territory and identity.[2]

The Ottoman amassing of Muhammad's relics, and the sultan's control over Islam's holiest cities, in turn catalyzed a plethora of new Prophet-centered devotional products that blossomed from the sixteenth to the nineteenth century. Illustrated pilgrimage guides and prayer litanies proved highly popular, in particular Muhyi al-Din Lari's (d. 1526–27 CE) *Futuh al-Haramayn* (Description of the Two Holy Cities) and al-Jazuli's *Dala'il al-Khayrat* (Proofs of Good Deeds).[3] Many other prayer miscellanies—generally classified under the rubric of *du'aname* (prayer book) or *du'a mecmuası* (prayer compendium)—were likewise made for a variety of patrons who wished to possess pocket-size manuals that facilitated pious thought and practice. Not infrequently, these types of devotional books included depictions of the Ka'ba and Muhammad's tomb; protective seals and amulets; images of Muhammad's genealogy, relics, and belongings; pink roses known as the rose of Muhammad (*gül-i Muhammmed*); and verbal icons known as *hilye*s. Taken together, these images served to recall prophetic geography and presence through the use of metaphor and synecdoche, two modes of abstraction that eventually supplanted the figural traditions of representing the Prophet that had been employed in earlier Islamic illustrated manuscripts.

A quintessentially Ottoman art form, the *hilye* blossomed from the end of the seventeenth century onward (and is experiencing a renaissance in Turkey today). Its graphic form was invented by the celebrated Ottoman calligrapher Hafız Osman (d. 1698 CE), who was inspired by Hakani's (d. 1606 CE) praise poem to the Prophet, entitled *Hilye-i Şerif* (The Noble Description), in which the author bemoans his incapacity to properly describe Muhammad's beauty with the rhyming rhetorical question: "How can I describe your characteristics / How can I explain your beauties?"[4] As a verbal icon or "physiognomic portrait,"[5] the *hilye* likewise embraces the inability to depict prophetic pulchritude. Instead, its graphic layout includes a textual description of Muhammad's physical and moral characteristics accompanied by qur'anic excerpts, the names of the four *rashidun*, and a range of other iconographic and textual contents. In essence, the *hilye* functioned as a contemplative device that enabled viewers to envision, approach, and commune with the Prophet, himself the object of his believers' devotion and love. The picture of Muhammad here is neither literal nor manifest; rather, it remains in the realm of the imaginative, whence it serves to stimulate a host of mental images and pious emotions.

Along with eulogistic poems, birth stories and festivals, ascension narratives, and other rituals, this rich and varied output of artistic expression coalesced into a larger corpus of Prophet-centered devotions in Ottoman lands during the early modern and modern periods. These oral, textual, and pictorial materials reflected and actively created a particular kind of "Ottoman piety" (*pietas ottomanica*) that was concerned, first and foremost, with Muslim devotees' wish to express their "love of the Prophet" (*aşk-ı nebi*).[6] Images of Muhammad in illustrated manuscripts, prophetic relics, pictured prayer books, and *hilyes* resulted from a creative mix of devotion and affection, revealing the extent to which Islamic belief systems were (and still are) predicated on the emotion of love—not merely doctrine. In this and other cases, Muslim piousness is a matter not only of belief and practice but also of reverence and affection.

Ottoman artistic expressions of praise and love of the Prophet essentially compose a Sunni form of mysticism. On the one hand, these more spiritualized methods of approaching the prophetic presence reveal the widespread influence of Sufism within Ottoman realms. On the other, they also highlight the fact that various methods of seeking blessing (*baraka*), guidance, protection, cure, and salvation could take on distinctly visual and material manifestations that served to strengthen and extend Muhammad's paradigmatic beauty and authority, to which Ottoman rulers claimed inheritance.

As a result, Ottoman Prophet-centered pietistic practices thrived at the fertile intersection of love and power. This was especially the case during and after the sixteenth century, when the ongoing project of differentiating Sunni from Shi'i Islam contributed to the articulation of contrasting identities across Islamic lands. For members of the House of Osman and Ottoman believers at large, carrying forward prophetic prerogatives and blessings was of paramount religious and political importance, and this urge catalyzed a burst of artistic products. At first, visual materials extended Turco-Persian book arts traditions; however, by the seventeenth century new artistic practices and products began to emerge, chief among them the collecting of relics and the production of *hilyes*. These contact objects and verbal icons display an especially strong preference for recalling Muhammad through synecdoche and simile, in the process heralding a decisive shift toward picturing the Prophet in nonliteral terms during the modern period.

Much like their Safavid counterparts, Ottoman rulers were lavish patrons of architecture, the decorative arts, and illustrated manuscripts. Sultans, princes, and other members of the cultured elite in Istanbul and other metropolitan centers of the empire took particular interest in painting and book arts.[7] These luxury products served both educational and commemorative purposes, and although they did not cater to large public audiences, they nevertheless reinforced an Ottoman politico-religious worldview within literate quarters.

From the sixteenth century onward, a variety of works were produced at and for the royal court in Istanbul. For example, Mehmed II (r. 1444–46 and 1451–81 CE) was fond of classical texts, antiques, and royal portraiture in both the painterly and medallic arts (which creatively combined European and Persianate styles), while Bayezid II (r. 1481–1512 CE) demonstrated an interest in compiling a variety of pictorial materials into albums.[8] By the mid-sixteenth century, Persian and Turcoman book painters had settled in Istanbul, and a new generation of Ottoman illustrators turned to producing manuscripts for sultans Süleyman (r. 1520–66 CE) and Murad III (r. 1574–95 CE). Under their and their successors' sponsorship, illustrated books glorified Ottoman military victories and the pedigree of the House of Osman. Beyond praising the dynasty's illustrious history and genealogy, Ottoman picture books made between the sixteenth and eighteenth centuries also commemorated lavish circumcision festivals or narrated religious tales for the edification of both young and mature readerships.[9]

Among the royal illuminati, Sultan Murad III proved to be a leading supporter of literature and book arts. The Ottoman monarch's reign heralded a burst of activity in these interrelated fields, as the calligrapher Mustafa 'Ali recorded with enthusiasm and pride, "In his current time of benevolence, men of knowledge live well and men of elegance are content. Men of the sciences and arts are appreciated, and praises and protection are bestowed upon eminent men of varied virtues. Learned men, poets, men of refinement, calligraphers, gilders, portrait painters, all the talented masses and chief [makers of] curious things are held in full esteem."[10]

During the last two decades of the sixteenth century, Sultan Murad III, his family, and his court also desired illustrated manuscripts that narrated and depicted Islamic religious history and the Prophet's biography. The most extensive and richly illustrated among these is a multivolume copy of al-Darir's *Siyer-i Nebi* (Biography of the Prophet), commissioned in 1594–95 CE by Murad III for his son and soon-to-be sultan Mehmed III (r. 1595–1603 CE).[11] That the illustrated manuscript was commissioned at the close of the sixteenth century suggests that it belonged to Murad III's efforts to renew the faith as the *hijri* millennium drew closer.[12]

The text's author, al-Darir, was a blind man from Erzurum.[13] Two centuries prior, he had found patronage at the Mamluk court under Sultan Barquq (r. 1382–99 CE), who requested that he produce a Turkish-language *sira*. Al-Darir combined parts of Ibn Ishaq's biography with other textual narratives (especially those by the elusive Abu'l-Hasan al-Bakri) and oral tales about Muhammad, with the aim of presenting the Prophet as the ultimate warrior-saint.

Written in simple Turkish prose and peppered with poetic verses, the text lent itself readily to oral narration and visual depiction.[14] For these reasons, the illustrated manuscript may have appealed to a particular demographic of the Ottoman court, most especially women and princes.[15] Moreover, that the text's sections on the Prophet's birth and ascension are noticeably long and detailed further suggests that the manuscript may have been read or consulted during birth (*mevlid*) and

THE PRAISEWORTHY ONE

ascension (*mi'rac*) commemorations, complementing the recitation of religious prayers and praise poems, which at times were accompanied by music.[16] Thus, this illustrated manuscript may have strengthened faith-based reading, viewing, and performance events in Ottoman courtly spheres during the early modern period.

With plenty of attention placed on Muhammad's miraculous deeds and military victories, the Ottoman illustrated copy of al-Darir's biography offers exuberant praise to the Messenger of Islam. Muhammad's birth inaugurates the heroic life of an entity whose existence had emanated from the light of God since time immemorial. In both text and image, the birth event is presented as an awakening that initiates the Prophet's radiant entry into the world (fig. 5.1).[17] The painting's artist cultivated the metaphor of divine light by depicting the baby Muhammad, whose facial features remain hidden under a small white veil, as bursting forth from a womb-shaped mandorla, from which a flaming aureole further illuminates the painting. This double halo extends upward, reaching a hanging lamp within a niche. Muhammad is flanked by his veiled mother, Amina, who points her finger to her mouth in a gesture of amazement while three angels welcome the swaddled infant with offerings. Finally, epigraphic bands above the doorways extend blessings (*tabarruk*), happiness (*sa'adat*), dominion (*dawlat*), and good fortune (*ni'mat*) to both the newborn Prophet and the viewers of this felicitous image.

The painting's iconography draws on a range of textual and visual sources. For example, both the radiant glow and the hanging lamp evoke the qur'anic "verse of light" (*ayat al-nur*, 24:35), whose terms for lamp (*zujjaj*) and torch (*siraj*) as well as the expression "light upon light" (*nur 'ala nur*) were interpreted by mystical exegetes as similes for Muhammad as the light of guidance (*nur al-huda*) into the world.[18] These pictorial devices also parallel depictions of the birth of the Prophet within Ilkhanid and Timurid illustrated histories (figs. 2.3 and 2.5), which in part explains the painting's inclusion of angels, hanging lamps, and the Prophet's flaming halo.[19] The Ottoman painting's divergences from its predecessors are also noticeable, however. The three key differences include three (and not two) angels in the birth scene; the visual emphasis on the Prophet's veil and the *nur Muhammad*; and the removal of subsidiary characters, with only the infant Muhammad, Amina, and three angels remaining in the Ottoman painting. In sum, over the course of three centuries, birth scenes came to extol Muhammad's veiled, radiant, and angelic qualities above all else, a pictorial development that also reflects a number of trends in Islamic religious traditions.

The production of literature in praise of the Prophet helped consolidate a range of images of Muhammad during the medieval period. Such textual iconographies were cultivated within al-Darir's *Biography of the Prophet*, in which the recounting of Muhammad's birth displays a range of allegorical amplifications. Among them, the author expends effort to describe the event as divinely ordained and angelically announced. For instance, the night before the Prophet's birth, the skies open, allowing angels and *huris* to flood down to earth.[20] The moment of birth heralds a blessed hour (*kutlu sa'at*) that is marked by absolute silence (*sessizlik*): even the seas and their waves come to a complete standstill.[21]

Al-Darir's text provides a lyrical, emotional account of Muhammad's silent, luminous birth.[22] The author records Amina as saying that the light that engulfed her and the city of Mecca was so overwhelming that her newborn was "lost" within it.[23] Moreover, the Prophet's birth is commemorated in verses uttered by Amina, including the rhyming lines, "A light emerged from my house to the heavens / until the entire world was completely filled with that light."[24] The rhetorical and visual metaphor of light thus holds pride of place in al-Darir's original text as well as in its illustrated copy.

While the concept of the *nur Muhammad* was widespread by the end of the sixteenth century, the Ottoman artist's decision to include three angels at Muhammad's side seems directly inspired by the text that frames the painting. The author tells us that three angels came to Amina on the Prophet's birth: one of them held a silver ewer, another a green basin, and the third a red silk cloth. The angel holding the basin approached Muhammad. It informed the Prophet that the basin represents the world, which is offered to him. It then instructed Muhammad to place his hand into the basin in order to determine in which clime he would reside.[25] Thereafter, Muhammad was ritually washed seven times with water from the ewer and wrapped in the red silk cloth, which contained a ring that left a mark of the seal of prophecy (*peygamberlik mührü*) on Muhammad's back.[26] This initiatory episode recalls descriptions of the splitting open of Muhammad's chest and the washing of his heart with pure water, while the impressing of the seal of prophecy on his back foreshadows his later recognition as a prophet by the Christian monk Bahira. Like the birth of the Prophet, these rites of purification and annunciation were also illustrated in earlier Islamic manuscripts (figs. 2.6, 2.7, and 2.9).

The text and painting of Muhammad's birth in al-Darir's *Biography of the Prophet* enrich the range of symbolic images that praise the Prophet's luminous and angelic entry into the world. These types of metaphors were developed early on in Turkish devotional literature, most especially in Süleyman Çelebi's *Mevlid-i Şerif* (The Noble Birth). Written in 1409 CE, this poem—which is also entitled *Vesilet'ün-Necat* (Means to Salvation)—proved popular in both literary and popular spheres. Its verses are cited in a number of later texts, including in al-Darir's biography of the Prophet. They likewise were recited during Ottoman celebrations of Muhammad's birth on 12 Rabi' I.

In *The Noble Birth*, Süleyman Çelebi employed lyrical Sufi language to develop the concept of a more mystical Muhammad. This moon-faced "beloved of God"[27] is, first and foremost, the devotees' primary "means to salvation," as the work's title clearly indicates. In addition to cultivating an image of the Prophet as embodied redemption, Süleyman Çelebi

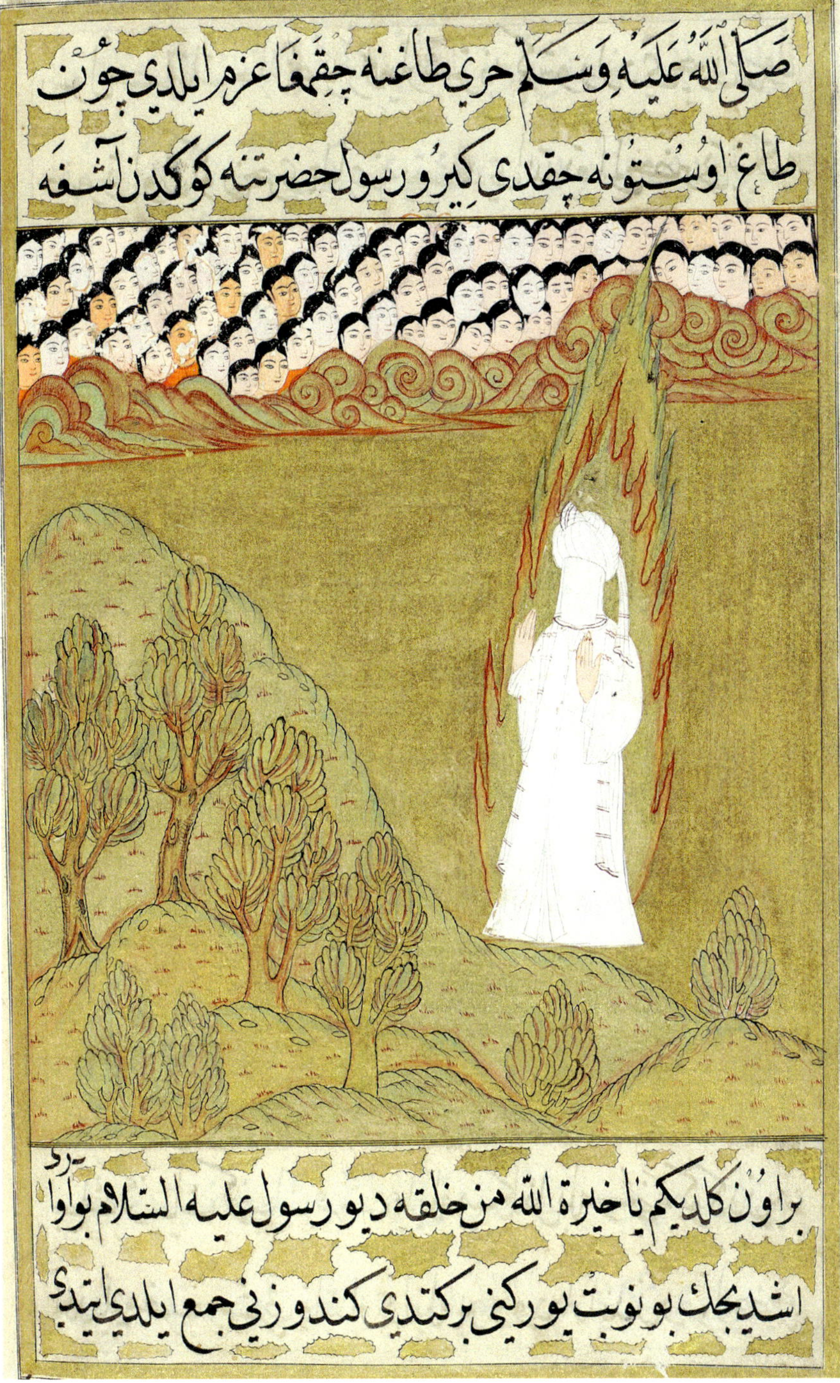

5.2. The Prophet Muhammad receives revelations at Mount Hira, al-Darir, *Siyer-i Nebi* (Biography of the Prophet), Istanbul, 1003 AH/1595–96 CE. Topkapı Palace Library, Istanbul, H. 1222, folio 158v. Photograph by Hadiye Cangökçe.

praises Muhammad's birth, which filled the entire known world with his light and purity (*nur ile safa*).[28] The text also repeatedly stresses that the Prophet serves as the quintessential intercessor (*şefi'*) and cure (*şifa*), if his followers diligently practice both prayer (*salat*) and love (*ışk*).[29] In this and other Ottoman texts and practices, praise for Muhammad conjoins doctrine and affection, as he serves as the living entity that unites the oneness of God and gnostic knowledge (*tevhid ü irfan*).[30] As the many texts, litanies, and images of the Ottoman Sunni-Sufi tradition strongly suggest, Muhammad was "internalized" by his followers at the religious and emotional level.[31]

The illustrated copy of al-Darir's *Biography of the Prophet* includes more than eight hundred paintings, two of which depict the pivotal moment of Muhammad's prophetic career: the qur'anic revelations (*wahy*) at Mount Hira. Both paintings of this sacred event shimmer brightly due to the exuberant use of gold pigment. While the first emphasizes the overwhelming presence of divine light, the second shows Muhammad's revelations on the mountain essentially as a luminous and angelic event (fig. 5.2).[32] Reaching new iconic heights, this painting sheds narrative specificity in order to immortalize the Prophet as the transcendent human carrier of God's celestial message.

While the attendant text describes a general confusion among Muhammad's companions as to his whereabouts,[33] the artist seized the occasion to wax poetic about the Prophet's supreme radiance, to which al-Darir devotes an entire chapter in his *Biography of the Prophet*.[34] This "prophetic light" (*peygamberlik nuru*), the reader is told, was among the first entities created by God as well as the procreant substance that generated all prophets sent into the world. As such, Muhammad exists as an archetypal "world of secrets" (*esrar 'alemi*) and "world of lights" (*nurlar 'alemi*),[35] two concepts that are pictorially integrated into the Ottoman painting via the Prophet's facial veil and flaming aureole. Even the trees, mountains, and clouds glow in the auric pigment of the *nur Muhammad*.

Ottoman writers and artists developed the idea that Muhammad was a "world of secrets" personified. Within the paintings of al-Darir's *Biography of the Prophet*, Muhammad's mystery is emphasized through his facial veil, which he wears even as an infant. In this illustrated manuscript, the veil distinguishes him from all other prophets, whose features are not concealed—although they, too, are surmounted by a flowing nimbus that visually indicates that they were created from the *nur Muhammad*. The use of the facial veil also sets Muhammad apart from his family members and companions. Indeed, Ottoman paintings most often render 'Ali without a facial veil, a practice that clearly differs from Safavid tactics of visually aligning these two protagonists, who are believed to be equally immersed in divine secrecy. Moreover, the Prophet's veil also functions as a marker for his proximity to God, as during his celestial ascension he crossed a number of curtains or veils. In his text, al-Darir states that there were twelve such veils (*perde*), each representing a concept, including power, glory, mercy, prophethood, and intercession.[36] The Prophet's facial veil thus fulfills at least three functions in Ottoman book arts: first, it represents Muhammad as a holy enigma that cannot be looked on; second, it differentiates him from, and elevates him above, all other monotheistic prophets, his companions, and his family members; and, third, it serves as a visual symbol of his ability to rise from the earth to the skies by crossing through the many conceptual veils that separate the realms.

Much like the facial veil, the *nur Muhammad* extends the prophetic corpus beyond literal forms of physical imagination and visualization.

 THE PRAISEWORTHY ONE

This primordial generative substance depicts the Prophet as the inception of the entire cosmos and divine revelation. Thus, the radiant Muhammad personifies the two luminaries: the moon and sun. This planetary analogy counts among the Prophet's many honorific epithets, most especially his title "the moon and sun of guidance" (*mah ü hurşid-i hüda*), as found in Süleyman Çelebi's *The Noble Birth*.[37] In the Mount Hira painting, Muhammad's full-body halo appears as if a planetary ring emitting light. The mention of this large aureole is also found within *The Noble Birth*, in which the author states that Muhammad was covered from head to toe (*başdan ayağa*) in a light that cast no shadow and represented theophany (*tecelli*) with radiance[38] It was no doubt for these reasons that the Ottoman painter showed Muhammad as a planet enveloped by the light of revelation—in other words, as qur'anic *light upon light* personified.

While the text and paintings in al-Darir's *Biography of the Prophet* depict Muhammad as a miracle-working warrior-saint who vanquishes his enemies and breaks the idols of paganism, his birth and revelations provided ideal occasions for Ottoman artists to demonstrate that the Prophet's coming into the world and his receiving of *wahy* cast a divine light on earth. Given the contents of al-Darir's text and the Ottoman mystical context of the manuscript's production, these uses of light also must be understood as metaphorical vehicles for intercession and salvation. Besides the yearly celebration of the Prophet's birth, at which time supplications were made to Muhammad, petitionary prayers are also transcribed by al-Darir, who included in his text an entire chapter entitled "Intercede for us, o Muhammad" (*Bize şefaʿat et ya Muhammed*).[39] Addressed in the first-person plural, the reader-viewers are invited to ask the Prophet to accept their prayers and to forgive them their sins because "there is no one but you who will help us" (*Bize senden başka yardım edecek kimse yoktur*).[40] Inscriptions later added to the Ottoman paintings by viewers also invoke Muhammad and ask him for intercession.[41] Taken as a whole, these many elements reveal the extent to which this Ottoman text and its pictorial contents were initially conceptualized and later used as channels for expressing love and faith in the Prophet, whose awesome powers included the ability to seek and secure salvation in the afterlife for pious members of his faith community.

The illustrated copy of al-Darir's *Biography of the Prophet* did not emerge ex nihilo. In addition to its Ilkhanid and Timurid precursors, a number of other manuscripts helped pave the way for this most important and extensive Ottoman pictorial program depicting the Prophet Muhammad. Indeed, about a decade earlier three illustrated copies of another text launched the Ottoman tradition of religious painting, to which the *Siyer-i Nebi* served as both heir and capstone. This text is Seyyid Lokman's *Zübdet'üt-Tevarih* (Quintessence of Histories), a historical account inspired by an Ottoman royal genealogical scroll.[42] Covering biblical and political history as well as the genealogy of the Ottoman sultans, each of the three illustrated copies of the *Quintessence*

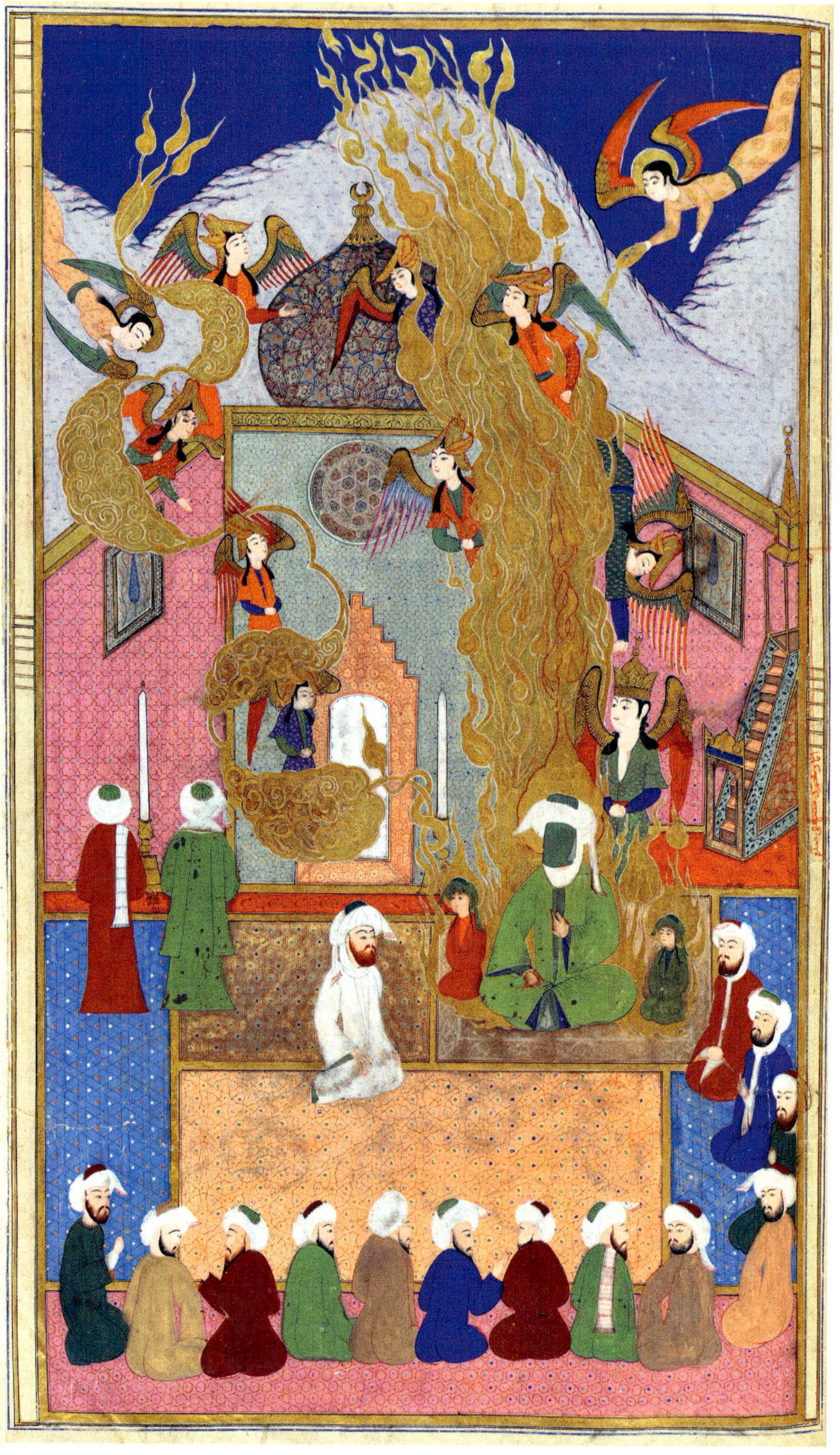

of Histories, made from 1583 to 1586 CE, includes between forty and fifty figural paintings that depict the prophets, caliphs, imams, and the first twelve Ottoman sultans. Highly expensive endeavors sponsored by elite members of the Ottoman court, these manuscripts draw a clear line connecting genesis, monotheistic history, Islamic prophecy, and the Ottoman dynasty's divinely ordained royal imperative.[43]

Fulfilling iconic rather than narrative purposes, each of the three manuscripts includes a single-page painting of the Prophet. Two of them,

THE PRAISEWORTHY ONE

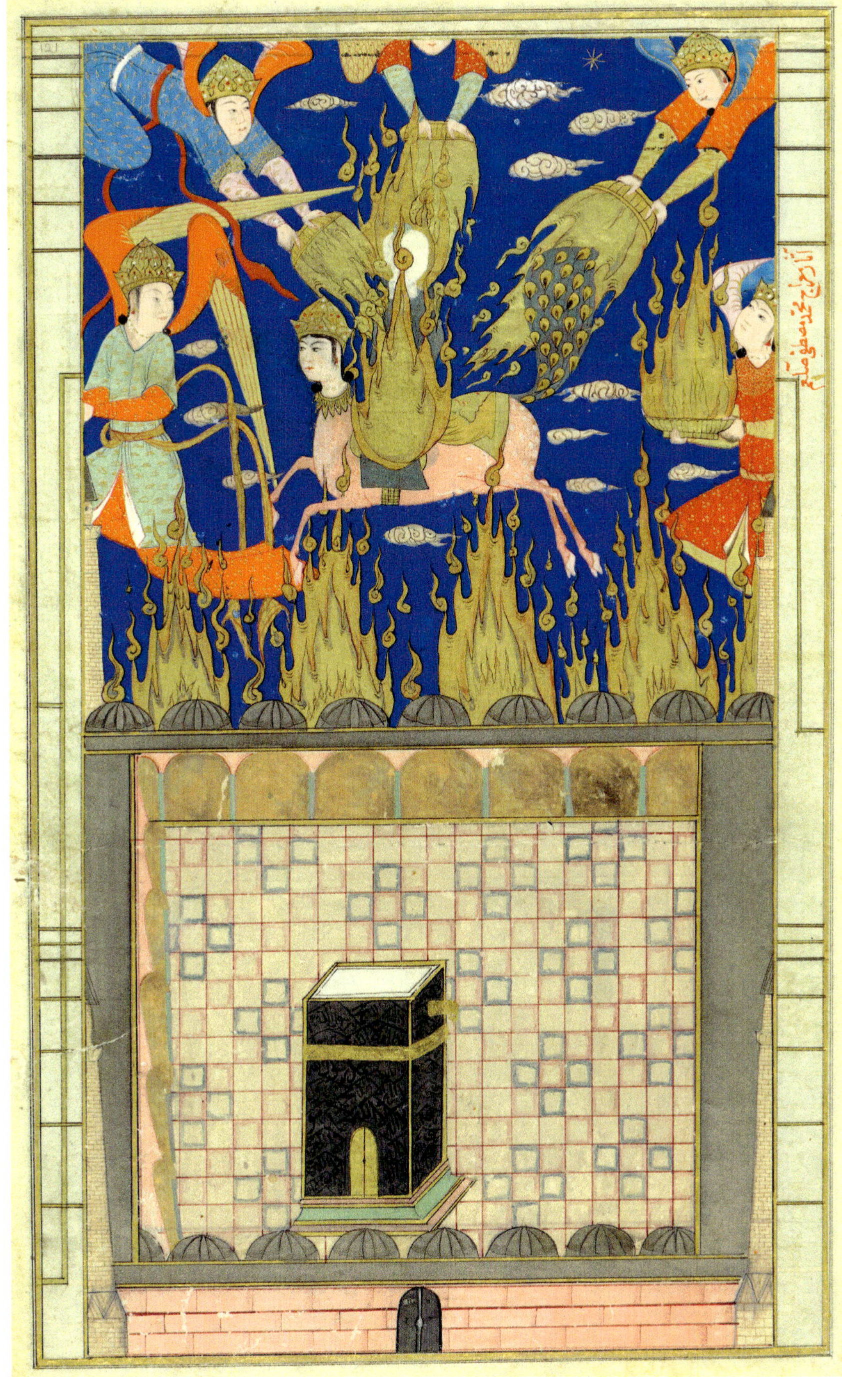

5.4. The Prophet Muhammad's celestial ascension, Seyyid Lokman, *Zübdet'üt-Tevarih* (Quintessence of Chronicles), Istanbul, 991 AH/1583 CE. Chester Beatty Library, Dublin, T414, folio 121r. © The Trustees of the Chester Beatty Library, Dublin.

including one dedicated to Grand Vizier Siyavuş Paşa (d. 1602 CE), depict Muhammad seated with his companions in a mosque-like space (fig. 5.3),[44] while the third represents the Prophet's heavenly ascent (fig. 5.4). Although the subject of the painting of the *mi'raj* is clear, the two audience scenes are not as easily identifiable—despite previous attempts to interpret the figures as Muhammad seated with his family and companions in the Dome of the Rock during his night journey (*isra'*).[45] In Islamic illustrated manuscripts, especially the Timurid *Books of Ascension* and al-Darir's *Biography of the Prophet*, this scene would include Buraq, who is noticeably missing here, as well as the prophets—but not

Muhammad's family and companions, who did not accompany him on his *isra'* to Jerusalem.[46] Instead, the audience scene in Seyyid Lokman's *Quintessence of Histories* is similar to a number of Timurid *majlis* paintings (especially fig. 3.1) while also anticipating Ottoman representations of Muhammad seated and speaking with his companions at other important moments of his prophetic career.[47]

A closer examination of Seyyid Lokman's textual description of the Prophet's life and deeds may prove fruitful in identifying the gathering scene illustrated in figure 5.3. The author's account of Muhammad's biography covers only five folios.[48] In a heavily abridged fashion, it describes Muhammad's *hijra* to Medina; his many battles, especially at Hudaybiyya; his conquest of Mecca, at which time he gathered all his companions, tribal leaders, and the people of Mecca; his farewell pilgrimage; and his death. This shortened *sira* includes only one sentence dedicated to Muhammad's *mi'raj*—three folios prior to the painting. The intervening folios are devoted to listing Muhammad's opponents; his moral and physical characteristics (*siffat*); and his habits and morals (*akhlaq*), including the fact that he would sit and chat with his companions and never refused to answer petitioners' questions. This latter section immediately precedes the painting, thereby suggesting that the rather nonspecific image of Muhammad seated among his entourage is intended to depict proper prophetic etiquette: namely, to sit peacefully as a community, to engage in constructive dialogue, and to politely respond to all queries posed.

The pattern of Muhammad's proper behavior is also suggested by the image's caption, located in the right vertical margin of the painting's frame. Written in red ink and flanking the *minbar*, the inscription reads, "The traces of Muhammad Mustafa, prayers and peace be upon him." Here, then, no direct mention of the *mi'raj* is made. Instead, of prime interest to the artist and reader-viewer are the "vestiges" (*athar*) of Muhammad's conduct as the Messenger of God and leader of his community. This painterly paradigm of prophetic politesse may have reflected Ottoman sociopolitical practices among the court's royal and elite members, including Grand Vizier Siyavuş Paşa, the manuscript's patron and owner.

The painting also could illustrate a theme of even greater interest to those active within the Ottoman palace: namely, relics associated with the prophetic corpus. Indeed, on the folio following the painting, Seyyid Lokman briefly recounts a story related to Muhammad's mantle, or *hırka*. The author informs his readers that the Prophet received his blessed *hırka* from God. Thereafter, it was kept in a chest that was passed on to the Ten Promised Ones (*al-'ashara al-mubashshara*), Muhammad's companions to whom paradise was promised. These individuals included Abu Bakr, 'Umar, 'Uthman, 'Ali, Talha, Zubayr, 'Abd al-Rahman b. 'Awf, Sa'd b. Abi Wakkas, Abu Ubayda b. Jarra, and Sa'id b. Zayd.

As a result, the painting also may depict an audience scene, as it intersects with the symbolic significance of the Ten Promised Ones and the prophetic *hırka* within Ottoman religious and political traditions. The image shows the Prophet surrounded by his companions, among whom the Ten Promised Ones may be counted. Muhammad is also accompanied by members of his family, including most likely ʿAli, who wears a white robe and kneels in front of the Prophet. Muhammad's young grandsons Hasan and Husayn, who flank him, also emit golden halos and partake in the Prophet's large flaming aureole. Conversely, and quite conspicuously, this golden flux of the sacred does not touch ʿAli, who remains compositionally distant and differentiated from the luminous threesome. Perhaps the artist's refusal to depict ʿAli as partaking in the *nur Muhammad* was a purposeful retort to Safavid pro-ʿAlid iconography.

Additionally, the Prophet's green robe and facial veil may have served to emphasize the "holy mantle" (*hırka-i şerif*) that is discussed in the manuscript's accompanying text. This relic-symbol of legitimate sovereignty came to be possessed by the Ottoman sultans, and, along with other prophetic relics, it was preserved in the Ottoman palace's collection of sacred trusts. From about 1700 CE onward, the mantle was worn during accession ceremonies, visited during religious rituals and feasts, and transported on military campaigns.[49] Muhammad's *hırka* also was represented in Ottoman illustrated prayer books (figs. 5.6–5.7), in which it symbolized the Prophet's political authority as passed down to and embodied by subsequent generations of Muslim rulers.

In addition to depicting good manners, faithful companionship, and legitimate rule, this painting may have gained further levels of meaning in an early modern Ottoman religious and political context. At this time, the Ten Promised Ones formed part of a growing Ottoman pro-Sunni rhetoric that posited itself against Safavid Twelver Shiʿism, which emphasized the spiritual supremacy of ʿAli and the imams. Especially during the mid-sixteenth century, the ten companions of the Prophet Muhammad (except for ʿAli) were vilified in Safavid ritual and public cursing.[50] Thus, for the Ottomans, reasserting the preeminence of the *ʿashara mubashshara* in both textual and pictorial traditions helped to create a counter concept opposing Shiʿi anti-Sunni cursing and glorification of the imams. Seyyid Lokman's text emphasizes these ten individuals through a narrative motif that promotes God-given sovereignty, and in their paintings Ottoman artists inserted these ten names into genealogical trees and "roses of the Prophet" (figs. 5.19 and 5.22). Figural painters, too, could recall these promised ones in their compositions while also visually excluding ʿAli, the figurehead of Safavid Shiʿism. This appears to be the case for the audience scene included in Seyyid Lokman's *Quintessence of Histories*, in which ʿAli sits alone and untouched by divine flux.

These interrelated textual and pictorial details suggest that the Ottoman audience scene serves to illustrate a number of contemporary discourses propelled by historical imagination. At first glance the painting appears to represent a past event (such as Muhammad meeting with the people of Mecca), his praiseworthy manners in social interactions, or the passing down of his blessed *hırka*. However, these pictorial tropes also describe Ottoman elite gatherings and ceremonial behavior along with the presence, preservation, and visitation of the prophetic mantle within palace quarters. Muhammad's *hırka* functioned as a tangible symbol of rulership passed down to the Ottoman rulers. Additionally, in Ottoman textual sources the *nur Muhammad* is described as generating human souls placed on a cosmic scheme, the highest among whom are granted the positions of caliphate and sultanate.[51] By depicting a social gathering in a mosque space ornamented with contemporary furnishings, emphasizing the Prophet's mantle relic, and highlighting 'Ali's removal from the luminous flux of the sultanate, the painter of the scene illustrated ideological support for the Ottoman sultans' prophetic inheritance and custodianship above and beyond all other Muslim claimants, in particular their Safavid Shi'i rivals to the east.

Another illustrated copy of Seyyid Lokman's text includes a painting that depicts the Prophet's celestial ascent instead of an audience scene with courtly and religious connotations (fig. 5.4).[52] The painting's subject is clearly identified as the "Traces of the Ascension of Muhammad Mustafa" in the upper right vertical margin. Interestingly, in the three illustrated manuscripts of the *Quintessence of Histories*, the images are provided with captions describing the scene as a "trace" or "vestige" (*athar* or *eser*) rather than an image (*surat*) or painting (*rasm* or *resim*) of the Prophet. This unusual, yet precise, choice of terminology raises the possibility that the manuscript paintings were intended to be viewed as vestiges of the Prophet rather than as figural representations. As a result, such depictions appear to have been conceptually linked to Muhammad's relics that were preserved in the Ottoman palace.

The painting's pictorial details are also unmistakable. Here, the Prophet rides a peacock-tailed Buraq above the Ka'ba's sacred (and equally lambent) enclosure in Mecca. Muhammad is accompanied by a group of angels from whose flaming platters golden light pours down to engulf his body. A blaze almost entirely subsumes Muhammad's green robe and white facial veil, causing him to appear more a light source than a corporeal entity. Such pictorial tactics of abstraction and disembodiment move Islamic traditions of prophetic representation one step closer to the nonfigural mode that became dominant in Ottoman lands during and after the seventeenth century.

In addition to displaying an innovative pictorial strategy, the painting also bears relevance to Ottoman discourses on religious power and political authority at the close of the sixteenth century. First, the Prophet is shown ascending above the Ka'ba, which, like Medina, was under the custodianship of the Ottoman sultans at this time. In the painting, the Ka'ba is covered in an Ottoman-style *kiswa*, or textile covering, on which the *shahada* is embroidered in zigzag patterns. These silk fabrics were often sent as royal gifts from Istanbul to Mecca and Medina.[53] The Topkapı Palace preserves more than six hundred Ka'ba hangings dating

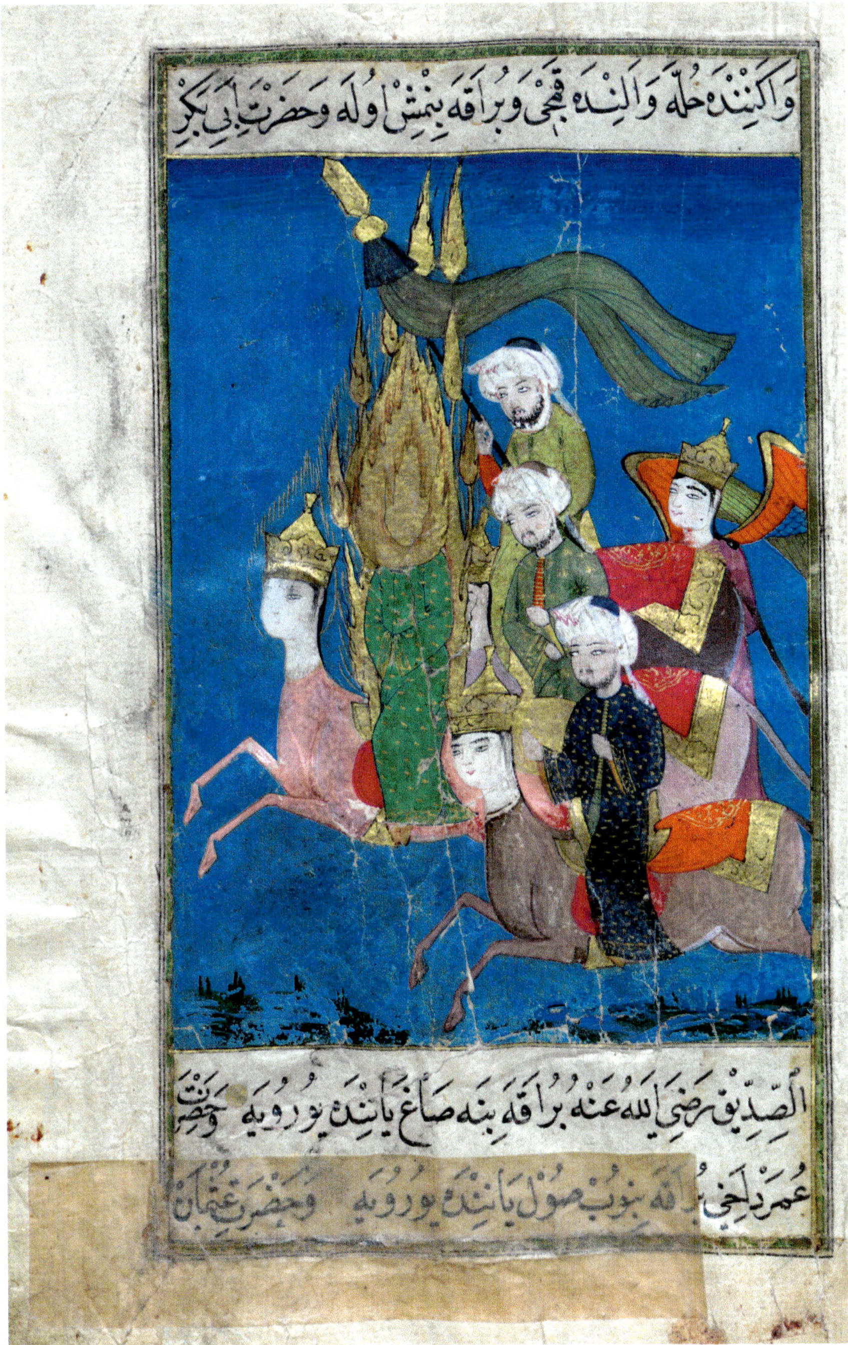

5.5. The Prophet Muhammad and his three companions ride *buraqs*, anonymous, *Ahval-i Kıyamet* (Conditions of Resurrection), possibly Istanbul, ca. 1550–1600 CE. Staatsbibliothek zu Berlin—Preussischer Kulturbesitz, Orientabteilung, Ms. Or. Oct. 1596, folio 49r.

from the sixteenth to the twentieth century, as well as golden rain gutters similar to the example depicted in the ascension painting.[54] These pictorial details thus panegyrize not only Ottoman imperial control of the *haramayn* but also the blessed items connected to the Prophet that were safeguarded in Ottoman palace collections. In addition, that the painting's *kiswa* includes the repeated *shahada* is noteworthy because contemporary Safavid paintings of the Ka'ba depict the holy structure ornamented with the Shi'i *walaya* instead (figs. 4.18–4.20). These ascension scenes hence could carry sectarian inflections when viewed within the dynamic and power-laden discursive systems of the early modern Islamic world.

Another painting of the Prophet's *mi'raj* included in an Ottoman-language manuscript copy of the *Ahval-i Kıyamet* (Conditions of Resurrection), made around 1550–1600 CE, experiments to an even greater extent with prophetic iconography and sectarian messaging (fig. 5.5). Anticipating and envisioning the impending *hijri* millennium, nonroyal Ottoman illustrated copies of the *Conditions of Resurrection* built on older Arabic-language apocalyptic texts while amplifying them with eschatological images, including the Antichrist, angels, heaven, and hell.[55] These Ottoman paintings provide vivid pictorial "signs of the hour" (*isharat al-sa'a*) while asserting the ascendancy—and thus the salvation—of the Sunni faith community. Going well beyond biographies, world histories, and genealogies, these illustrated tales describing the conditions of resurrection reveal the extent to which both the impending millennium and Ottoman-Safavid rivalries enabled new sectarian visions of the afterlife.[56]

The Ottoman painting of the Prophet in the *Conditions of Resurrection* advances an overtly pro-Sunni message that is not articulated in the accompanying text. The image illustrates the nineteenth chapter, which takes up the subject of *minbars* and specifies that the Prophet had a *minbar* made of red ruby. The text also notes that Muhammad rode Buraq at the front of his four companions, Abu Bakr, 'Umar, 'Uthman, and 'Ali, who likewise rode *buraqs*.[57] In this instance, the Ottoman recension of an older Arabic-language apocalyptical text clearly preserves mention of all four *rashidun*.[58] However, in creating a pictorial program for the text's more recent Turkish translation, the Ottoman painter clearly deemed it appropriate, perhaps even necessary, to depart from the text by omitting a depiction of 'Ali. Instead, the radiant Muhammad is accompanied by only three flying *rashidun*, not four. This type of tactical omission in Ottoman lands most likely served as a visual contraposition to 'Ali's ubiquitous presence as Muhammad's equal, even superior, in both life and afterlife in Safavid paintings of the sixteenth century. This process of pictorial excision must have sought to Sunnify the Prophet's character and status by effectively removing any possibility of grafting an oppositional Shi'i viewing system onto this apocalyptic image.

Within Ottoman book arts, a Sunni-inflected apocalyptic imagination also generated new visual articulations of the Prophet's nature and status. Among them is the ascension painting included in the *Conditions of Resurrection*, which depicts Muhammad wearing his green *hırka* as he rides Buraq alongside the three *rashidun*. While the Prophet's body emits cypress-shaped flashes of light, a gold blaze entirely subsumes his head and facial features. Unlike previous Islamic paintings, in which golden flames are poured onto the prophetic body by groups of angels bearing flaming platters, in this composition the *nur Muhammad* beams out from within. In this and other cases, Ottoman artists chose to abandon the conventions of depicting Muhammad's head in physical form or camouflaging his features by some device such as a facial veil. Instead, Muhammad's character, as represented by his head (and not his entire physical body), is shown as the wellspring—rather than the recipient—of divine light.

While these types of light metaphors for the prophetic corpus pervade Islamic and Ottoman texts, the head of fire was a pictorial invention of the late sixteenth century. Along with light and veil metaphors, it reveals the extent to which Ottoman artists creatively expanded the ways in which the prophetic corpus was conceptualized and visualized. This ongoing iconographic experimentation yielded nothing less than an uncoupling of Muhammad from his figural representation by 1600 CE.

Ottoman sultans, their families and entourages, and elite individuals encountered Muhammad in a variety of ways that transcended the figural arts. Other modes of prophetic representation emerged especially after 1517 CE, when Sultan Selim I defeated the Mamluks, thereby gaining the caliphate and custodianship of the *haramayn* as well as the Mamluk treasury, which included relics of the Prophet passed down via the ʿAbbasids. He also was given relics from the holy cities of Mecca and Medina by the Prophet's descendants ruling over the Hijaz. These objects were transferred from Cairo, Mecca, and Medina to Istanbul during the sixteenth century, and a number of other blessed items, whether transferred to Topkapı Palace or purchased by Ottoman rulers, further enriched the royal collections from the sixteenth until the early twentieth century. In sum, for about five hundred years of their history, the Ottomans were proud to possess objects that belonged to or were touched by Muhammad—a preservation effort that, following the 1924 CE transformation of the palace into a museum, continues today under the aegis of the Turkish Republic.[59]

During Ottoman times, efforts were made to accumulate the Prophet's relics because these were (and often still are) considered precious carriers of blessing for their owners and viewers. Relics catered to a range of devotional needs and served as centerpieces for prayers, ceremonies, and the religious holidays that punctuate the days and months of the Islamic ritual calendar. Additionally, such objects enabled Ottoman sultans in particular to lay claim to the Prophet's political legacy as quintessential leader of the Muslim *umma* by allowing them, quite literally, to follow in his footsteps and to carry his standard into battle. Thus, for the Ottomans, possessing prophetic relics was tantamount to securing the caliphate since Muhammad's relics were understood as portable forms of sacred territory as well as a means of distributing and preserving Muhammad's sensible presence in the world.[60]

The Prophet's relics included a variety of items classified as sacred trusts (*al-amanat al-mubaraka* or *mukaddes emanetler*), blessed objects (*tabarrukat*), traces or vestiges (*athar* or *eser*), estate items, and items left behind (*mukhallafat*). Objects that emitted particular *baraka*, or mystic virtue,[61] included both physical and artifactual remains. His physical vestiges consisted of hair strands, nail clippings, and teeth—that is, protein and calcium excrescences of the body, the removal of which did not threaten Muhammad's physical integrity on his death and burial—as well as footprints left on stones, which are essentially contact, or secondary, relics.[62] His personal accoutrements comprised clothing, such as his mantle and sandals, as well as everyday objects such as his ablutions basin and ewer, rosary, prayer mat, toothbrush, letters, signet ring, staff, swords, standards, and banners. Taken together, the Prophet's relics thus encompass his organic presence as a human being as well as his supreme status as the religious, political, and military leader of the early Muslim community.

During Ottoman times, Muhammad's relics were used in ceremonies conducted in Topkapı Palace, where they were held in a chapel-like room until the creation of a privy chamber during the rule of Sultan Mahmud II (r. 1808–39 CE). These relics were visited especially during the month of Ramadan, at which time various state officials were invited to partake in the ritual viewing, touching, and kissing of relics. Ritual practices in the privy chamber also involved the burning of candles and incense as well as the recitation of the Qur'an, hymns, and various prayers including the *tawarih*, supererogatory prayers uttered at night during the month of Ramadan.[63] So holy were these practices of visitation to the privy chamber that court observers, such as Ignatius Mouradgea D'Ohsson (d. 1807 CE), an Armenian diplomat in Swedish service, noted that for many in the royal milieu "the sanctity [of the chapel] seems to their eyes, as well as to those of the public, above even that of mosques."[64] While visits to Topkapı Palace's privy chamber remained a private, elite privilege, other relics, such as the Prophet's banner, were paraded through the streets of Istanbul before an awestruck public to the accompaniment of songs in his honor.[65] Muhammad's vestiges thus held a significant place in Ottoman palace practices and the public imagination at large.

While not objects of worship per se, these relics nevertheless served as intermediary devices through which to contemplate and approach the Prophet's spiritual being. They helped focalize their viewers' pious attention and also catalyzed a corpus of related visual arts, particularly during and after the seventeenth century, by which time the Ottoman royal collection of prophetic relics had grown substantially, and courtly traditions of ritual visitation had become relatively standardized.

The artistic products directly associated with or inspired by the Prophet's relics include chests, boxes and mounts, plaques and paintings, calligraphic panels and diagrams, and illustrated prayer books. The manuscripts, which were produced in numerous copies, typically include a selection of qur'anic *sura*s and petitionary prayers (*du'a*s) accompanied by a series of paintings of Muhammad's relics and seal-like designs. As religious miscellanies, these devotional books bear a variety of titles, including *du'aname* or *du'a kitabı* (prayer book), *du'a mecmuası* (prayer compendium), and *en'am-ı şerif* (the noble cattle, a title based on the sixth qur'anic chapter *surat al-in'am*).[66] They also tend to be

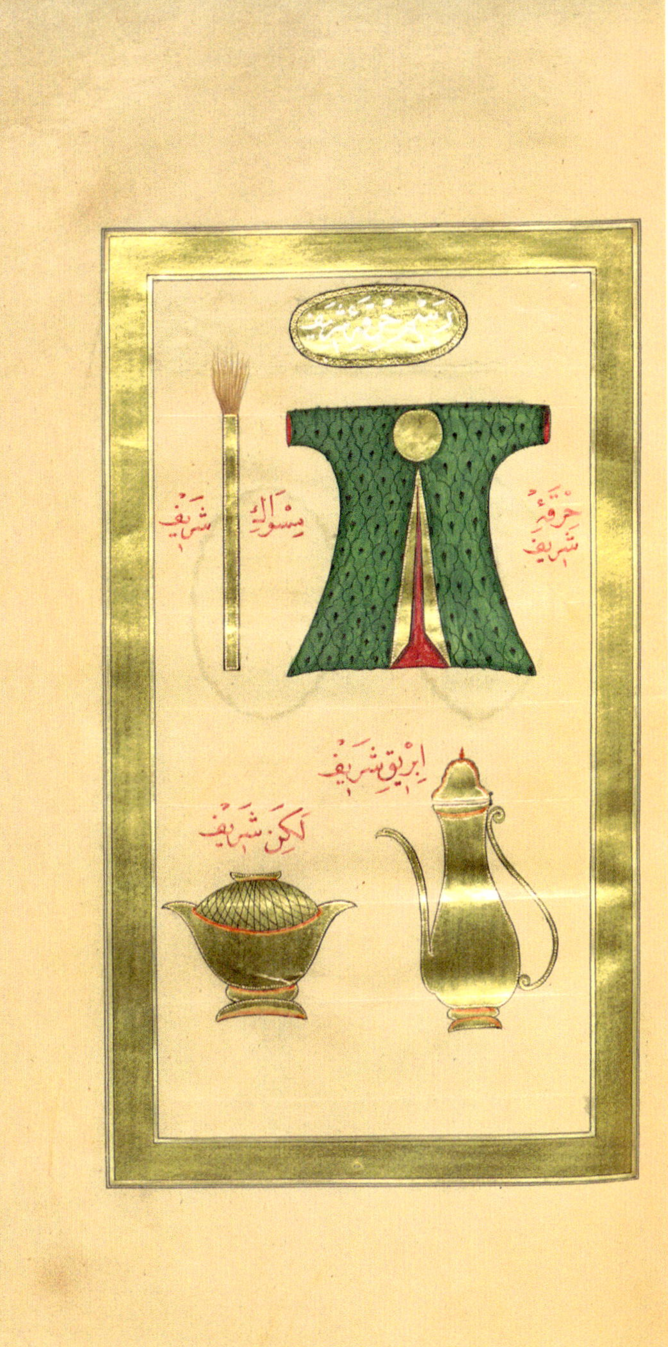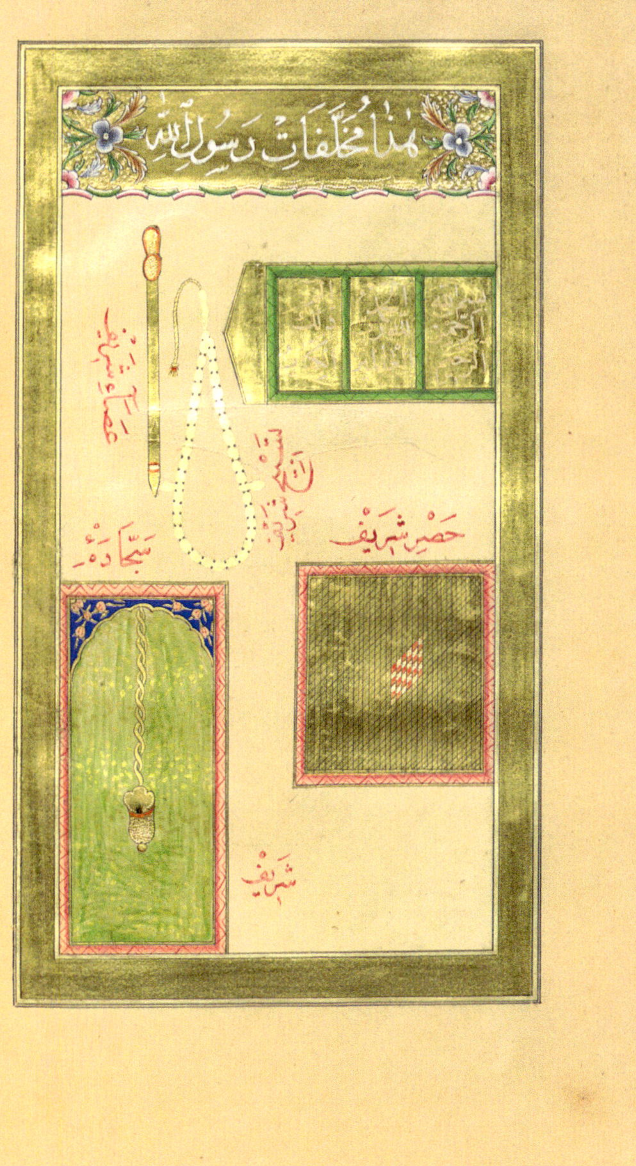

of rather portable size, acting as popular vade mecums for Ottoman individuals who wished to recite qur'anic and supplicatory prayers on various occasions.

In these small prayer books, the acts of seeing and touching were of paramount importance. To wit, a number of Ottoman prayer books include short how-to texts encouraging their readers to gaze on, touch, and kiss these visual representations at various times of the day and week. These types of interactions, the texts further inform us, help to unleash the images' latent *baraka* and thus enabled the manuscripts' owners to secure protection from a range of diseases and calamities.[67] The protective power of the illustrations and diagrams in Ottoman prayer books thus were believed to be activated by their viewers' intimate visual and physical encounters.

5.6. The Prophet Muhammad's personal items (*mukhallafat*), prayer book of Düzdidil, Istanbul, 1261 AH/1845 CE. Bayerische Landesbibliothek, Munich, Cod. Turc. 553, folios 206v–207r.

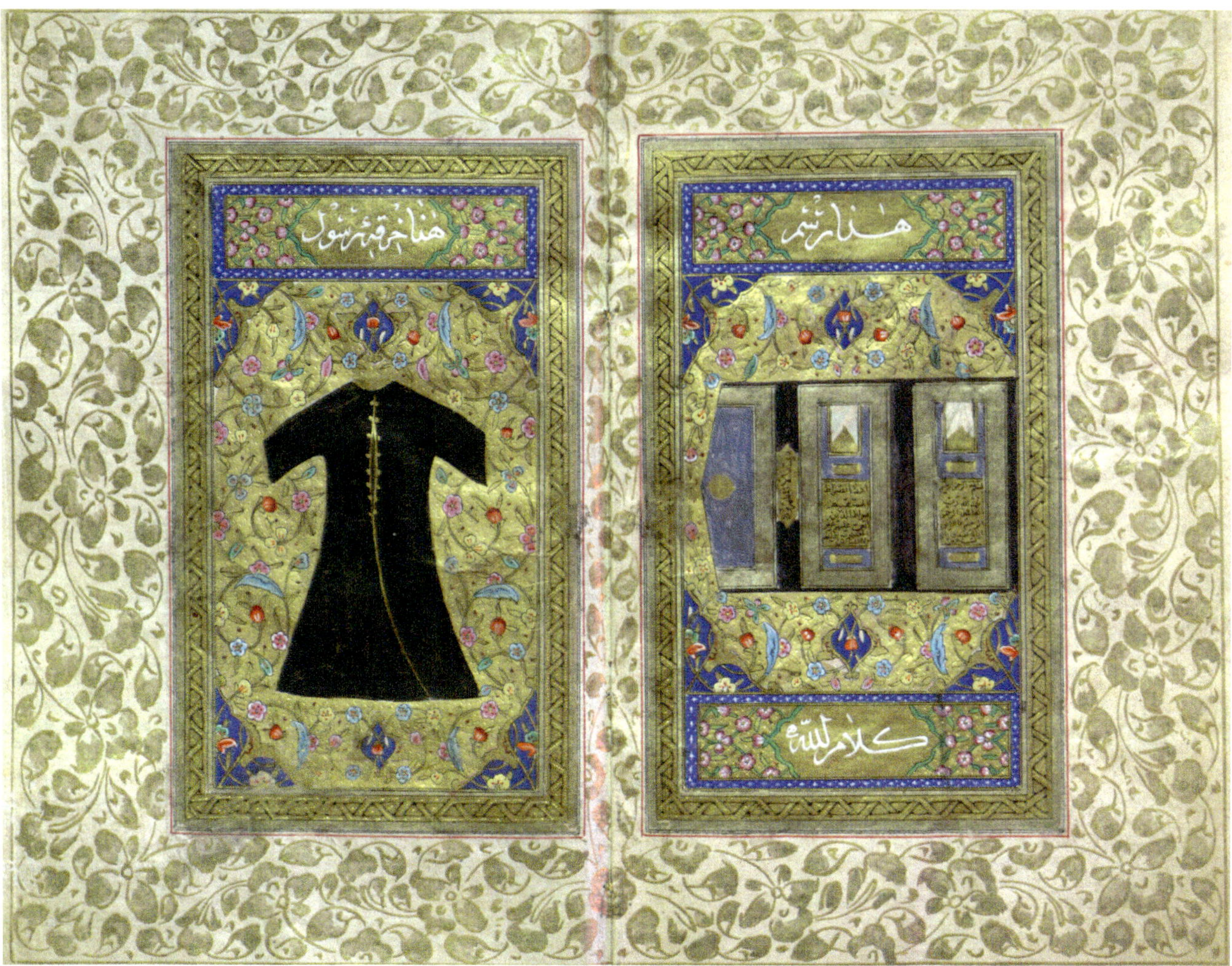

5.7. The Qur'an and the Prophet Muhammad's mantle, prayer book calligraphed by Mustafa al-Kutahi for an unnamed patron, Ottoman lands, 1185 AH/1771–72 CE. Special Collections Department, Bryn Mawr College Library, ms. BV#53, unfoliated.

Muhammad's relics fulfilled both pious and prophylactic functions, as did their depiction in illustrated prayer books. One manuscript made in 1845 CE for Düzdidil, the third-favorite official wife (*kadınefendi*) of Sultan Abdülmecid (r. 1839–61 CE), includes a depiction of some of the Prophet's personal items (fig. 5.6).[68] The double-page painting's caption (at top right) states, "These are the personal items (*mukhallafat*) of the Messenger of God." On the same page are represented various sacred objects, including a Qur'an, rosary, staff, mat, and prayer rug, while the left page illustrates the Prophet's mantle, toothbrush, ewer, and basin. Muhammad's mantle stands out due to its size, its brilliant green hue, and the gold oval cartouche identifying the image as an "illustration of the sacred mantle." Other Ottoman illustrated *du'aname*s include similar relics or else depict only the Qur'an and Muhammad's mantle, as is the case for a prayer book made in 1771 CE for an unnamed patron (fig. 5.7).[69]

While Muhammad used many of these items to perform prayer rites and maintain personal hygiene, the Qur'an and his mantle were set apart by their supreme symbolism in Islamic piety and politics across the centuries. They also were held in especially high esteem within Topkapı Palace during Ottoman times as Ottoman sultans were believed to be carrying forth and protecting the revealed word of God (*Kalam Allah*) as well as donning the mantle of divinely decreed rulership.

The Ottoman relics chamber preserved a number of parchment folios containing qur'anic verses, and some of these folios include later Ottoman notes attributing the Kufic script to 'Uthman b. 'Affan. One Kufic Qur'an believed to have been written in the hand of 'Uthman was sent from the Mamluk sultan Jaqmaq (r. 1438–53 CE) to the Ottoman sultan Murad II (r. 1421–44 and 1446–51) in 1440 CE,[70] while a bloodstained Kufic copy of the Qur'an that is believed to have been in 'Uthman's possession when he was killed was sent from the governor of Egypt to Istanbul in 1821 CE.[71] These material vestiges of prophetic and scriptural history stretch back to the earliest period of Islamic sacred history and thus carried a high degree of *baraka*. Moreover, by linguistic allusion they also praised the Ottoman dynasty, whose founding father, Osman I (r. 1299–1326 CE), shared the same name as this famous member of the *rashidun*.[72]

The presumably authentic 'Uthmanic codex played an important role in Islamic political life, as well. It was believed to have been passed down through generations of caliphs, from the Umayyads to the 'Abbasids, Mamluks, and Ottomans. Alongside the Prophet's *hırka*, it thus served as a prime symbol of temporal authority, in particular the caliphate. For these reasons, it was used in various court ceremonies. For example, at the 'Abbasid court the enthroned caliph would appear on special occasions carrying a copy of the Qur'an while wearing Muhammad's cloak.[73] During the medieval period, an 'Uthmanic Qur'an was also preserved in the main congregational mosque in Damascus, where it was kept in a cabinet and covered with a veil. This codex was touched and kissed by believers who wished to establish physical contact with the blessed manuscript; it also was sworn on by debtors as well as paraded around Damascus in order to protect the city's walls and thus forestall a Crusader invasion of the city in 1148 CE.[74]

The question of authenticity notwithstanding, possession of the 'Uthmanic codex enabled the transfer of these many symbolic messages to Topkapı Palace. The Ottoman sultans and members of the court could join a long and rich pedigree of sultanic guardianship of, and interaction with, this sacred relic of God's divine Logos. As Finbarr Barry Flood notes, this type of object highlights the "complex imbrications of oral narratives, textual artifacts, and material relics in fostering both the dispersal of and access to the sacred."[75] For Ottoman rulers, this sacred cachet was amassed in a large collection of prophetic relics, in which the Qur'an of 'Uthman functioned as a memento of revelation history, a metonym for the caliphate, a binding oath, and a carrier of divine protection and blessings.

Like God, the Qur'an is considered the best of guardians. Members of the Ottoman court therefore consulted holy scripture to seek assistance in daily affairs and find relief from pain, a positive method of "seeking guidance" (*istikhara*) that is still practiced by many Muslims.

Within the context of Ottoman prayer books, illustrations of the ʿUthmanic codex connect not only to the relic held in the palace collections but also to the qurʾanic verses selected for transcription within the manuscripts. Readers consulted these verses to secure aid, solace, or cure. This was certainly the case for the prayer book made for Düzdidil; the devotional miscellany was commissioned when this nineteen-year-old *kadınefendi* contracted tuberculosis, and the work functioned as a means to "search for forgiveness and a channel for entering paradise."[76] Moreover, a number of Ottoman-language petitionary prayers included in the manuscript are directly addressed to the Prophet and request that the doors of paradise be opened, while others are to be recited during the religious holidays of Ramadan and Berat.

The illustration of the ʿUthmanic codex within this royal prayer book thus functions as a pictorial proxy for the qurʾanic relic, which could convey its therapeutic *baraka* and secure paradise for an owner-viewer, like Düzdidil, stricken with illness. That such images were believed to hold curative—even salvific—powers that could be activated by their viewers' intent gaze is confirmed by internal evidence, including a short explanatory text in Düzdidil's *duʿaname* that informs the reader that whoever looks at a sacred seal from morning until night, or from night until morning, will be protected from disasters and saved from hell.[77] In Ottoman palace quarters, the ʿUthmanic codex and Muhammad's relics were believed to emit intercessory blessings when ritually viewed by their royal visitors, and such latent *baraka* evidently was thought to inhere in their visual representations, as well.

Besides the ʿUthmanic codex, the Prophet's mantle held pride of place among his relics. It was preserved in a special chamber, known as the "room of the sacred mantle" (*hırka-i şerif odası*), in Topkapı Palace. This room served as a space for contemplation and prayer from the end of the seventeenth century onward.[78] During the eighteenth and nineteenth centuries, when many illustrated prayer books were also produced, interactions with Muhammad's *hırka* occurred during enthronement ceremonies and Ramadan visitations. The prophetic mantle—which was present as both an artifactual relic and a representational image—therefore proved central to the political and devotional life of the Ottoman court.

As an item bearing political import, the *hırka* symbolized the Prophet Muhammad as the ruling body of his faith community. Textual sources inform us that the mantle was passed down by previous caliphs and either was found in Cairo or was given to Sultan Selim I by the Sharifs of Mecca on his defeat of the Mamluks in 1517 CE.[79] The mantle was reverently visited by later Ottoman rulers as a prelude to their accessions to the throne. For example, during their respective enthronement ceremonies, Sultan Ahmed II (r. 1691–95 CE) visited the room of the sacred mantle held in the Edirne palace, while Mustafa II (r. 1695–1703 CE) performed prayers at the *hırka* before heading to the mosque and shrine of Eyüp, where he viewed the Prophet's sword.[80] The mantle also accompanied some Ottoman sultans during their travels and war campaigns and was even worn by Sultan Mehmed III (r. 1595–1603 CE) at the siege of Eğri in 1596 CE.[81] As a result, by 1700 CE Muhammad's mantle acted as a symbol of legitimate sovereignty during accession ceremonies and also was believed to protect the sultan's physical body from harm. When donned by the sultan, the *hırka* metaphorically alloyed the body of the monarch to that of the Prophet. Albeit innovative, this Ottoman vestmental practice certainly merited its appellation as the "ancient custom of the great ancestors."[82]

The Prophet's mantle likewise contributed to the accomplishment of religious rituals at the Ottoman court, especially during Ramadan. On the fifteenth day of this holy month of fasting, the sultan, his family, and government officials took part in communal prayer in Hagia Sophia. Thereafter followed a pious visitation of the "felicitous mantle" (*hırka-i sa'adet*) in Topkapı Palace, at which time the mantle was uncovered, viewed, kissed, rubbed, and washed. This ceremony involved a number of specific rites, including the use of rose water (*gülsuyu*) to anoint the relic chamber and amber incense to infuse it with a pleasant scent. At times the rose water was used to ritually clean the mantle; at others, the *hırka*'s seams were lightly dipped in a basin thought to contain Zamzam water. This "water of the sacred mantle" (*ab-ı hırka-i şerif*)—whether concocted with rose essence or collected from the Zamzam well in Mecca—was stored in small bottles and offered as a gift to members of the court and other important officials, who used the liquid to break fast during the last two weeks of Ramadan or as a curative potion for illness.

In addition, the Ottoman sultan offered every visitor of the Prophet's mantle a muslin cloth (*tülbent*), and visitors brought with them their own handkerchiefs (*mendiller*). These small fabrics were rubbed on the mantle, thus rendering them sacred (*kutlu*). Some also included inscribed verses inviting their owners to kiss the mantle-imbued fabrics while requesting the Prophet's intercession for the Muslim community. At other times the Ottoman sultan and his entourage touched the Prophet's mantle without any intermediary object, kissing it directly with their lips and rubbing their faces and eyes with it.[83]

The *hırka* thus could be experienced via direct touch or the imbibing of relic water. These practices exhibit Ottoman Muslim devotees' wish to absorb, and even become one with, the symbolic being of the Prophet. Indeed, among all relics, Muhammad's *hırka* provided the most ideal object to incorporate political concepts and religious beliefs, acting as the mantle of a king and a prophet—a warrior and a man of God—at the same time.[84] Put simply, it functioned as a prime symbol for the Ottoman caliphate's worldly authority and Islamic pietism.

Ottoman prayer books that include images of the Prophet's sacred mantle were made during the eighteenth and nineteenth centuries, when ceremonial visits to the *hırka* formed a key part of court protocol and religious festivities. Illustrations depict the mantle in either black or green pigment, most likely because the robe was woven of black wool and wrapped in layers of green satin.[85] Moreover, in some manuscript paintings (as in fig. 5.7) the mantle is shown unfolded, as if inhabited by the spiritually real, yet physically absent, body of Muhammad himself. A quick glance or a sustained gaze at paintings of the Prophet's *hırka* may even lead the viewer to imagine herself the recipient of a warm embrace. For Düzdidil and others who suffered from sickness and pain, an image of the relic therefore could offer a visuospiritual channel by which to seek prophetic comfort and cure.

Through pictures of the mantle, Muhammad also could be conjured up as a talismanic force.[86] The apotropaic potential of these images is linked to the mantle's close relationship to the supplicatory panegyric ode entitled *Qasidat al-Burda* (The Mantle Ode), written by the Mamluk poet al-Busiri (d. ca. 1294–97 CE).[87] Indeed, the terms *hırka* and *burda* were used interchangeably for the Prophet's mantle, and thus the object and the devotional poem were closely related. Busiri's *Mantle Ode* (along with its translations and expansions) also functioned like Süleyman Çelebi's *Noble Birth* in that both texts were recited during the festival of the Prophet's birth.

Al-Busiri composed the *Mantle Ode* as a prayerful entreaty to the Prophet when he fell seriously ill. On reciting it, he experienced a dream vision of Muhammad, who placed his mantle on the author and miraculously cured him of his ailment. The text, endowed with great liturgical and spiritual power for Muslim devotees, thus was believed to engender the spiritual presence of the Prophet and to heal the ailments of those who read or heard it. A number of its verses also were thought to carry special properties (*khawass*) and benefits (*fada'il*) that could help cure diseases including epilepsy, colic, diarrhea, and hemorrhoids. For these reasons, particularly thaumaturgic verses were inscribed on pieces of paper, dissolved in rose water, and imbibed by supplicants as a form of prophetic medicine.[88]

The *Qasidat al-Burda*'s role as the prime mantle myth, text, and talisman most likely generated the actual relic of the Prophet's *hırka*. As Suzanne Stetkevych pointedly notes, "it was only a matter of time before an actual mantle became identified with the mythical one."[89] While the *hırka* proper certainly was thought to cure through rubbing, kissing, and imbibing, Ottoman painted images of the mantle also could be seen to function like the *Qasidat al-Burda*: that is, as a means of bringing a supplicant into the Prophet's spiritual company to secure his blessing and intercession and be healed by envisioning his contact relic. As both object and image, Muhammad's mantle thus offered therapeutic and talismanic protection to its Ottoman viewers and owners.

A number of other relics of the Prophet were kept in Topkapı Palace. Among them, special emphasis was placed on his noble footprint (*kadem-i şerif*) and pair of sandals (*na'layn*), which existed in various sizes and shapes.[90] These stone and leather relics were the frequent subjects of illustration in Ottoman prayer books. In one *du'aname*, for example, the foot- and sandal print are closely aligned by their balanced

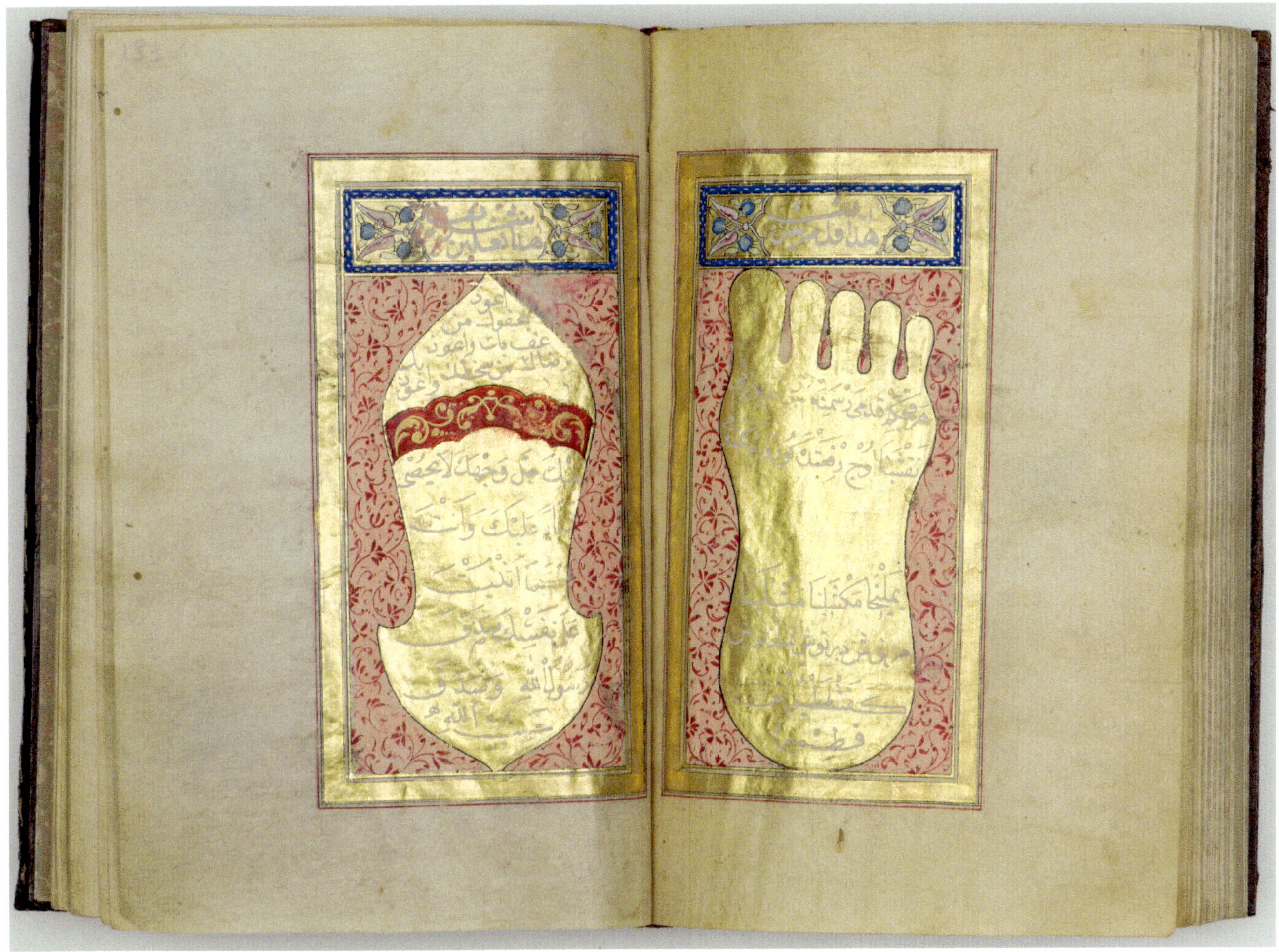

placement on facing folios (fig. 5.8). Identified by captions and placed on a pink background decorated with scrolling vines, the outlines are filled with gold paint and inscriptions written in white ink. In addition, both images display signs of wear—across the digits of Muhammad's foot, especially on the big toe, as well as above and across the red band of the sandal—suggesting that they, like the relics they represent, were not only viewed but touched.

The inscription within the footprint is divided into two parts. At the top, verses in Ottoman Turkish read, "Whenever I rub my face to the image of his [Muhammad's] footprint / Oh Naqşi, I see myself in the apogee of eminence."[91] The inscriber, whose nom de plume (*makhlas*) appears to be Naqşi, thus seeks spiritual elevation by rubbing his face on the painting of the Prophet's foot. At the bottom, another inscription lists the names of the Seven Sleepers of Ephesus—known in Arabic as *ahl al-kahf*, or people of the cave—and their dog, Qitmir. Frequently written on Ottoman amulets, mirrors, and other objects, the names of the Seven Sleepers are believed to protect persons and places from fire and ships from sinking.[92] In this instance, their names appear on Muhammad's footprint, suggesting that the image's amuletic qualities are inherently present as well as potentially unlocked or amplified through the process of devotional rubbing. This hypothesis is borne out by the

5.8. The Prophet Muhammad's footprint and sandal print, Ottoman lands, eighteenth or nineteenth century CE. Nasser D. Khalili Collection of Islamic Art, London, MSS 158, folios 132v–133r.

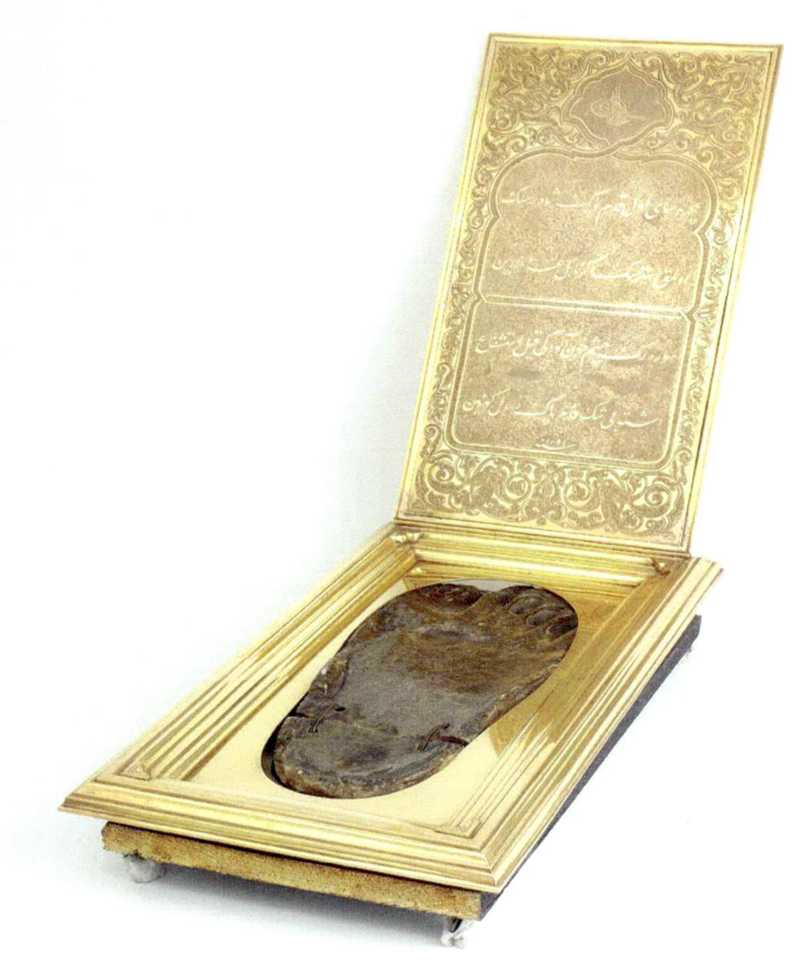

5.9. The Prophet Muhammad's footprint on stone in a gilt case commissioned by Sultan Abdülhamid II in 1294 AH/1877 CE. Topkapı Palace Museum, Istanbul, no. 21–195.

same manuscript's depiction of the seal of the Seven Sleepers, which informs its readers that rubbing the seal on one's face grants protection from hell and Satan and that gazing on it from morning until night or night until morning provides safety from calamities.[93] When it comes to the representational mode, therefore, Ottoman images of the Prophet's relics fulfill clear talismanic functions while also depicting a metonymic Muhammad as both *praesentia* and *potentia*.[94]

Paintings of Muhammad's footprint were inspired by stone relics housed within the palace collections as well as preserved in a number of mosques, madrasas, shrines, and tombs throughout Ottoman lands. As they came into the royal collections in Istanbul, these footprints were used in ritual practices. For instance, one stone imprint of Muhammad's right foot was brought from Tripoli to Istanbul, where its broken heel section was repaired with silver wires. Then, in 1877 CE, Sultan Abdül-hamid II (r. 1876–1909 CE) ordered a new gold cover to be made for it (fig. 5.9).[95] On the underside of the cover's lid, an inscription written in Ottoman Turkish invites the viewer to prayerfully rub his face on the footprint in order to secure healing (*istişfa*) thanks to the intercession of the "King of Prophets."[96] This written directive, which is placed directly on the object and is legible on its ritual opening and viewing, clearly

THE PRAISEWORTHY ONE

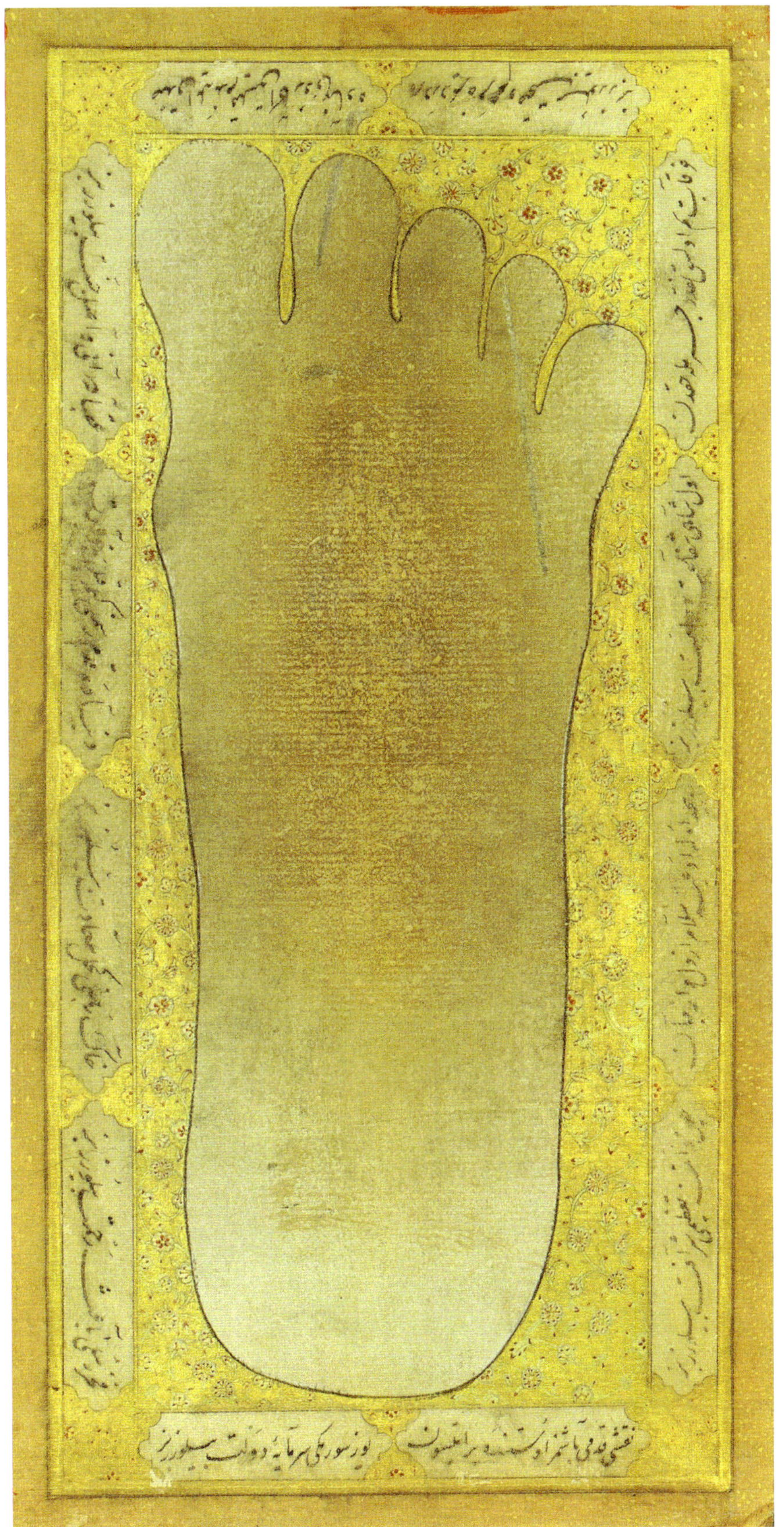

5.10. A drawing of the Prophet Muhammad's footprint on a card, Ottoman lands (probably Istanbul), eighteenth or nineteenth century CE. Topkapı Palace Museum, Istanbul, no. 21–640.

demonstrates that, within Ottoman quarters, Muhammad's footprints were prayed on, touched, and rubbed in order to release their therapeutic qualities.[97]

The Ottoman practice of piously rubbing Muhammad's relics carried over to book arts and paintings, as well. A number of images of his footprints in prayer miscellanies display signs of wear, as can be seen in figure 5.8, while some drawings mounted on cardboard exhibit a loss of pigment. One example, intended for affixing to a wall, includes cartouches along the outer rim (fig. 5.10).[98] The text contained within praises the Prophet and his intercession, with the final closing line reading, "May the painting of the foot be placed above our head, we consider rubbing our face a capital of fortune."[99] Evidently, a pious agent placed this relic-image at eye level (or even on the head) and rubbed it on his face in a physical action intended to secure good fortune (*devlet*). Thus, in Ottoman lands the Prophet's footprints and their associated depictions functioned as good luck charms.

Muhammad's footprints were closely linked to his sandals, a number of which were also housed in Topkapı Palace.[100] Images of the sandals were considered blessed and protective. As the double-page painting in figure 5.8 shows, they catered to liturgical practices, as well. Filling the inner ground of the sandal print's outline, the inscription records a Saying (Hadith) of the Prophet, which he addressed to God in his nighttime prayer during the middle of the month of Sha'ban: "I seek refuge in your forgiveness from your punishment, and I seek refuge in your pleasure from your annoyance, and I seek your refuge from yourself. I cannot praise you as fully as you deserve. You are exactly as you have defined yourself." This prayer of forgiveness counts among the most important *du'a*s recited by Muslims during *Laylat al-Bara'a* (The Night of Salvation), one of the holiest nights in the Islamic calendar, celebrated at mid-Sha'ban. Known in Turkish lands as *Berat Kandili*, this religious holiday finds believers seeking atonement for their sins and deliverance from hell. Practices include nighttime vigils requesting divine mercy and forgiveness, and, in Ottoman times, the pious visited and prayed on the Prophet's relics in royal quarters, as well. As a result, images of Muhammad's relics inscribed with holiday-specific *du'a*s suggest that Ottoman illustrated prayer books were used as oral recitation and relic-viewing manuals by devotees who celebrated Islamic religious holidays in the palace's relics chamber. That Qur'ans, prayer books, and other devotional manuscripts were originally stored in this "royal chapel" in turn strongly supports this hypothesis.[101]

From the fifteenth century onward, several of Muhammad's wooden and leather sandals were transferred to Topkapı Palace, where they were stored in the relics chamber and preserved in bejeweled boxes for both male and female members of the royal family.[102] The most famous among these was the sandal that was said to be held in the Ashrafiyya Madrasa in Damascus, which was sent to Istanbul in 1872 CE.[103] This sandal counts among the best documented of all of Muhammad's relics

THE PRAISEWORTHY ONE

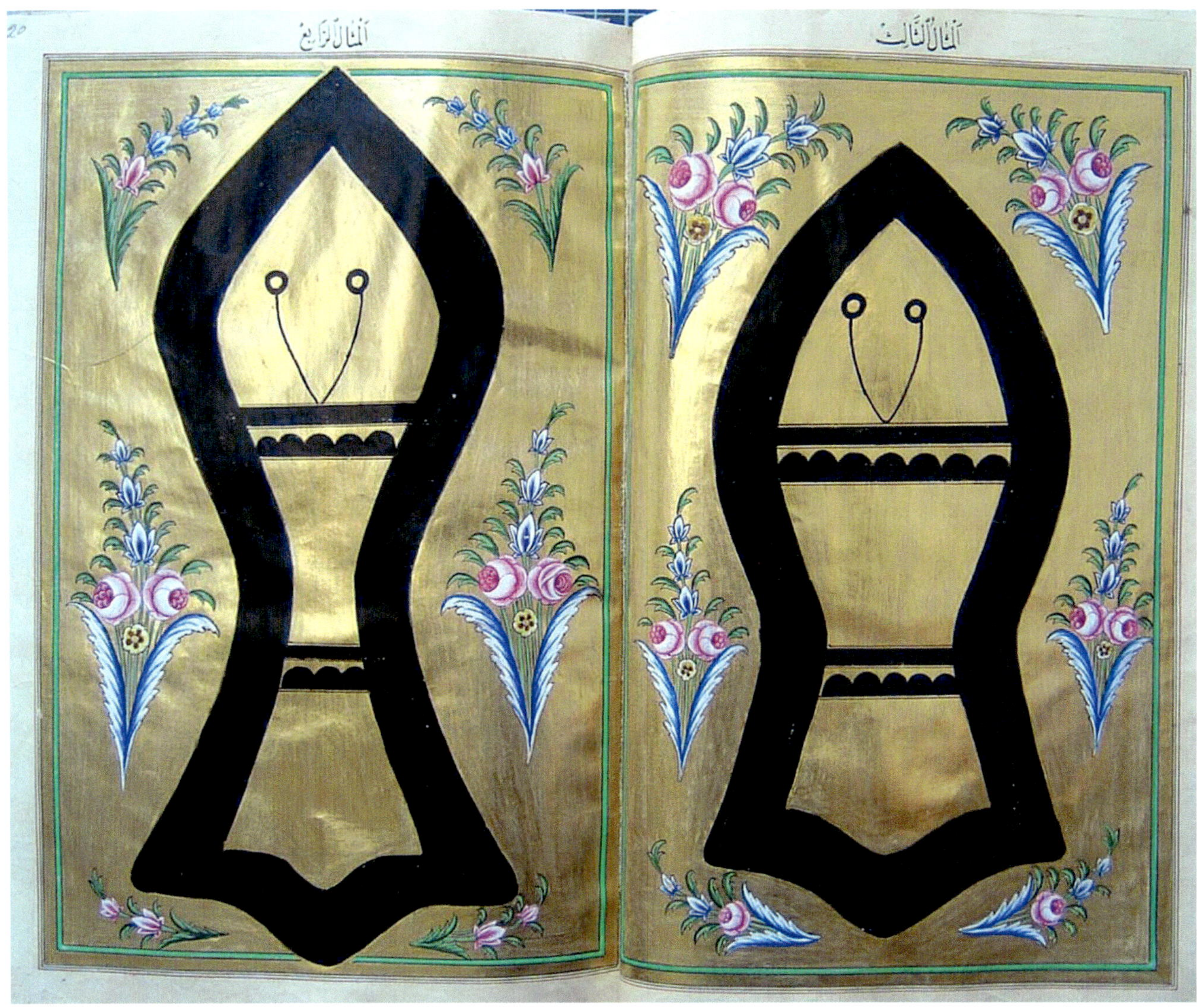

and inspired a veritable Damascene cult. It was housed in the madrasa until Timur's sack of the city in 1401 CE, at which time it disappeared. While still in Damascus, the sandal symbolized Hadith learning, the *'ulama'*, the building of colleges, and Sunni orthodoxy. During the medieval period, it also stimulated religious visitation to Damascus by pilgrims who sought the Prophet's intercession, via his sandal, to remedy problems and cure ills.[104] Its later rediscovery (or, more likely, its forgery) and acquisition by the royal palace in Istanbul thus helped to glorify the Ottoman sultans as guardians of the prophetic *sunna* and Islamic religious learning.

Individuals who could not visit Muhammad's original sandal in Damascus requested paper replicas of the original, which were created from the twelfth century onward.[105] A visual copy, or "similitude" (*mithal*), of the Prophet's sandal, especially if based on the original artifact, was thought to act as a particularly effective safeguard. Not the first or only text of its kind,[106] an Ottoman treatise entitled *Rawdat al-Safa fi Wasf Ni'al al-Mustafa* (The Garden of Purity in Describing the Pure One's Sandals) and composed around 1839–61 CE, includes eight slightly

5.11. The third and fourth representation (*mithal*) of the Prophet Muhammad's sandal, Ahmed Süleymanizade, *Rawdat al-Safa fi Wasf Ni'al al-Mustafa* (The Garden of Purity in Describing the Pure One's Sandals), Ottoman lands, ca. 1839–61 CE. Topkapı Palace Library, Istanbul, E.H. 1190, folios 19v–20r.

different representations of the sandal that show two straps crossing the foot and ankle along with two bands passing between the toes (fig. 5.11).[107] The structural details of the third and fourth similitudes of Muhammad's sandal are crisply outlined in black pigment on a gold ground ornamented with bouquets of pink flowers and roses.

In the third chapter, devoted to the properties (*khawass*) and benefits (*fawa'id*) of images of Muhammad's sandal, the treatise's author notes that these sandal designs protect against enemies and rebels as well as the devil and the evil eye; that they ease childbirth if a pregnant woman holds the image in her right hand; that one of the images should be placed on the location of pain to miraculously cure an illness; that an individual who wears the image in his turban will become a leader; that seafarers who place the image in their boats will be saved from shipwreck; and that the image of the blessed sandal protects a caravan from theft, a home from burning, soldiers from injury, and much more.[108] Supremely talismanic, visual representations of the Prophet's sandal print were widely considered a most effective and versatile form of prophetic prophylaxis—a popular belief that endures to the present day (figs. 6.22–6.24).

A plenitude of Islamic texts and poems also record the devotional practices of kissing and touching images of Muhammad's sandal in order to unleash its *baraka*, considered especially potent since his footwear is said to have rubbed against God's throne.[109] For example, the Andalusian poetess Himyariyya (d. 1242 CE) exclaims: "I shall kiss the image if I do not find a way to kiss the Prophet's sandal / and I rub my heart on it so that perhaps the burning thirst that rages in it may be quenched."[110] These verses speak to the devotee's urge for spiritual contact with the Prophet through image- and heart-based interactions.

These expressions of piety produced long-lasting visual and material evidence of religious engagement with images and relics related to the Prophet. While produced at various times and across Islamic lands (including west and sub-Saharan Africa), images of Muhammad's sandal that were kissed and rubbed emerge as a hallmark of the later Ottoman period. Many representations of the sandal can be found in illustrated pilgrimage guides, or on talismanic shirts, prayer carpets, and architectural tiles; some display wear while others invite physical contact. For instance, an Ottoman manuscript detailing the genealogy of the Prophet includes a representation that serves as the text's visual apex and closure (fig. 5.12). Here, the large outline of the sandal does not include any strap or band details. Instead, it is entirely filled with gold paint, several areas of which show wear suggestive of heavy devotional handling. That the *mithal* was touched and kissed is corroborated by the text contained in the cartouches surrounding the image. On the left, the Arabic-language verses command the viewer of the sandal image to kiss the *mithal* day and night, without arrogance. With slight textual variations, these verses also appear on Ottoman tiles from around 1600 CE,

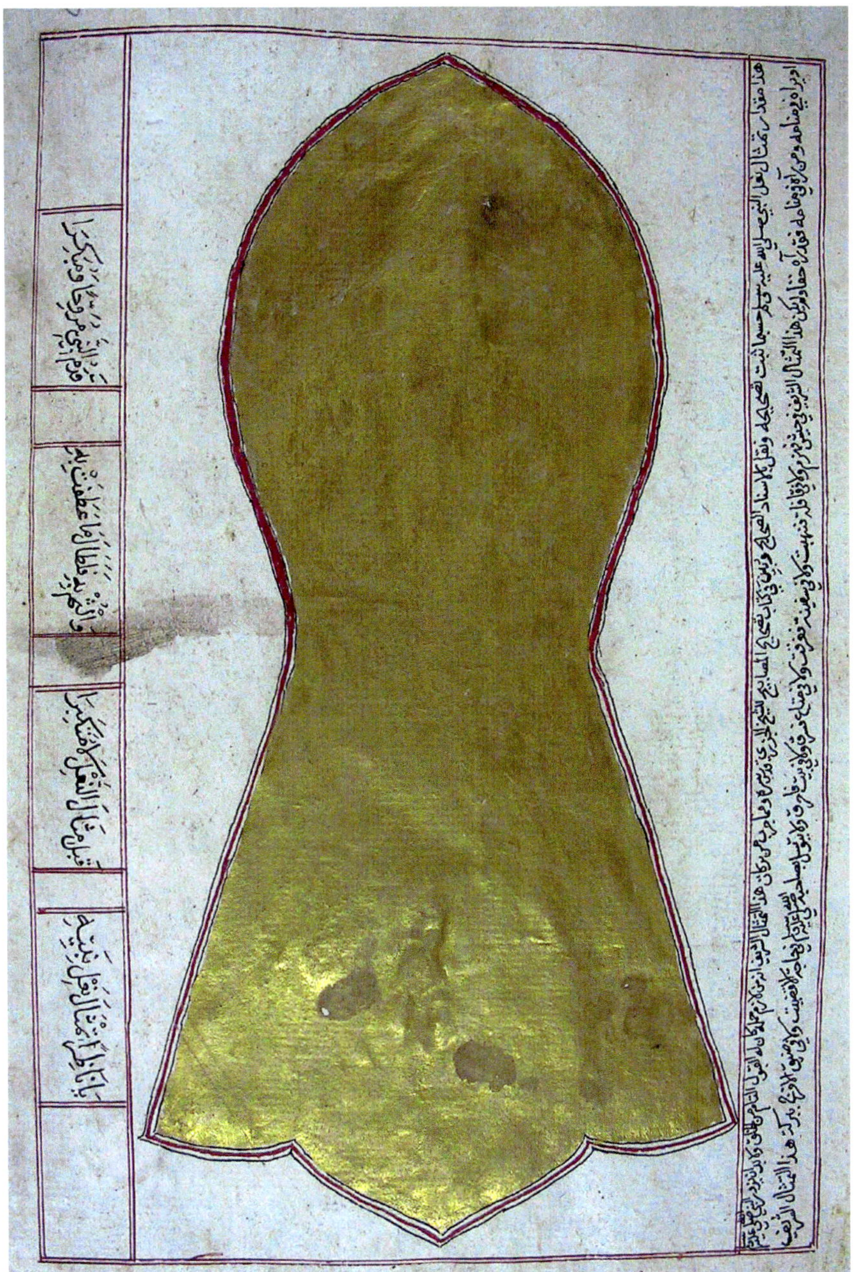

5.12. The Prophet Muhammad's sandal print, *Neseb'ün-Nebi* (Genealogy of the Prophet), Ottoman lands, eighteenth or nineteenth century CE. Süleymaniye Library, Istanbul, Esad Efendi 270, penultimate folio (manuscript unpaginated).

including the *mihrab* panel in the Darwishiyya Mosque in Damascus (fig. 5.13).[111]

This imperative to piety and humility is further elaborated on in figure 5.12. In the left panel, the text notes that the owner (*sahib*) of the representation will reap its many benefits. Among them, he will see the Prophet in his dreams, win battles against enemies, partake in caravans safe from theft, live in a home that will not burn, and travel on a ship that will not sink. As the text concludes, this noble representation (*al-timthal al-sharif*) is said to safeguard its possessor from all worries and troubles—a talismanic quality that, as the visual and textual evidence so clearly indicates, was thought to be unlocked via ardent and repeated viewing, touching, and kissing.

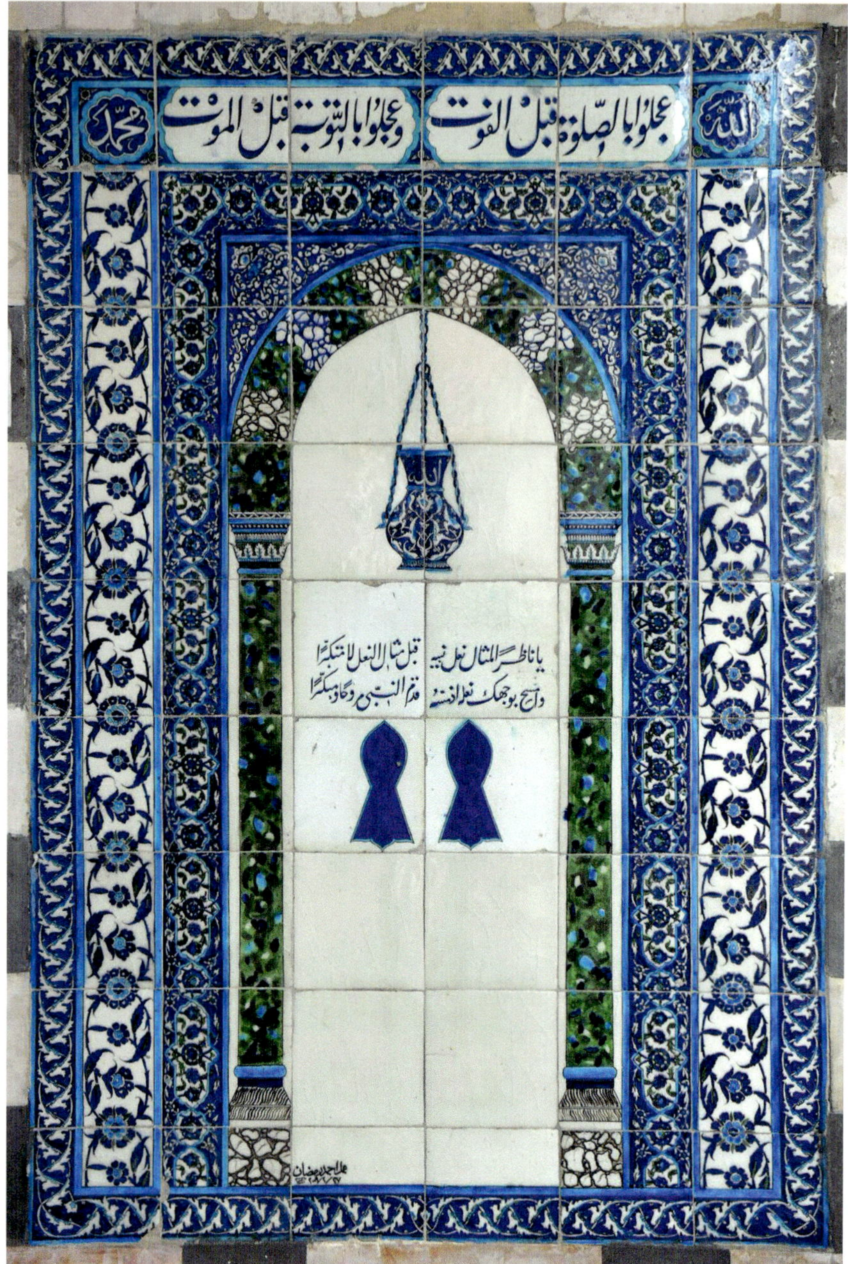

5.13. A depiction of the Prophet Muhammad's sandals on an Ottoman tile placed in the *mihrab* of the Darwishiyya Mosque, Damascus, Syria, ca. 1575–1600 CE (tile renovated and signed by Ahmad Ramadan in 2009). Photograph courtesy of Rania Ibrahim Kataf, 2017.

To date, scholarly discussions of religious images as objects of osculatory (kissing) urges have been largely limited to European Christian manuscript examples.[112] However, as these many prophetic relics and relic paintings reveal, the Ottoman accumulation and representation of sacred artifacts associated with Muhammad were joined by the related practices of touching and kissing, or using Zamzam water, rose water, and saliva as conduits for tasting or ingesting a blessed liquid. Believers thus activated the objects' and images' latent *baraka*, whose dust and pigment dregs touched the skin and entered devotees' bodies, thereby allowing them to become more prophet-like (both externally and internally). These practices in turn eroded images while also allowing the Prophet to gain a spiritually renewed life on the lips and within the flesh of members of his living community. While depicted through his relics

THE PRAISEWORTHY ONE

and relic paintings, a more metaphorical Muhammad—kissed, rubbed, and even imbibed—continued to thrive as the inner essence of those who wished to become one with his blessed traces.

From the seventeenth century onward, the Ottoman accumulation and depiction of Muhammad's relics became far more common than representational imagery, in the process reflecting and generating new methods of envisioning the Prophet in largely metonymic and nonfigural ways. At the same time, the viewing and washing of relics in prayer practices and the rubbing and kissing of images to secure protection and blessing also reveal the various interactive ways in which devotees approached the Prophet's physical and spiritual corpus. These tactile exercises were accompanied by yet another major Ottoman artistic innovation: the *hilye*. This popular type of verbal icon, which was made in a variety of forms, styles, and media, essentially provides a textual description of the Prophet. Transcending the figural mode, the *hilye* challenges pious viewers to contemplate the Prophet through visual and cognitive means that cultivate abstract thought and inner vision.

The term *hilye* was not an innovation of Ottoman Islamic culture. It can be traced to earlier Arabic-language texts that describe Muhammad's appearance (*hilya*) and miracles, most especially al-Tirmidhi's (d. 892 CE) *Al-Shama'il al-Muhammadiyya* (Muhammad's Characteristics) and al-Yahsubi's (d. 1149 CE) *Kitab al-Shifa bi Ta'rif Huquq al-Mustafa* (The Book of Healing by the Recognition of the Rights of the Chosen One). During the Ottoman period, these earlier texts inspired the creation of similar texts in Turkish, including a number of prose and verse *hilyes*.[113] The most famous among these is the *Hilye-i Şerif* (The Noble Description) composed by the poet Hakani (d. 1606 CE), which appears to have motivated the Ottoman calligrapher Hafız Osman (d. 1698 CE) to create a calligraphic diagram by the same name. As a result, the term *hilye* was quite versatile, indicating a likeness of the Prophet, a descriptive text or poem in his honor, or a schematic composition central to Islamic devotional art during the later Ottoman centuries.

The text most frequently inscribed within Ottoman *hilye*s is attributed to 'Ali, who describes Muhammad's physical and moral characteristics in both specific and vague terms. The Prophet is said to be neither tall nor short but of medium height; his hair is neither short nor curly; and his flesh is firm, his face round, his skin rosy, his eyes large and black, his lashes long, his bones strong, his shoulders broad, and his feet large. He is said to have had hair on his chest and stomach, and the seal of prophethood, resembling a pigeon's egg or a mole, was imprinted between his shoulders. In addition to these physical traits, Muhammad leaned forward while walking, spoke with a sincere tone, and was generous hearted, of a gentle nature, and well-liked.[114] In still another Hadith, the source for which remains rather opaque, the Prophet is recorded as encouraging his followers to contemplate his likeness after his death in order to "feel as if they have seen me" and to kiss and rub

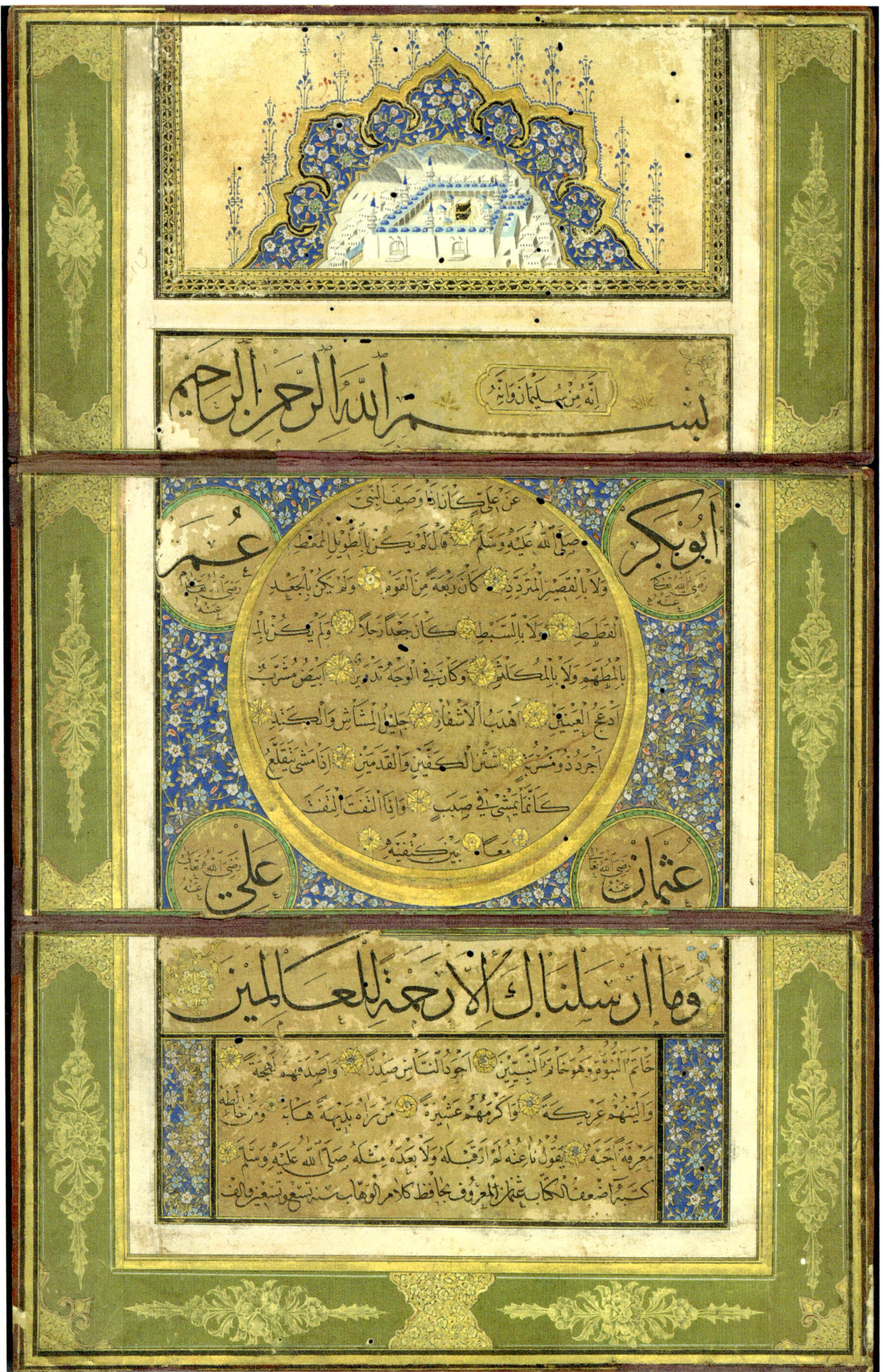

بسم الله الرحمن الرحيم
إنه من سليمان وإنه

أبو بكر
عمر
عثمان
علي

عن علي كان إذا وصف النبي صلى الله عليه وسلم قال لم يكن بالطويل الممغط ولا بالقصير المتردد كان ربعة من القوم ولم يكن بالجعد القطط ولا بالسبط كان جعداً رجلاً ولم يكن بالمطهم ولا بالمكلثم وكان في الوجه تدوير أبيض مشرب أدعج العينين أهدب الأشفار جليل المشاش والكتد أجرد ذو مسربة شثن الكفين والقدمين إذا مشى تقلع كأنما يمشي في صبب وإذا التفت التفت معاً بين كتفيه

وما أرسلناك إلا رحمة للعالمين

خاتم النبوة وهو خاتم النبيين أجود الناس صدراً وأصدقهم لهجة وألينهم عريكة وأكرمهم عشيرة من رآه بديهة هابه ومن خالطه معرفة أحبه يقول ناعته لم أر قبله ولا بعده مثله صلى الله عليه وسلم

his *hilye* to secure protection from hardship and disease.[115] Cultivating visual imagination through text and form, *hilye* texts and calligraphic compositions were considered doubly effective: they acted as meditative devices through which devotees could spiritually encounter Muhammad as well as powerful talismans necessitating physical interaction to activate their prophetic *baraka*.

A rather typical *hilye* composition by Hafız Osman includes a number of elements, as can be seen in an example made by the famed calligrapher in 1687–88 CE (fig. 5.14).[116] Originally executed on a single sheet of paper, the composition eventually was cut into three horizontal pieces and backed with leather, yielding a portable trifold whose interior was protected from dirt and the elements. Moreover, the blue-toned illumination and depiction of the Ka'ba in the top panel were most likely added during the eighteenth or nineteenth century. These later structural and decorative manipulations notwithstanding, the graphic layout of the original composition is clearly compartmentalized. The upper, or head (*başmakam*), segment contains the *bismillah*. A middle, or "belly" (*göbek*), section displays the *hilye* text surrounded by four roundels bearing the names of the *rashidun*, and a horizontal "belt" (*kuşak*) praises Muhammad with the qur'anic verse: "You were sent as nothing but mercy to all the universes" (22:107). The bottom, or "foot" (*etek*), section of the composition contains the rest of the *hilye* text, whose last line displays Hafız Osman's signature and the date of execution.[117] As the Turkish words for these structural sections reveal, the *hilye*'s components—from the head down to the belly, belt, and foot—were analogized both conceptually and semantically to human body parts. Bypassing figural representation while nevertheless sparking the believer's visual imagination, Ottoman *hilye*s helped to recall the Prophet's physicospiritual presence via the suggestive iconicity of verbal and graphic form.[118]

In designing the layout of his *hilye*, Hafız Osman appears to have tried to create a verbal icon of Muhammad, who is represented with contours, much like those in Ottoman paintings of the Prophet's mantle that visually hint at a human corpus extending its arms to envelop and give refuge to pious followers (fig. 5.7). Moreover, in his graphic rendering, the master calligrapher could have drawn on a number of antecedent visual sources, including Christian depictions of Jesus surrounded by the four evangelists as well as ground plans of Ottoman mosques showing a central dome supported by four pillars that are often equated with the *rashidun*.[119]

Beyond European saintly icons and Ottoman architectural plans, Hafız Osman also may have found inspiration in frontispieces to Sufi manuscripts, which frequently include a central roundel or medallion and horizontal panels of text.[120] Among the most popular, and possibly most influential, in this regard are Mamluk copies of al-Busiri's *Mantle Ode*, a number of which came into Ottoman possession after the conquest of Egypt in 1517 CE. These manuscripts include title pages with

FACING, 5.14. *Hilye* of the Prophet Muhammad calligraphed by Hafız Osman, Ottoman lands, 1099 AH/1687–88 CE. Special Collections, Hatcher Graduate Library, University of Michigan, Ann Arbor, Isl. Ms. 238.

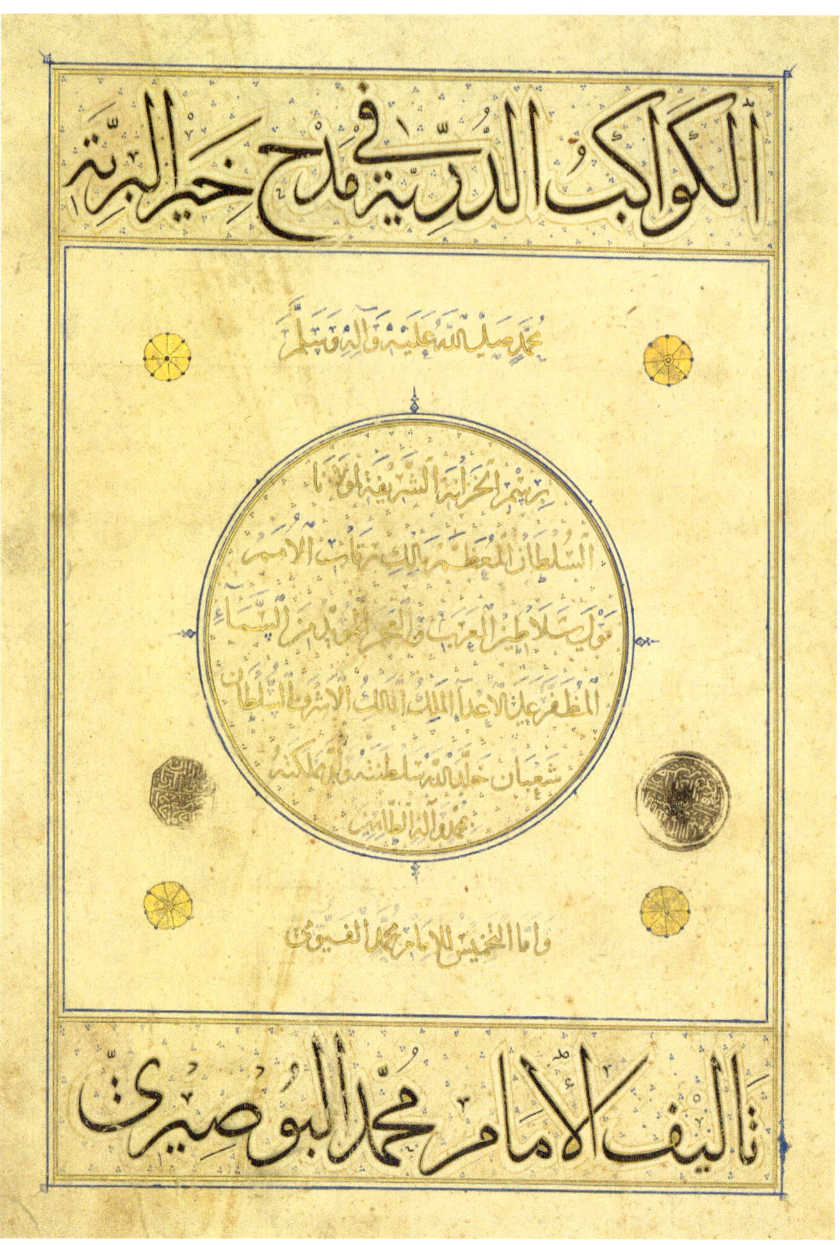

a compositional structure that parallels the typical layout of Ottoman *hilye*s. For example, one Mamluk copy of the *Mantle Ode*, dated 1308 CE, includes a dedication in its central roundel as well as the work's full title and the author's name in the top and bottom panels (fig. 5.15).[121] Four golden disk-shaped suns dazzle in the corners of the central register, in a pattern that appears to foreshadow the names of the *rashidun* inscribed within the roundels of Ottoman *hilye*s. That Ottoman *hilye*s might be structurally and symbolically connected to the *Mantle Ode* should come as no surprise given the text's popularity in Ottoman lands, its close connection to Muhammad's mantle relic, and its similar use as a prophetic talisman.

From the eighteenth century CE onward, Ottoman calligraphers creatively experimented with *hilye* compositions while nevertheless retaining the basic layout devised by Hafız Osman. Intended for hanging

THE PRAISEWORTHY ONE

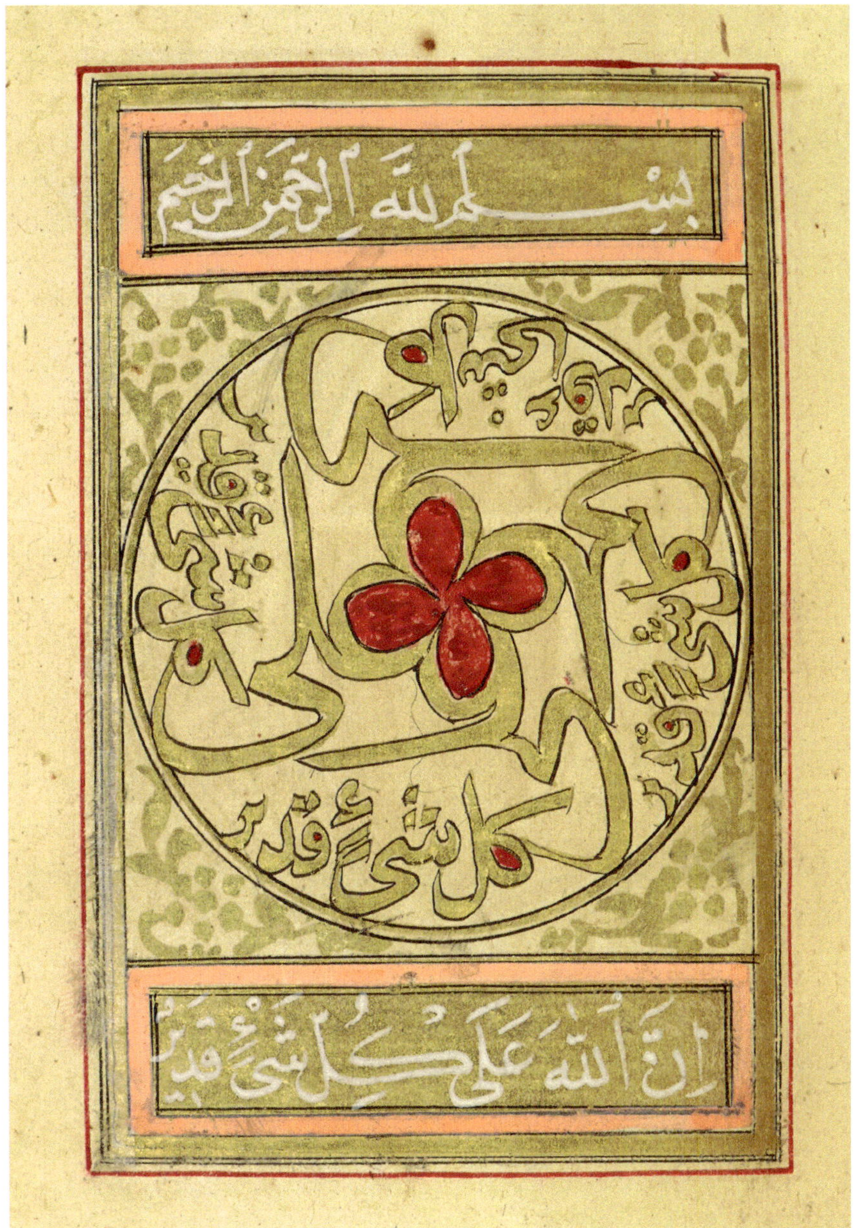

5.16. Seal of "Verily God has Power over Everything," Ottoman illustrated prayer book, Istanbul, 1194 AH/1780 CE. The Morgan Library, New York, M.950, folio 66r.

in (and thus protecting) a home, a number of *hilye*s were produced as large icons that were mounted on pasteboard or wood; some consisted of single panels while others were made as triptychs, with lateral doors that could be opened or closed depending on desire and occasion.[122] Still others were painted on a single or several folios within pocket-sized prayer books or were accompanied by *hilye*s of the *rashidun*, Hasan and Husayn, the Ten Promised Ones, or the Seven Sleepers. Moreover, some illustrated devotional manuals include depictions of the *hilye* that include a statement by al-Tirmidhi, to whom a Hadith about the benefits of rubbing and kissing Muhammad's resemblance is often attributed. In one prayer book, for example, the *hilye* is described in Ottoman Turkish as a blessed seal (*mühr-i şerif*) bearing a number of benefits (*feva'id*). Therefore, according to al-Tirmidhi, the believer should perform ablutions (*abdest*) with it in the morning; look at it during the evening to secure protection from hell; gaze at it during travel in order to ensure a safe journey; and look at it once annually to avoid death in that year.[123]

Whether placed on a wall or held in the hand, *hilye*s both large and small were considered protective devices that required their viewers to look at and interact with them. In this sense, they were not unlike seals, which were used in Ottoman (and other Islamic) practices of licit magic as a means to ward off the devil, the evil eye, and other tenebrous forces.[124] Their apotropaic qualities were channeled through metal objects and paintings, the latter frequently appearing as a series of seal designs following a *hilye* depiction within Ottoman illustrated books.

Along with seals of God's great name, Muhammad's prophethood, and Solomon, a rather popular version represents God's omnipotence (fig. 5.16).[125] The seal's circular perimeter encloses four or five repetitions of the Arabic phrase "[Verily God] has Power over Everything" (*[Inna Allah] ʿala kull shay qadir*). The rounded form of the letter *ʿayn* (of *ʿala*) creates a quatrefoil in the center of the composition, which is filled with red or pink pigment. The result thus combines a sphragistic (seal-like) impression with letter-like and floral shapes and reminds the viewer that, in the end, it is only God—and not fate, magic, or amulets—who wields ultimate power over all.

Sphragistic impressions migrated into the art of *hilye*-making during the eighteenth century (fig. 5.17).[126] At this time, several large-scale verbal icons meant for hanging on walls in private residences highlight the many intriguing intersections between amuletic compositions and word portraits of the Prophet. In a number of *hilye*s, the seal of God's omnipotence creates a cinquefoil around the name of Muhammad, which forms the center of this symbol of divine power. The descriptive *hilye* text has been relocated to the main roundel's outer frame, thereby occupying a status subsidiary to the seal and its invocations to God. Besides the names of the *rashidun* included in the four corner medallions, the names of Hasan and Husayn appear in the bottom left and right corners of the *hilye* composition while the names of the remaining members of the *ʿashara mubashshara* are inscribed within the curved *ya*s (of *ʿala*) of the five-petaled seal.

As mentioned previously, in this and other cases, the Ten Promised Ones could be interpreted as an Ottoman Sunni response to the Safavid glorification of the Shiʿi imams, creating an alternative prophetic genealogy for royal power and authority.

While *hilye*s functioned primarily as protective visuotextual devices with which to meditate on the Prophet's physical and moral attributes, they also intersected with other contemporaneous literary and artistic traditions—particularly those concerned with genealogy. Members of the House of Osman showed a keen interest in their own pedigree, which was believed to stretch back through many prophets and kings to Adam. As the "One of Noble Ancestry" (*asil al-jadd*),[127] Muhammad himself stood as the glorious pivot of this saintly-regal line. For these reasons, a number of *Silsilename*s (Books of Genealogy) stressing

5.17. *Hilye* of the Prophet Muhammad calligraphed by Abdulkâdir Şükri Efendi, Istanbul, ca. 1750–1800 CE. Sakıp Sabancı Museum, Istanbul, Turkey, inv. no. 400.

the Ottomans' prophetic-regal descent were produced from the late sixteenth century onward. Some were in the format of a scroll, while others were produced as codices; some were illustrated with portraits, while others were constructed of connecting lines, roundels, and other nonfigural devices; and still more used arboreal designs to represent the concept of the family or genealogical tree.[128]

As Emine Fetvacı has demonstrated, the emphasis on ancestral glory over individual achievement permeated the production of histori-cal works and serial portraits at the Ottoman court.[129] It also affected

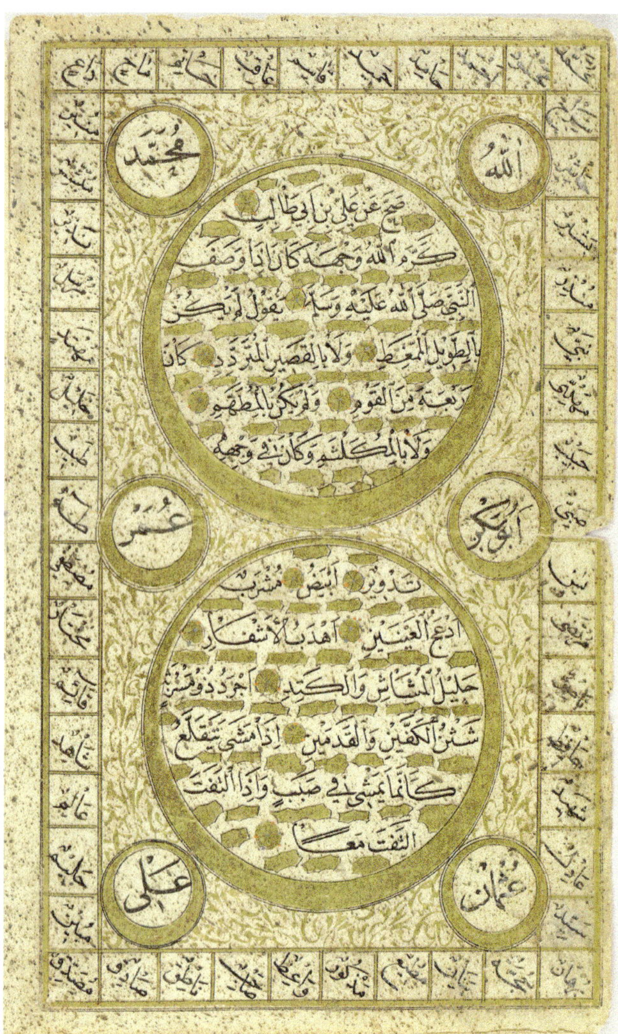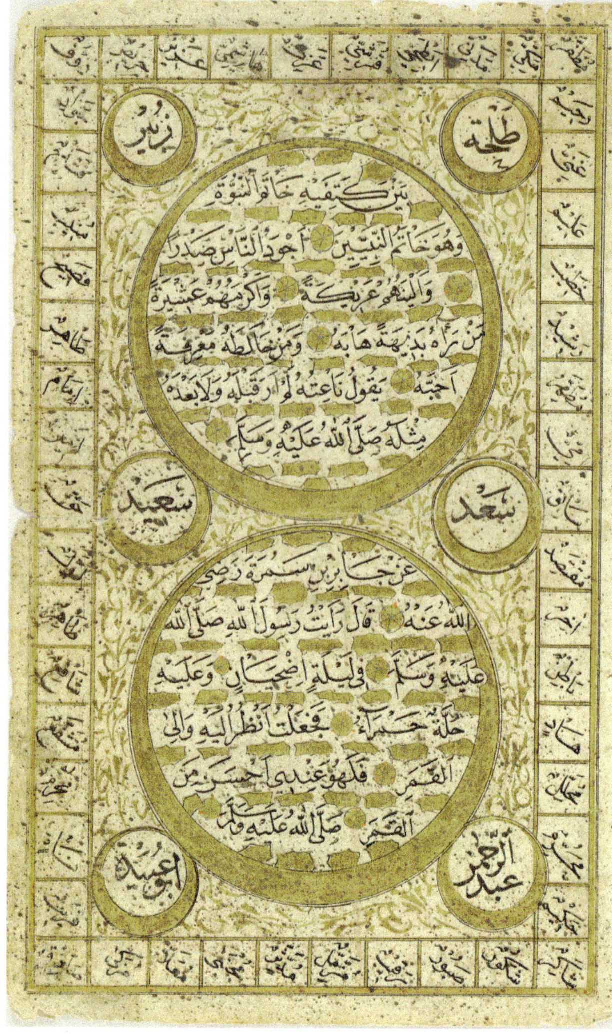

5.18. Double-page *hilye* of the Prophet Muhammad with the names of the *'ashara mubashshara* and the *asma' al-nabi* inscribed in a checkerboard frame, calligraphed by Isma'il Bosnavi, Ottoman lands, ca. 1700–1750 CE. Norma Jean Calderwood Collection of Islamic Art, Harvard Art Museums/Arthur M. Sackler Museum, 2002.50.119 and 2002.50.135.

Ottoman Islamic devotional art, particularly *hilye*s. The addition of the *'ashara mubashshara* was one mechanism by which to establish a connective chain of authority, as can be seen in a double-page *hilye* made around 1700–1750 CE (fig. 5.18).[130] Here, the names of the Ten Promised Ones are inscribed in medallions that appear to connect to both Muhammad and God in a graphic format that somewhat recalls the layout of genealogical books. In addition, the *hilye*'s frame is comprised of square cells that contain the names of the Prophet (*asma' al-nabi*), a verbal litany that aims to summon Muhammad in his complex totality. Finally, the lower omphalos on the left folio includes a statement attributed to the Prophet's companion Jabir b. Samra, who declares that to him Muhammad was more beautiful than the moon. This comparison is magnified through the lavish use of gold pigment and the multiple moons (*hilals*) that frame all the roundels in this double-page *hilye*.

On the backside of the *hilye*'s left folio also appears a genealogical tree, which the artist clearly intended as a companion for the verbal icon (fig. 5.19). The tree's composition visually echoes the verbal icon in its use of roundels, gold and black palette, and background filled with delicate

   THE PRAISEWORTHY ONE

flower-and-leaf designs. At its apex, Muhammad's name is inscribed within a cartouche. Much as the *hilye* shows the Prophet as a central protagonist surrounded by the *'ashara mubashshara*, the tree also includes the names of the Ten Promised Ones in the roundels stemming from branches that fan out in a semicircular fashion. These individuals are shown sharing the same patrilineal ancestor as Muhammad: 'Adnan, whose name is inscribed at the base of the tree. Thus, both the *hilye* and the genealogical tree not only glorify Muhammad's characteristics, prophetic status, and noble descent but also, just as significantly, serve as artistic opportunities to praise the Ten Promised Ones, who emanate from Muhammad's authority. Neither new nor unprecedented, this emphasis on Muhammad's connection to the *'ashara mubashshara* may have enabled Ottoman dynasts to similarly emphasize their own familial relations while crafting a royal pedigree that stretches back to prophetic ancestors that include Muhammad, Abraham, and Adam.[131]

Much like *hilye*s, a number of Ottoman illustrated *Books of Genealogy* made in Baghdad from the late sixteenth century onward place a double emphasis on prophetic pedigree and companionship.[132] This focus on Muhammad's noble origins enabled the Ottoman dynasty to legitimize itself as the final ruling dynasty within the prophetic line.[133] Additionally, through the inclusion of portrait medallions, a number of illustrated genealogies effectively combined paintings of prophets and rulers as found in illustrated manuscripts of the *Qisas al-Anbiya'* (Stories of the Prophets) and Seyyid Lokman's *Zübdet'üt-Tevarih* (Quintessence of Histories) (figs. 5.3–5.4). Popular well into the nineteenth century in both manuscript and print editions, these short, concise, and relatively affordable books were purchased by a well-to-do clientele interested in historical writing, genealogy, Ottoman history, and royal portraiture.

Illustrated *Books of Genealogy* provided yet another arena in which to develop prophetic iconography within an overarching Ottoman religious and political worldview. In many manuscripts, Muhammad takes center stage as the bridge between pre- and post-Islamic prophets and rulers. In these Ottoman genealogies, he is often shown seated within a genealogical roundel as well as surrounded by the four *rashidun* (fig. 5.20).[134] Here, as in almost all cases, the Prophet is visually differentiated from other depicted individuals by the inclusion of his white facial veil, which appears pinched at the top of his turban. Like other prophets (and unlike rulers), he also bears a flaming nimbus. At times, the aureole is contained within the borders of his portrait medallion. However, in the painting illustrated in figure 5.20 his radiance breaches the confines of the roundel, which has altogether disappeared, and encompasses the four *rashidun*, who are similarly engulfed in a lambent gold background.

The artist's iconographic strategy aims to show the Prophet's companions sharing in and carrying forth the *nur Muhammad* until it reaches the Ottoman monarchs. As possessors of the sultanate and caliphate, these contemporary rulers thus are understood as irradiating divine light and authority, much like the *rashidun*, their symbolic progenitors in prophetic power and companionship. Moreover, at least one *Book of Genealogy* shows a clear pro-Shi'i and pro-Safavid slant,[135] and one is left to wonder whether viewers of the painting illustrated in figure 5.20 may have purposefully smudged 'Ali in a visual act of sectarian cursing that has left dregs of brown pigment dripping from the beard of this figurehead of Shi'i Islam, who sits in the upper right corner of the quatrefoil. Whether the Prophet was depicted as surrounded by the *rashidun* or the *'ashara mubashshara*—but not the imams—this radiant esprit de corps proved ripe for cultivation in Ottoman genealogical

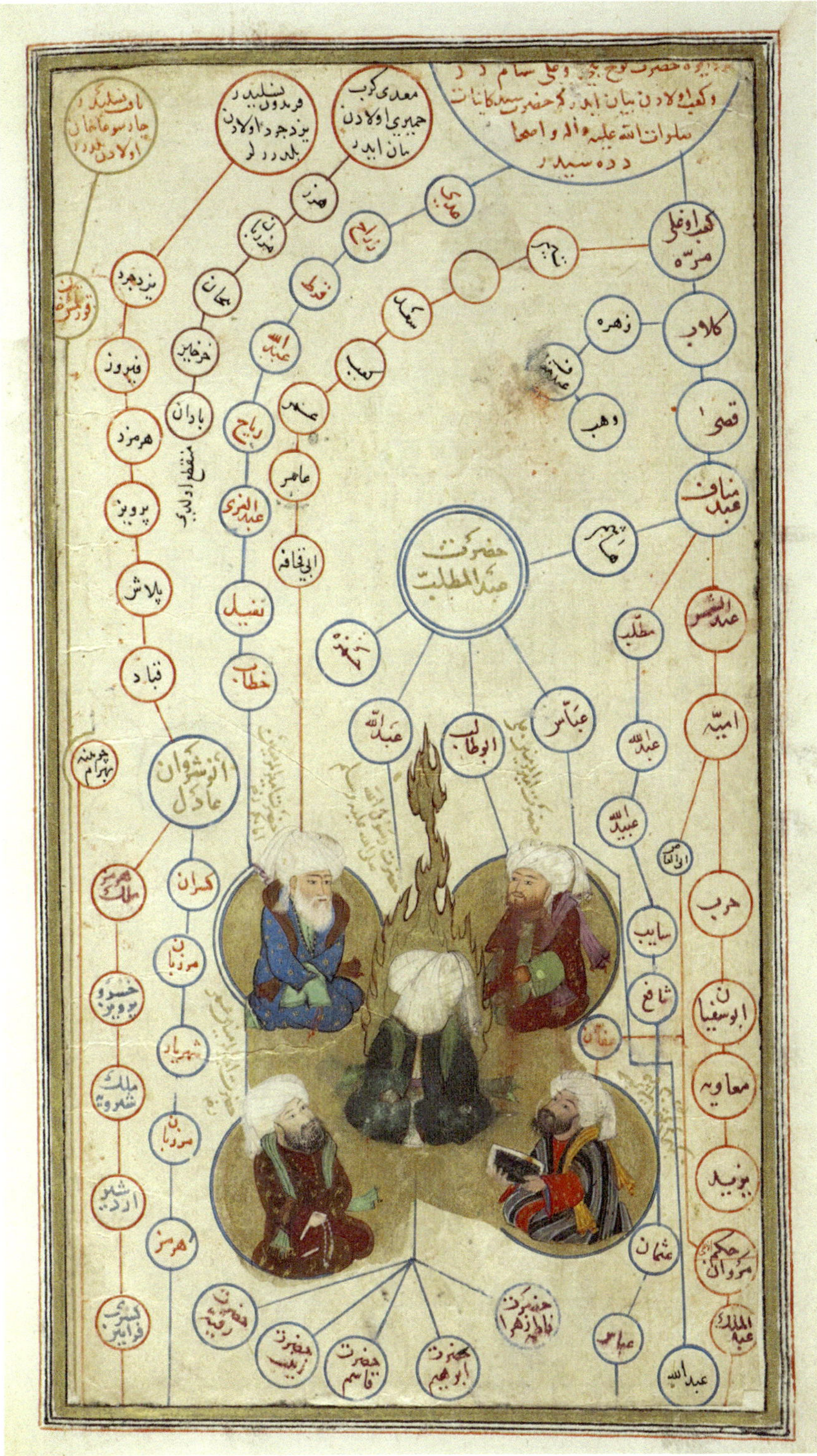

5.20. The Prophet Muhammad and the *rashidun*, text entitled *Zübdet'üt-Tevarih* (Quintessence of Chronicles) in the *Silsilename* (Genealogical Book) genre, Ottoman lands (probably Baghdad), ca. 1600–1650 CE. The Edwin Binney, 3rd, Collection of Turkish Art, Los Angeles County Museum of Art, M.85.237.38. Photo © Museum Associates/LACMA.

imagination and creative expression at a moment of increasing intra-Muslim dynastic competition.

The connections between Muhammad and the Ten Promised Ones were likewise elaborated in nonpictorial genealogies, as in a diagram included in an Ottoman miscellany of texts dated 1705–7 CE. In this compendium, pilgrimage treatises in prose and verse are accompanied

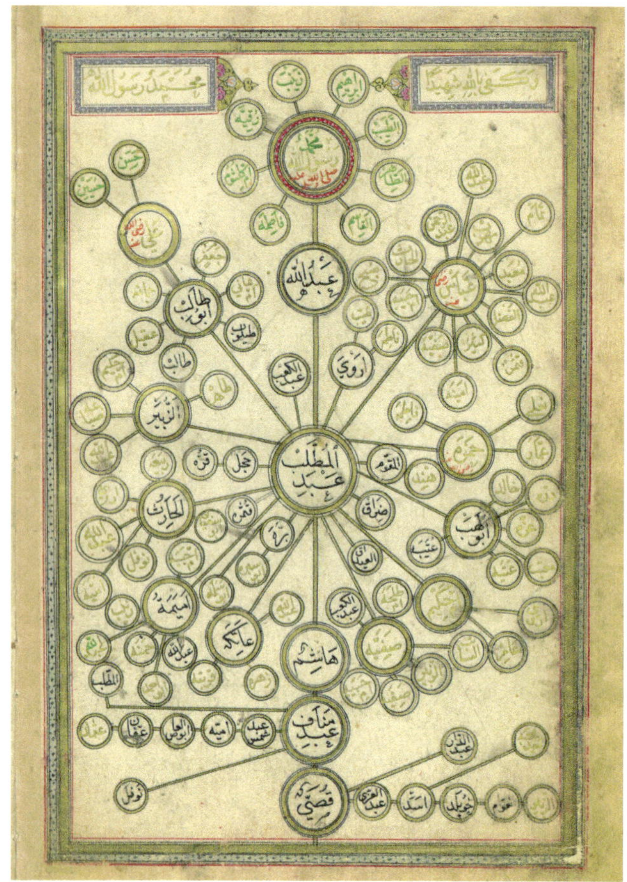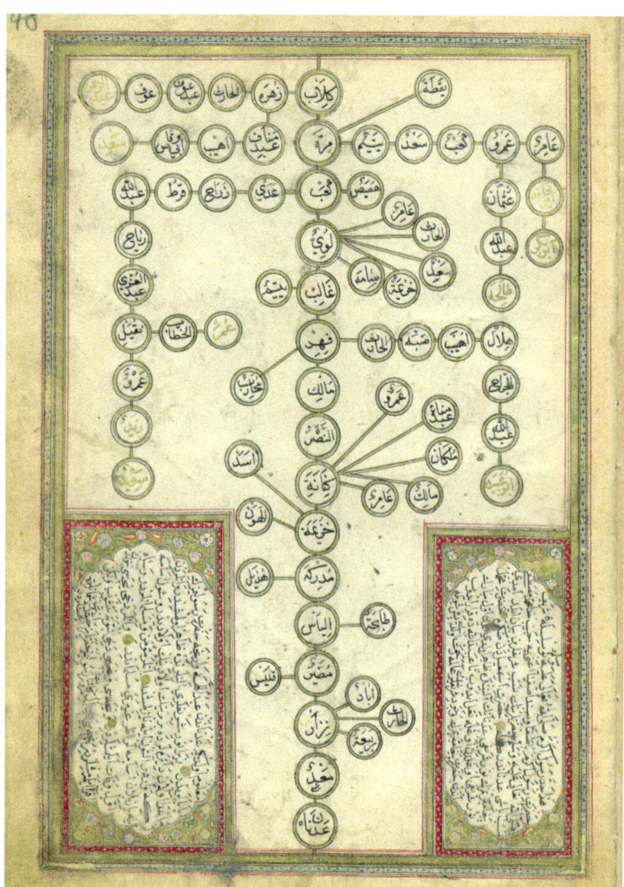

5.21. The Prophet Muhammad's genealogy, compendium of pilgrimage texts and *hilye*s, Ottoman lands, 1119–21 AH/1705–7 CE. Staatsbibliothek zu Berlin—Preussischer Kulturbesitz, Orientabteilung, Ms. Or. Oct. 1602, folios 47v–48r.

by a poem on the Prophet's characteristics and a treatise on Muhammad's pedigree. These texts are supplemented by a number of diagrams and images that depict heaven and hell, Mecca, Medina, and Jerusalem, Muhammad's foot- and sandal prints, two rose-shaped *hilye*s, and a double-page genealogy of the Prophet's ancestors (fig. 5.21).[136] Identified as a *neseb* (genealogy) and a *silsile-i şerif* (noble chain), this diagrammatic composition shows Muhammad as the ultimate link in a chain of patrilineal affiliations fashioned to resemble a rose bush or botanical specimen. Symbolized by a red confluence with *Muhammad* written in green ink, the Prophet stands at the very pinnacle of this Linnaean system.

On the left folio appear the *'ashara mubashshara*, whose pedigree stretches back to 'Adnan. That their names are executed in gold ink is no coincidence: indeed, the text in the lower two panels states that a "noble light" (*nur-i şerif*) appeared on 'Adnan's forehead, and this light was then passed down from father to son. These individuals whose names are written in gold ink, we are told, were faithful Muslims; those whose names are written in black either did not live long enough to witness revelations or refused to embrace Islam. As the diagram makes clear on a visual level, chief among these early Muslim believers are the Ten Promised Ones, whose names glow in a bright gold pigment representing the passing down of God's divine light. This light is shown as

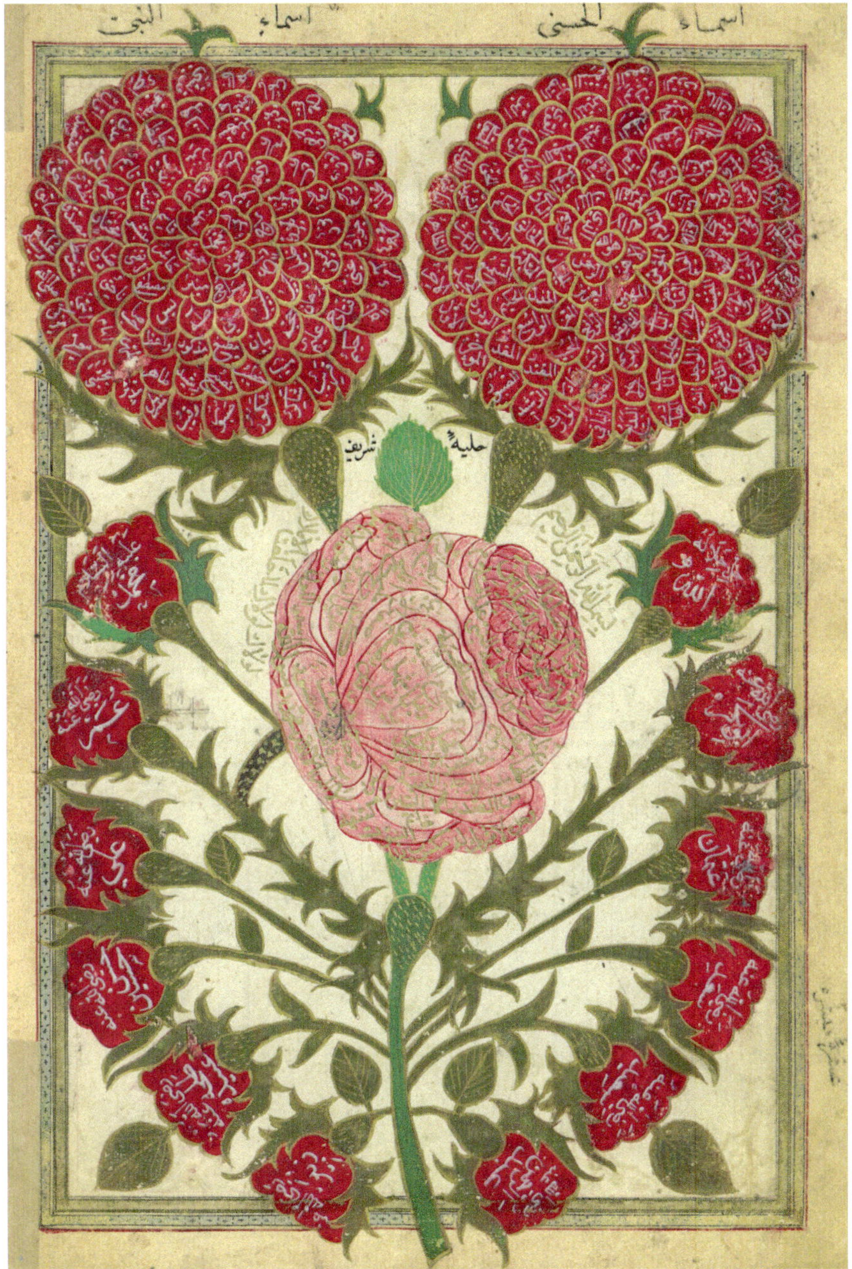

5.22. *Hilye* of the Prophet Muhammad in the shape of a pink rose, compendium of pilgrimage texts and *hilye*s, Ottoman lands, 1119–21 AH/1705–7 CE. Staatsbibliothek zu Berlin—Preussischer Kulturbesitz, Orientabteilung, Ms. Or. Oct. 1602, folio 48v.

inherited via tribal connections rather than a prophetic line, a strategy that may reflect an Ottoman interest in patrilineal relations. As a result, these types of genealogies not only accompanied *hilye*s but also intersected with the conceptualization of propheticofamilial relations within the royal House of Osman.

The link between verbal icons and genealogies can be found in another *hilye* of the Prophet, executed on the verso of the genealogy illustrated in figure 5.21. Rather than being shaped like a manuscript frontispiece, mosque ground plan, or amuletic quatrefoil, this *hilye* instead takes the shape of a large pink rose (fig. 5.22). The light pink rose in the composition's center includes 'Ali's verbal description of the Prophet inscribed in gold ink, which is difficult to read within the flower's petals.

To the right and left of the rose are also inscribed the *bismillah* and the *"Law laka"* *Hadith Qudsi* (Saying attributed to God) that states, "Were it not for you [oh Muhammad], I would not have created the heavenly spheres."

At the top of the composition, two fuchsia roses burst open, displaying petals inscribed with the names of God (on the right) and the Prophet (on the left). Twelve buds also sprout from the rose's green stem, creating a floral halo of sorts. Each of these buds is inscribed with the names of God, Muhammad, and the Ten Promised Ones, the latter clearly identified by the inscription *'ashara mubashshara* in the folio's right margin. Here, the inclusion of Muhammad's ten companions is evidently intended as a rejoinder to the genealogy executed in diagrammatic form on the other side of the folio.

In this instance, the *hilye* of the Prophet reasserts tribal stemmas through the genealogical flower rather than the genealogical tree. Even more importantly, the pink rose motif reflects the larger Ottoman urge to conceptualize the Prophet in entirely metaphorical terms. Transcending figural, synecdochal, and diagrammatic illustration, these color-based and floral similes in essence served to analogize Muhammad to a pink rose. Known as the "rose of the Prophet" (*gül-i peygamber*) and the "rose of Muhammad" (*gül-i Muhammed*), this concept of the prophetic corpus as a flower became quite popular in Ottoman Sufi traditions and artistic practices from the seventeenth century onward.[137]

While the appearance of pink roses in manuscripts and Qur'ans to some extent reflected an Ottoman rococo aesthetic at this time,[138] within religious arts they also must be understood as emanating from, and contributing to, creative depictions of Muhammad as the roseate juncture between the white light of revelation and the red blood of humanity, as well as the sweet-smelling flower of paradise whose prophetic beauty and curative qualities were passed down through generations of believers. Early Arabic descriptive texts, Persian poems, and Ottoman *hilye*s cultivated these rose allegories in order to develop a multisensory Muhammad who is called forth through his devotees' chromatic, gustatory, and olfactory perceptions.

In Ottoman artistic and religious traditions, the color pink was deployed in rose paintings and rose-tinted folios, while rose water was imbibed as a means of ingesting relic-contact liquid, as was the case for the water collected during the ritual cleaning of the Prophet's mantle and footprint. Muhammad also could be evoked through the burning of incense, particularly a mix known as the "incense of the Prophet" (*buhur-ı nebi*). This mixture, which combined ambergris, musk, and rose water, was burned in mosques, tombs, and the relics chamber in the Ottoman palace. Its recipe was quite similar to the "incense of the sultan" (*buhur-ı sultani*) and yielded an aroma that evoked both Prophet and king.[139] Much like the visual coupling of rose *hilye*s and genealogical

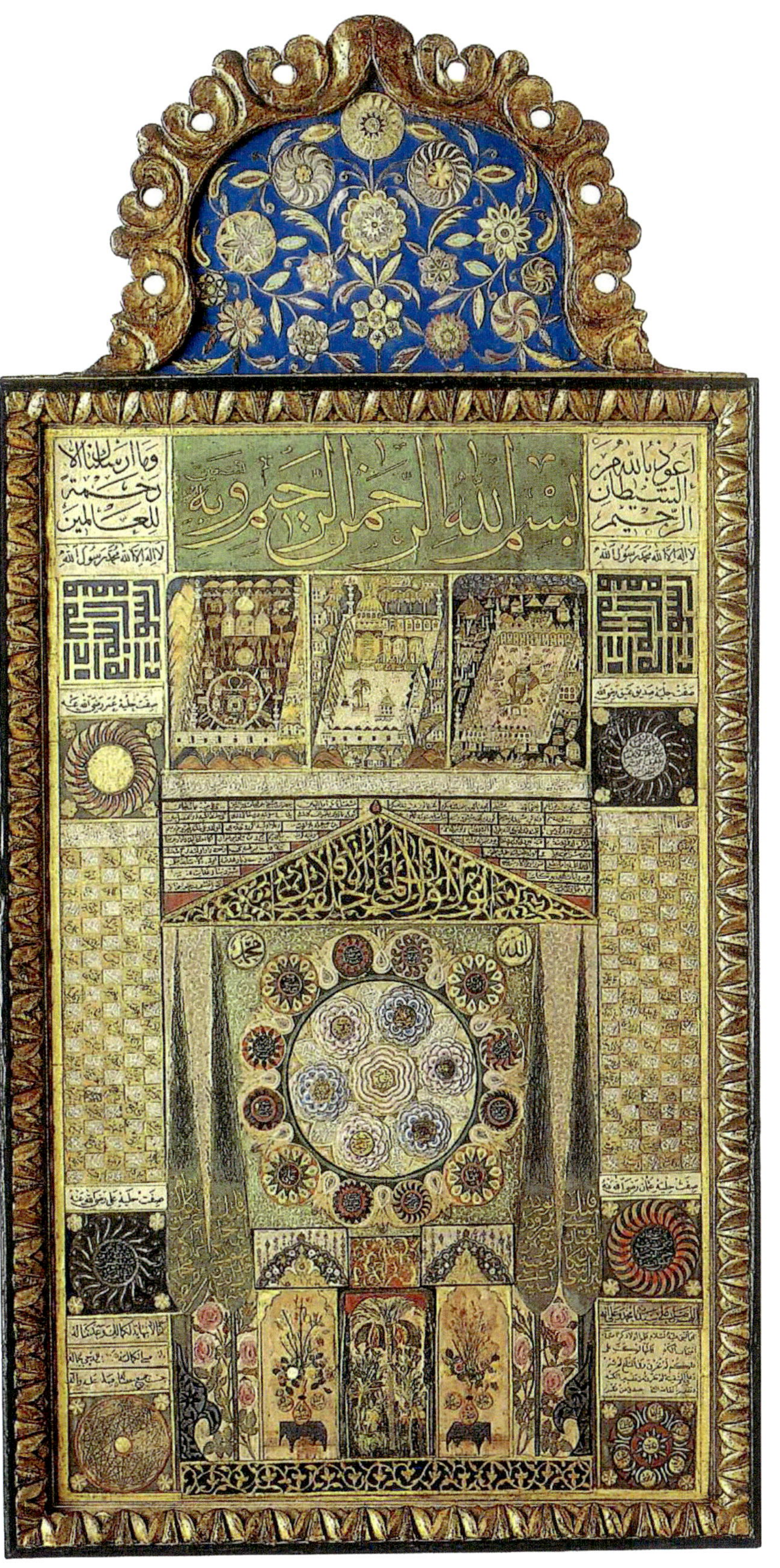

5.23. *Hilye* of the Prophet Muhammad, made of cut-out papers, black ink, and gold paint mounted on a panel measuring 50 x 32 cm, Ottoman lands, mid-eighteenth century CE. Sadberk Hanım Museum, Istanbul, 15501-Y.94.

diagrams, these Ottoman aromatics served to blend the sensible presence of apostleship and rulership.

In Ottoman lands, rose color, scent, water, and leaves were closely associated with Muhammad—still today, rose water is sold alongside other prophetic paraphernalia in stores abutting important Islamic shrines in Turkey—and the importance of the rose was not lost on European travelers, either. For example, writing during the second half of the sixteenth century, the herbalist and diplomat Ogier Ghiselin de Busbecq noted in his *Turkish Letters* that the Ottoman Turks "never allow rose-leaves to lie on the ground for they believe that the rose sprang from the sweat of Mahomet, just as the ancients thought that it came from the blood of Venus."[140] His observations certainly ring true: early Arabic texts and Ottoman poems, including Hakani's *Noble Description*, often compare Muhammad's perspiration to the scent of the rose.[141] In his *Biography of the Prophet*, moreover, al-Darir includes a story about Muhammad's "blessed scent" (*mübarek koku*). The anecdote describes a member of the Jewish community who caught a whiff of Muhammad as he walked by. He asked his identity and requested a sign of his divine selection, and so Muhammad displayed his seal of prophecy. Thereupon, the Jew immediately accepted Muhammad as a prophet. This short conversion narrative combines two common motifs—the seal and the scent of prophecy—to promote the superiority of Islam and its Messenger.[142]

Muhammad's finality is likewise emphasized in diagrammatic genealogies and rose *hilye*s. In both art forms, he acts as the ascendance and end point of a prophetic stemma. However, descending from his line (or stem) are often other individuals, symbols, and motifs, which serve to promote a range of religious notions.

Some Ottoman *hilye*s intended to provide protection to the faithful cultivate floral and amuletic metaphors. Among them, a mid-eighteenth-century *hilye* composed of minutely cut paperwork combines a range of devices and images, including Mecca, Medina, and Jerusalem (fig. 5.23).[143] In the composition's omphalos, an inner ring of multilayered flowers creates a rotational effect. Inscribed in the central flowers are the last few words of the *hilye* text. The outer ring of flowers contains the names of the Ten Promised Ones, topped by two roundels bearing the names of God and Muhammad. In the *hilye*, four other roundels, containing the names of the *rashidun*, appear as if swirling galaxies. Moving up the composition, immediately above the pediment-like structure, which includes the *"Law laka" Hadith Qudsi*, are several lines of text inscribed within horizontal panels. These lines do not include the *hilye* text attributed to 'Ali, as one might expect. Instead, an Ottoman text addresses the viewer directly, informing him or her that whoever looks at the *hilye* will be protected from all calamities and that his or her home will be shielded from sorrow and anger. The *hilye* panel, framed and thus intended for hanging in a home, explicitly encourages its beholders to partake in its prophylactic qualities by contemplating its designs and imagery.

This floral *hilye*'s amuletic qualities are strengthened by numerous other designs believed to exude talismanic power. For instance, the lower corners of the panel include, in the left, the star-shaped seal of Solomon and, in the right, the seal of the Seven Sleepers, above which an Ottoman text specifies that this particular amulet protects a home from burning and a ship from sinking.[144] Between these seals two vases flank a central date tree; while the tree may refer to the Prophet's house in Medina, the vases represent Gabriel, Michael, Israfil, and 'Azra'il, whose names are inscribed in small cartouches. (These four archangels often were included in Islamic talismans and Ottoman amuletic seals.) Moreover, the *hilye*'s vertical margins contain the names of God and Muhammad, whose pious recitation can bring peace and comfort to a devotee. The checkerboard layout recalls the talismanic magic square, a potent format in itself.[145] Finally, the upper right corner frames the proclamation, "I seek refuge in God from the cursed Satan." This prayer, in which an individual places his trust and safety in God, completes the *hilye*'s rich armory of protective texts, designs, and images.

In this and many other cases, the verbal icon of the Prophet does not simply constitute a nonfigural tactic of depicting Muhammad. The *hilye* offered a diagrammatic embrace, a genealogical metaphor, and a floral stand-in for the prophetic corpus. In the end, this quintessentially Ottoman visual device, denoting the unseen yet ubiquitous being and spirit of the Prophet, acted as the supreme talismanic refuge for Ottoman believers who sought a symbolic safe haven in their homes and daily affairs. And the ultimate refuge was understood as none other than the Prophet Muhammad himself.

Combining Sunni religious traditions and Sufi spiritual thought, many ceremonies, festivals, texts, images, diagrams, and amulets were joined in Ottoman Islamic practices from the late sixteenth to the nineteenth century. The production and accumulation of pietistic materials occurred in both Ottoman royal and nonroyal spheres. As a result, imaginative and devotional traditions linked to Muhammad began to reach a larger audience than in previous centuries, when visual systems were almost entirely restricted to illustrated manuscripts meant only for princely viewers. This rich corpus of visual artifacts at times reflected larger religious and political issues prevalent in early modern Ottoman lands, including the popularity of mystical forms of communion as well as anti-Safavid sectarian modes of speaking and seeing.

Ottoman rhetorical and visual traditions positioned the Prophet as a source of blessings and a subject of meditation on the divine. As an intercessory figure, Muhammad was commemorated and contemplated in manifold ways. In Ottoman lands, the creation of illustrated manuscripts was followed by the collection and depiction of relics as well as the production of *hilye*s. A hallmark of the last two decades of the sixteenth century in particular, illustrated manuscripts extended the written heritage of Islam into new artistic domains. In book paintings,

Muhammad is consistently depicted as a veiled and luminous entity, his facial features wholly invisible to viewers. At times, his entire head is subsumed in a flaming nimbus while at others his primordial radiance is shown extending to the *rashidun* and *'ashara mubashshara*. Still other instances omit 'Ali from the picture, even when he is mentioned in the accompanying text, or exclude him from prophetic radiance, a strategy no doubt intended as a subtle—yet overt—Ottoman Sunni contraposition to coeval Safavid Shi'i discourses about the Prophet, 'Ali, and the imams. Ottoman book arts depict Muhammad as cosmic light, veiled mystery, and the paragon of companionship, whose followers and legatees safeguard and embody the prophetic *sunna*.

The figural arts, however, largely ceded way to synecdochal and allegorical visual expression from the seventeenth century onward, at which time the amassing and visitation of Muhammad's relics proved central to political and religious ceremonies within Ottoman imperial quarters. In Topkapı Palace in particular, the 'Uthmanic codex enabled the sultans to promote themselves as the guardians of Islamic revelation while the Prophet's relics—most especially his mantle, footprint, and sandals—allowed them to figuratively, and sometimes quite literally, embody the prophetic presence by donning Muhammad's robe, imbibing water used to wash his footprints, and rubbing and kissing his sandals (and sandal prints) to activate their latent *baraka*. The desire to unleash the Prophet's mystic virtue prompted practices of haptic mediation, including wearing, imbibing, touching, and kissing—practices that betray Ottoman Muslim devotees' urge to approach and even merge with Muhammad, himself the personified channel through which one could access and harness a sacred power and source. Much as in practices of prophetic medicine (*tibb al-nabi*), this divine flux was considered protective and therapeutic for those who suffered from a variety of hardships and ailments, including the Ottoman royal wife Düzdidil, who sought solace and cure in her illustrated prayer book when she became afflicted by tuberculosis.

Abstracting the prophetic body one step further, Ottoman artists also created a variety of logograms known as *hilyes*. Hafız Osman, the genre's creator, may have been inspired by Byzantine icons, architectural ground plans, and frontispieces to mystical manuscripts when he developed this quintessentially Ottoman religious art form. While verbal icons of the Prophet reveal artists' movement toward conceptual representation and away from figuration, the *hilyes'* schematic appearance also invites viewers to engage in the mental act of good imagination (*husn al-tasawwur*), thereby combining a meditation on prophetic beauty with the cultivation of inner goodness.[146] At the same time, *hilyes* overlap with genealogical thought and talismanic arts, which thrived in Ottoman royal, elite, and popular spheres. Such symbolic intersections enabled members of the House of Osman to establish their rank in illustrious chains of command that descended along both prophetic and tribal lines. Artists also created *hilyes* as amuletic devices to protect an expanding group of consumers in their homes, at sea, and on the road. Much like the Prophet's relics, these devotional icons' thaumaturgic potential required their viewers' interactive participation, enabling them to cultivate a multisensory Muhammad along the way.

Transcending the more restrictive realms of literal description and figural representation, Ottoman pietistic and artistic practices revered Muhammad as an abstracted idea and ideal: absent yet existent, beautiful yet ineffable. Through the Prophet's vestigial remains and verbal icons, Ottoman devotees time and again aimed to conjure his presence, protection, and healing power. Such Ottoman Prophet-centered discourses, pictures, and objects thus generated a spectrum of creative images and artifacts meant to inspire and benefit the faithful. They likewise foreshadow modern and contemporary artistic depictions and commodities still sold in Turkey, artifacts that inventively reassert Ottoman visual traditions so as to enable patrons and consumers of religious art and goods to contemplate the Prophet's physical and moral traits, follow in his blessed traces, and seek his benediction and intercession through relics brimming with *baraka*.

1. Hakanî, *Hilye-i Saadet*, 50–51, line 132.

2. Faroqhi, *Pilgrims and Sultans*, 126, 181.

3. On illustrated *Futuh al-Haramayn* manuscripts, see Milstein, "Futuh-i Haramayn"; and, on the *Dala'il al-Khayrat*, see Daub, *Formen und Funktionen des Layouts in arabischen Manuskripten anhand von Abschriften religiöser Texte*, 133–70; and Witkam, "The Battle of the Images."

4. Hakanî, *Hilye-i Saadet*, 50–51, line 132: *Nice ta'rîf edeyim evsâfın / Nice şerh eyleyeyim eltâfın* (editor's transliteration).

5. Soucek, "The Theory and Practice of Portraiture in the Persian Tradition," 106–7.

6. Hagen, "The Emergence of a Pietas Ottomanica"; and *Aşk-ı Nebi*.

7. For an overview of Ottoman painting, see in particular Bağcı et al., *Ottoman Painting*; Fetvacı, *Picturing History at the Ottoman Court*; and Sims, "The Turks and Illustrated Historical Texts."

8. Rogers, "Mehmed the Conqueror: Between East and West"; Raby, "A Sultan of Paradox"; and Atıl, "Ottoman Miniature Painting under Sultan Mehmed II."

9. Genealogical books and religious tales will be discussed subsequently. For the illustrated history of Sultan Süleyman, see Atıl, *Süleymanname*; and for illustrated *Books of Circumcision,* see Atıl, *Levni and the Surname*; and Atıl, "The Story of an Eighteenth-Century Ottoman Festival."

10. Ali, *Mustafa Ali's Epic Deeds of Artists*, 165.

11. For further information on al-Darir, his *sira*, and the Ottoman illustrated copy of his text, see Hagen, "*Sira*, Ottoman Turkish," 589; Darir, *Kitab-ı Siyer-i Nebi*; Tanındı, *Siyer-i Nebî*; Garrett Fisher, "A Reconstruction of the Pictorial Cycle of the *Siyar-i Nabi* of Murad III"; and Grube, "The *Siyar-i-Nabi* of the Spencer Collection in the New York Public Library."

12. Fetvacı, *Picturing History at the Ottoman Court*, 43.

13. Erkan, "Darîr," 498.

14. For the *Siyer-i Nebi*'s poetic verses, see Egüz, "Erzurumlu Mustafa Darîr'in Sîretü'n-nebî'sindeki Türkçe Manzumeler."

15. Hagen, "*Sira*, Ottoman Turkish," 590.

16. For the *Siyer-i Nebi*'s sections on Muhammad's birth and ascension, see Darir, *Kitab-ı Siyer-i Nebi*, 1:235–60, 2:166–226.

17. Painting published in Tanındı, *Siyer-i Nebî*, miniature 3.

18. Böwering, "The Light Verse"; and Hermansen, "The Prophet Muhammed in Sufi Interpretations of the Light Verse," 224.

19. The *Siyer-i Nebi*'s paintings seem to be indebted to Ilkhanid and Timurid illustrated histories and *Mi'rajnama*s (Books of Ascension), which Ottoman artists may have consulted

in the palace library. For a discussion of the *Siyer-i Nebi*'s paintings of the ascension and their iconographical relationship to the Timurid *Mi'rajnama*, see Sims, "The Turks and Illustrated Historical Texts," 758.

20. Darir, *Kitab-ı Siyer-i Nebi*, 1:235–40.

21. Darir, *Kitab-ı Siyer-i Nebi*, 1:240–41.

22. Erkan, "Darîr," 498.

23. Al-Darir, *Siyer-i Nebi*, Topkapı Palace Library, Istanbul, H. 1221, folio 218v; and Darir, *Kitab-ı Siyer-i Nebi*, 1:242.

24. Al-Darir, *Siyer-i Nebi*, Topkapı Palace Library, Istanbul, H. 1221, folio 219v; and Darir, *Kitab-ı Siyer-i Nebi*, 1:242.

25. Al-Darir, *Siyer-i Nebi*, Topkapı Palace Library, Istanbul, H. 1221, folios 223r–224r; and Darir, *Kitab-ı Siyer-i Nebi*, 1:248.

26. Darir, *Kitab-ı Siyer-i Nebi*, 1:249.

27. Çelebi, *Mevlid-i Şerif*, 26, 23, and 33.

28. Çelebi, *Mevlid-i Şerif*, 28.

29. On the love verses included in the *Siyer-i Nebi*, see Egüz, "Erzurumlu Mustafa Darîr'in Sîretü'n-nebî'sindeki Türkçe Manzumeler," 388–94.

30. Çelebi, *Mevlid-i Şerif*, 23.

31. Waugh, "Following the Beloved," 78.

32. The manuscript includes two paintings of the revelations at Mount Hira. See al-Darir, *Siyer-i Nebi*, Topkapı Palace Library, Istanbul, H. 1222, folios 155r (Muhammad engulfed in light) and 158v (Muhammad engulfed in light and accompanied by angels). These two paintings are published in Tanındı, *Siyer-i Nebî*, miniatures 25–26. For a discussion of the first painting (H. 1222, f. 155r), see Gruber, "Between Logos (*Kalima*) and Light (*Nur*)," 251–52, fig. 14.

33. Darir, *Kitab-ı Siyer-i Nebi*, 1:486–88.

34. Darir, *Kitab-ı Siyer-i Nebi*, 1:31–37.

35. Darir, *Kitab-ı Siyer-i Nebi*, 1:35.

36. Darir, *Kitab-ı Siyer-i Nebi*, 1:32.

37. Çelebi, *Mevlid-i Şerif*, 77.

38. Çelebi, *Mevlid-i Şerif*, 31, 81.

39. Darir, *Kitab-ı Siyer-i Nebi*, 1:433–34.

40. Darir, *Kitab-ı Siyer-i Nebi*, 1:434.

41. For an inscription invoking Muhammad's intercession, see al-Darir, *Siyer-i Nebi*, Istanbul, 1594–95 CE, Chester Beatty Library, Dublin, T. 419, folio 172r. On this manuscript, see Minorsky, *The Chester Beatty Library*, 30–40.

42. The three illustrated manuscripts of the *Zübdet'üt-Tevarih* are: Chester Beatty Library (CBL), Dublin, T414; Topkapı Palace Library (TSK), Istanbul, H. 1321; and Museum of Turkish and Islamic Arts (TvIEM), Istanbul, no. 1973. On these manuscripts, see Renda, "The Miniatures of Silsilename, no. 1321 in the Topkapı Saray Museum Library"; and Renda, "New Light on the Painters of the 'Zubdet al-Tawarikh' in the Museum of Turkish and Islamic Arts in Istanbul." For these illustrated texts as initiating Ottoman religious painting in particular, see Renda, "The Miniatures of Silsilename, no. 1321 in the Topkapı Saray Museum Library," 484; Sims, "The Turks and Illustrated Historical Texts," 753; and Meredith-Owens, "Islamic Illustrated Chronicles," 33. For related pictorial genealogies, see Bağcı, "From Adam to Mehmed III: Silsilenâme."

43. Fetvacı, *Picturing History at the Ottoman Court*, 164–75.

44. Painting published in Renda, "The Miniatures of Silsilename, no. 1321 in the Topkapı Saray Museum Library," fig. 9; and Tanındı, *Siyer-i Nebî*, plate VIII. For a similar painting included in another copy of the manuscript, see Renda "New Light on the Painters of the 'Zubdet al-Tawarikh' in the Museum of Turkish and Islamic Arts in Istanbul," 188, fig. 3.

45. For the interpretation of these audience scenes as depicting the Dome of the Rock during the Prophet's ascension, see Renda, "The Miniatures of Silsilename, no. 1321 in the Topkapı Saray Museum Library," 488; and Renda, "New Light on the Painters of the 'Zubdet al-Tawarikh' in the Museum of Turkish and Islamic Arts in Istanbul," 188. This interpretation may be due to the depiction of the *mi'raj* in the CBL copy (see fig. 5.4) as well as the cartouche reading "An account of the deeds of the possessor of the ascension and Buraq" (*dhikr ahwal sahib al-mi'raj wa'l-buraq*) in the TvIEM copy (published in And, *Minyatürle Osmanlı-İslam Mitologyası*, 135). In this and other cases, however, the Prophet's titulature should be not understood as an identification of the painting's subject matter.

46. Séguy, *The Miraculous Journey of Mahomet*, plate 3; and Gruber, *The Timurid Book of Ascension (Mi'rajnama)*, figs. 3.5, 5.11.

47. See al-Darir, *Siyer-i Nebi*, Topkapı Palace Library, Istanbul, H. 1223, folios 26r and 28v.

48. Seyyid Lokman, *Zübdet'üt-Tevarih*, Topkapı Palace Library, Istanbul, H. 1321, folios 53v–58v.

49. Vatin and Veinstein, *Le sérail ébranlé*, 294–96; and Aydın, *Pavilion of the Sacred Relics*, 52–66.

THE PRAISEWORTHY ONE

50. Stanfield-Johnson, "The Tabarra'iyan and the Early Safavids," 64; and Calmard, "Les rituels shiites et le pouvoir."

51. Yıldız, "Ottoman Historical Writing in Persian, 1400–1600," 447–48; and Necipoğlu, *Architecture, Ceremonial, and Power*, 16.

52. On this manuscript, see Minorsky, *The Chester Beatty Library*, 21–25.

53. On Ottoman textiles sent from Istanbul to Mecca and Medina, see in particular Tezcan, "Ka'ba Covers from the Topkapı Palace Collection and Their Inscriptions"; İpek, "Ottoman *Ravza-ı Mutahhara* Covers Sent from Istanbul to Medina with the *Surre* Processions"; and al-Mojan, "The Textiles Made for the Prophet's Mosque at Medina."

54. On gold rain gutters held in the Topkapı Palace, see Aydın, *Pavilion of the Sacred Relics*, 166–69.

55. For the Ottoman Turkish text, see Yıldız, *Ahvâl-i Kıyâmet*; and, for the paintings, see Gruber, "Signs of the Hour," 49–52; And, *Minyatürle Osmanlı-İslam Mitologyası*, 240–65; and Milstein, *Miniature Painting in Ottoman Baghdad*, 79 and plates 1–2.

56. For a discussion of Safavid eschatological imagery, in particular last judgment and hell scenes, and how these contributed to sectarian visions of the afterlife during the second half of the sixteenth century, see Gruber, "Curse Signs."

57. Yıldız, *Ahvâl-i Kıyâmet*, 173.

58. For an earlier "Conditions of Resurrection" text in the Arabic language, see Wolf, *Muhammedanische Eschatologie*.

59. Aydın, *Pavilion of the Sacred Relics*; and Aydın, *Hırka-i Saadet Dairesi ve Mukaddes Emanetler*.

60. On relics as portable territory and establishing civilizational boundaries, see Wheeler, *Mecca and Eden*, 94–98; Wheeler, "Relics in Islam"; and Wheeler, "Collecting the Dead Body of the Prophet Muhammad," 54. On the "distribution of the sensible," see Rancière, *The Politics of Aesthetics*, 7–19.

61. Margoliouth, "The Relics of the Prophet Muhammad," 20.

62. On the exuviae of the Prophet, in particular his hair and nail clippings, see Flood, "Bodies and Becoming," 468.

63. For Ramadan rituals involving Muhammad's relics, see Aktaş, İstanbul'un 100 Âdeti, 141–44.

64. D'Ohsson, *Tableau général de l'empire othoman*, 2:398.

65. Aydın, *Pavilion of the Sacred Relics*, 11, 34–39; D'Ohsson, *Tableau général de l'empire othoman*, 2:386, 389; and Necipoğlu, *Architecture, Ceremonial, and Power*, 150–52.

66. On Ottoman illustrated prayer books, see especially Gruber, "A Pious Cure-All"; Bain, "The Late Ottoman En'am-ı Şerif"; Bain, "The En'am-ı Şerif"; Küçükbay, "Das sogenannte Dala'il ül-Khayrat"; Khameh-Yar, "Tasvir pardazi-yi asar-i mansub bi payambar-i Islam dar du'anamaha-yi musavvar-i 'usmani"; and Derman, *Calligraphies ottomanes*, 48, cat. no. 2; 52, cat. no. 4; 76, cat. no. 16; and 92, cat. no. 24. On the recitation of *surat al-in'am* in Ottoman mosques and the Topkapı Palace, see Ergin, "The Soundscape of Sixteenth-Century Istanbul Mosques," 206–8; and Ergin, "'Praiseworthy in That Great Multitude Was the Silence'," 126.

67. On these how-to texts accompanying amulet designs in Ottoman illustrated prayer books, see Gruber, "Power and Protection"; and Gruber, "'Go Wherever You Wish, for Verily You Are Well Protected.'"

68. This painting is reproduced in Küçükbay, "Das sogenannte Dala'il ül-Khayrat," 132. Also see the manuscript's entry in Rebhan, *The Wonders of Creation*, 218, cat. no. 79.

69. This unpublished Ottoman prayer book is held in Bryn Mawr College (ms. BV#53). It was calligraphed by Mustafa al-Kutahi and includes chapters and verses of the Qur'an along with the "beautiful names of god" (*al-asma' al-husna*). It does not include supererogatory prayers (*du'as*) in Ottoman Turkish. In addition to the depiction of the Qur'an and Muhammad's mantle at the close of the manuscript, this *du'aname* includes a number of seal designs.

70. Muhanna, "The Sultan's New Clothes," 192, 199. Muhanna notes that the Qur'an was sent with other luxury goods and that it signified Sunni Mamluk-Ottoman solidarity while also reinforcing the Mamluks' position as the ultimate preservers and arbiters of Islamic history.

71. Aydın, *Pavilion of the Sacred Relics*, 90–95.

72. While the 'Uthmanic codex was revered by the Ottomans, it nevertheless was considered defective and falsified in some Shi'i quarters. In these sectarian milieus, the 'Uthmanic codex was deemed to have been purged of mentions of 'Ali and his vicegerency (*walaya*), the *ahl al-bayt*, and the imams who had been included in an "original" Qur'an. This Qur'an—known as the Codex of 'Ali (*mushaf-i 'Ali*)—was believed to be triple in size and to have contained 'Ali's qur'anic commentary (for the most recent review of the topic, see Amir-Moezzi, "'Ali et le Coran," 680). Like the Ottomans, the Safavids also were interested in laying claim to Kufic copies of the Qur'an. However, the extant examples, whose authenticity also remains suspect, include putative signatures by the Shi'i imams rather than attributions to 'Uthman (on these Qur'ans, see Canby, "Early Qur'ans 'Signed' by the Shi'i Imams").

73. Déroche, "Written Transmission," 182.

74. Meri, "Aspects of Baraka," 47–49; and Meri, "Relics of Piety and Power in Medieval Islam," 116.

75. Flood, "Bodies and Becoming," 474.

76. Prayer book of Düzdidil, Bavarian State Library, Munich, Cod. Turc. 553, folios 101v and 220r (*ba'ith maghfirat wa wasilat dukhul al-jinna*).

77. Prayer book of Düzdidil, Bavarian State Library, Munich, Cod. Turc. 553, folio 203v. This explanation accompanies the "blessed seal of Ja'far al-Sadiq," located on folio 204r.

78. Vatin and Veinstein, *Le sérail ébranlé*, 294.

79. D'Ohsson, *Tableau général du l'empire othoman*, 2:390; and Darir, *Kitab-ı Siyer-i Nebi*, 3:669: here, the mantle is said to have been presented to Selim I at the same time as the keys to the *haramayn* were handed over to him.

80. Vatin and Veinstein, *Le sérail ébranlé*, 295.

81. Aydın, *Pavilion of the Sacred Relics*, 56–57, 63.

82. Vatin and Veinstein, *Le sérail ébranlé*, 296.

83. Darir, *Kitab-ı Siyer-i Nebi*, 3:664–71; D'Ohsson, *Tableau général du l'empire othoman*, 2:391–92; Aydın, *Pavilion of the Sacred Relics*, 36; and Flood, "Bodies and Becoming," 471.

84. On the mantle as the robe of the gazi and dervish, see Vatin and Veinstein, *Le sérail ébranlé*, 308.

85. Aydın, *Pavilion of the Sacred Relics*, 55.

86. See Staples, "Muhammad, a Talismanic Force"; and Gril, "Le corps du Prophète," 45.

87. The ode's full title is *Al-Kawakib al-Durriya fi Madh Khayr al-Bariyya* (Pearly Stars in Praise of the Best of Creation). For the text and its talismanic functions, see Stetkevych, *The Mantle Odes*; Stetkevych, "From Text to Talisman"; and Jeffery, *A Reader on Islam*, 605–20.

88. Stetkevych, "From Text to Talisman," 147, 150; Flood, "Bodies and Becoming," 473; and Abdulfattah, "Relics of the Prophet and Practices of his Veneration in Medieval Cairo," 86.

89. Stetkevych, "From Text to Talisman," 161–62.

90. For a discussion of Muhammad's footprints and sandals, see in particular Aydın, *Pavilion of the Sacred Relics*, 114–30; Aydın, "Peygamberimizin Mes ve Pabuçları"; Gruber, "The Prophet Muhammad's Footprint"; Gruber, "A Pious Cure-All," 134–37; Wheeler, *Mecca and Eden*, 78–80; Wheeler, "Relics in Islam," 108–10; and Abdulfattah, "Relics of the Prophet and Practices of his Veneration in Medieval Cairo."

91. In Ottoman Turkish: *Her kaçan-kim kademi resmine sü [rerim] yüzümi / Nakşiya evc-i rıf'atde görürüm kendümi*.

92. Porter, "Amulets Inscribed with the Names of the 'Seven Sleepers' of Ephesus in the British Museum," 126.

93. Ottoman prayer book, eighteenth or nineteenth century CE, Ottoman lands, the Nasser D. Khalili Collection of Islamic Art, London, mss. 158, folio 140v (textual directions for viewing and rubbing the seal of the "Seven Sleepers"); and manuscript mentioned in Safwat, *The Art of the Pen*, 49–50.

94. Brown, *The Cult of the Saints*, chaps. 5–6.

95. Illustrated in Aydın, *Pavilion of the Sacred Relics*, 119.

96. Aydın, *Hırka-i Saadet Dairesi ve Mukaddes Emanetler*, 122.

97. The Ottoman historian Evliya Çelebi (d. 1682 CE) records in his *Sehayatname* (Book of Travel) that there was a footprint of the Prophet in Mecca. This footprint was typically filled with rose water, and pilgrims to Mecca would collect the water and rub it on their faces (cited in Aydın, *Pavilion of the Sacred Relics*, 115). Moreover, these prints on stones must have been understood as bearing special attributes not only because they retained the physical trace of the Prophet but also because in Islamic lands stones were believed to carry miraculous powers (see Lewis, *Everyday Life in Ottoman Turkey*, 50; and on the worship of stones in Iran, see Donaldson, *The Wild Rue*, 148–54).

98. Illustrated in Aydın, *Pavilion of the Sacred Relics*, 120.

99. Aydın, *Hırka-i Saadet Dairesi ve Mukaddes Emanetler*, 120, 123.

100. Aydın, *Pavilion of the Sacred Relics*, 125–30.

101. Aydın, *Pavilion of the Sacred Relics*, 10, 262–64 (these manuscripts were eventually moved to the palace's manuscript library). For an Ottoman illustrated prayer book containing a painting of Muhammad's relics and Berat prayers, see Topkapı Palace Library, Istanbul, M.R. 275, folios 75r and 262r.

102. Aydın, "Peygamberimizin Mes ve Pabuçları," 15 (for the Queen Mother Pertevniyal's sandal relic box dated 1289 AH/1872 CE) and 17 (for the wooden sandal said to have been made by Dihya al-Kalbi). Pertevniyal also owned a prayer book; see Topkapı Palace Library, Istanbul, H. 100.

103. Wheeler, "Relics in Islam," 110; and Beyoğlu, "The Ottomans and the Islamic Sacred Relics," 41.

104. Meri, *The Cult of Saints among Muslims and Jews in Medieval Syria*, 109–11; Meri, "Relics of Piety and Power in Medieval Islam," 109; Dickinson, "Ibn al-Salah al-Shahrazuri and the Isnad," 483–84; and Schimmel, *And Muhammad Is His Messenger*, 40.

105. Meri "Relics of Piety and Power in Medieval Islam," 108.

106. For a review of texts and treatises on Muhammad's sandal, see Khameh-Yar, "Risalaha va Ta'lifati darbara-yi Na'layn-i Payambar."

107. On these straps and bands, see Tirmidhi, *Shamaal-il Tirmidhi*, 70–76; and Aydın, *Pavilion of the Sacred Relics*, 125. For a short preliminary discussion of the *Rawdat al-Safa fi Wasf Ni'al al-Mustafa* and its visual representations of Muhammad's sandals, see Gruber, "A Pious Cure-All," 135–37. This text is especially indebted to and extensively cites al-Maqqari's (d. 1631 CE) famous tract entitled *Fath al-Muta'al fi Madh al-Ni'al* (The Victory of the Sublime in Praise of the Sandals), printed copies of which also include variant designs of Muhammad's sandal (see St. Elie, "Le culte rendu par les Musulmans aux sandales de Mahomet").

108. Ahmed Süleymanizade, *Rawdat al-Safa fi Wasf Ni'al al-Mustafa* (The Garden of Purity in Describing the Pure One's Sandals), Ottoman lands, ca. 1839–61, Topkapı Palace Library, Istanbul, E.H. 1190, folio 9r.

109. Süleymanizade, *Rawdat al-Safa fi Wasf Ni'al al-Mustafa*, folios 8r–9v; and Aydın, *Pavilion of the Sacred Relics*, 126.

110. Cited in Schimmel, *And Muhammad Is His Messenger*, 40.

111. For the Darwishiyya sandal tile and another similar Ottoman tile of Damascene provenance, see Makariou, *Chefs d'oeuvre islamiques de l'Aga Khan Museum*, 200–201, cat. no. 72; and Arlı, "Depictions of 'Nalın-ı Şerif' (Holly Patten) on Ottoman Tiles," 280, fig. 3. Ottoman sandal tiles (without inscriptions) are also held in the Doris Duke Foundation for Islamic Art in Hawai'i (no. 48.76) and the Leighton House Museum in Kensington, London.

112. See in particular Rudy, "Kissing Images, Unfurling Rolls, Measuring Wounds, Sewing Badges and Carrying Talismans"; and Flood, "Bodies and Becoming," 470–71.

113. Taşkale and Gündüz, *Hz. Muhammed'in Özellikleri*, 21–27; and Erdoğan, *Türk Edebiyatında Manzum Hilyeler*.

114. Safwat, *The Art of the Pen*, 46; Zakariya, "The Hilye of the Prophet Muhammad," 16; Taşkale and Gündüz, *Hz. Muhammed'in Özellikleri*, 45–46; Schick, "The Iconicity of Islamic Calligraphy in Turkey," 213; and Schick, "The Content of Form," 189–93.

115. Taşkale and Gündüz, *Hz. Muhammed'in Özellikleri*, 18.

116. Gruber and Dimmig, *Pearls of Wisdom*, 80–81, cat. no. 58.

117. For the diagram's design and component terms, see Taşkale and Gündüz, *Hz. Muhammed'in Özellikleri*, 40–43.

118. See Schick, "The Iconicity of Islamic Calligraphy in Turkey."

119. See Necipoğlu, "The Süleymaniye Complex in Istanbul," 105, 110.

120. Tanındı, "Seçkin Bir Mevlevî'nin Tezhipli Kitapları."

121. Arberry, *The Chester Beatty Library*, cat. no. 4168; and Wright, *Islam: Faith, Art, and Culture*, 45, fig. 21. The title page also notes that this copy of the *Mantle Ode* is accompanied by the *takhmis* (expansion) of al-Fayyumi.

122. For Ottoman *hilye* icons and triptychs, see Gruber, "A Pious Cure-All," 127–28, and fig. 4.5; *Aşk-ı Nebi*, 172, cat. no. 65; Taşkale and Gündüz, *Hz. Muhammed'in Özellikleri*, 20, 38, 66, 106, 126, 141, 146, 147, 150, 161, and 188; Safwat, *The Art of the Pen*, 54–55; Alparslan, *Osmanlı Hat Sanatı Tarihi*, 133–34; and *In Pursuit of Excellence*, plate 38.

123. Undated illustrated prayer manual, eighteenth or nineteenth century, Ottoman lands, Topkapı Palace Library, Istanbul, E.H. 996, folios 10v–11r. The miscellany includes only Ottoman-language *du'a*s—no qur'anic *sura*s or *aya*s—and some are intended for celebrations of the New Year (folio 13v). Another minuscule seal mounted in glass includes a *hilye* accompanied by al-Tirmidhi's statement on the benefits of gazing on it; see Topkapı Palace Library, Istanbul, G.Y. 1500 (published in *Aşk-ı Nebi*, 128, cat. no. 23).

124. Porter et al., *Arabic and Persian Seals and Amulets in the British Museum*; and Porter, "Islamic Seals."

125. On the seal of God's omnipotence, see Gruber, "A Pious Cure-All," 240–45; and on the seal of Solomon, see Dawkins, "The Seal of Solomon."

126. Reproduced in Taşkale and Gündüz, *Hz. Muhammed'in Özellikleri*, 128; and *Sakıp Sabancı Museum Collection of the Arts of the Book and Calligraphy*, 314–15, cat. no. 168. The lower horizontal panel in this *hilye* includes the *Hadith Qudsi* (Saying attributed to God) that states: "Were it not for you [oh Muhammad], I would not have created the celestial spheres."

127. Muhammad's descent from 'Adnan, the legendary ancestor of pure Arabs, and Adam, the first man, conferred great honor, as did his Hashemite tribal affiliation. On Muhammad's genealogy, see Ibn Ishaq, *The Life of Muhammad*, 3; Watt, "The Materials Used by Ibn Ishaq," 26, 32; Varisco, "Metaphors and Sacred History"; and Asani and Abdel-Malek, *Celebrating Muhammad*, 66, 102.

128. On the family tree as a textual and visual concept, see Klapisch-Zuber, *L'ombre des ancêtres*; and Klapisch-Zuber, "The Genesis of the Family Tree."

129. Fetvacı, *Picturing History at the Ottoman Court*; and Fetvacı, "From Print to Trace."

130. McWilliams, *In Harmony*, 251–52, cat. no. 117A–B.

131. For an antecedent Arabic-language poem and genealogical tree on Muhammad and the Ten Promised Ones, see al-Dirini's (d. 1294–95 CE) *Kitab al-Shajara fi Dhikr Nasab al-Nabi wa'l-'Ashara* (Süleymaniye Library, Istanbul, Ayasofya 4348). The text mainly extols the virtues of the Prophet and the *'ashara mubashshara*. Its genealogical tree (folios 38v–39r) is dated to 801 AH/1398–99 CE and comprises a zigzag diagram showing a main line from Adam to Muhammad, whose offshoots are the Ten Promised Ones. On this text and genealogical tree, see Binbaş, "Structure and Function of the Genealogical Tree in Islamic Historiography," 506–9, 542, and fig. 5.

132. On Ottoman genealogies, of which about a dozen survive in international collections, see in particular Aygan, "Osmanlılarda Silsile Geleneği ve Resimli Hanedan Silsilenameler"; Bayram, "Musavvir Hüseyin Tarafından Minyatürleri Yapılan ve Halen Vakıflar Genel Müdürlüğü Arşiv'inde Muhafaza Edilen Silsile-Name"; Bayram, "Medallioned Genealogies"; Bağcı, "From Adam to Mehmed III"; Necipoğlu, "The Serial Portraits of Ottoman Sultans in Comparative Perspective"; Renda, "The Miniatures of Silsilename, no. 1321 in the Topkapı Saray Museum Library"; Milstein, *Ottoman Miniature Painting in Baghdad*, 36–42, 111–13 (cat. nos. 48–55); Sims, "The Turks and Illustrated Historical Texts," 752–53, fig. 8; and *Aşk-ı Nebi*, 192–93, cat. no. 82.

133. Bağcı, "From Adam to Mehmed III," 195, 198.

134. Binney, *Turkish Treasures from the Collection of Edward Binney, 3rd*, 89–94, cat. no. 57; and Milstein, *Miniature Painting in Ottoman Baghdad*, 113, cat. no. 54. Like many other illustrated *Books of Genealogy*, the manuscript appears to have been produced during the reign of Mehmed III (i.e., ca. 1595–1600 CE). However, the last five paintings appear to have been added at a later date.

135. See the pro-Shi'i *Book of Genealogy* held in the Ethnography Museum, Ankara, inv. no. 8457. In this manuscript, Muhammad is depicted at the Ka'ba with the angel Gabriel and Imam 'Ali rather than surrounded by the *rashidun*. Both the Prophet and 'Ali bear white facial veils and flaming nimbi. In addition, the manuscript emphasizes and depicts the twelve imams and Safavid monarchs. On this manuscript, see Bayram, "Ankara Etnografya Müzesi'ndeki Madalyonlu Silsile-nâme'de Doğu Anadolu ve Batı Asya"; Bayram, "Musavvir Hüseyin Tarafından Minyatürleri Yapılan ve Halen Vakıflar Genel Müdürlüğü Arşiv'inde Muhafaza Edilen Silsile-Name," 318, fig. 42; and Taner, "'Caught in a Whirlwind,'" 227–50.

136. For a highly similar compendium of texts and diagrams dated 1123 AH/1711 CE, see Süleymaniye Library, Istanbul, Nuruosmaniye 3709. The treatise on the Prophet's genealogy (*kitab shajarat al-nabi*) includes a genealogical tree (folios 17v–18r) and a rose-shaped *hilye* (folio 18v) that appear to have been copied after the earlier representations illustrated in figs. 5.21–5.22.

137. For a discussion of Ottoman rose texts and images, and their intersections with Ottoman Sunni-Sufi spirituality, see Gruber, "The Rose of the Prophet."

138. Demiriz, *Osmanlı Kitap Sanatında Doğal Çiçekler*; Demiriz, "On Rococo-Decorated Manuscripts in the Sadberk Hanım Museum"; and Taşkale, "Kur'an-ı Kerîm'de Açan Çiçekler."

139. Ergin, "The Fragrance of the Divine," 87–88.

140. De Busbecq, *The Turkish Letters of Ogier Ghiselin de Busbecq*, 28.

141. Gruber, "The Rose of the Prophet," 223–24; and Schimmel, *And Muhammad Is His Messenger*, 35.

142. Darir, *Kitab-ı Siyer-i Nebi*, 1:477–79. Elsewhere, al-Darir relates a story in which Muhammad perspired from his awe of God. God then created a gem from that bead of sweat. He split the gem in two and used both halves to create his divine pen (*kalem*) and throne (*'arş*). These sweat gems are thus shown as God's generative substance (see Darir, *Kitab-ı Siyer-i Nebi*, 1:35).

143. Image reproduced in Taşkale and Gündüz, *Hz. Muhammed'in Özellikleri*, 21; Çağman, *Kat'ı*, 250–51; and Bilgi, *Gönülden bir Tutku*, 81.

144. On the seal of Solomon, see Dawkins, "The Seal of Solomon."

145. For a general discussion of magic squares (*wafq*, *buduh*, or *jadwal*), see Cammann, "Islamic and Indian Magic Squares."

146. On the *hilye* as a conceptual representation, see Safwat, *The Art of the Pen*, 47; and on *hilye*s promoting "good imagination," see Cooperson, "Images without Illustrations," 8.

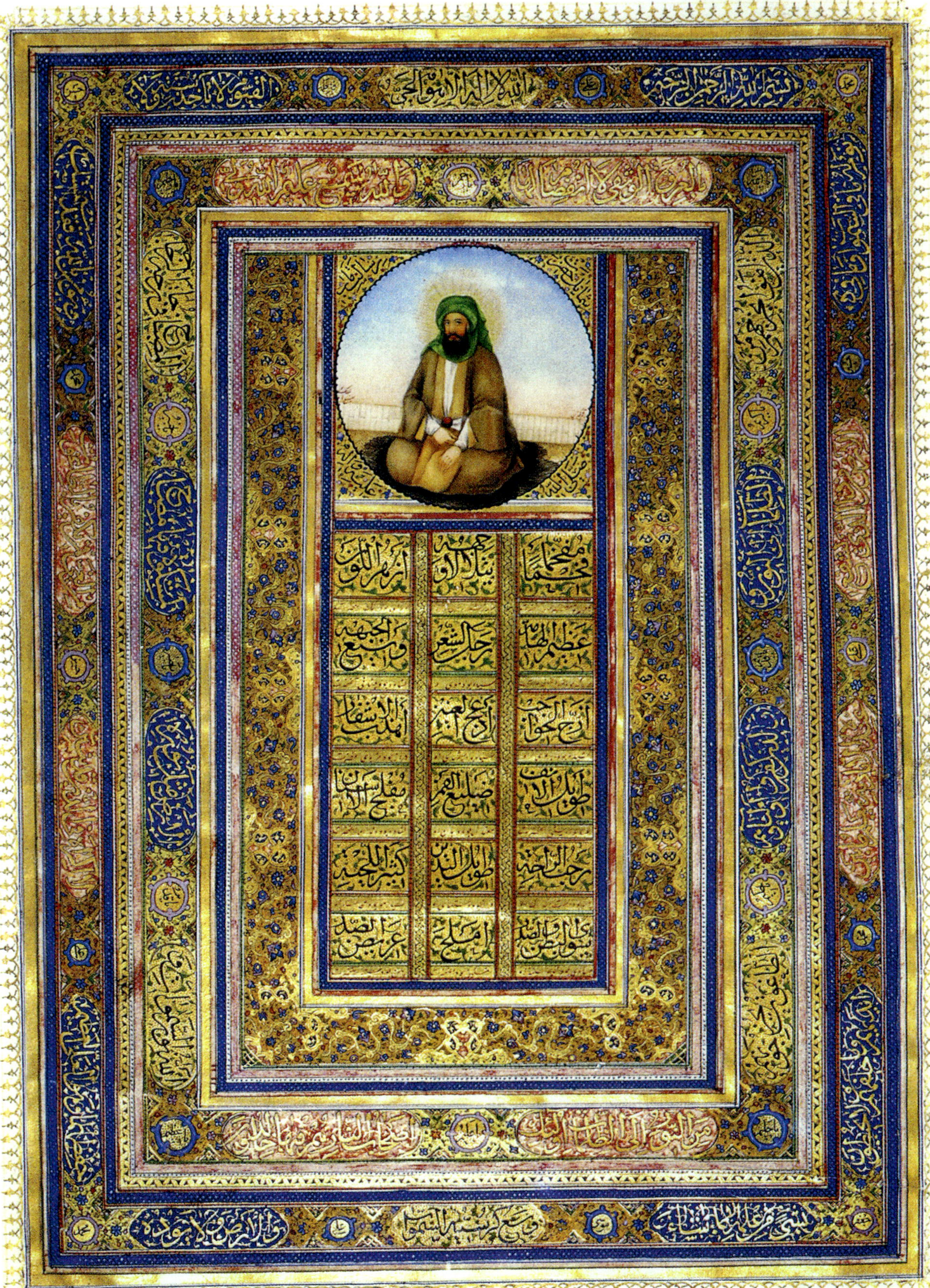

The onset of modernity did not bring the production of images of Muhammad—figural or abstract—to a halt. Indeed, since the nineteenth century, depictions of the Prophet have extended both tradition and innovation. In more recent years, they also have tended to reflect anxieties and concerns related to the supposed prohibition of prophetic depictions. Despite changes to traditions of figural representation and the rise of public narratives that condemn such images, Islamic artistic practices of representing Muhammad continue to the present day. These images emerge from cultural settings marked by both iconophilic and iconoclastic impulses. Such divergent directions within global Muslim communities should not be understood as mutually exclusive. To the contrary, they have existed side by side, much as the appeal of representational images has waxed and waned in different times and places.[2]

Artistic approaches to depicting Muhammad creatively respond to a broad range of ever-evolving sociopolitical needs and aesthetic sensitivities; as a result, modern images of the Prophet are quite a mixed lot. Indeed, while Islamic depictions of Muhammad may display a certain unity in diversity,[3] their sheer heterogeneity complicates any overarching narrative about the trajectory of prophetic iconography. One can surmise that images of the Prophet developed from medieval verism to modern abstraction, culminating in their reduction, removal, and even prohibition in the modern and contemporary periods. While the visual evidence, if selectively chosen, may point in this general direction, a scholarly inquiry that presumes this foregone conclusion inevitably will present an oversimplification of Islamic pictorial practices, which display a range of complexities well into the present era.

In order to highlight the plurality and interconnectedness of Islamic traditions of representing the Prophet during the modern period, it is of paramount importance to shed a teleological approach based on rigid geocultural taxonomies, despite the utility and allure of such methods in organizing and discussing a large body of disparate material. Instead, an investigation that explores images of the Prophet through cross-cultural framings may prove more fruitful and nuanced, even in its untidy intricacies.

A flexible comparative methodology also helps to pinpoint a number of commonalities between pictorial motifs as found in modern and contemporary images of the Prophet made across the globe. In this regard, three major thematic strands emerge: the continuation and diversification of veristic depictions of Muhammad; the development of

Light the world, too long in darkness, with Muhammad's radiant name.[1]

Muhammad Iqbal (d. 1938)

FACING, 6.1. Pictorial *hilya* of the Prophet Muhammad, painted by Saniʿ al-Mulk, Tehran, Iran, ca. 1862 CE. Islamic Period Museum, Tehran, Iran, no. 4982.

pictorial strategies that further abstract the prophetic corpus; and the ongoing popularity of Muhammad's relics, along with their commodification as pilgrimage souvenirs and talismans. Thus, while both naturalistic and allegorical depictions of Muhammad serve to extend Islamic book painting traditions into the contemporary period, the more recent boom in prophetic paraphernalia and mass-produced religious goods proves entirely novel.

The great majority of veristic depictions of Muhammad stems from Persian lands. While such images prove almost nonexistent elsewhere in the Islamic world, they have thrived in Iran from the nineteenth century to the present day. To a large extent, these images continue long-lasting pictorial traditions, stretching back to the fourteenth-century illustrated *Compendium of Chronicles* and Safavid paintings of a more sectarian bent. During the Qajar (1785–1925 CE) and Pahlavi (1925–79 CE) periods, Iranian artists inherited and innovated on premodern motifs while experimenting with new media, especially oil on canvas, and mass reproduction as enabled by the printing press, which emerged in Iran during the nineteenth century.[4] As a result, during the modern period images of Muhammad no longer were confined to the relatively private and restricted domain of book arts. To the contrary, with their sizes now enlarged and copies multiplied, such depictions once and for all entered the public sphere, where they were used during devotional meditation, illustrated storytelling, Shi'i passion plays, and shrine visitation.

Further expanding both media and meanings, many more images and objects were produced in Iran during the postrevolutionary period (from 1979 CE). Some items depict the Prophet as an enlightened adult, while others show him as a smiling adolescent; some draw on premodern Persian pictorial traditions, while others freely borrow from and adapt European Christian iconography and Oriental photographs. To a certain degree, Iranian postage stamps, stickers, posters, postcards, and carpets tend to reflect the state-sponsored—and often conspicuously pro-Shi'i—worldview of the Islamic Republic, revealing the extent to which prophetic portraiture has intermingled with sectarian messaging systems since the adoption of Shi'ism as the official religion of Iran in 1501 CE. Their Shi'i inflections notwithstanding, contemporary Iranian images of Muhammad and other prophetic products were, and continue to be, used in both private and public arenas—despite the image-adverse discourses that have dominated public discussions of the subject since the 2005–6 Danish *Jyllands-Posten* cartoon controversy and the 2015 assassination of cartoonists at the Paris-based offices of the French satirical newspaper *Charlie Hebdo*.[5]

While a number of Iranian images depict the Prophet in a veristic fashion, many others camouflage his facial features with a white veil or burst of light. Tendencies to abstract the prophetic corpus antedate the modern period, stretching back to Safavid and Ottoman times. In late Ottoman and modern Turkish devotional arts, the Prophet also continued to be represented as a pink rose and through verbal icons known as *hilye*s. At times, he even was reduced to a small ball. Muhammad's corporeality went through a further reduction in manuscript paintings made on the Indian subcontinent during the eighteenth and nineteenth centuries, in which he is frequently depicted as a flaming nimbus. Last but not least, in modern Arab lands and within contemporary Muslim communities worldwide, the Prophet is almost never depicted with discernible corporeal features. Instead, a general avoidance of figural representation impels the use of other pictorial devices, including his scripted name *Muhammad* and flying steed Buraq. From artfully written calligrams to his mythical animal stand-in, the Prophet frequently figures as an "absent presence"[6] alluded to through creative hints and insinuations.

From the Balkans to Bengal and beyond,[7] Muhammad's relics collectively act as a common visual means of recalling and commemorating his life and being. While the Prophet's garments, accoutrements, and foot- and sandal prints were popular during the premodern period, in more recent times these visual vestiges have contributed to increasingly aniconic Prophet-centered devotions in the Islamic world. To a large degree, Muhammad's relics and physical impressions function as metonymic—rather than abstract or allegorical—visual devices: they represent material parts and marks, often highlighted and displayed in isolation, in order to signify a prophetic whole and endow it with greater significance.[8] Besides their synecdochal evocation of the Prophet, relics also provide *baraka*-imbued centerpieces within religious festivals and pilgrimages to holy sites, such as the Dome of the Rock in Jerusalem, Eyüp Shrine in Istanbul, and the Qadam Rasul (Prophet's footprint) Shrine in Delhi, all of which house examples of the Prophet's blessed footprints on stone.[9]

More recently, a desire to own copies and souvenirs of Muhammad's relics has precipitated a thriving market for the religious commodities and protective amulets that are offered for sale in the vicinity of shrines. These aniconic prophetic vestiges and paraphernalia cater to a broad consumer base during various "seasons of demand,"[10] thanks to the technologies of mass reproduction, pilgrimage practices, and the global tourism industry. Within contemporary Islamic consumerist and gift-giving cultures, such objects are embedded in a larger system of sacred consumption, in which the notion of the sacred results from a human behavioral and affective investment process that endows prophetic depictions with ontological meaning and efficacy in daily affairs.[11]

Whether depicted on painted icons, printed posters, or relic trinkets, Muhammad has been imagined in many ways since the nineteenth century. Veristic, abstract, and metonymic depictions of the Prophet engage with older pictorial paradigms, to which they add creative twists. They also embrace new visual vocabularies, some of which are neotraditional while others cull from European sources. Still others respond to global artistic and manufacturing trends, from abstract expressionism to digital novelties that circulate in international markets. Employing a multitude of iconographies and technologies, Muslim artists and communities across the globe have turned the figure—and notion—of Muhammad into nothing less than a global phenomenon, wherein depictions of the Prophet partake in a wide range of visual and material cultures. In these many contexts, the Prophet Muhammad fulfills various roles—apostle of God, doyen of his community, and spiritual force for protection and healing—while also stimulating the entire human sensorium and thus quickening religious affect in the eyes, hearts, and minds of his followers.[12]

CREATIVE TWISTS: VERISTIC IMAGES OF MUHAMMAD IN MODERN IRAN

While illustrated manuscripts were made in Iran well into the nineteenth century, a great number of depictions of Muhammad spread beyond the relatively private confines of the book arts. They began to appear in different formats and media, particularly as stand-alone icons divorced from written narratives, large-scale oil paintings used in illustrated storytelling practices, and posters, postcards, and carpets that decorated religious shrines, gathering halls, and private homes. Moving forward into the twentieth century, and especially after the 1979 revolution, depictions of the Prophet fully burst into the public sphere, where they came to ornament stamps, stickers, and even a five-story mural in Tehran.[13] Such highly visible art forms allowed cultural producers and consumers to send and receive a range of religious and political messages within the Iranian public sphere, in which images of Muhammad helped to craft an "imagined community."[14] In this larger social setting, rhetorical and visual strategies promoted consensus and cohesion—and hence greater personal attachment to both religion and state.

To a large extent, modern Iranian innovations in prophetic portraiture benefited from experiments with art and technology during the reign of Nasir al-Din Shah (1848–96).[15] This Qajar monarch embraced and sponsored the modern practices of photography and print technology, which thrived during the second half of the nineteenth century.[16] Nasir al-Din also cultivated traditional artistic forms, including Shi'i devotional arts and performances, such as passion plays (*ta'ziyya*s) reenacting the battle of Karbala.[17] Additionally, he is well known for his interest in European history, art, and culture; his many trips to Europe; and his founding of the School of Fine Arts (Dar al-Funun) in Tehran, where students read European texts in Persian translation and copied European paintings for local patrons.[18] As a result, between around 1850 and 1900 CE, Iranian artists creatively synthesized Persian motifs with European artistic styles and methods of production, elaborating new depictions of human subjects, among them the Prophet Muhammad. Such images served to extoll Iran's Persian-Islamic past while propelling its religiopolitical future via strategic engagement with new media and models.

Persian verbal icons stand out as one of the more notable inventions in the field of prophetic representation during the Nasirid period.[19] These representational devices function as holy images, combining a

THE PRAISEWORTHY ONE

written description and figural representation of a revered individual, typically the Prophet Muhammad or Imam 'Ali.[20] At times, the icon is identified as a *shama'il*—that is, a representation of a saintly personage's "features"—a term that finds its genesis in medieval Islamic "proofs" (*dala'il*) and "characteristics" (*shama'il*)—texts that praise the Prophet's physical and moral qualities.

Qajar pictorial icons to a certain extent recall Ottoman *hilye*s insomuch as they function as pious contemplative devices with text organized in a diagrammatic format. Ottoman *hilye*s, however, remain entirely aniconic. On the rare occasion when they include nonwritten content intended to recall the Prophet, such content usually consists of allegorical motifs and geographic markers, such as the pink rose and illustrations of Mecca and Medina. Nineteenth-century Iranian artists thus seem to have drawn inspiration from Islamic *shama'il* texts as well as antecedent and coeval Ottoman *hilye* traditions, which they supplemented by inserting a figural image into their compositions. This hybrid "imagetext"[21] strongly suggests that the figurative mode was considered a sine qua non of devotional imagination for Persian painters and viewers, a mode of visual-emotional engagement that both antedates and postdates the Qajar period.

One pictorial *hilya* of the Prophet made in about 1862 CE typifies the ways in which text and image were creatively combined to produce devotional icons in late nineteenth-century Iran (fig. 6.1).[22] Here, text encircles the composition's several frames and creates a checkerboard pattern below a roundel containing an unveiled and haloed Muhammad, who kneels while returning the viewer's gaze. In the four corners surrounding the roundel, an inscription identifies the icon as a *shama'il* of Muhammad, himself the "repository of prophethood" (*shama'il-i hazrat-i risalat-ma'ab*). However, in this and other cases, the term *shama'il* does not simply mean "characteristics" or "attributes." Rather, as a Qajar neologism describing this innovative "imagetext" product, the term is best translated as an "icon" that includes a pictorial representation. In other words, the Qajar *shama'il* icon essentially comprises a figural expansion of the Ottoman *hilye* tradition.

The texts included in the *shama'il* illustrated in figure 6.1 include descriptive terms, personal names, and qur'anic verses. The checkerboard contains a number of expressions describing the Prophet's physical features, including his "luminous face," "radiant color," "wide forehead," "arched eyebrows," "black eyes," "long eyelashes," "thick beard," and "broad chest." These nouns and adjectives are not placed within sentences, as they are in Ottoman *hilye*s. Instead, they appear as a litany to be ritually recited; acting as a "behavioral trigger,"[23] they probably prompted viewers to utter praises to the Prophet as they gazed on and read the icon. The descriptions have been calligraphed within a lattice structure reminiscent of a magic square, a key pattern in Islamic occult arts. Much like Muhammad, magic squares are often conceptualized as intercessory, protective entities.[24]

The icon's other textual contents also strongly hint at its talismanic character and uses. For example, the two outer borders include the qur'anic "throne verse" (2:255, *ayat al-kursi*) and "light verse" (24:35, *ayat al-nur*), inscribed within cartouches, as well as the beautiful names (*al-asma' al-husna*) of God and the names of Muhammad, his family, and the imams within small circles. In addition to the prophetic metaphor of light and the Shi'ification of the icon, the inclusion of the "throne verse" is noteworthy. This verse praises God as the eternal and omnipotent intercessor for humankind, and, as such, is considered especially protective. For this reason, the "throne verse" is the most popular qur'anic verse for transcription in Islamic talismanic objects.[25] Its insertion into a pictorial icon of the Prophet is thus suggestive in at least two ways: first, it echoes Muhammad's own "talismanic force"[26] in guiding, protecting, and healing devotees, and, second, it hints at the icon's role as an amuletic object, whose blessings and prophylactic qualities were perhaps believed to be enhanced through the viewer's sustained reading, reciting, and gazing.

Beyond such sensorial activities, European travelers to Iran inform us that Iranian devotees physically prostrated themselves and kissed icons of the Prophet and 'Ali, as if in adoration of the saintly figure. For example, Charles Wills, who visited Iran in 1866–81 CE, writes, "The painting of portraits of Mohammed, Ali, Houssein, and Hassan . . . is almost a trade in itself, though the representation of the human form is contrary to the Mahommedan religion, and the saints are generally represented as veiled and faceless figures. Yet in these particular cases, custom has over-ridden religious law, and the Schamayul (or portrait of Ali) is common."[27] Not merely functioning as contemplative devices, Qajar *shama'il*s were made in plentiful numbers as complements to modern Persian cultural and religious practices that involved seeking protection and performing prayer.

Popular interactions with images were not limited to the domain of the hoi polloi, however. To the contrary, they benefited from top-down sponsorship, emanating from the pinnacle of society—royal spheres. For example, the painterly image of Muhammad shown in figure 6.1 is signed by Abu'l-Hasan Ghaffari, Nasir al-Din Shah's court painter, known as Sani' al-Mulk. Famous for portraits of his royal patron and other powerful individuals at the Qajar court, Sani' al-Mulk made this pictorial icon of the Prophet for Nasir al-Din Shah. It was placed in the palace repository and brought out once a month so that the ruler could ritually gaze on the image of Muhammad, as if he were peering at the "new moon."[28]

This *shama'il* thus belongs to a larger corpus of meditational images that provide evidence for Qajar Perso-Islamic spiritual practices of seeking favor and blessings from a holy person by gazing on his likeness. As Mohammad Ali Amir-Moezzi has demonstrated, the aim of visually meditating on (*tafakkur*) and facing (*wajha*) a blessed icon is to lead the devotee from the realm of the illusory (*batil*) to the realm of

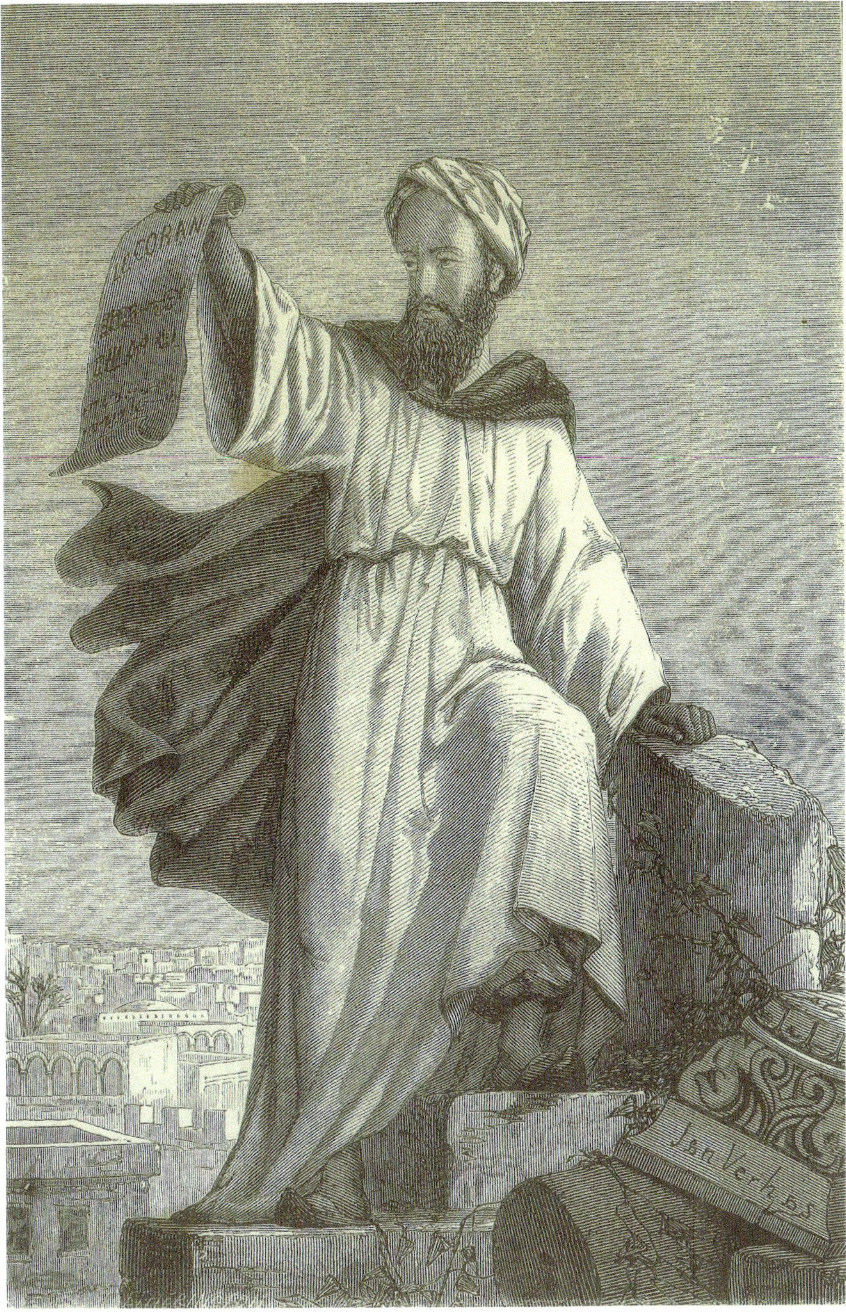

6.2. The Prophet Muhammad holding the Qur'an, illustration by Jan Verhas (1834–1896 CE) included in Louis Figuier's (1819–1894 CE) *Vie des savants illustres du moyen âge* (Paris: Lacroix, 1867), 2.

the real (*haqq*), where a vision of the eye leads to a vision of the heart.[29] An exoteric image thus is thought to precipitate an esoteric experience, much as a tangible picture is used to activate mental visualization. Figural images of the Prophet thus may have been used as pictorial aides within the larger practice of securing mystical visions of the heart, a theme discussed in detail in chapter 3.

Stretching beyond Iran, Qajar illustrated *hilya*s also seem to be indebted to the European painterly arts. For instance, Sani' al-Mulk traveled to Italy, where he spent time in the major academies and museums in Rome, Florence, Venice, and the Vatican. There, he made oil and watercolor copies of famous paintings, including depictions of Christ's ascension and Raphael's *Madonna di Foligno*.[30] The *shama'il* in figure

6.1 includes a painting of the Prophet within a tondo frame, a format encountered by the artist during his visits to European museums. Other *shama'il*s of the period also include cherubs in grisaille, a technique of painting in a grayish color that emulates relief sculpture. On at least one occasion, a bejeweled grisaille icon of 'Ali was worn around the neck of Nasir al-Din.[31] If produced in enamel or metal and encrusted with gems, figural icons also could function as suspended portrait medals (*nishan* or *hama'il*), the latter linked to Qajar orders of merit and European chivalric arts—and hence, more broadly, to practices of political recognition, ceremonial gift-giving, and international diplomacy.[32] Whether made as paintings on paper or relief images on medals, icons of Muhammad and 'Ali also formed part of court protocol and regalia, acting as heraldic devices in both prayer and politics.

Other Qajar and Pahlavi images amplify the Prophet's figural presence while showcasing the various ways in which Persian artists adopted and adapted European pictorial prototypes in order to creatively expand the range of prophetic iconography within Islamic artistic traditions. While some modern painters culled from premodern Persian book arts, for centuries manuscript paintings emerged from manifold interactions with global art forms. Displaying Western influence, Persian images depicting the Prophet reveal an indebtedness to Christian religious iconography, as is most evident in the comparison of scenes depicting Christ's nativity and Muhammad's birth (figs. 2.3–2.5). Persian artists turned to Christian imagery and European painterly techniques well before the nineteenth century; however, over the course of the nineteenth century, European representations of Muhammad grew in number and eventually reached Iran, where they were copied and transported into new semiotic terrain.[33]

A number of European depictions of the Prophet (and Jesus Christ) have been copied and altered in Iran since the nineteenth century. A corpus of images represents Muhammad as a bearded, mature adult standing on a hilltop, while another shows him as a beardless youth who tilts his head and smiles.[34] The first corpus of adult images comprises adaptations of an image of Muhammad made by the Belgian painter Jan Verhas (1834–96 CE), which was included in Louis Figuier's (1819–94 CE) *Vie des savants illustres du moyen âge*, published in Paris in 1867 (fig. 6.2). Covering the lives of eminent learned men of the Middle Ages, Figuier's text also includes a chapter on "The State of Sciences in the Arab Nations from the Capture of Alexandria to the Thirteenth Century." The printed image of Muhammad functions as a frontispiece to this section, in which Figuier lauds the Prophet as "the first and principal founder of this memorable revolution [Islam]. He also had great intellectual and moral qualities, which comprise true superiority. Moreover, he had a certain genius. This man was Muhammad."[35] Through both text and image, Verhas and Figuier offer unadulterated praise of the Prophet, a positive approach not unusual within European literate milieus during the nineteenth century. As John Tolan has observed, these tropes

    THE PRAISEWORTHY ONE

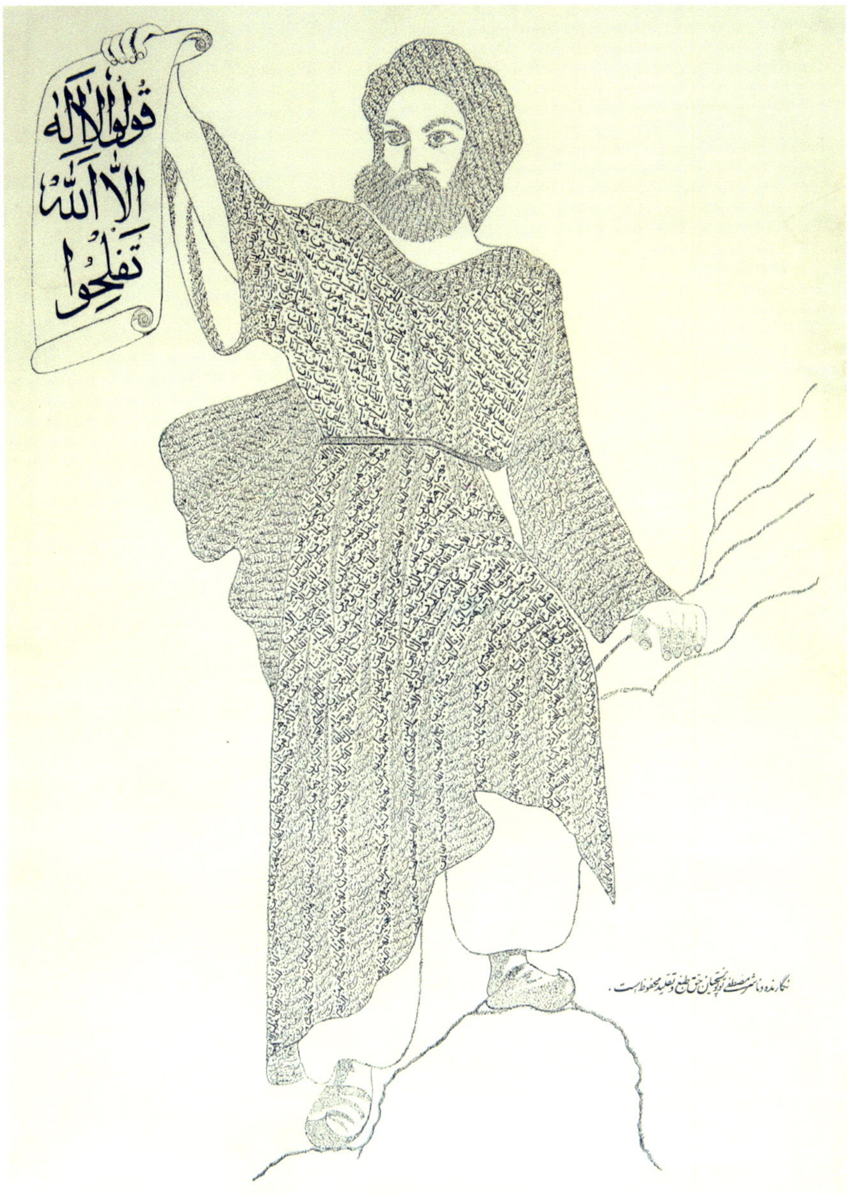

6.3. The Prophet Muhammad holding the Qur'an, illustration and print by Mustafa Tutunchiyan, Iran, ca. 1900–1950 CE. Frederick de Jong Collection, National Museum of World Cultures, Amsterdam, 7031–33.

"allowed a relatively objective and irenic appreciation of the importance of the Prophet and of Islam on the stage of world history, avoiding the bitter religious polemics that had so often colored European discourse on Islam."[36]

Through their visual lexicon, artists such as Jan Verhas imagined the Prophet as similar to Moses—that is, within a discernably "Mosaic mould"[37]—but with a detectable Orientalist twist. For example, in figure 6.2 Muhammad stands on high ground and receives divine commandment, with cape fluttering in the wind and curled-toe sandals upturned to the sky. In Verhas's composition, however, what would be Moses's tablet, inscribed with the Ten Commandments, transforms into an unwound scroll bearing the words "Le Coran" and several lines of pseudo-Arabic script. Through a number of Oriental attributes, most especially the cape and sandals, the European artist depicted Muhammad, a world prophet of a "certain genius," as if he were an Arabian Moses, an apostle who climbed high and experienced communication with God. Enlightened, elevated, and bearing divine writ, Moses and Muhammad certainly share prophetic similarities, and, here, within one image, they conjoin in their iconographies, too.

This cross-cultural encounter in image-making became ever more rich and complex once Verhas's printed image of Muhammad migrated to Iran sometime during the late nineteenth century. By 1900 CE, Iranian-European diplomatic, scholarly, cultural, and artistic relations were thriving, as were photography and the printing press. Many French-language history books were imported into Iran, translated into Persian, and assigned in schools. Histories of Louis XIV and Napoleon Bonaparte proved especially popular,[38] and therefore Figuier's *Vie des savants illustres du moyen âge* must have appealed to Iranian adolescent students and adult readers conversant in French and interested in learning more about the great men of world history. Without a doubt, Figuier's illustrated book belongs to larger Iranian efforts to access publications and images dealing with world history—from ancient times to the modern period—particularly those that might harmonize well with Islamic religious and civilizational history.

Jan Verhas's depiction of the Prophet, as included in Figuier's text, was copied in Iran sometime during the first half of the twentieth century. Made by a certain Mustafa Tutunchiyan, a designer and printer who signed his name and claimed image and printing copyright, the work depicts the Prophet (wearing his curled-toe sandals) standing on a mountaintop displaying an unwound scroll proclaiming God's all-encompassing unity (fig. 6.3). In a creative twist on Verhas's image, Tutunchiyan inscribed the proclamation "Say 'There is no god but God' and you will attain salvation" on the scroll. He also filled Muhammad's robe with minute handwritten verses from the Qur'an, insinuating that the Prophet is fully enwrapped in holy scripture. These textual adaptations praise the salvific potential of Islamic monotheism and exalt Muhammad's special status, calling to mind his honorific epithets the "enshrouded one" (*al-muddaththir*) and the "enwrapped one" (*al-muzzammil*).[39]

This depiction of the Prophet is transplanted from its European milieu of production, its interpretations strategically altered by Iranian artists and viewers. When such images leave their original cultural zones, they undergo a process of transvaluation,[40] in this case an imagining of Muhammad not just as a man "of a certain genius" but, much more importantly, as the ultimate embodiment of holy scripture and the pathway to paradise. His roles are thus magnified in terms of their religious and eschatological import by Iranian creative entrepreneurs who produce their own images within a call-and-response system of artistic production that at times responds to European Oriental imagery.

Iranian artists like Tutunchiyan acted as "Orientalism's interlocutors"[41] by speaking with and to Europe in the field of image production. Not merely derivative or imitative, modern Iranian images of the

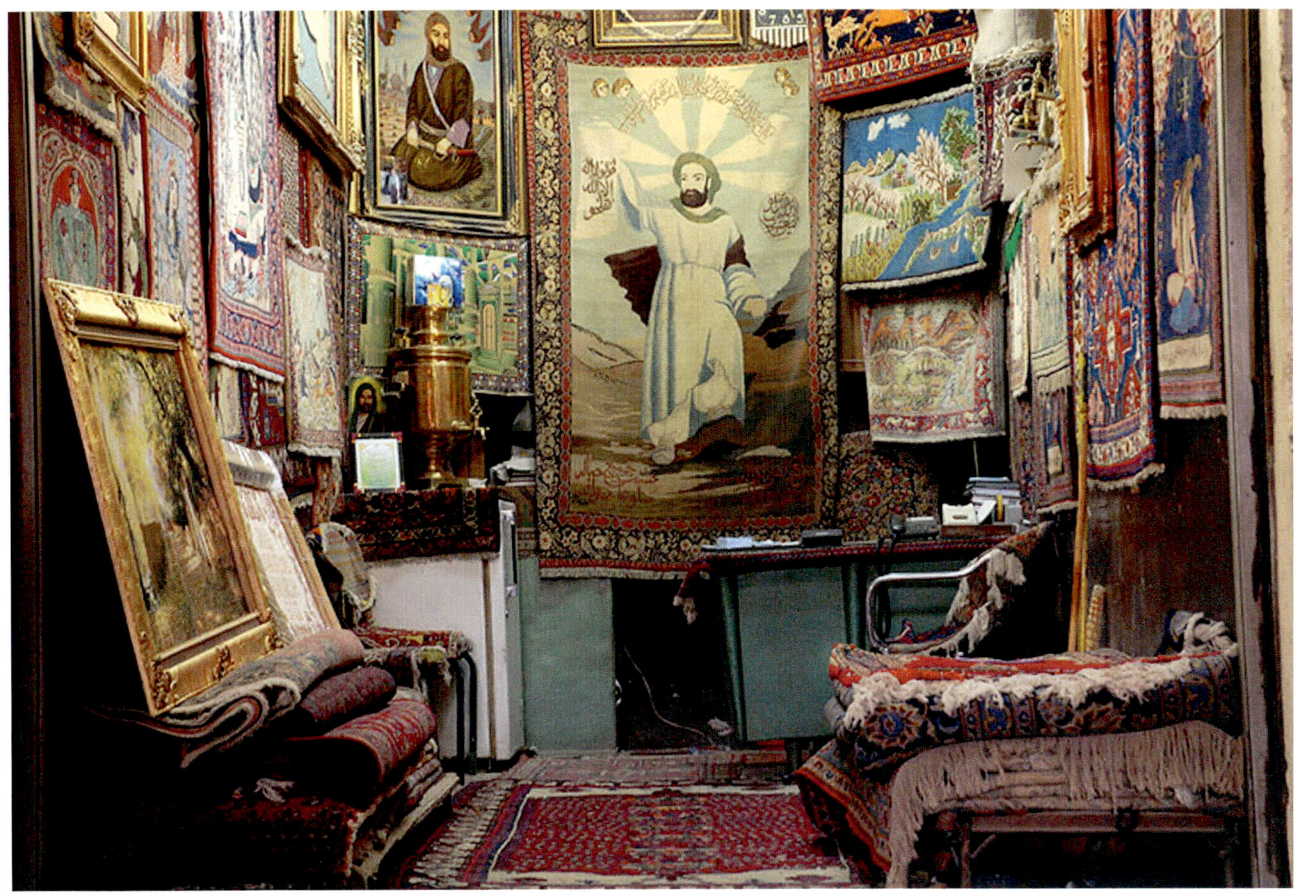

6.4. Store selling carpets with figural designs, including one depicting the Moses-like Muhammad, Tehran, Iran, 2006 CE. Photograph by Kamyar Adl, courtesy of Elizabeth Puin.

Prophet must be understood as belonging to a dialogic global matrix of artistic production and exchange. What is more, the broad Iranian acceptance of—indeed, the popularity of—these Moses-like images of Muhammad is attested to by works in many artistic media, including metal standards and carpets (fig. 6.4).[42]

Although originally derived from Verhas's composition, Iranian images of Muhammad standing and displaying scripture were frequently augmented with other motifs. Among the mass media of the mid-twentieth century, printed books and posters extend this European type of prophetic iconography even as they illustrate more local religious themes, including Shi'i heroes and Persian shrine visitation.[43] One such poster, which draws on and alters a European pictorial paradigm while expanding its Shi'i-Islamic symbolic vocabulary, again depicts the Prophet standing, holding scripture, and wearing curled-toe sandals, as in Verhas's original image (fig. 6.5). Here, Muhammad holds an open book (rather than an unfurled parchment), identified as the "glorious Qur'an" (*Qur'an-i majid*) across two of its folios. While the Qur'an—in both its codex (*mushaf*) format and its inscriptional content[44]—attests to the Prophet as the recipient of God's revelations, the green banner in Muhammad's left hand highlights his role as a victorious leader in battle. Furthermore, this ceremonial accoutrement of war and object relic of the Prophet is inscribed with "Victory is from God and triumph is near" (*nasr min Allah wa fath qarib*), a qur'anic verse (61:13)

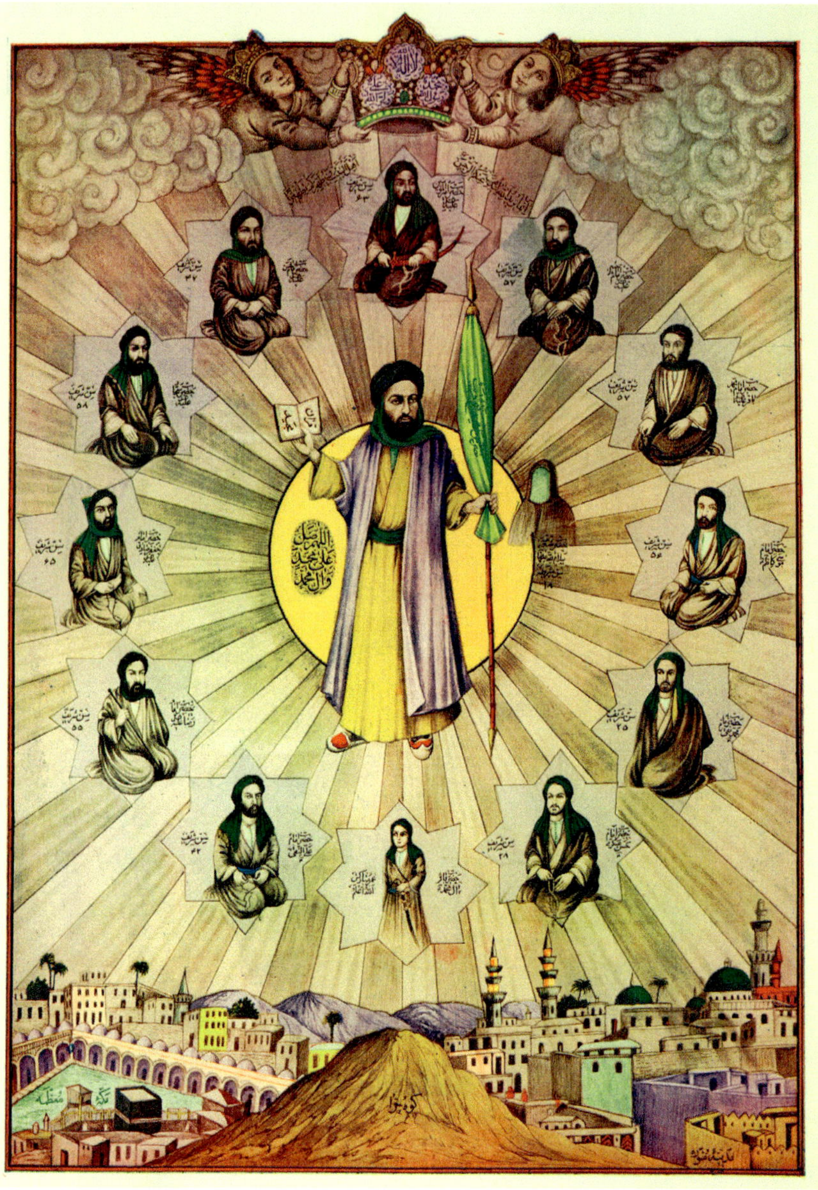

that promises power and protection in situations of confrontation and
hardship.

Besides the addition of the codex and banner, which endow Verhas's
original composition with a further Islamic tinge, the poster has been
Shi'ified through the incorporation of a panoply of motifs. Immediately
behind the Prophet, the sun bathes the central protagonist in the *nur
Muhammad*, a visual argument for the Prophet's preexistiential light.
Just as importantly, the large yellow disk also features, on the left, a seal-
like epigraph offering prayers for Muhammad and his family (*al-i Muhammad*) and, on the right, an ethereal bust portrait of a veiled Fatima,
who floats like a celestial apparition at the edge of the burst of light. The
inscription's sphragistic shape resembles Muhammad's own "seal of
prophecy" and therefore should be understood as an abstract emblem
of political authority. Its textual contents, moreover, extend Muhammad's prestige and jurisdiction to his daughter, family members, and

   THE PRAISEWORTHY ONE

descendants, particularly the twelve imams, each of whom is represented sitting within an eight-pointed star, as if a constellation of luminaries.

At the apex, a kneeling 'Ali holds the sword Dhu'l-Fiqar as he hovers immediately above Muhammad, a hierarchical position of superiority found in Persian Shi'i images that both antedate and postdate the poster. The conjunction of Muhammad's prophecy (*nubuwwa*) and 'Ali's vicegerency (*walaya*) is further articulated by the jewel-encrusted Kayanid crown held aloft by two angels in swirls of clouds.[45] A symbol of Qajar kingship, this crown also includes the Shi'i *walaya*, inscribed within three medallions. Much like the inclusion of 'Ali, whose facial features appear strikingly similar to those of Muhammad, the *walaya* aligns the Prophet and his son-in-law, making them an inseparable whole. Last but not least, on either side of 'Ali appears the qur'anic verse of purification (33:33: *ayat al-tathir*), which reads, "God desires to remove impurities from you, o members of the house (*ahl al-bayt*), and to cleanse and bring out the best in you." The mention of the *ahl al-bayt* in this verse is often interpreted in Shi'i exegetical texts as referring to the five "pure members" (*panj tan*) of the Prophet's family, who are believed to act as an ark of salvation and entryway to paradise.[46]

The poster combines the Kayanid crown, a symbol of Qajar temporal rule, with pictorial and rhetorical devices that praise the superiority and purity of the *ahl al-bayt* and imams. As a complex totality, this Persian Shi'i Islamic "imagetext" aims to represent Muhammad as a sacred light source illuminating the cosmos as well as crowning the three geographic locales of qur'anic revelation: Mecca, Medina, and Mount Hira. Muhammad also stands in the companionship of Fatima, known as the "radiant one" (*al-zahra'*), while his light rays generate the imams, who likewise are conceptualized as star-like "silhouettes of light" (*ashbah-i nur*). Partaking in the Prophet's radiance (*nur*) and perfection (*'isma*), these fourteen "infallibles" (*ma'sum*)—Muhammad, Fatima, and the twelve imams—are believed in Twelver Shi'ism to be immune from error and sin.[47]

In this nineteenth-century poster, prophetic enlightenment and infallibility are bolstered by a sectarian theological armature and the Kayanid crown, the signature emblem of the Qajar dynasty's right to rule in the land of Iran. Long gone is Verhas's Moses-like Muhammad, holding a parchment and standing on a mountaintop. Instead, Muhammad—although still wearing his curled-toe sandals—emerges as a Persian Shi'i prophetic sun king, crowned in majesty and wreathed by a constellation of infallible progeny. This sectarian apotheosis boasts a European picture as its original source, and yet the visual prototype has been transcended in highly strategic ways in order to position the Qajar dynasts as carrying forth the prophetic legacy. This tactic of coopting European iconography and overlaying it with highly legible Persian Shi'i motifs underscores the fact that artistic creation in Islamic lands has remained a dynamic process during the modern period, especially in the field of prophetic iconography. Looking westward while also turning

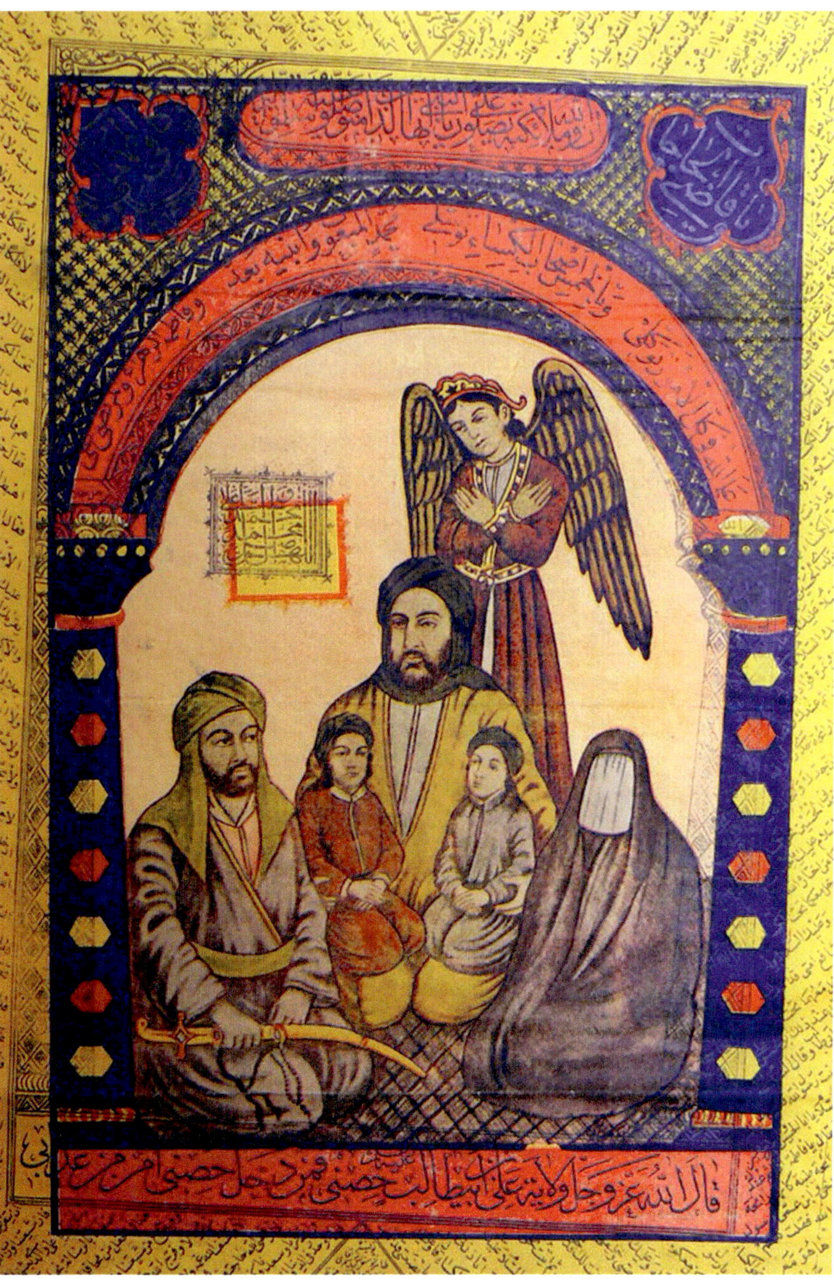

within, Qajar artists depicted Muhammad through visual tropes that, in a number of cases, overtly reassert discourses on Shi'i traditionalism and Iranian rulership.

Posters like the one illustrated in figure 6.5 hung in the private homes of well-to-do individuals and/or in religious buildings. In devotional contexts and milieus, these types of visuals likely served to focus prayer and meditation, like icons placed in Iranian shrines today (despite official injunctions that discourage their presence and use in the public sphere).[48] With their emphasis on the imamate in particular, these types of Iranian posters may well have ornamented the interior walls of Shi'i mausoleums dedicated to the Prophet Muhammad's descendants (*imamzada*s), which are scattered around the country.

　　THE PRAISEWORTHY ONE

In addition to posters, postcards have been printed from the Qajar period to today. Often framed, surrounded by prayers written on paper or chiseled in metal, postcards accompany votive offerings and are placed in public drinking fountains and shrines.[49] In more religious environments, these pictorial commodities transcend the profane sphere of capitalist exchange to function as blessed—and highly singularized—icons central to acts of worship.[50] Among the many mass-produced icons, postcards and broadsides often depict Muhammad and ʿAli singly, or show the five members of the Prophet's household (*ahl al-bayt* or *panj tan*) sitting together and accompanied by the angel Gabriel (fig. 6.6).[51] What is particularly intriguing about icons that represent the "Holy Five" or "Holy Pentad" is the fact that they emerged during the Qajar period, suggesting that, as is the case for other prophetic images of the period, they may have been influenced by Christian images of the Holy Family that depict Jesus flanked by Mary and Joseph, with Gabriel in attendance.[52] These modern Iranian images that celebrate Muhammad as a paterfamilias—rather than depict him singly or coupled with ʿAli, as is most typical for Safavid paintings—were possibly inspired by European *sacra famiglia* icons. The family members who accompany the Prophet embody the principle of human intimacy and hence act as a powerful "engine for spiritual elevation."[53]

Besides promoting family (rather than celibacy) as a model for emulation, *ahl al-bayt* icons also help to reinforce a sectarian worldview within Iranian Shiʿi contexts. The expression *ahl al-bayt* appears twice in the Qur'an, and its use in the qur'anic verse of purification (33:33) often appeared alongside the *Hadith al-Kisa'* (Saying of the Cloak) and narratives about ʿAli's investiture at Ghadir Khumm, which collectively assert the superiority of Muhammad's household alongside ʿAli's hereditary right to rule.[54] In its various iterations, the *Hadith al-Kisa'* describes Muhammad taking his family members under the protection of his robe and declaring them his pure supporters and confidants. The qur'anic verse of purification and an extended version of the Saying of the Cloak appear inscribed on the *ahl al-bayt* broadside illustrated in figure 6.6. These texts record Muhammad as reminding his followers, "Their flesh is my flesh and their blood is my blood. Whoever hurts them, hurts me." Additionally, the curved arch that creates a protective canopy above the five protagonists includes a prayer that encourages the viewer to place his or her trust in Muhammad and the *ahl al-bayt* in order to secure God's favor and protection.

This overtly pro-ʿAlid icon must have functioned as a spiritual refuge, through which and with which devotees sought to secure blessings and protection. It therefore must have been considered capable of transmitting *baraka* and warding off the evil eye. Indeed, amuletic objects inscribed with the names of members of the *panj tan* or displaying their likenesses were quite popular during the Qajar period.[55] These Shiʿi pictorial talismans could be used in private homes or shrines.

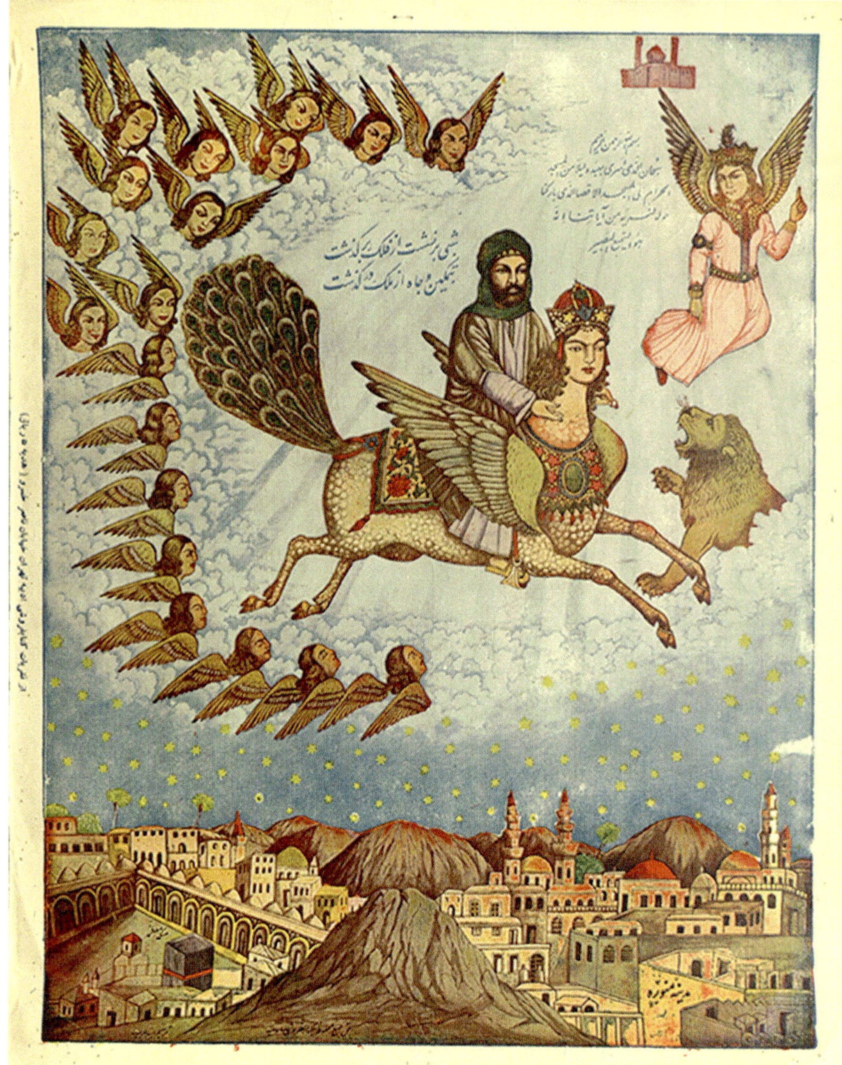

Others, made as mirrors or small boxes, functioned as memory aids for Sufi novices training in spiritual seeing, prayer, and meditation and included directions on how to "activate" the icon through daily looking and kissing.[56] Whether in private homes, Shiʻi shrines, or Sufi milieus, modern Iranian veristic images of Muhammad girdled by his family members enjoyed a host of visual-physical interactions, from intense gazing to devotional kissing. Although such images were mechanically reproduced in substantial quantities, it is patently clear that their aura remained undiminished in the eyes and minds of their beholders.[57]

While the inclusion of the imams and *ahl al-bayt* effectively signal a sectarian semantic bracketing of images of Muhammad, still other twentieth-century Iranian printed images are likewise "infused with Shiʻism."[58] They represent the Prophet within the larger cultural landscape of modern and contemporary Iran, in which both Persian poetry and international politics play a significant role in the formation of religious and social identities. For example, a Pahlavi-period poster made in Tehran around 1950 depicts Muhammad's celestial ascent (*miʻraj*) through the heavens (fig. 6.7).[59] The composition draws on earlier Shiʻi

Safavid and Qajar pictorial traditions, in which the Prophet is depicted as encountering ʿAli as a leonine angel to whom he offers his signet ring (*khatam*) in order to receive authority and blessings (fig. 3.21).[60] This overtly Shiʿi rendering of the ascension narrative has continued unabated in the visual culture of contemporary Iran, where a five-story mural of the *miʿraj* painted in Tehran in 2008 shows a similar encounter between the ascending Prophet and the leonine ʿAli.[61] During past centuries and well into the present day, the coupling of Muhammad and his son-in-law (whether in human or animal form) has proved an enduring image for pro-Shiʿi narratives of the Prophet's life and miracles.

In the mid-twentieth-century poster, Muhammad is shown riding the peacock-tailed Buraq above the same landscape included the apotheosis poster illustrated in figure 6.5. This repeated landscape reveals that the prophetic terrain of Mecca, Medina, and Mount Hira could be used in a variety of mass-produced compositions. Other details include the angel Gabriel—who flutters in the upper right while wearing an Iranian amuletic armband (*bazuband*) and gesturing that God is singular (*tahlil*)—and the large crescent-like formation of cherubs on the left.[62] Moreover, to the right of Gabriel appears the qurʾanic verse at the very heart of the ascension narrative: the "verse of the night journey" (17:1: *ayat al-israʾ*), which mentions a journey from the "sacred mosque" (*al-masjid al-haram*) to the "faraway mosque" (*al-masjid al-aqsa*). Although the expression *al-masjid al-aqsa* has been interpreted in various ways, the location it mentions is most frequently identified as Jerusalem—and, more specifically, the Dome of the Rock, where Muhammad is believed to have left a footprint on the rocky outcrop when he ascended into the skies.[63]

The expression *al-masjid al-aqsa* as included in the qurʾanic inscription may have prompted the poster's creator to include what at first glance might appear to be a small—and thus faraway—depiction of the Dome of the Rock hovering near the upper right corner. However, the pinkish building includes two prominent minarets and a pointed dome, while the Dome of the Rock has no minarets and a rounded dome. Instead, the structure closely resembles the Shiʿi shrines of Najaf and Karbala, where imams ʿAli and Husayn, respectively, are interred. Most intriguingly, then, a building at the heart of Shiʿi pilgrimage appears as the ultimate goal of Muhammad's celestial journey—a pinnacle that, like God, emits radiance that illuminates the skies and reaches earth.

In addition to the leonine ʿAli and shrine structure, which doubly promote the Shiʿi faith through angelic and architectural analogies, Persian poetic verses included to the left of the Prophet's head add a Sufi tinge to the overall composition. The verses, which praise Muhammad, are drawn from the preface to Saʿdi's *Bustan* (Fruit Orchard), a Sufi Persian text beloved by Iranians. Like many other Persian texts that include preliminary encomia to the Prophet and his *miʿraj*,[64] these verses describe Muhammad riding Buraq and traversing the celestial spheres (*aflak*) until he reaches a status and rank beyond that of the

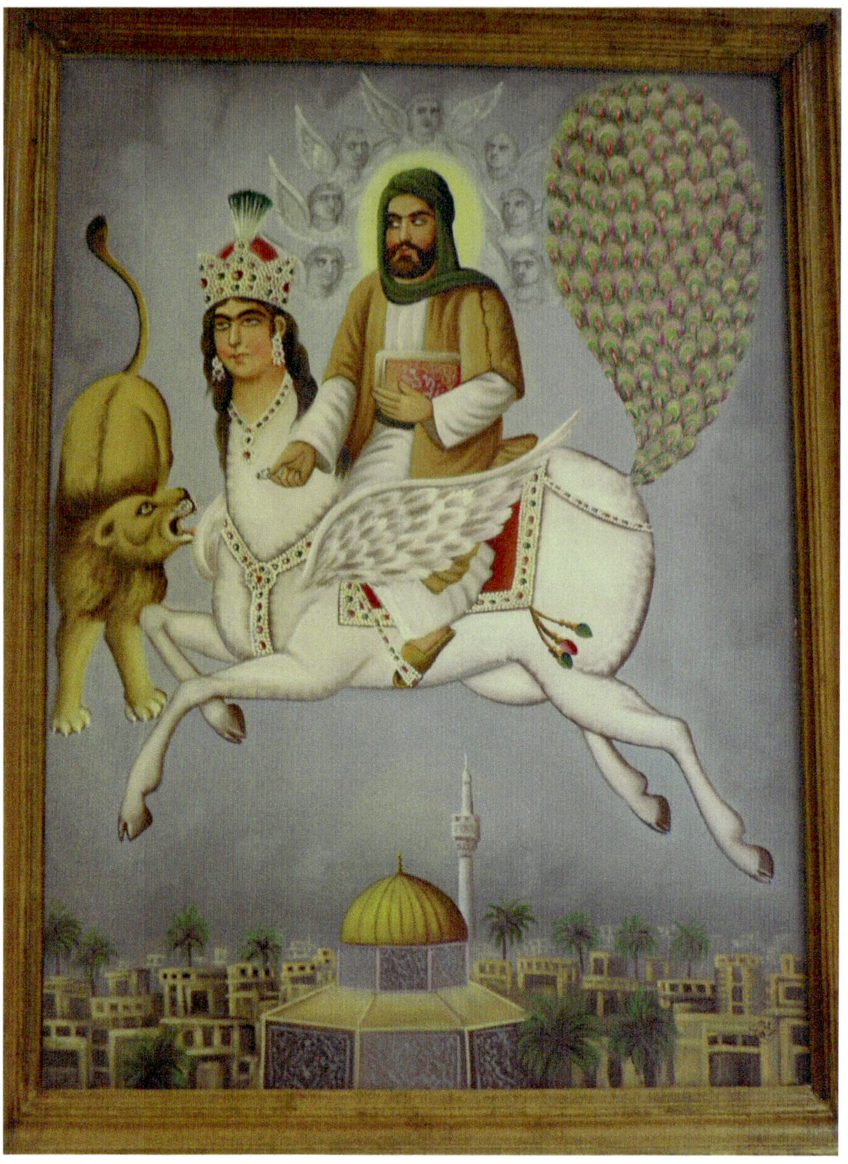

angel Gabriel.[65] In addition to lauding the prophetic ascent, these poetic verses recall the journeys of Sufi mystics as they embarked on their own quests toward ultimate spiritual unity (*tawhid*) and gnostic knowledge (*ma'rifat*).[66] The poster thus couples a Shi'ified ascension image with *ayat al-isra'* and Sa'di's ascension verses, thereby creating a larger synthesis that typifies Shi'i Iranian devotional life, literature, and pictorial arts from the early modern period to today.

Still other contemporary Iranian images of the Prophet's ascent seem to be entangled with domestic and international politics. Such is the case for a painting made around 1998 by the Iranian artist Muhammad Hamidi (fig. 6.8). While the central composition is rather typical of Shi'i Iranian *mi'raj*-cum-lion images, the landscape at the bottom of the image has been altered in a revealing manner: Muhammad does not rise above Mecca, Medina, or Mount Hira; instead, he hovers above a depiction of Jerusalem's Dome of the Rock, which is readily recognizable due to its golden dome and blue revetment tiles. Although ascension tales describe the Prophet's ascent to the skies from this domed structure housing his footprint, the great majority of Islamic *mi'raj* paintings depict Muhammad ascending above Mecca—not Jerusalem.[67]

The question thus arises: if there did not exist a strong tradition of representing the Dome of the Rock in Persian ascension images, why did the Iranian painter Hamidi make such an overt—and innovative—pictorial alteration during the late 1990s? Although one could point to a possible desire to maintain fidelity to textual sources or a wish to exalt Jerusalem as a pilgrimage site and eschatological city,[68] a number of religiopolitical discourses prevalent in postrevolutionary Iran suggest other reasons for his inclusion of the Dome of the Rock—chief among them rhetoric about "freeing" the third-holiest city in Islamdom.

After the Iranian revolution, Iranian leaders such as Ayatollah Ruhollah Khomeini (1979–89 CE) and President Mahmud Ahmadinejad (2005–13 CE) imagined the Islamic Republic of Iran as the prime liberator of oppressed Muslim communities worldwide, including Palestinians living in Jerusalem. During the Iran-Iraq War (1980–88 CE) a prominent Iranian slogan exclaimed, "the road to Jerusalem goes through Karbala," asserting that an Iranian offensive in Iraq served as a prelude to delivering Jerusalem from imperial occupation in the form of international Zionism. For these reasons, during the 1980s and 1990s countless paintings, posters, murals, maquettes, stamps, paper money, and other Iranian visual representations depicted the Dome of the Rock as the beating heart of the international *umma*, the final target of Iranian military engagement, and the architectural embodiment of Palestinian victimhood and martyrdom.[69] Thus, within Hamidi's ascension painting, Muhammad's *mi'raj* serves to visually reclaim the Dome of the Rock within an overarching Shi'i soteriological narrative.

During the first decade of the twenty-first century, Iranian anti-Israel sentiments became increasingly bellicose, and Ahmadinejad became well known for his inflammatory remarks about the "Zionist regime." In one infamous 2005 speech, he declared that the "regime occupying Jerusalem must vanish from the page of time," a statement that often was mistranslated in English-language media as equivalent to "Israel must be wiped off the map."[70] Possibly deliberate mistranslations notwithstanding, this type of statement proved central to Ahmadinejad's political rhetoric on Palestinian self-determination. However, to many Iranians the president's rather obsessive focus on the Palestinian issue served as a tactic for diverting attention from severe domestic problems, including electoral disputes and waves of political dissent that were violently repressed.

Hamidi's *mi'raj* painting, which was created between the Iran-Iraq War and the rise of Ahmadinejad, thus bears witness to shifting Iranian discourses about Jerusalem as well as the changing manner in which images function as "codes by which our interpretive attention makes them meaningful."[71] The many coded meanings of the Dome of the Rock within contemporary Iranian depictions of Muhammad's *mi'raj* invite an array of exegetical explanations, including sectarian readings and political narratives concerned with global Muslim deliverance and redemption.

These many veristic Iranian images, made from the Qajar period onward, depict Muhammad as an adult male with visible facial features, stressing the Prophet's physical maturity and integrality. His representation is often bracketed by a number of textual and visual devices that generate larger meanings and discourses. For instance, the Qajar period witnessed the emergence of pictorial icons that acted as "imperial effigies"[72] within elite practices of pious meditation. Moreover, although some representations continued older Persian iconographic traditions, modern Iranian artists made creative use of European visual sources, including Figuier's irenic depiction of the Prophet, which was adopted and adapted in myriad ways. The most notable developments surrounding these new or translocated images include the addition of Islamic motifs, such as the Qur'an and prophetic geography, as well as the insertion of elements particularly central to the Shi'i cause, including the imams, *ahl al-bayt*, 'Ali as a leonine angel, Shi'i architectural structures, and other sites of Iranian contemporary political yearning, such as the Dome of the Rock in Jerusalem. In the end, these many modern Iranian images of Muhammad, made from the nineteenth century to today, depict the Prophet as the central object of his devotees' spiritual affection, as the radiant centerpiece of the imamate, and as the salvific leader in all matters pertaining to both faith and state.

A MUHAMMADAN REALITY: VISUAL ABSTRACTIONS AND METAPHORS

While veristic images have thrived in Iran since the thirteenth century, depictions of the Prophet that transcend naturalistic depiction have proven most popular within global Islamic cultural settings from the eighteenth century to today. In many Arab, Persian, Turkish, Indian, Southeast Asian, and even American paintings, posters, calligraphic compositions, and other visual materials, Muhammad's physical image undergoes a visual process of partial or complete disembodiment. Additionally, a range of pictorial attributes and emblems are used to allude to his spiritual presence.

The Prophet's corporeality is rendered somewhat invisible or immaterial through the pictorial devices of the facial veil and aureole, the latter at times so overpowering that it subsumes the entirety of his physical presence, which in turn becomes a flaming nimbus. Beyond the reduction or camouflaging of Muhammad's corporeal likeness, a number of other iconographic symbols serve as parts that summon the whole. Engaging in the open-ended semantic processes of allegory, synecdoche, and metonymy, a number of images evoke the Prophet through calligrams and verbal icons as well as by his relics and his animal stand-in, Buraq. Taken altogether, these diverse pictorial strategies coalesce into what might be best called implicative images that render Muhammad physically absent yet spiritually present—that is, as an all-pervasive mythic reality.

The notion that Muhammad exists as a greater "truth" (*haqiqa*) is found in various Islamic cultures, especially Sufistic ones. Known as the "Muhammadan truth" (*al-haqiqa al-muhammadiyya*), this concept postulates that the Prophet's corporeal form comprises only one facet of his cosmic selfhood. Writers from medieval times to today posit that Muhammad was covered by a human form, under which was hidden his inner, eternal being, known as *al-haqiqa al-muhammadiyya*.[73] This blessed effusion is believed to couple the Prophet's earthly being with divine flux, thereby generating a "complete man" (*al-insan al-kamil*), the archetype of the universe and humanity.[74] How this inner essence—or "Muhammadan reality"—should be conceptualized remained a fluid notion in the domains of imagistic thought and pictorial production. Bypassing the limitations of notional literalism and physical representation, such mystical conceptions of the prophetic spirit and body generated images of a brilliant, ethereal, and even cosmic Muhammad. These types of allegorical representations also intersected with, and not infrequently were a direct creative outcome of, artists' drives to avoid strictly mimetic depiction, itself a pictorial practice that (today perhaps more than ever) is avoided in Muslim cultural spheres.

Within Iran, various images of Muhammad thrived side by side during the modern period, revealing the extent to which prophetic portraiture has tended to fluctuate, even in the same place and time. During the Qajar period, for example, a number of freestanding icons, book illustrations, paintings (on shrine walls or large canvases), and prints depicted Muhammad with his facial features visible or veiled.[75] Not mutually exclusive, these depictive forms suggest a moving mosaic—rather than a strict, unchanging rule—that determined which pictorial practices were considered proper, and which taboo. In overtly pro-Shiʿi texts and icons, a veiled Muhammad is at times accompanied by the veiled figures of ʿAli, Hasan, and Husayn. Such is the case for printed copies of Bazil's (d. 1712 CE) *Hamla-yi Haydari* (Lion's Attack), a Persian versified account of the life, battles, and miracles of Imam ʿAli, nicknamed as the "lion" (*haydar*) of God. Much like Ibn Husam's (d. 1470 CE) equally pro-ʿAlid *Khavarannama* (Book of Eastern Exploits),[76] the *Hamla-yi Haydari* was produced as an illustrated manuscript and printed book in Persian and Indian lands especially during the eighteenth and nineteenth centuries.

While coeval Indian copies reduce Muhammad to a flaming nimbus (fig. 6.11), Persian printed books tend to depict the Prophet and his family as fleshed but veiled, as can be seen in a colored illustration of the Mubahala included in a copy of Bazil's text printed in Iran in 1904 CE (fig. 6.9).[77] In Shiʿi spheres, the presence of Muhammad's family during his disputation with the Christians of Najran—an episode discussed in detail in chapter 4—provides ultimate proof of the superiority of Islam as well as ʿAli's and his descendants' right to rule. Whereas Ilkhanid and Safavid painters depicted all of the protagonists unveiled (figs. 4.5–4.6), Qajar artists included facial coverings for not only the Prophet but also his son-in-law (who here kneels while holding his bifurcated sword, Dhu'l-Fiqar) and two young grandsons (who sit on Muhammad's lap). Combined with the solar disk and flaming aureoles, the facial veils serve to differentiate these four radiant and mysterious protagonists from their adversaries, who sport Christian headgear and whose facial features remain visible to onlookers.

　　THE PRAISEWORTHY ONE

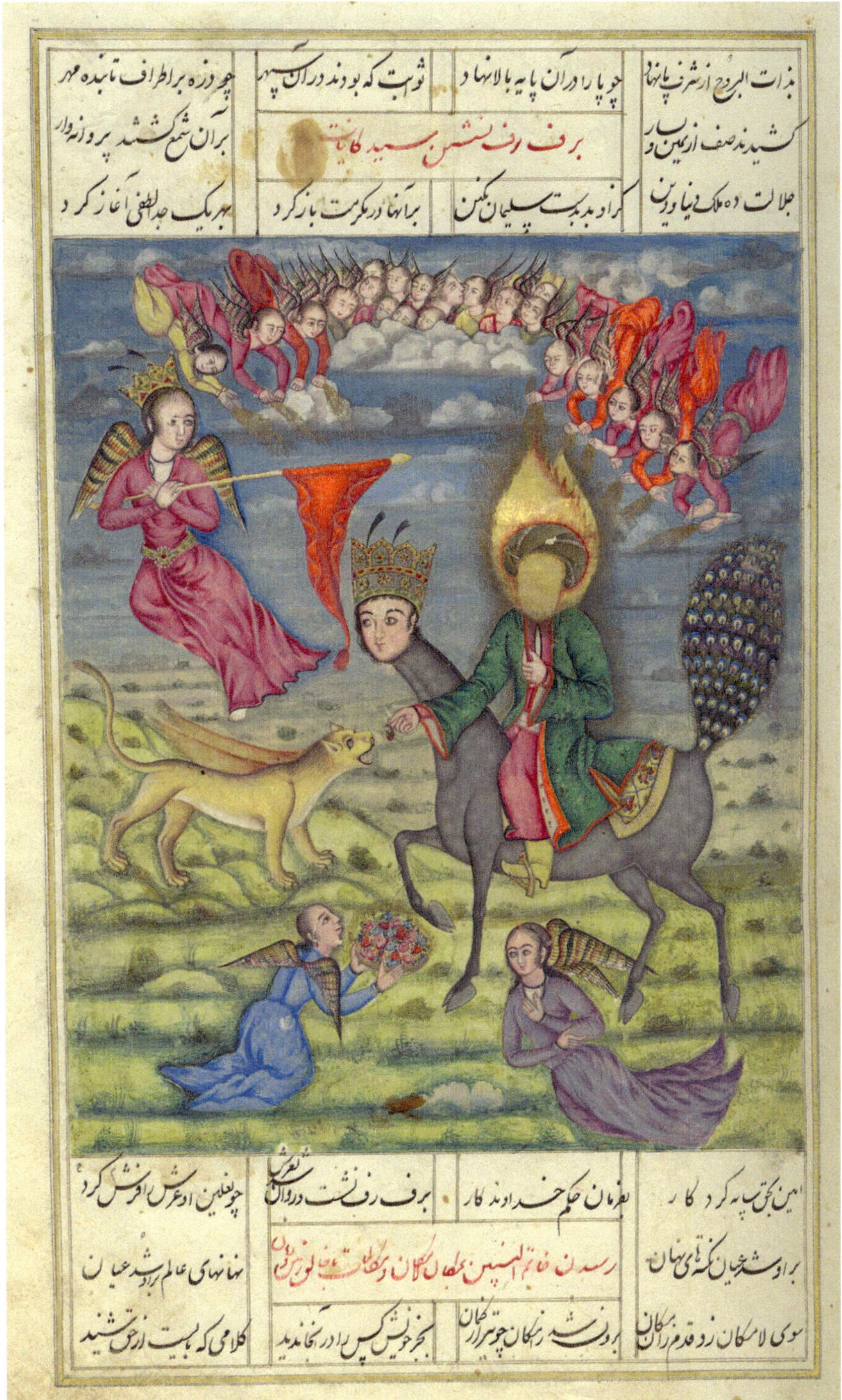

6.10. The Prophet Muhammad riding Buraq, Bazil, *Hamla-yi Haydari* (Lion's Attack), probably Kirman, Iran, 1248 AH/1833–34 CE. Anne S. K. Brown Military Collection, Brown University Library, Providence, RI, manuscript unnumbered.

In this and other cases, the veil cannot be considered a restriction on representing human figures (since they indeed are depicted in the composition) or the result of a ban on images of Muhammad (as the veil is also applied to his family members). Instead, the veil must be understood as a visual metaphor for the passing down of divine light—from God to Muhammad and onward to his male progeny, in accordance with a Shi'i religious worldview. This sacred *nur* is not to be shared by Christian antagonists, and it cannot be confronted directly by the viewer, lest it overwhelm his or her eyesight.

Persian poets before Bazil developed the metaphorical potential of the veil (*hijab* or *parda*) as a necessary boundary or chasm between a devotee and his beloved. For example, in his *Makhzan al-Asrar* (Treasury of Secrets), the poet Nizami (d. 1209 CE) lauds Muhammad: "Be the secret behind the curtain of mystery. We all are asleep, but you awake."[78] In addition, in his *Yusuf va Zulaykha* (Joseph and Potiphar's Wife), the great Persian poet Jami (d. 1492 CE) states that, "Such is the beauty whose splendor is everywhere and because of which the loved ones of the world are veiled from view. Wherever you see a veil, that is what is being concealed."[79] In these revealing lines, both Nizami and Jami observe that whenever we see a veil we should realize that it conceals sublime beauty and love, which cannot be grasped by the human eye and which remain unfathomable to the human intellect. The veil therefore does not merely hide or handicap; to the contrary, it mirrors the viewer's own optical and cognitive limitations.

In still other cases, Muhammad's facial veil disintegrates even further into a radiant source, as is the case in an illustrated copy of Bazil's *Lion's Attack* completed in 1833–34 CE (fig. 6.10). This manuscript was commissioned by the Qajar prince Ibrahim Khan, who served as Fath 'Ali Shah's governor in the eastern Iranian city of Kirman, where he actively sponsored the city's architecture.[80] A rare example of book arts attributable to his patronage, this princely provincial copy of Bazil's epic text includes a number of paintings depicting 'Ali's battles, in which the imam's facial features are consistently covered by a white facial veil that looks like fabric pleated around the protagonist's turban. Muhammad, for his part, is differentiated from 'Ali (and all other depicted characters) by a flaming golden facial veil, which fans out and merges with a double halo poured onto the Prophet's head by angels flying above. Following the by-then traditional Shi'i *mi'raj* pictorial trend, Muhammad is shown encountering the leonine 'Ali, to whom he offers his signet ring, as he rides the peacock-tailed Buraq.

In the painting's accompanying verses, Bazil describes Muhammad as dismounting Buraq to ride *rafraf* (a flying carpet of sorts) onward to the domain of illocality (*la-makan*), where his sandals will touch the throne of God. The poet also uses a range of poetic metaphors to describe the Prophet, including sun (*mihr*) and torch (*sham'*). The Persian word *mihr* carries many other meanings, among them love, friendship, and affection. Moreover, in Persian lands, one of the Prophet's honorific epithets is *mihr-i shari'at*, or "sun of law,"[81] while Arab, Turkish, and other Muslim poets also refer to Muhammad as the "sun of reality" and the "sun of virtue."[82] Like writers waxing poetic, the Qajar painter appears to prefer a solar metaphor insomuch as he, too, wishes to describe the Prophet as emanating divine light, grace, and justice as well as an ontological mystery that remains unknown, imperceptible, and thus invisible to the mortal gaze.

Like the artist's creative decision to set the facial veil alight, Muhammad's double halo is rather unusual. On the one hand, the halo's

 THE PRAISEWORTHY ONE

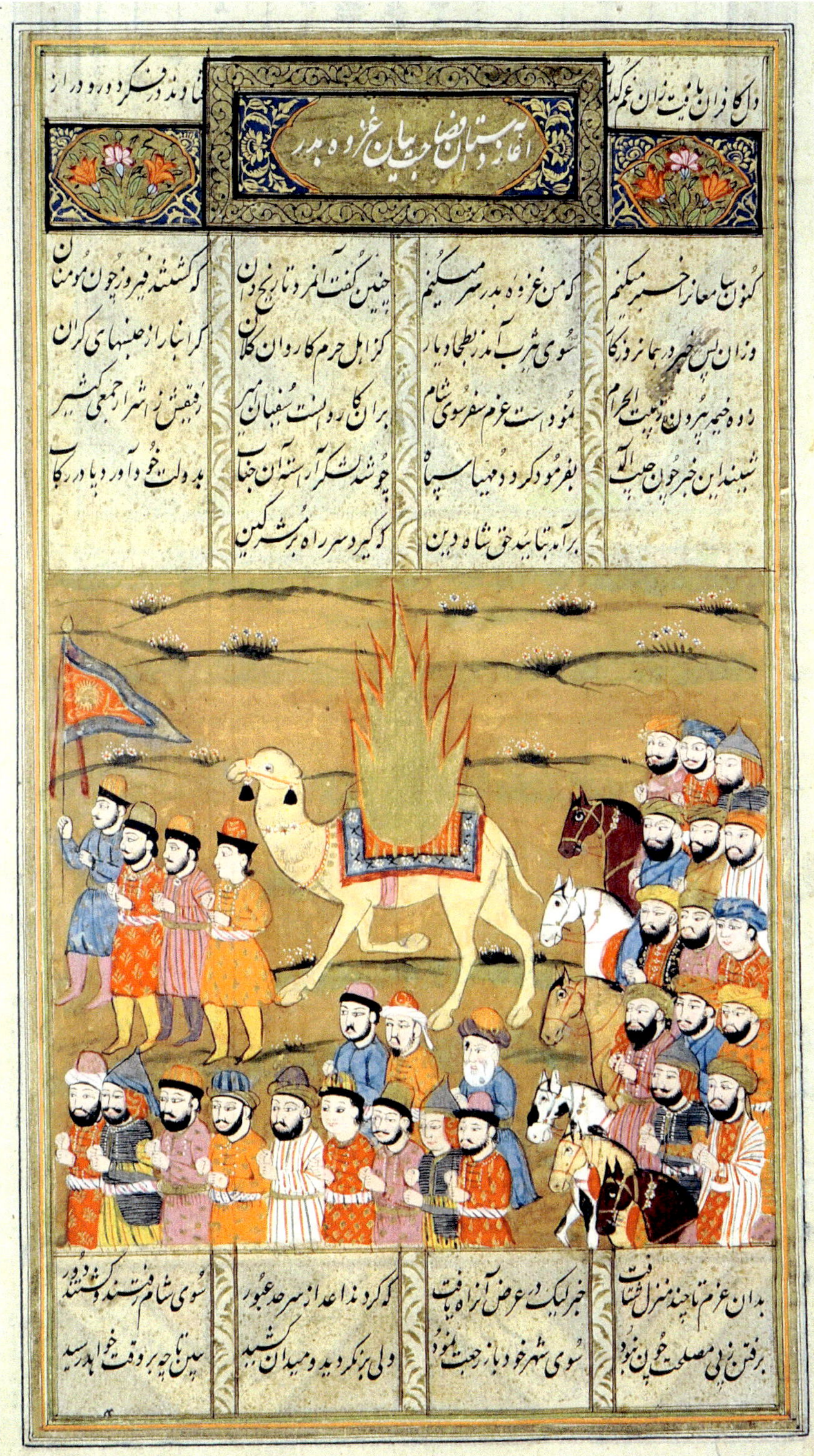

6.11. The Prophet Muhammad, represented as a flaming nimbus, rides a camel en route to the battle of Badr, Bazil, *Hamla-yi Haydari* (Lion's Attack), Kashmir, 1223 AH/1808 CE. Bibliothèque nationale de France, Paris, Suppl. Persan 1030, folio 71r.

duplication may point to the qur'anic expression "light upon light" (24:35: *nur 'ala nur*). However, within a sectarian context, the halo's doubling seems to point to Muhammad and 'Ali as sharing the same radiant soul, a spiritual copresence found in earlier Safavid paintings in which the veiled heroes are shown inhabiting the same physical body (fig. 4.10). Muhammad thus comes to encompass the "two lights" (*nurayn*) as he incorporates both himself and 'Ali—that is, prophecy (*nubuwwa*) and vicegerency (*walaya*)—within an overarching Shi'i rhetorical and visual framework of meaning.[83] In this intriguing Qajar painting made in Iran's eastern provinces, Muhammad is therefore depicted as doubly lit, his face and head acting as the repository and conjunction of divine mystery, radiance, and authority.

This Qajar Iranian painting is located on an iconographic spectrum somewhere between the white facial veil and the flaming halo, the latter overtaking the former in geographical areas closer to the Indus Valley. Moving eastward, the Prophet undergoes a further process of disembodiment, especially in nineteenth-century manuscript paintings made in Kashmir, which either fully omit his physical presence or represent a flaming nimbus in his physical stead.[84]

A number of manuscripts of Bazil's *Lion's Attack*, which was quite popular on the Indian subcontinent, include cycles of paintings depicting Muhammad's and 'Ali's lives and deeds. In one Kashmiri illustrated copy made in 1808 CE, the Prophet is consistently shown as a flaming nimbus, as can be seen in a painting that depicts his departure for the battle of Badr (fig. 6.11). Riding a camel en route to the military confrontation, Muhammad is accompanied by soldiers on foot and on horseback. His companions and soldiers are fully fleshed: their bodies are adorned with robes, their hands make fists or hold reins, and their facial features and beards are clearly discernible. On the other hand, the Prophet's presence is merely insinuated by the flaming nimbus "seated" on the quadruped in the center of the composition. The aureole's red outline further pushes the nimbus to the foreground while distinguishing it from the background's hilly landscape.

Centrally placed and larger in scale than the composition's other elements, the flaming aureole hints at an ontological hierarchy of being for the Prophet, in which he is shown as unshackled from the laws of nature. Moreover, while this abstracting device enables the artist to sidestep figural imagery (here, solely in the case of Muhammad), it also conveys a number of important concepts that relate to the prophetic corpus, itself considered superior in its celestial origins and inner constitution. As discussed previously, in various Islamic texts and devotional practices, Muhammad was analogized to divine light, inspiring the notion of the *nur Muhammad*. This metaphorical process seeks to align the Prophet with God, the "effuser of lights" (*qa'id al-anwar*) and the "light of reality" (*nur al-haqiqa*)[85] as well as "the one who illuminates the hearts of believers with guidance."[86] In addition to creating a symbolic parallel to God through light similes, a number of philosophers, theologians, and mystical writers developed the notion that God possesses a "body" (*jism*) but not a "form" (*sura*) and argued that God's "body" consists in a beacon of light.[87] In these textual elaborations, God is portrayed as a perceptible yet incorporeal entity delivering enlightenment and revelation, much like the Prophet Muhammad.

Poets of the Persianate tradition from the medieval period onward likewise offer a picture of God as limitless light, freed from the bonds of accident and matter. For example, in his *Makhzan al-Asrar* (Treasury of Secrets), Nizami describes Muhammad's encounter with God on the night of his ascension:

> He saw the sign of that Light (*ayat nuri*) that knows no decline,
> With eyes which were beyond imagination (*khiyal*)
> The vision of Him is free from accident and matter (*bi-ard va jawhar*)
> Because He is beyond accident and matter.[88]

In these stanzas, Nizami stresses that human optical perception and imaginative faculty cannot grasp God, who is limitless in matter and dimension. Similarly, in his *Yusuf va Zulaykha* (Joseph and Potiphar's Wife), Jami declares that God is "free of the bonds of appearances,"[89] and that God's essence "is exempt of quality, quantity, and all spatial attributes. Intellect stands baffled before the essence of God: it is quite inept to pursue Him along that path."[90] This conjunction of antipodal elements, positing mass against form and visibility against invisibility, is resolved by means of a rhetorical strategy that depicts God's epiphanic form (*mazhar*) as a cosmic aggregation of sacred luminescence.

This same metaphor of "illuminated effusion" holds true for the Prophet within modern Persianate painterly arts. In the case of figure 6.11, the nineteenth-century Kashmiri artist created a theophanic equivalent within his composition by using the language of form and color in lieu of figural representation. In this and other cases, the blazing nimbus characterizes Muhammad's proximity to the divine by using the "body-without-form" modality—that is, a formula that depicts an entity that is visible and material yet freed from the limitations of vision, space, and physicality. This said, the nimbus's red outline may in turn point to the blood of humanity or the blood clot (*'alaq*) that engenders all of creation (Qur'an 96). As a consequence, the painting's artist may be articulating, through both form and color, Muhammad's evolving nature as it inches closer to a formless God and further away from mimetic literalism. The figurative mode here cedes to a more abstract coalescence of light and blood, divinity and humanity.

This pictorial process of distancing the prophetic corpus from its fleshed form has pervaded the greater Muslim world during the modern period. Beyond Persianate spheres, techniques of visual abstraction developed within Ottoman lands as well. Late Ottoman and contemporary Turkish artists, as well as artists inspired by Ottoman creative practices, often show a distinct preference for the *hilye* as a means of depicting Muhammad through a descriptive text placed within circular and rectangular registers, a devotional calligraphic tradition discussed at length in chapter 5. A number of illustrated manuscripts and printed books continued Ottoman book art traditions, although their figural representations underwent a clear and decisive process of condensation that, much like the *hilye* tradition, placed inscribed text within geometric form to symbolically evoke the Prophet's complete being. Although this mode of abstraction underscores the modern tendency to avoid figural imagery, it also highlights the ways in which artists and viewers activated their imaginative faculties in order to picture a more metaphorical Muhammad, believed to exist before, above, and beyond his physical materialization on earth.

In Ottoman lands, the illustrated multivolume copy of al-Darir's *Biography of the Prophet*, made in 1594–95 CE, offers the most important pictorial cycle of the Prophet, in which he is depicted as a corporeal figure whose face is covered by a white facial veil (figs. 5.1–5.2). The next most important codex-based repository of images of Muhammad is the illustrated manuscripts and printed books of the *Muhammediyye* (Muhammad Poem) written by the Ottoman Sufi practitioner and poet Mehmed Yazıcıoğlu (d. 1451 CE). The *Muhammad Poem* is a Turkish verse biography of the Prophet that includes approximately nine thousand verses written in the form of rhyming couplets.[91] Highly popular among a broad Ottoman readership as well as recited in various ritualistic, cultic, and political contexts,[92] its text covers the beginning of the world, the biography of the Prophet, judgment day, and heaven and hell. It thus effectively combines the fields of cosmology, prophetology, and eschatology.

From the sixteenth century onward, many manuscript and printed copies of the *Muhammad Poem* featured a range of illustrations, including elaborate depictions of the Prophet's banner of mercy (*liwa' al-hamd*). Nineteenth-century examples draw on a rich repertoire of paintings, particularly the pictorial program of al-Darir's *Biography of the Prophet*. Unlike manuscripts of the latter text, copies of Yazıcıoğlu's *Muhammad Poem* never include depictions of a physical Prophet wearing a facial veil—or, for that matter, any human figure whatsoever. Instead, they illustrate Muhammad's *hilye*, his relics and accoutrements, and the prophetic cities Mecca and Medina,[93] a synecdochal method of expression typical of late Ottoman religious arts.

Two illustrated manuscripts of Yazıcıoğlu's *Muhammad Poem*, made in 1822 and 1844 CE, stand out for having been made by hand (rather than print, which was widespread at this time) and for including more than fifty images each. They also showcase one of the strategies developed by late Ottoman artists who depicted the life and deeds of the Prophet while cautiously avoiding figural representation. Like many coeval illustrated printed copies, the volume made in 1822 CE depicts a number of biographical episodes, among them Muhammad's military campaigns. In these dynamic yet minimalistic compositions, figural representations are entirely absent, despite the fact that the textual narrative describes the heroic feats of the human protagonists of the early Muslim period.

In these manuscripts of the *Muhammad Poem*, viewers instead are confronted with gold circles, flags, bows, and arrows, as can be seen in the depiction of the battle of Uhud (fig. 6.12).[94] Each gold circle is marked with an inscription identifying one of Muhammad's companions (*ashab*). On the left, Abu Bakr, 'Umar, and 'Ali are identified by inscriptions as they fight other circles, which are identified as the opposing Quraysh. 'Ali's name is placed within a circle surmounted by the gilt and bifurcated Dhu'l-Fiqar, a special object attribute that places him apart from the melee. Finally, on the right, the large red flag is identified as the noble standard (*sancak*) of the Prophet; bows and arrows stand in for the Muslim archers who, although initially successful in their advances, disobeyed Muhammad's orders, left their posts, and were attacked by the enemy, causing the Muslim forces a major setback at this critical moment of the early Muslim-Meccan wars.[95]

While the inscriptions in almost all of the circles are well preserved and hence decipherable, one of the roundels adjacent to the red standard has heavily abraded paint. Despite the damage, the red inscription remains legible and reads: "The Messenger of God" (*rasul Allah*). The red pigment of Muhammad's honorific epithet has been smudged into the gilt background of the roundel. It is likely that the artist used gold paint inside the circle to differentiate Muhammad from his nonluminous companions and enemies. While the radiance of the pigment probably points to his preexistential light, the gold circle offers a geometric parallel to the flaming nimbus used in depictions of the Prophet within Kashmiri illustrated manuscripts produced at the same time (as in fig. 6.11).

This golden prophetic roundel shows damage that cannot be interpreted as the result of a viewer's urge to expunge figural imagery, which is entirely absent in the image and throughout the manuscript's visual program. Instead, this representation of a radiant Muhammadan circle appears to show the effects of devotional kissing, touching, and rubbing—a tactile tradition of encounter that is well attested to in Ottoman relics visitation, how-to manuals describing the process of unleashing the *baraka* of the Prophet's relics and seals in prayer books, and other images and designs that show patterns of devotional wear.[96] The viewer's determination to come into contact with Muhammad and to activate his prophetic blessings is therefore not restricted to iconic and synecdochal representations. Rather, it is also found in narrative depictions, like that of the battle of Uhud, that are populated by abstract circles in lieu of figural imagery.

As noted by Tobias Heinzelmann, late Ottoman artists who illustrated the *Muhammad Poem* tended to adopt both older and contemporary *hilye* traditions, in which the Prophet's physical and moral description is written within a roundel.[97] To a certain degree, the inscribed circles in the depiction of the battle of Uhud indeed recall the *hilye* format, with Muhammad's honorific epithet placed in a central omphalos (*göbek*) while the names of his companions, especially the four rightly guided caliphs, show similarities to painted *hilye*s in Ottoman illustrated prayer books and calligraphed panels placed in Ottoman mosques. They also recall schematic depictions of military formations as included in premodern illustrated war tactic (*furusiyya*) manuscripts.[98]

On the one hand, the Muhammadan circle thus functions as a metaphorical omphalos: that is, as a womblike locus of generation. This cosmic circle is self-enclosed and bears no endpoint; like the Prophet, it is a complete and total entity, with no discernible beginning or end. It also evokes the outline of seal impressions, among them the seal of prophecy that served as physical evidence of Muhammad's special status as God's envoy to humankind. As a generative omphalos, microcosmos, and imprimatur of apostleship, the Muhammadan circle thus creates a link to the realm of the divine through a symbolism that is deliberately distant from mimetic representation, which is studiously avoided in all pictorial programs of Ottoman manuscripts and printed books of the *Muhammad Poem*.

Somewhat like later Brechtian theatrical techniques, this estrangement or alienation effect aims to defamiliarize viewers and therefore make them more critically and actively aware of the viewing process. Within the visual arts, this procedure of making something other, strange, or foreign causes transformation not only within the field of iconography but also in the realm of consciousness, where the human imagination is invited to reach for a cosmic form of cogitation while the physical body vanishes from view.[99] Comprising the flaming nimbus, golden roundel, and other visual stratagems, techniques of abstraction have altered the arc of Islamic pictorial traditions while influencing viewers' optical-cognitive encounters with Muhammad. Over and again, these visual strategies accentuate the Prophet's sublime, unseen otherness in both being and beauty.

Stretching to the present day, the Muhammadan circle has made a comeback in contemporary Islamic artistic settings through creative revivals of the Ottoman *hilye* tradition. During the last decade, these aniconic icons have become pervasive in Turkey, where exhibitions of the "blessed hilye" (*hilye-i şerif*) and other objects representing "love of the Prophet" (*aşk-ı nebi*) have been hosted in Hagia Sophia, the Topkapı Palace Museum, and many other venues in Istanbul and throughout the country.[100] These public displays of Prophet-centered piety reveal that, within Turkey, Islamic religious arts have been folded within the ideological apparatus of the Sunni-Islamist Justice and Development Party (AKP) while also benefiting from the financial backing of the Ministry of Religious Affairs. In addition to their instrumentalization in the public sphere, *hilye*s continue to be produced for and used by individual Turkish patrons, some of whom tend toward Sufism and thus prefer more private and less politicized forms of spiritual expression.

Moreover, the art of the *hilye* has spread throughout the world, particularly to England and the United States. In their new geocultural environments, verbal icons of Muhammad tend to be made by master calligraphers for private contemplation by a diverse clientele, both Muslim and non-Muslim, who wish to own one of Islam's most distinct artistic forms. Contemporary revivals of the *hilye* tradition highlight the extent to which calligraphers inventively engage with and update Islamic visual devotions to the Prophet while maintaining the contours of cultural continuity within a highly diverse global system of art production.[101]

One such practitioner is Mohamed Zakariya (b. 1942 CE), an American Muslim scholar of Islamic book arts and Arabic-script calligrapher who resides in the Washington, DC, area. Zakariya trained in Istanbul under the master calligrapher Hasan Çelebi, who granted him his diploma (*icazet*) in 1988 CE. Since then, Zakariya has produced many calligraphies, ranging from Eid stamps for the US Postal Service to large-scale *hilye*s commissioned by international patrons. He also has written the most accessible English-language scholarly article on the *hilye*, outlining its symbolic meanings, literary features, formal structure, and history within Islamic calligraphic arts.[102]

Over the years, Zakariya has followed Ottoman *hilye* traditions in developing his own calligraphic oeuvre. For example, a large, richly

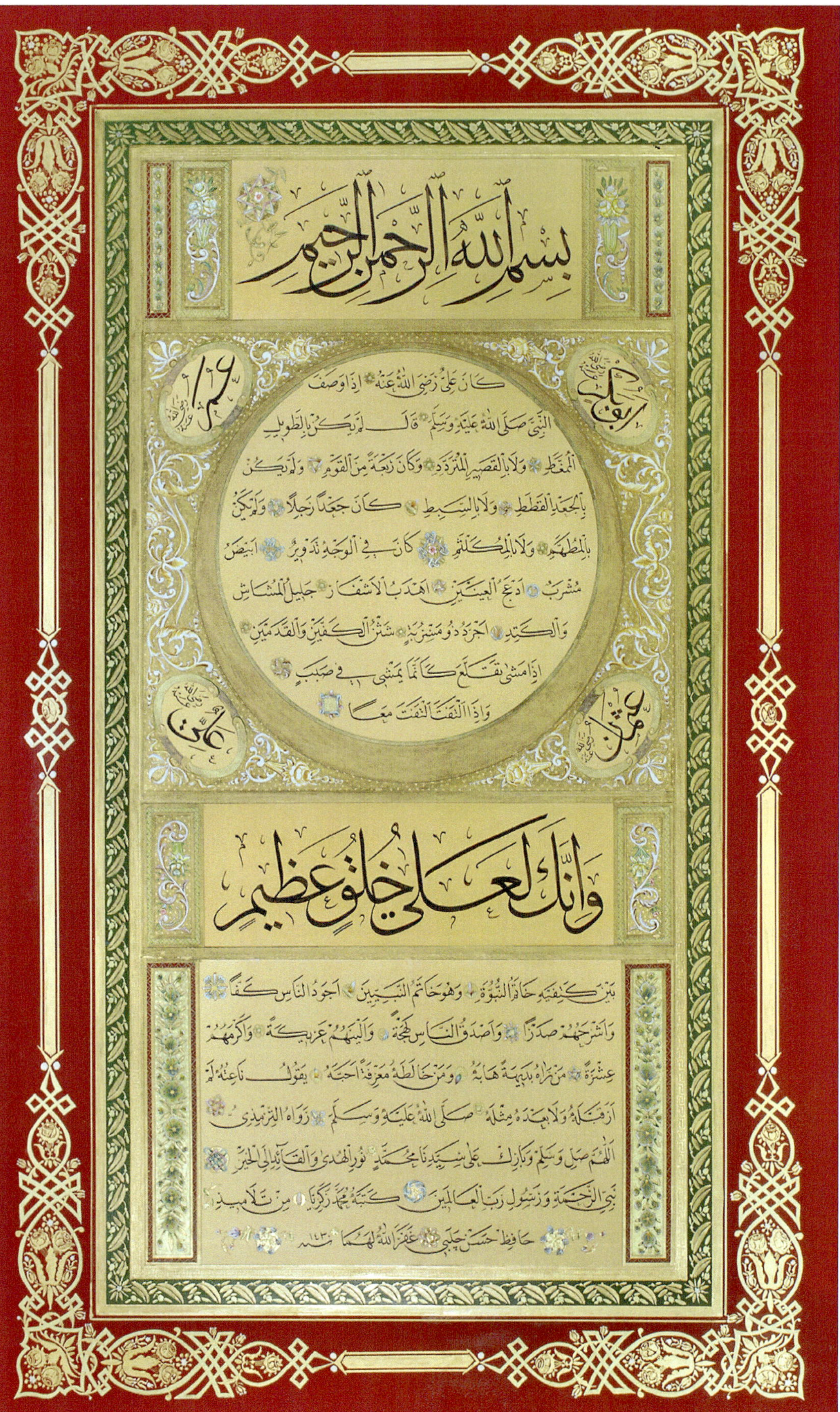

بسم الله الرحمن الرحيم

كان علي رضي الله عنه اذا وصف النبي صلى الله عليه وسلم قال لم يكن بالطويل الممغط ولا بالقصير المتردد وكان ربعة من القوم ولم يكن بالجعد القطط ولا بالسبط كان جعدا رجلا ولم يكن بالمطهم ولا بالمكلثم كان في الوجه تدوير ابيض مشرب ادعج العينين اهدب الاشفار جليل المشاش والكتد اجرد ذو مسربة شثن الكفين والقدمين اذا مشى تقلع كانما يمشي في صبب واذا التفت التفت معا

وإنك لعلى خلق عظيم

بين كتفيه خاتم النبوة وهو خاتم النبيين اجود الناس كفا واشرحهم صدرا واصدق الناس لهجة والينهم عريكة واكرمهم عشرة من رآه بديهة هابه ومن خالطه معرفة احبه يقول ناعته لم ار قبله ولا بعده مثله صلى الله عليه وسلم رواه الترمذي اللهم صل وسلم وبارك على سيدنا محمد نور الهدى والقائد الى الخير نبي الرحمة ورسول رب العالمين كتبه محمد زكريا من تلاميذ حافظ حسن چلبي عفر الله لهما آمين

illuminated composition completed in 2010 CE (fig. 6.13)—entitled *Red Hilye* due to the deep tint of its burnished paper—is executed in three cursive scripts. Like most *hilye*s of past centuries, its texts praise the Prophet's physical and moral features by citing 'Ali's famous description and transcribing the qur'anic verse "And truly [Muhammad] you are of an exalted nature / of great moral character (*khulq*)."[103] In Islamic thought, the Arabic term *khulq*, which refers to the Prophet's character or nature, is often juxtaposed with his *khalq*, or beautiful physical form of creation, the latter dependent on and reflecting the former.[104] The *hilye*'s diagrammatic and textual representation of Muhammad's *khalq* circumvents Muhammad's corporeality in order to more faithfully convey his *khulq*. The *hilye*, as an exercise in depiction, thus should be considered a deliberate move from the literal to the abstract, from the physical to the spiritual.

At the bottom of *Red Hilye*, Zakariya includes a statement related by al-Tirmidhi. It asks for divine blessings on the Prophet with the vocative prayer: "O God, have mercy on our master Muhammad. Grant him peace and bless him. He is the light of guidance, and the foundation of what is good, the prophet of mercy, and the messenger of the Lord of the Worlds." The Prophet's epithets "light of guidance" (*nur al-huda*), "foundation of what is good" (*qa'id ila'l-khayr*), "prophet of mercy" (*nabi al-rahma*), and "messenger of the lord of the worlds" (*rasul rabb al-'alamin*) glorify above all Muhammad's radiance, righteousness, clemency, and apostleship. While the lavish gold illumination of *Red Hilye* might point to the Prophet's sacred brilliance through color symbolism, its monumental size aims to reflect Muhammad's larger-than-life qualities, both moral and physical.

In Zakariya's personal, artistic, and scholarly estimation, the *hilye* is a powerful art form because it "can refresh the heart and mind. It gives us, so many generations later, a kind of intimacy with the Prophet as though we had known him. To see him in this way is to allow him to show the way."[105] For Zakariya, the *hilye* is also about achieving an elevation of the soul. In this regard, he notes, "One of the great concepts of what we can call Islamic-style spirituality is that of nearness—one draws near to God, with the Prophet as guide on this life journey."[106] For practitioners and devotees, the *hilye* thus acts much like the Prophet: as a sober guide for reaching proximity with God.

Above all, Zakariya emphasizes that the *hilye* must not be considered a form of idolatry, as it is not worshipped per se. Rather, this type of art form must be understood as enabling believers to discover a "better position from which to appreciate the Prophet's message and learn more, thereby increasing one's love and appreciation for Muhammad—the beloved of God—beyond all bounds of time and place."[107] These lovingly written works, which Zakariya often creates to the accompaniment of European classical music, are thus thought to be spiritually moving in both their optical and oral dimensions.

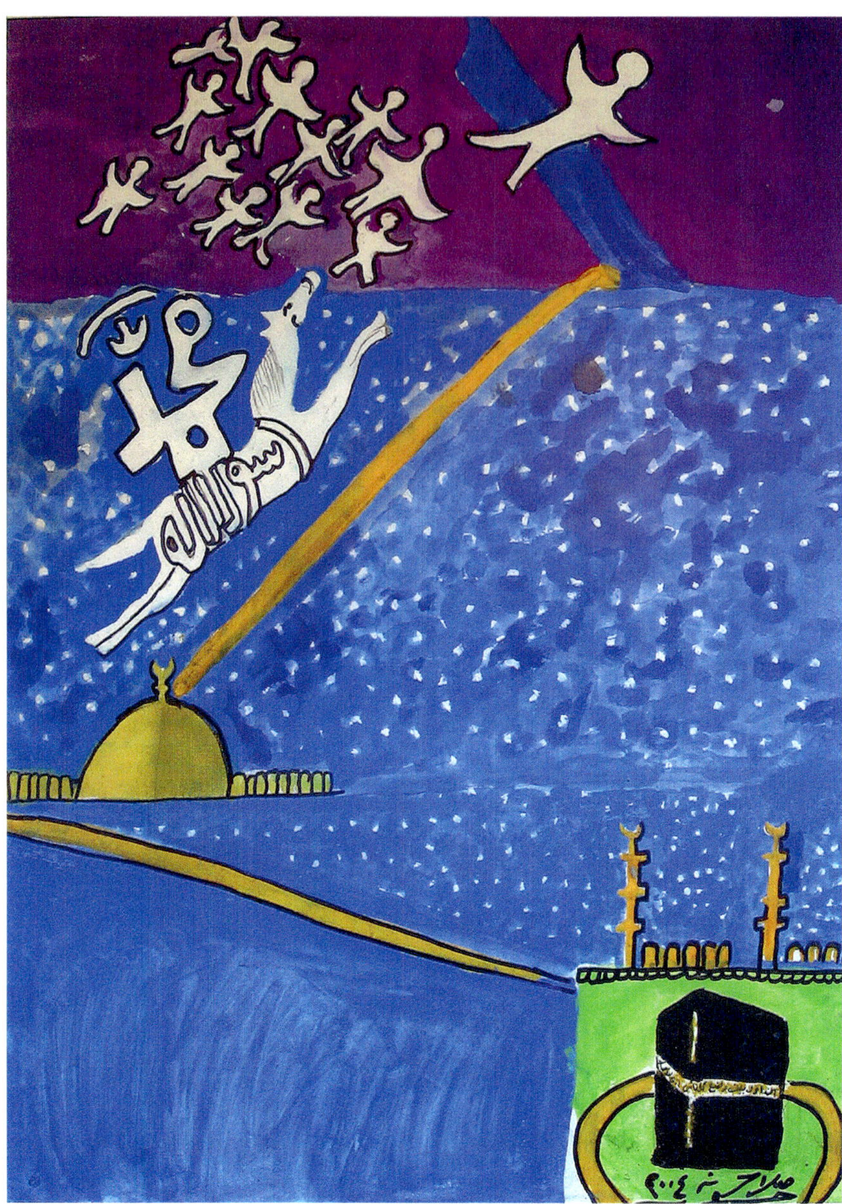

Muhammad, music, and the visual arts share transcendent qualities, especially when conceived of in allegorical terms. Thus, metaphorical representations of the Prophet encompass a wide array of abstractions. In addition to the veil, flaming nimbus, Muhammadan circle, and
*hilye*s, artists in the Islamic world often prefer to transcribe Muhammad's name as beautifully shaped calligraphy. A calligram—scripted
text molded into various evocative forms—often "at first sight appears to
be plain text, and yet is perceived and treated as an image."[108] This type
of word portrait at times has exited the realm of calligraphic arts to find
an important place within pictorial practices, even within premodern
Persian manuscript paintings.[109]

Calligrams of Muhammad's name also appear in contemporary
Islamic works of art, including a watercolor painting made in 2004 CE
by Salah Hassuna (fig. 6.14).[110] An Egyptian self-taught painter, Hassuna

(b. 1935 CE) first worked as a baker before he turned to painting in 1970 CE. Since then, this so-called Picasso of Egypt has gained fame for his naive style, which is reminiscent of Egyptian wall paintings, many of which commemorate the annual *hajj* to Mecca or praise Muhammad as the warrior of Islam.[111] In Hassuna's painting, the Prophet is depicted as a calligram, the letters of his name forming a corporeal mass that is "seated" on Buraq, here rendered as a leaping horse rather than a winged, human-headed mount. Its body does not comprise the parts or limbs of various animals but is instead inscribed with the words "Messenger of God" (*rasul Allah*). Taken together with the Muhammad calligram, the leaping protagonist and his mount come together to embody the second clause of the proclamation of faith (*shahada*): "Muhammad is the Messenger of God." The calligraphic mode serves two complementary purposes in Hassuna's composition: first, it strives to conjure the Prophet's presence in a nonphysical manner, and, second, it bears witness to his exalted status, itself one of the foundations of the Islamic faith.

Hassuna's painting of a pictographic Muhammad riding Buraq during the night of his ascension is not unique. Indeed, a number of posters printed in India and Pakistan make use of the same trope.[112] What is innovative about Hassuna's painting, however, is its emphasis on movement rather than stasis. The painter's use of dynamic gold lines is clearly meant to draw viewers' eyes from the Ka'ba in Mecca to the Dome of the Rock in Jerusalem, from where Muhammad, accompanied by angelic silhouettes, leaps through the skies and stars en route to God. These energetic lines tell a story, almost like the movement of laser pointers across a screen; in this way, they emulate pedagogical practices of show-and-tell and anticipate graphic novels and other forms of sequential art that employ words and images—as well as their conjunction, pictographs—as expressive media.[113] Hassuna's painting is thus pictographic and narrative, free of human representation and yet bursting with vitality.

The work's pedagogical underpinnings relate to an argument in favor of pictorial representation that has been articulated in Egypt since the early twentieth century.[114] Despite a widely held belief in the permissibility and even benefits of depicting human beings, the artist shunned the figural mode in his depiction of the Prophet and angels. This strategy of abstraction allowed Hassuna to focus on Muhammad's name, meaning "The Praiseworthy One," itself believed to exude luminescence and bestow blessings.

Like Hassuna, the modern thinker Muhammad Iqbal (d. 1938 CE) encourages his readers to write the Prophet's personal name: "Light the world, too long in darkness, with Muhammad's radiant name."[115] Moreover, stretching back centuries, medieval Persian poets such as Farid al-Din 'Attar (d. 1220 CE) lauded Muhammad's name, focusing their attention especially on its two constituent *m*'s (*mim*s). Like his Sufi colleagues in poetry, 'Attar considered the double *m* in Muhammad's name to be generative of both the here and the hereafter:

> Both worlds are from the two *m*'s of his name.
> The world, *'alam*, has only one *m* as provision,
> But Muhammad has got two *m*'s in his name.
> Definitely one world is from one of his *m*'s
> And the other world from the other half.[116]

This Muhammadan *mim* is at the center of Hassuna's painting, in which the first *m* composes the Prophet's head and the second his haunch. At a purely visual level, these two *mim*-graphemes insinuate a human body from head to midriff.

At the symbolic level, the letter *m* also encourages abstract thought by inviting viewers to draw on the centuries-long Islamic tradition of mystical speculation on the various meanings of the letter *m*—especially its interpretation as one of the disconnected letters (*al-huruf al-muqatta'a*) that open several chapters of the Qur'an. For example, the second *sura* of the Qur'an begins with the letters *alif-lam-mim*. Exegetes and letter mystics (*hurufis*) have interpreted this triad of letters as pointing to God's names and epithets, particularly *al-rahim* (The Merciful) and *Allah latif majid* (God, Gentle, Glorious).[117] In addition to its link to divine attributes, the letter *m* is also considered the most important letter of Muhammad's name. Consequently, as Annemarie Schimmel notes, "the mystics' speculations about it are almost endless."[118] For Sufis, the Muhammadan *mim* indicates the Prophet's heavenly name, Ahmad (The Most Praised), or the earthly—one could even say *mim*-ed—version of God's own name, Ahad (The Singular). The *m* in Muhammad's name therefore comes to represent the circle of mercy and creation, the most brilliant point of the compass, and the pole of existence, for which the Prophet acts as the ultimate embodiment of divine fiat.[119] It is this mystical Muhammadan *mim* that ascends to God in Hassuna's ascension painting.

Beyond visual abstractions and lettrist metaphors, the Prophet may altogether disappear from representation, the only hint of his presence indicated by Buraq. This mythical flying steed serves not only as the vehicle for Muhammad's heavenly ascent but also, more significantly, as the animal stand-in for his corporeal being.[120] Over the centuries, Muslim writers have highlighted Buraq's role in the Prophet's *mi'raj* as a means of proving that Muhammad's celestial ascension was not merely a dream vision or spiritual voyage: after all, flying steeds carry concrete bodies, not amorphous spirits.[121] This opinion is clearly put forth by Ibn Kathir (d. 1373 CE), who clarifies that Muhammad "was carried on Buraq, a shining white animal. This indicates a physical journey, because the soul does not need a means of transportation of this nature."[122]

Within pictorial images, Buraq's presence also serves as proof of Muhammad's prophecy and corporeality—that is, of his high status and bodily mass. Artists across the Islamic world have depicted the Prophet's

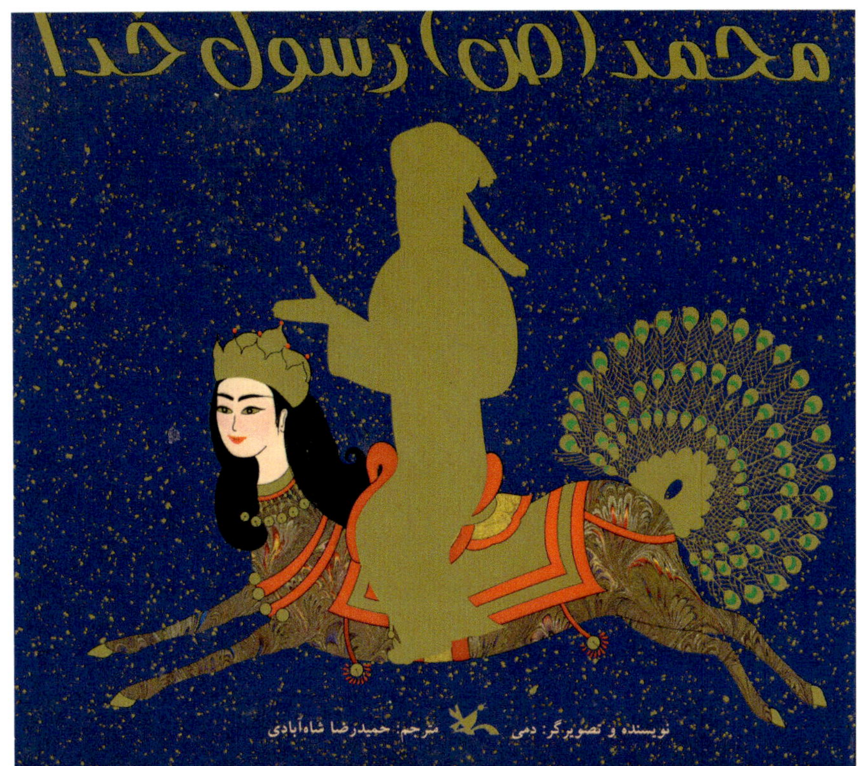

6.15. Front cover of the Persian translation of Demi's *Muhammad*, Institute for the Intellectual Development of Children and Young Adults, Tehran, Iran, 2009 CE.

steed from the early fourteenth century to the present day. In early illustrations, Buraq appears centaur-like, with a human torso and without wings (fig. 2.16); in more recent centuries, its features have become distinctly female, its head and neck ornamented with precious gems. Regardless of its pictorial variations, Buraq's primary raison d'être remains carrying (a corporeal) Muhammad through the heavens, and hence its depiction has remained closely intertwined with the history of prophetic iconography.

In eighteenth- and nineteenth-century Kashmiri manuscript painting, Muhammad's physical body underwent a process of abstraction and even excision—leaving Buraq to ascend with only a levitating nimbus of gold flames or in a solitary fashion, with no human protagonist or visual allegory in sight. More recently, twentieth-century Indo-Persian posters show Buraq as a winged, bejeweled female mount, alone or carrying a pink rose emblazoned with Muhammad's name, itself a motif that shares similarities with Hassuna's ascension painting. In these popular posters, Buraq is at times shown between the Ka'ba in Mecca and the Prophet's mosque in Medina, while at others it is also flanked by Imam Husayn's horse, Dhu'l-Janah.[123] In Shi'i settings, a heroic steed thus intimates Husayn's physical presence, as well.

Beyond Arab and Persianate lands, images of Muhammad and Buraq can be found from North America to Southeast Asia. A number of these images, and the products on which they appear, cater not only to adults but also to a younger demographic; they include graphic novels, coloring books, miscellaneous juvenilia, and even wooden sculptures. One contemporary children's book artist, whose nom de plume is Demi, turned her attention to the Prophet's life story in 2003 CE, when she collaborated with a New York City publisher to create a picture-book biography entitled *Muhammad*, which was subsequently translated into Persian and published in Iran six years later (fig. 6.15). The book's radiant cover depicts the Prophet as an outline filled with gold leaf while Buraq's body is filled with marbled paper. Throughout the interior illustrations, the outline of Muhammad's robe, turban, face, hands, and feet is discernible—though physical details remain entirely camouflaged by the addition of gilding. According to National Public Radio's Michele Norris, "Demi faced the challenge of writing and illustrating a biography about someone whose image she couldn't portray, out of respect for the religion's beliefs. She decided to draw his outline only, blending him to the background on some pages or using gold foil to represent his shape on others."[124]

The manner in which Demi faced the challenge of creating a contemporary illustrated children's book on Muhammad's life reveals a number of artistic strategies that respond to various ideas about what is and what is not considered permissible in Islam. Created before the Danish cartoon controversy of 2005–6 and the ISIS massacre of cartoonists at the Paris offices of *Charlie Hebdo* in 2015, Demi's *Muhammad* of 2003 might not have seen the light of day had it been pitched to a publisher in more recent years. After all, immediately before the publication of Jytte Klausen's 2009 book *The Cartoons That Shook the World*, Yale University Press removed historical Islamic images of the Prophet in response to vaguely articulated domestic security and foreign policy risks.[125] Klausen was quick to note that she received no threats, stating, "When you suppress something like the illustrations in my book . . . you are taking something away from readers. You are denying access to important information and by denying that access, you shut down dialogue."[126] She also criticized Yale University Press for catering to the "most extreme sections of Islamist movements," thus reinforcing such groups in their positions and militancy.

In 2003, Demi did not face the same fears and anxieties around images of the Prophet that caused the excision of images from Klausen's work and that have so afflicted our postcartoon era. Instead, the award-winning children's-book artist, who is famous for her many illustrated biographies of saints and heroes belonging to the world's religions and civilizations, practiced her craft with relative artistic freedom. She did so, however, "out of respect for the religion's beliefs," which are widely understood as shunning figural images of the Prophet.

Demi's own artistic methods reveal the extent to which she herself actively drew on, altered, and (one could even say) censored a corpus of historical images of the Prophet in order to fit contemporary discourses about Islamic aniconism. Looking more closely at her depictions of Muhammad, it becomes clear that she harvested Safavid ascension imagery and Ottoman paintings of al-Darir's *Biography of the Prophet*

   THE PRAISEWORTHY ONE

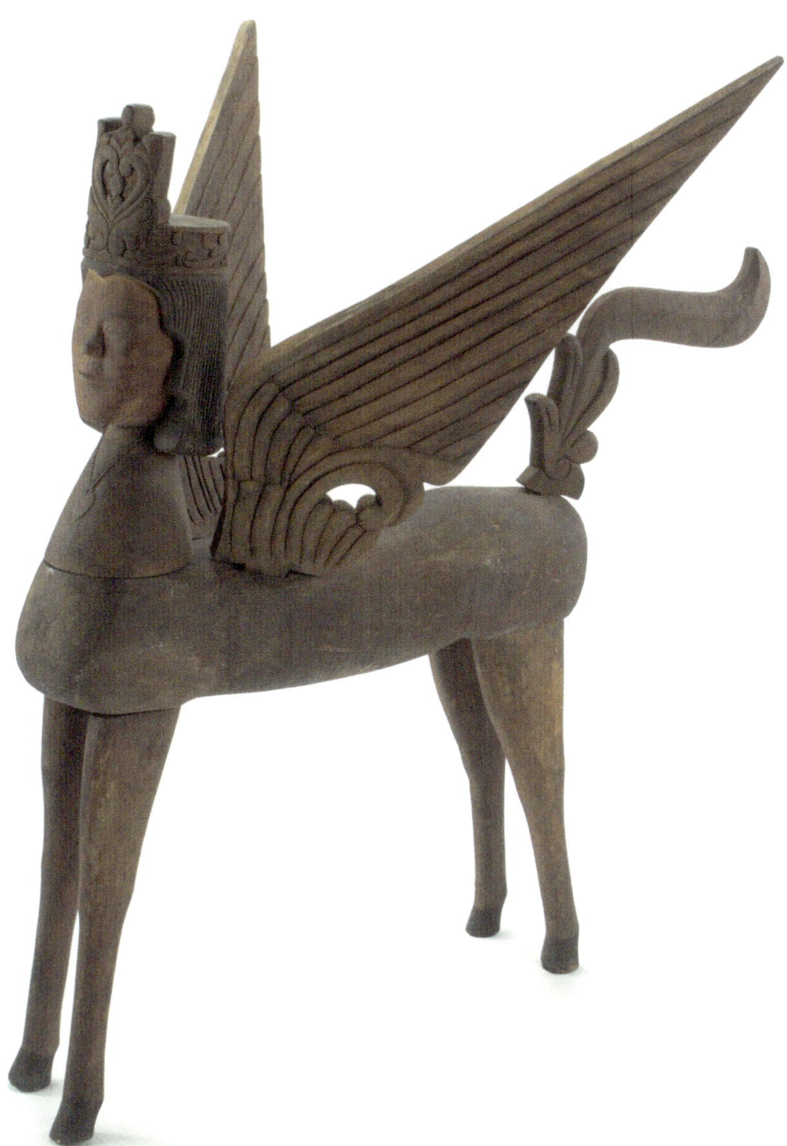

(figs. 5.1 and 5.2), only to overlay a thick gold foil on the entirety of the Prophet's physical outline, flesh-colored hands, facial features, and facial veil. Instead of showing the Prophet's face or body, as was the case in Safavid and Ottoman painterly traditions, Demi gave preference to the gold nimbus as used in later Indo-Persian book arts (fig. 6.11), which she contoured to Muhammad's physical silhouette. The artist's act of culling Ottoman and Safavid pictorial traditions and aligning them to later Kashmiri visual abstractions yields an innovative, syncretistic iconography. This new gilded prophetic silhouette is nothing if not a "new serial position,"[127] as it flows forth from centuries of representing Muhammad in Islamic lands. However, despite its harking back to tradition, it is driven by contemporary beliefs in some spheres—both Muslim and non-Muslim—that figural images of the Prophet must not or cannot exist.

This blending of old and new has continued throughout the Islamic world, including in Southeast Asia. In a most creative twist, three-dimensional sculptures of Buraq have been made since the early decades of the twentieth century in Muslim-majority communities in the southern Philippines and Indonesia.[128] In addition to their use as parade floats, dancing dolls, pull-toys, and tombstones, Buraq sculptures can be made in large sizes. For instance, one large wooden sculpture of the flying steed measures over one meter in height (fig. 6.16). The razor-sharp wings and windblown tail give it a soft yet slick look, while the locks of hair and heart-shaped pendant suggest that Buraq, in this case at least, is considered a female mythical creature. In still other cases, pairs of male and female Buraq sculptures are brightly painted and covered with mirrors and colored cloth.[129]

The Buraq sculpture in figure 6.16 was made during the first half of the twentieth century in Mindanao, the southernmost major island in the Philippines, which is home to a significant Muslim population. The Maranao people are known for their three-dimensional Buraqs, some of which are painted, with others left plain.[130] Many Muslim Filipinos (especially the Maranao) and Indonesians (based in the city of Lombok) use these sculptures of Buraq in ceremonial activities, including weddings, circumcisions, and celebrations of the Prophet Muhammad's ascension.[131] Often, they carry a rider—typically a child or a bride—in a religious festival or wedding procession. Accompanied by music, singing, and dancing, Buraq can also be made as a large, hollow doll animated by four dancers, as is most notably the case for the Burokan (Buraq) festivals of Cirebon, a city on the north coast of Java, Indonesia.[132] In Cirebon's Burokan festivals, other dancing dolls depict elephants, monkeys, tigers, and horses, thereby revealing the extent to which the Muslim festivals of Southeast Asia subsume non-Islamic creative practices, particularly the Southeast Asian arts of music, dance, and puppetry. In such traditions, Muhammad no longer remains the sole rider of Buraq; children and brides figuratively attain quasiprophetic prestige while embarking on their own journeys into adulthood and marriage.

Marked by embodiment and plasticity, images of Buraq showcase the adaptability of the representational arts in Islam as they relate to the Prophet Muhammad. Such images extend beyond paintings and posters to include American picture books, Southeast Asian wooden floats, and richly painted Pakistani trucks.[133] While Buraq may serve as a surrogate and emissary—or even animal metaphor—for Muhammad within more image-shunning milieus, its image nevertheless belongs to a long history of Islamic figurative arts in which a versatile system of give and take yields a range of pictorial abstractions that, in the end, are intended to function as visual proxies for the Prophet. Not infrequently, iconographic inventions complement, reiterate, and even reinforce aniconic urges. Such is the case for the iconographic devices of the facial veil, flaming nimbus, Muhammadan circle and *mim*, *hilye*, calligram, and Buraq. These abstracting motifs, however, should not be considered evidence solely of a self-regulating urge to eschew figuration within the

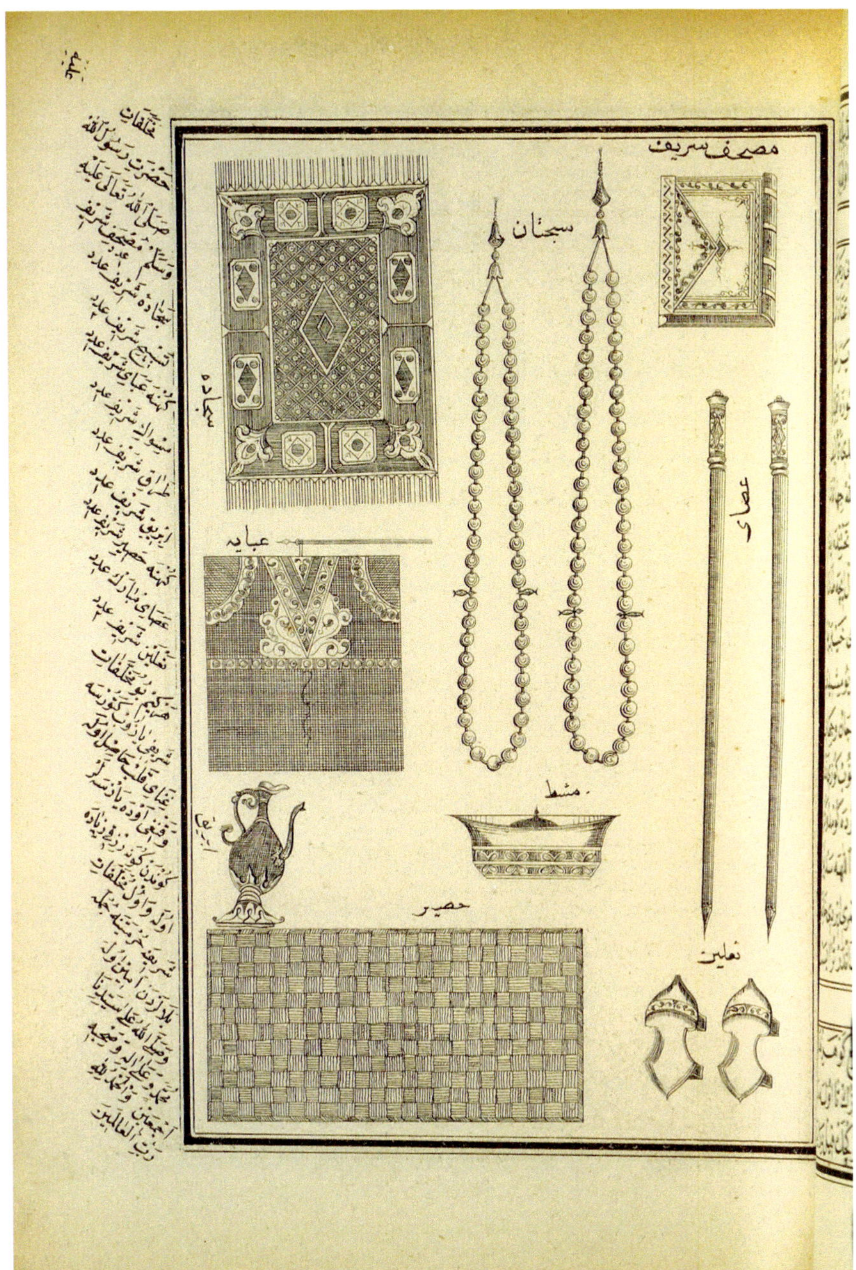

6.17. The Prophet's relics, Mehmed Yazıcıoğlu, *Muhammediyye* (Muhammad Poem), Istanbul, 1297 AH/1879–80 CE. Bibliothèque nationale de France, Smith Lesouef 9905, p. 215.

modern and contemporary Islamic world. Much more critically, they must be understood as paying tribute to artists' thoughtful and creative efforts to represent a greater Muhammadan reality, unbound from time and space, and, at times, eclipsing the human body itself.

The gradual move away from figuration catalyzed other depictive strategies that have sought to evoke the Prophet's presence, blessings, and protection. Today, the most common of these are Muhammad's relics and object attributes. Such Islamic religious commodities are produced en masse, especially in Turkey, and they can be purchased from online Islamic fashion stores catering to international consumers. Widespread belief in the efficacy of ready-made objects depicting the traces

PROPHETIC
PARAPHERNALIA:
RELICS AS PROTECTIVE
COMMODITIES

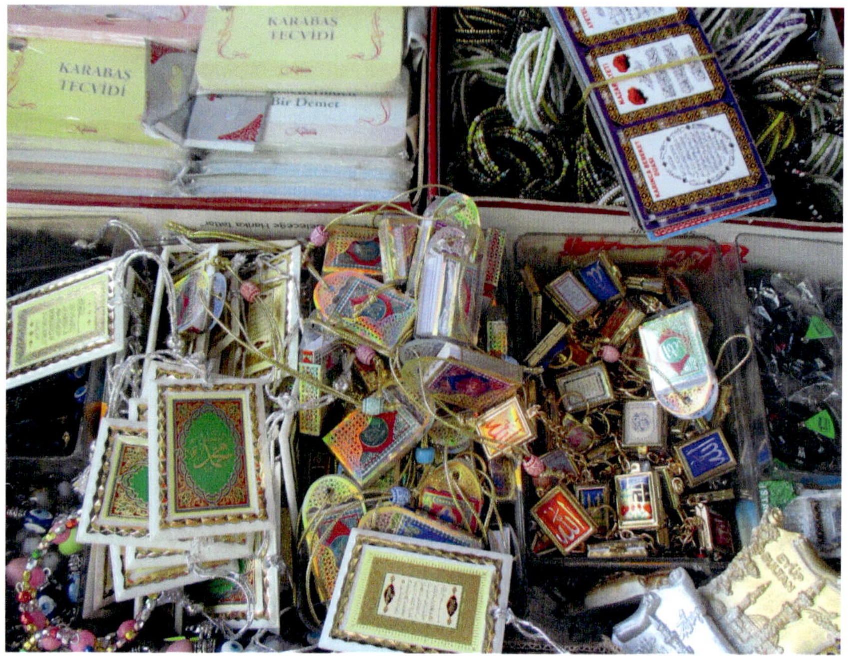

6.18. Various religious goods, including miniature Qur'ans, devotional books, and laminated cards inscribed with Muhammad's name and a variety of prayers, in a devotional goods store close to the Eyüp shrine, Istanbul, Turkey, 2015 CE. Photograph by author.

and belongings of the Prophet has prompted their production as amulets, laminated cards, posters, necklaces, and wall decals, among other forms. As protective paraphernalia, these items contribute in lively ways to religious material culture and the talismanic arts in Islam at the dawn of the twenty-first century.

The production of representations of the Prophet's accoutrements (*mukhallafat*) as well as imprints of his foot (*qadam*) and sandal (*ni'al*) began in Ottoman lands during the sixteenth century, and a noticeable upsurge in their representation in illustrated devotional texts and prayer books occurred over the course of the eighteenth and nineteenth centuries (figs. 5.8–5.12). For instance, Yazıcıoğlu's *Muhammad Poem*—which includes depictions of the Qur'an and Muhammad's staff, sandals, mat, prayer rug, ablutions ewer and basin, rosaries, and robe—extended the rather exclusive book arts tradition to a greater public sphere thanks to print technology (fig. 6.17; also see figs. 5.6 and 5.7).[134] Whether represented through manual or mechanical production, the Prophet's relics were thought to have protective qualities that could be activated by the devotional gaze, kiss, and touch of viewers. For instance, the marginal text in figure 6.17 itemizes all of Muhammad's relics and instructs readers to make written lists of them, placing copies in their houses in order to attain all of their hearts' desires, secure protection from every calamity, and increase sustenance from day to day. These "blessed items" (*tabarrukat*) did not lose—and still today, have not lost—their aura, thanks in large part to the power afforded to optical perception, tactile apprehension, and manual duplication.[135]

The creation of objects similar to late Ottoman artistic renditions of Muhammad's relics has continued to the present day, albeit with differences dictated by their means of manufacture, loci of consumption,

THE PRAISEWORTHY ONE

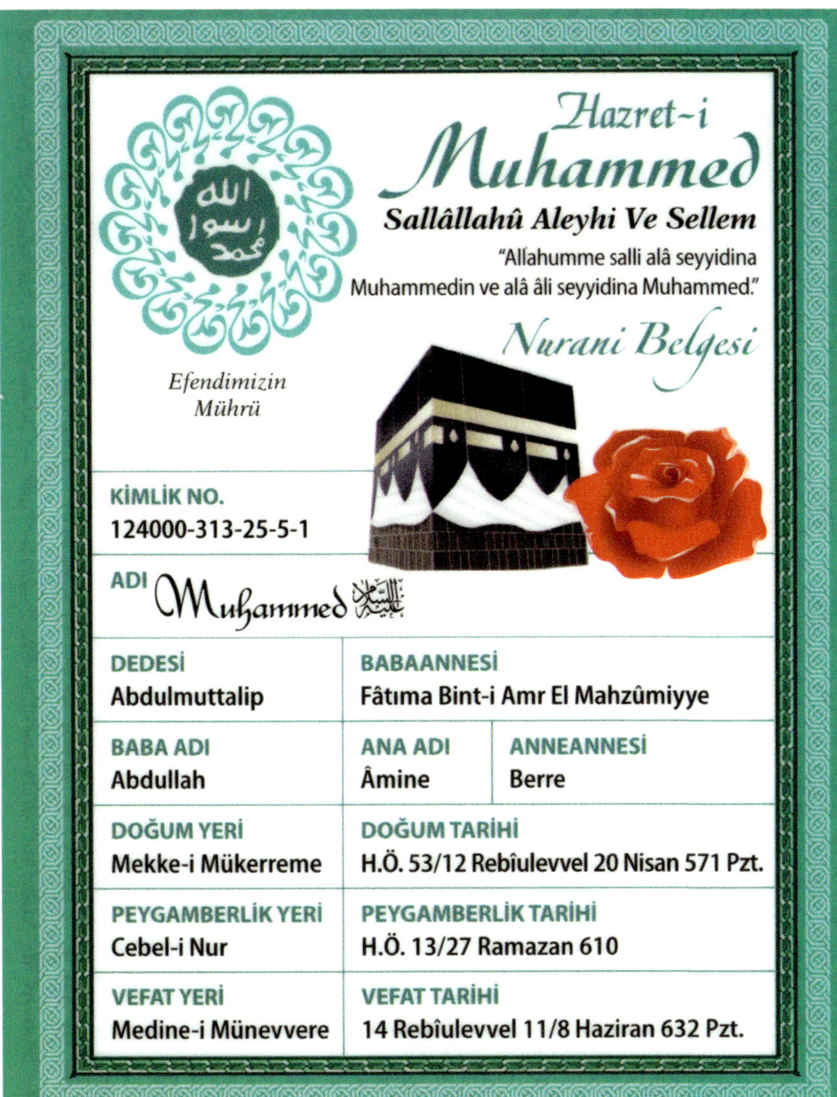

6.19. Recto of a laminated *hilye* card of the Prophet Muhammad purchased at a devotional goods store close to the Eyüp shrine, Istanbul, Turkey, 2015 CE. *Hilye* card in author's collection and photograph courtesy of Sally Bjork.

and devotional uses. Among the most popular items offered for sale in Turkish stores of "*hajj* goods" (*hac malzemeleri*) are miniature Qur'ans, prayer books, and small laminated cards arranged in the format of a Turkish government-issued ID (fig. 6.18).[136] These pocket-size religious objects often depict Muhammad's blessed "seal of prophecy" (*mühr-i şerif*), his sandal or sandal print (*nalın-ı şerif*), and his footprint (*kadem-i şerif* or *ayak izi*) on their rectos. On their versos, texts explicating the merits (*faziletler*) of these marks and relics inform their owners that they must look at, touch, and kiss these images in order to unleash their many powers, which include protection from the evil eye, whispers of the devil, and enemy attack. These cards, we are further told, make childbirth less painful for women, enable devotees to see Muhammad in their dreams, stop ships from sinking, protect houses from theft and fire, and provide cures for illness. Finally, they directly relate to a number of seal, sandal print, and footprint prayers published on Turkish imams' Facebook pages and blogs, which provide further commentary on the many virtues of owning these religious commodities and encourage their followers to direct devotional obeisance to the Prophet as part of their daily routines.

The most widespread version of these laminated cards enumerates the Prophet Muhammad's physical characteristics (fig. 6.19).[137] While some similar cards identify this type of latter-day *hilye* as a personal identification card (*nüfus cüzdanı*), others, such as this example, bear the title "radiant document" (*nurani belgesi*).[138] Often, Muhammad's seal impression and a roundel of his calligraphed name fill the upper left corner of the card, in lieu of a Turkish citizen's photograph. The Ka'ba and a rose accompany this synecdochal and scripted portrait of Muhammad, offering viewers further pictorial allegories for the Prophet through a sacred geographic marker and heavenly scented flower.

In addition to these visuals, the front of the card provides textual information about Muhammad's parents and grandparents, his birth and death places and dates, as well as the place and date of his appointment to prophecy (*peygamberlik*). On the back, the Prophet's "radiant document" also notes his civil status as married; his religion as Islam; his tribe as Qurayshite; the color of his face as radiant (*nurani*) and glowing (*parlak*); his eyes and hair as black; and his size as not too tall and not too short—all physical descriptors traditionally found in Islamic *hilye* texts and Ottoman *hilye* paintings and panels (figs. 5.14, 5.22, and 5.23). Last but not least, the ID card's number (*kimlik no.*) is given as 124000–313–25–5–1, which recalls the number of prophets (124,000), apostles (313), Muslim prophets (twenty-five), leading Abrahamic prophets (Abraham, Moses, David, Jesus, and Muhammad), and the last prophet of all, Muhammad. Through charged numerical symbolism, this contemporary Turkish "radiant document" serves to celebrate Muhammad's prophetic pedigree and supreme standing within a long line of illustrious apostles sent by God to humankind.

Judging from the material evidence and online news stories, the production of contemporary *hilye* cards dates only from about 2011. While these new (and very affordable) devotional commodities certainly appeal to a middlebrow religious market, they also are connected to Turkish president Recep Tayyip Erdoğan's and the AKP's efforts to conspicuously Islamize Turkey's public sphere, including through the large-scale construction of mosques and the establishment of religious schools whose stated goal is to cultivate a new "pious generation."[139] Intriguingly, some *hilye* cards made in 2012 provide the names of the Prophet's children, including a boy named Tayyip. Turkish opposition politicians and news outlets were quick to point out that Muhammad did not have a male child sharing the same surname as Turkey's then prime minister.[140] Exactly how such a felicitous—yet erroneous—insertion came to be remains unknown; nevertheless, this *hilye* brouhaha provides telling evidence of the more curious conjunctions of prophetic paraphernalia and religious politics in contemporary Turkey.

Turkish *hilye* cards typically are sold in religious goods stores at Islamic sacred sites, including the Eyüp shrine in Istanbul and the Hacı Bayram mosque in Ankara. Once purchased, these mass-produced items are carried in pockets and hung on walls, in the hopes of bringing protection and blessings to individuals, homes, stores, and restaurants. Furthermore, *hilye* cards are used as invitations to celebrations of the Prophet's birthday (*mevlid*) and are offered as gifts during the holy month of Ramadan. They thus circulate within religiously charged zones and more widely during festive seasons. During Islamic holidays in particular, these "sign-vehicles" function as a larger "communicative event" that, although occurring between individual actors, bears the imprint of institutional patterns of power and domination.[141] *Hilye* cards—much like other devotional goods belonging to global religious cultures—therefore allow humans to communicate according to a symbolic language that promotes the ontological efficacy of the divine. However, overlaps in systems and behaviors raise complicated questions about "religious authority, the moral economy of public display, and the dynamics of capitalist penetration."[142] In sum, such prophetic paraphernalia triangulate various points of reference within Turkey's religious, political, and economic spheres of activity.

Other Muhammadan merchandise is meant to be worn on or suspended from the body. For example, also offered for sale around the Eyüp shrine, which preserves a footprint of the Prophet in stone, are necklaces and ornaments that represent the Prophet's seal and his sandal print (fig. 6.20). Some of these metalwares are long enough to be worn around the neck while others are relatively short and therefore can be suspended from a bag or bookshelf, or, if miniaturized, a cell phone. Without exception, the seal of the Prophet bears the Arabic imprimatur "Muhammad is the Messenger of God" (*Muhammad rasul Allah*), scripted in a lapidary form to emulate the Prophet's chiseled bezel ring. However, the sandal (*ni'al*) frequently is misidentified as a "foot" (*qadam*), as is the case in figure 6.20. On the one hand, this error may be due to the two prints' relative interchangeability; on the other, their Turkish manufacturers are uncomfortable with Arabic script, which was abandoned in favor of Latin script after the Turkish parliament passed an alphabet reform law in 1928.[143]

The occasional linguistic slipup notwithstanding, these prophetic trinkets offer material testimony to Muhammad's authority as a divinely ordained ruler as well as commemoration of the miraculous traces of his life. If worn visibly, they also transform Muhammad into a brand name of sorts. In the streets of Turkey and beyond, such items can be made to replace the tags of international fashion houses, emphasizing their wearers' commitment to the Islamic faith and their dedication to service and humility. Moreover, due to their low cost—indeed, each of these ornaments fetches a price no higher than a few dollars—such wares have much to say about their buyers' socioeconomic class: those

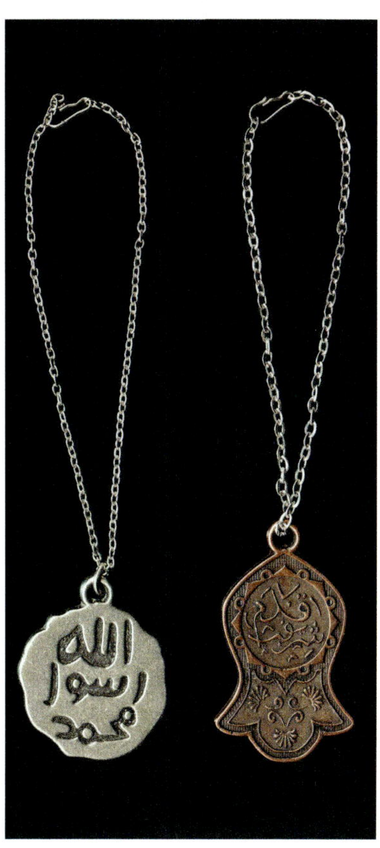

6.20. Necklaces (or hanging ornaments) of Muhammad's seal of prophecy and sandal print (here misidentified as his footprint), purchased at a devotional goods store close to the Eyüp shrine, Istanbul, Turkey, 2015 CE. Pendants in author's collection and photograph courtesy of Sally Bjork.

6.21. The black flag of ISIS (Islamic State in Iraq and Syria) inscribed with the *shahada* and ornamented with Muhammad's seal of prophecy. Image in the public domain.

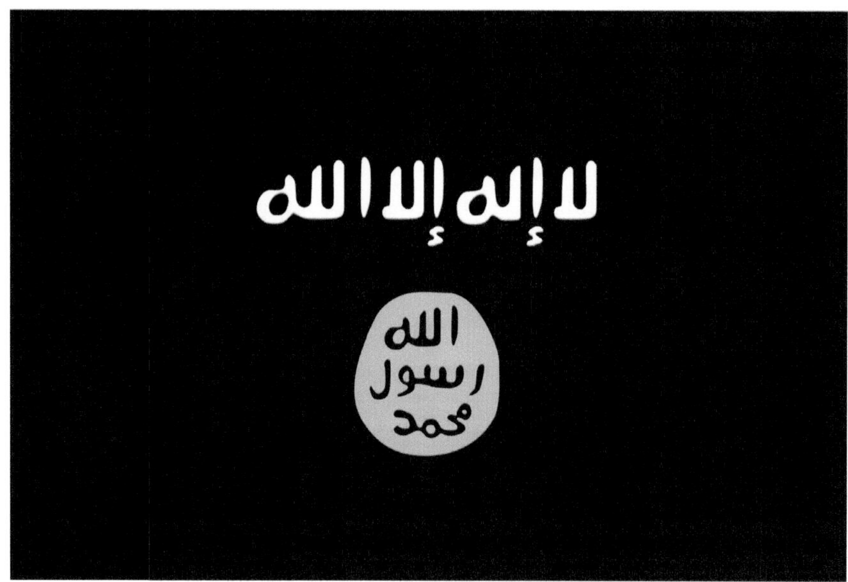

who purchase, own, wear, and display such items do not belong to the Turkish Muslim bourgeoisie and upper class, whose male members prefer to wear Rolexes and whose female members fold Versace and Armine silk scarves into fashionable, color-coordinated head covers.

The metal pendants of Muhammad's seal and sandal print also hark back to Ottoman depictions of his prophetic traces as included most especially in illustrated prayer books of the eighteenth and nineteenth centuries (figs. 5.11–5.13). Efforts to revive Ottoman artistic heritage and its religious modes pervade contemporary Turkey, where Ottoman forms stipple mosque architecture, the arts of calligraphy, marbling, jewelry-making, and even popular soap operas.[144] In the field of religious goods, this type of neo-Ottomanism—some might say even Ottomania—cultivates an aesthetic of nostalgic devotion and public display of piety. Moreover, in Istanbul's cityscape, the consumption of such goods tends to be localized in sacred assemblages or religious neighborhoods (such as Eyüp); simultaneously, it is energized by business networks across Turkey's nationwide neoliberal marketplace.[145] The seal and sandal-print pendants count among these types of Islamic neo-Ottoman goods, allowing their wearers to declare their adherence to the Prophet's heritage along with their admiration of Turkey's imperial past.

A pious neo-Ottoman artistic tendency undergirds the production of these religious goods, which reflect the Sunni-Islamic platform of the ruling AKP party and largely cater to devout middle- and lower-class Turkish Muslim citizens. However, because these pendants have been made only during the last few years, one cannot omit the likelihood of Jihadi or even ISIS-friendly buyers. After all, t-shirts, hoodies, and baseball caps imprinted with pro-ISIS messages and Muhammad's seal of prophecy were offered for sale in Istanbul's Islamist gift shops in 2014 (that is, more or less at the same time that these pendants emerged in stores of religious goods).[146] Although such stores were shut down,

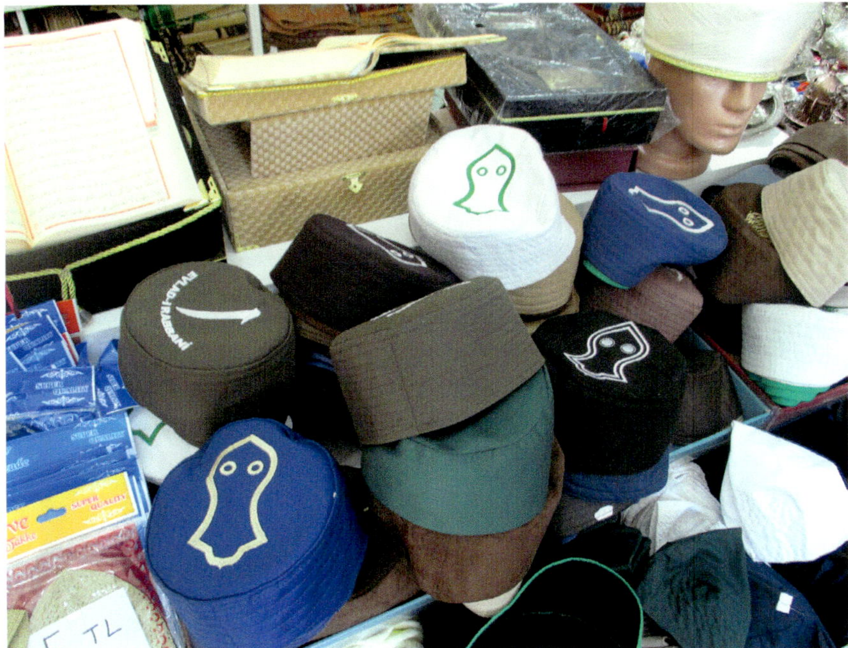

6.22. Turban hats embroidered with sandal print designs, offered for sale at a devotional goods store close to the Eyüp shrine, Istanbul, 2015 CE. Photograph by author.

pro-ISIS vestments and goods combining prophetic insignia with militant motifs still can be found on the Turkish market today.

Moreover, the fact that Muhammad's seal is included on ISIS merchandise made in Turkey should not come as a surprise, as the very same prophetic symbol ornaments the black flag of ISIS (fig. 6.21).[147] This logo is borrowed from the letters attributed to the Prophet's hand, which are now held in the relics display in Topkapı Palace in Istanbul.[148] Although most likely nineteenth-century forgeries, Muhammad's letters include his seal impression created by a signet ring. As such, the seal impression functions as a visual shorthand for prophetic authority, to which ISIS claims inheritance.

Thus, beyond its use by pious Muslim consumers, the pendant of Muhammad's seal also can be considered "Jihadi bling" within pro-ISIS circles. Evidently, the Prophet's imprimatur is increasingly marshaled in service of the material and visual culture of contemporary Islamic militancy, within which it is used to catalyze a variety of symbolic discourses on authenticity, authority, and supremacy. Muhammad's seal is thus employed in the business of Jihadi fashion and decor by ISIS in its massive effort to assert global Islamic sovereignty via claims to prophetic bona fides.

Leaving aside Jihadi attempts to "seal" the prophetic *sunna*, Muhammad's other relics and traces appeal to more mystically minded devotees interested in improving strength and peace of body, mind, and character. Of prime importance in this regard is the sandal print, which today is produced in many media, ranging from small-scale stickers and pendants to tote bags and hats. For instance, today stores abutting the Eyüp shrine complex in Istanbul sell Qur'ans, Ottoman turbans, and hats embroidered with a minimalistic outline of the Prophet's sandal print (fig. 6.22). This simple graphic form emulates late Ottoman sandal-print images, in which the two circles represent the riveting of the shoe's two straps between the toes (figs. 5.8 and 5.11–5.13).

The same sandal-print hats are offered for international purchase at Shukr Islamic Clothing, which also caters to the Turkish market.[149] On its website, the company promotes its cotton sandal-print turban hats with the tagline, "Be proud of your Islamic identity and complete your modest outfit with a quality *kufi*, hat or cap." The same website even includes a "customer guide" that provides a detailed explanation of the meanings and benefits of the Prophet's sandals, which reads in part:

> The depiction of the noble Prophetic sandals has had a special place in the hearts of Muslims since it points to one of the needs of their tremendous Prophet (Allah bless him and give him peace), and since it inspires in them the utmost humility toward his high rank (Allah bless him and give him peace). Because of this, they took care to record this depiction, and to draw it, and they sometimes even placed it under their turbans, to feel their complete subservience to the tremendousness of this most noble Messenger (Allah bless him and give him peace). They also hung this depiction in their houses, seeking *baraka* from it. . . . May the best of blessings and peace be upon the owner of these blessed sandals.[150]

Such hats are promoted as "capping" the Muslim man's humble outfit. At its apex, the sandal externalizes its wearer's decency, humility, and selflessness, as if he were the dust under Muhammad's feet. Through this visual symbolism, the owner also declares his adherence and submission to the Prophet's authority, for which the sandal print has served as an indexical mark since the medieval period. Finally, Muhammad's sandal—as well as the many drawings and copies that have been produced throughout the Islamic world over the centuries—is believed to dispel troubles, guard against the evil eye, alleviate illness, and, more generally, impart *baraka* to its viewers and owners. Embroidered onto hats, the sandal print thus is interpreted as functioning as a neutralizer and palliative—that is, as preventive medicine in visual form. This seeking out of prophetic inoculation highlights a widespread belief in the protective virtues of proper vestment as expressed both within and outside of Islamic cultures.

As can be seen in figure 6.22, in Eyüp's stores of devotional goods these turban hats are accompanied by others inscribed with an *alif* (letter *a*) and the inscription "*Evlad-ı Rabbani.*" These "sons" (*evlad*) are the followers of Ahmad Sirhindi, known as Imam Rabbani, a prominent *shaykh* of the Naqshbandi order who died in 1624 CE.[151] In contemporary Turkey, the "sons of Rabbani" are a group of Sufis who consider their practice an orthodox form of mysticism that is compatible with Sunni norms and principles. Rabbani's followers believe in the notions of "unity of being" (*wahdat al-wujud*) and "unity of vision" (*wahdat al-shuhud*) as well as the ontological superiority of the Prophet's creation, itself referred to as the "Muhammadan reality" (*haqiqat-i Muhammadi*). Much as in other Islamic mystical traditions, according to

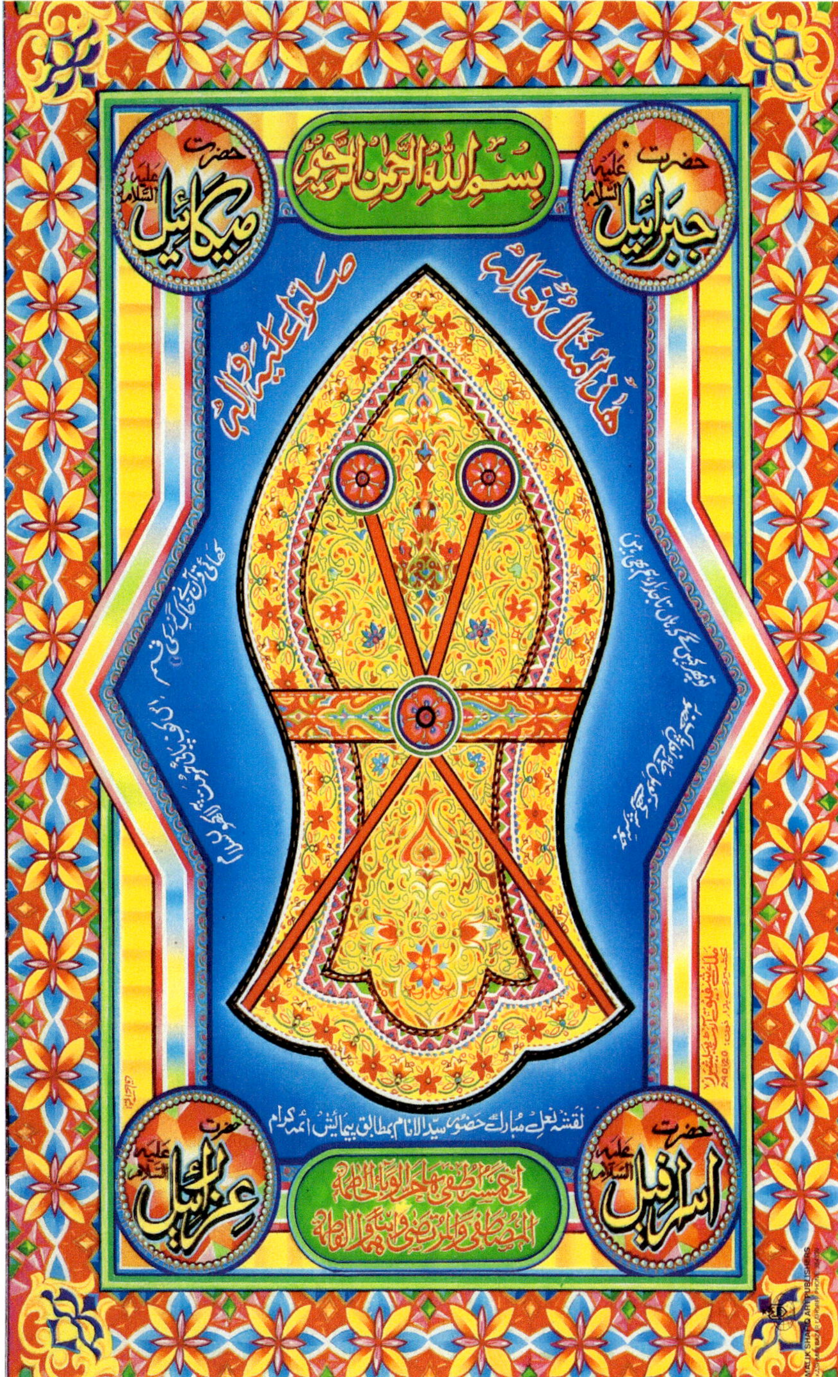

6.23. Poster of Muhammad's sandal print, Lahore, Pakistan, mid-twentieth century CE. Museum Fünf Kontinente, Munich, 99–320.394. Photograph by Marietta Weidner.

this Sunni-Sufi conceptualization the Prophet must not be considered merely a hylomorphic entity: that is, a simple conjunction of matter and form. Rather, he exists as a larger, immaterial spiritual being that effuses holiness, perfection, and life throughout time. To the sons of Rabbani and other Sunni devotees of a Sufi bent, the Prophet's sandal as imprinted on turban hats and tote bags allows individuals to craft visibly "Muslim looks" within the contemporary global fashion system.[152] Moreover, this synecdochal motif eschews literal depiction, thereby allowing the properly outfitted pious man and woman to imagine—even don and carry—a more emblematic and timeless Muhammad.

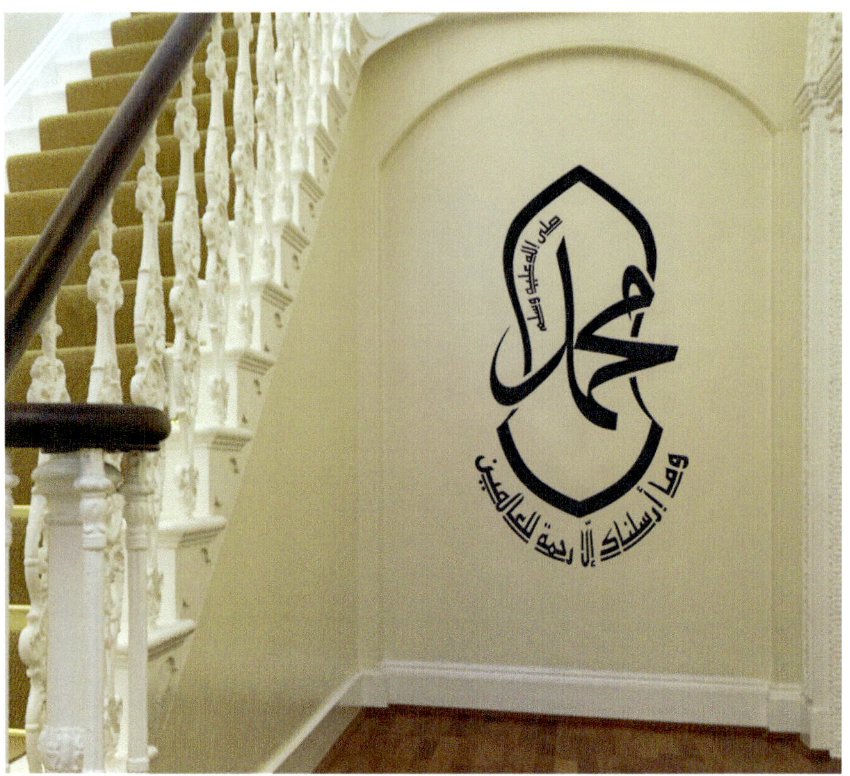

Across the Islamic world, images of the Prophet's sandals also fulfill apotropaic functions since they promote Muhammad as a larger talismanic force. For instance, posters made on the Indian subcontinent around the middle of the twentieth century reproduce the "similitude" (*mithal*) of the Prophet's footprint and sandal print (fig. 6.23).[153] Verses in Urdu command the viewer to recite a prayer of benediction in order to activate the image's many blessings, which include protection from disaster and physical harm. The brightly colored sandal print poster also includes text that exalts the viewers' humble subservience: "If I could find the pure sandal of the Prophet to place on my head, then would I say: 'Yes! I, too, wear a crown!'"[154] In addition to this pious expression of utmost humility, the poster follows a traditional talismanic format—which includes the four archangels, whose names (Gabriel, Michael, Israfil, and 'Azra'il) are inscribed within roundels in the poster's corners.

Today, other sandal prints are digitally designed and printed as large-scale decals (fig. 6.24).[155] These wall accents in praise of the Prophet feature symbolic outlines thought to protect both home and body. In her decal shown in figure 6.24, the artist Fawzia Ghafoor Khawaja combines the amuletic sandal print with Muhammad's calligraphed name and the qur'anic verse "And We have not sent you but as a mercy to the worlds" (21:107), which frequently appears on *hilye*s. Here, the London-based designer draws on a mature tradition of Islamic art as she notes, "Our mission is to make modern Islamic décor more accessible, bringing fresh ideas and products that present a new perspective to the traditional Islamic art we know quite well."[156] In this sandal-print decal, Fawzia turned to the devotional arts dedicated to the

THE PRAISEWORTHY ONE

Prophet by combining Muhammad's scripted name, the qur'anic verse found on *hilye*s, and visual representations of the Prophet's sandal print. In doing so, she enables her consumers to express their personal piety within largely domestic confines, where they use this type of Islamic décor to beautify an interior space—to a certain extent in the hope of reaping prophetic blessings, mercy, and protection.

The type of inventive behavior evidenced by the wall decal attests to the tradition-forming power of replication as it intersects with the human desire for variety.[157] From the printing press to digital design, modern technological inventions allow for a diversification of forms while catalyzing new liturgies of production and consumption within religious registers. In this regard, Muhammad's prophetic paraphernalia result from, and reinforce, an "authorized language" pertaining to depictions of the Messenger of Islam. This language produces a dominant culture and ideology through a range of consumer goods that coalesce to form a normative, legitimate, and thus orthodox position.[158] Consequently, today's images of the Prophet reveal that individuals operating in many (but not all) public and private spheres subtly avoid or altogether reject figuration. Such artistic habits have emerged from both the embrace and the abandonment of centuries of Islamic pictorial practices.

Taken altogether, modern and contemporary Islamic representations of the Prophet do not offer a simple, cohesive, or unilinear narrative. However, if one were to endeavor to find a unifying strand in this rich miscellany, it would be the simple fact that veristic images have tended to fade from view since about 1800 CE. Such a conclusion, however, would disregard the mass manufacture of unveiled portraits of Muhammad that were a staple of Persian pictorial tradition from around 1300 CE to the Danish cartoon controversy of 2005–6, after which Iranian top-down efforts to curb portraits of saints at public sites—including shrines, cemeteries, and street processions—attest to the increasing influence of more conservative Muslim discourses promoting the avoidance (or even prohibition) of figural imagery, especially of the Prophet Muhammad. While indebted to older image-shunning urges, which certainly have marked parts of the Islamic world in different times and places, this more recent narrative about Islamic aniconism must be understood for what it is: a newly formulated contraposition that, albeit couched in Islamic tradition, above all emerges from, and responds to, the ideological contests unfolding on today's international stage.

Leaving aside these more recent efforts at cultural and religious differentiation, it nevertheless remains clear that modern Islamic depictions of Muhammad display much versatility. Moreover, they are imbricated in global art systems, in which artists freely practice their trade while creatively mining a shared iconographic repertoire. Veristic images of the Prophet made in Iran during the twentieth century—some of which feature pictorial origins that can be traced to European printed and photographic sources—provide the clearest example of this phenomenon. Such to-and-fro in the field of the figural arts calls into question overly rigid conceptual dichotomies and undermines inherited art-historical paradigms, chief among them the taxonomic labels "European art" and "Islamic art." Thus, Euro-Iranian pictorial encounters help to uncover points of correlation rather than points of divergence, a phenomenon that can be marshaled against various (Muslim and non-Muslim) discourses that seek to self-otherize or anathemize Islamic art, religion, and culture.

Islamic traditions of representing the Prophet nevertheless do display various idiosyncrasies, which often blossom from dynamic conjunctions in the fields of theology, poetry, and the painterly arts. For example, Iranian veristic portraits of Muhammad were produced as pictorial icons that were respected, kissed, and gazed on. They were not worshipped per se; rather, they were revered in ways that parallel both doctrinal notions of propriety and poetic expressions of love. Moreover, while some Iranian images of the Prophet drew on premodern Persian manuscript paintings, a number of others show the influence of European sources. These pictorial templates were not reproduced wholesale by Iranian artists. To the contrary, European images were overtly Islamized and Shi'ified through a range of recognizable motifs, including the insertion of the Qur'an, 'Ali as a leonine angel, the *ahl al-bayt* and imams, and Shi'i holy sites. Beyond modifying images of Muhammad to promote a more sectarian worldview—as was done during the Safavid period—Iranian artists at times have embedded their compositions in the political discourses of their time, from postrevolutionary calls to "free" the Dome of the Rock in Jerusalem to government-sponsored artistic endeavors that reasserted the Prophet's beauty and legacy after the Danish cartoon controversy of 2005–6.

Today more than ever, images of Muhammad intensify the sensitive domains of religion and politics. This was not always the case, however. Before the turn of the twenty-first century, representations of the Prophet reflected more personal and spiritual desires. Far removed from today's image wars, such depictions catered to more quietist desires within the quotidian habits of devotees who wished to conjure a greater Muhammadan reality. Stressing his timelessness and freedom from physicality, more conceptual approaches to the Prophet's ontology catalyzed a range of nonveristic images. Such images resulted from processes of pictorial abstraction, in which artists creatively exploited the metaphorical potential of various pictorial motifs, including, among others, the facial veil, flaming nimbus, Muhammadan circle and *mim*, *hilye*, calligram, and his mythical proxy, Buraq. While the facial veil presents the Prophet's being as a sacred mystery hidden from his viewers' eyes, the flaming nimbus depicts him as the source of divine revelation and lights. Abstracting the physical body even further, the Muhammadan circle presents the Prophet as a complete microcosmos, while the *mim* glorifies him as the circle of creation, highlighting the importance of letter-based modes of expression within Islamic literate cultures. Last but not least, both the *hilye* and the calligram function as hybrid image-texts and somber guides to contemplation, at times "setting the world alight" with Muhammad's radiant name. Generally indebted to more mystically inclined modes of expression, these visual metaphors labor to establish a "compact of communicability"[159] with a beloved prophet, who, although physically absent, remains ever-present in the minds and eyes of his followers.

Another hallmark of mystical cultures, Muhammad's relics have held pride of place in Ottoman artistic traditions since the sixteenth century. While in the premodern period such synecdochal motifs were confined to painting and the book arts, in today's Turkey they have captured a corner of the market for Islamic religious goods. Produced as intimate and portable vade mecums, these affordable commodities reveal the extent to which Muhammad—through his objects and relics—exerts a larger talismanic force that is believed to protect and cure those in possession of his traces and signs. Some (of a Marxist bent) might call such objects the stuff of "proletarian material culture,"[160] while others might classify them as "working-class kitsch" that draws on a fully matured cultural tradition and a deep reservoir of accumulated experience in order to monetize simulacra of "real" culture.[161] Regardless of one's valuation of such items, it is clear that the Muhammadan merchandise produced in Turkey today is considered potent, especially when it reaches the stage of "terminal commoditization,"[162] at which time an item exits the market and finds a permanent home. Whether eventually carried on the body or affixed to a wall, these prophetic paraphernalia organize both public and private affections. They also create visibly "Muslim looks." On the one hand, such fashions stress humility over opulence for a middle- to lower-class religious demographic; on the other, they enable the crafting of Jihadi identities within and beyond Turkish borders. In the end, these types of objects circulate widely as they cater to practices from prophetic medicine to the newest trends in Islamist militancy.[163]

Through and through, images and symbols of Muhammad partake in a larger behavioral complex, which includes the practices of making, procuring, giving, seeing, thinking, and feeling.[164] They function as communicative signs and create a shared flow among like-minded individuals, thereby creating a larger community of belief, one not bound by national, geographic, linguistic, or ethnic borders. Through canonization and multiplication—that is, through their commonly accepted "authorized language"—these pictorial materials come together to create a normative view of what is permitted and what is forbidden within contemporary representations of the Prophet. More recent years have witnessed a strong uptick in the avoidance in figural depiction in favor of synecdochal representation, through which Muhammad's facial features eventually yield to inscribed sandal prints. Moving from head to toe, today's prophetic commodities thus craft a particular brand of Islamic religious material and visual culture for our contemporary world.

1. Cited in Schimmel, *As through a Veil*, 174n17.

2. Flood, "Between Cult and Culture," 641.

3. For the (rather spiritualist) scholarly discourse on Islamic art as displaying unity in diversity, see especially the publications linked to the 1976 World of Islam Festival, including Burckhardt, *Art of Islam*.

4. For a general discussion of the early Iranian printing press, see Marzolph, "Early Printing History in Iran (1817–ca. 1900)."

5. On the Danish cartoon controversy, see Klausen, *The Cartoons That Shook the World*; and Flood, "Inciting Modernity?"

6. On Muhammad as an "absent presence" in contemporary Islamic popular imagery, see Centlivres and Centlivres-Demont, "Une présence absente."

7. On the "Balkans-to-Bengal complex," see Ahmed, *What Is Islam?*, 32.

8. On the isolated material sign or motif as identifying a whole and endowing it with significance, see Potts, "Sign," 32.

9. Gruber, "The Prophet Muhammad's Footprint"; Hasan, "The Footprint of the Prophet"; and Welch, "The Shrine of the Holy Footprint in Delhi."

10. On the notion of "seasons of demand" for the selling and purchasing of Islamic religious commodities, see Starrett, "The Political Economy of Religious Commodities in Cairo."

11. On "sacred consumption" and sacredness as the result of an "investment process," see Belk, Wallendorf, and Sherry, "The Sacred and the Profane in Consumer Behaviour," 9 and 13.

12. On the use of images and the human sensorium to stimulate religious affect, see Morgan, *The Sacred Gaze*, 52.

13. For a discussion of depictions of Muhammad on Iranian stamps, see Gruber, "Prophetic Products," 264–68, figs. 3–4; and on the five-story mural painted in Tehran in 2008, see Gruber, "Images of Muhammad in and out of Modernity"; and Gruber, "Reclaiming the Prophet Muhammad in Iran."

14. For the support and spread of nationalism through an imagined cohesive body politic, see Anderson, *Imagined Communities*.

15. On Nasir al-Din Shah and his rule, see Amanat, *Pivot of the Universe*.

16. On the arts of the Nasirid period, see Diba and Ekhtiar, *Royal Persian Paintings*, 239–67.

17. On *ta'ziyya*s, see, inter alia, Chelkowski, *Ta'ziyeh*; Chelkowski, *From Karbala to New York*; and Beeman, *Iranian Performance Traditions*.

18. On the Dar al-Funun, its development, and its curriculum, see Ekhtiar, "Nasir al-Din Shah and the Dar al-Funun"; Ekhtiar, "The Dar al-Funun"; and Ekhtiar, "From Workshop and Bazaar to Academy," especially 58–61, on art training in the "Western Mode."

19. On the expression "pictorial *hilya*," see Ekhtiar, "Infused with Shi'ism," 110.

20. For another Qajar pictorial *hilya* of Muhammad (holding a sword and identified as *shama'il-i hazrat-i rasul*), see Zoka, *Life and Works of Sani' al-Mulk (1814–1866)*, 42, 145–46, plate 80A (misidentified as 'Ali); and for a pictorial *hilya* of 'Ali, see Vernoit, *Occidentalism*, 64, cat. no. 32 (CAL 60).

21. For "imagetexts" that combine visual and textual motifs, see Morgan, *The Sacred Gaze*, 65–66.

22. This icon is published in Ekhtiar, "Infused with Shi'ism," 110–12, plates 35–36; Zoka, *Life and Works of Sani' al-Mulk (1814–1866)*, 43, 146–47, plates 81A–B; Newid, *Der schiitische Islam in Bildern*, 170, fig. B6; and Amanat, "Court Patronage and Public Space," 430, fig. 21.9 (in which the icon is misidentified as 'Ali).

23. On objects as "focalizers" and "behavioral triggers" of piety and devotion, see Starrett, "The Political Economy of Religious Commodities in Cairo," 61.

24. On magic squares, see Cammann, "Islamic and Indian Magic Squares, Parts 1–2."

25. For a general survey of qur'anic verses used in Islamic talismans and amulets, including *ayat al-kursi*, see Leoni, "Sacred Words, Sacred Power."

26. Staples, "Muhammad, a Talismanic Force." Another clearly talismanic *shama'il*—which includes depictions of Muhammad (seated on Buraq), 'Ali, Hasan, and Husayn, along with magic squares and designs—is held in the Library of the Shrine of Fatima in Qom (painting no. 904).

27. Wills, *Persia as It Is*, 125. Wills also visited a private house where he witnessed individuals prostrating in front of a large portrait of 'Ali. He notes: "Before this picture they prostrated themselves, kissing it and paying it profound adoration, while they mumbled their prayers."

28. Zoka, *Life and Works of Sani' al-Mulk (1814–1866)*, 43.

29. Amir-Moezzi, "Icon and Meditation," 32–33.

30. Zoka, *Life and Works of Sani' al-Mulk (1814–1866)*, 27.

31. The portrait medallion was worn by Nasir al-Din on the 27th of Rabi' I 1273/1857. See Zoka, *Life and Works of Sani' al-Mulk (1814–1866)*, 42, 145–46, plates 80A–B.

32. On Qajar medals, see Soucek, "The Visual Language of Qajar Medals"; and Piemontese, "The Statutes of the Qajar Orders of Knighthood."

33. For the most recent scholarship on representations of the Prophet Muhammad in European literary and artistic traditions, see, in particular, Shalem et al, *Constructing the Image of Muhammad in Europe*; Saviello, *Imaginationen des Islam*; and the articles in Gruber and Shalem, *The Image of the Prophet Between Ideal and Ideology.*

34. For a discussion of twentieth-century Iranian "Young Muhammad" images, which adapt an Orientalist photograph of a young Arab boy from 1905–6, see Centlivres and Centlivres-Demont, "Une étrange rencontre"; Centlivres and Centlivres-Demont, "The Story of a Picture"; Grabar and Natif, "The Story of the Portraits of the Prophet Muhammad"; Shatanawi, *Islam at the Tropenmuseum*, 170–72; Gruber, "Images of Muhammad *In and Out* of Modernity," 18–26; and Gruber, "Prophetic Products," 282–89. In addition to this well-studied case, at least two other European images influenced Iranian depictions of Muhammad as a boy or young man. The first is Harold Copping's depiction of Jesus Christ as the "Good Shepherd" (see Puin, *Islamische Plakate*, 3:903, J-3 and 975, fig. 55), and the second is a French print of about 1850–80 that depicts Muhammad standing among the great men of the world. Iranian representations of the "Young Muhammad" that adapt European images deserve further analysis and will be discussed in a future study.

35. Figuier, *Vie des savants illustres du moyen âge*, 2.

36. Tolan, "Impostor or Lawgiver?," 269; and Tolan, "European Accounts of Muhammad's Life."

37. As John Wansbrough has noted, it is not surprising to find a "Moses paradigm" within Islamic prophetology, as the "historical portrait of the Arabian prophet conforms to a pattern composed partly of the Qur'anic data on prophethood, in character emphatically Mosaic, and partly of motifs drawn from a narrative tradition typically associated with men of God"; see "Emblems of Prophethood," 78. Additionally, as Jane Dammen McAuliffe underscores, "virtually every major element in Muhammad's prophetic vocation finds its counterpart in the life of Moses," including, among others, God's gift of a holy book and the final triumph of the faithful; see McAuliffe, "Connecting Moses and Muhammad," 331–32.

38. For a list of European books translated into Persian and assigned for reading at Tehran's Dar al-Funun, see Ekhtiar, "The Dar al-Funun," 317–19.

39. Rubin, "The Shrouded Messenger," 99. These two appellations are derived from the titles of chapters (*suras*) 73 and 74 of the Qur'an and have been interpreted as praise terms for the Prophet as well as metaphors denoting him as "covered" or "loaded" with prophethood.

40. Appadurai, "Introduction: Commodities and the Politics of Value," 23.

41. This expression is borrowed from Beaulieu and Roberts, "Orientalism's Interlocutors."

42. For this Moses-like image of Muhammad within an Iranian metal standard (*'alam*), see Newid, *Der schiitische Islam in Bildern*, 173, fig. B7; within a poster, see Puin, *Islamische Plakate*, 3:904, plate J-4; and for the figural carpet illustrated in fig. 6.4, see Puin, *Islamische Plakate*, 3:968, fig. 41.

43. For Qajar printed books and pilgrimage scrolls that depict Shi'i themes and sites, see Marzolph, "The Pictorial Representation of Shi'i Themes in Lithographed Books of the Qajar Period"; and Marzolph, "From Mecca to Mashhad"; and on depictions of the Prophet in Qajar lithographed books in particular, see Boozari, "Shama'il-i payambar dar kitabha-yi chap-i sangi-yi dawra-yi qajar."

44. For a discussion of the codex as visually differentiating the Qur'an from the scroll format of the Torah, see Déroche "Written Transmission," 176. Déroche also notes that early Qur'ans in the oblong format were perhaps meant to be visually differentiated from Bibles executed in a vertical format.

45. On the Kayanid crown used in Qajar coronation ceremonies, see Amanat, "The Kayanid Crown and Qajar Reclaiming of Royal Authority"; and Doka, "Crown v. In the Qajar and Pahlavi Periods."

46. Sharon, "*Ahl al-Bayt*," 171–72; and Suleman and Jiwa, "Shi'i Art and Ritual," 16.

47. For an overview of the Islamic doctrine of *'isma* (infallibility, purity, immunity from error and sin) as extended to the prophets (in Sunnism) and the imams (in Shi'ism), see in particular Andrae, *Die Person Muhammeds in Lehre und Glaube seiner Gemeinde*, 124–74.

48. For a detailed discussion of Shi'i icons as "focalizers" into devotion, rather than as objects of worship, see Flaskerud, *Visualizing Belief and Piety in Iranian Shiism*. For a discussion of recent Iranian attempts to curb or even ban their presence and use in shrines and streets, see Gruber, "Prophetic Products," 262. Although such images helped to focus devotees' attention, others were actually worshipped during the Qajar period. For example, Nasir al-Din Shah founded a circle whose main goal was to venerate icons (*shama'il*) of 'Ali. Elaborate rituals were staged around these images at the royal court, while other icons—especially large-scale cloth paintings (*pardas*)—were carried in processions, kissed, and used for storytelling in the *ta'ziyya* performances that were sponsored by Nasir al-Din Shah. Lastly, at the latter's death, the monarch's image was displayed with that of Imam 'Ali. Ekhtiar, "Exploring *Ahl al-Bayt* Imagery in Qajar Iran (1785–1925)," 147; Chelkowski, "Narrative Painting and Painting Recitation in

Qajar Iran," 101; Chelkowski, "Popular Arts," 94; and Diba, "Images of Power and the Power of Images," 43.

49. For a photograph of framed postcard icons placed in an Iranian public water fountain (*saqqakhana*), see Allan, *The Art and Architecture of Twelver Shi'ism*, 60, plate 2.16.

50. On spheres of exchange and the process of singularization, see Kopytoff, "The Cultural Biography of Things," 71–77.

51. For the same icon, see Newid, *Der schiitische Islam in Bildern*, 199, fig. D8.

52. On the *ahl al-bayt* as the "Holy Family" or "Holy Five" and its link to the Christian Holy Family, see Sharon, "*Ahl al-Bayt*," 173; and, on the "Holy Pentad," see Suleman and Jiwa, "Shi'i Art and Ritual," 16. For a further discussion of modern Iranian icons of Muhammad and 'Ali, see Fontana, *L'Iconografia dell'Ahl al-Bayt*, 47–56, figs. 52–61; Newid, *Der schiitische Islam in Bildern*, 189–201; Ekhtiar, "Exploring *Ahl al-Bayt* Imagery in Qajar Iran (1785–1925)," 150–52; and Kleiber, "Expression populaire et devotion shi'ite," 66–70.

53. Gril, "Le Prophète en famille," 29, 69 (*moteur d'élévation spirituelle*).

54. Sharon, "*Ahl al-Bayt*," 183.

55. Vesel, "Talismans from the Iranian World," 264.

56. Amir-Moezzi "Icon and Meditation," 30; Kleiber, "Expression populaire et devotion shi'ite," 68–69; and Ekhtiar, "Exploring *Ahl al-Bayt* Imagery in Qajar Iran (1785–1925)," 146.

57. Contra Benjamin, "The Work of Art in the Age of Mechanical Reproduction," 223.

58. Expression borrowed from Ekhtiar, "Infused with Shi'ism."

59. For the same poster, see Puin, *Islamische Plakate*, 2:540–43, cat. no. J-6a, and 3:906, plate J-6a. The Harvard poster includes an attribution to the artist. However, it reproduces a drawing by Husayn Zaydi Latifi, a late-Qajar-era artist known as Sayyid 'Arab; on Sayyid 'Arab, see Puin, *Islamische Plakate*, 2:435–39, and 3:845.

60. 'Ali is also known as the "lion of God" (*asadullah* and *shir-i khuda*) and therefore is depicted as an angelic lion, especially within *mi'raj* narratives and images. See Shani, "The Lion Image in Safavid *Mi'raj* Paintings"; Gruber, "When *Nubuvvat* Encounters *Valayat*"; and Boozari, "Persian Illustrated Lithographed Books on the *Mi'raj*." For a broader discussion of leonine symbolism in Shi'i figural and calligraphic arts, see the contributions by Zarcone, Shani, Khosronejad, and Suleman to Khosronejad, *The Art and Material Culture of Iranian Shi'ism*.

61. For a detailed discussion of this mural, see Gruber, "Images of Muhammad *In and Out* of Modernity."

62. On *bazuband*s, see Gandy, "Inscribed Silver Amulet Boxes"; and Maddison and Savage-Smith, *Science, Tools and Magic*, 144–47.

63. On the many interpretations of the term *al-masjid al-aqsa*, see in particular Busse, "Jerusalem in the Story of Muhammad's Night Journey and Ascension"; Bevan, "Mohammed's Ascension to Heaven"; and Hasson, "The Muslim View of Jerusalem."

64. For a selection of Persian poetic ascension texts, see Ranjabar, *Chand Mi'rajnama*.

65. The verses read, "One night he rode and traversed the celestial sphere / he reached an honor and place beyond the angel."

66. Hanaway, "Some Accounts of the *Mi'raj* of the Prophet in Persian Literature," 558.

67. For a discussion of paintings depicting Muhammad's ascension over Mecca, see Gruber, "The Prophet Muhammad's Ascension (*Mi'raj*) in Islamic Art and Literature, 1300–1600," 255–63 (section on "Ka'ba-*Mi'raj* Compositions").

68. Roxburgh, "Pilgrimage City," 767.

69. Gruber, "Jerusalem in the Visual Propaganda of Post-Revolutionary Iran."

70. Ram, *Iranophobia*, 89, 168n98; Amirpur, "Iran's Policy towards Jewish Iranians and the State of Israel," 387; and Hooglund, "Decoding Ahmadinejad's Rhetoric on Israel," 198–203, especially 199–200, for a critical discussion of the content and language of Ahmadinejad's statement.

71. Brown, "Thing Theory," 4.

72. Flaskerud, *Visualizing Belief and Piety in Iranian Shiism*, 30.

73. Rubin, "The Shrouded Messenger," 99.

74. Rubin, "Nur Muhammadi," 125.

75. There exist many Qajar and post-Qajar depictions of the veiled Prophet. For a selection of paintings, murals, and other objects, see in particular Ekhtiar, "Infused with Shi'ism"; Ekhtiar, "Exploring *Ahl al-Bayt* Imagery in Qajar Iran (1785–1925)," 146, 149–50; and Boozari, "Shama'il-i payambar dar kitabha-yi chap-i sangi-yi dawra-yi qajar."

76. A number of modern illustrated manuscripts of Ibn Husam's *Book of Eastern Exploits* include depictions of the veiled Prophet. However, the text was produced as an illustrated manuscript as early as the last quarter of the fifteenth century. For more information on the author, text, and illustrated manuscripts, see Ibn Husam, *Khavaran Nameh*; and for Qajar-period illustrated copies, see Ekhtiar, "Infused with Shi'ism," 104–5, 129–33, plates 25–29.

77. Bazil, *Kitab-i Hamla-yi Haydari*, 43.

78. Nizami, *Makhzanol Asrar*, 109, line 285.

79. Jami, *An Allegorical Romance*, 5.

   THE PRAISEWORTHY ONE

80. Soroush, "Zahir al-Dawla, Ebrahim Khan."

81. Steingass, *A Comprehensive Persian-English Dictionary*, 1353, viz. "*mihr.*"

82. Schimmel, *As through a Veil*, 186, 290n171.

83. Some Shi'is believe that entire chapters were omitted from the Qur'an; these include *surat nurayn* (the chapter of the two lights) and *surat al-walaya* (the chapter of vicegerency), both of which discuss 'Ali's elevated rank. For a review of these discussions, see Amir-Moezzi, *The Divine Guide in Early Shi'ism*, 79–91.

84. See Ådahl, "A Copy of the Divan of Mir 'Ali Shir Nava'i," 9, fig. 8; 11, fig. 11.

85. Al-Ghazali, *The Niche of Lights*, 1, 23.

86. Al-Yahsubi, *Muhammad*, 127.

87. Van Ess, *The Youthful God*, 8.

88. Nizami, *Makhzanol Asrar*, 103, 200–202.

89. Jami, *An Allegorical Romance*, 4.

90. Jami, *An Allegorical Romance*, 2.

91. Heinzelmann, *Populäre religiöse Literatur und Buchkultur im Osmanischen Reich*, 165. Yazıcıoğlu wrote his *Muhammad Poem* in Arabic under the title *Magharib al-Zaman* (Sunset of Time) before he translated it into Turkish.

92. For example, the Ottoman polymath Evliya Çelebi notes that Yazıcıoğlu's *Muhammad Poem* was memorized and recited, much like the Qur'an. Additionally, copies of the text were considered holy relics, were recited over Yazıcıoğlu's grave, and were even used in the accession ceremonies of two Ottoman sultans during the nineteenth century (see Heinzelmann, *Populäre religiöse Literatur und Buchkultur im Osmanischen Reich*, 316–22).

93. Heinzelmann, *Populäre religiöse Literatur und Buchkultur im Osmanischen Reich*, 120–21.

94. Illustrated in Heinzelmann, *Populäre religiöse Literatur und Buchkultur im Osmanischen Reich*, 509, fig. 3.34.

95. For a further discussion of the battle of Uhud (625 CE), see Ibn Ishaq, *The Life of Muhammad*, 370–91; Lings, *Muhammad*, 180–94; and Armstrong, *Muhammad*, 187–90.

96. For a more detailed discussion of Ottoman tactile interventions, see chapter 5; Gruber, "In Defense and Devotion"; and Flood, "Bodies and Becoming."

97. Heinzelmann, *Populäre religiöse Literatur und Buchkultur im Osmanischen Reich*, 200–201.

98. For a thirteenth-century illustrated war tactic (*furusiyya*) manuscript published as a facsimile, see Fakhr-i Mudabbir, *Adab al-Harb wa'l-Shaja'a*, in particular 285–288 for comparative diagrams of military formations.

99. On the "alienation" or "estrangement" effect (*Verfremdungseffekt*) and making "strange" or "other" (*Umheimlich*) in Bertolt Brecht's plays, see Carney, *Brecht and Critical Theory*, 14–22.

100. For the 2012 *hilye* exhibition in Hagia Sophia, see the many press releases online, including at http://www.yenisafak.com/aktuel/hilye-i-serif-sergisi-ayasofyada-acildi-377923 (accessed May 17, 2018); and for the 2014 *Aşk-ı Nebi* show in Topkapı, see the catalogue *Aşk-ı Nebi*.

101. On the maintenance of the contours of cultural continuity in modern Islamic art, see Bhabha, "Another Country," 31; and on Islamic art as partaking in global systems of art, see Lowry, *Oil and Sugar*, 10.

102. Zakariya, "The Hilye of the Prophet Muhammad."

103. Qur'an 68:4: *wa innaka la'ala khuluqin 'adhimin.*

104. On *khalq* and *khulq* in descriptions of the Prophet's body and character, see Gril, "Le corps du Prophète," 39.

105. Zakariya, "The Hilye of the Prophet Muhammad," 21.

106. Author's interview with Mohamed Zakariya, December 7, 2015.

107. Author's interview with Mohamed Zakariyya, December 7, 2015.

108. Schick, "The Iconicity of Islamic Calligraphy in Turkey," 211; and Schick, "The Content of Form," 189–93.

109. For a calligram of Muhammad's name represented in a painting included in a western Indian manuscript dated 1441 CE, see Gruber, "Between Logos (*Kalima*) and Light (*Nur*)," 246, fig. 11.

110. For more about Salah Hassuna and his art, see Gysi, *Geschichten, Bilder*; and for other Islamic calligrams of Muhammad's name produced as popular posters, see Puin, *Islamische Plakate*, vol. 3, fig. D-28; Centlivres and Centlivres-Demont, "Une présence absente," 150–51; and Centlivres and Centlivres-Demont, *Imageries populaires en Islam*, 27–31, figs. 7–14.

111. For pilgrimage paintings, see Parker, *Hajj Paintings*; and Michot, "Les fresques du pélerinage au Caire"; and for a 2012 Islamist mural of Muhammad—shown from the back and topped by a calligram of his name—riding on horseback with the qur'anic proclamation "Indeed, we are sufficient for you against the mockers" (15:95), see Abaza, "The Dramaturgy of a Street Corner," fig. 4.

112. For posters showing Muhammad as a calligram riding Buraq made in Pakistan and India, see Centlivres and Centlivres-Demont, *Imageries populaires en Islam*, 46, fig. 35; and Saeed,

Muslim Devotional Art in India, 46, fig. 2.4. For posters of Buraq alone, see Shatanawi, *Islam at the Tropenmuseum*, 200–201.

113. On the use of pictographs in sequential art, see Eisner, *Comics and Sequential Art*, 8–10.

114. For the Egyptian Grand Mufti (chief judge) Muhammad ʿAbduh's opinion (*fatwa*) in favor of pictorial representation, in which he praises the pedagogical and religious benefits of images and sculptures, see Ramadan, "'One of the Best Tools for Learning,'" 149; and Vernoit, "The Visual Arts in Nineteenth-Century Muslim Thought," 31.

115. Schimmel, *As through a Veil*, 174.

116. Schimmel, *As through a Veil*, 193.

117. Massey, "Mysterious Letters." Beyond the interpretation of the Qur'an's disconnected letters as abbreviations for God's names and epithets, they also have been understood as stand-ins for the *basmala* or initials for the reciters of the Qur'an. For the letters' abbreviation of the *basmala*, see most especially Bellamy, "The Mysterious Letters of the Koran."

118. Schimmel, "The Primordial Dot," 355.

119. On the *mim* of Muhammad's name as the "circle of empire," "circle of mercy," and "most brilliant center of the compass," see Nizami, *Makhzanol Asrar*, 97 (line 120), 98 (line 129), 106 (line 235); and on Muhammad as the "pole" (*qutb*) of creation, see Ernst, "Muhammad as the Pole of Existence," 136.

120. For a discussion of Buraq in literary and artistic traditions, see, inter alia, Gruber, "Al-Buraq"; and Arnold, "Buraq."

121. Gruber, "Al-Buraq," 40.

122. Ibn Kathir, *Tafsir Ibn Kathir*, 5:574.

123. Centlivres and Centlivres-Demont, *Imageries populaires en Islam*, 46; Centlivres and Centlivres-Demont, "Une présence absente," 160–64; Centlivres-Demont, "La bataille de Kerbela (680/61H.) dans l'imagerie populaire chiite," especially 116–17, figs. III.4–7; and Saeed, *Muslim Devotional Art in India*, 51, fig. 2.6

124. Norris, "Demi's 'Muhammad.'"

125. Klausen, *The Cartoons That Shook the World*.

126. "Jytte Klausen on Yale University and the Danish Cartoons," *Free Speech Debate*, April 17, 2014, http://freespeechdebate.com/en/media/jytte-klausen-on-yale-university-and-the-danish-cartoons/ (accessed May 17, 2018). Despite Klausen receiving no threats, the cartoons were considered blasphemous in various parts of the Islamic world. For a study of reactions in Indonesia, which included articulations of the notion of "blasphemy," see Keane, "Freedom and Blasphemy."

127. Kubler, *The Shape of Time*, 64.

128. For comparative Buraq sculptures made in Nigeria and India, see von Folsach, Lundbæk, and Mortensen, *Sultan, Shah, and Great Mughal*, 237, cat. no. 237, and 16, cat. no. 40; and Bernus-Taylor, *L'étrange et le merveilleux en terres d'Islam*, 291, plate 193.

129. For a female Buraq sculpture (which belongs to a male-female pair) made in Lombok, Indonesia, see Johnson Museum of Art, Cornell University, 2007.069.002, http://museum.cornell.edu/collections/asian-pacific/indonesia/female-buraq (accessed May 17, 2018).

130. Sakili, *Space and Identity*, 191. Additionally, it has been suggested that the "flourishing carving industry of religious images for Catholic Filipinos may have encouraged the making of such sculptures" (Chong et al, *Devotion and Desire*, 96, fig. 95).

131. Gowing, *Muslim Filipinos*, 61 (on descriptions of Buraq), 133–34 (on dancing dolls).

132. For photographs and videos of Cirebon Burokan processions, see "Burokan," August 9, 2011, http://disparbud.jabarprov.go.id/wisata/dest-det.php?id=363; and "Kesenian BuroQ Gebang Cirebon," September 12, 2012, http://www.youtube.com/watch?v=vTWxoGq6q_M (a number of child-bearing Buraq dolls arrive at minute 1:04).

133. Pakistani trucks include talismanic representations of Buraq as a metaphor for the truck's journey as well as other motifs that protect the driver from the evil eye (*nazar*). These trucks also propagate the Islamic faith or exhort the benefits of prayer. See Elias, *On Wings of Diesel*, 192 (on Buraq); and Elias, "Truck Decoration and Religious Identity," 63, which lists maxims that refer to Muhammad's celestial journey, including "prayer is the path to salvation" and "prayer is the ascent (*miʿraj*) of the believer."

134. Published in Berthier and Zali, *Livres de parole*, 183, cat. no. 126.

135. On the aura of objects and their "tactile apprehension" in particular, see Benjamin, "The Work of Art in the Age of the Mechanical Reproduction," 243.

136. There exist a number of Turkish companies that produce *hajj* goods and laminated devotional cards. Chief among them is Tevhid Seda, the country's leading wholesale provider of Islamic religious goods.

137. Numerous articles about Muhammad's ID card can be found on Turkish news websites by using the search term *Hz. Muhammed'e nüfus cüzdanı*. For a critical discussion of these types of Turkish ID cards and state-sponsored religious practices in Turkey today, see in particular http://www.sozcu.com.tr/2017/yazarlar/yilmaz-ozdil/insanda-biraz-utanma-olur-1743213/ (accessed May 17, 2018).

138. The expression *nurani belgesi* is linguistically awkward, suggesting that the card's manufacturer was not fully conversant in either Arabic or Ottoman Turkish.

139. Orhan Kemal Cengiz, "Erdogan's Reforms Meant to Educate 'Pious Generation,'" *Monitor*, June 24, 2014, http://www.al-monitor.com/pulse/originals/2014/06/cengiz-produce-religious-generations-erdogan-akp-islamist.html (accessed May 17, 2018).

140. "Hz. Muhammed'in oglunun adı Tayyip mi?," *Radikal*, October 10, 2012, http://www.radikal.com.tr/politika/hz-muhammedin-oglunun-adi-tayyip-mi-1103536/ (accessed May 17, 2018).

141. Hall, "Encoding, Decoding," 90–92.

142. Starrett, "The Political Economy of Religious Commodities in Cairo," 66.

143. On Turkish educational and alphabet reforms, see, most especially, Fortna, *Learning to Read in the Late Ottoman Empire and the Early Turkish Republic*.

144. For the television series *Muhteşem Yüzyıl* (Magnificent Century), which dramatizes the life of Sultan Süleyman (d. 1566), see Carney, "A Dizi-ying Past."

145. On Eyüp as an urban "assemblage" of material piety, see Hammond, "Matters of the Mosque"; and on neo-Ottomanism, see Walton, "Practices of Neo-Ottomanism."

146. John Hall, "Inside the ISIS Gift Shop," *Mail Online*, June 24, 2014, http://www.dailymail.co.uk/news/article-2666854/Inside-ISIS-gift-shop-Online-jihadist-spring-summer-collection-shocks-internet.html (accessed May 17, 2018).

147. Kashmira Gander, "Isis Flag: What Do the Words Mean and What Are Their Origins?," *Independent*, July 6, 2015, http://www.independent.co.uk/news/world/middle-east/isis-flag-what-do-the-words-mean-and-what-are-its-origins-10369601.html (accessed May 17, 2018). Additionally, ISIS military uniforms were made in Turkish sweatshops until 2016; see Isabel Hunter and Salem Rizk, "'Child Slaves' Making Uniforms for ISIS," *Mail Online*, June 6, 2016, http://www.dailymail.co.uk/news/article-3597143/Child-slaves-making-uniforms-Isis-Inside-Turkish-sweatshop-children-young-nine-work-12-hours-day-stitching-combat-gear-used-battle-Islamic-State.html (accessed May 17, 2018).

148. Aydın, *Pavilion of the Sacred Relics*, 95–101.

149. For men's sandal print "turban hats," see *Shukr Islamic Clothing*, http://www.shukronline.com/mh0202.html (accessed May 18, 2018).

150. "The Prophet Muhammad's Sandal," *Shukr Islamic Clothing*, http://www.shukronline.com/the-prophets-sandal.html (accessed May 18, 2018).

151. On Imam Rabbani and Islamic mysticism, see, in particular, Karaman, *İmam-ı Rabbânî ve İslâm Tasavvufu*; and Schimmel, *Islam in the Indian Subcontinent*, 93–95. The Evlad-ı Rabbani also manage a Facebook page with almost two thousand members: https://www.facebook.com/%C4%B0MAM-I-RABBAN%C4%B0-EVLADI-123844027713032/ (accessed May 18, 2018).

152. On Islamic vestmental systems and the crafting of "Muslim looks," see Akou, "Building a New 'World Fashion'"; and Tarlo, *Visibly Muslim*.

153. Elias, "Islam and the Devotional Image in Pakistan," 120–24, and figs. 8.1–8.2; and for a similar sandal print poster, see Centlivres and Centlivres-Demont, *Imageries populaires en Islam*, 32, fig. 16; and Centlivres and Centlivres-Demont, "Une présence absente," 156.

154. Elias, "Islam and the Devotional Image in Pakistan," 122, fig. 8.2.

155. The wall decal is sold in a number of different sizes, the largest of which measures 127 x 68.6 cm. See the sandal print decal information at *Simply Impressions*, http://www.simplyimpressions.com/collections/traditional-text/products/mercy-to-mankind-mohammad (accessed May 18, 2018).

156. "About Us," *Simply Impressions*, http://www.simplyimpressions.com/pages/about-us (accessed May 18, 2018).

157. Kubler, *The Shape of Time*, 82.

158. On "authorized language" in religious registers and the use of consumer goods in the production of an orthodox position, see Bourdieu, "Authorized Language"; and Bourdieu, "The Market of Symbolic Goods," 129.

159. Morgan, *The Sacred Gaze*, 83.

160. Arvatov and Kiaer, "Everyday Life and the Culture of the Thing," 125.

161. Greenberg, "Avant-Garde and Kitsch," 11.

162. Kopytoff, "The Cultural Biography of Things," 75; and Brown, "Thing Theory," 7.

163. On the "traffic of criteria" in mass-produced commodities, see Appadurai, "Introduction: Commodities and the Politics of Value," 54.

164. On the consumption of objects as part of a larger "behavioral complex," see Belk, Wallendorf, and Sherry, "The Sacred and the Profane in Consumer Behaviour," 32.

وصول النبي صلى الله عليه وسلم الى مقام القربة واشارة جبريل انه مقام القربة
وقال له اسجد فسجد صلى الله عليه وسلم وقال رايت الحق تعالى وجل جلاله بعين قلبي

حضرت محمد عليه السلام مقام قربة اولاشدی وجبرائيل عليه السلام بو مقام قربة دور تب اشارت ايلادی و سجده ايلا دیدی حضرت رسول صلى الله عليه وسلم
دنی حقه سجده ايلادی وبی کوکل کوزی الحق تعالی حضرتلرنی کوردم دیدوکی حالدر

[illegible]
[illegible]
[illegible]
[illegible]
[illegible]
[illegible]
[illegible]

[illegible]

[illegible]

CONCLUSION

In the fall of 2015, the Iranian artist Shahpour Pouyan (b. 1980), who lives and works in New York City, held an exhibition at the Copperfield Gallery in London. The exhibition, *History Travels at Different Speeds*, included a series of sixteen miniatures made between 2008 and 2015. Pouyan's compositions reproduce famous premodern Turco-Persian book paintings, which the artist manipulated by extracting all representations of humans and animals. After digitally removing the depicted animate beings, he repainted the areas that they had occupied, using the processes and pigments of medieval book painters. At times, he reconstituted a natural landscape to "coax the unspoken from the background," while at others he included swaths of black pigment to create in his viewers a "discomfort evoked by these images, now devoid of their mythic and historic characters."[1]

I visited Pouyan's exhibition in the throes of finishing this book. While I wandered through the gallery, the figureless folios loomed large even in their diminutive formats. One of his miniature paintings caught my eye (fig. C.1). Before me was a folio of the famous Timurid *Mi'rajnama* (Book of Ascension) of about 1436 CE, with its recognizable Uighur script contained in the main text frame.[2] At the top, a gold caption in Arabic identifies the subject as Muhammad prostrating in prayer on his arrival at the "station of proximity" (*maqam al-qurba*), where he experiences a vision of God with the "eye of his heart." Pouyan omitted the Prophet in his full physical form, genuflecting in the light of divinity, as Muhammad appears in the original Timurid composition (fig. C.2). Instead, a large rectangular field of purplish black now overwhelms the painting's frame.

At first glance, it would be easy to interpret Pouyan's work as a scathing commentary on the bowdlerization of Islamic representations of Muhammad in a world fraught with conflicts over the image of Islam and its prophet. The artist readily admits as much: the black rectangle mourns a lost artistic heritage, from which contemporary Muslims are increasingly disconnected and alienated. Additionally, Pouyan explains that the black rectangle is intended to recall the stroke of the Iranian censor's black pen, which blotches out the skin of women printed on the labels of imported commercial products.[3] In this miniature, however, it is Muhammad's own flesh that has been blackened by redaction.

However, the monochromatic field that hovers in the Prophet's stead aims toward much more than making Muhammad off-limits or taboo. For Pouyan, this color-field painting in miniature format strives to depict God and the Prophet as out of sight and out of bounds—and

A question is [already] half of knowledge (*al-su'al nisf al-'ilm*).

Saying attributed to the Prophet Muhammad

FACING, C.1. Shahpour Pouyan, *After, the Prophet Muhammad Bows before the Lord's Radiance*, mixed media on Japanese rice paper, 53 × 47 cm (20 ⅞ × 18 ½ in.), 2012. Image courtesy of the artist and Copperfield Gallery, London.

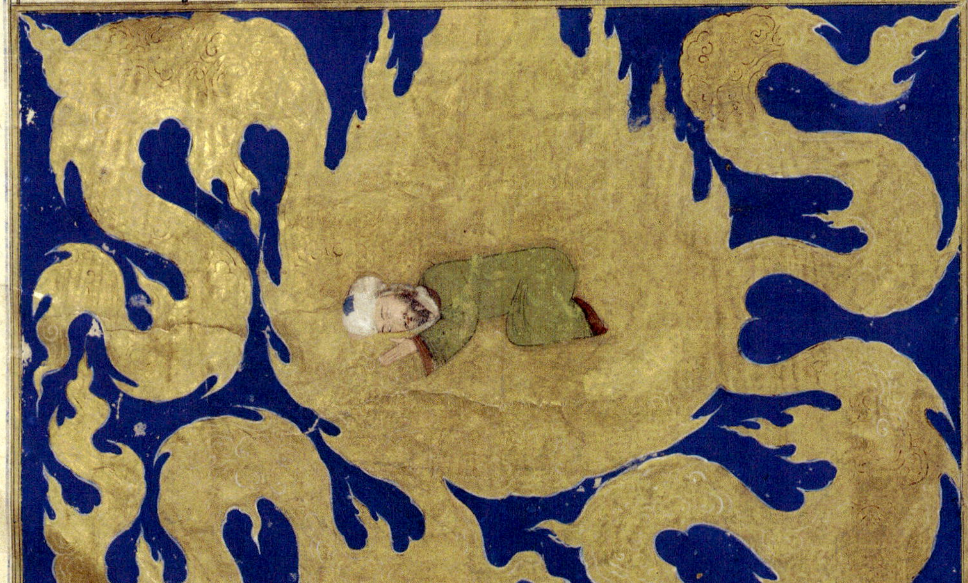

حضرت محمد عليه السلام مقام قرب اولسه وجبرائيل عليه السلام دو مقام قرب دولر ديو اشارت ايلدوكي و بجان ايلدو دو حضر رسول الله عليه السلم
دخى حقه سجد ايدوب كوكل كوز ريله حق تعالى حضرتلرني كوردم ديدوكي خبردر

[central text block in stylized script — not legibly transcribable] therefore transcendent. Per the artist's own account, the rectangle conveys an eeriness and sense of loss, and it remains open to multiple readings. One way to interpret this field of color is by looking to the artist Mark Rothko (1903–70), the abstract expressionist painter known for his color-field compositions. In his youth, Pouyan studied and viewed Rothko's canvas paintings in the Tehran Museum of Modern Art, and the Iranian artist stresses that the purplish black hue in his revised miniature of Muhammad purposefully mimics the deeply toned purple and maroon canvas paintings hanging in the Rothko Chapel in Houston, Texas.[4] There, in a modern ecumenical chapel built in 1971, viewers do not confront figural images of Jesus or other representational imagery. Instead, they are surrounded by fourteen large-scale monochromatic canvases painted in deep, serene blackish mauves, hues that shimmer and change as sunlight streams into the building through a central dome.

Working within their own traditions, both Pouyan and Rothko attempted to capture divine otherness through painterly techniques typically associated with abstract expressionism and color-field painting. For both artists, this modernist artistic language captures the "urgency of the transcendent experience."[5] On the one hand, for Rothko and his admirers, the abstract purplish tones allow an interfaith sanctuary to have a soothing effect on its visitors while inviting them to gaze on the beyond: what bypasses the realm of figuration, the limitations of eyesight, the here and now, and divisions of faith. As Dominique de Menil, the chapel's patron, remarked during the opening ceremony, "we are cluttered with images and only abstract art can bring us to the threshold of the divine."[6] In this center of worship, an individual belonging to any faith community (or none) can contemplate absolute otherness through a series of amorphous fields of color whose melancholy tones do not sink the spirit but rather elevate it.

Despite its omission of figuration, Pouyan's Muhammad overlaid in crimson-black hues offers its own religious sanctuary of sorts. Its transcendence of form invites the viewer to a psychological ascension, surpassing the limits of vision in a manner reminiscent of the Prophet's own *mi'raj* into the heavenly spheres. Here, Muhammad is shown as leaving behind time, space, and physicality itself, challenging the painting's viewers to do likewise. This alternative interpretive reading reveals the double-edged nature of the process of abstraction while also highlighting potentially contradictory views on Islam and its visual arts: while to some this blackened aniconic field may result from Islam's putative ban against figural representation, to others it stands as the ultimate sign of modernity, unshackled from the literalism of the figural mode. To still others, it may prove a productive encounter between innovation and tradition, blurring facile binaries along the way.

What stands out most in this scenario is the extent to which discourses on modernity stress abstraction over figuration, or figuration over figurelessness, claiming one's superiority to the other, depending on need and circumstance. In our postcartoon world, Euro-American teleological discourses that affirm the pictorial image (rather than abstraction) as an index of modernity tend to argue that Islamic cultures prove a medieval "evolutionary failure with moral overtones."[7] Within such polemical framings, modernity and morality are allowed to some but not to others—and when it comes to questions of morality, the use and abuse of depictions of the Prophet is the one tactic that has over and again proved ethically suspect.

Today, images of Muhammad have been caricatured and mocked, rejected and banned, reasserted and treasured. These contradictory stances and reactions reveal much more about contemporary ideologies than they do about Islamic artistic traditions. In the surviving corpus of Islamic images dating back to the thirteenth century, the Prophet is shown in an array of modes: as a sacred king, a veiled mystery, and a talismanic force. These pictorial strategies reflect the skills and creativity of many Muslim artists who lived and worked within their own religious, cultural, and political settings. Over the course of more than a millennium, Islamic textual and visual depictions have attempted to convey Muhammad as a "welter of differences,"[8] embodying qualities that his followers have most desired to see, praise, and emulate.

As much as they act as barometers of Muslim life and thought, Islamic images of the Prophet also offer a cautionary tale about how we go about posing questions, and in what ways we can begin to answer them. For example, in querying Pouyan's Rothko-like twist on an Islamic depiction of Muhammad, some may conclude that it provides an instance of Islamic iconoclasm, while others may see in it an abstracted form of modernism. For his part, Pouyan claims to adopt and enact both possibilities, refusing to accept either as the primary drive for or destination of his oeuvre. Like many artists who came before him, Pouyan has created an image that reflects his own artistic agency and agenda. Its many possibilities invite us to move beyond hackneyed discourses on Islam's so-called image problem to pose more nuanced questions about Islamic practices of representing the Prophet Muhammad. In their complex totality, such images offer us a richly textured tale that travels at different speeds and remains half-told, its conclusion still to be written.

NOTES

1. See a description of the fall 2016 exhibition at http://www.copperfieldgallery.com/shahpour-pouyan-history-travels-at-different-speeds.html (accessed May 17, 2018).

2. On the Timurid *Book of Ascension*, see chapter 2, figs. 2.20–2.22.

3. Shahpour Pouyan, interview with author, December 5, 2015, New York City.

4. Barnes, *The Rothko Chapel*; de Menil, *The Rothko Chapel*.

5. Stoker, "The Rothko Chapel Paintings and the 'Urgency of the Transcendent Experience'"; and on abstraction as an "expression of spiritual transcendentalism" in scholarly discourses about European modernist and premodern Islamic art, see Flood, "Picasso the Muslim," 56.

6. Menil, *The Rothko Chapel*, 19.

7. Flood, "Inciting Modernity?," 56.

8. Donner, "Muhammad and the Debates on Islam's Origins in the Digital Age," 33.

Abaza, Mona. "The Dramaturgy of a Street Corner." *Jadaliyya*, January 25, 2013. http://www.jadaliyya.com/pages/index/9724/the-dramaturgy-of-a-street-corner.

'Abd al-Mun'im, 'Amru. *Al-Sahih min Qissat al-Isra' wa'l-Mi'raj*. Tanta: Dar al-Sahaba, 1413/1993.

Abdel-Malek, Kamal. *Muhammad in the Modern Egyptian Popular Ballad*. Leiden: Brill, 1995.

Abdulfattah, Iman. "Relics of the Prophet and Practices of His Veneration in Medieval Cairo." *Journal of Islamic Archaeology* 1, no. 1 (2014): 75–104.

Abel, Armand. "Bahira." In *The Encyclopaedia of Islam*, edited by P. Bearman, Th. Bianquis, C. E. Bosworth, E. van Donzel, and W. P. Heinrichs, 922–23. 2nd ed. Leiden: Brill, 1986.

Abrahamov, Binyamin. "Fakhr al-Din al-Razi on the Knowability of God's Essence and Attributes." *Arabica* 49, no. 2 (April 2002): 204–30.

Ådahl, Karin. "A Copy of the Divan of Mir 'Ali Shir Nava'i of the Late Eighteenth Century in the Lund University Library and the Kashmiri School of Miniature Painting." In *Persian Painting from the Mongols to the Qajars: Studies in Honour of Basil W. Robinson*, edited by Robert Hillenbrand, 3–18. London: I. B. Tauris, 2000.

Aflaki. *The Feats of the Knowers of God (Manaqeb al-'arefin)*. Translated by John O'Kane. Leiden: Brill, 2002.

Afsaruddin, Asma. "Where Earth and Heaven Meet: Remembering Muhammad as Head of State." In *The Cambridge Companion to Muhammad*, edited by Jonathan Brockopp, 180–98. New York: Cambridge University Press, 2010.

Ahmadi, Nozhat. "The Role of Dreams in the Political Affairs of the Safavid Dynasty." *Journal of Shi'a Islamic Studies* 6, no. 2 (Spring 2013): 177–98.

Ahmed, Shahab. "Ibn Taymiyyah and the Satanic Verses." *Studia Islamica* 87 (1998): 67–124.

———. *What Is Islam?: The Importance of Being Islamic*. Princeton, NJ: Princeton University Press, 2015.

Akou, Heather Marie. "Building a New 'World Fashion': Islamic Dress in the Twenty-First Century." *Fashion Theory* 11, no. 4 (2007): 403–22.

Aktaş, Uğur. *İstanbul'un 100 Âdeti*. Istanbul: İstanbul Büyükşehir Belediyesi, 2013.

Algar, Hamid. "Devotional Practices of the Khalidi Naqshbandis of Ottoman Turkey." In *The Dervish Lodge: Architecture, Art, and Sufism in Ottoman Turkey*, edited by Raymond Lifchez, 209–27. Berkeley: University of California Press, 1992.

———. "The Naqshbandi Order: A Preliminary Survey of Its History and Significance." *Studia Islamica* 44 (1976): 123–52.

Ali, Mustafa. *Mustafa Ali's Epic Deeds of Artists: A Critical Edition of the Earliest Ottoman Text about the Calligraphers and Painters of the Islamic World*. Edited and translated by Esra Akın. Leiden: Brill, 2011.

Ali, Wijdan. "From the Literal to the Spiritual: The Development of the Prophet Muhammad's Portrayal from 13th Century Ilkhanid Miniatures to 17th Century Ottoman Art." In *Proceedings of the 11th International Congress of Turkish Art (Utrecht, The Netherlands, August 23–28, 1999)*, edited by Machiel Kiel, Nico Landman, and Hans Theunissen, 1–24. Utrecht: University of Utrecht, 2001.

Allan, James. *The Art and Architecture of Twelver Shi'ism: Iraq, Iran, and the Indian Sub-Continent*. Oxford: Azimuth Editions, 2012.

Allen, Terry. "Aniconism and Figural Representation in Islamic Art." In *Five Essays on Islamic Art*, 17–37. Sebastopol, CA: Solipsist, 1988.

Allsen, Thomas. "Changing Forms of Legitimation in Mongol Iran." In *Rulers from the Steppe: State Formation on the Eurasian Periphery*, edited by Gary Seaman and Daniel Marks, 223–41. Los Angeles: University of Southern California, 1991.

———. *Commodity and Exchange in the Mongol Empire: A Cultural History of Islamic Textiles*. Cambridge: Cambridge University Press, 1997.

Alparslan, Ali. *Osmanlı Hat Sanatı Tarihi*. 2nd ed. Istanbul: Yapı Kredi Yayınları, 2004.

Al-Alwani, Taha Jaber. "Fatwa Concerning the United States Supreme Courtroom Frieze." *Journal of Law and Religion* 15, nos. 1–2 (2000–2001): 1–28.

Amanat, Abbas. "Court Patronage and Public Space: Abu'l-Hassan Sani' al-Mulk and the Art of Persianizing the Other in Qajar Iran." In *Court Cultures in the Muslim World*, *Seventh to Nineteenth Centuries*, edited by Albrecht Fuess and Jan-Peter Hartung, 408–44. London: Routledge, 2010.

———. "The Kayanid Crown and Qajar Reclaiming of Royal Authority." *Iranian Studies* 34, nos. 1–4 (2001): 17–30.

———. "*Meadows of the Martyrs*: Kashifi's Persianization of the Shi'i Martyrdom Narrative in Late Timurid Herat." In *Culture and Memory in Medieval Islam: Essays in Honour of Wilfred Madelung*, edited by Farhad Daftary and Josef Meri, 250–75. London: I. B. Tauris in association with the Institute of Ismaili Studies, 2003.

———. *Pivot of the Universe: Nasir al-Din Shah Qajar and the Iranian Monarchy, 1831–1896*. Berkeley: University of California Press, 1997.

Amir, Mahmud. *Iran dar Ruzgar-i Shah Isma'il va Shah Tahmasb Safavi*. Edited by Ghulam Riza Tabataba'i. Tehran: Bunyad-i Mawqufat-i Duktur Mahmud Afshar Yazdi, 1370/1991.

Amir-Moezzi, Mohammad Ali. "'Ali et le Coran (aspects de l'imamologie duodécimaine XIV)." *Revue des Sciences Philosophiques et Théologiques* 98 (2014): 669–704.

———. *The Divine Guide in Early Shi'ism: The Sources of Esotericism in Islam*. Albany: State University of New York Press, 1994.

———. "Icon and Meditation: Popular Art and Sufism in Imami Shi'ism." In *The Art and Material Culture of Iranian Shi'ism: Iconography and Religious Devotion in Shi'i Islam*, edited by Pedram Khosronejad, 25–45. London: I. B. Tauris, 2012.

———. "The Imam in Heaven." In *The Spirituality of Shi'i Islam: Beliefs and Practices*, 169–91. London: I. B. Tauris, 2011.

———. "Notes à propos de la *walaya* imamite (aspects de l'imamologie duodécimaine, X)." *Journal of the American Oriental Society* 122, no. 4 (October–December 2002): 722–41.

———. "The Pre-existence of the Imam." In *Divine Guide in Early Shi'ism: The Sources of Esoteriscism in Islam*, translated by David Streight, 29–59. Albany: State University of New York Press, 1994.

———. "Some Remarks on the Divinity of the Imam." In *The Spirituality in of Shi'i Islam: Beliefs and Practices*, 103–21. London: I. B. Tauris, 2011.

———. *The Spirituality of Shi'i Islam*. London: I. B. Tauris, 2011.

———, ed. *Le voyage initiatique en terre d'Islam: Ascensions célestes et itinéraires spirituels*. Louvain: Peeters, 1996.

Amirpur, Katajun. "Iran's Policy towards Jewish Iranians and the State of Israel: Is the Present Iranian State Islamofascist?" *Die Welt des Islams* 52, nos. 3–4 (2012): 370–99.

Amitai, Reuven. "Mongol Imperial Ideology and the Ilkhanid War against the Mamluks."

In *The Mongols in Islamic Lands: Studies in the History of the Ilkhanate*, article XII, 57–72. Aldershot: Ashgate/Variorum, 2007.

Amitai-Press, Reuven. "Sufis and Shamans: Some Remarks on the Islamization of the Mongols in the Ilkhanate." *Journal of the Economic and Social History of the Orient* 42, no. 1 (1999): 27–46.

Anawati, George. "Le nom suprême de Dieu." In *Atti del terzo Congresso di Studi Arabi e Islamici*, 7–58. Naples: Istituto Universitario Orientale, 1967.

And, Metin. *Minyatürle Osmanlı-İslam Mitologyası*. Istanbul: Akbank, 1998.

Anderson, Benedict. *Imagined Communities: Reflections on the Origin and Spread of Nationalism*. Rev. ed. London: Verso, 2006.

Andrae, Tor. *Die Person Muhammeds in Lehre und Glauben seiner Gemeinde*. Stockholm: Norstedt & Söner, 1918.

Appadurai, Arjun. "Introduction: Commodities and the Politics of Value." In *The Social Life of Things: Commodities in Cultural Perspective*, edited by Arjun Appadurai, 3–63. Cambridge: Cambridge University Press, 1986.

Arberry, Arthur, Mojtaba Minovi, and Edgar Blochet. *The Chester Beatty Library: A Catalogue of the Persian Manuscripts and Miniatures*. 3 vols. Dublin: Hodges, Figgis, 1959–62.

Arjomand, Said Amir. *The Shadow of God and the Hidden Imam: Religion, Political Order, and Societal Change in Shi'ite Iran from the Beginning to 1890*. Chicago: University of Chicago Press, 1984.

Armstrong, Karen. *Muhammad: A Short Biography*. New York: Harper Collins, 1992.

Arlı, Belgin Demirsar. "Depictions of 'Nalın-ı Şerif' (Holly Patten) on Ottoman Tiles." In *14th International Congress of Turkish Art (Paris, Collège de France, 19–21 September 2011)*, edited by Frédéric Hitzel, 273–82. Paris: Collège de France, 2013.

Arnold, Thomas. "Buraq." In *Painting in Islam: A Study of the Place of Pictorial Art in Muslim Culture*, 117–22. New York: Dover, 1965.

———. *Painting in Islam: A Study of the Place of Pictorial Art in Muslim Culture*. New York: Dover, 1965.

Arvatov, Boris, and Christina Kiaer. "Everyday Life and the Culture of the Thing (Toward the Formulation of the Question)." *October* 81 (1997): 119–28.

Asani, Ali, and Kamal Abdel-Malek. *Celebrating Muhammad: Images of the Prophet in Popular Muslim Poetry*. Columbia: University of South Carolina Press, 1995.

Asatryan, Mushegh. "An Early Shi'i Cosmology: *Kitab al-ashbah wa'l-azilla* and Its Milieu." *Studia Islamica* 110 (2015): 1–80.

Ashrafi-Aini, M. M. "The School of Bukhara to c. 1550." In *The Arts of the Book in Central Asia, 14th–16th Centuries*, edited by Basil Gray, 248–72. Boulder, CO: Shambhala Publications, 1979.

Aşk-ı Nebi: Doğumunun 1443. Yılında Hz. Peygamber / Love for the Prophet: The Prophet Muhammad on the 1443th Anniversary of his Birth. Istanbul: Kültür Sanat Basımevi, 2014.

Ateş, Ahmed. "Un vieux poème romanesque persan: Récit de Warqah et Gulshah." *Ars Orientalis* 4 (1961): 143–52.

Atıl, Esin. *Levni and the Surname: The Story of an Eighteenth-Century Ottoman Festival*. Istanbul: Koçbank, 1999.

———. "Ottoman Miniature Painting under Sultan Mehmed II." *Ars Orientalis* 9 (1973): 103–20.

———. "The Story of an Eighteenth-Century Ottoman Festival." *Muqarnas* 10 (1993): 181–200.

———. *Süleymanname: The Illustrated History of Süleyman the Magnificent*. New York: H. N. Abrams, 1986.

Aubin, Jean. "La politique religieuse des safavides." In *Le Shî'isme imâmite*, edited by Toufic Fahd, 235–44. Paris: Université de Strasbourg, 1970.

———. "Revolution chiite et conservatisme: Les Soufis de Lahejan, 1500–1514. Études safavides II." *Moyen Orient et Océan Indien* 1 (1984): 1–40.

Aydın, Hilmi. *Hırka-i Saadet Dairesi ve Mukaddes Emanetler*. Istanbul: Kaynak Kitaplığı, 2004.

———. *Pavilion of the Sacred Relics: The Sacred Trusts, Topkapi Palace Museum, Istanbul*. Istanbul: Light, 2004.

———. "Peygamberimizin Mes ve Pabuçları: Nalın-ı Saâdet." *Tarih ve Düşünce* 4 (2001): 4–25.

Ayğan, Abdurrahim. "Osmanlılarda Silsile Geleneği ve Resimli Hanedan Silsilenameler." PhD diss., Mimar Sinan Fine Arts University, 2017.

Ayoub, Mahmoud. *The Qur'an and Its Interpreters*. Albany: State University of New York Press, 1984.

'Ayyuqi. *Varqa va Gulshah-i 'Ayyuqi*. Edited by Zabih Allah Safa. Tehran: Tehran University Press, 1343/1964.

Azarpay, Guitty. "Crowns and Some Royal Insignia in Early Iran." *Iranica Antiqua* 9 (1972): 108–15.

Babayan, Kathryn. "The Cosmological Order of Things in Early Modern Safavid Iran." In *Falnama: The Book of Omens*, edited by Massumeh Farhad with Serpil Bağcı, 245–55. Washington, DC: Arthur M. Sackler Gallery, Smithsonian Institution, 2009.

———. *Mystics, Monarchs, and Messiahs: Cultural Landscapes of Early Modern Iran*. Cambridge, MA: Harvard University Press, 2002.

———. "The Safavid Synthesis: From Qizilbash Islam to Imamite Shi'ism." *Iranian Studies* 27, nos. 1–4 (1994): 135–61.

Baer, Eva. "The Ruler in Cosmic Setting: A Note on Medieval Islamic Iconography." *Islamic Art and Architecture* 1 (1981): 13–19.

Bağcı, Serpil. "From Adam to Mehmed III: Silsilenâme." In *The Sultan's Portrait: Picturing the House of Osman*, edited by Ayşe Orbay, 188–201. Istanbul: İşbank, 2000.

Bağcı, Serpil, Filiz Çağman, Günsel Renda, and Zeren Tanındı. *Ottoman Painting*. Translated by Ellen Yazar. Ankara: Kültür ve Turizm Bakanlığı Kütüphaneler ve Yayınlar Genel Müdürlüğü, 2010.

Bahari, Ebadollah. "The Sixteenth-Century School of Bukhara Painting and the Arts of the Book." In *Society and Culture in the Early Modern Middle East: Studies on Iran in the Safavid Period*, edited by Andrew Newman, 251–64. Leiden: Brill, 2003.

Bain, Alexandra. "The En'am-ı Şerif: Sacred Text and Images in a Late Ottoman Prayer Book." *Archivum Ottomanicum* 19 (2001): 213–38.

———. "The Late Ottoman En'am-ı Şerif: Sacred Text and Images in an Islamic Prayer Book." PhD diss., University of Victoria, 1999.

Al-Bal'ami, Muhammad. *Tarikh-i Bal'ami*. Edited by Muhammad Taqi Bahar. Tehran: Zavvar, 1381/2002.

Baqli, Ruzbihan. *The Unveiling of Secrets: Diary of a Sufi Master*. Translated by Carl Ernst. Chapel Hill, NC: Parvardigar, 1997.

Barnes, Susan. *The Rothko Chapel: An Act of Faith*. Austin: University of Texas Press, 1989.

Barrett, C. K. "The Holy Spirit in the Fourth Gospel." *Journal of Theological Studies* 1, no. 1 (April 1950): 1–15.

Barry, Michael. *Figurative Art in Medieval Islam and the Riddle of Bihzâd of Herât (1465–1535)*. Paris: Flammarion, 2004.

Barthes, Roland. "The Reality Effect." In *The Rustle of Language*, translated by Richard Howard, 141–54. New York: Hill and Wang, 1986.

Bartholeyns, Gil, et al. "Des raisons de détruire une image [Why destroy an image]?" *Images Re-vues* 2 (2005): 1–20.

Bashear, Suliman. "Riding Beasts on Divine Missions: An Examination of the Ass and Camel Traditions." *Journal of Semitic Studies* 32, no. 1 (Spring 1991): 37–75.

Bashir, Shahzad. "Narrating Sight: Dreaming as Visual Training in Persianate Sufi Hagiography." In *Dreams and Visions in Islamic Societies*, edited by Özgen Felek and Alexander Knysh, 233–47. Albany: State University of New York Press, 2012.

Baumann, Brian. "By the Power of Eternal Heaven: The Meaning of Tenggeri to the Government of the Pre-Buddhist Mongols." *Extrême-Orient, Extrême-Occident* 35 (2013): 233–84.

Bayram, Sadi. "Ankara Etnografya Müzesi'ndeki Madalyonlu Silsile-nâme'de Doğu Anadolu ve Batı Asya." In *VIIIth International Congress on Turkish Art: Ankara, 11–15 October 1976*, vol. 2, 645–57. Ankara: Tarih Kurumu Basımevi, 1981.

———. "Medallioned Genealogies (*Silsilenâme's*)." In *Vth International Congress on Turkish Art: Budapest, 22–27 September 1975*, 3–7. Budapest: Hungarian National Museum, 1975.

———. "Musavvir Hüseyin Tarafından Minyatürleri Yapılan ve Halen Vakıflar Genel Müdürlüğü Arşiv'inde Muhafaza Edilen Silsile-Name." *Vakıflar Dergisi* 13 (1981): 253–338.

Bazil. *Kitab-i Hamla-yi Haydari*. Tehran: Imam 'Ali Museum of Religious Arts, 1385/1965.

Beaulieu, Jill, and Mary Roberts. "Orientalism's Interlocutors." In *Orientalism's Interlocutors: Painting, Architecture, Photography*, edited by Jill Beaulieu and Mary Roberts, 1–18. Durham, NC: Duke University Press, 2002.

Beeman, William. *Iranian Performance Traditions*. Costa Mesa, CA: Mazda, 2011.

Beffa, Marie-Lise. "Le concept de *tänggäri*, 'ciel' dans l'*Histoire secrète des Mongols*." *Etudes mongoles et sibériennes* 24 (1993): 215–36.

Belk, Russell, Melanie Wallendorf, and John F. Sherry Jr. "The Sacred and the Profane in Consumer Behaviour." *Journal of Consumer Research* 16, no. 1 (1989): 1–38.

Bellamy, James. "The Mysterious Letters of the Koran: Old Abbreviations of the Basmalah." *Journal of the American Oriental Society* 93, no. 3 (July–September 1973): 267–85.

Benjamin, Walter. "The Work of Art in the Age of Mechanical Reproduction." *Illuminations* (1968): 217–51.

Berghe, Louis van den. "Les scènes d'investiture sur les reliefs rupestres de l'Iran ancien: Évolution et signification." In *Orientalia Iosephi Tucci Memoriae Dicata III*, edited by Giuseppe Tucci, Gherardo Gnoli, and Lionello Lanciotti, 1513–31. Rome: Istituto italiano per il Medio ed Estremo Oriente, 1988.

Bernus-Taylor, Marthe. *L'étrange et le merveilleux en terres d'Islam*. Paris: Réunion des Musées Nationaux, 2001.

Berthier, Annie, and Anne Zali. *Livres de parole: Torah, Bible, Coran*. Paris: Bibliothèque nationale de France, 2005.

Bevan, Anthony Ashley. "Mohammed's Ascension to Heaven." In *Studien zur Semitischen Philologie und Religionsgeschichte (for Julius Wellhausen on the Occasion of his 70th birthday, May 17, 1914)*, edited by Karl Marti, 51–61. Giessen: Von Alfred Töpelmann, 1914.

Bevan Jones, L. "The Paraclete or Mohammed: The Verdict of an Ancient Manuscript." *The Moslem World* 10, no. 2 (1920): 112–25.

Beyoğlu, Süleyman. "The Ottomans and the Islamic Sacred Relics." In *The Great Ottoman-Turkish Civilization*, edited by Kemal Çiçek, vol. 4, 36–44. Ankara: Yeni Türkiye, 2000.

Bhabha, Homi. "Another Country." In *Without Boundary: Seventeen Ways of Looking*, edited by Fereshteh Daftari, 30–35. New York: Museum of Modern Art, 2006.

Bilgi, Hülya. *Gönülden Bir Tutku: Sevgi Gönül Hat Koleksiyonu / A Heartfelt Passion: The Sevgi Gönül Calligraphy Collection*. Istanbul: Vehbi Koç Foundation, 2004.

Binbaş, Evrim. "Structure and Function of the Genealogical Tree in Islamic Historiography (1200–1500)." In *Horizons of the World: Festschrift for İsenbike Togan*, edited by Evrim Binbaş and Nurten Kılıç-Schubel, 465–544. Istanbul: Ithaki, 2011.

Binney, Edwin. *Turkish Treasures from the Collection of Edward Binney, 3rd*. Portland: Portland Art Museum, 1979.

Binyon, Laurence, J. V. S. Wilkinson, and Basil Gray, eds. *Persian Miniature Painting, Including a Critical and Descriptive Catalogue of the Miniatures Exhibited at Burlington House, January–March, 1931*. New York: Dover, 1971.

Birkeland, Harris. *The Legend of the Opening of Muhammad's Breast*. Oslo: I Kommisjon Hos Jacob Dybwab, 1955.

Al-Biruni, Abu Rayhan Muhammad ibn Ahmad. *Al-Athar al-Baqiyya 'an al-Qurun al-Khaliyya*, edited by Parviz Azkayi. Tehran: Miras-i Maktub, 1385/2001.

———. *The Chronology of Ancient Nations*. Edited and translated by Edward Sachau. London: W. C. Allen, 1879.

Bjelajac, David. "Masonic Fraternalism and Muhammad among the Lawgivers in Adolph A. Weinman's Sculpture Frieze in the United States Supreme Court (1931–1935)." In *The Image of the Prophet between Ideal and Ideology: A Scholarly Investigation*, edited by Christiane Gruber and Avinoam Shalem, 357–81. Berlin: De Gruyter, 2014.

Blair, Sheila. "Calligraphers, Illuminators, and Painters in the Ilkhanid Scriptorium." In *Beyond the Legacy of Genghis Khan*, edited by Linda Komaroff, 167–82. Leiden: Brill, 2006.

———. *A Compendium of Chronicles: Rashid al-Din's Illustrated History of the World*. Edited by Julian Raby. Nasser D. Khalili Collection of Islamic Art 27. Oxford: Nour Foundation and Oxford University Press, 1995.

———. "Invoking the Prophet Muhammad through Word, Sound, and Image: Verbal, Vocal, and Visual Images in the Religious Arts of Islam." *Religion and the Arts* 20 (2016): 29–58.

———. "Patterns of Patronage and Production in Ilkhanid Iran: The Case of Rashid al-Din." In *The Court of the Ilkhans, 1290–1340*, edited by Julian Raby and Teresa Fitzherbert, 39–62. Oxford: Oxford University Press, 1994.

———. "The Religious Art of the Ilkhanids." In *The Legacy of Genghis Khan: Courtly Art and Culture in Western Asia, 1256–1353*, edited by Stefano Carboni and Linda Komaroff, 104–33. New York: Metropolitan Museum of Art, 2002.

Blochet, Edgar. *Catalogue des manuscrits persans*. Paris: Imprimerie Nationale, 1905–1934.

Boespflug, François. "Un étrange spectacle: Le buisson ardent comme théophanie dans l'art occidental." *Revue de l'Art* 97, no. 1 (1992): 11–31.

———. *Le Prophète de l'islam en images: Un sujet tabou?* Montrouge: Bayard, 2013.

Boozari, Ali. "Persian Illustrated Lithographed Books on the *Mi'raj*: Improving Children's Shi'i Beliefs in the Qajar Period." In *The Prophet's Ascension: Cross-Cultural Encounters with the Islamic Mi'raj Tales*, edited by Christiane Gruber and Frederick Colby, 252–68. Bloomington: Indiana University Press, 2009.

———. "Shama'il-i payambar dar kitabha-yi chap-i sangi-yi dawra-yi qajar [Icons of the Prophet in Lithographed Books of the Qajar Period]." *Faslnama-yi Farhang-i Mardum* 35–36 (2011): 125–48.

Bourdieu, Pierre. "Authorized Language: The Social Conditions for the Effectiveness of Ritual Discourse." In *Language and Symbolic Power*, edited by John Thompson, translated by Gino Raymond and Matthew Adamson, 107–16. Cambridge, MA: Harvard University Press, 1991.

———. "The Market of Symbolic Goods." In *The Field of Cultural Production: Essays on Art and Literature*, edited by Randal Johnson, 112–41. New York: Columbia University Press, 1993.

Bourriaud, Nicholas. *PostProduction. Culture as Screenplay: How Art Reprograms the World*. New York: Has and Sternberg, 2002.

Böwering, Gerhard. "The Light Verse: Qur'anic Text and Sufi Interpretation." *Oriens* 36 (2001): 113–44.

Boyle, John Andrew. "Rashid al-Din: The First World Historian." *Iran* 9 (1971): 19–26.

Brack, Yoni. "Mediating Sacred Kingship: Conversion and Sovereignty in Mongol Iran." PhD diss., University of Michigan, 2016.

Broadbridge, Anne. *Kingship and Ideology in the Islamic and Mongol Worlds*. Cambridge: Cambridge University Press, 2008.

Brockopp, Joanthan. "Muhammad the Peacemaker, Muhammad the Warrior: Visions of Islam's Prophet after 9/11." In *Muhammad in the Digital Age*, edited by Ruqayya Yasmine Khan, 35–56. Austin: University of Texas Press, 2015.

Brosh, Na'ama, and Rachel Milstein. *Biblical Stories in Islamic Painting*. Jerusalem: Israel Museum, 1991.

Brown, Bill. "Thing Theory." *Critical Inquiry* 88, no. 1 (2001): 1–22.

Brown, Peter. *The Cult of the Saints: Its Rise and Function in Latin Christianity*. Chicago: University of Chicago Press, 1981.

Bruner, Jerome. "Past and Present as Narrative Constructions." In *Narration, Identity, and Historical Consciousness*, edited by Jürgen Straub, 23–43. New York: Berghahn Books, 2005.

Burckhardt, Titus. *Art of Islam: Language and Meaning.* Translated by Peter Hobson. London: World of Islam Festival Publications, 1976.

Busse, Heribert. "Jerusalem in the Story of Muhammad's Night Journey and Ascension." *Jerusalem Studies in Arabic and Islam* 14 (1991): 1–40.

Cachia, Pierre. *Popular Narrative Ballads of Modern Egypt.* Oxford: Clarendon, 1989.

Çağatay, Neşet. "The Tradition of Mavlid Recitations in Islam, Particularly in Turkey." *Studia Islamica* 28 (1968): 127–33.

Çağman, Filiz. *Kat'ı: Cut Paper Works and Artists in the Ottoman World.* Istanbul: Aygaz, 2014.

Calhoun, Craig Jackson. "The Radicalism of Tradition: Community Strength or Venerable Disguise and Borrowed Language?" *American Journal of Sociology* 88, no. 5 (March 1983): 886–914.

Calmard, Jean. "Les rituels shiites et le pouvoir. L'imposition du shiisme safavide: eulogies et malédictions canoniques." In Études Safavides, edited by Jean Calmard, 109–50. Paris: Institut français de recherche en Iran, 1993.

Cammann, Schuyler. "Islamic and Indian Magic Squares, Part 1." *History of Religions* 8, no. 3 (1969): 181–209.

———. "Islamic and Indian Magic Squares, Part 2." *History of Religions* 8, no. 4 (1969): 271–99.

Campbell, Joseph. *The Hero with a Thousand Faces.* 3rd ed. Novato, CA: New World Library, 2008.

Canby, Sheila. "Early Qur'ans 'Signed' by the Shi'i Imams." In *People of the Prophet's House: Artistic and Ritual Expressions of Shi'i Islam,* edited by Fahmida Suleiman, 97–105. London: Azimuth Editions in association with The Institute of Ismaili Studies and in collaboration with the British Museum's Department of the Middle East, 2015.

Canby, Sheila, Deniz Beyazit, Martina Rugiadi, and Andrew Peacock. *Court and Cosmos: The Great Age of the Seljuks.* New York: Metropolitan Museum of Art, 2016.

Canepa, Matthew. *The Two Eyes of the Earth: Art and Ritual of Kingship between Rome and Sasanian Iran.* Berkeley: University of California Press, 2009.

Capezzone, Leonardo. "Un Miracolo di 'Ali ibn Abi Talib: I Versi Attributi ad al-Sayyid al-Himyari e il Modello Storiografico delle Fonti Relative al *Radd al-Shams.*" *Supplemento no. 2 alla Rivista degli Studi Orientali* 71, *In Memoria di Francesco Gabrieli (1904–1996)* (1997): 99–112.

Carney, Joshua. "A Dizi-ying Past: 'Magnificent Century' ('*Muhteşem Yüzyil*') and the Motivated Uses of History in Contemporary Turkey." PhD diss., Indiana University, 2015.

Carney, Sean. *Brecht and Critical Theory: Dialectics and Contemporary Aesthetics.* London: Routledge, 2005.

Çelebi, Süleyman. *Mevlid-i Şerif = Vesilet'ün-Necat,* edited by Vedat Sağlam et al. Istanbul: Birlik Yayın-Dağıtım, 1996.

Centlivres-Demont, Micheline. "La bataille de Kerbela (680/61H.) dans l'imagerie populaire chiite: langage et symbols." In *La multiplication des images en pays d'Islam: De l'estampe à la television (17è–20è siècle),* edited by Bernard Heyberger and Silvia Naef, 103–17. Würzburg: Ergon, 2003.

Centlivres, Pierre, and Micheline Centlivres-Demont. "Une étrange rencontre: la photographie orientaliste de Lehnert et Landrock et l'image iranienne du Prophète Mahomet." *Etudes Photographiques* 17 (2005): 5–15.

———. *Imageries populaires en Islam.* Geneva: Georg, 1997.

———. "Une présence absente: Symboles et images populaires du Prophète Mahomet." *Derrière les images,* edited by Roland Kaehr, Marc-Olivier Gonseth, and Jacques Hainard, 139–70. Neuchâtel: Musée d'ethnographie, 1998.

———. "The Story of a Picture: Shiite Depictions of Muhammad." *ISIM Review* 17 (Spring 2006): 18–19.

El-Cheikh, Nadia Maria. "Muhammad and Heraclius: A Study in Legitimacy." *Studia Islamica* 89 (1999): 5–21.

Chelkowski, Peter, ed. *From Karbala to New York: Ta'ziyeh on the Move.* Special issue, *Drama Review* 188 (Winter 2005).

———. "Narrative Painting and Painting Recitation in Qajar Iran." *Muqarnas* 6 (1989): 98–111.

———. "Popular Arts: Patronage and Piety." In *Royal Persian Paintings: The Qajar Epoch, 1785–1925,* edited by Layla Diba and Maryam Ekhtiar, 90–97. London: I. B. Tauris, 1998.

———. *Ta'ziyeh: Ritual and Drama in Iran.* New York: New York University Press, 1979.

Chih, Rachida. "La célébration de la naissance du Prophète (*al-Mawlid al-nabawî*): aperçus d'une fête musulmane non canonique." *Archives de sciences sociales des religions* 178/2 (2017): 177–94.

Chittick, William. "The Perfect Man as the Prototype of the Self in the Sufism of Jami." *Studia Islamica* 49 (1979): 135–57.

Chodkiewicz, Michel. "Quelques aspects des techniques spirituelles dans la *tariqa* Naqshbandiyya." In *Naqshbandis, cheminements et situation actuelle d'un ordre mystique musulman,* edited by Marc Gaborieau, Alexandre Popovic, and Thierry Zarcone, 69–82. Istanbul: ISIS, 1990.

Choksy, Jamsheed. "Sacral Kingship in Sasanian Iran." *Bulletin of the Asia Institute,* n.s., 2 (1988): 35–52.

Chong, Alan. *Devotion and Desire: Cross-Cultural Art in Asia. New Acquisitions.* Singapore: Asian Civilizations Museum, 2013.

Coffey, Heather. "Encountering the Body of Muhammad: Intersections between *Mi'raj* Narratives, the *Shaqq al-Sadr,* and Dante's *Divina Commedia* in the Age before Print." In *Constructing the Image of Muhammad in Europe,* edited by Avinoam Shalem, 33–86. Berlin and Bonn: Walter de Gruyter, 2013.

Colby, Frederick. "The Early Imami Shi'i Narratives and Contestation over Intimate Colloquy Scenes in Muhammad's *Mi'raj.*" In *The Prophet's Ascension: Cross-Cultural Encounters with the Islamic Mi'raj Tales,* edited by Christiane Gruber and Frederick Colby, 141–56. Bloomington: Indiana University Press, 2010.

———. *Narrating Muhammad's Night Journey: Tracing the Development of the Ibn 'Abbas Ascension Discourse.* Albany: State University of New York Press, 2008.

Cook, Michael. *Commanding Right and Forbidding Wrong in Islamic Thought.* Cambridge: Cambridge University Press, 2000.

———. "Did the Prophet Muhammad Keep Court?" In *Court Cultures in the Muslim World: Seventh to Nineteenth Centuries,* edited by Albrecht Fuess and Jan-Peter Hartung, 23–29. London: Routledge, 2011.

Cooperson, Michael. "Images without Illustrations: The Visual Imagination in Classical Arabic Biography." In *Islamic Art and Literature,* edited by Oleg Grabar and Cyntia Robinson, 7–20. Princeton, NJ: Markus Wiener, 2001.

Corbin, Henri. *The Man of Light in Iranian Sufism.* New Lebanon, NY: Omega, 1994.

———. "The Visionary Dream in Islamic Spirituality." In *The Dream and Human Societies,* edited by Gustave von Grunebaum and Roger Caillois, 381–408. Berkeley: University of California Press, 1966.

Cornell, Henrik. *The Iconography of the Nativity of Christ.* Uppsala: Uppsala University Press, 1924.

Curtis, Vesta. "Royal and Religious Symbols on Early Sasanian Coins." In *Current Research in Sasanian Archaeology, Art and History,* edited by Derek Kennet and Paul Luft, 137–47. BAR International Series 1810. Oxford: Archaeopress, 2008.

Dakake, Maria. "Hiding in Plain Sight: The Practical and Doctrinal Significance of Secrecy in Shi'ite Islam." *Journal of the American Academy of Religion* 74, no. 2 (June 2006): 324–55.

Daniel, Elton. "Bal'ami's Account of Early Islamic History." In *Culture and Memory in Medieval Islam: Essays in Honor of Wilfred Madelung,* edited by Farhad Daftary, 163–88. London: I. B. Tauris, 2003.

Dankoff, Robert. *Evliya Çelebi in Bitlis: The Relevant Section of the Seyahatname.* Leiden: Brill, 1990.

Darir, Mustafa. *Kitab-ı Siyer-i Nebi: Peygamber Efendimizin Hayatı.* Edited and translated by Mehmet Faruk Gürtunca. 3 vols. Istanbul: Sağlam Kitabevi, 1977.

Daub-Wiebke, Frederike. *Formen und Funktionen des Layouts in arabischen Manuskripten anhand von Abschriften religiöser Texte: al-Busiris Burda, al-Gazulis Dala'il und die Sifa' von Qadi 'Iyad.* Wiesbaden: Harrassowitz, 2016.

Dawkins, J. M. "The Seal of Solomon." *Journal of the Royal Asiatic Society* (October 1944): 145–50.

De Busbecq, Ogier Ghiselin. *The Turkish Letters of Ogier Ghiselin de Busbecq, Imperial Ambassador at Constantinople, 1554–1562.* Translated by Edward Seymour Forster. Oxford: Clarendon, 1968.

De Fouchécour, Charles-Henri. *Moralia: Les notions morales dans la littérature persane du 3e/9e au 7e/13e siècle.* Paris: Recherche sur les Civilisations, 1986.

De Menil, Dominique. *The Rothko Chapel: Writings on Art and the Threshold of the Divine.* New Haven, CT: Yale University Press, 2010.

Demiriz, Yıldız. "On Rococo-Decorated Manuscripts in the Sadberk Hanım Museum." *Palmet: Sadberk Hanım Müzesi Yıllığı* 3 (2000): 65–76.

———. *Osmanlı Kitap Sanatında Doğal Çiçekler.* Istanbul: Yorum Sanat, 2005.

Derman, M. Uğur. *Calligraphies ottomanes: Collection du Musée Sakıp Sabancı, Université Sabancı, Istanbul.* Paris: Réunion des Musées Nationaux, 2000.

Déroche François. "Written Transmission." In *The Blackwell Companion to the Qur'an,* edited by Andrew Rippin, 172–86. Malden, MA: Blackwell, 2006.

De Voragine, Jacobus. *The Golden Legend: Readings on the Saints.* Translated by William Granger Ryan. Princeton, NJ: Princeton University Press, 1993.

De Vos, Idris. *Eloge du Prophète: Anthologie de poésie religieuse, poems choisis.* Arles: Berque, 2011.

De Waele, Éric. "L'investiture et le triomphe dans la thématique de la sculpture rupestre sassanide." In *Archaeologia Iranica et Orientali: Miscellanea in Honorem Louis Vanden Berghe,* edited by Leon de Meyer and Ernie Haerinck, 811–30. Ghent: Peeters, 1989.

Diba, Layla. "Images of Power and the Power of Images." In *Royal Persian Paintings: The Qajar Epoch, 1785–1925,* edited by Layla Diba and Maryam Ekhtiar, 30–49. London: I. B. Tauris, 1998.

Diba, Layla, and Maryam Ekhtiar. *Royal Persian Paintings: The Qajar Epoch, 1785–1925.* Brooklyn: Brooklyn Museum of Art in association with I. B. Tauris, 1998.

Dickinson, Eerik. "Ibn al-Salah al-Shahrazuri and the Isnad." *Journal of the American Oriental Society* 122/3 (2002): 481–505.

Dickson, Martin, and Stuart Cary Welch. *The Houghton Shahnameh.* 2 vols. Cambridge, MA: Harvard University Press, 1981.

D'Ohsson, Ignatius Mouradgea. *Tableau général de l'empire othoman, divisé en deux parties, dont l'une comprend la législation mahométane, l'autre, l'histoire de l'Empire othoman.* 8 vols. Paris: Imprimerie de Monsieur, 1971.

Doka, Yahya. "Crown v. In the Qajar and Pahlavi Periods." In *Encyclopaedia Iranica Online.* http://www.iranicaonline.org/articles/crown-v (published December 15, 1993).

Donaldson, Bess Allen. *The Wild Rue: A Study of Muhammadan Magic and Folklore in Iran.* London: Luzacand, 1938.

Donner, Fred. "Muhammad and the Debates on Islam's Origins in the Digital Age." In *Muhammad in the Digital Age,* edited by Ruqayya Yasmine Khan, 16–34. Austin: University of Texas Press, 2015.

Dozy, Reinhart. *Dictionnaire détaillé des noms des vêtements chez les arabes.* Amsterdam: J. Müller, 1845.

Dschingis Khan und seine Erben: Das Weltreich der Mongolen. Heidelberg: Vernissage, 2005.

Dutton, Yasin. "*Amal v. Hadith* in Islamic Law: The Case of *Sadl al-Yadayn* (Holding One's Hands by One's Sides) When Doing the Prayer." *Islamic Law and Society* 3, no. 1 (February 1996): 13–40.

Eberhard, Wolfram, and Pertev Naili Boratav. *Typen Türkisher Volksmärchen.* Wiesbaden: F. Steiner, 1953.

Eckmann, Janos, trans. *Nehcü'l-Feradis.* Edited by Semih Tezcan and Hamza Zülfikar. Ankara: Türk Dil ve Tarih Yüksek Kurumu, 1995.

Egüz, Esra. "Erzurumlu Mustafa Darîr'in Sîretü'n-nebî'sindeki Türkçe Manzumeler." PhD diss., Istanbul University, 2013.

Eisner, Will. *Comics and Sequential Art: Principles and Practices from the Legendary Cartoonist.* New York: Norton, 2008.

Ekhtiar, Maryam. "The Dar al-Funun: Educational Reform and Cultural Development in Qajar Iran." PhD diss., New York University, 1994.

———. "Exploring *Ahl al-Bayt* Imagery in Qajar Iran (1785–1925)." In *People of the Prophet's House: Artistic and Ritual Expressions of Shi'i Islam,* edited by Fahmida Suleman, 146–54. London: Azimuth Editions in association with the Institute of Ismaili Studies in collaboration with the British Museum's Department of the Middle East, 2015.

———. "From Workshop and Bazaar to Academy: Art Training and Production in Qajar Iran." In *Royal Persian Paintings: The Qajar Epoch, 1785–1925,* edited by Layla Diba and Maryam Ekhtiar, 50–65. Brooklyn: Brooklyn Museum of Art in association with I. B. Tauris, 1998.

———. "Infused with Shi'ism: Representations of the Prophet in Qajar Iran." In *The Prophet between Ideal and Ideology: A Scholarly Investigation,* edited by Christiane Gruber and Avinoam Shalem, 97–112. Berlin: De Gruyter, 2014.

———. "Nasir al-Din Shah and the Dar al-Funun: The Evolution of an Institution." *Iranian Studies* 34, no. 1 (2001): 153–63.

Ekhtiar, Maryam, Priscilla Soucek, Sheila Canby, and Navina Haidar. *Masterpieces from the Department of Islamic Art in the Metropolitan Museum of Art.* New York: Metropolitan Museum of Art, 2011.

Elias, Jamal. *Aisha's Cushion: Religious Art, Perception, and Practice in Islam.* Cambridge, MA: Harvard University Press, 2012.

———. "Islam and the Devotional Image in Pakistan." In *Islam in South Asia in Practice,* edited by Barbara Metcalf, 120–32. Princeton, NJ: Princeton University Press, 2009.

———. "Mevlevi Sufis and the Representation of Emotion in the Arts of the Ottoman World." In *Affect, Emotion, and Subjectivity in Early Modern Muslim Empires: New Studies in Ottoman, Safavid, and Mughal Art and Culture,* edited by Kishwar Rizvi, 185–209. Leiden: Brill, 2017.

———. "On Wings of Diesel: Spiritual Space and Religious Imagination in Pakistani Truck Decoration." *RES: Anthropology and Aesthetics* 43 (2003): 187–202.

———. *On Wings of Diesel: Trucks, Identity, and Culture in Pakistan.* Oxford: Oneworld, 2011.

———. "Truck Decoration and Religious Identity: Material Culture and Social Function in Pakistan." *Material Religion* 1, no. 1 (March 2005): 48–71.

Erdoğan, Mehtap. *Türk Edebiyatında Manzum Hilyeler.* Istanbul: Kitabevi, 2013.

Ergin, Nina. "The Fragrance of the Divine: Ottoman Incense Burners and their Context," *Art Bulletin* 96, no. 1 (2014): 70–97.

———. "'Praiseworthy in that Great Multitude Was the Silence': Sound/Silence in the Topkapı Palace, Istanbul." In *Resounding Images: Medieval Intersections of Art, Music and Sound,* edited by Diane Reilly and Susan Boynton, 109–33. Turnhout: Brepols, 2015.

———. "The Soundscape of Sixteenth-Century Istanbul Mosques." *Journal of the Society of Architectural Historians* 67, no. 2 (June 2008): 204–21.

Erkan, Mustafa. "Darîr." In *İslam Ansiklopedisi.* Vol. 8, 498–99. Istanbul: Türkiye Dinayet Vakfı, 1993.

Erkmen, Aslıhan. "The Visualization of Shaykh Safi al-Din Ishaq Ardabili: A Unique Illustrated Copy of the *Safvat al-Safa* at the Aga Khan Museum Collection and Its Illustrations." *Iranian Studies* 50, no. 1 (2017): 45–77.

Ernst, Carl. "It's Not Just Academic: Writing Public Scholarship in Middle Eastern and Islamic Studies." *Review of Middle East Studies* 45, no. 2 (Winter 2011): 164–71.

———. "Muhammad as the Pole of Existence." In *The Cambridge Companion to Muhammad,* edited by Jonathan Brockopp, 123–38. New York: Cambridge University Press, 2010.

———. *Ruzbihan Baqli: Mysticism and the Rhetoric of Sainthood in Persian Sufism*. Richmond, VA: Curzon, 1996.

Eschraghi, Armin. "'I Was a Hidden Treasure.' Some Notes on a Commentary Ascribed to Mulla Sadra Shirazi: *Sharh Hadith: 'Kuntu Kanzan Makhfiyyan. . . .'*" In *Islamic Thought in the Middle Ages: Studies in Text, Transmission and Translation in Honour of Hans Daiber*, edited by Anna Akasoy and Wim Raven, 91–99. Leiden, Brill, 2008.

Ettinghausen, Richard. *Arab Painting*. Geneva: Albert Skira, 1977.

———. "Persian Ascension Miniatures of the Fourteenth Century." In *Convegno di Scienze Morali Storiche e Filologiche, Symposium on Orient and Occident during the Middle Ages, May 27–June 1, 1956*, 360–83. Rome: Accademia nazionale dei Lincei, 1957. Republished in Richard Ettinghausen, *Islamic Art and Archaeology: Collected Papers*, edited by Myriam Rosen-Ayalon, 244–68. Berlin: G. Mann, 1984.

Fakhr-i Mudabbir, Muhammad b. Mansur. *Adab al-Harb wa'l-Shaja'a*. Edited by Ahmad Suhayli Khwansari. Tehran: Intisharat-i Iqbal, 1346/1967.

Farès, Bishr. *L'art sacré chez un primitif musulman*. Cairo: Institut français d'archéologie orientale, 1955.

———. "Une miniature nouvelle de l'école de Bagdad datée 614 Hég./1217–8 figurant le Prophète Muhammad." *Bulletin de l'Institut d'Egypte* 28 (1947): 259–62.

Farhad, Massumeh, with Serpil Bağcı, eds. *Falnama: The Book of Omens*. Washington, DC: Arthur M. Sackler Gallery, Smithsonian Institution, 2009.

Faroqhi, Suraiya. *Pilgrims and Sultans: The Hajj under the Ottomans, 1517–1683*. London: I. B. Tauris, 1994.

Fetvacı, Emine. *Picturing History at the Ottoman Court*. Bloomington: Indiana University Press, 2013.

———. "From Print to Trace: An Imperial Ottoman Portrait Book and Its Western European Models." *Art Bulletin* 95, no. 2 (June 2013): 243–68.

Figuier, Louis. *Vie des savants illustres du moyen âge*. Paris: Librairie Internationale, 1867.

Firdawsi, Hakim Abu'l-Qasim. *Firdussi Liber regum qui inscribitur Schahname*. Edited by Johann Vullers and Samuel Landauer. Leiden: Brill, 1877.

Fitzherbert, Teresa. "'Bal'ami's Tabari': An Illustrated Manuscript of Bal'ami's *Tarjama-yi Tarikh-i Tabari* in the Freer Gallery of Art, Washington (F59.16, 47.19 and 30.21)." 2 vols. PhD diss., University of Edinburgh, 2001.

———. "Religious Diversity under Ilkhanid Rule c. 1300 as Reflected in the Freer Bal'ami." In *Beyond the Legacy of Genghis Khan*, edited by Linda Komaroff, 390–406. Leiden: Brill, 2006.

Flaskerud, Ingvild. *Visualizing Belief and Piety in Iranian Shiism*. New York: Continuum, 2012.

Flatman, Joe. *Ships and Shipping in Medieval Manuscripts*. London: British Library, 2009.

Flood, Finbarr Barry. "Between Cult and Culture: Bamiyan, Islamic Iconoclasm, and the Museum." *Art Bulletin* 84, no. 4 (December 2002): 641–59.

———. "Bodies and Becoming: Mimesis, Mediation, and the Ingestion of the Sacred in Christianity and Islam." In *Sensational Religion: Sensory Cultures in Material Practice*, edited by Sally Promey, 459–93. New Haven, CT: Yale University Press, 2014.

———. *Islam and Image: Polemics, Theology and Modernity* (forthcoming, 2019).

———. "Inciting Modernity?: Images, Alterities, and the Contexts of 'Cartoon Wars.'" In *Images That Move*, edited by Patricia Spyer and Mary Steedly, 41–72. Santa Fe, NM: SAR Press, 2013.

———. "Light in Stone: The Commemoration of the Prophet in Umayyad Architecture." In *Bayt al-Maqdis, Part Two: Jerusalem and Early Islam*, edited by Jeremy Johns, 311–59. Oxford Studies in Islamic Art 9. Oxford: Oxford University Press, 2000.

———. "Picasso the Muslim." *RES: Anthropology and Aesthetics* 67–68 (2016–17): 45–60.

Fontana, Maria Vittoria. *Iconografia dell'Ahl al-Bayt: Immagini di arte persiana dal XII al XX secolo*. Naples: Istituto Universitario Orientale, 1994.

Forbes Manz, Beatrice. *Power, Politics, and Religion in Timurid Iran*. Cambridge: Cambridge University Press, 2007.

Fortna, Benjamin. *Learning to Read in the Late Ottoman Empire and the Early Turkish Republic*. New York: Palgrave Macmillan, 2011.

Gandy, Christopher. "Inscribed Silver Amulet Boxes." In *Islamic Art in the Ashmolean Museum*, edited by James Allan, 155–66. Oxford: Oxford University Press, 1995.

Garrett Fisher, Carol. "A Reconstruction of the Pictorial Cycle of the *Siyar-i Nabi* of Murad III." *Ars Orientalis* 14 (1984): 75–94.

Gätje, Helmut. *The Qur'an and Its Exegesis: Selected Texts with Classical and Modern Muslim Interpretations*. Berkeley: University of California Press, 1976.

Gaube, Heinz. *Arabosasanidische Numismatik*. Braunschweig: Klinkhardt and Biermann, 1973.

Gero, Stephen. "The Legend of the Monk Bahira, the Cult of the Cross, and Iconoclasm." In *La Syrie de Byzance à l'Islam, VIIe–VIIe siècles*, edited by Pierre Canivet and Jean-Paul Rey-Coquais, 47–58. Damascus: Institut français de Damas, 1992.

Ghabin, Ahmad. "The Quranic Verses as a Source for Legitimacy or Illegitimacy of the Arts in Islam." *Der Islam* 75, no. 2 (1998): 193–225.

Al-Ghazali, Abu Hamid. *The Name and the Named: The Divine Attributes of God*. Edited by Tosun Bayrak and with an introduction by William Chittick. Louisville, KY: Fons Vitae, 2000.

———. *The Niche of Lights*. Translated by David Buchman. Provo, UT: Brigham Young University Press, 1998.

———. *The Ninety-Nine Beautiful Names of God: Al-Maqsad al-Asna fi Sharh Asma' Allah al-Husna*. Edited and translated by David Burrell and Nazih Daher. Cambridge: Islamic Texts Society, 2011.

Ghiasian, Mohamad Reza. "The 'Historical Style' of Painting for Shahrukh and Its Revival in the Dispersed Manuscript of *Majma' al-Tawarikh*." *Iranian Studies* 48, no. 6 (2015): 871–903.

Gimaret, Daniel. "Ru'yat Allah." In *Encyclopaedia of Islam*. 2nd ed. BrillOnline Reference Works. http://referenceworks.brillonline.com/browse/encyclopaedia-of-islam-2 (accessed May 18, 2018).

Gleave, Robert. "Muhammad and Personal Piety." In *The Cambridge Companion to Muhammad*, edited by Jonathan Brockopp, 103–22. Cambridge: Cambridge University Press, 2010.

———. "The Hadith as a Means of Edification and Entertainment." In *Muslim Studies*, edited by S. M. Stern, translated by C. R. Barber and S. M. Stern, vol. 2, 145–63. Chicago: Aldine, 1971.

Golombek, Lisa. *The Timurid Shrine at Gazur Gah*. Toronto: Royal Ontario Museum, 1969.

Gonnella, Julia, Friederike Weis, and Christoph Rauch. *The Diez Albums: Contexts and Contents*. Leiden: Brill, 2017.

Gowing, Peter. *Muslim Filipinos—Heritage and Horizon*. Quezon City: New Day, 1979.

Grabar, Oleg. "Islam and Iconoclasm." In *Early Islamic Art, 650–1100: Constructing the Study of Islamic Art*, vol. 1, 43–56. Burlington, VT: Ashgate, 2005. Originally published in *Iconoclasm*, edited by Anthony Bryer and Judith Herrin, 45–52. Birmingham: Center for Byzantine Studies, 1977.

———. "Islamic Art: Art of a Culture or Art of a Faith?" *Art and Archaeology Research Papers* 11 (June 1978): 1–6.

———. "Pictures or Commentaries: The Illustrations of the *Maqamat* of al-Hariri." In *Studies in Art and Literature of the Near East in Honor of Richard Ettinghausen*, edited by Peter Chelkowski, 85–104. Salt Lake City: University of Utah Press, 1974.

———. "Reflections on the Study of Islamic Art." *Muqarnas* 1 (1983): 1–14.

———. *Sasanian Silver: Late Antique and Early Medieval Arts of Luxury*. Ann Arbor: University of Michigan Art Museum, 1967.

———. *The Shape of the Holy: Early Islamic Jerusalem*. Princeton, NJ: Princeton University Press, 1996.

———. "The Umayyad Dome of the Rock in Jerusalem." *Ars Orientalis* 3 (1959): 33–62.

Grabar, Oleg, and Sheila Blair. *Epic Images and Contemporary History: The Illustrations of the Great Mongol Shahnama*. Chicago: University of Chicago Press, 1980.

Grabar, Oleg, and Mika Natif. "The Story of the Portraits of the Prophet Muhammad." *Studia Islamica* 96 (2003): 19–38.

Gramlich, Richard. *Die Wunder der Freunde Gottes. Theologien und Erscheinungsformen des islamischen Heiligenwunders.* Wiesbaden: Franz Steinder, 1987.

Gray, Basil, ed. *The Arts of the Book in Central Asia, 14th–16th Centuries.* Boulder, CO: Shambhala, 1979.

Green, Nile. "The Religious and Cultural Roles of Dreams and Visions in Islam." *Royal Asiatic Society* 13, no. 3 (2003): 287–313.

Greenberg, Clement. "Avant-Garde and Kitsch." In *Art and Culture: Critical Essays*, 3–21. Boston: Beacon, 1965.

Gril, Denis. "La commémoration de la naissance du Prophète *(mawlid al-nabi).*" In *La Nativité et le temps de Noël: XVIIe-XXe siècle*, edited by Régis Bertrand, 189–202. Aix-en-Provence: Publications de l'Université de Provence, 2003.

———. "Le corps du Prophète." *Revue des mondes musulmans et de la Méditerranée* 113–114 (November 2006): 37–57.

———. "Le Prophète en famille." In *Family Portraits with Saints: Hagiography, Sanctity, and Family in the Muslim World*, edited by Catherine Mayeur-Jaouen and Alexandre Papas, 27–72. Berlin: Klaus Schwarz, 2014.

Grube, Ernst. "The *Siyar-i-Nabi* of the Spencer Collection in the New York Public Library." In *Atti del Secondo Congresso Internazionale di Arte Turca*, 149–76. Naples: Istituto Universitario Orientale, Seminario di Turcologia, 1965.

Gruber, Christiane. "Al-Buraq." In *Encyclopaedia of Islam*. 3rd ed. BrillOnline Reference Works. http://referenceworks.brillonline .com/browse/encyclopaedia-of-islam -3 (accessed May 18, 2018).

———. "Between Logos (*Kalima*) and Light (*Nur*): Representations of the Prophet Muhammad in Islamic Painting." *Muqarnas* 26 (2009): 1–34.

———. "Curse Signs: The Artful Rhetoric of Hell in Safavid Iran." In *Locating Hell in Islamic Traditions*, edited by Christian Lange, 297–335. Leiden: Brill, 2016.

———. "'Go Wherever You Wish, for Verily You are Well Protected': Seal Designs in Late Ottoman Prayer Books." In *Visions of Enchantment: Occultism, Spirituality, and Visual Culture*, edited by Daniel Zamani, 23–35. London: Fulgur, 2018.

———. *The Ilkhanid Book of Ascension: A Persian-Sunni Devotional Tale.* London: I. B. Tauris, 2010.

———. "The Ilkhanid *Mi'rajnama* of ca. 1317–35 as an Illustrated Sunni Prayer Manual." In *The Prophet's Ascension: Cross-Cultural Encounters with the Islamic Mi'raj Tales*, edited by Christiane Gruber and Frederick Colby, 27–49. Bloomington: Indiana University Press, 2010.

———. "Images of Muhammad *In and Out* of Modernity: The Curious Case of a 2008 Mural in Tehran." In *Visual Culture in the Modern Middle East: Rhetoric of the Image*, edited by Christiane Gruber and Sune Haugbolle, 2–31. Bloomington: Indiana University Press, 2013.

———. "Images of the Prophet Muhammad: Brief Thoughts on Some European-Islamic Encounters." In *Seen and Unseen: Visual Cultures of Imperialism*, edited by Sanaz Fotouhi and Esmaeil Zeiny, 34–52. Leiden: Brill, 2017.

———. "In Defense and Devotion: Affective Practices in Early Modern Turco-Persian Manuscript Paintings." In *Emotion and Subjectivity in the Art and Architecture of Early Modern Muslim Empires*, edited by Kishwar Rizvi, 95–123. Leiden: Brill, 2017.

———. "Jerusalem in the Visual Propaganda of Post-Revolutionary Iran." In *Jerusalem: Idea and Reality*, edited by Suleiman Mourad and Tamar Mayer, 168–97. London: Routledge, 2008.

———. "The Keir *Mi'raj*: Islamic Storytelling and the Picturing of Tales." *Central Eurasian Studies Review* 4, no. 1 (Winter 2005): 35–39.

———. "Power and Protection: Late Ottoman Seal Designs." *Hadeeth al-Dar* 38 (2013): 2–6.

———. "Prophetic Products: Muhammad in Contemporary Iranian Visual Culture." *Material Religion* 12, no. 3 (September 2016): 259–93.

———. "The Prophet Muhammad's Ascension (*Mi'raj*) in Islamic Art and Literature, 1300–1600." PhD diss., University of Pennsylvania, 2005.

———. "The Prophet Muhammad's Footprint." In *Ferdowsi, the Mongols, and the History of Iran: Art, Literature and Culture from Early Islam to Qajar Persia*, edited by Robert Hillenbrand, Andrew Peacock, and Firuza Abdullaeva, 297–305. London: I. B. Tauris, 2013.

———. "A Pious Cure-All: The Ottoman Illustrated Prayer Manual in the Lilly Library." In *The Islamic Manuscript Tradition: Ten Centuries of Book Arts in Indiana University Collections*, edited by Christiane Gruber, 117–53. Bloomington: Indiana University Press, 2009.

———. "Questioning the 'Classical' in Persian Painting: Models and Problems of Definition." *Journal of Art Historiography* 6 (June 2012): 1–25.

———. "Reclaiming the Prophet Muhammad in Iran." *Newsweek*, January 31, 2015. http:// www.newsweek.com/reclaiming-prophet -muhammad-iran-303526.

———. "The Rose of the Prophet: Floral Metaphors in Late Ottoman Devotional Art." In *Envisioning Islamic Art and Architecture: Essays in Honor of Renata Holod*, edited by David Roxburgh, 227–54. Leiden: Brill, 2014.

———. "Signs of the Hour: Eschatological Imagery in Islamic Book Arts." *Ars Orientalis* 44 (2014): 40–60.

———. *The Timurid Book of Ascension (Mi'rajnama): A Study of Text and Image in a Pan-Asian Context.* Valencia, Spain: Patrimonio Ediciones, 2008.

———. "When *Nubuvvat* Encounters *Valayat*: Safavid Paintings of the Prophet Muhammad's *Mi'raj*, ca. 1500–1550." In *The Art and Material Culture of Iranian Shi'ism: Iconography and Religious Devotioin in Shi'i Islam*, edited by Pedram Khosronejad, 46–73. London: I. B. Tauris, 2012.

Gruber, Christiane, ed. *The Image Debate: Figural Representation in Global Cultural Contents.* London: Gingko Library, 2019.

Gruber, Christiane, and Frederick Colby, eds. *The Prophet's Ascension: Cross-Cultural Encounters with the Islamic Mi'raj Tales.* Bloomington: Indiana University Press, 2010.

Gruber, Christiane, and Ashley Dimmig. *Pearls of Wisdom: The Arts of Islam at the University of Michigan.* Ann Arbor: Kelsey Museum of Archaeology, University of Michigan, 2014.

Gruber, Christiane, and Avinoam Shalem, eds. *The Image of the Prophet between Ideal and Ideology: A Scholarly Investigation.* Berlin: De Gruyter, 2014.

Günther, Sebastian. "Fictional Narration and Imagination within an Authoritative Framework: Toward a New Understanding of Hadith." In *Story-telling in the Framework of Non-Fictional Arabic Literature*, edited by Stefan Leder, 433–71. Wiesbaden: Harrassowitz, 1998.

Guthrie, A., and E. F. F. Bishop. "The Paraclete, Almunhamanna and Ahmad." *The Muslim World* 41, no. 4 (October 1951): 251–56.

Gysi, Sandra. *Geschichten, Bilder: Die Welt des Salah Hassouna.* Zurich: Völkerkundemuseum der Universität Zürich, 2005.

Hagen, Gottfried. "The Emergence of a Pietas Ottomanica." Lecture delivered at the second Great Lakes Ottoman Workshop, DePaul University, Chicago, IL, September 23–24, 2005.

———. "The Imagined and the Historical Muhammad." *Journal of the American Oriental Society* 129, no. 1 (2009): 97–111.

———. "Sira, Ottoman Turkish." In *Muhammad in History, Thought, and Culture: An Encyclopedia of the Prophet of God*, edited by Coeli Fitzpatrick and Andrew Walker, vol. 2, 585–97. Santa Barbara: ABC-CLIO, 2014.

Hakanî, Mehmet Bey. *Hilye-i Saadet.* Edited by İskender Pala. Istanbul: Kapı Yayınları, 2008.

Hall, Stuart. "Encoding, Decoding." In *The Cultural Studies Reader*, edited by Simon During, 90–103. London: Routledge, 1993.

Hammond, Timur. "Matters of the Mosque: Changing Configurations of Buildings and Belief in an Istanbul District." *City:*

Analysis of Urban Trends, Culture, Theory, Policy, Action 18, no. 6 (2014): 679–90.

Hanaway, William. "Some Accounts of the Mi'raj of the Prophet in Persian Literature." In Cultural Horizons: A Festschrift in Honor of Talat S. Halman, edited by Jayne Warner, 555–60. Syracuse, NY: Syracuse University Press, 2001.

Harper, Prudence. Silver Vessels of the Sasanian Period. Vol. 1. New York: Metropolitan Museum of Art, 1981.

———. "Thrones and Enthronement Scenes in Sasanian Art." Iran 17 (1979): 49–64.

Hasan, Perween. "The Footprint of the Prophet." Muqarnas 10 (1993): 335–43.

Hasson, Izhak. "The Muslim View of Jerusalem—the Qur'an and Hadith." In The History of Jerusalem: The Early Muslim Period, 638–1099, edited by Joshua Prawer and Haggai Ben-Shammai, 349–85. New York: New York University Press, 1996.

Hauglid, Brian. "On the Early Life of Abraham: Biblical and Qur'anic Intertextuality and the Anticipation of Muhammad." In Bible and Qur'an: Essays in Scriptural Intertextuality, edited by John Reeves, 87–105. Leiden: Brill, 2004.

Hawting, G. R. "The Literary Context of the Traditional Accounts of Pre-Islamic Arab Idolatry." Jerusalem Studies in Arabic and Islam 21 (1997): 21–41.

Heath, Peter. The Thirsty Sword: Sirat 'Antar and the Arabic Popular Epic. Salt Lake City: University of Utah Press, 1996.

Heidemann, Stefan. "The Representation of the Early Islamic Empire and Its Religion on Coin Imagery." In Court Cultures in the Muslim World: Seventh to Nineteenth Centuries, edited by Albrecht Fuess and Jan-Peter Hartung, 30–53. London: Routledge, 2011.

Heinzelmann, Tobias. Populäre religiöse Literatur und Buchkultur im Osmanischen Reich: Eine Studie zur Nutzung der Werke der Brüder Yazıcıoğlı. Würzburg: Ergon, 2015.

Heller, Bernhard. Die Bedeutung des arabischen 'Antar-Romans für die vergleichende Literaturkunde. Leipzig: H. Eichblatt, 1931.

Hermansen, Marcia. "The Prophet Muhammed in Sufi Interpretations of the Light Verse (Ayat Nur 24:35), Part II." Islamic Quarterly 42, no. 2 (1998): 218–27.

Hillenbrand, Robert. "The Arts of the Book in Ilkhanid Iran." In The Legacy of Genghis Khan: Courtly Art and Culture in Western Asia, 1256–1353, edited by Stefano Carboni and Linda Komaroff, 134–67. New Haven, CT: Yale University Press, 2002.

———. "The Frontispiece Problem in the Early 13th-Century Kitab al-Aghani." In Central Periphery? Art, Culture and History of the Medieval Jazira (Northern Mesopotamia, 8th–15th Centuries), edited by Lorenz Korn and Martina Müller-Wiener, 199–207. Wiesbaden: Reichert Verlag, 2017.

———. "The Iconography of the Shahnama-yi Shahi." In Safavid Persia: The History and Politics of an Islamic Society, edited by Charles Melville, 53–78. London: I. B. Tauris, 1996.

———. "Images of Authority on Kashan Lustreware." In Islamic Art in the Ashmolean Museum, part 1, edited by James W. Allan, 167–98. Oxford: Oxford University Press, 1995.

———. "Images of Muhammad in al-Biruni's Chronology of Ancient Nations." In Persian Painting from the Mongols to the Qajars: Studies in Honour of Basil W. Robinson, edited by Robert Hillenbrand, 129–46. London: I. B. Tauris, 2000.

———. "Muhammad as Warrior Prophet: Images from the World History of Rashid al-Din." In The Image of the Prophet between Ideal and Ideology: A Scholarly Investigation, edited by Christiane Gruber and Avinoam Shalem, 65–75. Berlin: De Gruyter, 2014.

———. "The Schefer Hariri: A Study in Islamic Frontispiece Design." In Arab Painting: Text and Image in Illustrated Arabic Manuscripts, edited by Anna Contadini, 117–34. Leiden: Brill, 2007.

Hobsbawm, Eric. The Invention of Tradition. Edited by Eric Hobsbawn and Terence Ranger. Cambridge: Cambridge University Press, 1983.

Hodgson, Marshall. "Islâm and Image." History of Religions 3 (1964): 220–60.

Hoffman, Valerie. "Annihilation in the Messenger of God: The Development of a Sufi Practice." International Journal of Middle East Studies 31 (1999): 351–69.

Hoffman-Ladd, Valerie. "Devotion to the Prophet and His Family in Egyptian Sufism." International Journal of Middle East Studies 24, no. 4 (November 1992): 615–37.

Hooglund, Eric. "Decoding Ahmadinejad's Rhetoric on Israel." In Navigating Contemporary Iran: Challenging Economic, Social and Political Perceptions, edited by Eric Hooglund and Leif Stenberg, 198–214. London: Routledge 2013.

Hosein, Hidayat. "A Translation of the Ash-Shama'il of Tirmizi." Islamic Culture 8 (April 1934): 273–89.

Howorth, Henry. History of the Mongols from the 9th to 19th Century, Part III, The Mongols of Persia. London: Longmans Green, 1888.

Hoyland, Robert. "Writing the Biography of the Prophet Muhammad: Problems and Solutions." History Compass 5, no. 2 (2007): 581–602.

Hussain, Amir. "Images of Muhammad in Literature, Art, and Music." In The Cambridge Companion to Muhammad, edited by Jonathan Brockopp, 274–92. Cambridge: Cambridge University Press, 2010.

Ibn 'Arabi, Muhyi al-Din. On the Mysteries of Bearing Witness to the Oneness of God and Prophethood of Muhammad. Translated by Aisha Bewley. Chicago: KAZI Publications, 2002.

Ibn Bazzaz. Safvat al-Safa: dar Tarjumah-i Ahval va Aqval va Karamat-i Shaykh Safi al-Din Ishaq Ardabili. Edited by Ghulam Riza Tabataba'i Majd. Tehran: Intisharat-i Zaryab, 1376/1997.

Ibn Dihya, Abu'l-Khattab. Al-Ibtihaj fi Ahadith al-Mi'raj. Edited by Rafa't F. 'Abd al-Muttalib. Cairo: Maktabat al-Khaniji, 1417/1996.

Ibn Husam. Khavaran Nameh: A Masterpiece of Iranian Literature and Painting (15th c.). With an introduction by Saeed Anvari, translated by Muhammad Savoji. Tehran: Ministry of Culture and Islamic Guidance with the Cultural Heritage Organization, 2002.

Ibn Ishaq. The Life of Muhammad: A Translation of Ishaq's Sirat Rasul Allah. Translated by Alfred Guillaume. Lahore: Pakistan Branch, Oxford University Press, 1955.

Ibn al-Kalbi, Hisham. The Book of Idols. Princeton, NJ: Princeton University Press, 1952.

———. Les idoles de Hicham Ibn al-Kalbi. Edited and translated by Wahib Atallah. Paris: Librairie C. Klincksieck, 1969.

Ibn Kathir. Tafsir Ibn Kathir (Abridged). Edited by Safiur-Rahman al-Mubarakpuri. Riyadh: Darussalam, 2000.

Ibn Sirin, Muhammad. Le grand livre de l'interprétation des rêves. Edited by Youssef Siddik. La Tour d'Aigles: Ed. de l'Aube, 2005.

Ibn Warraq, ed. The Quest for the Historical Muhammad. Amherst: Prometheus Books, 2000.

Inal, Güner. "Miniatures in Historical Manuscripts from the Time of Shahrukh in the Topkapi Palace Museum." In Timurid Art and Culture: Iran and Central Asia in the Fifteenth Century, edited by Lisa Golombek and Maria Subtelny, 103–15. Leiden: Brill, 1992.

———. "Some Artistic Relationships between the Far and Near East as Reflected in the Miniatures of the Gami' at-Tawarih." Kunst des Orients 10 (1975): 108–43.

———. "Some Miniatures of the Jami' al-Tavarikh in Istanbul, Topkapi Museum, Hazine Librayr no. 1654." Ars Orientalis 5 (1963): 163–75.

In Pursuit of Excellence: Works of Art from the Museum of Turkish and Islamic Arts, Istanbul. Istanbul: Ahmet Ertuğ, 1993.

İpek, Selin. "Ottoman Ravza-i Mutahhara Covers Sent from Istanbul to Medina with the Surre Processions." Muqarnas 23 (2006): 289–316.

İpşiroğlu, Mazhar Şevket. Saray-Alben: Diez'sche Klebebände aus den Berliner Sammlungen. Wiesbaden: F. Steiner, 1964.

'Isa, Ahmad Muhammad. "Muslims and Taswir." The Muslim World 45, no. 3 (July 1955): 250–68.

———. Painting in Islam: Between Prohibition and Aversion. Istanbul: Waqf for Research on Islamic Art and Culture, 1996.

Jami. *An Allegorical Romance: Yusuf and Zulaikha.* Translated by David Pendlebury. London: Octagon, 1980.

Jeffery, Arthur. "The Quest of the Historical Muhammad." In *The Quest for the Historical Muhammad,* edited by Ibn Warraq, 339–57. Amherst: Prometheus Books, 2000.

———. *A Reader on Islam: Passages from Standard Arabic Writings Illustrative of the Beliefs and Practices of Muslims.* 'S-Gravenhage: Mouton and Co., 1962.

Kadoi, Yuka. "The Mongols Enthroned." In *The Diez Albums: Contexts and Contents,* edited by Julia Gonnella, Friederike Weis, and Christoph Rauch, 243–75. Leiden: Brill, 2017.

Kaptein, N. J. G. *Muhammad's Birth Festival: Early History in the Central Muslim Lands and Development in the Muslim West until the 10th/16th Century.* Leiden: Brill, 1993.

Al-Karaki (al-Husayn Muhaqqiq al-Thani, known as). *Nafahat al-Lahut fi La'n al-Jibt wa'l-Taghut.* Edited by Muhammad Hassun. Qum: Manshurat al-Ihtijaj, 1423/2002–3.

Karaman, Hayreddin. *İmam-ı Rabbânî ve İslâm Tasavvufu.* Istanbul: Nesil, 1992.

Katz, Jonathan. "Dreams and Their Interpretations in Sufi Thought and Practice." In *Dreams and Visions in Islamic Societies,* edited by Özgen Felek and Alexander Knysh, 181–97. Albany: State University of New York Press, 2012.

———. *Dreams, Sufism and Sainthood: The Visionary Career of Muhammad al-Zawâwî.* Leiden: E. J. Brill, 1996.

Katz, Marion Holmes. *The Birth of the Prophet Muhammad: Devotional Piety in Sunni Islam.* London: Routledge, 2007.

———. "The Prophet Muhammad in Ritual." In *The Cambridge Companion to Muhammad,* edited by Jonathan Brockopp, 139–57. Cambridge: Cambridge University Press, 2010.

Keane, Webb. "Freedom and Blasphemy: On Indonesian Press Bans and Danish Cartoons." *Public Culture* 21, no. 1 (2009): 47–76.

Kessler, Herbert. *Spiritual Seeing: Picturing God's Invisibility in Medieval Art.* Philadelphia: University of Pennsylvania Press, 2000.

Khaleghi-Motlagh, Dj. "'Ayyuqi.'" In *Encyclopaedia Iranica Online.* http://www.iranicaonline.org/articles/ayyuqi-a-poet (published December 15, 1987).

Khalidi, Tarif. *Images of Muhammad: Narratives of the Prophet in Islam across the Centuries.* New York: Doubleday, 2009.

Khameh-Yar, Ahmad. "Risalaha va Ta'lifati darbara-yi Na'layn-i Payambar," http://ganjineh.kateban.com/post/2451 (accessed May 18, 2018).

———. "Tasvir pardazi-yi asar-i mansub bi payambar-i Islam dar du'anamaha-yi musavvar-i 'usmani." *Nama-yi Baharistan* 1 (1392/2012): 184–97.

Khaza'ili, Muhammad. *Sharh-i Bustan.* Tehran: Sazman-i Intisharat-i Javidan, 1984.

Khazanov, Anatoly. "Muhammad and Jenghiz Khan Compared: The Religious Factor in World Empire Building." *Comparative Studies in Society and History* 35, no. 3 (July 1993): 461–79.

Khosronejad, Pedram, ed. *The Art and Material Culture of Iranian Shi'ism: Iconography and Religious Devotion in Shi'i Islam.* London: I. B. Tauris, 2012.

Kia, Chad. "Sufi Orthopraxis: Visual Language and Verbal Imagery in Medieval Afghanistan." *Word and Image* 28, no. 1 (2012): 1–18.

Kinberg, Leah. "Literal Dreams and Prophetic Hadiths in Classical Islam: A Comparison of Two Ways of Legitimation." *Islam* 70 (1993): 279–300.

King, G. R. D. "Islam, Iconoclasm, and the Declaration of Doctrine." *Bulletin of the School of Oriental and African Studies* 48 (1985): 267–77.

Al-Kisa'i, Muhammad ibn 'Abdallah. *Tales of the Prophets.* Translated by Wheeler Thackston. Chicago: KAZI Publications, 1997.

Klapisch-Zuber, Christiane. "The Genesis of the Family Tree." *I Tatti Studies in the Italian Renaissance* 4 (1991): 105–29.

———. *L'ombre des ancêtres: essai sur l'imaginaire médiéval de la parenté.* Paris: Fayard, 2000.

Klausen, Jytte. "Art History and the Contemporary Politics of Depicting Muhammad: The Case of the Danish Cartoon Controversy." In *Muhammad in the Digital Age,* edited by Ruqayya Yasmine Khan, 57–82. Austin: University of Texas Press, 2015.

———. *The Cartoons That Shook the World.* New Haven, CT: Yale University Press, 2009.

Kleiber, Liliane. "Expression populaire et devotion shi'ite." *La revue des musées de France* 4 (2006): 64–71.

Kleinmichel, Sigrid. *Die Geburt des Propheten Muhammad: Drei Dichtungen aus Mittelasien.* Wiesbaden: Reichert, 2009.

Kohlberg, Etan. "Some Imami Shi'i Views on the *Sahaba.*" In *Belief and Law in Imami Shi'ism,* edited by Etan Kohlberg, 143–75. Aldershot: Variorum, 1991.

Kopytoff, Igor. "The Cultural Biography of Things: Commoditization as Process." In *The Social Life of Things: Commodities in Cultural Perspective,* edited by Arjun Appadurai, 64–91. Cambridge: Cambridge University Press, 1986.

Korkhmazian, Emma. *Toros Taronatsi.* Yerevan: Erebouni, 1984.

Korkhmazian, Emma, and Hravard Hacopian. "L'enluminure de l'Arménie Majeure." In *La miniature arménienne: Collection du Maténadaran,* edited by Tamara Mazaéva and Hratchia Tamrazyan, 34–46. Erevan: Naïri, 2006.

———. "Greater Armenia." In *Armenian Miniatures of the 13th and 14th Centuries from the Matenadaran Collection,* Yerevan, edited by Emma Korkhmazian, 9–18. Leningrad: Aurora, 1984.

Kotwicz, Wladyslaw. "Formules initiales des documents mongols aux XIII-e et XIV-e ss." *Rocznik Orjentalistyczny* 10 (1934): 131–57.

Kubler, George. *The Shape of Time: Remarks on the History of Things.* New Haven, CT: Yale University Press, 1962.

Küçükbay, Emine. "Das sogenannte *Dala'il ül-Khayrat*: Eine Untersuchung der Handschrift [Cod. turc. 553] der Bayerischen Staatsbibliothek, München." Master's thesis, Ludwig-Maximilians-Universität, 2010.

Lewis, Raphaela. *Everyday Life in Ottoman Turkey.* London: Batsford, 1971.

Lambton, Ann. "Early Timurid Theories of State: Hafiz Abru and Nizam al-Din Shami." *Bulletin d'Études Orientales* 30 (1978): 1–9.

Lange, Christian. "'On That Day when Faces Will Be White or Black' (Q3:106): Towards a Semiology of the Face in the Arabo-Islamic Tradition." *Journal of the American Oriental Society* 127, no. 4 (2007): 429–45.

Laoust, Henri. "Le role de 'Ali dans la sira chiite." *Revue des Etudes Islamiques* 30 (1962): 7–26.

Latour, Bruno. "What Is Iconoclash? Or Is There a World Beyond the Image Wars?" In *Iconoclash: Beyond the Image Wars in Science, Religion, and Art,* edited by Bruno Latour and Peter Weibel, 14–37. Cambridge, MA: MIT Press, 2002.

Le Gall, Dina. "Forgotten Naqshbandis and the Culture of Pre-modern Sufi Brotherhoods." *Studia Islamica* 97 (2003): 87–119.

Leites, Adrien. "*Sira* and the Question of Tradition." In *The Biography of Muhammad: The Issue of Sources,* edited by Harald Motzki, 49–66. Leiden: Brill, 2000.

Leoni, Francesca. "Sacred Words, Sacred Power: Qur'anic and Pious Phrases as Sources of Healing and Protection." In *Power and Protection: Islamic Art and the Supernatural,* edited by Francesca Leoni, 53–66. Oxford: Ashmolean Museum, 2016.

Levy, Reuben. *The Tales of Marzuban.* Bloomington: Indiana University Press, 1959.

Lings, Martin. *Muhammad: His Life Based on the Earliest Sources.* Rochester, VT: Inner Traditions International, 1983.

L'Orange, Hans Peter. *Studies on the Iconography of Cosmic Kingship in the Ancient World.* Oslo: Aschehoug, 1953.

Lory, Pierre. *Le rêve et ses interpretations en Islam.* Paris: Albin Michel, 2003.

———. "La vision du Prophète en rêve dans l'onirocritique musulmane." In *Autour du regard. Mélanges Gimaret,* edited by Éric Chaumont, 189–212. Louvain: Peeters, 2003.

Lowry, Glenn. *Oil and Sugar: Contemporary Art and Islamic Culture.* Toronto: Institute for Contemporary Culture, Royal Ontario Museum, 2009.

Madadpur, Muhammad, Zahra Ja'fari, and 'Ali Asghar Shirazi. "Fihrist-i Mawzu'i va Tahlili-i Kutub-i Tasviri dar Majmu'a-yi nusakh-i khatti-yi Kitabkhana-yi Madrasa-yi ʻAli-yi Shahid-i Mutahhari (Sipahsalar-i Sabiq).” *Nagara: Faslnama-yi Tahlili-Pazhuhashi* 25, no. 3 (1385/2006): 29–33.

Maddison, Francis, and Emilie Savage-Smith. *Science, Tools and Magic*. Part 1, *Body and Spirit, Mapping the Universe*. Nasser D. Khalili Collection of Islamic Art 12. London: Nour Foundation, 1992.

Al-Majlisi, Muhammad Baqir ibn Muhammad Taqi. *Bihar al-Anvar*. Vol. 41. Tehran: Dar al-Kutub al-Islamiyya, 1970.

Makariou, Sophie, ed. *Chefs d’oeuvre islamiques de l’Aga Khan Museum*. Paris: Musée du Louvre, 2007.

Al-Maktaba al-Shamila (The complete library). http://shamela.ws/rep.php/main (accessed May 18, 2018).

Al-Maliji, ʻArif Qasim Amin. *Asma’ al-Nabi fi’l-Qur’an wa’l-Sunna*. Cairo: ʻAlam al-Fikr, 1999.

Margoliouth, David. “The Relics of the Prophet Muhammad.” *The Moslem World* 27 (1937): 20–27.

Marzolph, Uli. “Early Printing History in Iran (1817–ca. 1900).” In *Middle Eastern Languages and the Print Revolution: A Cross-Cultural Encounter*, edited by Eva Hanebutt-Benz, Dagmar Glass, and Geoffrey Roper, 249–68. Westhofen: WVA, 2002.

———. “From Mecca to Mashhad: The Narrative of an Illustrated Shiʻi Pilgrimage Scroll from the Qajar Period.” *Muqarnas* 31 (2014): 207–42.

———. “The Pictorial Representation of Shiʻi Themes in Lithographed Books of the Qajar Period.” In *The Art and Material Culture of Iranian Shiʻism: Iconography and Religious Devotion in Shiʻi Islam*, edited by Pedram Khosronejad, 74–103. London: I. B. Tauris, 2012.

Massé, Henri. *Croyances et coutumes persanes, suivies de contes et chansons populaires*. Paris: Librairie Orientale et Américaine, 1938.

Massey, Keith. “Mysterious Letters.” In *Encyclopaedia of the Qur’an*. BrillOnline Reference Works. http://referenceworks .brillonline.com/browse/encyclopaedia -of-the-quran (accessed May 18, 2018).

Massignon, Louis. “La Mubahala de Médine et l’hyperdulie de Fatima.” In *Opera Minora*, edited by Youakim Moubarac, vol. 1, 550–72. Beirut: Dar al-Maaref, 1963.

Masuya, Tomoko. “Ilkhanid Courtly Life.” In *The Legacy of Genghis Khan: Courtly Art and Culture in Western Asia, 1256–1353*, edited by Linda Komaroff and Stefano Carboni, 75–103. New York: Metropolitan Museum of Art, 2002.

———. “The *Miʻradj-nama* Reconsidered.” *Artibus Asiae* 67, no. 1 (December 2007): 39–54.

Mathews, Thomas, and Avedis Sanjian, *Armenian Gospel Iconography: The Tradition of the Glajor Gospel*. Washington, DC: Dumbarton Oaks Research Library and Collection, 1991.

Mathews, Thomas, and Alice Taylor. *The Armenian Gospels of Gladzor: The Life of Christ Illuminated*. Los Angeles: J. Paul Getty Museum, 2001.

Mazaéva, Tamara, and Hratchia Tamrazyan, eds. *La miniature arménienne: Collection du Maténadaran*. Erevan: Naïri, 2006.

Mazzaoui, Michel. “A ‘New’ Edition of the *Safvat al-safa*.” In *History and Historiography of Post-Mongol Central Asia and the Middle East: Studies in Honor of John E. Woods*, edited by Judith Pfeiffer and Sholeh Quinn, 303–10. Wiesbaden: Harrassowitz, 2006.

McAuliffe, Jane. “Connecting Moses and Muhammad.” In *Books and Written Culture of the Islamic World: Studies Presented to Claude Gilliot on the Occasion of His 75th Birthday*, edited by Andrew Rippin and Roberto Tottoli, 326–40. Leiden: Brill, 2015.

———. “The Prediction and Prefiguration of Muhammad.” In *Bible and Qur’an: Essays in Scriptural Intertextuality*, edited by John Reeves, 107–31. Leiden: Brill, 2004.

McWilliams, Mary, ed. *In Harmony: The Norma Jean Calderwood Collection of Islamic Art*. Cambridge, MA: Harvard Art Museums, 2013.

Meier, Fritz. “Invoking Blessings on Muhammad in Prayers of Supplication and When Making Request.” In *Essays on Islamic Piety and Mysticism*, translated by John O’Kane, 549–88. Leiden: Brill, 1999.

Meisami, Julie Scott. “The Past in Service of the Present: Two Views of History in Medieval Persia.” In “Cultural Processes in Muslim and Arab Societies: Medieval and Early Modern Periods,” edited by Ehud R. Toledano. Special issue, *Poetics Today* 14, no. 2 (Summer 1993): 247–75.

Melikian-Chirvani, Assadullah Souren. “Le roman de Varqe et Golshah: Essai sur les rapports de l’esthétique littéraire et de l’esthétique plastique dans l’iran pré-mongol, suivi de la traduction du poème.” *Ars Asiatiques* 22 (1970): 1–264.

Melville, Charles. “Between Tabriz and Herat: Persian Historical Writing in the 15th Century.” In *Iran und iranisch geprägte Kulturen: Studien zum 65. Geburtstag von Bert G. Fragner*, edited by Markus Ritter, Ralph Kauz, and Birgitt Hoffmann, 28–38. Wiesbaden: Dr. Ludwig Reichert, 2008.

———. “The Illustration of History in Safavid Manuscript Painting.” In *New Perspectives on Safavid Iran: Empire and Society*, edited by Colin Mitchell, 163–97. London: Routledge, 2010.

———. “The Mongol and Timurid Periods, 1250–1500.” In *Persian Historiography*, edited by Charles Melville, 155–208. London: I. B. Tauris, 2012.

———. “Padshah-i Islam: The Conversion of Sultan Mahmud Ghazan Khan.” In *Persian and Islamic Studies in Honour of P. W. Avery, Pembroke Papers 1*, edited by Charles Melville, 159–77. Cambridge: University of Cambridge Press, 1990.

Melville, Charles, and ʻAbbas Zaryab. “Chobanids.” In *Encyclopaedia Iranica Online*. http://www.iranicaonline.org/articles /chobanids-chupanids-pers (published December 15, 1991).

Membré, Michele. *Relazione di Persia (1542)*. Edited by Gianroberto Scarcia. Naples: Istituto Universitario Orientale, 1969.

Meredith-Owens, Glyn Munro. “Islamic Illustrated Chronicles.” *Journal of Asian History* 4 (1970): 20–34.

Meri, Josef. “Aspects of Baraka (Blessings) and Ritual Devotion among Medieval Muslims and Jews.” *Medieval Encounters* 5, no. 1 (1999): 46–69.

———. *The Cult of Saints among Muslims and Jews in Medieval Syria*. Oxford: Oxford University Press, 2002.

———. “Relics of Piety and Power in Medieval Islam.” *Past and Present* 206, suppl. 5 (2010): 97–120.

Meserve, Ruth. “The Uses of Blood in Traditional Inner Asian Societies.” In *Religion, Customary Law, and Nomadic Technology*, edited by Michael Gervers and Wayne Schlepp, 35–50. Toronto Studies in Central and Inner Asia 4. Toronto: Joint Center for Asia Pacific Studies, 2000.

Michot, Jean. “Les fresques du pélerinage au Caire.” *Art and Archaeology Research Papers* 13 (1978): 7–21.

Milstein, Rachel. “Futuh-i Haramayn: Sixteenth-Century Illustrations of the Hajj Route.” In *Mamluks and Ottomans: Studies in Honour of Michael Winter*, edited by David Wasserstein and Ami Ayalon, 166–94. London: Routledge, 2006.

———. *Miniature Painting in Ottoman Baghdad*. Costa Mesa, CA: Mazda, 1990.

Milstein, Rachel, Karin Rührdanz, and Barbara Schmitz. *Stories of the Prophets: Illustrated Manuscripts of the Qisas al-Anbiya’*. Costa Mesa, CA: Mazda, 1999.

Minorsky, Vladimir. *The Chester Beatty Library: A Catalogue of the Turkish Manuscripts and Miniatures*. Dublin: Hodges, Figgis, 1958.

———. “The Poetry of Shah Ismaʻil I.” *Bulletin of the School of African and Oriental Studies* 10, no. 4 (1942): 1006a–1053a.

Mirkhwand. *The Rauzat-us-Safa or Garden of Purity*. Translated by Edward Rehatsek. Delhi: Idarah-i Adabiyat-i Delli, 1982.

Moin, Azfar. *The Millennial Sovereign: Sacred Kingship and Sainthood in Islam*. New York: Columbia University Press, 2012.

Al-Mojan, Muhammad. “The Textiles Made for the Prophet’s Mosque at Medina: A Preliminary Study of their Origins, History, and Style.” In *The Hajj: Collected Essays*, edited by Venetia Porter and Liana Seif, 184–94. London: British Museum, 2013.

Morabia, Alfred. "Surnaturel prodiges prophétiques et incubation dans la ville de l'envoyé d'Allâh." *Studia Islamica* 42 (1975): 93–114.

Morgan, David. *The Sacred Gaze: Religious Visual Culture in Theory and Practice*. Berkeley: University of California Press, 2005.

Morgan, David O. "Persian Historians and the Mongols." In *Medieval Historical Writing in the Christian and Islamic Worlds*, edited by David Morgan, 109–24. London: School of Oriental and African Studies, 1982.

Morris, James. "The Spiritual Ascension: Ibn 'Arabi and the Mi'raj, Part I." *Journal of the American Oriental Society* 107 (1987): 629–52.

———. "The Spiritual Ascension: Ibn 'Arabi and the Mi'raj, Part II." *Journal of the American Oriental Society* 108 (1988): 63–77.

Mostaert, Antoine, and Francis Woodman Cleaves. *Les lettres de 1289 et 1305 des ilkhan Argun et Öljeitü à Philippe le Bel*. Cambridge, MA: Harvard University Press, 1962.

———. "Trois documents mongols des Archives Secrètes Vaticanes." *Harvard Journal of Asiatic Studies* 15, nos. 3–4 (December 1952): 419–506.

Muhanna, Elias. "The Sultan's New Clothes: Ottoman-Mamluk Gift Exchange in the Fifteenth Century." *Muqarnas* 27 (2010): 189–207.

Naef, Silvia. *Y a-t-il une "question de l'image" en Islam?* Paris: Téraèdre, 2004.

Nagel, Tilman. *Allahs Liebling: Ursprung und Erscheinungsformen des Mohammedglaubens*. Munich: Oldenbourg, 2008.

Nasr, Seyyed Hossain. "The Sufi Master as Exemplified in Persian Sufi Literature." *Iran* 5 (1967): 35–40.

Nasrallah Munshi, Abu'l-Ma'ali. *Tarjuma-yi Kalila va Dimna*. Edited and with an introduction by Mujtaba Minovi. Tehran: University of Tehran Press, 1343/1924–25.

Natif, Mika. "The Painter's Breath and Concepts of Idol Anxiety in Islamic Art." In *Idol Anxiety*, edited by Josh Ellenbogen and Aaron Tugendhaft, 41–55. Stanford, CA: Stanford University Press, 2011.

Necipoğlu, Gülru. *Architecture, Ceremonial, and Power: The Topkapi Palace in the Fifteenth and Sixteenth Centuries*. Cambridge, MA: MIT Press, 1991.

———. "Framing the Gaze in Ottoman, Safavid, and Mughal Palaces." *Ars Orientalis* 23 (1993): 303–42.

———. "An Outline of Shifting Paradigms in the Palatial Architecture of the Pre-modern Islamic World." *Ars Orientalis* 23 (1993): 3–24.

———. "The Serial Portraits of Ottoman Sultans in Comparative Perspective." In *The Sultan's Portrait: Picturing the House of Osman*, edited by Ayşe Orbay, 22–65. Istanbul: İşbank, 2000.

———. "The Süleymaniye Complex in Istanbul: An Interpretation." *Muqarnas* 3 (1985): 92–117.

Newid, Mehr Ali. *Der schiitische Islam in Bildern: Rituale und Heilige*. Munich: Edition Avicenna, 2006.

Nicholson, Reynold. "An Early Arabic Version of the *Mi'raj* of Abu Yazid al-Bistami." *Islamica* 2, no. 3 (1926): 402–15.

———. *The Mystics of Islam*. London: Routledge and K. Paul, 1963.

Nikitine, B. "Essai d'analyse du *Safvat-us-safa*." *Journal Asiatique* 245 (1957): 385–94.

Nizami. *The Haft Paykar, a Medieval Persian Romance*. Translated by Julie Scott Meisami. Oxford: Oxford University Press, 1995.

———. *Makhzanol Asrar: The Treasury of Mysteries of Nezami of Ganjeh*. Translated by Gholam Hosein Darab. London: A. Probsthain, 1945.

Norris, Michele. "Demi's 'Muhammad': Author, Artist Brings Tale of Islam to Children." *All Things Considered*, National Public Radio, September 18, 2003. http:// www.npr.org/templates/story/story .php?storyId=1433867.

Nwyia, Paul. *Exégèse coranique et language mystique: Nouvel essai sur le lexique technique des mystiques musulmans*. Beirut: Dar al-Machreq, 1970.

Ohlander, Erik. "Behind the Veil of the Unseen: Dreams and Dreaming in the Classical and Medieval Sufi Tradition." In *Dreams and Visions in Islamic Societies*, edited by Özgen Felek and Alexander Knysh, 199–213. Albany: State University of New York Press, 2012.

Okhravi, Rasoul, and Morteza Djamali. "The Missing Ancient Lake of Saveh: A Historical Review." *Iranica Antiqua* 38 (2003): 327–44.

Otto-Dorn, Katharina. "Das seldschukische Thronbild." *Persica* 10 (1982): 149–203.

Padwick, Constance. *Muslim Devotions: A Study of Prayer-Manuals in Common Use*. London: SPCK, 1961.

Pancaroğlu, Oya. "Resimli ve tasvirli el yazmaları." In *Türkiye Selçukluları ve Beylikler Dönemi Uygarlığı*, edited by Ali Uzay Peker and Kenan Bilici, vol. 2, 575–85. Ankara: Turkish Ministry of Culture and Tourism, 2006.

———. "Signs in the Horizons: Concepts of Image and Boundary in a Medieval Cosmography." *RES: Anthropology and Aesthetics* 43 (Spring 2003): 31–41.

———. "A World unto Himself: The Rise of a New Human Image in the Late Seljuk Period (1150–1250)." PhD diss., Harvard University, 2000.

Paret, Rudi. "Das islamische Bilderverbot und die Schia." In *Festschrift Werner Caskel zum siebzigsten Geburstag 5. März 1966*, edited by Erwin Gräf, 224–32. Leiden: Brill, 1968.

Parker, Ann. *Hajj Paintings: Folk Art of the Great Pilgrimage*. Washington: Smithsonian Institution Press, 1995.

Pavet de Courteille, Abel. *Mirâdj-Nâmeh, Récit de l'Ascension de Mahomet au Ciel Composé A.H. 840/1436–1437*. Amsterdam: Philo, 1882.

Peters, F. E. "The Quest of the Historical Muhammad." *International Journal of Middle East Studies* 23, no. 3 (August 1991): 291–315.

Peterson, Erik. "Das Schiff als Symbol der Kirche." *Theologische Zeitschrifi* 6 (1950): 77–79.

Pfeiffer, Judith. "Conversion Versions: Sultan Öljeytü's Conversion to Shi'ism (709/1309) in Muslim Narrative Sources." *Mongolian Studies* 22 (1999): 35–67.

———. "Reflections on a 'Double Rapprochement': Conversion to Islam among the Mongol Elite during the Early Ilkhanate." In *Beyond the Legacy of Genghis Khan*, edited by Linda Komaroff, 369–89. Leiden: Brill, 2006.

Piemontese, Angelo. "The Statutes of the Qajar Orders of Knighthood." *East and West* 19, nos. 3–4 (September–December 1969): 431–73.

Porter, Venetia. "Amulets Inscribed with the Names of the 'Seven Sleepers' of Ephesus in the British Museum." In *Word of God, Art of Man: The Qur'an and Its Creative Expressions*, edited by Fahmida Suleman, 123–34. Oxford: Oxford University Press in association with the Institute of Ismaili Studies, 2007.

———. "Islamic Seals: Magical or Practical?" In *Magic and Divination in Early Islam*, edited by Emilie Savage-Smith, 179–200. Aldershots, UK: Ashgate Variorum, 2004.

Porter, Venetia, Robert Hoyland, Alexander Morton, and Shailendra Bandhare. *Arabic and Persian Seals and Amulets in the British Museum*. London: British Museum, 2011.

Porter, Yves. *Peinture et arts du livre: Essai sur la littérature technique indo-persane*. Louvain: Peters, 1992.

Potter, Lawrence. "Sufis and Sultans in Post-Mongol Iran." *Iranian Studies* 27, nos. 1–4, (1994): 77–102.

Potts, Alex. "Sign." In *Critical Terms for Art History*, edited by Robert Nelson and Richard Shiff, 20–34. 2nd ed. Chicago: University of Chicago Press, 2003.

Puin, Elisabeth. *Islamische Plakate: Kalligraphie und Malerei im Dienste des Glaubens*. 3 vols. Dortmund: Orientkunde, 2008.

Quinn, Sholeh. "Coronation Narratives in Safavid Chronicles." In *History and Historiography of post-Mongol Central Asia and the Middle East, Studies in Honor of John E. Woods*, edited by Judith Pfeiffer and Sholeh Quinn, 311–31. Wiesbaden: Harrassowitz, 2006.

———. "The Dreams of Shaykh Safi al-Din and Safavid Historical Writing." *Iranian Studies* 29, nos. 1–2 (Winter–Spring 1996): 127–47.

———. *Historical Writing during the Reign of Shah 'Abbas: Ideology, Imitation, and Legitimacy in Safavid Chronicles*. Salt Lake City: University of Utah Press, 2000.

Quinn, Sholeh, and Charles Melville. "Safavid Historiography." In *Persian Historiography*, edited by Charles Melville,

209–25. A History of Persian Literature 10. London: I. B. Tauris, 2012.

Al-Qushayri, 'Abd al-Karim ibn Hawazin. *Epistle on Sufism: Al-Risala al-Qushayriyya fi 'Ilm al-Tasawwuf.* Translated by Alexander Knysh. Reading, UK: Garnet, 2007.

Al-Rabghuzi, Nasir al-Din ibn Burhan al-Din. *The Stories of the Prophets: Qisas al-Anbiya', An Eastern Turkish Version.* Translated by H. E. Boeschoten, J. O'Kane, and M. Vandamme. 2 vols. Leiden: Brill, 1995.

Raby, Julian. "Opening Gambits." In *The Sultan's Portrait: Picturing the House of Osman,* 64–95. Istanbul: İş Bankası, 2000.

———. "A Sultan of Paradox: Mehmed the Conqueror as a Patron of the Arts." *Oxford Art Journal* 5, no. 1 (1982): 3–8.

Rahman, Fazlur. "Dream, Imagination, and 'Alam al-Mithal." In *The Dream and Human Societies,* edited by Gustave von Grunebaum and Roger Caillois, 409–19. Berkeley: University of California Press, 1966.

Ram, Haggai. *Iranophobia: The Logic of an Israeli Obsession.* Stanford, CA: Stanford University Press, 2009.

Ramadan, Dina. "'One of the Best Tools for Learning': Rethinking the Role of 'Abduh's Fatwa in Egyptian Art History." In *A Companion to Modern African Art,* edited by Gitti Salami and Monica Blackmun Visonà, 137–53. Malden, MA: John Wiley and Sons, 2013.

Rambelli, Fabio, and Eric Reinders. "What Does Iconoclasm Create? What Does Preservation Destroy? Reflections on Iconoclasm in East Asia." In *Iconoclasm: Contested Objects, Contested Terms,* edited by Stacy Boldrick and Richard Clay, 15–33. London: Ashgate, 2007.

Rancière, Jacques. *The Politics of Aesthetics: The Distribution of the Sensible.* Translated by Gabriel Rockhill. London: Continuum, 2004.

Ranjabar, Ahmad. *Chand Mi'rajnama.* Tehran: Amir Kabir, 1372/1952.

Rasheed, Ghulam Dastagir. "The Development of Na'tia Poetry in Persian Literature." *Islamic Culture* 39, no. 1 (January 1965): 53–69.

Rashid al-Din. *Geschichte Gazan Hans.* Edited by Karl Jahn. London: Luzac, 1940.

———. *Jami' al-Tawarikh (Iran wa Islam).* Edited by Muhammad Rushan. Tehran: Miras-i Maktub, 2013.

Réau, Louis. "La nativité et l'adoration des images." In *Iconographie de l'art chrétien,* vol. 2, part 2, 213–55. Paris: Presses universitaires de France, 1955–59.

Rebhan, Helga. *The Wonders of Creation: Manuscripts of the Bavarian State Library from the Islamic World.* Wiesbaden: Harrassowitz, 2010.

Redford, Scott. "Portable Palaces: On the Circulation of Objects and Ideas about Architecture in Medieval Anatolia and Mesopotamia." In *Mechanisms of Exchange: Transmission in Medieval Art and Architecture of the Mediterranean, ca. 1000–1500,* edited by Heather Grossman and Alicia Walker, 382–412. Medieval Encounters 18. Leiden: Brill, 2013.

Renda, Günsel. "The Miniatures of Silsilename, no. 1321 in the Topkapı Saray Museum Library." *Sanat Tarihi Yıllığı* 5 (1972–73): 481–95.

———. "New Light on the Painters of the 'Zubdet al-Tawarikh' in the Museum of Turkish and Islamic Arts in Istanbul." In *IVème congrès international d'art turc,* 183–200. Aix-en-Provence: Université de Provence, 1976.

Reynolds, Gabriel Said. *The Qur'an and Its Biblical Subtext.* London: Routledge, 2010.

Reza'i, Muhammad Javad, and Mahdi Dasht Bozorgi. "A Study of the Verse of Mubahalah." *Journal of Shi'a Islamic Studies* 2, no. 1 (Winter 2009): 69–83.

Rice, David Storm. "The Aghani Miniatures and Religious Painting in Islam." *Burlington Magazine* 95, no. 601 (April 1953): 128–35.

Rippin, Andrew. "The Function of *Asbab al-Nuzul* in Qur'anic Exegesis." *Bulletin of the School of Oriental and African Studies* 51, no. 1 (1988): 1–20.

———. "Al-Zarkashi and al-Suyuti on the Function of the 'Occasion of Revelation' Material." *Islamic Culture* 59, no. 3 (July 1985): 243–58.

Robinson, Basil. *A Descriptive Catalogue of the Persian Paintings in the Bodleian Library.* Oxford: Clarendon, 1958.

———. *Fifteenth-Century Persian Painting: Problems and Issues.* New York: New York University Press, 1991.

———. *Islamic Painting and the Arts of the Book.* London: Faber and Faber, 1976.

———. *Persian Painting in the John Rylands Library: A Descriptive Catalogue.* 2nd ed. Totowa, NJ: Sotheby Parke Benet, 1980.

———. "The Turkman School to 1503." In *The Arts of the Book in Central Asia, 14th–16th Centuries,* edited by Basil Gray, 215–58. Boulder, CO: Shambhala, 1979.

———. "Two Illustrated Manuscripts in the Malek Library." In *Content and Context of Visual Arts in the Islamic World: Papers from a Colloquium in Memory of Baysunghur's Library Richard Ettinghausen, Institute of Fine Arts, New York University, 2–4 April 1980,* edited by Priscilla Soucek, 91–97. University Park: Pennsylvania State University Press, 1988.

Rogers, J. Michael. "Approval and Disapproval of Images in Islam." In *The Topkapı Saray Museum: The Albums and Illustrated Manuscripts,* 21–24. Boston: Little, Brown, 1986.

———. *Arts of Islam: Masterpieces from the Khalili Collection.* London: Thames and Hudson, 2010.

———. "The Genesis of Safawid Religious Painting." In *Vth International Congress of Iranian Art and Archaeology, Tehran-Isfahan-Shiraz, 11th–18th April 1968,* 2 (1968): 167–188. Tehran: Ministry of Culture and Arts. Republished in *Iran* 8 (1970): 125–40.

———. "Mehmed the Conqueror: Between East and West." In *Bellini and the East,* edited by Caroline Campbell and Alan Chong, 80–97. New Haven, CT: Yale University Press, 2005.

Roggema, Barbara. *The Legend of Sergius Bahira: Eastern Christian Apologetics and Apocalyptic in Response to Islam.* Leiden: Brill, 2009.

Roux, Jean-Paul. "Tängri. Essai sur le ciel-dieu des peuples altaïques (premier article)." *Revue de l'histoire des religions* 149, no. 1 (1956): 49–82.

Roxburgh, David. "Concepts of the Portrait in the Islamic Lands, c. 1300–1600." In *Dialogues in Art History, from Mesopotamian to Modern: Readings for a New Century,* edited by Elizabeth Cropper, 119–37. Studies in the History of Art 74. Washington, DC: National Gallery of Art, 2009.

———. "Heinrich Friedrich von Diez and his Eponymous Albums: Mss. Diez A. Fols. 70–74." *Muqarnas* 12 (1995): 112–36.

———. "Micrographia: Toward a Visual Logic of Persianate Painting." *RES: Anthropology and Aesthetics* 43 (Spring 2003): 12–30.

———. *The Persian Album, 1400–1600: From Dispersal to Collection.* New Haven, CT: Yale University Press, 2005.

———. "Persian Drawing, ca. 1400–1450: Materials and Creative Procedures." *Muqarnas* 19 (2002): 44–77.

———. "Pilgrimage City." In *The City in the Islamic World,* edited by Salma Khadra Jayyusi, Renata Holod, Attilio Petruccioli, and André Raymond, 753–74. Leiden: Brill, 2008.

———. *Prefacing the Image: The Writing of Art History in Sixteenth-Century Iran.* Leiden: Brill, 2001.

Rubin, Uri. *The Eye of the Beholder: The Life of Muhammad as Viewed by the Early Muslims.* Princeton, NJ: Darwin, 1995.

———. "More Light on Muhammad's Pre-existence." In *Books and Written Culture of the Islamic World: Studies Presented to Claude Gilliot on the Occasion of His 75th Birthday,* edited by Andrew Rippin and Roberto Tottoli, 288–311. Leiden: Brill, 2015.

———. "Muhammad's Message in Mecca: Warnings, Signs, and Miracles." In *The Cambridge Companion to Muhammad,* edited by Jonathan Brockopp, 39–60. Cambridge: Cambridge University Press, 2010.

———. "Nur Muhammadi." In *Encyclopaedia of Islam.* 2nd ed. BrillOnline Reference Works. http://referenceworks.brillonline.com/browse/encyclopaedia-of-islam-2 (accessed May 18, 2018).

———. "Pre-existence and Light: Aspects of the Concept of Nur Muhammad." *Israel Oriental Studies* 5 (1975): 62–119.

———. "The Shrouded Messenger: On the Interpretation of *al-Muzzammil* and *al-Muddaththir.*" *Jerusalem Studies in Arabic and Islam* 16 (1993): 96–107.

Rudy, Kathryn. "Kissing Images, Unfurling Rolls, Measuring Wounds, Sewing Badges and Carrying Talismans: Considering Some Harley Manuscripts through the Physical Rituals They Reveal." *Electronic British Library Journal* Article 5 (2011): 1–56.

Ruggles, Fairchild D., ed. *Islamic Art and Visual Culture: An Anthology of Sources.* Malden, MA: Wiley-Blackwell, 2011.

Rührdanz, Karin. "The Illustrated Manuscripts of *Athar al-Muzaffar*: A History of the Prophet." In *Persian Painting from the Mongols to the Qajars: Studies in Honour of Basil W. Robinson*, edited by Robert Hillenbrand, 201–16. London: I. B. Tauris, 2000.

———. "Die Miniaturen des Dresdener 'Falnameh.'" *Persica* 12 (1987): 1–56.

Rüstem, Ünver. "The Afterlife of a Royal Gift: The Ottoman Inserts of the *Shahnama-i Shahi*." *Muqarnas* 29 (2002): 245–337.

Saʿdi. *Morals Pointed and Tales Adorned: The Bustan of Saʿdi.* Translated by G. M. Wickens. Toronto: University of Toronto Press, 1974.

Saeed, Yousuf. *Muslim Devotional Art in India.* New Delhi: Routledge, 2012.

Safi, Omid. *Memories of Muhammad: Why the Prophet Matters.* New York: HarperOne, 2009.

Safwat, Nabil. *The Art of the Pen: Calligraphy of the 14th to 20th Centuries.* Nasser D. Khalili Collection of Islamic Art 5. New York: Nour Foundation in association with Azimuth Editions and Oxford University Press, 1992.

Sakili, Abraham. *Space and Identity: Expressions in the Culture, Arts and Society of the Muslims in the Philippines.* Quezon City: Asian Center, University of the Philippines, 2003.

Sakıp Sabancı Museum Collection of the Arts of the Book and Calligraphy. Istanbul: Sakıp Sabancı Museum, 2012.

Saviello, Alberto. *Imaginationen des Islam: Bildiche Darstellungen des Propheten Mohammed im westeuropäischen Buchdruck bis ins 19. Jahrhundert.* Berlin: De Gruyter, 2015.

Sayyid, Ayman Fuʾad. *Dar al-Kutub al-Misriyya bayna al-ams waʾl-yawm waʾl-ghad.* Cairo: al-Haʾya al-ʿAmma li-Dar al-Kutub waʾl-Wathaʾiq al-Qawmiyya, 2008.

Schick, İrvin Cemil. "The Content of Form: Islamic Calligraphy between Text and Representation." In *Sign and Design: Script as Image in Cross-Cultural Perspective (300–1600 CE)*, edited by Brigitte Miriam Bedos-Rezak and Jeffrey Hamburger, 173–94. Washington, DC: Dumbarton Oaks, 2016.

———. "The Iconicity of Islamic Calligraphy in Turkey." *RES: Anthropology and Aesthetics* 53–54 (Spring–Autumn 2008): 211–24.

Schimmel, Annemarie. *As through a Veil: Mystical Poetry in Islam.* New York: Columbia University Press, 1982.

———. *Islam in the Indian Subcontinent.* Leiden: Brill, 1980.

———. *And Muhammad Is His Messenger: The Veneration of the Prophet in Islamic Piety.* Chapel Hill: University of North Carolina Press, 1985.

———. *Mystical Dimensions of Islam.* Chapel Hill: University of North Carolina Press, 1975.

———. "The Primordial Dot: Some Thoughts about Sufi Letter Mysticism." *Jerusalem Studies in Arabic and Islam* 9 (1987): 350–56.

———. *Die Träume des Kalifen: Träume und ihre Deutung in der islamischen Kultur.* Munich: C. H. Beck, 1998.

Schmitz, Barbara. "Bukhara VI: The Bukharan School of Miniature Painting." In *Encyclopaedia Iranica Online.* http://www.iranicaonline.org/articles/bukhara-vi (accessed May 18, 2018).

Schmitz, Barbara, and Ziyaud-Din Desai. *Mughal and Persian Paintings and Illustrated Manuscripts in the Raza Library, Rampur.* New Delhi: Rampur Raza Library, 2006.

Schussman, Aviva. "The Legitimacy and Nature of *Mawlid al-Nabi* (Analysis of a *Fatwa*)." *Islamic Law and Society* 5, no. 2 (1998): 214–34.

Séguy, Marie-Rose. *The Miraculous Journey of Mahomet: Miraj Nameh, BN, Paris Sup Turc 190.* Translated by Richard Pevear. New York: G. Braziller, 1977.

Sells, Michael. *Early Islamic Mysticism: Sufi, Qurʾan, Miʿraj, Poetic and Theological Writings.* New York: Paulist, 1996.

Shalem, Avinoam, et al. *Constructing the Image of Muhammad in Europe.* Berlin: De Gruyter, 2013.

Shani, Raya. "Calligraphic Lions Symbolising the Esoteric Dimensions of ʿAli's Nature." In *The Art and Material Culture of Iranian Shiʿism: Iconography and Religious Devotion in Shiʿi Islam*, edited by Pedram Khosronejad, 122–58. London: I. B. Tauris, 2012.

———. "Illustrations of the Parable of the Ship of Faith in Firdausi's Prologue to the *Shahnama*." In *Shahnama Papers* I, edited by Charles Melville, 1–40. Cambridge: University of Cambridge, 2006.

———. "The Lion Image in Safavid *Miʿraj* Paintings." In *A Survey of Persian Art*, vol. 18, edited by Abbas Daneshvari, 265–426. Costa Mesa, CA: Mazda, 2005.

Sharon, Moshe. "*Ahl al-Bayt*—People of the House." *Jerusalem Studies in Arabic and Islam* 9 (1986): 169–84.

Shatanawi, Mirjam. *Islam at the Tropenmuseum.* Arnhem, Netherlands: LM, 2014.

Shaykh al-Mufid. *Kitab al-Irshad: The Book of Guidance into the Lives of the Twelve Imams.* Translated by I. K. A. Howard. Qom: Ansariyan Publications, 2001.

Shenkar, Michael. *Intangible Spirits and Graven Images: The Iconography of Deities in the Pre-Islamic Iranian World.* Leiden: Brill, 2018.

———. "Royal Regalia and 'Divine Kingship' in Pre-Islamic Central Asia." *Parthica* 19 (2017): 55–74.

Shiro, Ando. "Gazorgahi, Mir Kamal-al-Din Hosayn." In *Encyclopaedia Iranica Online.* http://www.iranicaonline.org/articles/gazorgahi- (published December 15, 2000).

Siddiqi, Muhammad Iqbal. *Ninety-Nine Names of Prophet Muhammad.* Lahore: Kazi Publications, 1998.

Sims, Eleanor. "The *Nahj al-Faradis* of Sultan Abu Saʿid ibn Sultan Muhammad ibn Miranshah: An Illustrated Timurid Ascension-Text of the 'Interim Period.'" *Journal of the David Collection* 4 (2014): 89–147.

———. "The Turks and Illustrated Historical Texts." In *Fifth International Congress of Turkish Art*, edited by G. Fehér, 747–72. Budapest: Akadémiai Kiadó, 1978.

Simpson, Marianna Shreve. *The Illustration of an Epic: The Earliest Shahnama Manuscripts.* PhD diss., Harvard University, 1978.

———. "In the Beginning: Frontispieces and Front Matter in Ilkhanid and Injuid Manuscripts." In *Beyond the Legacy of Genghis Khan*, edited by Linda Komaroff, 213–47. Leiden: Brill, 2006.

———. "Manuscripts and Mongols: Some Documented and Speculative Moments in East-West/Muslim-Christian Relations." *French Historical Studies* 30, no. 3 (Summer 2007): 351–94.

———. "The Pattern of Early *Shahnama* Illustration." *Ars Orientalis* 1 (1982): 43–53.

———. "The Role of Baghdad in the Formation of Persian Painting." In *Art et société dans le monde iranien*, edited by Chahryar Adle, 91–116. Paris: Recherche sur les Civilisations, 1982.

Soroush, Mehrnoush. "Zahir al-Dawla, Ebrahim Khan." In *Encyclopaedia Iranica Online.* http://www.iranicaonline.org/articles/zahir-al-dawla-ebrahim-khan (published March 4, 2011).

Soucek, Priscilla. "Armenian and Islamic Manuscript Painting: A Visual Dialogue." In *Treasures in Heaven: Armenian Art, Religion, and Society*, edited by Thomas Matthews and Roger Wieck, 115–31. New York: Pierpont Morgan Library, 1998.

———. "An Illustrated Manuscript of al-Biruni's *Chronology of Nations*." In *The Scholar and the Saint: Studies in Commemoration of Abuʾl-Rayhan al-Biruni and Jalal al-Din al-Rumi*, edited by Peter Chelkowski, 103–68. New York: New York University Press, 1975.

———. "The Life of the Prophet: Illustrated Versions." In *Content and Context of Visual Arts in the Islamic World: Papers from a Colloquium in Memory of Richard Ettinghausen, Institute of Fine Arts, New York University, 2–4 April 1980*, edited by Priscilla Soucek, 193–218. University Park: Pennsylvania State University Press, 1988.

———. "The Theory and Practice of Portraiture in the Persian Tradition." *Muqarnas* 17 (2000): 97–108.

———. "The Visual Language of Qajar Medals." In *Islamic Art in the 19th Century: Tradition, Innovation, and Eclecticism*, edited by Doris Behrens-Abouseif and Stephen Vernoit, 305–31. Leiden: Brill, 2006.

Soudavar, Abolala. *The Aura of Kings: Legitimacy and Divine Sanction in Iranian Kingship*. Costa Mesa, CA: Mazda, 2003.

Spuler, Bertold. *History of the Mongols: Based on Eastern and Western Accounts of the Thirteenth and Fourteenth Centuries*. Translated by Helga and Stuart Drummond. Berkeley: University of California Press, 1972.

St. Elie, Anastase-Marie de. "Le culte rendu par les Musulmans aux sandales de Mahomet." *Anthropos* 5 (1910): 363–66.

Stanfield-Johnson, Rosemary. *Ritual Cursing in Iran: Theology, Politics and the Public in Safavid Persia*. London: Tauris Academic Studies, 2015.

———. "The Tabarra'iyan and the Early Safavids." *Iranian Studies* 37, no. 1 (March 2004): 47–71.

Staples, W. E. "Muhammad, a Talismanic Force." *American Journal of Semitic Languages and Literatures* 57, no. 1 (January 1940): 63–70.

Starrett, Gregory. "The Political Economy of Religious Commodities in Cairo." *American Anthropologist* 97, no. 1 (1995): 51–68.

Stchoukine, Ivan. "La peinture à Baghdad sous Sultan Pir Budaq Qara-Qoyunlu." *Arts Asiatiques* 25 (1972): 3–18.

———. *Les peintures des manuscrits tîmûrides*. Paris: Imprimerie Nationale, 1954.

———. "Qasim ibn 'Ali et ses peintures dans les *Ahsan al-Kibar*." *Arts Asiatiques* 28 (1973): 45–54.

Steingass, Francis. *A Comprehensive Persian-English Dictionary*. New Delhi: Munshiram Manoharlal, 2000.

Stern, S. M. "A New Volume of the Illustrated Aghani Manuscript." *Ars Orientalis* 2 (1957): 501–3.

Stetkevych, Suzanne Pinckney. "From Text to Talisman: Al-Busiri's *Qasidat al-Burda* (Mantle Ode) and the Supplicatory Ode." *Journal of Arabic Literature* 37, no. 2 (2006): 145–89.

———. *The Mantle Odes: Arabic Praise Poems to the Prophet Muhammad*. Bloomington: Indiana University Press, 2010.

Stoker, Wessel. "The Rothko Chapel Paintings and the 'Urgency of the Transcendent Experience.'" *International Journal for Philosophy of Religion* 64, no. 2 (October 2008): 89–102.

Strothmann, Rudolf. "Die Mubahala in Tradition und Liturgie." *Islam* 33 (1958): 5–29.

Subtelny, Maria. "Art and Politics in Early 16th Century Central Asia." *Central Asiatic Journal* 26, nos. 1–2 (1982): 121–48.

———. "Badi'-al-Zaman," In *Encyclopaedia Iranica Online*. http://www.iranicaonline.org/articles/badi-al-zaman-b (published December 15, 1988).

———. "The Cult of 'Abdallah Ansari under the Timurids." In *Gott ist schön und Er liebt die Schönheit: Festschrift für Annemarie Schimmel*, edited by Alma Giese and Christoph Bürgel, 377–406. Bern: Peter Land, 1994.

———. "The Jews at the Edge of the World in a Timurid-Era *Mi'raj-nama*: The Islamic Ascension Narrative as Missionary Text." In *The Prophet's Ascension: Cross-Cultural Encounters with the Islamic Mi'raj Tales*, edited by Christiane Gruber and Frederick Colby, 50–77. Bloomington: Indiana University Press, 2010.

———. "Scenes from the Literary Life of Timurid Herat." In *Logos Islamikos: Studia Islamica in Honorem Georgii Michaelis Wickens*, edited by Roger Savory and Dionisus Agius, 137–55. Toronto: Pontifical Institute of Mediaeval Studies, 1984.

Subtelny, Maria, and Anas Khalidov. "The Curriculum of Islamic Higher Learning in Timurid Iran in the Light of the Sunni Revival under Shah-Rukh." *Journal of the American Oriental Society* 115, no. 2 (April–June 1995): 210–36.

Suhrawardi. *The Philosophy of Illumination*. Edited and translated by John Walbridge and Hossein Ziai. Provo, UT: Brigham Young University Press, 1999.

Suleman, Fahmida, and Shainool Jiwa. "Shi'i Art and Ritual: Contexts, Definitions, and Expressions." In *People of the Prophet's House: Artistic and Ritual Expressions of Shi'i Islam*, edited by Fahmida Suleman, 13–29. London: Azimuth Editions in association with the Institute of Ismaili Studies in collaboration with the British Museum's Department of the Middle East, 2015.

Al-Suyuti, 'Abd al-Rahman ibn Abi Bakr. *Al-Riyad al-Aniqa fi Sharh Asma' Khayr al-Khaliqa* (The Beautiful Gardens: Explanation of the Names of the Best of Creation). Beirut: Dar al-Kutub al-'Ilmiyya, 1405/1985.

———. *Le mawlid. Fatwa sur la celebration de la naissance du Prophète*. Translated by Fayçal Znati and Introduction by Tayeb Chouiref. Wattrelos: Editions Tasnîm, 2014.

Szilágyi, Krisztina. "Muhammad and the Monk: The Making of the Christian Bahira Legend." *Jerusalem Studies in Arabic and Islam* 34 (2005): 169–214.

Al-Tabari, Muhammad ibn Jarir. *La chronique de Tabarî: Histoire des envoyés de Dieu et des rois*. Translated by Hermann Zotenberg. Paris: Al-Bustane, 2002.

———. *Muhammad in Mecca*. Translated by Montgomery Watt and M. V. McDonald. Albany: State University of New York Press, 1988.

Takim, Liyakat. "From *Bid'a* to *Sunna*: The *Wilaya* of 'Ali in the Shi'i *Adhan*." *Journal of the American Oriental Society* 120, no. 2 (2000): 166–77.

Talbot Rice, David. *The Illustrations to the "World History" of Rashid al-Din*. Edited by Basil Gray. Edinburgh: Edinburgh University Press, 1976.

Taner, Melis. "'Caught in a Whirlwind': Painting in Baghdad in Late Sixteenth-Early Seventeenth Centuries." PhD diss., Harvard University, 2016.

Tanındı, Zeren. "Seçkin Bir Mevlevî'nin Tezhipli Kitapları." In *M. Uğur Derman Armağanı: Altmışbeşinci Yaşı Münasebetiyle Sunulmuş Tebliğler / M. Uğur Derman Festschrift: Papers Presented on the Occasion of his Sixty-Fifth Birthday*, edited by İrvin Cemil Schick, 513–36. Istanbul: Sabancı University, 2000.

———. *Siyer-i Nebî: İslâm Tasvir Sanatında Hz. Muhammed'in Hayatı*. Istanbul: Hürriyet Vakfı Yayınları, 1984.

Tarlo, Emma. *Visibly Muslim: Fashion, Politics, Faith*. Oxford: Berg, 2010.

Taşkale, Faruk. "Kur'an-ı Kerîm'de Açan Çiçekler." In *M. Uğur Derman Armağanı: Altmışbeşinci Yaşı Münasebetiyle Sunulmuş Tebliğler / M. Uğur Derman Festschrift: Papers Presented on the Occasion of his Sixty-Fifth Birthday*, edited by İrvin Cemil Schick, 537–52. Istanbul: Sabancı University, 2000.

Taşkale, Faruk, and Hüseyin Gündüz. *Hz. Muhammed'in Özellikleri: Hat Sanatında Hilye-i Şerîfe / Characteristics of the Prophet Muhammed in Calligraphic Art*. Istanbul: Kültür Yayınları, 2006.

Tatar, Sarolta. "The Festive Beverages of the Khans." In *Altay Dünyasında Gündelik Hayat (Proceedings of the 46th Meeting of the Permanent International Altaistic Conference)*, edited by Gülzemin Özrenk Aydın, 457–62. Ankara: Türk Dil Kurumu, 2007.

Taylor, Alice. "Armenian Illumination under Georgian, Turkish, and Mongol Rule: The Thirteenth, Fourteenth, and Fifteenth Centuries." In *Treasures in Heaven: Armenian Illustrated Manuscripts*, edited by Thomas Mathews and Roger Wieck, 84–103. New York: Pierpont Morgan Library, 1994.

Ter Haar, Johan. "The Importance of the Spiritual Guide in the Naqshbandi Order." In *The Legacy of Mediaeval Persian Sufism*, edited by Leonard Lewisohn, 311–21. London: Khaniqahi Nimatullahi Publications, 1992.

Tezcan, Hülya. "Ka'ba Covers from the Topkapı Palace Collection and their Inscriptions." In *Word of God, Art of Man: The Qur'an and Its Creative Expressions*, edited by Fahmida Suleman, 227–38. London: Institute of Ismaili Studies, 2007.

Thackston, Wheeler. *Album Prefaces and Other Documents on the History of Calligraphers and Painters*. Studies and Sources in Islamic Art and Architecture, Supplements to *Muqarnas* 10. Leiden: Brill, 2001.

———. "The Paris Mi'rajnama." *Journal of Turkish Studies* 18 (1994): 263–99.

Al-Tirmidhi, Muhammad ibn ʿIsa. *Shamaal-il Tirmidhi: Characteristics of the Holy Prophet Muhammad, Sallallahu ʿAlayhi Wasallam*. Edited by Muhammad Zakariyya. Karachi: Idaratul Quran, 1993.

———. *Shamaʾil al-Nabi*. Edited by Mahir Yasin Fahl. Beirut: Dar al-Gharb al-Islami, 2000.

Titley, Norah. *Miniatures from Persian Manuscripts: A Catalogue and Subject Index of Paintings from Persia, India, and Turkey in the British Library and the British Museum*. London: British Museum Publications, 1977.

Tolan, John. "European Accounts of Muhammad's Life." In *The Cambridge Companion to Muhammad*, edited by Jonathan Brockopp, 226–50. Cambridge: Cambridge University Press, 2010.

———. "Impostor or Lawgiver?: Muhammad through European Eyes in the 17th and 18th Centuries." In *The Image of the Prophet between Ideal and Ideology: A Scholarly Investigation*, edited by Christiane Gruber and Avinoam Shalem, 261–69. Berlin: De Gruyter, 2014.

Touati, Houari, ed. *De la figuration humaine au portrait dans l'art islamique*. Leiden: Brill, 2015.

———. "Le régime des images figuratives dans la culture islamique médiévale." In *De la figuration humaine au portrait dans l'art islamique*, 1–30. Leiden: Brill, 2015.

Uluç, Lale. "The *Majalis al-ʿUshshaq*: Written in Herat, Copied in Shiraz, Read in Istanbul." In *M. Uğur Derman Armağanı: Altmışbeşinci Yaşı Münasebetiyle Sunulmuş Tebliğler / M. Uğur Derman Festschrift: Papers Presented on the Occasion of his Sixty-Fifth Birthday*, edited by İrvin Cemil Schick, 569–602. Istanbul: Sabancı Universitesi, 2000.

———. *Turkman Governors, Shiraz Artisans, and Ottoman Collectors: Sixteenth Century Shiraz Manuscripts*. Istanbul: Türkiye İş Bankası Yayınları, 2006.

Van Ess, Joseph. *The Youthful God: Anthropomorphism in Early Islam, the University Lecture in Religion at Arizona State University*. Tempe: Arizona State University, 1988.

Van Reenen, Daan. "The *Bilderverbot*, A New Survey." *Der Islam* 67, no. 1 (1990): 27–77.

Al-Varavini, Saʿd al-Din. *Kitab-i Marzubannama*. Edited by Muhammad Qazvini. Tehran: Furughi, 1984.

Varisco, Daniel. "Metaphors and Sacred History: The Genealogy of Muhammad and the Arab 'Tribe.'" *Anthropological Quarterly* 68, no. 3 (July 1995): 139–56.

Vatin, Nicolas and Gilles Veinstein. *Le sérail ébranlé: Essai sur les morts, dépositions et avènements des sultans ottomans (XIVe-XIXe siècle)*. Paris: Fayard, 2003.

Vermeulen, Urbain. "L'Apparition du Prophète dans la *Sirat ʿAntar*." *Quaderni di Studi Arabi* 7 (1989): 153–61.

Vernoit, Stephen. *Occidentalism: Islamic Art in the 19th Century*. Nasser D. Khalili Collection of Islamic Art 23. London: Nour Foundation in Association with Azimuth Editions and Oxford University Press, 1997.

———. "The Visual Arts in Nineteenth-Century Muslim Thought." In *Islamic Art in the 19th Century: Tradition, Innovation and Eclecticism*, edited by Doris Behrens-Abouseif and Stephen Vernoit, 19–35. Boston: Brill, 2006.

Vesel, Shiva. "Talismans from the Iranian World: A Millenary Tradition." In *The Art and Material Culture of Iranian Shiʿism: Iconography and Religious Devotion in Shiʿi Islam*, edited by Pedram Khosronejad, 254–75. London: I. B. Tauris, 2012.

Von Folsach, Kjeld. *For the Privileged Few: Islamic Miniature Painting from the David Collection*. Copenhagen: David Collection, 2007.

Von Folsach, Kjeld, Torben Lundbæk, and Peder Mortensen, eds. *Sultan, Shah, and Great Mughal: The History and Culture of the Islamic World*. Copenhagen: National Museum, 1996.

Von Gladiss, Almut. *Die Freunde Gottes: Die Bilderwelt einer persischen Luxushandschrift des 16. Jahrhunderts*. Berlin: Preussischer Kulturbesitz, 2005.

Von Grunebaum, Gustav. *Muhammadan Festivals*. New York: Schuman, 1951.

Al-Wahidi, Abuʾl-Hasan ʿAli ibn Ahmad. *Al-Wahidi's Asbab al-Nuzul*. Louisville: Fons Vitae, 2008.

Waldman, Marilyn Robinson. *Prophecy and Power: Muhammad and the Qurʾan in the Light of Comparison*. Sheffield: Equinox, 2012.

Walton, Jeremy. "Practices of Neo-Ottomanism: Making Space and Place Virtuous in Istanbul." In *Orienting Istanbul: Cultural Capital of Europe?*, edited by Deniz Göktürk, Levent Soysal, and İpek Türeli, 88–100. London: Routledge, 2010.

Wansbrough, John. "Emblems of Prophethood." In *Quranic Studies: Sources and Methods of Scriptural Interpretation*, 53–84. Oxford: Oxford University Press, 1977.

———. *Quranic Studies: Sources and Methods of Scriptural Interpretation*. Oxford: Oxford University Press, 1977.

Al-Waqidi, Abu ʿAbdallah Muhammad ibn ʿUmar. *The Life of Muhammad: al-Waqidi's Kitab al-Maghazi*. Edited and translated by Rizwi Faizer. London: Routledge, 2011.

———. *Muhammed in Medina: Das is Vakidi's Kitab alMaghazi*. Translated by J. Wellhausen. Berlin: G. Reimer, 1882.

Warner, Arthur George, and Edmond Warner. *The Sháhnáma of Firdausí*. London: Kegan Paul, Trench, Trübner and Co., 1905.

Watt, W. Montgomery. *Bell's Introduction to the Qurʾan*. Edinburgh: Edinburgh University Press, 1970.

———. "His Name is Ahmad." *Muslim World* 43, no. 2 (April 1953): 110–17.

———. "The Materials Used by Ibn Ishaq." In *Historians of the Middle East*, edited by Bernard Lewis and P. M. Holt, 23–34. London: Oxford University Press, 1962.

———. *Muhammad: Prophet and Statesman*. London: Oxford University Press, 1961.

Waugh, Earle. "Following the Beloved: Muhammad as Model in the Sufi Tradition." In *The Biographical Process: Studies in the History and Psychology of Religion*, edited by Frank Reynolds and Donald Capps, 63–85. The Hague: Mouton, 1976.

———. *The Munshidin of Egypt: Their World and Their Song*. Columbia: University of South Carolina Press, 1989.

———. "The Popular Muhammad: Models in the Interpretation of an Islamic Paradigm." In *Approaches to Islam in Religious Studies*, edited by Richard Martin, 41–58. Tucson: University of Arizona Press, 1985.

Weismann, Itzchak. *The Nashbandiyya: Orthodoxy and Activism in a Worldwide Sufi Tradition*. London: Routledge, 2007.

Welch, Anthony. "The Shrine of the Holy Footprint in Delhi." *Muqarnas* 14 (1997): 166–78.

Wheeler, Brannon. "Collecting the Dead Body of the Prophet Muhammad: Hair, Nails, Sweat and Spit." In *The Image of the Prophet between Ideal and Ideology: A Scholarly Investigation*, edited by Christiane Gruber and Avinoam Shalem, 45–61. Berlin: De Gruyter, 2014.

———. *Mecca and Eden: Rituals, Relics, and Territory in Islam*. Chicago: Chicago University Press, 2006.

———. "Moses." In *The Blackwell Companion to the Qurʾan*, edited by Andrew Rippin, 248–65. Malden, MA: Blackwell Publishing, 2006.

———. *Moses in the Quran and Islamic Exegesis*. London: Routledge Curzon, 2002.

———. "Relics in Islam." *Islamica* 11 (Summer/Fall 2004): 107–12.

White, Hayden. "The Value of Narrativity in the Representation of Reality." In *The Content of Form: Narrative Discourse and Historical Representation*, 1–25. Baltimore: Johns Hopkins University Press, 1987.

Widengren, Geo. *Muhammad, the Apostle of God, and His Ascension*. Wiesbaden: Otto Harrassowitz, 1955.

Williams, Rebecca. *Muhammad and the Supernatural: Medieval Arab Views*. London: Routledge, 2013.

Wills, Charles. *Persia as It Is*. London: S. Low, Marston, Searle, and Rivington, 1886.

Witkam, Jan Just. "The Battle of the Images: Mekka vs. Medina in the Iconography of the Manuscripts of al-Jazuli's *Dalaʾil al-Khayrat*." In *Theoretical Approaches to the Transmission and Edition of Oriental Manuscripts, Proceedings of a Symposium Held in Istanbul March 28–30, 2001*, edited by Judith Pfeiffer and Manfred Kropp, 67–82. Beirut: Orient-Institut, 2007.

Wolf, Maurice, ed. and trans. *Muhammedanische Eschatologie (Kitab Ahwal al-Qiyama)*. Leipzig: F. A. Brockhaus, 1872.

Wood, Barry. "The *Tarikh-i Jahanara* in the Chester Beatty Library: An Illustrated Manuscript of the 'Anonymous Histories of Shah Isma'il'." *Iranian Studies* 37, no. 1 (2004): 89–107.

Woodman Cleaves, Francis. "The Mongolian Documents in the Musée de Téhéran." *Harvard Journal of Asiatic Studies* 16, nos. 1–2 (June 1953): 1–107.

Woods, John. "The Rise of Timurid Historiography." *Journal of Near Eastern Studies* 46, no. 2 (April 1987): 81–108.

Wright, Elaine. *Islam: Faith, Art, and Culture. Manuscripts of the Chester Beatty Library*. London: Scala, 2009.

Al-Yahsubi, 'Iyad ibn Musa. *Kitab al-Shifa bi-Ta'rif Huquq al-Mustafa.*

Edited by 'Ali Muhammad al-Bajawi. Cairo: 'Isa al-Babi al-Halabi, 1977.

———. *Muhammad, Messenger of Allah: Ash-Shifa of Qadi 'Iyad*. Translated by Aisha Abdarrahman Bewley. Inverness, Scotland: Madinah, 1991.

Yalman, Suzan. "'Ala al-Din Kayqubad Illuminated: A Rum Seljuq Sultan as Cosmic Ruler." *Muqarnas* 29 (2012): 151–86.

———. "Building the Sultanate of Rum: Memory, Urbanism, and Mysticism in the Architectural Paronage of 'Ala al-Din Kayqubad (r. 1220–1237)." PhD diss., Harvard University, 2010.

Yıldız, Osman. *Ahvâl-i Kıyâmet: Orta Osmanlıca Dönemine Ait Bir Dil Yadigârı*. Istanbul: Şûle Yayınları, 2002.

Yıldız, Sara Nur. "Ottoman Historical Writing in Persian, 1400–1600." In *Persian Historiography*, edited by Charles Melville, 436–502. Vol. 10 of *A History of Persian Literature*. London: I. B. Tauris 2012.

Yusupova, Maylyuda. "Evolution of Architecture of the Sufi Complexes of Bukhara." In *Bukhara: The Myth and the Architecture*, edited by Attilio Petruccioli, 121–32. Cambridge, MA: Aga Khan Program for Islamic Architecture, 1999.

Zakariya, Mohamed. "The Hilye of the Prophet Muhammad." *Seasons* (Autumn–Winter 2003–2004): 13–22.

Zarcone, Thierry. "*Mevlid Kandili*: La fête de la naissance du Prophète en Turquie." In *Penser, agir et vivre dans l'Empire ottoman et en Turquie: Études réunies pour François Georgeon*, edited by Nathalie Clayer and Erdal Kaynar, 307–20. Paris: Peeters, 2013.

Zeitlin, Irving. *The Historical Muhammad*. Cambridge: Polity, 2007.

Zoka, Yahya. *Life and Works of Sani' al-Mulk (1814–1866)*. Edited by Cyrus Parham. Tehran: Tehran University Press, 2003.

References to images are in italics.

'Abbasid, 13, 36, 37, 52, 213, 269, 273
'Abdallah, 99
'Abdallah b. Mas'ud, *113, 114,* 115
'Abdallah ibn al-Zubayr, 43
'Abd al-Malik, 43
'Abd al-Mu'min b. Muhammad, *45,* 46
'Abd al-Muttalib *91,* 92, 94, *95,* 96
'Abd al-Rahman b. 'Awf, 264
Abdülhamid II, Sultan, *278*
'Abdullah, 89
Abdülmecid, Sultan, 272
'Abidin, Zayn al-, *221,* 224
Abraham/Abrahamic, 3, 13, 16, 72, 73, 74, 75,
  86, 90, 107, 122, 127, 132, 220, 240, 294, 354
Abru, Hafiz-i: *Majma' al-Tawarikh*
  (Quintessence of Chronicles),
  84, 94–97, *95,* 111, 168, *169*
Abu Bakr, *14, 15,* 45, 47, 60, 61, 69, 70, *140,* 148,
  154, 160, 161, 162, *198,* 203, 211, 220, 222, 228,
  230, 234, *235,* 236, 242, 244, 264, *267,* 268, *339*
Abu Jahl, *113, 114,* 115, 130
Abu'l-Hasan Ghaffari (aka Sani'
  al-Mulk), *310,* 316–17
Abu'l-Qasim Rabib al-Din, 52, *57*
Abu Sa'id, 127
Abu Talib, 103, 105
Abu Ubaya b. Jarra, 264
Abyssinian, 70
Adam, 13, 253, 290, 294
'Adnan, *293, 296*
Aflaki, Shams al-Din Ahmad: *Manaqib
  al-'Arifin* (The Feats of the Know-
  ers of God), 172, *173,* 174, 175, 177–78
ahl al-bayt, 18, 61, 70, 71, 77, *177,* 178, 179,
  204, 206, 207, 208, 215, 218, 219, 223,
  227, 229, 323, 325, 326, 330, 362
Ahmadinejad, Mahmud, President, 329
Ahmed II, Sultan, 274
Ahval-i Kıyamet (Conditions of
  Resurrections), *267,* 268
'A'isha, 165–66
'alam al-mithal (realm of likenesses), 19, 142, 151, 175, 192
Alexander the Great, 92
Alexandria, 13, 318
'Ali (Imam), 15, 19, 20, *45,* 47, 61, 70, 71, 75, *140,*
  148, 161–62, 164, 170, *176, 177,* 178, 179, 180,
  184, 186, 188, *189, 190, 198,* 201, 202, 203,
  204, 205, 206, 207–8, 208–9, *210,* 211, *212,*
  213, 214, *215, 216,* 217, 218, 219, 220, *221,* 222,
  223, 224, *225, 226, 227,* 228, 229–40, *231, 232,*
  235, 237, 239, 241, 242, 243, 244, 245–46, 260,
  262, 264, 265, 266, 268, 285, 294, *295,* 297,
  300, 302, 315, 316, 318, *322, 323, 324, 325,* 327,
  330, *331, 332, 333,* 334, 335, 336, *339,* 343, 362

'Ali, Mirza, 204, *205, 206*
'Ali, Mustafa, 256
'Ali b. Abi Talib, 207
'Ali b. Husayn Kashifi Safi: *Rasha-
  hat-i 'Ayn al-Hayat* (Dewdrops
  from the Elixir of Life), 162
Allah, 12, 43, 103, 105, 118, 119, 144, 145, 149,
  160, 222, 273, 290, 321, 345, 346, 355, 358
Allen, Terry, 28, 29
Amina, 89, *91,* 92, 94, *95,* 96–7, *252,* 257, *258*
Amir-Moezzi, Mohammad Ali, 316
Anatolia, 46, 172
Andalusia, 10, 282
angels: celestial rooster, *128,* 129, 130;
  half-fire and half-snow, *129,* 130
aniconism, 28, 30, 43, 313, 315,
  341, 348, 350, 361, 373
Ankara, 355
Ansari, 'Abdallah, 153
Ansari, Khwaja 'Abdallah, 152–54, *152,*
  160, 164; *Kitab al-'Arba'in* (Forty Had-
  ith), 153; *Munajat* (Supplications), 153
'Antara b. Shaddad, 44
Arabo-Sasanian, *43*
archangels, 301, 360. *See also* 'Azra'il;
  Israfil; Gabriel; Michael
Arch of Nushirvan, 97
Ardabil, 179, 182, 183
Ardabili, Shaykh Safi al-Din, 178–92,
  181, 183, 185, 187, 211, 214
Armenia, 92, *93,* 105, *106,* 270
asbab al-nuzul (explanation of occasions for revelation), 111, 116
Ashrafiyya Madrasa, 280
asma' al-nabi (names of the Prophet), 2, 3,
  7, 69, 86, 157, *292; aftab-i jan* (sun of life),
  186; Ahmad (The Most Praised One, The
  Most Praiseworthy One), 3, 86, 89, 90, 346;
  asil al-jadd (one of noble ancestry), 290;
  bashir (bearer of glad tidings), 3; *janab-i
  rasalat-panah* (His Excellency the Refuge
  of Prophecy), 236; *khatam al-nabiyyin* (seal
  of prophets), 3, 16, 71, 182; *mah ü hurşid-i
  hüda* (the moon and sun of guidance), 11,
  261; *al-Masih* (Messiah or Anointed One),
  86, 107; *mihr-i shari'at* (sun of law), 334; *al-
  muddaththir* (the enshrouded one), 208, 320;
  al-muzzammil (the enwrapped one), 208,
  209, 320; *nabi al-rahma* (prophet of mercy),
  343; *nadhir* (warner [of hell and calami-
  ties]), 3; *nur al-huda* (light of guidance), 69,
  98, 257, 343; *qa'id ila'l-khayr* (foundation of
  what is good), 343; *al-rahim* (the merciful), 346; *rasul Allah* (messenger of God),
  339, 345; *rasul rabb al-'alamin* (messenger

of the Lord of the Worlds), 103, 343; *sahib
  al-taj* (possessor of the crown), 61, 64
Astarabad, 225
Astarabadi, Nizam al-Din: *Athar al-Muzaffar*
  (Traces/Exploits of the Victorious), 200,
  225, 226, 227, 231, 232, 238, 239, 241, 242
'Attar, Farid al-Din: *Tazkirat al-Awliya'*
  (Biographies of Saints), 164–65, 345–46
'Ayyuqi: *Varqa wa Gulshah* (Varqa and
  Gulshah) 44, *45,* 46, 47, 48, 49, 50–51, 52, 61
Azerbaijan, 52, 92
Azhar, al-, 26
'Azra'il, 301, 360

Babylon, 88, 89
Badi' al-Zaman, 147, 154
Baghdad, 13, 36, 52, *53, 57,* 58, 68, 69,
  88, 172, *173,* 175, *176, 177,* 294, 295
Bahira, 16, 89–90, 99, 100, 103, *104,*
  105, 106–7, *108,* 109, 117, 124, 258
Bakri, Abu'l-Hasan al-, 256
Bal'ami, al-, 90; *Ta'rikh al-Rusul wa'l-Muluk*
  (History of Messengers and Kings), 84, 100,
  101, 102, 111, *112, 113, 114,* 115–16, 118, 120, 234
Balkans, 313
Banu'l-Nadir, 111, 116, *117,* 118, 122, 233
Baqli, Ruzbihan: *Kashf al-Asrar* (Un-
  veiling of Secrets), 146, 162
baraka (blessings), 6, 255, 269–85,
  287, 302, 303, 313, 325, 340, 358
Barquq, Sultan, 256
Barry, Michael, 29
Barzuya, 68
Battle of Badr, 111, *112, 113, 114,* 115, 116, 122,
  229, 230, 231, 232, 233, 240, *335,* 336
Bayezid II, Sultan, 256
Bayqara, Sultan Husayn, 147, 151, 153, 154, 164
Baysunghur, 68
Bazil: *Hamla-yi Haydari* (Lion's At-
  tack), *331, 332, 333, 334, 335,* 336
Bengal, 313
Bible, 86
Bilal, 15, 70, *140, 148,* 166, 172, *173*
Birkeland, Harris, 102
Biruni, al-: *Al-Athar al-Baqiyya 'an al-
  Qurun al-Khaliyya* (Chronology of
  Ancient Nations), *82,* 84, 86, *87,* 88,
  91, 215, 216, 217, 218, 219, 220, 221
bismallah, 43
Bistami, Abu Yazid al-, 10, 145
Bistami, Bayazid, 154
Bitikchi, Khwajah Sayf al-Din Muzaffar, 225
Blair, Sheila, 58
Bonaparte, Napoleon, 320
Boniface VIII, Pope, 121

CHRISTIANE GRUBER is Professor of Islamic Art at the University of Michigan, Ann Arbor. Her primary field of research is Islamic painting, in particular illustrated books of the Prophet Muhammad's ascension. She is author of *The Timurid Book of Ascension (Mi'rajnama): A Study of Text and Image in a Pan-Asian Context* and *The Ilkhanid Book of Ascension: A Persian-Sunni Devotional Tale*. She is editor (with Frederick Colby) of *The Prophet's Ascension: Cross-Cultural Encounters with the Islamic Mi'raj Tales* and (with Avinoam Shalem) *The Image of the Prophet Between Ideal and Ideology: A Scholarly Investigation*.